BURT REYNOLDS

PUT THE PEDAL TO THE METAL

What is Blood Moon Productions?

"Blood Moon, in case you don't know, is a small publishing house on Staten Island that cranks out Hollywood gossip books, about two or three a year, usually of five-, six-, or 700-page length, chocked with stories and pictures about people who used to consume the imaginations of the American public, back when we actually had a public imagination. That is, when people were really interested in each other, rather than in Apple 'devices.' In other words, back when we had vices, not devices."

—The Huffington Post

Award-Winning Entertainment About
American Legends, Hollywood Icons, and the Ironies of Fame.

www.BloodMoonProductions.com

BURT REYNOLDS

PUT THE PEDAL TO THE METAL

DARWIN PORTER & DANFORTH PRINCE

BURT REYNOLDS
PUT THE PEDAL TO THE METAL

Darwin Porter and Danforth Prince

www.BloodMoonProductions.com
Manufactured in the United States of America

ISBN 978-1-936003-63-1

Cover & Book Designs by Danforth Prince
Distributed worldwide through National Book Network
(www.NBNBooks.com)

national book network

PREVIOUS WORKS BY DARWIN PORTER
PRODUCED IN COLLABORATION WITH BLOOD MOON

BIOGRAPHIES

Kirk Douglas, More Is Never Enough

Playboy's Hugh Hefner, Empire of Skin

Carrie Fisher & Debbie Reynolds
Princess Leia & Unsinkable Tammy in Hell

Rock Hudson Erotic Fire

Lana Turner, Hearts & Diamonds Take All

Donald Trump, The Man Who Would Be King

James Dean, Tomorrow Never Comes

Bill and Hillary, So This Is That Thing Called Love

Peter O'Toole, Hellraiser, Sexual Outlaw, Irish Rebel

Love Triangle, Ronald Reagan, Jane Wyman, & Nancy Davis

Jacqueline Kennedy Onassis, A Life Beyond Her Wildest Dreams

Pink Triangle, The Feuds and Private Lives of Tennessee Williams, Gore Vidal,
Truman Capote, and Famous Members of their Entourages.

Those Glamorous Gabors, Bombshells from Budapest

Inside Linda Lovelace's Deep Throat,
Degradation, Porno Chic, and the Rise of Feminism

Elizabeth Taylor, There is Nothing Like a Dame

Marilyn at Rainbow's End, Sex, Lies, Murder, and the Great Cover-up

J. Edgar Hoover and Clyde Tolson
Investigating the Sexual Secrets of America's Most Famous Men and Women

Frank Sinatra, The Boudoir Singer. All the Gossip Unfit to Print

The Kennedys, All the Gossip Unfit to Print

The Secret Life of Humphrey Bogart (2003)

Humphrey Bogart, The Making of a Legend (2010)

Howard Hughes, Hell's Angel

Steve McQueen, King of Cool, Tales of a Lurid Life

Paul Newman, The Man Behind the Baby Blues

Merv Griffin, A Life in the Closet

Brando Unzipped

Katharine the Great, Hepburn, Secrets of a Lifetime Revealed

Jacko, His Rise and Fall, The Social and Sexual History of Michael Jackson

Damn You, Scarlett O'Hara,
The Private Lives of Vivien Leigh and Laurence Olivier
(co-authored with Roy Moseley)

FILM CRITICISM
Blood Moon's 2005 Guide to the Glitter Awards
Blood Moon's 2006 Guide to Film
Blood Moon's 2007 Guide to Film, and
50 Years of Queer Cinema, 500 of the Best GLBTQ Films Ever Made

NON-FICTION
Hollywood Babylon, It's Back!
Hollywood Babylon Strikes Again!
Staten Island's Historic Magnolia House
Volume One, Celebrity and the Ironies of Fame

NOVELS
Blood Moon,
Hollywood's Silent Closet,
Rhinestone Country,
Razzle Dazzle
Midnight in Savannah

OTHER PUBLICATIONS BY DARWIN PORTER
NOT DIRECTLY ASSOCIATED WITH BLOOD MOON

NOVELS

The Delinquent Heart
The Taste of Steak Tartare
Butterflies in Heat
Marika (a roman à clef based on the life of Marlene Dietrich)
Venus (a roman à clef based on the life of Anaïs Nin)
Bitter Orange
Sister Rose

CUISINE

Food For Love, Hussar Recipes from the Austro-Hungarian Empire,
with collaboration from the cabaret chanteuse, Greta Keller

A Word About Phraseologies:

Since we at Blood Moon weren't privy to long-ago conversations as they were unfolding, we have relied on the memories of our sources for the conversational tone and phraseologies of what we've recorded within the pages of this book.

This writing technique, as it applies to modern biography, has been defined as "conversational storytelling" by *The New York Times*, which labeled it as an acceptable literary device for "engaging reading."

Some people have expressed displeasure in the fact that direct quotes and "as remembered" dialogue have become a standard—some would say "mandatory"—fixture in pop culture biographies today.

Blood Moon is not alone in replicating "as remembered" dialogues from dead sources. Truman Capote and Norman Mailer were pioneers of direct quotes, and today, they appear in countless other memoirs, ranging from those of Eddie Fisher to those of the long-time mistress (Verita Thompson) of Humphrey Bogart.

Best wishes to all of you, with thanks for your interest in our work.

Danforth Prince, President,
Blood Moon Productions

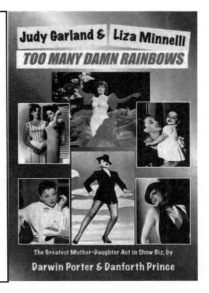
Judy and Liza were the greatest, most colorful, and most tragic mother-daughter saga in show biz history. They live, laugh, and weep again in the tear-soaked pages of this remarkable biography from the entertainment industry's most prolific archivists, Darwin Porter and Danforth Prince. They've compiled a compelling "post-modern" spin.

Their memorable stories unfold through eyewitness accounts of the typhoons that engulfed them. They swing across glittery landscapes of euphoria and glory, detailing the betrayals and treachery which the duo encountered almost daily. There were depressions "as deep as the Mariana Trench," suicide attempts, and obsessive identifications on deep psychological levels with roles that include Judy's Vicky Lester in *A Star is Born* (1954) and Liza's Sally Bowles in *Cabaret* (1972).

Lesser known are the jealous actress-to-actress rivalries. Fueled by klieg lights and rivers of negative publicity, they sprouted like malevolent mushrooms on steroids.

For millions of fans, Judy will forever remain the cheerful adolescent (Dorothy) skipping along a yellow brick road toward the other side of the rainbow. Liza followed her down that hallucinogenic path, searching for the childhood, the security, and the love that eluded her.

Judy Garland, an icon whose memory is permanently etched into the American psyche, continues to thrive as a cult goddess. Revered by thousands of die-hard fans, she's the most poignant example of both the manic and depressive (some say "schizophrenic") sides of the Hollywood myth. A recent film portrayal by Renée Zellweger helped promote and perpetuate her image.

Deep in her 70s, Liza is still with us, too, nursing memories of her former acclaim and her first visit as a little girl to her parents at MGM, the "Dream Factory," during the Golden Age of Hollywood.

Softcover, approximately 650 pages, with photos, available everywhere in 2020. ISBN 978-1-936003-69-3

CONTENTS

CHAPTER THREE

BURT'S STRUGGLES AS A BIT PLAYER IN THE EARLY DAYS OF TELE-VISION

HOW HIS VIOLENT TEMPER ALMOST IMPLODED HIS SCREEN CAREER BEFORE IT EVEN GOT LAUNCHED.

RIVERBOAT: BURT LANDS HIS BIGGEST ROLE AS A "DUMB-DUMB WHISTLE BLOWER," FREQUENTLY TANGLING WITH HIS CO-STAR, DARREN MCGAVIN

AUDIE MURPHY: HOW WORLD WAR II'S MOST DECORATED AMERICAN HERO THREATENED TO KILL BURT REYNOLDS

SPENCER TRACY: WHAT REALLY HAPPENED DURING THAT DRUNKEN NIGHT HE SPENT WITH BURT?

ANGEL BABY: BURT LANDS A SMALL MOVIE ROLE IN HIS FIRST FEATURE FILM.

JOAN BLONDELL LEARNS WHY BURT IS NICKNAMED "HOT PANTS."

CHAPTER FOUR

WHAT EVER HAPPENED TO BABY JANE? HOW BURT INAUGURATED AND SUSTAINED BRIEF, NEUROTICALLY CHARGED AFFAIRS WITH BETTE DAVIS AND HER NEMESIS, JOAN CRAWFORD

ARMORED COMMAND: BURT PLAYS A SOLDIER IN A WORLD WAR II FILM THAT EVEN THE STUDIO'S HIGHEST-OCTANE PRESS AND PUBLICITY COULDN'T SAVE

MARLON BRANDO: BURT'S FEUD WITH, AND HIS STRIKING RESEMBLANCE TO

GUNSMOKE: BURT, BORED WITH THE UNRELIEVED MONOTONY OF ANOTHER MINOR ROLE, PLAYS A HALF-BREED BLACKSMITH NAMED QUENTIN.

CHAPTER FIVE

CHAPTER SIX

CHAPTER TWELVE

CHAPTER THIRTEEN

THIS BOOK IS DEDICATED TO
BURT REYNOLDS

who told the story of his own life on TV to millions, and privately, directly to his friends.

Our task involved rounding up his hundreds of confessions and insights delivered over the course of many decades. They were humorous, mocking, self-deprecating, full of angry tirades, and/or filled with love and devotion for those who stood by him in stormy weather.

TAKING RISKS: *At Long Last Love* (1975)

Burt celebrates the music and lyrics of Cole Porter with,
left to right: Cybill Shepherd,
Madeline Kahn, and Duilio del Prete.

CHAPTER ONE

THE EVERGLADES
As an Adolescent "Florida Boy,"
Burt Roams the Alligator Swamplands

In Off-Season, When the "Snowbirds" Fly North,
He Breaks into Palm Beach Mansions, Including
MAR-A-LAGO
for Parties with His Friends

EXPLORING HETEROSEXUALITY
How a Buxom 42-year-old "Cougar" Initiates & Sustains
a Sexual Affair with Fourteen-Year-Old Burt

BURT IMPREGNATES A CHEERLEADER
She's Rich, She's Socially Connected, and Her Mother
Succeeds at Making EVERYTHING Better

GRIM REAPERS
Wedged Beneath a Cement Truck with Burt Inside,
His Father's Buick is "Decapitated."
Pulled from the Wreckage, He's Stitched Together, Barely Alive

THE DEATH OF SATURDAY'S HERO
As a Hung-Over College Football Star
with a Promising Future,
Burt Is Injured So Badly on the Field that as a Player,

HE'S OUT OF THE GAME FOR LIFE

The Everglades...The boyhood playground for Buddy Reynolds

The future movie star, Burton Leon Reynolds, Jr.,
known during his childhood as "Buddy," claimed, "My life didn't really
begin until I moved to Florida at age ten, settling north of Palm Beach."
That was immediately after World War II in 1946.

His father—a factory worker and war hero known as "Big Burt," Burt
Sr., and/or Burt Milo Reynolds—had bought a Ford fresh from the reacti-
vated postwar automobile factories of Detroit. With Buddy in the back seat,
and with his wife beside him in front, they migrated south to a new home
and a new life. Buddy's older sister, Nancy Ann, would follow later.

They were fleeing the cold winters of Lansing, Michigan, and Buddy
was thrilled to be doing so, even though he'd heard that Florida was crawling with poisonous snakes and alligators.

Before settling into Florida, "Big Burt" had led a rather nomadic life.
He'd been born and had grown up on a Cherokee Indian Reservation in
western North Carolina. His mother had been a full-blooded Cherokee.
She had fallen in love and married a forest ranger assigned to the reservation where she had settled. That meant that Burt Reynolds, future movie
star, was part Native American.

When "Big Burt" was just a baby, his mother and father had moved to
Los Angeles. John Burton Reynolds, his father, bought a ranch-style house
at Silver Lake and found a job working for a railway line. He saved enough
money to buy a wagon and a team of horses.

The Reynolds home in Los Angeles was near Mack Sennett's Keystone
Comedies, turning out silent films. For five dollars a day, paid to him as
an extra, young "Big Burt" appeared a few times on the silver screen years

before Burt himself made his film debut.

As a teenager, Big Burt patronized a café, Larsen's Bakery, where his mother worked as a waitress. Her customers included Mary Pickford, Charlie Chaplin, Fatty Arbuckle, Douglas Fairbanks, Sr., and Mabel Normand.

Tiring of California, teenaged Big Burt migrated to the Escalante Valley in Utah, where he briefly owned a 320-acre cattle ranch. It was near the town of Zane, named for Zane Grey, the most famous writer of Western films in Hollywood.

In Utah, enduring many mishaps, Big Burt held down tough jobs that included working as a ranch hand, rounding up cattle, and blasting tunnels through rock for Utah's fast-developing network of railways.

Finally, realizing that ranch work was not for him, "Big Burt" moved his family back to Lansing, Michigan.

He got a job shoveling coal in a factory run by the Ford Motor Company. There, he made a friend, Wade Miller, who would go hunting in the forests of Northern Michigan with him on weekends, following in the footsteps of Ernest Hemingway, who used to hunt in these forests.

One Saturday, Wade took Big Burt home to meet his family. They included six brothers and one sister, Harriet Fernette, nicknamed "Fern." Born in 1902, she was four years older than Big Burt—being twenty-six as opposed to his twenty-two.

A registered nurse, she worked the night shift at the Lake City Hospital. She was tall and with dark skin and a shapely figure and long brunette hair.

She and Big Burt gravitated to each other at once. She was husband hunting, and he was "the best thing" she'd seen so far.

That Monday morning at work, Big Burt told Wade, "I plan to marry your sister and become the father of her children."

And so he did.

A daughter, Nancy Ann, was born to the couple in 1930. In spite of the nationwide Depression, Big Burt always kept food on the table, even though

Buddy's parents, Big Burt and Fern, who gave birth to an untamed boy.

millions of out-of-work Americans were on a very lean diet. He took whatever job he could find—digging ditches, unloading steel at an auto plant.

As a wife, he found Fern very quiet, but very strong, a woman of iron will. "She only pretended I was the boss," he said. "At times, I felt she really wore the pants."

Late in 1934, their next child was still-born. Early in 1936, Fern became pregnant again with her final child, born on November 11 of that year. It was the future movie star, Burt Reynolds.

"He looked like such an innocent little boy," his father said. "He turned out to be a hellraiser."

Burt was born in Lansing, Michigan, but for reasons of his own, he frequently claimed that he entered the world in Waycross, Georgia.

This picture was the first time "Baby Burt" posed for a camera. Later in life, he jokingly said, "My legs are still the same today."

In addition to his Cherokee blood, his parents had a mixture of Dutch, English, and Scottish ancestry. In Florida, Burt was thought to be Italian, and he never bothered to correct that misconception.

Big Burt was drafted into the Army in 1941, and that December, America entered World War II, following the Japanese attack (on December 7, 1941) on Pearl Harbor.

Burt, with his mother and sister, went to live for two years at Fort Leonard Wood, Missouri, where Big Burt was stationed. When he wasn't in school, young Burt explored the Ozarks, fancying himself "a copperhead killer" and modern-day Huck Finn. He was not afraid to explore mysterious caves in the mountains, but never ventured more than a mile into their dark recesses.

In 1944, Big Burt and his fellow soldiers were sent to the south of England, where they later joined in the D-Day landings in June of that year on the beaches of Normandy in the north of France, Seventy percent of his regiment was killed by the Nazis.

Later, he fought again in the Battle of the Bulge, where Hitler's forces staged their last violent penetration of Allied forces, with some inglorious belief that the Führer might rule again in Paris.

When the war in Europe ended, young Burt, his mother, and his sister hoped that Big Burt would be sent home. But he wasn't. He was shipped to join the occupying forces in Japan after that nation surrendered after two atomic bombs virtually obliterated the cities they fell on in August of 1945. Briefly, he became part of the American Army occupying Japan, but in November, just a few months later, he was sent home. While Big Burt was at war, Burt, along with his mother and sister, had moved back to Michigan, occupying a small house.

Burt recalled his father's homecoming like a scene evoking the Samuel Goldwyn movie, *The Best Years of Our Lives* (1946), starring Fredric March and Myrna Loy.

With his sister, he waited inside the house, allowing his mother to rush out for a private and very emotional greeting with her returning war hero.

Later, Big Burt shook his son's hand, gave him a ten-dollar bill, and told him to "get lost." Then he retreated with Fern for a long visit with her in the bedroom.

***

During the "second honeymoon" that followed Big Burt's return to his family in Michigan, he met George Putnam, the owner of nearly one-hundred vacant lots in the small fishing village of Riviera Beach. A real estate developer, he was impressed with Big Burt and wanted to designate him as the general contractor for a series of housing units being planned as shelter for the military men returning from the battlefields of Europe and the Pacific with their fast-growing children (i.e., the "Baby Boomer" generation.)

BACK HOME FOR KEEPS

Big Burt and Fern were not the only couple who reunited passionately after World War II.

The illustration above promoted Oneida Silver Flatware as tangible evidence of the good life that awaited men and women committed to raising a family after the deprivations of wartime.

Young Burt frolicking in the snows of Michigan shortly after his father's homecoming.

In contrast to what he sometimes told fans checking his credentials as a *bona fide* southerner, he was NOT born in Waycross, Georgia, as he often claimed during the peak of his redneck phase.

En route south from Michigan to Florida, a young Burt saw the Atlantic Ocean for the first time and stopped in Jupiter, Florida, for a hamburger and coke with his family. Jupiter was only a truck stop back then, and he could not have known that in time it would become his future home.

***

Incorporated in 1922, Riviera Beach in Palm Beach County is today a predominantly African-American city. But when the Reynolds family drove into it, it was filled mainly with "poor white folks" and a coven of Italian fishermen.

Their first home was a small, rusty trailer dating from 1934 that was propped up on cement blocks in a seedy trailer park called "Star Camp." Neighbors were mostly refugees from the north, hoping to find a new life in South Florida.

On his third day in town, Big Burt accepted the job that had previously been offered by the construction contractor, erecting cheap little Cape Cod-style cottages on a stretch of empty lots north of town.

Big Burt himself purchased the first house his men built for $8,000 on a G.I. loan. By now, Nancy Ann, Burt's sister, had come to live with them. She and Buddy occupied the two attic rooms, sharing the bathroom downstairs with their parents.

When the school year began in September, Fern accompanied her son to the small elementary school to enroll him. It was in the adjoining community of Lake Park, which had never recovered from the devastation of

6

a 1928 hurricane that had destroyed the Florida building boom. Back then, it was known as "Kelsey City," planned as a Utopia by a multi-millionaire from Ohio whose dream involved developing it into a rival of Palm Beach. That dream was swept away by the violent winds.

In lieu of the meat dishes they'd grown up on in Michigan, the Reynolds family's main source of protein became fresh fish, a foodstuff they now consumed almost every night. Accompanied by her young son, Fern bought the catch of the day from local fishermen, all of whom assumed that she and her young son were Italian.

"The so-called white trash lived in Riviera Beach," Burt Reynolds recalled years later. "And the rich folks lived seven miles to the south in ritzy Palm Beach. When I was a little older—say, about fourteen—I journeyed there to be inducted into the chamber called Facts of Life."

With what was left of the summer, Burt set out to discover the natural landscape, the white sandy beach that stretched along the Atlantic Coast of Florida to the east, and the mysterious swampland to the west known as the Florida Everglades.

"Earlier in my life, I had been Huck Finn in the Ozarks. Now I became the Huck Finn of Florida, setting out every day on a voyage of discovery. Instead of the Mississippi, I had the Atlantic Ocean."

Often, he had the beach to himself, except for the fiddler crabs that emerged from between the densely intertwined mangrove roots. He soon became a very young "beach bum," fascinated by the bluish green salt water shimmering under the hot sun, with fluffy clouds overhead. He grew accustomed to the squawking of the seagulls during their search for food.

At times, he imagined himself as a shipwrecked castaway, having escaped from a sinking pirate ship offshore. On some moonlit nights after supper, he'd go to the beach and light a fire from the driftwood and papers he'd collected earlier.

During the day, he wore only what he called "sawed-off jeans" without underwear. When no one was around, he'd discard the jeans and run naked along the beach.

"Of course, later on, when I was a grown man," he said, "I took off all my clothes and posed naked before the world."

Some of the settlers were known as "conchs." That name derived from a local mollusk with a trumpet-shaped shell. [*The same word was applied to the fisherfolk, sailors, merchants, and blockade-runners who settled into Key West to the south.*] "They spoke with a clipped accent, like a foreign language to me," Burt said. "The debauchery of Key West would be discovered by me when I was a little older and more experienced."

When all the prefab tract homes were built, and with money saved, Big Burt opened a small sundry store and café near the big warehouses where fish were gutted and cleaned. It stood on Blue Heron Boulevard just before Singer Island Bridge. Its location was designated with a hand-painted sign advertising GOOD FOOD.

Breakfast was a key event during the course of any given day. As a pre-teen, young Burt waited tables, serving bacon and eggs with grits, along with plenty of hot coffee.

The faces of many of the clients there were weathered and humorless, as most of them had faced rough lives on the sea. Two of the regular diners had lost their legs to sharks.

Beginning at 6AM, country-western music blared from the jukebox, usually about love gone wrong, a state of affairs that a mature Burt would know all too well and too many times.

Lunch hour mostly focused on hamburgers and French fries served with Fern's cole slaw. By four o'clock, the little dive shut down for the day.

That was when Burt headed for the beach, where he'd become en-chanted with the skies over Florida with their endless streaks of lights, sometimes a molten orange or pink, or—often early in the morning, blues and reds.

As each day faded into memory, he looked forward to the adventure of tomorrow.

***

"How would I characterize my years as an early teenager growing up on Riviera Beach?" Burt asked.

Fun in the Sun on Riviera Beach in the early 1950s before the bikini came into vogue.

"Here goes: Daily brawls with the local thugs, car wrecks, speeding, an abortion, an affair with an older woman when I was fourteen, ass-beating by Big Burt, jail time, adopting a brother, a racing champ—and a football hero. Not bad for a kid, wouldn't you say?"

"I got beaten up at home and every time I stepped out the door," Burt said. "A gang of local thugs were always after me, ready to bloody my nose. They heard I was part Italian, part Indian, so I was called 'Greaseball' or 'Mullet.'"

"One time, I came home all bloody and bruised. Mom was a nurse, so she tended to me. But Big Burt attacked me, calling me a 'sissy boy.' He gave me a word of advice."

"In any fight, make sure you're the one standing," he told his son.

"One thing I knew not to do—and that was to cry." Burt said. "Dad told me if he ever caught me crying, he'd beat the shit out of me."

"As I grew up, I was a bit of a smart-ass," Burt claimed. "I went to school with my T-shirt sleeves rolled up to show off my muscles. I used a lot of Vaseline on my thick black hair."

"My mom said I had two different moods—mad and madder. I'd take on all comers, even the biggest bullies. Of course, these thugs often whipped my ass. I knew that somewhere within me lurked a sensitive boy, but I had to keep that part of me hidden from the world. Only when I became an actor, could I reveal that side of me to the world."

"At home, I lived in terror of Big Burt," his son said. "He never hugged me in my entire life, much less a kiss, not even a peck on the cheek. My mother didn't hug or kiss me either. I guess they loved me in their fashion. They just didn't show it. But their love for each other was great, although it lasted only sixty-five years."

"Big Burt had that old theory—spare the rod, spoil the child. His rod was a big black leather strap. My young ass became very acquainted with it. Once, he heard me talking back to my mom. The next thing I knew, I was knocked through the closet door, fading into unconsciousness."

"The last thing I remembered was my mom yelling, 'Don't kill him!'"

"As a kid, I discovered the world of the movies, little knowing at the time that I would devote my life to the film world," Burt said. "Amazingly, my parents let me go to the local movie house for the 12:30 first showing in the afternoon, and I'd still be there for the last show which started at 11PM. Mom packed sandwiches for me."

"At the movies, I could escape into a world of fantasy, blotting out the harsh realities of my life. First, I was hung up on Westerns, but soon gravitated to more adult fare. Roy Rogers, the 'King of the Cowboys,' was my favorite, and I later got to know him personally. I also liked that singing cowboy, Gene Autry."

"I fell under the spell of Betty Grable, the blonde bombshell, the biggest box office attraction of World War II and the favorite pinup girl of G.I.s fighting in the trenches."

"Betty inspired different feelings in different men," Burt said. "I later got to know George Hamilton and work with him in film. He had this half-brother named Bill Porter. He, too, was an ardent Betty Grable fan. I wanted to fuck her, Bill wanted to be her. Lloyds of London insured her legs for a million dollars. From what I heard, and though Bill admired Grable, he believed that his own legs were lovelier."

"My all-time favorite on the screen was not Grable, but Cary Grant," Burt said. The epitome of the 'debonair man about town' magnet for the ladies, a gentleman of class and style. I longed to grow up to be like him."

Adolescent fantasy: Betty Grable in a publicity photo for *The Farmer Takes a Wife* (1953)

"Years later, I got to meet him in Hollywood," Burt said. "As it turns out, he wasn't a ladies' man at all. His tastes lay elsewhere, and he thought I was the greatest thing since sliced bread."

***

When all those prefab houses were built for the Riviera Beach contractor, Big Burt needed another job and became a policeman. When the chief of police died of a heart attack a few years later, his job was offered to Big Burt at a salary of one-hundred dollars a week.

Winter was coming, which meant an annual invasion of "snowbirds" from the North. Big Burt was convinced, with some degree of bitterness, that whereas rich people went to Palm Beach, his town got the riff-raff—or in his words—"the

Young Buddy Reynolds had a hero: The singing cowboy, Roy Rogers, posed here in a publicity shot with his "Queen of the Cowgirls," Dale Evans.

fruits, the hopheads, the cooze peddlers, the pimps, and the gamblers."

Gold Coast gamblers also came south. Although gambling was illegal, it flourished. Blown in on some winter blast from Jersey City, "Slick Willie" (Bill Minta) controlled most of the gambling in the north of Palm Beach County.

One day, he arrived at Big Burt's office with a paper bag stuffed with money—maybe as much as $20,000, and plopped it directly in the center of Big Burt's desk. "I want you to ignore what I do this winter, big guy," he said. "Got that?"

Big Burt roared out from behind his desk, grabbled Willie by the collar, and dragged him out the front door, along with the money bag.

Pointing his gun at his head, he stuffed a wad of bills into Willie's mouth and commanded him to eat it. When he refused, Big Burt made a threatening move to suggest that if he didn't, he'd blow his head off.

At this moment, Burt, who stopped in at the police station every afternoon, was walking home from school. He was astonished to see Slick Willie gagging on that money, and eventually, vomiting.

That was the last bribe the chief of police was ever offered.

When not arresting people for drunkenness, vagrancy, or gambling, Big Burt tried to control "the wild streak in my boy." As he told Fern, "I don't know what crap he gets into when he leaves the house. At times, I hear he takes stupid dares like a stuntman in the movies. He goes crazy, or so I'm told, but not around me. He knows I won't stand for it."

One night, Burt, along with three schoolmates, stole a rental car from a tourist. The oldest of the boys, Arlie Rae Davis, was the driver, with one of the boys up front and with Burt and the other boy in the back. They jump-started the stolen car and roared north on U.S. 1 at 100 miles an hour.

Big Burt chased after them in his squad car, and Davis finally pulled off to the side of the road. Everyone in the car, including young Burt, was thrown into jail that night.

Big Burt kept them there for two days and nights, feeding them bread and water. Fern arrived daily with food for her son and the other three boys, but Big Burt never gave it to the kids.

Illegal gambling, attempted bribery, and Big Burt did not get along well, as young Buddy discovered during a visit to his father's police headquarters one day after school.

He ate what he wanted himself, giving the rest to his three police officers.

It wasn't until two years later before Big Burt finally let his son drive the family car again, and then only to run an errand for his mother.

"I had to go to the grocery store on the corner," Burt said. "It was only three blocks away. But I went eighty-five miles an hour." As he later reflected, "This must have been a rehearsal for *Smokey and the Bandit.*"

***

When Burt was twelve years old, he "adopted" a brother, Jimmy Hooks, a year older than him. As schoolboys, he and Burt bonded, and, whenever Burt was attacked as a "Mullet," Jimmy helped defend him. They soon became the best of friends, spending their days and nights together.

"We both went barefoot, as did most school boys," Burt said. "Who could afford shoes?" Besides, it was Florida."

"I used to think of myself as Huck Finn," Burt said. "Jimmy became my Tom Sawyer. We had all sorts of adventures. Jimmy knew this fisherman who took us out to sea on his boat. I learned to fish, although I didn't know one fish from the other. We explored the Everglades, and even swam in a river with alligators. It's a wonder we weren't eaten alive."

"Often, guys would make fun of Jimmy because of his partial clubfoot," Burt said. "I would help Jimmy beat up those jerks."

"He never wanted me to see his home and meet his mother," Burt said. "I knew his parents had never married, and his no-good dad had bolted even before Jimmy was born. I also found out that his mother almost aborted him. In her racket, which was prostitution, a kid didn't fit in."

"Finally, I insisted on going home with Jimmy one afternoon," Burt said.

He lived in a two-room shanty that had once been used by construction workers. It stood in a field of weeds and garbage, including one old Ford pickup in retirement."

Jimmy's mother, Betty Lou Hooks, was the ugliest woman Burt had ever

Buddy, age 12 in 1948, was called "Greaseball" or "Mullet" by the local gang members when they were not beating him up.

seen. She was drunk and had stringy bleached hair, two missing front teeth, and was at least thirty pounds overweight. She was dressed only in her bra and panties and didn't bother to get a robe.

In the other room, Burt could see some man in his forties sprawled nude on a bed. Jimmy's bed, without sheets and covered with some dirty blankets, filled a corner of the same room.

For no reason at all, Betty Lou started pounding her son for some alleged infraction. "Soon, that bastard in the bedroom stumbled out and kicked Jimmy, who was lying on the floor, fending off the blows," Burt said. "I grabbed him and practically carried him out the door. We headed to my home."

At his house, Burt came in through the back door, entering the kitchen with Jimmy. His mother was at the stove, preparing supper. "Mom, this is Jimmy," Burt said. "He is my new brother. I'm moving him in."

All she said was, "Wait until your father gets home."

When Big Burt came through the door an hour later, Burt defiantly announced the presence of the new arrival. He might have expected his father to explode, but he didn't. "Both you had better follow house rules—or out go the two of you," he said.

He paraded the boys upstairs and into Burt's attic bedroom. His meager wardrobe was in a closet nearby, and Big Burt threw open its door. He separated the clothes into two sections and said. "Those on the right belong to my son, the clothes on the left to you, Jimmy boy. I know about your mother. I've arrested her on two or three occasions for solicitation. She can't bring up a son. You're welcome here. I'll drive by tonight and tell the bitch you've moved in here. I won't allow her to come here to see you, however."

"Don't worry about that," young Burt said. "From what I saw, I think she'll be glad to get rid of Jimmy."

Jimmy moved in, and he had such a winning personality that he immediately won over both Fern and Big Burt. Unlike young Burt, he helped with the household chores, mowed the lawn, and even planted a small garden in back. He also planted flowers in front of the house.

In time, Big Burt and Fern legally adopted him.

As the months went by, Young Burt grew tired of Jimmy, who always wanted to go home in the afternoon after school to see what he could do for Fern.

That domestic scene didn't appeal at all to Burt's sense of adventure, and he turned elsewhere for amusement. "Let me be frank," Burt once said. "I liked to get into trouble. Call me a Hell's Angel."

When Burt turned fourteen, he began to hang out with two of the toughest guys at school, Fred Jackman, an arrival from the Blue Ridge Mountains of North Carolina, and Chuck Hopper, a Florida boy whose father was in jail for shooting a man during a botched robbery in Miami.

Unlike Burt and more like Jimmy, Fred and Chuck had no parental supervision. Burt envied their freedom and thrill seeking, dreading to go home to what he called "the police state."

Jimmy usually returned every afternoon after school to help Fern with chores around the house. She was always bragging on him, praising him for being such a good son. Jimmy also won the approval of Big Burt, who was never known to strike him or beat him.

Burt began to resent Jimmy, feeling he had stolen the love of his parents that rightly belonged to him. He came to believe that Jimmy, not him, was the son his parents had always wanted.

Young Burt was often a reluctant participant in some of the schemes of Fred and Chuck, who plotted adventures that were sometimes so outrageous that they got locked up in the larger jail in West Palm Beach.

Fred and Chuck talked of kidnapping a young girl and taking her west along the lonely road leading to the Everglades. Somewhere along the way, they would repeatedly rape her, then dump her with the hope that she'd get home by herself. "That is," Chuck claimed, "Unless the gators eat her for breakfast."

Burt felt that was far too extreme, and he would never do that, but he said nothing, not wanting to be called a sissy.

A few weeks later, he came up with another daring scheme, one that appealed to Burt's sense of rebellion: All three of them would run away from home.

Before they could do that, they needed money. "Those guys turned to me, the *putz*," Burt said. "I was supposed to get them the dough, and I said I would."

The following afternoon, he rode with Big Burt to the café to pick up Fern. She was finished for the day, leaving her waitress, Jeanne, to clean up, put everything away, and lock the door.

Fern got into the family's car with the paper bag she always carried with the day's receipts. She sat in the front seat, placing the bag on the back seat with Burt. When she wasn't looking, he reached into the bag and removed a stack of bills, a sum that he later learned was a hundred dollars.

He stuffed the bills into his jeans. When they reached the house, he darted upstairs to count the money and to pack some clothing in a pillow case he planned to take on the road early the next morning.

From down below, he heard Fern crying when Big Burt and Jimmy came in the door. She told Burt that Jeanne had stolen all the day's receipts. Big Burt was furious and set off to hunt her down and arrest her.

Plagued with guilt, Burt nonetheless continued with his plan to run away the following morning. He couldn't allow Jeanne to take the blame. Slipping out of the house at 5AM, he taped the money, with a note, to the steering wheel of the family car.

His note read: "I TOOK THE MONEY. I'M RUNNING AWAY. LOVE TO MOM."

When Burt met up with Fred and Chuck, "They were seriously pissed off at me for leaving the money behind but decided we would run away anyway." The three boys then hitched a ride north to the nearest train station where they slipped into a freight car.

They thought it would stop somewhere along the coast, but it hauled them all the way to Allendale, South Carolina. When it pulled into the station there, the boys jumped off.

As they headed toward the center of town, they must have looked suspicious, because the local sheriff stopped them and searched them. Tired and hungry, they had no money, so he arrested them on a charge of vagrancy and locked them up in a cell in the local jail.

When teenaged and rebellious Buddy Reynolds ran away from home, he found solace, shelter, and some degree of understanding from a family of itinerant crop pickers. Although no photos exist of their historical selves, this scene from John Ford's 1940 film classic, *The Grapes of Wrath*, replicates the impoverished straits of the clan that young Burt almost made his life with.

"At least we got some food in our gut," Burt said. "We were starving."

The next morning, the sheriff surprised them with his deal. During the day, they would be driven to the large field of a local farmer, where tomatoes were being harvested. They would pick tomatoes for three dollars a day and be transported back to their cells at night. That arrangement would remain in effect until they earned enough money for bus fare back to Florida.

Picking tomatoes, Burt worked side by side with a beautiful, sixteen-year-old Mary Hays. "She liked me, and I dug her," he said. "She reminded me of Gene Tierney in that movie I saw, *Laura* (1944)."

For their noonday lunch, Mary invited Burt to join her and her family. There, he met her father, mother, and two very young brothers and three sisters. All of them lived in a battered old truck, which they rode in from state to state, wherever there were crops to harvest or oranges or apples to pick.

Joining them, Burt ate fried salt pork and potatoes—naturally, there were plenty of fresh tomatoes, too. He bonded with the family, especially the mother and father. "Throughout this very humble meal, Mary's beautiful eyes never left me. She gazed upon me like I was some God fallen from heaven. Mr. and Mrs. Hays were beaming, too."

At the end of the lunch, he was shocked when Mr. Hays invited him to come and join their gypsy-like family as they migrated from state to state harvesting crops as "pickers."

"It was not the life I envisioned for myself, and I had to turn him down," Burt said.

He regretted his refusal only because it meant tearing himself away from the adoring eyes of Mary. "It was the first time in my life when I felt real lust coming from a girl, who obviously had the desires of a woman. I would spend the rest of my life seeing lust in the eyes of countless women."

"By the time I left, it was obvious to me that Mr. and Mrs. Hays, not to mention Mary, had picked me out as a future husband."

Fred, Chuck, and Burt were driven back to the Allendale jail, where news awaited them. The sheriff informed them that Big Burt had wired three railway tickets, and that they were to be on the train in the morning heading back to Florida. From Riviera Beach, he had called every sheriff's office along the coast, rightly believing that the boys would eventually get arrested.

They rode the train to its southernmost terminus, then hitched the rest of the way to Riviera Beach. He told Fred and Chuck goodbye and that he would see them soon. Actually, he had decided they were not the kind of guys he wanted to hang out with anymore.

At his house, he decided to knock on the door, as he feared he might receive a hostile reception as his homecoming.

Fern threw open the door and ran into his arms, hugging and kissing him, a first for him. Big Burt stood in the door, eyeing him skeptically.

"Why don't you get your ass in here?" his father asked. "Mom's already got supper on the table."

As Burt walked into the small dining room, he noticed Jimmy at table. He said nothing. In fact, most of the meal was silent, except for such requests as "pass me the mashed potatoes."

"I was home again, but somehow, I was different. I was just a teenager, but I was beginning to feel like a man, with the needs of a man. I was ready for my next act. Time to leave the boy behind."

***

"Jimmy Hooks and I should have been friends, almost like real brothers, for life," Burt said. "But it didn't work out that way. We slept in the same bed every night, but as time moved on, our interests diverged."

"When I went to New York, I didn't see much of him. I know he got married. When I hooked up with him again in Florida, I didn't think his wife liked me."

"Later, in Hollywood, when I became a movie star, she wrote a lot of letters, telling me I should send Jimmy money. The way I figured it, I'd done enough for him."

"We drifted apart."

***

As he entered high school, Burt was envious of "those cool cats," the Lettermen. They wore white buck shoes like Pat Boone and had letters on their sweaters. Burt saw them walking the halls with their arms around a pretty girl.

"I was still "Mullet," he said, a reference to the derisive name assigned to him—even though he was the son of the local chief of police.

"One day, I was challenged to a footrace with the best athlete in school, Vernon ("Flash") Rollison. Here was my one chance. If I didn't take it, I knew I'd be 'Mullet' until I graduated from high school. Fool that I was, I accepted."

The next day, Burt showed up barefoot on the football field, and was astonished to see nearly every member of the two-hundred members of the student body assembled in the bleachers as if for the biggest football game of the season. Flash shook his hand, as Burt told him, "Only a fool would race you. Try not to leave me more than half a mile behind."

"I promise," Flash answered.

"I noticed his track shoes with spikes," Burt said, "in contrast to my bare feet."

Burt went into his four-point "racer's starter stance." At the signal, they were off. "His spikes made sounds when they plowed the earth, and my feet were soundless," Burt said.

In the beginning of the race, it appeared that Flash was winning, as the crowds cheered him on, and as Burt fell hopelessly behind.

Suddenly, a determination came over me like I never had felt before," Burt said. "Something hit me like a bolt of lightning. I was imbued with a final burst of energy that sent me flying to the goalpost. I passed Flash like a speeding racecar, forgetting to tell him, 'Eat my dust!'"

The crowd roared its approval. "My days as 'Mullet' were over."

The next day, "The Lettermen" who used to ignore him suddenly wanted to be his friend. He earned a new nickname: "White Lightning."

The school's top athlete, Richard Dalton Howser, nicknamed "Peanut" because of his small stature, approached Burt: "We could use a guy like you on the football team."

"Why not?" Burt said.

"Show up for practice tomorrow at three o'clock," Peanut said. "I think you've got what it takes. You sure can run."

"Saturday's Hero was born that day," Burt recalled.

***

"I didn't know a damn thing about football when I started to play the game," Burt said, "but I became a star athlete. I didn't know a damn thing about acting, but I became a movie star. Hey, this is America. You can do whatever you

Although at first, he didn't like football very much, Burt later came to love it, partly because of how it helped him release his aggressions and anger, and partly because it made him a BMOC (Big Man on Campus,)

The photo above shows Burt in 1953 at Palm Beach High School with Homecoming Queen Mary Alice Sullivan.

set your mind to, or at least that's what I was told growing up."

In the locker room at our school, the coach gave me my practice jersey," Burt said. "It was green and white. I knew where the helmet went, but what about those hip and shoulder pads? If you get confused with your thigh pads, you might end up a soprano."

"I took to football like a pig to shit," he said. "The gut-busting tackles, the colliding helmets with brain concussions, running like you've got a firecracker exploding in your rosebud—it's my kind of game—not for the faint of heart."

Burt's first game was against Riviera Junior High. He played alongside his newly minted friend, "Peanut," as quarterback.

[Peanut, aka Richard Dalton Howser, might have been too small to play college football, but he was the best athlete at Burt's school.

In time, after changing his sports-related focus to baseball, he became manager of the New York Yankees, and later the Kansas City Royals, eventually guiding them to the franchise's first World Series title in 1985.]

Burt came to like the roar of the crowd in the stands, the cute cheerleaders urging him on, and the blasts of the school band.

"Before I took up football, I took out my aggression in fistfights," Burt said. "But for the most part, when I played football, I used up those aggressive hormones that made me raging mad."

"Any honest coach will tell you that football is beastly, brutal, and nasty. I also find that football is also a release from a young man's sexual frustration."

"The language of football is filled with sexual references," Burt said. "Before a big game, your coach will tell you to go out on the field 'and fuck those bastards.' You're told to 'take that ball and stick it down their throats or up their asses.' My coach was fond of saying, 'go out there and knock their dicks off.' Or else he'd say, when you go for that touchdown, 'drop your load when you've made it.' Another favorite line was, 'stick it in their hole.'"

"Being a football hero had its advantages—according to Burt. "All the pretty girls go for a football hero. High school girls don't like bookworms. They're hot for athletes, especially those who can stuff a jockstrap."

His sex education began with Margie Amole, the cheerleader sexpot. "She taught me about French kissing. I tried for her lips, but she kept her mouth wide open. It took me a while to realize she was waiting for my tongue."

The guys in the locker room talked about their sexual adventures, but Burt thought they were exaggerating. "I had not been inducted yet."

With Barbara Jane Moody, he learned how to fondle a girl's breasts.

With Clara Mae Dean, he learned what awaited a young man whose hand traveled up a girl's skirt.

He put on twenty pounds and admitted, "I became an animal on the field. My coach, Rod Whittington, told me I'd be starting as halfback when September came."

***

While still in high school, Burt made a new best friend, and this time it would last a lifetime: Kreig Mustiane, nicknamed "Mo" because he was part Mohawk, came into his life. They played football, baseball, and basketball together. Mo was poor. His father had deserted him, and his mother worked as a sales clerk, making twenty-five dollars a week. They lived modestly.

Mo wanted to go to college, but there was no money and no scholarship.

[He didn't do badly, however. After accepting a job at an electrical company, he rose within its ranks and, at his peak, had 150 men working under his supervision.]

Back when he and Burt were teenagers, they viewed South Florida, especially the Everglades, as their playground. Burt used to jump fifty feet off the bridge over the Boynton Beach inlet, as Mo collected a quarter from each of the tourists who gaped at his feat. Sometimes, the pair would end up with as much as six dollars, often ten dollars on a Sunday.

They frequented the Everglades, dodging alligators and poisonous snakes. In an airboat, Burt would "bulldog" a deer—that is, jump out of the boat and grab a deer around its neck. "You had to be careful that one of those sharp horns didn't ruin your love life."

In the Everglades, they often visited a hermit, Trapper Nelson, known as "Tarzan of the Loxahatchee River."

"He taught me how to handle a live rattler by grabbing its neck, and also how to trap and skin wild animals," Burt said.

[For a while, the reclusive eccentric operated a small zoo attracting tourists until state authorities closed it down in 1960.

By 1968, Trapper was dead, killed by a shotgun blast into his stomach. Was it murder or suicide?]

The boys' most daring adventure derived from when they untied an inflated blimp near a local garage and hung onto it as it became airborne. Whereas Mo dropped off at ten feet above the earth, Burt hung on until twenty-five feet before he let go and fell back to earth.

Fortunately, he fell onto a soft surface. Had he fallen onto concrete or jagged rock, *Smokey and the Bandit* would have been made with another actor.

Decades later, during any of his extended periods in Florida, Burt had lunch with Mo once a week. "Mo didn't give a fuck about Hollywood. Throughout our lives together, I was always his good friend Buddy—not Burt Reynolds, movie star."

***

PALM BEACH

Invariably cited as one of the richest and most decadent cities in the world, Palm Beach played a role in the sexual education of Burt as an underaged sex object to wealthy women. Here's a fast overview of other ultra-jaded residents of what some purists call "an affluent branch of Gomorrah."

The Empress of Palm Beach, Marjorie Merriweather Post, holding a replica of the crown of the Empress of Iran.	Cosmetics mogul Estée Lauder had been a regular on the Palm Beach circuit for decades. After THE DONALD arrived to sweep up Mar-a-Lago, she was photographed in 1986 at a charity event in Palm Beach with his then-wife, Ivana Trump.

Doris Duke, heiress to a tobacco and aluminum fortune, with playboy Porfirio Rubirosa, She had a voracious sexual appetite and married him partly because of his "Rubba Hosa," the nickname of his endowment, for which he was celebrated.	Kennedys Three (left to right) Joe, Jr., Joe Sr, and Jack (JFK), frequent winter residents of Palm Beach. Sometimes, the ambassador passed women along to his young sons.

Heavy petting with cheerleaders was as far as Burt had gone in making love to girls, often in the back seat of the family car, whenever Big Burt would lend it to him. He knew there was much more to love-making than that, but in the 1950s, most girls, except for the school prostitute, did not go all the way. The refrain was, "We'll have to wait until we get married to do that."

When he wasn't working aboard fishing boats in drydock, or diving for quarters, Burt spent his free time strolling along Palm Beach to the south. Once, he walked its entire twelve-mile stretch, passing the gilded mansions of the rich, the often famous, and the sometimes notorious.

Tabloid newspapers described the place as Palm Beach Babylon, a decadent city brimming with sex and scandal. He read one column which claimed that Palm Beach was where "Sodom met Gomorrah."

It was truly the American version of the French Riviera, though far more subdued. Mostly, it came alive in the winter, with champagne-and-caviar parties whose guest lists included socialites, heiresses, diplomats, politicians, corporate leaders, and the merely rich. The bootlegger, Joseph Kennedy, with his brood, visited in December. The rumor had spread that no debutante was safe from the young Kennedy boys—Jack, Bobby, and Teddy.

The queen of them all was Marjorie Merriweather Post, whose fortune (amassed through the hawking of breakfast cereal) had led to the creation of Mar-a-Lago, the most fabulous mansion on Florida's Gold Coast.

When he got a little older, Burt thought he might join the coven of gigolos who descended every winter to prey on the rich socialites.

The best-known stud was the Dominican playboy, Porfirio Rubirosa, who eventually married the two richest women in the world, tobacco heiress Doris Duke and the Woolworth heiress Barbara Hutton.

Burt was too young to drink, but he was always welcomed at the bar-café Alibi. It was owned by Trevor Howell, a former police officer who was a friend of Big Burt. The swanky Worth Avenue crowd stopped off here.

Burt's favorite drink was what Howell called an "orange fizz," freshly squeezed juice mixed with club soda.

Once, he spotted a famous local resident, Estée Lauder, the cosmetics queen. She was accompanied by an extraordinarily handsome young man who looked young enough to be her son. But at one of the sidewalk café tables, the couple didn't act like mother and son, unless it was incestuous.

Burt once spotted Joe Kennedy, the family patriarch. He had a reputation for seducing many young women, later passing them on to his sons. Once, JFK came into the bar with a woman that Howell told him was Flo

Pritchett, who would later marry Earl E. T. Smith, mayor of Palm Beach. She was rumored to have continued her poolside trysts with JFK, even during the course of her marriage.

Burt was at Alibi one afternoon, when JFK, handsome and charismatic, arrived. He was in a bathing suit, as was his companion, the movie star, Peter Lawford.

"The women at the bar wanted to be picked up by these handsome guys," Burt said. "They were rumored to have three-ways, and I hadn't even had a two-way. According to gossip, JFK was said to let Lawford "service" him on occasion. The actor was known to pick up beach boys and specialized in lifeguards."

One day, Burt wandered across the street from Alibi to a small antique store with a window display containing a replica of a three-masted schooner. It fascinated him. He stood a long time just gazing upon it and fantasized that one day he might be the skipper of such a vessel, sailing the seas of the world, stopping in at exotic ports of call.

After he'd stood there for about twenty minutes, the owner of the store came out to speak to him. She was blonde-haired, blue-eyed, and quite buxom, wearing a rather revealing white dress that was cut low. He later recalled, "She looked like Marilyn Monroe might have looked in her mid-forties. She smelled good, too, no doubt an expensive perfume."

"Do you want to be a sailor one day, young man?" she asked.

At first, he didn't answer, just taking in her figure, with its slim waist and Betty Grable legs. She wore very steep high heels and had a soft, soothing voice that sounded like an imitation of Ava Gardner.

When he introduced himself, she recognized his name at once. She'd read about him in the sports page of the local newspaper. He was mildly surprised that she kept up with high school sports. "Your father is chief of police at Riviera Beach, isn't he?" She seemed very well-informed.

He told her he was a diver at the old pier up the street and earned quarters from tourists who watched him dive. He also said he earned extra money by baiting the hooks of wealthy men from the North who came South to Florida in the winter for fishing, often in The Bahamas.

"I do half-gainers and jackdives—that's dive jive."

She invited him inside, giving him a coke as she walked him around her shop, which was filled with rare curiosities she'd gathered from her world travels.

Apparently, she'd once been married to a wealthy businessman in Florida. She was divorced now and had not remarried.

[Years later, he learned that she'd been involved in some sort of scandal when her husband caught her in bed with his thirteen-year-old son from an earlier mar-

riage.]

After thanking her, he excused himself to go diving for more of those quarters. About an hour later, he noticed her standing in back of the crowd watching him dive. He tried to put on his most spectacular show for her. He wished he'd worn more revealing swimwear than his baggy old trunks.

He'd noticed that her shop opened at ten that morning, and he was standing outside the next day waiting for her. He'd dressed in his newest pair of jeans, a white shirt, and leather boots his parents had given him for Christmas.

She didn't seem surprised that he was waiting for her to open up, and she invited him inside, offering him a choice of coffee or hot chocolate in her little kitchen at the rear of the store.

"You look wonderful," she said. "Very handsome. You're becoming quite a man. I bet you want to be in Western movies like Roy Rogers."

"I've never considered acting, but I am a show-off, both in my dives and on the football field."

"Your dives are spectacular, and I enjoyed watching you yesterday. You had a friend going around collecting tips for you, but I had an appointment and didn't get to give you my tip." From the cash register, she removed a ten-dollar bill.

"I can't take this much money," he said. "I usually get a quarter."

"My sweet young man, you're worth a hell of a lot more than some quarter. Take it! I know you need it. There's only one thing you must promise me. Do not tell your father that you know me. He and I had a run-in one day, and he wouldn't want his son associating with me."

"It's a promise," he answered. "It'll just be our secret."

Before he left, she invited him for dinner at 5:30 that upcoming Saturday afternoon. "We'll sit on my balcony and have a sundowner. A boy of your age should learn to drink. It's sadistic to make boys wait until they're twenty-one."

He told his parents that he'd earned enough money with the fishing boats and diving to take a girl on a date, with food at a hot-dog stand and a movie later.

For dinner, she had prepared Florida lobster, and he had his first glass of wine. Later, they walked along the moonlit beach, and she held his hand. His heart was beating faster and faster, as he knew where the evening was headed. He was a virgin, and she obviously was a woman of the world. He was afraid to confess his inexperience.

Before the night ended, he was surprised that she seemed delighted in his innocence. "You'll find I'm the best teacher you will ever have." She was very oral, exploring every crevice of his body. "She even went down on me," he said. "A couple of homo guys on the football team wanted to do that to me, but never a woman. When I got in the saddle, I had her moaning and groaning, and I felt I was a natural."

"She told me what she wanted, and I complied," he said. "I didn't understand what thrill she got from me biting her nipples. It hurt her, but that is what she begged for, and I went along with it. Her lips were marshmallow soft, her thighs creamy. Later in the night, she wanted oral sex performed on her, and she taught me how to do it, a lesson I would use for the rest of my life."

Burt's affair with the older woman stretched on for nearly a year during his term as a high schooler.

She gave him money, often a hundred dollars at a time, and he told his parents he was one of the young boys or men who hired out their services to wealthy tourists, who paid them to travel on a rented yacht to The Bahamas. He claimed he was a cabin boy, keeping the rooms cleaned, washing dishes and serving drinks, for which he was paid $300 a week.

His parents seemed pleased with that and demanded that he save the money for college.

Some days, he would be away for a week to ten days, claiming he was working as a cabin boy on rented yachts. During those prolonged times, he was living with his older lover at her beach house in Palm Beach.

"My lady friend became my teacher in the language of love," he said. "It was heaven, as she was always ready to make love, but as time went by, our roles changed."

After several months, I was no longer the innocent, virginal fourteen-year-old. I was becoming the man of the house, and I began to take charge as I did in all my future relationships."

"As it turned out, she didn't go for that," he said. "She wanted that inexperienced young boy who had stood longingly outside her antique store looking in the window."

"One night, ten months after I met her, she gave me my walking papers after a night of love making. She told me I would always have a place in her heart, but it was time for me to move on. I had been replaced with this kid in the ninth grade."

"There were no hard feelings when I left, although I begged her to let me stay," he said. "She had made a man out of me, and for that I would always be grateful to her. We stayed in touch for several years, and when I was in Florida I sometimes visited her—not for sex, but just for an update on what I was doing."

"And then one day she left Palm Beach for somewhere, and I never knew what happened to her. She may have gotten into trouble for her love of young boys, but I'm not sure."

"With all my acquired experience, I set about looking for love—if not that, then sex. I had come of age, and I wanted to be in charge of my next relationship."

"When I became a movie actor, I was cast into a film with the suntanned George Hamilton. Once afternoon, when we were waiting to do a scene together, we chatted casually about the first time we got laid."

"What a coincidence. When he was a young boy in Palm Beach, he, too, lost his virginity to my older lady friend, that 42-year-old blonde-haired sexpot who deflowered teenage boys."

"At least George and I had something in common. Otherwise, our taste in women was different, as he dated—actually more than dated—every gal from Lynda Byrd Johnson to Imelda Marcos, the co-dictator of the Philippines. The only woman we agreed upon to seduce was Elizabeth Taylor."

***

Autumn had already come to the north when Burt returned to Palm Beach High School to begin his second year. His thoughts were on becoming a football hero instead of concentrating on his studies.

His coach, Bobby Riggs, suggested that he might be eligible for a football scholarship to college if he buckled down with his studies, especially algebra, biology, English, and history.

He took his advice and later claimed that he completed both his sophomore and junior year in one school term. If he did, this was most unusual.

For the next several months, he buckled down, concentrating on just study hall and football, which occupied all his time, at least for a while.

Although in the future, he would display his body for world consumption, he was never pleased with it. His complaint was that his upper body was too long, his legs too short. When he went to buy some new jeans, he bought a pair more suited for a man who stood five feet, seven.

Even with constant studying, he was only an average student, if that. Because he was such a football hero, he felt that many of his teachers who might have given him a "D" marked down a "B" instead.

On the football field, he became known as a terror. "When an incoming player tried to block me, I just knocked him down and left my tracks on his stunned face as I plunged forward."

"I pissed off a lot of guys," he admitted. "If I felt someone had done me wrong, I'd square off and slug it out with them, even if they were bigger than me. On the football field, I took out my anger by being real aggressive.

I never truly understood why I had so much hatred in me, when I fought someone, I battled to kill, and I almost mean that, but not quite."

Once, when a player called me a fag, I not only knocked the sucker out, but started to gouge his eyes out until the coach pulled me off him."

"I was the fastest guy on the field," he said. "Because of my short legs, I had to run three times as fast as the other players. The roar of the crowd in the stands seemed to provide an extra bundle of energy to me."

"Being a football hero, I had many brighter students helping me with my lessons," he claimed. "Of course, I also had my enemies, many referring to me as smart-alecky. But I made headlines in the sports pages. A typical one might read—PALM BEACH DELIVERS 13-0 BLOW AS REYNOLDS CARRIES 18 TIMES.

By the end of the football season, he was named All-Southern as a fullback in 1953, and in 1954, First Team All-State.

"As every football hero in every high school knows, guys like me attract the girls," Burt said. "Most of them just wanted to date me, but our team had one gal who would offer more. Let's call her Betty Lou. She had large, firm breasts and was a blonde. She was from Miami, but her stepfather had moved with her to Riviera Beach. There was no mother—rumor had it that her stepfather was banging her. I think before the season ended, she'd screwed the entire team except for two guys who I think secretly made it with each other."

"When summer came, it was time for fun. In those days, all those mansions in Palm Beach closed down. But our gang, mostly boys but with some girls, too, often broke in to party."

"We didn't like the Kennedy compound, too damn austere. The Dodge mansion was one of our most frequented places to throw a party. Years later, when I became a movie star and visited Florida, Mrs. Dodge would invite me to her parties. The first time I arrived, she offered to show me around. But, as it turned out, I knew the place better than she did."

"Our favorite place, though, was Mar-a-Lago, that palace built by Marjorie Merriweather Post, the cereal queen. We used the kitchen there to roast hot dogs or fry hamburgers. Our drink of choice was 'Purple Passion'—vodka and grape juice."

"We played music and danced, especially to the sound of Fats Domino or Bo Diddley. We found Eddie Fisher a bore. Later, if the girl were willing, we retired to one of the luxurious bedrooms. Not everyone wanted to surrender the pink. Most girls would kiss you while you whacked off. Remember, it was the '50s, the Eisenhower years."

"Late in 1952 and deep into '53, I was hopping from bed to bed, but not falling in love. Put another way, you might say I was doing the 100-

27

yard dash from conquest to conquest, whatever girl made herself available."

"Everything changed during my senior year, as a beautiful rich girl entered my life."

***

Her name was Mary Alice Sullivan, and she was not only the prettiest girl at Palm Beach High School, but the sexiest. She was the chief cheerleader, and it was inevitable that she'd meet the school's football hero, "Buddy" Reynolds.

Mary Alice Sullivan Firestone was notorious even as Burt Reynolds' date in high school.

Later, she generated headlines in tabloids throughout Florida:

"When I came up to her to introduce myself," he recalled, "I tried to be as virile as possible. What a sight she was: Sloe-eyes, full bosom, succulent red lips, Miss America legs, a slim waist, even dimples."

Her first words to him were, "I'll save my wildest cheers for you."

She stood before him in her school sweater and "a skirt so short I could see all the way to Atlanta," he said.

In November, she was dismissed from the cheerleaders after performing cartwheels during the Saturday afternoon game. She'd performed this spectacular stunt before, only this time with a difference: Either deliberately or with calculation, she didn't wear any panties. She was removed from the squad for this indiscretion but reinstated later when her mother offered to make a generous contribution to expanding the gym.

Several months went by before Buddy, as Burt was known, summoned enough courage to ask Mary Alice out. In those days, boys from Riviera Beach did not date girls from ritzy Palm Beach. It was an unwritten rule.

To his surprise, she said, "A date! I thought you'd never ask. I figured I'd have to ask you. I was beginning to suspect you liked boys."

At the agreed-upon time of seven o'clock, he drove up to her family mansion in Palm Beach, walked through the iron gates, and rang the doorbell, expecting it to be answered by a butler in tails.

He was surprised when her mother opened the door. She was elegantly gowned and was as beautiful as her daughter, wearing a diamond necklace and a sable coat around her shoulders. It was obvious that she was leaving to attend some gala event in the city.

"You must be Buddy Reynolds," she said. "I'm Mary Alice's mother. You're the Cherokee Indian football player. If you ever call on my daughter again—and I hope you don't—please used the servants' entrance at the rear of the house."

"Thanks for putting me in my place," he said. "I won't make that mistake again."

"See that you don't," she said, brushing past him as her chauffeured Rolls-Royce pulled up to drive her away.

He walked into the foyer where he was greeted by a uniformed maid. "I've summoned Mary Alice," she said.

As he remembered it, "It was the hottest date of my life, unlike any girl I had ever gone out with, that babe didn't believe wasting time with a lot of chit-chat like 'How are you doing in school?'"

"She was a young love goddess who made it clear that she was ready and rarin' for some action on my part," he said. "Before the night ended, I found her body had only one imperfection—and that was two deformed fingers on her left hand. I discovered that when she unzipped my pants while I was driving and reached in to fondle my penis and jiggle my balls."

In his first memoir, he disguised Mary Alice's identity, calling her "Constance Phipps." He referred to her as "a joke-cracking clown, rebellious, athletic, wild, and crazy. I thought I was pretty daring until I met her. Constance was into advanced calculus."

After only an hour at the party they attended, she asked her girlfriend, the hostess, if she could use one the guest rooms upstairs. Permission granted."

On their way up the stairs, she turned to him and said, "I need to get fucked tonight…real bad."

"I'm the man to do it," he answered.

It was a night of love-making he would remember forever, even after he'd seduced half the beautiful women in Hollywood. As he bragged later to two friends on the football team, "Mary Alice knows how to give a guy a good time. She massaged my tits, and I returned the favor. We both nibbled each other's tits like rabbits chewing lettuce. I put my fingers to work in that bush of hers, turning her into a bundle of writhing ecstasy. She stroked my lusting monster before she placated it."

"Shut up!" one of his teammates said. "You're giving me a hard-on."

Another player told him. "You're gonna end up writing porn."

Despite her mother's objections, Burt continued to date Mary Alice. "I never went to the front door ever again. She had to have it every day. Since she thought I was a full-blooded Cherokee, she called me 'Tomahawk.' We became inseparable. Our schoolmates wee jealous of all the attention we were getting."

In Burt's second memoir, he referred to Mary Alice as "Betty Lou." This time, he described her as a "knockout whose knockers were always bouncing because she never wore a bra. She was a genuine free spirit with the most incredible body I've ever seen."

He didn't relate in his memoir that for a time, he seduced her beautiful but snobbish mother, too. "Mrs. Sullivan was gorgeous, with an earthy sense of humor," he wrote.

When Mary Alice attended a weekend retreat in Miami Beach with her girlfriends from school, Mrs. Sullivan invited Burt over for dinner. It was a repeat of his involvement as a fourteen-year-old with that owner of the antique store.

When he got there, he found no husband, no servants, and soon realized they were alone in the house. He was invited not only to spend the night, but the entire weekend.

As he later relayed to his friends, "She was the mistress of the oral arts. She even sucked my toes, a first for me. Even Mary Alice didn't do that. I concluded that many older dames like to devour teenage boys young enough to be their sons. Maybe Freud could explain it. These two seductions of me by older women sparked a life-long fascination of mine. I don't mean to suggest that I screwed them exclusively, as I had plenty of young stuff, too. During that weekend with Mrs. Sullivan, I don't think she ever allowed me to put on my clothes even once."

"I was the luckiest boy at Palm Beach High, the centerpiece of a mother-daughter combo that went on for many months. Mary Alice never found out about her mom and me. Then, as Mary Alice and I were reigning as King and Queen of the Junior Prom, my world came tumbling down."

"She was in my arms, and we were dancing to the sound of 'Harbor Nights' when I got the bad news."

She whispered in his ear, "I'm pregnant."

"I felt the roof of the auditorium had fallen on me. What to do? No one must find out.

Mary Alice Sullivan and Buddy Reynolds were named best all-around couple in the Palm Beach High School Class of 1954. We all know what happened to Buddy, but Mary Alice gained some fame of her own. She married tire company heir Russell Firestone and divorced him in a nationally publicized case.

30

What would Big Burt and Fern say? What would Mrs. Sullivan say?"

On the way home, she was silent as he tried to formulate a plan.

Later that night, he bought a case of beer, and he and a fellow footballer sat under a bridge and drank all night. Before morning's glow, he had decided what to do.

He would drive her to Georgia, where the age limit was sixteen, and get married. But the next day, when he went to the Sullivan house, the maid told him that Mrs. Sullivan and Mary Alice had gone on a three-week vacation in Havana.

Four weeks later, Mary Alice was back at school, but her dating of him had stopped. She appeared friendly but avoided seeing him alone. He went over to her home where Mrs. Sullivan received him at the servants' entrance. She told him that Mary Alice had had an abortion in Havana, since the procedure was illegal in Florida at the time.

That early evening marked the end of Burt's affair with both the mother and the daughter.

[As the years went by, Burt on occasion saw Mary Alice, but only for catch-up chats. She was thrilled when he became a movie star, and often bragged about her early dates with him.

"We continued to bond because each of us in different ways became notorious," he said.

Burt followed key moments of her life, and some of her exploits, in the newspapers, beginning in 1961 when she married Russell A. Firestone, Jr., the handsome, polo-playing heir to the Firestone tire-and-rubber fortune. He was the grandson of Harvey S. Firestone, the founder of the company, one of the first global makers of automobile tires. Along with Henry Ford and Thomas Edison, he had been in a very special triumvirate, the Millionaire's Club.

To Burt, it appeared to be a fairytale marriage until trouble set in. The marriage, as it turned out, was filled with adultery on both sides, along with cruelty, investigations by detectives, and ultimately, a scandalous divorce where all sorts of charges were aired.

The presiding judge, James R. Knott, said, "The divorce case has enough scandal

Daredevil and sports hero; Burt as a high school heartthrob.

to make Dr. Freud's hair curl. Mr. Firestone seems to have the erotic zeal of a satyr, and Mrs. Firestone never met a beach boy she didn't want to seduce."

The divorce was finally granted in 1967.

As the years went by, Burt watched in sympathy as his former girlfriend endured one scandal after another, including a major drug arrest while married to her second husband, John Asher, a Kentucky oil company executive.

Her mother had told her, "You can't marry that Indian, Burt Reynolds, because he will never amount to a hill of beans. Marry only rich men and use Jacqueline Bouvier as your role model."

Burt's high school affair with Mary Alice went public twenty years after it had faded. Merv Griffin arrived in Palm Beach to film a pilot for a hoped-for TV series called Take Me Home Again. *It was about movie stars going back to their hometowns and meeting figures from their pasts.*

In her forties, and as part of his show, Mary Alice appeared in a skimpy white bikini with the same measurements she'd had in high school.

Griffin asked her, "I understand that you and Burt Reynolds dated in high school."

"We did more than that, Merv," Mary answered. "I was a virgin until five minutes after I met this horndog."

Merv signaled for his cameraman to halt. "We can't say that on television. Let's clean it up and try again."

When the camera was turned on them again, he asked, "I heard that you used to date Burt Reynolds in high school."

"That's right, Merv," Then she pointed to a curved palm tree in her garden. "He used to lay me against it and bang my brains out."

Founded before the Civil War, FSU was a former all-girls' school. When Burt arrived on campus, he found FSU still had "more than a dozen girls for every guy like me. I made a bet with a pal that I'd have two dozen of them before Christmas."

The respected and in some places legendary football coach, Ted Nugent, spotted the sports potential of Burt Reynolds as a college player early and easily.

***

By the time Burt was graduated from Palm Beach High School, he was offered fourteen university scholarships. Each of the talent scouts associated with those offers believed that he might excel at college football and go on to become a professional player.

One of the most tempting offers came from Notre Dame, but he turned it down because he wanted to stay in South Florida, attending the University of Miami in Coral Gables.

The most impressive coach he met was Bear Bryant, who showed up in his trademark houndstooth fedora and plaid jacket. He was head coach at the University of Alabama's football team.

[During his 25-year tenure there, Bryant amassed six national championships and thirteen conference championships.]

A talent scout for the Baltimore Colts also sized him up. "He even followed me into the shower after football practice to size me up even more," Burt claimed. "The Detroit Lions were also on my tail."

His friend, "Peanut" Howser, had been given a baseball scholarship to Florida State University at Tallahassee. He invited Burt to drive north with him to check out the campus and to meet with head coach Ted Nugent.

Founded in 1851, FSU was the oldest college in Florida.

FSU football rookie Burt Reynolds...known for breaking the collarbone and ribs of his fellow players.

Nugent, a native of Lawrence, Massachusetts, was not only a coach, but an innovator, and is credited in football legend for the development of the "I Formation," which made its debut in 1950. He put FSU on the map, his football record at Florida State 34-28-1.

After talking with Nugent for almost an hour, Burt changed his mind about Miami, and signed with FSU, which offered him a scholarship.

Nugent impressed him with his plan to create a major football team at FSU to take on the bigger, most prestigious colleges.

Lee Corso, as a sports announcer, years after his football "misadventure" on the field of FSU with Burt Reynolds.

"He was my roomie, and in his Green Hornet, we were named Batman and Robin," Burt said.

Burt, jokingly or otherwise, claimed that he was convinced to sign when Nugent told him that FSU's student body was noted for the rather odd demographic of fourteen girls to every guy. Up until 1948, it had been an all-girls' school.

On the first week of tryouts, an astounding 400 guys showed up, but Nugent narrowed those down to three dozen, of which Burt was among the chosen few.

"Nugent was one hell of a coach," Burt said. "There was no Army sergeant putting privates through tougher shit than he did us. Brutal as hell. Whatever good play I pulled off, he demanded more. Some guys couldn't take it and dropped out, but I stayed there for the duration—my season in hell."

[Nugent eventually succeeded in getting FSU to play such big teams as Auburn University in Auburn, Alabama, which dated from 1856. As a side note about Auburn University, historians have noted that four years after it opened, it lost almost all of its enrollment, as its male students enlisted in the Confederate Army. Tragically, many of them were killed.]

Even as a freshman, Burt made the varsity squad, becoming a running back in his freshman year, a left halfback as a sophomore.

The university's Sports Information Office, in September of 1955, listed Burt as weighing 171 pounds and standing five feet, nine inches tall.

"In my first game, I viewed myself as a Roman gladiator," Burt said. "I sized up the competition, and focused on this quarterback, Vic Prinzi. He was sort of runty, and, even though he was Italian, I labeled him 'Gandhi in a football jersey.'"

"I aimed to take him down. We collided and he ended up in the hospital with two broken ribs and a broken collarbone. That knocked him out for the season. Believe it or not, Vic and I became the best of friends. Obviously, he forgave me, and I visited him every day in the hospital."

"I worked my balls off playing football, and I also hit the books. At first, I was girl crazy, but I had to control that. I knew that the way out of poverty for me was becoming a football star. I hadn't thought about acting in those days. If I failed, I knew I'd end up in Riviera Beach and become a school janitor or work on some fishing boat and being a 'Mullet' for the rest of my life. Not only that, but football was helping me release all this aggression within me—and I had plenty of that."

One of the highlights of Burt's college football year occurred not on the field, but in a movie house. The team was set to travel to Louisville, Kentucky by bus the following morning. But the coach invited all the team to the local movie house that was showing Marlon Brando in *On the Waterfront* (1954).

"After the movie, all the guys on the team told me I was a dead-ringer for Brando. I kept hearing, 'You look just like him.' Actually, I wasn't flattered. I didn't want to look like somebody else, because I thought of myself as an original. Besides, I heard that he'd fucked that gay playwright, Tennessee Williams, to get cast in *A Streetcar Named Desire*."

"And so it began that night in Tallahassee," Burt said. "For the next twenty years, all I heard was how much I looked like Brando. In my future, 'Mumbles' would cost me a lot of money for jobs I lost because a director considered me too much of a lookalike. I grew to hate the conceited bastard."

During Burt's sophomore year, he roomed with Lee Corso, who was destined to become a famous coach and sports announcer. He was known as "Sunshine Scooter," because of his speed on the football field as a punt and kick returner.

Although not a big bruiser like some of the players, Corso, according to Burt, could play both offense and defense. As a starting quarterback, he broke passing records for his day. Many of them remained, unbroken, for three decades.

"The girls were after us, as we were named Batman and Robin, driving around in his metallic green Chevrolet called the Green Hornet."

"We flew to Texas in 1955 to play the Sun Bowl in El Paso."

Before the game with Texas, Burt and Corso crossed the Mexican border into Juárez, even though the coach had told them to get a good

Two views of who Burt identified as "the man who destroyed my football career," Fob James.

When his own football career ended, he became a right-wing religious extremist, elected as governor of Alabama.

night's sleep. They partied all night with the *putas* and returned to El Paso at dawn.

Both of them hit the football field with no sleep, and Corso broke his fibula *[the more slender of the two long bones of the lower leg]* and ended up in the hospital. Burt fumbled every move, and FSU lost to Texas 47-20.

[Corso was too small to play professional football, so he became a coach, mainly at the University of Louisville and at Indiana University in Bloomington.

In 1987, he migrated to ESPN as an analyst for that network's Saturday College GameDay, shaping the words "not so fast, my friend," into a national catchword.]

Burt was set to make the run of his life, dashing fifty-four yards from scrimmage. But he was tackled on the one-yard line, that move costing FSU the game. Nugent never wanted Burt to forget that.

Unknown to him at the time, he was tackled by Fob James, who turned out to be a world-class sprinter, a hundred-meter champion.

[Fob James became governor of Alabama in 1995 until 1999, following racist George Wallace in office. James became a right-wing extremist mired in controversy, particularly about his religious beliefs. Burt once saw him on television, attacking the theory of evolution by imitating a slump-shouldered ape turning into an upright human.

Burt also heard James on TV bragging about his exploits in college football, talking about "How I ran down this guy and tackled him, even though he could have qualified for the Olympics."

"He called me 'this guy,' and didn't identify me as Burt Reynolds. I guess he figured his hard-assed fans would not be impressed that he tackled some candy-assed actor. I'm sure those tough guys in Alabama think all actors are fags, as they like to call gay men."]

***

My football career was destroyed by my fucking up my body…big time," Burt claimed. "It all began with a knee injury on the field."

He was performing well in a game in which FSU was up against Georgia Tech. As he related, "I started returning a punt upfield, I cut to the right and went down in excruciating pain. I felt like my knee had been hit with an ax."

He was carried off the field on a stretcher and felt embarrassed because none of the other athletes had collided with him. "No other player was even close to me when I had the accident."

Very foolishly after an examination of his knee, he asked to be put back into the game. Big mistake. "I banged my knee up even worse, I ground it into hamburger and gristle."

Although he was warned never to play again, he convinced the coach to let him play in the last two games of the season. But, as he admitted to himself, "I had slowed down, my displays of speed and power on the field gone with the wind. In the last game of the season, I fucked up my knee royally. Goodbye football hero. Goodbye career. I was toast."

***

Burt was always reckless behind the wheel, and he admitted that as a teenager, he'd destroyed three cars in a short time. The third accident almost proved fatal.

It was amazing that Big Burt kept turning the family car over to him. He recalled that his first major accident occurred when he was driving an old Plymouth that belonged to his father. He was going 105 mph in a heavy downpour, coming home from a hot date where "the gal almost went all the way, but not quite."

Recklessly, he wondered what would happen on a wet tar road if he jerked the wheel to see if it would slide. It didn't. "Then, I decided to give it a real jerk. As he did, the car spun around on the wet pavement, and the door flew open on the driver's side. "I winged out of it like an eagle in flight."

Fortunately, he didn't land on cement but on the soft sand beside a small body of water. Then, as if with a life of its own, the Plymouth continued down the road until it hit a royal palm. He had no broken bones, just some bruises. He was seventeen years and had to face Big Burt that night.

"I dreaded going home and feared that Big Burt would beat the shit out of me." That didn't happen.

"He looked at me with all the disappointment a father can have when confronting his errant boy," Burt said.

"You're one damn crazy kid," Big Burt said. "I guess I should be grateful that you're still alive." Then he turned and walked away.

A far more serious accident occurred on Christmas Eve in 1955 when Burt was racing home in Big Burt's 1953 Buick.

He was traveling at 105 mph in 45 mph speed zone when he spotted a red dome light flashing and heard a siren wailing. When he finally stopped the car, he confronted John Kirk, Jr., the son of the sheriff in Palm Beach. He was known to both Burt and his father. Burt asked if he could be forgiven, but Kirk gave him the ticket anyway, saying, "I'm not a big football fan."

Angry at himself for getting caught, Burt detoured down a dirt road. "I put the pedal to the metal, as I'd so often do in my future. Once again, I was breaking speed records. I was god damn defiant."

Suddenly, a flatbed truck with its lights on was in the middle of the road. It turned out that four men were stealing cement blocks from Rinkers, a large construction company.

Impulsively, he knew that even if he hit the brakes, the car

After its wreckage, Burt's car looked something like this. It's a miracle he survived. That night he nearly died, and he ended up minus his spleen.

wouldn't stop in time and his head might be severed. Instead, he ducked under the dashboard of the Buick just before it rammed into the narrow space beneath the pavement and the steel underbelly of the truck. The impact ripped off the top of Burt's car and crumpled it into something resembling an accordion.

"I got smashed like a sardine in the mangled sheet metal between the cement blocks."

He was pinned in a fetal position beneath the Buick's steering wheel. It took the local police seven and a half hours to extricate his body from the crumpled wreckage.

As he learned later, his spleen had burst, he'd injured both knees again, had four broken ribs, and had made "mincemeat" of his shoulder.

At first, he didn't know the extent of his injuries. In his cramped position, his blood had coagulated. But when he was unpinned from the wreckage and stood up, it came pouring out of his mouth.

He was hustled into an ambulance and rushed to a hospital. As it turned out, he knew one of the medics, Thomas Price, who had been in his class at Palm Beach High School. *En route* to the emergency room, Price took Burt's hand and prayed for him all the way there as he faded in and out of consciousness.

As it turned out, Lynn Fort, the high school doctor at Palm Beach High, was on duty there at the time. He quickly examined Burt and turned to the staff. "Get him into the operating room at once. He's dying."

Burt passed out, and he seemed to be drifting into pink clouds, as he'd remember it later. He regained consciousness at one point during the seven and a half-hour operation, and he heard a nurse say, "He's going fast."

Dr. Fort straddled him at one point and administered CPR, which no doubt saved his life.

When he woke up many hours later, Big Burt and Fern were at his bedside. Dr. Fort had informed them earlier that there was a chance that their son might spend the rest of his life in a wheelchair.

The nurse told him that he had been given nearly sixty stitches. "Think of it as a big zipper," she said.

At home recovering on January 1, 1956, Burt lay in bed and wondered, "What in hell am I going to do with the rest of my life? My football days are over!"

CHAPTER TWO

BURT SHACKS UP WITH
MARILYN MONROE,
GETS INVITED TO A POKER NIGHT WITH
ELVIS PRESLEY,
& OFFERS REFUGE TO **RIP TORN** WHEN HE'S HOMELESS

STAGE DIVAS WITH AGENDAS OF THEIR OWN:
JOANNE WOODWARD & CAROL LAWRENCE
AFTER FALLING IN LOVE TWICE, BURT GETS REJECTED TWICE

HOW TO AUDITION ON BROADWAY, AKA
SEX & THE GREAT WHITE WAY

WILLIAM INGE & TENNESSEE WILLIAMS
HOW TWO OF THE 20TH CENTURY'S MOST INFLUENTIAL PLAYWRIGHTS
TRIED TO SEDUCE AND MANIPULATE BURT BUT EVENTUALLY DUMPED
HIM FOR WARREN BEATTY

BURT's FEUD WITH GORE VIDAL
THEIR VIOLENT ARGUMENT AFTER A DRUNKEN EVENING OF
LITERARY BITCHERY

TEA & SYMPATHY with LINDA DARNELL
PERFORMING ONSTAGE AS A CLOSETED HOMOSEXUAL, BURT
ACCOMPANIES THE DOOMED CELEBRITY ON A SUMMER STOCK TOUR AS
HER BEDMATE & HANDLER

GRETA GARBO
BURT REJECTS A MYSTERIOUS OLDER WOMAN'S AMOROUS ADVANCES.

PALM BEACH STATE
COLLEGE

Burt, as he looked after his migration from FSU to Palm Beach State College. "My life was changed forever."

The coach at FSU, Tom

Nugent, was willing to let Burt keep his football scholarship until he was graduated, in spite of the fact that his body injuries would keep him permanently off the field. Although Nugent offered him a scholarship-saving role as one of his assistants, Burt rejected the offer, telling Nugent, "What would I do? Hand out jockstraps?"

He decided to return to Riviera Beach and enroll at Palm Beach Junior College. *[Known today as Palm Beach State College, it had been founded in 1933 as the first public junior college in the state. Because the college had had a nomadic existence, moving from one location to another, it was nicknamed "The Little Orphan College."]*

"My first day there marked the low point in my life so far," he claimed. "My dreams of football glory had been shattered—in essence, I would have to reinvent myself."

He was the last student to enroll, and many of the classes were already filled. Since there were still openings in art appreciation and English literature courses, he signed up for them.

His most charismatic and gifted teacher, nicknamed "the Pied Piper of English Literature," was Watson B. Duncan III. "He became my mentor and changed the direction of my life forever," Burt said.

Until that point in his life, Burt had never read a work of fiction. If called upon in high school to submit a book report, he read the book's jacket, nominally altered whatever it said, and submitted it as his own, original work.

In this new environment, each student was assigned a different book to review. Burt drew J.D. Salinger's *Catcher in the Rye*. Published in 1951 and later to become a world-wide sensation and major bestseller that influenced an entire generation of postwar teenagers and twenty-somethings, its theme revolved around angst, alienation, and isolation.

Burt identified with the novel's protagonist, Holden Caulfield, a symbol of teenage rebellion, and he related to the colloquial speech patterns of that era—"flit" for a homosexual, "snowing" for sweet-talking, and "necking" for kissing.

The novel would inspire millions, including one fan, George H.W. Bush. On the downside, at least in the immediate aftermath of its release, it became the most censored book in high schools and libraries.

"After *Catcher*, I became an avid reader of books for the rest of my life, starting out with two long tomes, *Forever Amber* and *Gone With the Wind*," Burt said. Years later, when I became an acrtor, I thought I'd make a tremendous Rhett Butler in a remake of *Gone With the Wind*."

"In class, Duncan was mesmerizing," Burt said. "When he read *Othello*, he became the character. When he read *Hamlet*, he was Hamlet, giving a better performance than Laurence Olivier. Of course, at that time, I had never seen Olivier."

The class also concentrated on the works of Shakespeare, Byron, Keats, Chaucer, Shelley, Milton, and Elizabeth Barrett Browning.

When summer came, Duncan became an actor, appearing annually in plays at the Shakespeare Festival in Stratford, Ontario.

For his students' stage production that year, Duncan announced that the school's Theater Club would stage a performance of *Outward Bound*. Then he walked over to Burt's desk: "I want you to show up for rehearsals at three this afternoon in the auditorium."

"I'm not an actor," Burt protested.

"But you've got fire in your belly—that's what is needed. Show up!"

At first reluctant to follow the mandate, Burt finally gave in, saying, "What the hell." He didn't expect to be cast.

At the rehearsal, he was given only one line to speak from the play's character of Tom Prior. After he said only three words, Duncan jumped up from his chair. "The part is yours! Here's your chance to show your classmate that you're not some dumb jock."

Burt was amazed to discover that his role as the downtrodden alcoholic was the lead. He'd never seen a play before, but he was an avid movie fan. He'd already seen the film adaptation of *Outward Bound*. Entitled *Between Two Worlds* (1944), it had starred John Garfield, Paul Henreid, Sydney Greenstreet, and Eleanor Parker. In his environment with this new professor, Burt had been assigned the role portrayed onscreen by Garfield.

[The original Broadway version of Outward Bound, *first performed in 1923 and written by Sutton Vane, had starred Alfred Lunt and Leslie Howard.]*

A combination of fantasy and drama, its plot focuses on seven passengers aboard an ocean liner who did not know where they were—or where they were going. It seems they are dead but don't know it. Actually, they have arrived at Judgment Day, where it will be determined if they're headed for Heaven or Hell.

"During rehearsals, I began to hang out with a whole new group of kids," Burt said. "These wannabe actors detested football jocks and made fun of them. The boys wanted to be James Dean, the girls Carroll Baker."

"Hanging out with this group, I found I had a talent to amuse. Since

QUESTION:
WHAT WAS THE STAGE PRODUCTION THAT "BIT" BURT REYNOLDS WITH THE ACTING BUG?

It was a metaphysical/spiritual drama about a ship carrying passengers between the world of the living and the afterlife.

Burt played the male lead--the part made famous in various movie adaptations by both Leslie Howard and John Garfield.

And from that unlikely beginning on a junior college stage, he went on to New York.

everybody said I looked like Marlon Brando, I began to imitate him, giving a mocking interpretation. I was even better as Gabby Hayes."

"Duncan supported me and believed in me as no one had ever before," Burt continued. "Other than my own father, I came to love this man."

Burt later interpreted the opening night of *Outward Bound* as "one of the great thrills of my life. At curtain call, I basked in the adulation, the applause, the attention. I was a male peacock, strutting and showing off my feathers. Duncan was right. I could act...and how. Opening night marked the emergence of a new man. Burt Reynolds, young male actor."

At the end of the school term, Burt won the 1956 Florida State Drama Award, which was a first prize scholarship to Hyde Park Playhouse in New York State.

Doc Ringer, the owner of Ringer's Cement Company, gave him $5,000 in damages. He was the owner of the truck that Burt had crashed into, although it had been stolen at the time of his accident. "In spite of that, he was very generous to me. With all that money," Burt said. "I bought a white Dodge. I was heading for New York."

Eventually, he told his parents about his plan. Whereas Fern promised to pray for him, Big Burt told him, "You're out of your mind. What a silly little dope you are. Don't you know all actors are fags? The other night I arrested two guys in the men's toilet in the park. They were having sex with each other. Is that the kind of son I've raised? A queer?"

Despite his parents' objections, Burt headed north in his new Dodge, vowing not to crash it. He didn't tell Duncan, but he didn't really plan to devote his life to being an actor. He was thinking he might become a parole officer. Big Burt would approve of that profession.

He viewed the upcoming summer "as a lark, a time to have fun and meet girls, perhaps fall in love."

***

Burt arrived at the Hyde Park Playhouse in a town famously associated with Franklin and Eleanor Roosevelt. Summer stock productions would be presented here for three decades, bringing cultural life to residents of the Hudson Valley. The tradition lasted until 1987, when the theater—a converted barn—burned down.

Once, the land and building had been part of the Vanderbilt Farm, a site with 50,000 chickens, 21 Belgian workhorses, and other animals, too. Its hay barn had been converted into a theater that won praise from its most famous visitor, Eleanor Roosevelt herself. "I cannot think of a more delightful setting than these old Vanderbilt barns, with a clock tower in the middle of the square."

The first play presented here had been *Gigi* in 1954, followed by George Bernard Shaw's *Pygmalion, The Caine Mutiny,* and Oscar Wilde's *The Importance of Being Ernest.*

"Buddy Reynolds" (aka Burt) was the second "Buddy" listed in the playhouse's roster of stars who eventually appeared here. "Buddy Rogers," the second husband of silent screen star Mary Pickford, had once performed here. A director claimed that "Miss Pickford kept calling from Hollywood to make sure none of the female members of the cast got too close to her Buddy boy."

Other stars who appeared at the Hyde Park Playhouse included Olivia de Havilland and her sister, Joan Fontaine, Joanne Woodward, Duke Ellington, George Jessel, Van Johnson, *I Love Lucy's* Vivian Vance, Ann Sothern, Eleanor Parker, Christopher Reeve, and Jason Robards.

Burt's first role there was in the comedy, *My Three Angels,* which had opened on Broadway in 1953. The play starred character actor Walter Slezak and was directed by José Ferrer. In a minor role, Darren McGavin was cast. The same actor would later co-star with Burt in the TV series, *Riverboat.*

Based on a French play, *My Three Angels* was set in 1900 in French Guiana and depicted the interaction among three prisoners and the local population of French-speaking colonists. *[A movie had been based on this play*

To the deep regret of culture hounds throughout New York State, a suspicious fire destroyed the Hyde Park Playhouse in 1987. Among those who mourned was Burt Reynolds.

and released as We're No Angels (1955)]

Although the roles assigned to Burt were small at first, often no more than walk-ons, he got to meet a lot of actors, some of them former stars, and all of them beyond their "expiration dates."

In 1950, Celeste Holm, star of *Gentleman's Agreement* (1947) and *All About Eve* (1950), had opened on Broadway in *Affairs of State.* During Burt's time here, she migrated to the Hyde Park Playhouse to reprise her stage role.

Holm was at home on the stage, having created a sensation as Ado Annie in Rodgers and Hammerstein's ground-breaking *Oklahoma! (1943)* on Broadway.

"She was a clever woman and a warm and darling personality, unlike many of the dragons I would encounter in my future," Burt said.

A native of North Carolina, Shepperd Sturdwick had been in the original Broadway cast of that landmark musical, and he, too, had journeyed to Hyde Park to repeat his role. He was a familiar face to movie-going Burt, who had seen him in such films as *Joan of Arc* (1948) with Ingrid Bergman and in *All the King's Men* (1949) with Broderick Crawford.

Burt's next role was also small. *Anniversary Waltz* was a comedy, set within a Manhattan apartment, that had opened on Broadway at the Broadhurst Theatre in 1954. Its title derived from a 1941 Decca recording by Bing Crosby.

Its star was the Bronx-born actress, Sylvia Sidney, who had risen to fame in Hollywood in the 1930s in a series of motion pictures that had starred Gary Cooper, Spencer Tracy, Henry Fonda, Fredric March, and Cary Grant. In 1949, she'd been labeled "box office poison." At this point in her career, she was accepting whatever roles she could get.

"Sylvia was born in 1910 and might have been one of those older dames I seduced as a kid," Burt said. "But nothing happened. I don't think she even knew I existed."

A minor play, *The Spa*, featured another walk-on by Burt. Local audiences flocked to see it because it starred two in-the-news celebrities, Gloria Vanderbilt and Turhan Bey.

Who was Celeste Holm? As an established star who happened to interact with then-neophyte Burt Reynolds onstage at the Hyde Park Theater, she was kind to him, nurturing him through his inaugural jitters.

Holm (left) is depicted above with Bette Davis in a famous clad-in-mink scene from *All About Eve* (1950).

She, of course, was not only an actress, but in time, an author, fashion designer, heiress, and socialite. *[Miss Vanderbilt had been a media sensation ever since the 1930s when she became the centerpiece of the most famous custody battle in American history.]*

Wisdom and the ravages of time: Sylvia Sydney, one of Burt's acting colleagues at the Hyde Park Playhouse, in the 1930s (left) and in 1988.

Known as "The Turkish Valentino," or "Turkish Delight," Turhan Bey sustained a film career that lasted from 1941 to 1953. In the 1940s, he appeared on the screen many times as an exotic foreigner. *[He had once been foolishly cast as a Chinaman opposite Katharine Hepburn in* Dragon Seed *(1944).]* Off screen, he became known for his seduction of Hollywood goddesses who included Lana Turner.

"Both of these stars were beyond my lowly status in the theater," Burt said, "so I was royally ignored in their august presence."

When Burt met Miss Vanderbilt, she had already divorced her second husband, the composer, Leopold Stokowski, and had married director Sidney Lumet.

She was known for a string of affairs with men who included Marlon Brando, Frank Sinatra, and—among others—Howard Hughes. After her divorce from Stokowski in 1955, she married author Wyatt Emory Cooper in 1963, and they had two sons, Carter Cooper and Anderson Cooper, who eventually evolved into the CNN News anchor. In 1988, when he was 23, Carter plunged to his death by jumping out the 14th-floor window of the family's apartment in Manhattan.

***

Bus Stop, a hit play by William Inge, had opened on Broadway in 1955 and had run for 478 performances. It had starred Kim Stanley and Albert Salmi, with Harold

Gloria Vanderbilt in the early 1940s with her then-husband, Leopold Stokowski, longtime Music Director of the Philadelphia Orchestra.

Clurman directing.

It was one of the first Broadway plays Burt ever saw. He bought a standing room ticket and was immediately captivated by the role of the dumb cowboy, Bo Decker, a brash, naïve young stud with boorish manners. Bo was in obsessive pursuit of Cherie, a "hill country" nightclub singer forced to work cheap dives.

The play unfolds in the bus station of a rural Kansas town during a snowstorm in which passengers are stranded.

Burt was delighted when he heard that the Hyde Park Playhouse planned to mount its own production of *Bus Stop*, and that he'd be cast in it alongside Jocelyn Brando, Marlon's older sister. She would play one of the lead female roles: Grace Hoyland, the fortyish owner of a cheap little diner who is still pretty but fading in a hard-bitten way. Her part called for her to "have a passionate side to her nature, and to love both a good fight and the attention of a good man."

Jocelyn's best-known role had been in the movies, when she'd starred as Glenn Ford's doomed wife in the *film noir,* The Big Heat (1953), directed by Fritz Lang.

She was seventeen years older than Burt, but he avidly pursued her, and she was not immune to his boyish charm. Of course, the moment he was introduced to her, she delivered the line he'd come to expect—"You look so much like Marlon. Did anybody ever point that out to you?"

"Never!" he lied.

After three nights, she relinquished herself to his seductive powers. "She was such a nice lady, but I was rather rough on her in bed," he later confessed to William Inge. "I wasn't just screwing her but getting back at Marlon for no fault of his own. I suffered from losing roles because I looked so much like her brother—and that made me hate him. It would take Dr. Freud to explain it, but I was pounding Jocelyn when I wanted to

Jocelyn Brando with her brother, Marlon. Burt seduced the sister but hated the brother because his looks were often compared to the famous actor's. "I lost many a job because of that comparison," Burt lamented.

be pounding my fists into Marlon."

Inge traveled north from Manhattan to Hyde Park to see this new production of his play. He came backstage after the show, inviting Burt to join him for drinks and dinner. Burt eagerly accepted, not knowing if his part in the play's upcoming film adaptation had been cast yet. *Variety* had previously reported that Marilyn Monroe had signed to play Cherie on the screen.

Burt hoped to charm Inge into using his influence to get the star-making role for him. When they first met, the playwright was at the peak of his success on Broadway, not only because of *Bus Stop,* but also with *Come Back, Little Sheba* and *Picnic.*

"That night I really turned on my macho charm," Burt said. "Maybe too much of it. The end result was that Inge fell in love with me, or at least had the hots for me. He stayed in Hyde Park for three more days, following me around like a puppy dog with his tongue hanging out."

"Thank god he was shy and didn't put the make on me," Burt said. "I was actually 'courting' him, but avoiding the bedroom if that made sense."

When Inge left, he made Burt promise that he'd come to visit him in Manhattan. "He even promised to write a play just for me."

Burt later admitted that as a young actor, he seriously considered the casting couch, whose pain, embarrassments, and rewards were available to both wannabe actresses and their male counterparts, too. Burt had been told that Rock Hudson had become a superstar thanks to some degree on his auditions on casting couches, as had Marilyn Monroe.

Burt didn't think of himself as a male whore and kept reminding himself that it might not be that difficult. "Maybe all I'd have to do is lie on the sofa, perhaps looking at the centerfold of *Playboy* while Inge did his thing. We'd see. It was not something I was looking forward to, let me tell you."

***

Plain and Fancy had been a musical hit when it opened for the first time on Broadway in 1954. One of the first depictions of the Amish people in American pop culture, it was a rousing, robust, and charming musical that included re-enactments of an old-fashioned "Pennsylvania Dutch" wedding and a barn

William Inge, then one of Broadway's leading playwrights, was falling in love with young Burt.

48

dance

Its lead actress was a blonde about thirty-five years old. Every night her friend, a younger blonde who looked like Jayne Mansfield, showed up, waiting in the wing, to dispense praise, support, and affirmation.

"I developed a crush on the Mansfield clone, feeling I had to have her. I invited her to dinner, and she accepted, but only if the show's star could come along too."

"The more the merrier," he said, not meaning it, although his statement turned out to be true.

Throughout the duration of the play, he frequently hung out with them. He was eventually invited back to their hotel room for a three-way. Both women had sex with him and sex with each other. He found it erotic, watching them make love to each other, then inviting him to join them.

One night, after his return to his room, his roommate, Don Charles, asked, "What is it like to make love to two dykes?"

"What in hell do you mean?" I've never heard a woman called a dyke."

"Oh God, you naïve kid. A dyke is a lesbian."

"That's news to me."

"Don't be embarrassed," Charles said. "A lot of men get off watching lesbians make love. Why don't you let me join in some night before the show ends? While the girls are making love, I'll let them watch you fuck me. A deal?"

"No deal," Burt said. "Not only did I learn what the word dyke means, I also found out that my roommate likes to get plowed."

"That's show business, darling."

"At the end of the run of the play, those two hot-to-trot blondes moved on," Burt said. "I thought about what I found seductive in a woman, and of my attraction for older women. Even Ben Franklin praised the glory of seducing older females. I was also equally attracted to young things. I found older women easier to seduce. You have to put up a fight with young things to get their panties off."

Land of The Plain and Fancy

While appearing on stage in *Plain and Fancy*, Burt was learning what actors do when the curtain falls.

"I enjoyed a romp with two beautiful lesbians and learned that my roommate was gay."

There was a footnote to the season's

final performance of *Plain and Fancy*. It involved Alexis Smith and her actor husband, Craig Stevens, who showed up as members of the audience. The news backstage was that they were planning to take *Plain and Fancy* on a national tour, and they were scouting to see if any of the Hyde Park cast might be suitable as a member of the troupe they were forming for a coast-to-coast tour scheduled for the summer of 1955.

After the curtain descended on the Hyde Park production for the last time, Smith and Stevens came backstage and invited Burt to dinner.

Alexis Smith with Craig Stevens. Burt opted not to become their toy boy on a national tour.

He recalled it as "a most flirtatious evening, with Craig flirting with me as much as Alexis. Unfortunately, I'd already been booked into another show and had to turn them down. Even so, those two lovebirds invited me back to their hotel for a hot session. I was mildly intrigued but rejected their offer."

"Years later, I learned the dope on that pair. Alexis could get Craig to fuck her only if he were being fucked by a man at the same time. Ah, show business...Ain't it wonderful?"

***

One bright, sunny afternoon during the run of *Plain and Fancy,* Burt met another performer who would play a major role in getting him launched as an actor. He was on his way out of the theater barn when he spotted her in the parking lot getting out of her car.

Instantly intrigued, he approached her. "Hi, I'm Buddy Reynolds."

"Hi, yourself," she said. "I'm Joanne Woodward. I saw you performing last night, and you were just great—but your role could have been bigger."

"A girl after my own heart," he answered.

"Your voice sounds like you're from the South," she said. "I'm a Southerner, too, from Georgia."

"Georgia, that's my neighbor to the north," he said. "I'm from Florida, a little fishing village to the north of ritzy Palm Beach."

"I'm working hard to get rid of my Southern drawl," she said. "One director in New York told me I sound like I'm spittin' cotton having finished a lunch of chittlin' bread and collards."

"You sound perfect to me, a dream walking," he said.

"If only I could convince directors of that. I'm an actress, named after Joan Crawford but spelled J-O-A-N-N-E."

"Let's go have a cup of coffee. My treat," he said, taking her arm. "I suspect this is going to be the beginning of a beautiful friendship."

"You stole that line from the closing reel of *Casablanca*," she said. "That's what Bogie said to Claude Rains after sending Ingrid Bergman off in that plane."

"You nailed me." He looked at her provocatively. "Perhaps I'll nail you just to retaliate."

"Dream on, *honey chile*," she said. "Let's have that cup of coffee and see how it goes. I have to warn you. You came into my life a little too late. You see. I already have a boyfriend. He's away right now on a job."

"You mean, you *had* a boyfriend," Burt answered. "After we've had our second cup of coffee, we'll talk about how to get rid of the loser."

Those two cups of coffee lasted an hour and a half as they got to know each other. It turned out that she was from Thomasville, a once-thriving winter resort in southern Georgia before better transportation opened up the glories of Florida to winter visitors.

She told him amusing stories about her life. When she was nine years old, she was part of the mob who descended on Atlanta in 1939 for the premiere of *Gone With the Wind*. Its star, Vivien Leigh, cast as Scarlett O'Hara, arrived in a limousine with her lover, Laurence Olivier.

"I opened the rear door and jumped right into Olivier's lap," she said. "I sure startled him. I told him, 'I'm gonna be an actress, not just any actress but a great one.'"

"Okay," he said. "I'm your director, com-manding you to get the hell out of my car... and fast! I'll critique your performance." After she'd landed outside on her feet, he slammed the door in her face, ordering the driver to move on.

Both Burt and Woodward knew William Inge. Whereas Burt had just met him, Woodward had been the understudy to both of the leading ladies, Kim Stanley and Janice Rule, at the time of *Picnic's* 1953 opening on Broadway

She failed to mention that there was another young actor in that drama, Paul New-

Joanne Woodward with Paul Newman, a publicity photo for *The Long, Hot Summer.*

51

man, who had become her boyfriend despite his status at the time as a married man.

There arose a sour note in their chat when she said, "I don't know if anyone has ever told you this, but you have an amazing resemblance to Marlon Brando."

"Never heard that one before," he answered. "But there's a difference: I'm a better actor than Brando. Inge told me I was."

"Oh, that Bill," she said. "He just wants to get into your pants."

As they talked, he became more and more attracted to her graceful charm, pixie face, and inquisitive green eyes. "I felt I was falling in love with her," he later recalled.

She invited him to drive over with her that night from Hyde Park to the nearby home of a friend of hers.

He eagerly accepted the invitation, although their visit evolved into a violent and very upsetting disaster.

***

With Joanne Woodward in the passenger seat, Burt drove up in front of a dignified and imposing mansion known as Edgewater, in the village of Barrytown, in Dutchess County, 104 miles north of Manhattan. Its front was graced with manicured gardens and locust trees.

[Built about 1824 with a monumental colonnade of six Doric columns, and looking out across a lawn to the Hudson River, it was described by historians as an example of "the combined dignity and subtle grace that marked the houses of the Federal Era."]

"This is the home of Gore Vidal, the writer. Perhaps you've heard of him."

"Can't say that I have," Burt answered. "I've only started to read books."

At the door, they were welcomed by Harold Austen, who Burt gathered was Vidal's lover or companion, perhaps both. He was strangely dressed, wearing a fringed cowboy jacket like the one Buffalo Bill wore in the 1950 movie, *Annie Get Your Gun.*

Burt followed Austen and Woodward into the living room, where a drunken Vidal did not

Gore Vidal's historic estate, Edgewater. Burt faced toxic venom from the author and owner, and a sexual pass from his lover/companion.

get up. Woodward went over and kissed him.

"This is Buddy Reynolds," she said, as Burt extended his hand, which Vidal failed to shake. "Don't you think he looks like Marlon Brando, whom you know?"

"Another Brando clone," Vidal said. "Hollywood must be overpopulated by a horde of Brando clones or else James Dean wannabes."

"Thanks for the plug," Burt said sarcastically.

In contrast, Austen was most attentive, hovering over Burt. "Don't listen to Gore," he said. "With your good looks and male flash, I think you'll become the biggest box office star in Hollywood."

"Cut the shit, Howard," Vidal said. "Why encourage mediocrity?"

"Don't be cruel, darling," Woodward said. "After all, you told Paul (Newman) that he'd go far."

"Paul is gorgeous," Vidal said. "He can make it just on those beautiful blue eyes of his. I wanted him for myself until you moved in on him. Don't get me wrong. You know I love you, but I'm jealous of how you stole him from me."

"I don't understand," Burt said. "You've got Howard here. He looks like a fine young man to me. What would you need with Joanne's boyfriend?"

"I don't want to get confessional with a stranger, but Howard and I have a mutual agreement. We're free to indulge our tastes in outside meat."

"I've already staked out Buddy for the night," Austen said, possessively.

Burt looked surprised. Did he hear right? Was Woodward setting him up for something?

The rest of the evening went downhill from there. Whenever Burt tried to be witty or say something he thought was clever, Vidal attacked with his razor-sharp tongue, spewing venom.

"What did you think of *The City and the Pillar?*" Vidal asked.

"That was the novel Gore wrote," Woodward said. "Its homosexual theme stirred up a lot of controversy."

"Sorry, but I've never heard of it."

Gore Vidal, circa 1945, with his competitors and "frenemies," Truman Capote (center) and Tennessee Williams (right.)

"Too bad," Vidal said. "Did you read *Other Voices, Other Rooms* by that lisping faggot, Truman Capote?"

"Never heard of him either," Burt said. "I do know William Inge. In fact, when I hook up with him again in New York, I'm gonna ask him to write a Broadway play in which I can star."

"So, you're Bill's latest conquest," Vidal said. "He promises dozens of handsome young men he'll write a star vehicle for them. Don't count on it. Tennessee Williams makes the same promises to young men, too."

"I know of him," Burt said. "I saw *A Streetcar Named Desire*, mainly because everybody says I look like Brando."

"At least you're not totally illiterate," Vidal said. If you ever meet Tenn, he'll probably promise to write a play for you, too. Bill and Tenn are attracted to guys who look like you, sorta handsome but rough, and more than a little dumb. In the theater, guys like you will have to get used to pulling off your shorts."

"Not me!" Burt protested. "I want to get ahead with my talent."

"Don't be so god damn sanctimonious," Vidal said. "It makes me sick. Howard, get me another Scotch. You should read more, Buddy boy. Here at Edgewater, I've been reading Apuleius and Petronius. Reading them is like

Casting directors often rejected, but sometimes accepted, Burt for roles because of his resemblance to the better-known (and older) Marlon Brando.

In the trio of photos above, Marlon is in the middle, Burt at the top and bottom. What do you think?

54

turning on a lightbulb in my head. Sometimes, late at night, I plow through Meredith." *[George Meredith (1828-1909) was an English novelist and poet of the Victorian era. He was nominated for the Nobel Prize in Literature seven times.]*

"I even read the novels of Sir Walter Scott," Vidal continued. "Actually, I'm thinking of writing my own version of *Count Robert of Paris*. For a special treat, I turn to the novels of Thomas Love Peacock. If only I'd been named Gore Love Peacock, I'd have been an overnight literary sensation."

Norman Mailer in 1948. Was he really Gore Vidal's temporary *pissoir*?

Then he turned to confront Burt. "What are you reading now?"

"*The Naked and the Dead* by Norman Mailer. It's a great World War II drama. Have you heard of it?"

"Heard of it? Are you kidding?" Vidal said. "Norman and I have this ongoing literary feud. A few weeks ago, I took the drunken ass to this party in Manhattan. He stumbled in, gave a speech, and then passed out on the floor. I had had a lot to drink that night and had to take a piss. He was the ideal toilet for me. I pissed on him. Otherwise, Norman and I are great friends."

As the evening sunk lower, and as Vidal drank more, he turned again on Burt, challenging him. "What makes you think you can make it as an actor? There are construction workers prettier than you."

Fearing he could no longer hold his temper, Burt got up and headed to the kitchen to get more ice, hoping that would cool him down. Austen followed him.

As Burt stood at the kitchen sink removing ice cubes, Austen came up behind him and enclosed him in his arms. "I think I've fallen in love with you. You admired by cowboy jacket. It'll be yours if you come upstairs to my bedroom."

Burt later wrote in a memoir, "I picked up Howard and airmailed him into the living room where he landed at Vidal's feet."

Back in the room, he grabbed Woodward's arm. "C'mon, babe, let's get the hell out of here."

She blew kisses at Vidal as they headed out the door.

En route back to Hyde Park, he asked her, "Did I make a good impression?"

"*Honey chile*, Gore and Howard will never forget Buddy Reynolds."

***

Although Joanne Woodward was planning to appear in a play at Hyde Park, she was still negotiating the terms of her employment there. During that period, she continued to see Burt, despite the social fiasco at Edgewater. He had come to believe that she had a crush on him. He later wrote, "I thought I could blow her boyfriend out of the tub."

That fantasy ended when Burt was introduced to Paul Newman, who had come up from New York City for the weekend.

"When I met this good-looking guy with the bluest eyes ever invented, I knew I would never get Joanne. The competition was too great. Not only that, but he was one of the nicest guys I'd ever met. The two of them disappeared after I met him. By Monday morning, Paul was gone, and I realized that the best I could do with Joanne was to be her friend."

When he saw her later that day, she asked, "What did you think of Paul?"

"I think I'm in love," he told her. "If you ever decide to dump him, I'm next in line."

"I hope you're joking," she said.

Woodward thought Burt needed an agent, and she used her influence to get Maynard Morris, a powerhouse at MCA, to sign and represent him. In time, Morris would play a crucial role in the careers of such stars as Gregory Peck, Charlton Heston, singer Robert Goulet, and Paul Newman himself.

Maynard later met with director Wynn Handman and somehow managed to get Burt cast in *Tea and Sympathy*, even though the role had already been offered to Mark Rydell, at that time a star of soap operas.

[Mark Rydell survived the rejection and went on to become a director in Hollywood, turning out such Oscar-nominated hits as Cinderella Liberty *(1973) with James Caan, and* On Golden Pond *(1983) with Jane and Henry Fonda co-starring with Katharine Hepburn.*

"I would have been ideal cast as the sailor in Cinderella Liberty," *Burt said. "Maybe Rydell was still pissed off at me."]*

***

Tea and Sympathy had first opened on Broadway in 1953 in a production directed by Elia Kazan. It had co-starred Deborah Kerr and John Kerr (no relation). A student at a New England preparatory school is accused of being effeminate and is targeted for persecution after sunbathing with a professor.

Laura, the star of the play, is married to a cold, hyper-masculine, and emotionally distant instructor at the prep school. She opposes the shaming of the boy.

Burt had not seen the original stars on Broadway but attended a later production with a cast that included Joan Fontaine and Anthony Perkins.

Later, *Tea and Sympathy* was revived at the Neighborhood Playhouse in Manhattan. It had long been associated with acting coach Sanford Meisner, who was inspired by the techniques of Stanislavsky as an alternative to Method acting being taught by Lee Strasberg at the Actors Studio.

Alumni of the Playhouse included Kim Basinger, Robert Duval, Betty Garrett, Farley Granger, Tammy Grimes, Diane Keaton, Steve McQueen, Gloria Vanderbilt, and Grace Kelly.

Burt learned that the fading movie queen of the 1940s, Linda Darnell, was taking over the role of Laura that had originated with (and been forever defined by) Deborah Kerr.

Burt had hoped that he'd be assigned the male lead that had already starred John Kerr and later, Tony Perkins. Instead, he was assigned the role of Al, a macho, dim-witted jock who –with good but misguided intentions—teaches the gay teenager how to talk, walk, and act more masculine.

His scenes involved very little interaction onstage with Darnell, and she had little to do with him, other than treating him politely.

[After the box office failure of Forever Amber *(1947), a "bodice-ripper" based on a best-selling romance novel by Kathleen Winsor, Darnell's star was setting. Increasingly depressed, and sinking into alcoholism, this "Yellow Rose" of Dallas, Texas, was just coming down from a divorce from her second husband and had not yet married her third.]*

For his performance in The Neighborhood Playhouse version of *Tea and Sympathy*, Burt got his first review in *The New York Times*. "Buddy Reynolds looks like Marlon Brando without the fishmonger's gestures or mumbling. He steals scenes, he gets the laughs. We see a job on the horizon."

During the play's run on Off-Broadway, Darnell had often showed up at least half drunk, but managed to go on anyway.

The tabloids had described her many lovers in the 1940s, including

Kirk Douglas, Howard Hughes, Milton Berle, Darryl F. Zanuck, Joseph Mankiewicz, and a chicken farmer, Rudolph Sieber, otherwise known as "Mr. Marlene Dietrich."

When its run at the Neighborhood Playhouse ended, its producers decided to take *Tea and Sympathy* on the road, touring across the country in key cities. This time, Burt was offered the male lead (the role that John Kerr had played on Broadway) with the understanding that Darnell had agreed to continue in the role of Laura. He'd have key scenes with her, including a seduction episode in which she delivers the drama's most famous line: "Years from now, when you talk about this…and I know you will…please be kind."

On the road, Burt found that Darnell had a weak, insecure, and vulnerable side to her, but, like a Mrs. Jekyll and Dr. Hyde, she could turn violent at times, throwing objects, cursing, and denouncing everybody around her.

It was when she displayed her softer side that she needed him at her side, sharing her fears. "The theater is a whole new world for me," she confessed, "and it terrifies me. Laura is a difficult part, and I'm so afraid and so nervous I have to have a drink or two before going on."

"Linda felt at this point in her career that the stage offered more opportunities for her than Hollywood where Fox had dropped her," Burt said. "She was deeply troubled. On top of everything else, the IRS

NEIGHBORHOOD PLAYHOUSE
SCHOOL OF THE THEATRE

In anticipation of the Neighborhood Playhouse's stage revival of the film classic, *Tea and Sympathy*, its publicity department made ample use of the screen image of its star, Linda Darnell, whose options for playing the "big leagues" by then had faded.

The portrait that appears below was snapped at around the time she was hired for *Tea and Sympathy*. She portrayed the empathetic wife of the school coach, bolstering the confidence of a high school student. Burt got to be her co-star in the road tour.

The upper photo shows Darnell as she appeared in the morale-building *Yank* magazine, in association with the U.S. Armed Forces, in 1944.

was moving in on her for failure to pay back taxes. Agents were threatening to take what little she had left. It was at those times of her greatest fear that she needed me to make love to her."

On the road with Darnell, Burt recalled "My job was to keep Linda sober enough to go on, to drive the tour bus, to screw her at least once a night—and, oh yes—to play my role."

She praised his love-making, telling him, "I chose you because I hate weak men. I've got more balls than most men do. I've had all the good things any woman could desire, and a lot of the bad things no woman wants."

[Burt was saddened to learn the final chapter of the Linda Darnell saga. Broke, drunk, deeply depressed, and on the verge of homelessness, on April 10, 1965, she was invited to move temporarily into the Glenview, Illinois home of her former secretary.

On her second night in town, as she was deep in an alcohol-sodden sleep on the couch in the second-floor apartment's living room, a fire broke out. But whereas the secretary and her daughter escaped, Darnell was set on fire. With burns that charred 80% of her body, she was transferred to the burn unit of Chicago's Cook County Hospital. She died soon after that.]

***

After returning to Manhattan, following a summer tour of *Tea and Sympathy*, Burt rented a cold-water flat on West 81st Street near the Hayden Planetarium. It was no more than a broom closet, but it was all he could afford. He needed to find a job and soon, as he had less than two hundred dollars in the bank.

"In my tiny little box, I could do almost anything from my bed—shave, cook my meals, even take a piss if I were Forrest Tucker."

[Many readers of Burt's memoirs might not have understood that oblique reference to Forrest Tucker. Burt was commenting on the size of Tucker's penis. That raised a question: How did Burt know the size of Tucker's penis?

ANSWER: Burt had joined a gym to keep his body in shape in case a role called for him to go shirtless, as so many did. At the gym, he had met Tucker. "Forrest seemed to believe that if you've got it, flaunt it," Burt said. "He paraded around the gym bare-assed until everybody got a look. If Forrest hadn't made a living in films and on TV, he could have been a star in porn," Burt said.]

During that low-income period of his life, Burt would try out for any acting job he heard about. Between gigs, he worked at a series of odd jobs. His first was as a dishwasher at Schrafft's, where he was eventually promoted to waiting tables.

Later, in the weeks before Christmas, the Post Office hired extra help, and he got better pay delivering Yuletime packages.

Then, but for only two nights, Burt worked as a bartender at a tavern in Greenwich Village called Julius. He was fired on the second night after the manager accused him of being "too generous in pouring a drink."

He consumed most of his meals at Horn & Hardart's Automat on West 42nd Street. Platters of prepared food would be released from behind a glass door after consumers inserted coins or tokens into a slot. If funds were really low, you could do what out-of-work people did. They took a cup of hot water, poured in some catsup, stirred it up, and, presto: tomato soup. Sliced lemons were available, without charge, for tea drinkers. Presto! Lemonade.

To sharpen his acting skills, Burt signed up for classes with Wynn Handman, who had directed him in *Affairs of State* at the Hyde Park Playhouse. In time, he would praise him as a far better

Two views of Frank Gifford: Top photo: as a football star in 1952 and (lower photo) with his wife, TV talk show host, Kathie Lee Gifford, in 1992.

teacher than the more famous Lee Strasberg at the Actors Studio.

During Burt's first day in class, he met some of his fellow students and gravitated to Frank Gifford, the star of the New York Giants. They had coffee together after class, and Burt shared his tattered dream of becoming a football hero until he "destroyed my body in one foolish move after another."

Gifford would go on to become an Emmy Award-winning sportscaster and the husband of TV host Kathie Lee Gifford.

The next day at class he met Carol Lawrence. "If anybody could help me get over my crush on Joanne Woodward, it was Carol. She was lovely and talented but married to some guy named Cosmo Allegretti. Their marriage would be annulled, and she'd go on to marry singer Robert Goulet."

When she met Burt, she was on the dawn of her greatest success, playing Maria in the Broadway stage version of *West Side Story* (1957).

Burt liked to think he would make a better boyfriend than any of her current ones, including husbands. That would be confirmed when he read her 1990 autobiography, *Carol Lawrence: The Backstage Story*. In it, she accused Goulet of being an alcoholic and abusing their children.

"There was a dark side to Goulet," Burt said. "He and I became friends. I forgave him for taking Carol from me."

Red Buttons was in his acting class, too, and Burt liked him a lot in spite of his tricky name. "Red came up the hard way, taking that curious name when he was an entertaining bellhop at this joint in the Bronx. His hair was red, and he wore shiny buttons on his uniform—hence the name. Better than Aaron Chwatt, I guess. With Robert Alta, he worked the 'Borscht Belt' in the Catskills, which catered to a Jewish clientele."

Carol Lawrence with her husband, Broadway star Robert Goulet.

From Buttons, Burt learned that the well-known director, Joshua Logan, was in town casting roles for his upcoming movie, *Sayonara* (1957), which was already set to star Marlon Brando. Buttons thought he would be ideal for the supporting male lead.

Behind Buttons' back, Burt slipped out and went to where Logan was auditioning actors. Whereas Buttons had already made an appointment for himself the following day, Burt arrived unannounced and uninvited.

Red Buttons in 1965...no longer the comic bellhop.

Logan looked him up and down before asking, "Who in hell are you?"

"Buddy Reynolds," he said. "I'm here to test for *Sayonara.*"

"This is not a film about two brothers," Logan said. "You look just like Marlon's younger brother. Get out!"

Going down in the elevator, Burt shocked the other passengers. "That fucking Marlon Brando. Some day I'm gonna kill that son of a bitch."

[Buttons showed up the next day to audition and got the role. Not only that, but he won both a Golden

Joshua Logan. He rejected Burt because he looked too much like Marlon Brando.

Globe and an Oscar for Best Supporting Actor.]

That brief confrontation with Logan was just the beginning of a series of lost jobs Burt suffered because of his uncanny resemblance to Brando. "I kept hearing about how much I looked like him time and time again," Burt said. "One director told me if he needed Brando, he'd hire the real thing. I wanted to smash his face in."

Of course, it didn't help that Burt walked the streets of Manhattan wearing jeans, a white T-shirt, a leather jacket, and boots, an outfit that Brando had immortalized in the 1954 movie, *The Wild One.*

Many fans, believing they were spotting Brando, stopped Burt on the street and asked for his autograph. He never refused, but in lieu of a standardized autograph, he wrote: "FUCK YOU! LOVE, MARLON"

He continued his classes with Wynn Handman. Every day, students were assigned a premise to improvise, making up their own dialogue. In a typical exercise, Handman asked Burt to enter a room to greet his friends, who were waiting to welcome him back from the Korean War, where the character he portrayed had been blinded in action.

Marlon Brando in *The Wild One* (1954).

Burt was always annoyed by how moviegoers confused him with Marlon Brando.

Marlon accused him of copy-catting his style.

When he came into the room, there was nothing but blackness. Then lights were switched on, as his friends crowded around him, patting him on the back and welcoming him home.

"SURPRISE! SURPRISE!"

For reasons he never figured out, and as part of his spontaneous improvisation, he went ballistic. He started screaming at his classmates, even striking some of them. He ordered them to get out of the room and shoved some of them out the door. "I kicked a few asses," he recalled.

As if suddenly realizing he must have appeared insane, he fled from the classroom and stayed away for two weeks, fearing that "I was coming unglued. The pressure of trying to make it in New York was proving too much."

Two weeks later, he returned to class, feeling ashamed. Handman greeted him warmly. "That was one hell of an improvisation."

The next day, Handman told him that the actor/director John Forsythe was holding auditions to cast a revival of *Mister Roberts* that would be staged at the New York City Center. The play had been a big hit when it opened in 1948 starring Henry Fonda as Lieutenant Roberts. *[Fonda had also starred in the 1955 movie version.]*

Arrangements were made for Burt to be auditioned by Forsythe the following afternoon. Forsythe knew the script well, as he'd played *Mister Roberts* on its road tour, and had filled in for Fonda when he left the production to make a film in Hollywood. Like Burt himself, Forsythe had also waited tables in Manhattan during his struggling early years.

In 1953, Forsythe had starred in the Broadway stage version of *The Teahouse of the August Moon*, but had lost the movie role to Glenn Ford, who had feuded with his co-star, Marlon Brando, during the shoot.

Forsythe and Burt clicked, and the director assigned him, for $85 a week, one of the play's minor roles as a soldier. Three weeks of general rehearsals began almost immediately, even though the production's star, Charlton Heston, was still in Hollywood completing *The Ten Commandments* for Cecil B. DeMille.

About a week later, Burt spotted Heston, who had finally arrived. As Burt later quipped, "He came to Broadway directly after parting the Red Sea."

When Forsythe took Burt over to introduce him to Heston, the younger actor took three steps, tripped, and fell down on his face—"Some impression I made," he said.

"I was both awed and jealous of the man everybody called Chuck," Burt said. "He had

Whereas then-newbie Burt had a supporting role in the stage revival of *Mister Roberts*, the diva and star of the show was the "oblivious to Burt's charm" Charlton Heston.

Heston is depicted above as he appeared in ancient Roman drag in the namesake role of *Ben-Hur* (1959)

a no-nonsense attitude toward work, and took direction well from Forsythe, a major actor himself. This Chuck guy had a sculpted physique, which inspired me to work harder at the gym."

"Even before the play opened, Heston became seriously pissed off," Burt said. "In his lean days, he'd been a nude model, and someone had taken frontal shots of him. Pictures of his dick were being hawked on Times Square. This has happened to so many actors, including Gary Cooper. Maybe that's why he became known as the 'Montana Mule.'"

"I tried to bond with Heston, but failed miserably," Burt said. "I heard that he told Forsythe that he found me 'too cocky.' I, too, have been asked several times to pose for nude photographs, but I turned down the offers."

On the second night of the *Mister Roberts* revival, William Inge showed up and renewed the contact he had made with Burt at Hyde Park. He was most gracious when he came backstage, although "He probably pissed off Chuck when he came up to me first to congratulate me on my performance," Burt said.

After the show, and after their dinner together, Burt feared he'd have to deal with an invitation to come home with the playwright for a session on the casting couch.

That didn't happen. Instead, Inge extended an invitation to a party he was hosting at his apartment on Riverside Drive for the following night. The guest list included other actors appearing in shows on Broadway, so it was clearly understood that it would be a late-night event. As described to Burt by Inge, "I have a special female guest I want you to meet."

After the curtain went down on *Mister Roberts* that Saturday, Burt headed at once to Inge's apartment, where the shindig had already begun. Many other guests began to arrive, some of them celebrities whose faces were familiar to him, others unknown.

Kim Stanley arrived with her boyfriend, Brooks Clift, brother of film star Montgomery Clift. Burt made the rounds, meeting the stage actress Barbara Baxley, the literary agent Audrey Wood (who represented both Inge and Tennessee Williams), and the character actress Mildred Dunnock. Geraldine Page made an appearance, as did Shirley Booth.

Burt was dazzled by all this talent until he spotted a woman who looked about fifty, wearing a yellow blouse, black pants, and sunglasses. She patted the seat beside her on the sofa and motioned for him to sit down. At first, he was reluctant to do so, but there was something compelling about her…

She began to ask about his life and appeared genuinely interested. It seemed that everybody at the party came over and tried to talk to her, but she showed no interest in pursuing a conversation with anybody but Burt.

Her hair was tied back with a lace ribbon, and she spoke with a slight foreign accent, her "whiskey voice" very seductive.

Burt kept looking at her breasts through the translucent silk of her yellow blouse, as it was obvious that she did not wear a brassiere. Noticing his intense concentration on her breasts, she said with a bemused smile, "My eyes are up here."

In the dim light of the party, she was quite luminous.

Years from that night when he talked about meeting her, and he would, he found it hard to describe her—that is, until he read a description of her from the famous photographer, Cecil Beaton: "Her eyes are like those of an eagle's, a pale mauve blue. The skin on her neck and chest is of the finest grain, as shiny as marble. Her long legs are like those of a girl of fifteen, her skin a deep apricot in colour."

As she settled back on the sofa, Burt kept lighting one cigarette after another for her. She had a way of being all consuming, attracting all his attention, as if nobody else in the room existed but the two of them.

She listened sympathetically to his dreams of becoming a star. "With your personal charm and looks, I think you can rise to the top," she said. "Of course, you'll attract a lot of interest from fans who will want to pry into your private life. If you live long enough and continue your career, people one day may even write books about your life. Chances are, these books will be an unflattering portrait. There's a way to handle it, however: You don't have to read the books about yourself, and you can pretend they don't exist. If the books emerge after your death, what does it matter? At that point, you'll be beyond caring."

He described his football days, his dangerous car crashes, his summer tour with Linda Darnell.

"But that's enough about me," he finally said. *[Ironically, that phrase would become the title of his second memoir.]* "What about you?"

With a sigh, she answered, "There is so little to tell…It's been a boring life. I'm often compared to a hummingbird. I might land in your hand and linger for only a moment, and then I flutter away, never to return."

At one point, she reached for his hand: "Darling," she said. "I find this party boring. The only person who interests me is you. Why don't you come home with me? If you're hungry, I can fry you a potato omelette with just a little bit of peanut oil—not too much."

"Perhaps after a peaceful night, we'll fly to Venice tomorrow," she said. "The tourists have mainly gone now. I can't abide Venice when it's overrun with sightseers."

"No, thanks," he said. "I'd better go home and get some rest. Busy day tomorrow."

"Too bad," she said. "It could have been an enchanting evening like one of those nights I used to spend with John Gilbert."

He kissed her hand and left after thanking Inge for the invitation.

Walking back to his dreary hotel, he wondered who this John Gilbert was.

The next morning at around 9AM, his phone rang. It was Inge. "What's the matter with you, Burt? You made the history books last night. You're the only man who ever turned down Greta Garbo."

"Oh, my God," he said.

He could think of nothing for the rest of the day, but he felt he should be forgiven for not recognizing Garbo. He'd heard of her, but she'd faded from the screen when he was only three or four years old. In Riviera Beach, they did not hold Garbo movie revivals.

Greta Garbo, from around the time of her flirtatious encounter with Burt.

In time, at the New Yorker Theatre in Manhattan and at a movie house in downtown Los Angeles, he would see *Grand Hotel* and *Mata Hari* (both released in 1932) and *Camille* (1937). He'd even learned who John Gilbert was. *[One of the greatest on-screen lovers in the history of silent pictures, Gilbert had fallen madly in love with the elusive Garbo.]*

"Who knows?" Burt later asked. "If I'd gone home with Garbo, become her lover, gone to Venice with her…would that have become my only claim to fame?"

***

"Back in the 1950s, many of us were trying to break into the theater. A songwriter might say we were fighting for love and glory," Burt said. Then he cited as fellow travelers along the road to stardom "that handsome devil," George Peppard; "that little devil," Steve McQueen; "Mr. Blue Eyes," Paul Newman; and "Blondie," Robert Redford.

"The one guy who had all of us beat had the oddball name of Rip Torn," Burt claimed. "He was the best actor in New York,"

One afternoon, Burt spotted Torn sitting in the corner of a coffeeship in Manhattan's Theater District. As Burt walked by his table, Rip said, "C'mon and join me. You're the only guy in here who's not wearing a black turtleneck, and I need someone to talk to."

[Burt positioned their inaugural meeting at Child's, a diner/coffeeshop on West 46th Street. In the mid-1950s, dozens of actors, mostly those who were tired after hours of looking for a gig, used to hang out at there. Shelley Winters might show up with the latest "boy stud" she'd snared, perhaps Christopher Jones, who

would later marry actress Susan Strasberg. "Chris knew one way to attract attention," Burt said. "He wore the tightest pair of pants in Manhattan, so tight you could tell he wasn't circumcised."]

From that day forth, the two men bonded and became the best of friends. Rip had been kicked out of his room for failure to pay back rent, and Burt invited him to move in with him, "If you don't mind being a bit cramped."

Two views of actor Rip Torn

When he was young (left photo) and, as a struggling actor, temporarily homeless, Burt took him in.

[At that point, Burt was living in Gorpy Towers, a building on West 44th Street that gave him a little more space. "Rip moved in and had to share my small bed," Burt said. "He didn't even ask if I were gay."]

Soon, the two actors were playing basketball at the YMCA, or trying to lose their Southern accents under the tutelage of vocal coach Al Malver.

Within a few days, each man learned where the other originated before migrating to New York. In Texas, Rip's father, "Tiger" Torn, promoted, as part of an ongoing advertising campaign, the consumption of black-eyed peas. *[They had evolved into traditional New Year's Day staple because of their reputation for bringing good luck.]* Torn's mother, Thelma, was the aunt of actress Sissy Spacek.

Rip also had a pregnant wife, 18-year-old Ann Wedgeworth, and he was trying to earn enough money to send for her.

One afternoon, Rip asked Burt if he would be his counterpart in a reading scheduled the following day at the Actors Studio in front of Elia Kazan and Lee Strasberg. Burt agreed and the two men studied together, practicing a passage from Tennessee Williams' play *Camino Real*.

The following day, with Rip beside him, Burt entered the studio, claiming, "I was so nervous I felt I was sitting on firecrackers. Despite an awkward start, the reading was going smoothly until Rip stopped in the middle of a line and threw the script toward Strasberg, who was sitting in the front row next to Kazan.

Then he yelled out, "God damn it," and stormed out of the studio.

Strasberg yelled to Burt, "Go after him! He's terrific!"

Burt ran into the street, nearly getting hit by a car. It took a lot of convincing to get Rip to return to the studio, but after some coaxing, he came back. Both Kazan and Strasberg gave him their approval of—and praise for—his reading. But before he would join Actors Studio, he insisted on their signing up "Buddy Reynolds" too.

Strasberg reluctantly agreed to that in order to get Rip.

After that temperamental outburst, Rip's career took off "like a fox after a chicken." He was cast as an understudy to Alex Nichol, who was starring on Broadway as the repressed homosexual, Brick, in Tennessee Williams' *Cat on a Hot Tin Roof*. Eventually, after Nichol left that production, Ben Gazzara had starred as his replacement. Then Rip took over the part. *[Eventually, Paul Newman starred in the screen adaptation opposite Elizabeth Taylor as Maggie the Cat.]*

In the same year (1956), Rip was also cast in the film version of Williams' controversial *Baby Doll*.

` *[Later, in yet another Williams' play,* Sweet Bird of Youth, *Rip played the son of Boss Finley, with the leads going to Paul Newman and Geraldine Page. Both of these stars would also appear in the play's film adaptation. In 1963, Rip married Page.]*

"I soon dropped out of the Actors Studio," Burt said. "Everyone seemed to think Strasberg was the Second Coming—not me. You could take all that crap about Method Acting, painfully exploring the depths of your soul—and shove it where the sun don't shine."

"I learned more about watching actors like Rip Torn, Jack Lemmon, or Mildred Dunnock emote than I ever did from Strasberg," Burt said.

***

In dire need of cash, Burt was told that Roseland was hiring more bouncers, and he decided to apply for a job there. He headed for Manhattan's theater district on West 52nd Street for an interview with the manager.

He'd heard that Roseland was a legend in New York, and that many famous stars had performed there, including Glenn Miller, Louis Armstrong, Harry James, Tommy Dorsey, and Ella Fitzgerald, among countless others.

It was a multi-purpose club known for its dances, but also for a variety of other events, everything from "jazz weddings" to female prizefights. *Time* magazine defined it as "a purple-and-cerise tentlike décor that creates a definite harem effect."

Burt was told that male members of the staff—bouncers, bartenders, waiters—could make a lot of extra money renting themselves out as gigolos to the rich women who came to dance there. He was informed that movie gangster George Raft and the silent screen heartthrob, Rudolph Valentino, got their start that way, using the place as a means to support themselves during low points of their early careers in show-biz.

The manager of the club looked like a cheap imitation of Darryl F. Zanuck, head of 20th Century Fox. "He inspected me like I was a piece of meat," Burt said.

"You look too small to be a bouncer at Roseland," he told Burt. "I like tough, big, beefy burly guys."

"I bet I'm tougher than any bouncer you have on your staff," Burt protested.

Tough, crowded with drunks, and sometimes a lot of fun, Roseland was the nightlife venue that every NYC resident under 40 had frequented at least once.

Here's how it looked in 1956, around the time Burt Reynolds worked here as a security guard, bouncer, and "breaker-up of fistfists."

In response, the manager, known only as "Buck," summoned his head bouncer to his office. In about five minutes, Tony Galento, nicknamed "Two Ton," came in.

After checking him out, Burt turned to the manager. "Do I have to beat the shit out of this slab of ass to get the job?"

All of a sudden, Galento lurched toward Burt, grabbed him by the collar, lifted him off the ground, and threw him against a nearby table and chair.

Rising to his feet, Burt charged Galento. But, as he wrote in a memoir, "Tony caught me like a line drive and put me into a headlock, jeopardizing what few brains I had left."

Galento turned to Buck. "This stupid kid has got guts. Give him the job."

As Burt learned later, Galento was famous in boxing circles for his June 1939 bout with Joe Louis, the heavyweight champ of the world. Before the bout, Galento had told the press, *"I'll moida da bum!"*

That didn't happen. The fourth round was brutal, and Galento seemed to have no defense, leaving himself open for an invasion from Louis' relentless battering. Blood was pouring from the boxer's eyes, nose, and right cheek.

Later, Galento told Max Baer, a former champ himself, that he would have clobbered Louis, but his manager told him to fight clean.

"I fight dirty," Galento claimed. "I knee, butt, gouge, bite, and hit below the belt, and I often kick a guy in his balls. When he falls to the floor,

I jump on him while he's still writhing in agony over my assault on his *cojones*. I leave him screaming in pain. As you can see, I don't follow the Marquis of Queensberry rules, or whatever that English fag was called."

On his second night on the job, Burt met and befriended another bouncer and struggling actor, Jack DeMave, Jr., who wasn't as fierce or unbalanced.

[The actor, Jack DeMave, Jr. should not be confused with his famous father, Jack De Mave Sr. (1904-1968), a well-known boxer. Born in Holland, De Mave Sr. had been a leading contender for Heavyweight Boxing Champion. Clifford Odets, the playwright, was so inspired by him that he wrote a play, Golden Boy, *based on the Dutch-born prize-*

Jack DeMave, as Ranger Bob Ericson, posed here with Lassie, from the era when he was a key player on that TV series.

fighter's life. William Holden launched his movie career playing that boxer in the play's 1939 film adaptation. It co-starred Barbara Stanwyck, whom Holden had bedded off-screen.]

"I didn't last long as a bouncer at Roseland," Burt said. "It was the toughest job I ever had. On a rowdy Saturday night, at least five or six fights—on one drunken night, a total of ten—would break out. Jack, Tony, and me to the rescue."

"Most often, some jerk would look at the three of us and head straight for me," Burt said. "We were on the second floor, and I often ended up locked in an embrace with the fucker as we tumbled down the stairs. The job prepared me for my future work as a stuntman on TV."

On one particularly bad night, a 30-year-old drunk from the Bronx, a truck driver, went tumbling down the stairs with Burt. The driver nearly broke his neck. An ambulance was summoned to rush him to the hospital. The following week he filed a million-dollar lawsuit against Roseland.

When Burt showed up for work the next evening, Galento called him aside. "Buck has fired you. We can't take a chance with a hothead like you, kid. You never learned what Jack and I know: Knock the fucker out at the top of the stairs—don't tumble down with him. You'll live longer that way."

As Burt was packing up his gear and changing his clothes in the locker room, DeMave came in. "Sorry you were fired. Let's stay friends. I don't plan to be a bouncer for long. You didn't know this, but I'm a member of

Actors Studio, although I've never seen you there. I heard you'd joined."

"Yeah, but I think I'm gonna drop out," Burt said. "Strasberg and I aren't making love, so to speak."

"Do me a favor," DeMave said. "I've got to do a reading tomorrow at four o'clock. Please come over and offer your support."

"You've got yourself a deal," Burt said. "It's not that I have anything else to do. But imagine that…Jack DeMave, an actor."

"Oh, just make sure you show up. I'll tell you who my leading lady's gonna be at my reading: Marilyn Monroe!"

"Yeah, right," Burt said, sarcastically. "I'll be there to see you and Miss Monroe. It'll probably be some pig."

***

Obsessed with erotic thoughts on the night before his visit to the Actors Studio, Burt could not get Marilyn Monroe out of his mind. "Unless Jack DeMave was bullshitting, I'm gonna meet Marilyn herself tomorrow afternoon."

Ever since he'd seen her emote in *Niagara* (1953), he claimed that "I've had the hots for her." He still remembered her performance in that *film noir* with a sexual glow that was almost fiery.

[Unlike most other films of that genre, Niagara *was in Technicolor. The camera had obsessively followed her body around, focusing on it in bed, where it was obvious that she was nude under the sheets. She was seen emerging from the shower, wrapping a towel around her nudity. All of this was hot stuff for Hollywood in the 1950s.]*

When he'd gone to see *Gentlemen Prefer Blondes* (1953), Burt had sat through three screenings. "She made her co-star, big-busted Jane Russell, look like a butch lesbian." He thought her rendition of "Diamonds Are a Girl's Best Friend," the sexiest song ever performed onscreen, rivaling Rita Hayworth's *"Put the Blame*

The brooding, menacing film that first exposed Burt Reynolds to the charms of Marilyn Monroe: *Niagara* (1953).

71

on Mame," in *Gilda* (1946).

The following afternoon, as Burt was walking down Broadway, heading for the Actors Studio, he spotted Marilyn at once, deliberately falling in step beside her. He introduced himself as Buddy Reynolds, and told her that her acting partner, Jack DeMave, had invited him to observe their reading onstage in front of Lee Strasberg.

"That's wonderful," she said. "Glad to meet you."

"I can't believe it," he answered. "Here I am walking along beside Marilyn Monroe. I'm so surprised. I thought you'd attract a mob."

"Do you want to see me become Marilyn Monroe?" She was wearing a raincoat with her blonde hair covered with a scarf. She wore sunglasses and no makeup at all. Then she reached into her purse, withdrew a tube of lipstick and heavily applied it to her luscious lips. She removed the scarf from her head, ruffled her hair, and took off the raincoat, handing it to him. Then she unbuttoned the top four buttons of her blouse and pranced ahead of him, assuming the same walk she had presented onscreen in *Niagara*.

Within minutes, she was mobbed. It took five policemen to get her safely inside the door of Actors Studio.

During her reading, Burt sat next to Carroll Baker, who did not seem aware of his existence. Baker's eyes were focused attentively on Marilyn and DeMave.

Marilyn had chosen some of Laura's lines from Tennessee Williams' *The Glass Menagerie,* with DeMave playing the Gentleman Caller.

When it was over, Baker spoke to Burt for the first time. She obviously viewed Marilyn as stiff competition. "If Marilyn's lips aren't gyrating, she's winching her shoulders or swinging her fuzzy pink tits or making that sucking fish-pucker mouth. Everything about her says 'I'm yours! Take me!'"

Then Marilyn went into a huddle with Strasberg, and DeMave sought out Burt. "I've got to report to work at Roseland. I told Marilyn you'd take her back to the apartment where she's staying."

"I'd be honored," Burt said. "You're one swell actor. I didn't know you had it in you."

After finishing with Strasburg, Marilyn came up to Burt, "Let's get the hell out of here. Back to my place."

On the street, she signed autographs as he hailed a taxi. In a memoir, Burt admitted to encountering Marilyn on the street, but omitted any details after that. He did reveal what happened after that to a number of friends, including William Inge.

Over dinner, Marilyn said, "I'd like you to spend the night, but first, I have to ask you something."

"Fire away," he answered.

"Are you a pansy?"

"Hell no!" he said, surprised at her use of such a word. "I'm a macho man."

"I think most male actors are pansies," she said. "Strasberg told me that acting is a feminine art. It attracts the type of male who wants to put on makeup, dress up in costume, and play-act, strutting around like a preening peacock and pretending emotions. Frankly, I think nearly all actors are gay, or at least have a strong gay streak racing through their blood stream. Do you consider Tony Curtis masculine? Monty Clift? I could go on and on."

Blonde Venus: Marilyn Monroe, circa 1953. She wanted Burt to prove he was not gay.

"I'm not like those guys," he said. "I'm the real deal."

She looked at him flirtatiously. "You men like to brag on yourselves so much."

She told Burt she'd be leaving soon to film Inge's *Bus Stop.* She also told him that the role of the lusty but dumb cowboy had been sought by a number of other actors. Rock Hudson had wanted to do it, but his studio wouldn't release him. Paul Newman, Ralph Meeker, and even Elvis Presley had coveted the role, too.

"Hell, Marilyn, throw my hat into the ring," Burt said. "I saw Albert Salmi do it on Broadway, and I think it would be a perfect vehicle to introduce me on the screen. You and I would heat up the sheets."

Later that night, after three bottles of champagne, it was time to go to bed. He stripped down and crawled under the sheets as she stood at the window, staring out. After *"Gentlemen Prefer Blondes,* I told my agent that I'd sucked my last cock in Hollywood."

"So sorry to hear that," he said from the bed.

"I didn't finish," she said. "I told him that I'd sucked my last cock in Hollywood to get a part. Now I do it only when I want to."

"Glad to hear that," he said.

That night, Burt joined the long roster of Marilyn's lovers. They included both John and Robert Kennedy, Marlon Brando, Robert Mitchum, John Huston, Frank Sinatra, Milton Berle, Yul Brynner, Darryl F. Zanuck, Paul Newman, James Dean, and even Elvis Presley.

Glancing away from the window, she surveyed her figure in a mirror. "People tell me I'm narcissistic and in love with myself. But I think any actor who has to go out and perform for applause must have some self-love."

"I couldn't agree more," Burt answered. "You can't love anybody unless you love yourself—at least that's what Linda Darnell thinks."

Then he got out of bed and, completely nude, walked over and enclosed her in his protective arms. "Let's make love."

As she slipped into bed with him, she asked, "Do you think I'm pretty?"

"The prettiest girl in the history of Hollywood," he assured her.

As he would agree, even a hundred women later, "Making love to Marilyn Monroe was the highlight of my erotic life."

Burt would always remember waking up the next morning with Marilyn in bed asleep beside him. He had an early appointment to see the foreman of a company that loaded and unloaded cargo ships at the Port of New York.

He looked back at her as she lay in bed. Her ample breasts were exposed in the morning light. He knew she was a troubled star, but at this very moment, she looked at peace with herself and the world.

Fully dressed, he tiptoed from the room and headed down in the elevator, getting soaked up in the crowd of New Yorkers rushing to work.

***

Burt was hired as a dock worker, loading and unloading cargo. "You had to be damn careful with those shipments from the Banana Republics to the South. Some of those stalks of bananas had deadly tarantulas lurking inside."

He worked with weather-beaten men, some of whom had served prison sentences. Many had journeyed north under arduous conditions from such countries as Guatemala and Honduras.

"At lease it kept my muscles tuned, and I was proud to work shirtless, showing off my physique," Burt said. "I didn't want any flab to accumulate."

One of his fellow workers, Bruce Thompson, had been a nude male model before he turned thirty-five. He told Burt that gay men came down to the docks to make contact with well-built men. "Many gays prefer construction workers or well-muscled men who work the docks. I sometimes hook up with one of them and earn a lot of extra bread."

"Not for me," Burt said.

He'd been on the job for only two weeks when he spotted this well-dressed man checking him out. "He was the only man on the docks wearing a suit and tie. He was standing only ten feet away, and couldn't take his eyes off me," Burt said. "I was tempted to walk over to him and punch him in the nose. In fact, I did go over to confront him. I asked him, 'What are you looking at, motherfucker?'"

"I was checking you out to offer you a job as a stuntman on live TV," he answered. "Name's Gary Olden. There's a job on a TV series called *Frontiers of Faith* broadcasting on Sunday morning."

"Sorry," Burt said. "I thought you had another job in mind."

"I'm not gay, and it's a legit offer. Pays $132 for about two minutes of work. All you have to do is jump through a candy-glass window."

"I'm your man," Burt said.

As it turned out, "the cruiser's" offer was genuine, and the show he'd described was legitimate. [*Running as a TV series from 1951 to 1970,* Frontiers of Faith, *featuring non-denominational testimonials of religious faith, included cameos from stars such as Sal Mineo, Martin Balsam, Ruby Dee, Mildred Dunnock, Arthur Hill, and Cicely Tyson.*]

"My gig lasted only two minutes, and I made off with $132, enough to pay the rent on my cold-water flat and buy a lot of hamburgers," Burt said.

At the end of the shoot, the talent agent congratulated him. "You must have had some sort of athletic background. You were perfect—very agile, very convincing. There's a lot of live television shows being shot in New York, and I can get you stunt work, maybe one or two jobs a week. It pays about the same as what you earned today, maybe a lot more if the stunt is really dangerous."

"Hell, sign me up," he answered. "It sure beats unloading bananas. What have I got to lose—only my life?"

"So I became a stuntman," Burt said. "If a director needed a man to take a fall down the stairs, call on me. I didn't realize my short career as a bouncer at Roseland paid off. There, I learned to tumble down the stairs with a drunken jerk stirring up trouble at the club."

"In some of my stunt work, I'd be given a line or two of dialogue before I was thrown off a roof. I had roles like diving into a water tank, fighting in the ring with a heavyweight, rolling off the hood of a speeding car… whatever. Serious accidents could have befallen me, but I escaped the bullet."

"I became the most convincing stuntman in New York when it came to getting bounced off the wall, and I was also a master at taking a nosedive."

"All of this work was preparing me for the day I'd play an actual stuntman in *Hooper,* a film I'd make with that adorable little filly, Miss Sally Field."

"In another job, I had to pretend to be stabbed by a sharp knife before I plunged over a cliff onto the jagged rocks below. I went over the cliff but landed on a platform with a mattress. Of course, that was off-camera."

The most substantial stunt job Burt got was where he was set on fire in *M Squad*, part of NBC's TV crime series, an episode called *Pete Marashi*. Its star was Lee Marvin, a New Yorker born and bred. "I thought I was the macho man until I met this

Lee Marvin in action before going with Burt to pick up women who think Burt is the REAL Marlon Brando.

walking dynamo, all lean and mean with an air of menace hovering over him," Burt said. "He had a deep voice that meant trouble."

From 1957 to 1960, Marvin had starred in M Squad as Detective Frank Ballinger. *[Produced in part by Marvin's Latimer Productions, its main sponsor was Pall Mall cigarettes, which hired Marvin to promote their brand in many of the series' commercials. Other sponsors included General Electric and Bulova watches. Lee Marvin, by the way, had been named in honor of Confederate General Robert E. Lee, one of his distant ancestors.*

Marvin and Burt had something in common. When both of them were teenagers, they used the Florida Everglades as their playground. Marvin went there to hunt puma, wild turkey, and bobwhite.

During World War II, Marvin had joined the U.S. Marines. But during the Battle of Saipan against the Japanese, he was hit by machine gun fire. It had severed his sciatic nerve, forcing him to spend a year in government hospitals.

After the war, he opted to become an actor, and studied at the American Wing Theater on the G.I. Bill.

Burt had seen him in two movies, most definitely that revved-up motorcycle classic, The Wild One (1953) opposite Marlon Brando.

That same year, Burt had also seen The Big Heat in which Marvin immortalized himself in an iconic scene by tossing a pot of scalding coffee into the face of Gloria Grahame.

In the 1950s, police dramas occasionally featured Marvin. They included Dragnet *and* Checkmate. *The best of them,* M Squad, *focused on Marvin's portrayal of a tough undercover police officer who was utterly cool but with a potential for violence. The series was shot in a gritty* film noir *style. Marvin's hard-nosed character of Frank Ballinger became the archetype for many tough, big-hearted crime fighters ranging from Hammet's Sam Spade to Raymond Chandler's Philip Marlow.]*

Burt appeared in "The Teacher," an episode of *M Squad* that aired in January of 1959. The character he played was Pete Marashi. Detective Ballinger goes after a gang of toughs who are terrorizing a trade school in Chicago. The gang leader (portrayed by Tom Laughlin) is "Sharpy Sharpies." Burt plays "Pistol Pete," who is on his shit list for blabbing to the police. There's trouble ahead.

Marvin bonded with Burt, and—at the end of one day's shoot—he approached him and invited him out with him for a night on the town. "You don't have to tell me that you're shit-faced tired of hearing people tell you that you look like Marlon Brando. But tonight, your looks can work to our advantage. We'll go to some pick-up bar on a *poontang* hunt. I'll go over to two of the hottest-looking dames and tell the bitches that you ARE Marlon Brando. I bet you they'll be our *putas* for the rest of the evening."

"I'm game," Burt said.

***

His next job was his most dangerous to date.

At long last, his dangerous stunt work was augmented with an entire page of dialogue. The director set up the scene for him: Burt's character is trapped in a fire and to escape from it, he has to jump out the window. He falls into an alley where, unseen by the camera, a 12"-deep pool of water will extinguish the flames.

Rip Torn had spent many hours prepping Burt for the lines he'd deliver, and the director had carefully and frequently rehearsed Burt in what he was to do. In those days, fire suits had not been fully developed, and still had many flaws in their design.

Prepped and psyched for his big scene with Ford, Burt reported to work. He'd told Rip the night before, "I expect to get a Best Supporting Actor Emmy for my death scene."

According to Burt, "I was already burning, lit up brighter than a Christmas tree. Then I jumped out of the window and into the puddle bath below."

Then, as actor Paul Ford held him in his arms, the character he played was supposed to die.

[During the course of his career, Ford would be nominated for three Emmy Awards. Directors knew that despite of his talent, Ford had trouble remembering his lines, a trait that made him a poor candidate for live TV. When Burt met him, Ford had recently scored a big hit as Horace Vandegelder opposite Shirley Booth in the 1958 screen version of The Matchmaker.*]*

To that point, Burt had never asked his parents to view any of his television appearances, but for this one, he notified Big Burt and Fern about seeing the episode on TV. Since they didn't own a television set, they went over to his Aunt Edna's to see the broadcast.

The episode represented Ford's first live TV appearance and he was visibly shaken. After he rushed over to embrace Burt's dying character, and as the camera zoomed in on him in a close-up, Ford for-

Paul Ford (center) with Phil Silvers (left) and Diana Dors on the *Phil Silvers Show* (aka *Sergeant Bilko*; 1955-59).

got his lines, and began improvising something unrehearsed instead. As the camera rolled, he said, "If the kid had survived, he might have said…"

Burt, horizontal and (supposedly) dying, reacted with horror as Ford delivered lines which had otherwise been assigned to him (Burt) as part of his big scene. "All my frigging lines," Burt said. "He hogged them all. It would be a long time before I asked Big Burt and Fern to watch me on TV."

***

In 1958 and 1959, in addition to episodes within Lee Marvin's *M Squad*, Burt found work in scattered episodes of other TV series broadcast over ABC, CBS, or NBC.

In most of these he was a stuntman, although he was sometimes assigned a leading role. An example included *Flight*, a TV anthology broadcast between 1958 and 1959. It focused on the science of aviation, usually during wartime. Burt appeared on two of its episodes, "Master Sergeant" and "Eve for Victory," the latter co-starring Robert Anderson.

Another popular TV anthology in which he appeared was the *Schlitz Playhouse*, broadcast between 1951 and 1959. In it, CBS featured major film stars (Anthony Quinn, Charlton Heston, and Irene Dunne) as well as an occasional theatrical legend (one of whom was Helen Hayes).

Burt watched its episodes whenever he could. One of them ("The Unlighted Road," released in 1955), starred James Dean, filmed shortly before his death.

Another included Burt's future friend, Fred Astaire, in his 1957 TV debut in an episode entitled "The Life You Save."

In yet another episode ("You Can't Win "Em All") Burt co-starred with the 1940s heartthrob, Guy Madison in a tale involving a professional football player who can't admit that his playing days are over. "It was a story that hit too close to home for comfort," Burt said.

Burt Reynolds (left) in an episode of his first ever TV series. It was named *Flight*.

Released as a public awareness enhancement for the aviation prowess of the U.S. military, it thrived during the early days of television.

He followed that with an appearance in an episode of *The Lawless Years,* a crime drama series for NBC. Set in the Roaring '20s, the series starred James Gregory and Robert Karnes.

Burt's episode was entitled "The Payoff," in which he played the second male lead. Its plot spun around a girl-friend who is murdered after she dumps a bootlegger during the violence associated with Prohibition.

That was followed with a gig in an episode of the western TV series named *Pony Express.* Its theme underscored the dangers of a job as a rider delivering mail during the turbulent 1860s.

In Burt's episode ("The Good Samaritan"), he played a character named Adam. In that role, he was called upon to perform what evolved into an unexpectedly dangerous stunt.

"It didn't go as planned," Burt said. "I rode into the shot as another guy was shooting at me. I was supposed to get off my horse as fast as I could and prepare for a gunfight. Instead, with my foot caught in the stir-rup, the animal bolted. I could have easily broken my neck, but I managed to unhook my booted foot before I was dragged to my death."

"I thought the shot, unrehearsed as it was, added to the tension of the story. But then I hobbled over to the director, near death and with a sore ass, and he said, 'Can you shoot that again?'"

"I practically punched him out. 'You gotta be kidding!' I said."

***

Burt had known Buster Nash in Florida and had attended school with him, back when Nash entertained dreams of becoming a sound engineer in Hollywood, and back when Burt still nursed dreams of becoming a football hero.

"Buster was music crazed, and I was girl crazed, and we never became real friends, but liked each other a lot," Burt said.

After Nash migrated from Florida to Hollywood, Burt never heard from him again. But one afternoon, Burt found himself standing in line outside the Paramount Theater in New York City's Times Square. At the time, it was dominated by a fifty-foot cutout of Elvis advertising his film debut in *Love Me Tender* (1956).

HISTORY'S HEROES RACING DEATH ON THE BLAZING OVERLAND TRAIL

PONY EXPRESS

TONIGHT and Every Thursday 8:30 P. M. on Ch. 7 ALL FIRST RUNS, FULLY SPONSORED EVERY WEEK BY

ALBUQUERQUE LUMBER CO. on
KOAT-TV Channel 7

As a TV series, *Pony Express* enlarged its viewer base by encouraging local sponsors to subsidize some of the production costs.

The poster that's replicated above brought the attention of local TV owners to the programming of the series, two episodes of which featured Burt Reynolds at the debut of his TV career.

Its premiere was scheduled for the following night, and local police had erected barricades to control ticket-buyers, who waited in lines which stretched around the block. *[It had been announced in newspapers that Elvis would make a personal appearance at the film's premiere.]*

What happened next was one of those odd coincidences that witnesses remember years later with a sense of wonder. Burt was moving south along Broadway. Near the corner of 46th Street, he spotted Nash coming toward him.

The two men hugged each other and went off to have coffee together to discuss, "What in hell has been going on with you?"

Burt spoke first, revealing his work as a stunt man. Nash reprised with news that he was in town for the premiere of *Love Me Tender.* He'd worked on the acoustics of that film during its filming in Hollywood.

"Elvis is hosting a poker game tonight in his hotel suite, and he said I could bring someone," Nash said. "Wanna come?"

"Do I? I'd give my right nut to meet Elvis Presley. He's the sensation of the decade. Forget Pat Boone, that goody-two-shoes. And forget Eddie

Fisher singing about his papa, too."

"Before you meet Elvis, there's just one thing…" Nash told him. "Elvis rules the night. Whatever he says, goes. He takes no lip."

"Okay by me," Burt answered. "If he asks, I'll wipe the shit off his blue suede shoes, even if he steps in a pile of it. "

***

That night, in his suite, Elvis emerged from his bedroom wearing a pair of jockey shorts. He shook Burt's hand and was warm, friendly, and welcoming. Nash told him that Burt, too, was a "good ol' Southern boy."

Elvis then introduced Burt to five other guys, informing him that they were from Tennessee.

Then he asked Burt what he did for a living. "Hustle your ass? Bootlegger? Bouncer? Bellhop? Waiter? Actor?"

"You've nailed me on the last try. Right now, I'm doing mostly stunt work, risking my neck on live TV. You know, jumping off roofs, crashing through windows."

"Sounds like fun," Elvis said. "So both of us are breaking into the movie business. I want to be taken seriously as an actor, but my manager, Col. Tom Parker, and me are having some different ideas about what kind of scripts I should do."

Elvis related that a few months before, in Hollywood, he had heard that Marilyn Monroe wanted to meet him. During the phone conversation that followed, he invited her to his suite. When she got there, he learned about her next picture (i.e., *Bus Stop*). According to Elvis, "The more she talked about it, the more I wanted to play this sexy dumb cowboy named Bo."

Burt did not reveal that he, too, knew Marilyn and that he, too, had wanted to portray the character of Bo.

"Could you just see it on the marquee—Elvis Presley and Marilyn Monroe in *Bus Stop*," Elvis said. "There would be stampedes at box offices across America."

"But the Colonel was totally opposed to it," Elvis said. "He says it was written by some fag named William Inge. That's not the kind of picture he wants

Elvis Presley told Burt that Marilyn Monroe was not his type.

for me. He wants me to star in silly, romantic musicals."

"Maybe you and Marilyn will do some other movie together," Burt said. "I think the two of you would make a great team."

"Perhaps," Elvis said, not concealing the skepticism in his voice. "Frankly, and this may surprise you, but I don't think there's that sexual chemistry I thought might exist between the two of us. Of course, I took her to bed. No big deal. She's not my type. She's too tall and too inexperienced. I like shorter, more innocent girls, and youngers ones, too."

"I had also wanted to play Brick," Elvis continued, "in *Cat on a Hot Tin Roof* opposite Elizabeth Taylor, but the Colonel said it was another fag role, this one written by Tennessee Williams. The Colonel claims that my fans would desert me in droves."

"Well, if the Colonel objects to gays, he'd better keep you out of the movie business," Burt said. "I've heard that more than half the men who make movies bat for the other team."

"I can deal with it," Elvis said.

"In the middle of the poker game, Elvis interrupted his play and called over one of his gofers. "Chase, I heard that the new Chryslers have gone on the market today."

"They have," Chase responded. "I walked by one of their showrooms today. They look great!"

Elvis signaled to another of his gofers to fetch his pants, draped across an armchair in a corner. He reached into its pocket and removed what looked like a wad of thousand-dollar bills. Without counting them, he told Chase, "Go to that showroom and buy me a new Chrysler. Within two hours, I want the latest model parked in the garage of this hotel."

"Any particular color?" Chase asked.

"How in hell do I know which color?" Elvis asked. "Buy me one. Got that? If you don't come back in two hours, I'll stick a firecracker up your ass. Now get out!"

Then he turned to Burt. "I want to go for a spin on the streets of Manhattan tonight, when it's late and the crowds are gone."

At the end of the poker game, Elvis was declared the winner. Nash had warned Burt, "Let Elvis win. That's the rule of the house."

Before he left his hotel suite, Elvis scratched his crotch and turned to Burt. "I like you. You're a good ol' Southern boy. What's your name again? I'm bad with names."

"My friends call me Buddy. I'm Burt Reynolds."

"You've got something," Elvis said. "I don't know what…but something. So you're an actor? One day your name might be in lights on 42nd Street."

"Perhaps," Burt said. "But I don't think my picture will be advertised with a fifty-foot cutout."

"A word of advice," Elvis said. "The 'Burt' will have to go. There's already a Burt Lancaster." Then he took time out to order his gofer to call room service for some fried chicken, served with banana and peanut butter sandwiches.

Then he turned once again to Burt. "I've got it! I can see it on a marquee right now. LASH DURANGO."

"Great!" I'll go to a lawyer and have it changed tomorrow. Wonderful to meet you, Elvis. You're a great guy."

"That's what they tell me. The babes are crazy for me. I can't escape them. They mob me...find me sexy."

"And you're complaining?" Burt asked. "Goodbye, Elvis. Any time you need another hand at poker, I'm ready, willing, and able."

"Thanks...and good night to you, Lash."

***

Perhaps thinking it would damage his macho image, Burt was never candid about his relationship with either Tennessee Williams or William Inge, the two hottest playwrights of the 1950s. *[They had once been lovers.]*

But although Burt acknowledged knowing them in his memoirs, he omitted the details of his intimate links to them and how passionately he wished to star in some of their stage plays and screen adaptations.

Each of the two playwrights became so enamored of Burt that they promised to write, specifically for him, a play that they'd tailor-make specifically for his particular image.

Inge—in his own words—had been "intoxicated by Burt" even since he'd met him at the Hyde Park Playhouse.

Even before meeting Burt, Inge had written plays (*Picnic* and *Bus Stop)* that Burt considered could be, or could have been, star-making vehicles for him. He had been mesmerized by the script of *Picnic,* which he'd missed out on, partly because of its timing.

[Picnic had opened on Broadway in 1953, too early for Burt to have been able to make any reasonably convincing claim on it. During its early months, it had featured Ralph Meeker in the male lead of Hal Carter, the charming drifter who arrives in a small Kansas town and sends the blood pressure of several local women soaring.

Meeker's counterpart in Picnic's *film adaptation was interpreted by William Holden who, at the age of thirty-seven, protested that he was too old to play Hal.]*

Even as late as 1961, Burt wanted to play Hal so much that he agreed to portray him in a stage version of *Picnic* at the Cherry Country Playhouse in Traverse City, Michigan.

Burt also lost out on what he called "my alltime dream role," that of Bo Decker, a brash young cowboy who lusts after Cherie, a stripper/singer. He'd met Marilyn Monroe weeks before she headed to Hollywood to star in *Bus Stop's* film version.

Rock Hudson had wanted to play the lead, but Universal wouldn't release him. Paul Newman, plus a horde of other actors, each thought they'd be ideal as Bo. Burt told Inge, "I was born to play Bo. It's as if you had my image in mind when you wrote it."

At one point, as their relationship intensified in the late 1950's, Burt was seeing Inge three or four times a week. The playwright said he was writing his latest play (*A Loss of Roses*), and that he believed that Burt would be ideal as its male lead on Broadway. It was the story of a boy growing up in a small town in Kansas. He meets and falls in love with an older, and far more seasoned female show biz veteran.

It seemed, however, that Burt was not performing sexually, or not putting out at all, for Inge. Eventually, the playwright's lusty thoughts became focused instead on a hot new discovery named Warren Beatty, the older brother of actress Shirley MacLaine. He seemed to exude sex appeal and macho charm for the physically lack-luster Inge.

In 1959, Inge was forty-six years old. Inge interpreted Beatty as a heartthrob the moment he met him. In fact, he liked to think of this very heterosexual actor as his *protégé*. When Beatty entered Inge's life, his dreamy yearnings for Burt faded with the arrival of this new boy in town. If he could not have Beatty in bed (and

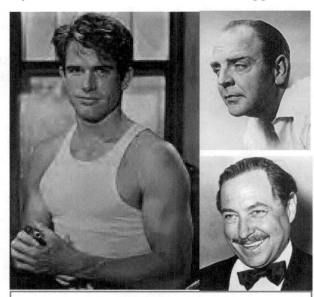

Warren Beatty (left) with (right side, top) his admirers, William Inge and (right side, bottom) Tennessee Williams.

When these two gay playwrights met Warren Beatty, thoughts of Burt Reynolds drifted away like a summer cloud.

the jury is still undecided on that issue), he at least could love him by re-creating his image in his upcoming play, *A Loss of Roses.*

In the play, Kenny, aged 21, is described as a "nice-looking boy who wears a mysterious look of misgiving on his face as though he bears some secret resentment that he has never divulged and has perhaps never admitted to his consciousness."

Often, playwrights have little to do with casting, but Inge had power in that domain because he'd put up $100,000 of his own money to produce the play.

It was a sad day for Burt when Inge told him that he'd cast the role not with him, but with Beatty.

Burt's first reaction was, "Who in hell is this little two-bit hustler, Warren Beatty?"

That day, his friendship with Inge ended on a sour note.

Burt later attempted to renew it when he heard that Inge—still mesmerized by Beatty—was writing a screenplay for him called *Splendor in the Grass,* in which he would co-star with Natalie Wood. In Beatty's case, he would do more than co-star.

Variety reported that *Splendor* would mark the screen debut of Warren Beatty. Elia Kazan was named as the director of a story of two frustrated lovers set in 1939 Kansas.

At the last minute, Burt tried to contact Inge about casting him, if not as the male lead, then at least in some key role, even though he had not read the script. But by that time, Inge had changed his phone number.

Burt then read that even before the release of *Splendor,* Inge was hard at work adapting a novel *All Fall Down,* written by James Leo Herlihy, into a screenplay. In a few months, it would go into production with leading ladies Eva Marie Saint and Angela Lansbury.

"Oh well, "Burt told his friend, Rip Torn. "I lost out, a familiar Hollywood story. I guess there's always Tennessee Williams. Let's face it…He's a bigger name even that Inge. I'd have been great playing Brick on the screen opposite Elizabeth Taylor as Maggie the Cat." *[He was referring to the 1958 film adaptation of Tennessee's play,* Cat on a Hot Tin Roof."*]*

***

Burt would always remember the first time he met Tennessee Williams, who never made any best-dressed list. *[If someone every dared to criticize his apparel, Tennessee would say, "Who in hell do you think I am? Adolphe Menjou?"]*

At the time, Williams was attired in a baggy, grayish suit with stains on the collar, a red silk scarf, and a tie that no tourist, not even in Honolulu, would dare to wear. He was shorter than Burt had imagined, standing about five feet, eight inches, and he looked like he weighed no more than 150 pounds.

"I understand from Bill Inge that you're a hustler, working your way up the Broadway ladder rung by rung."

"Bill misinformed you," Burt said. "I've hustled all my life, but not in a sexual way."

"Nonsense," Williams said. "Everything we see, do, feel, and experience is sexual. Without our sexual thoughts, which occur at least every three minutes in the male brain, what would life be? How do you expect to advance yourself if not on the casting couch? I saw you perform tonight in *Mister Roberts,* one of several other guys. You are possibly interesting as a talent who needs a lot of work and development of technique. But you seem to have no more than hundreds of other young men, pounding the streets of Broadway looking for a gig."

"That's encouraging," Burt answered.

"Cut the sarcasm," Williams said. "I'm telling you the truth. In this world of today, there isn't time for Norma Desmond illusions."

"Okay, I'm a good-looking guy that some people find sexy. I have a certain talent, but I might get ahead with my sheer audacity."

"That's probably an accurate appraisal, so let's be friends. But first, tell me: What are you angling for? You want to play Brick in a road tour of *Cat on a Hot Tin Roof.* But if not that, then what?"

"I'll be blunt if you want me to lay my cards on the table," Burt said.

"Let's avoid the clichés," Williams answered.

"What actor wouldn't want to play Brick?" Burt said. "Paul Newman, Rip Torn, Ralph Meeker. Inge told me there's a strong possibility that Hollywood is going to film your novella, *The Roman Spring of Mrs. Stone.* The male lead is that of an Italian gigolo, pursuing an older actress in Rome."

"I look more Italian than any of those other guys. Newman is, in fact, Jewish. I want you to consider me for the role. It could launch my career in films."

"And why should I do that for you?" Williams asked. "What do you have to offer me?"

"I'm not so crude as to say 'my dick,'" Burt answered. "Most actors on Broadway would offer you that. I can offer friendship—take it or leave it."

"Let's go for a nude swim at the YMCA," Williams said. "That way I can enjoy your family jewels even though I'm not allowed to touch them."

As Burt later recalled, "Swimming in the nude with Tennessee Williams was the beginning of a beautiful friendship that lasted as long as a plucked wildflower."

"On our next night out, he took me to this decaying townhouse in the East Village that had been subdivided into apartments," Burt said. "We went in to discover about thirty mostly young men and women there. The air was laden with the heavy smell of pot. One well-muscled young man was lying nude in the middle of the floor, as various men and women took turns fellating him."

"Later, when I had to go to the bathroom after drinking two beers, I discovered two nude women in the bathtub," Burt said. "One was going down on the other, and they just ignored me. I did my business, zipped up, and came back into the room."

At this point, Tennessee seemed bored with the party, and suggested that they leave at once. A taxi took them to a midtown hustler bar called the Haymarket. The clientele consisted of sellers of male flesh and buyers of male flesh.

"Word soon got out that Tennessee Williams was in the bar," Burt said. "A parade of young men, probably many out-of-work actors, paraded by our table, each of them hoping to be tomorrow's Marlon Brando or a replacement for the late, lamented James Dean."

And so it went for Burt and Tennessee Williams, as they made the rounds of pointless parties with stoned guests, years before the marijuana-soaked 1960s had even arrived.

One late afternoon, however, was different. Burt was invited to Williams' hotel. "Here it comes," he told Rip Torn.

But when he got there, he was pleasantly surprised that there would be no attempt at seduction. Instead, the playwright read passages from his novella, *The Roman Spring of Mrs. Stone*. The gigolo (Poolo) was more enticing than Burt had imagined. "In Riviera Beach in Florida where I grew up, people thought I was Italian."

"The passage was lyrical," Burt recalled, "a predator gigolo in pursuit of a fifty-ish woman who is lonely and vulnerable, needing love but looking for it in all the wrong places. The part called for an actor who could be powerfully seductive but narcissistic and ruthlessly destructive."

"Poolo is me," Burt said after Williams put down the script. "I can play him right down to my toenails."

Then news arrived about some emergency bursting forth from Williams home in Key West. It revolved around Frankie Merlo, Williams' long-time lover, the man on whom he had based the character of Stanley Kowalski.

Williams abruptly abandoned both Burt and Manhattan, heading for Key West where he handled whatever problems had arisen there. But then, instead of returning immediately to New York, he opted to spend a few days alone in San Juan. At the time, he and Merlo were feuding.

During Williams' absence, Burt told Rip Torn, "The role of Poolo is practically in the bag for me."

Burt, however, was not alone in his pursuit of the role of Poolo. Somehow, probably through Bill Inge, Warren Beatty, Burt's adversary, learned that Williams was in residence, alone, at the San Juan Hilton.

For weeks, Beatty had been practicing his Italian accent. Abruptly, he flew to San Juan to seek out the playwright.

Here, the story grows murky, as there are many versions of what happened next between Tennessee and Beatty. But a few days later, when they flew out of San Juan together, the role of Poolo had been assigned to Beatty.

Shooting was to begin in Rome. Mrs. Stone would be portrayed by Vivien Leigh, who had won an Oscar for her interpretation of an earlier (tragic) Tennessee Williams' heroine, Blanche DuBois in *A Streetcar Named Desire*.

Burt never heard from Williams again. Later, he learned through Dorothy Kilgallen's column that *The Roman Spring of Mrs. Stone* had been cast with Leigh and Beatty.

Burt was heartbroken, but, at his young age, he recovered quickly. He made a decision: To become a movie star, he'd have to give up his pursuit of aging, fickle, middle-aged playwrights and take some other road.

"There must be another way," he said.

***

Stunt jobs dried up for Burt during the summer of 1959. Most television stations were broadcasting re-runs, with the understanding that live filming wouldn't begin until the fall.

Consequently, Burt returned to Riviera Beach for a reunion with his parents. Then he headed over to Tampa, working the rest of the summer as a counselor at Camp Keystone.

In September, when he returned to New York, he found that live TV was a thing of the past, and that an army of actors, technicians, directors, producers, and agents had begun a mass migration toward the palm trees of Hollywood.

Burt opted to join them, bidding his friends goodbye. "I'm going to tell that god damn Marlon Brando to move over," he said. "He's gonna be replaced by the New Boy, the hottest man in town...Burt Reynolds!"

CHAPTER THREE

BURT'S STRUGGLES AS A BIT PLAYER IN THE EARLY DAYS OF TELEVISION

Portraying Minor Characters in Forgettable Series,
He Plods On, and On, and ON

HOW BURT'S VIOLENT TEMPER

Almost Imploded His Screen Career Before It Got Launched

RIVERBOAT

Burt Lands His Biggest Role as a "Dumb-Dumb Whistle Blower," Tangling with His Scene-Stealing Co-Star, Darren McGavin

AUDIE MURPHY

Why World War II's Most Decorated American Soldier Threatened to Kill Burt Reynolds in a Hollywood Gym

SPENCER TRACY

What Really Happened that Drunken Night He Spent with Burt?

ANGEL BABY

Burt Lands a Small Role in his First Feature Film

JOAN BLONDELL

Learns Why Burt is Nicknamed "Hot Pants"

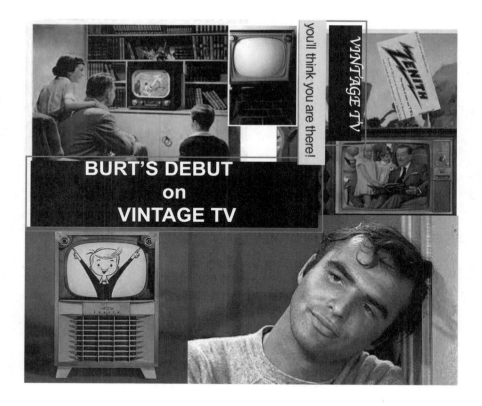

you'll think you are there!

VINTAGE TV

ZENITH

BURT'S DEBUT on VINTAGE TV

In 1958, Burt found himself winging from New York to Los Angeles in a seat next to an actor (George Maharis) he'd be competing with as part of a screen test for an upcoming May-December romantic comedy entitled *But Not for Me*.

Burt's agent had arranged for him to be tested for its role of the second male lead, a part that called on him to portray a young Method actor named Gordon Reynolds.

Set for a 1959 release, *But Not for Me* would star Clark Gable, 57, playing an aging Broadway producer, running into trouble with his latest script.

[Clark Gable, once "The King of Hollywood," had two more pictures in him before he joined the completely unglued Marilyn Monroe to film The Misfits *(1961), co-starring with Montgomery Clift in a script written by her alienated husband, Arthur Miller.]*

In the plot, his 22-year-old secretary, Carroll Baker, an aspiring actress, falls in love with Gable in spite of their age differences. In a reversal of the usual Hollywood plot, the young girl chases after the older man. Of course, as could be anticipated, the secretary realizes at the end that she's really in love with the young actor, the role being sought by Burt.

Burt was not the only contender for the second male lead. Both Maharis and a young actor from Santa Monica, Barry Coe, would also in the running.

Coe had had a minor role in Elvis Presley's *Love Me Tender* (1956) but had gained greater exposure when he had starred as the lustful Rodney Harrington in the original *Peyton Place* (1957), based on the best-selling novel by Grace Metalious.

Maharis was eight years older than Burt and had appeared in such Off-Broadway productions as Edward Albee's *The Zoo Story* and Jean Genet's *Deathwatch.*

Although they were competing for the same role, Maharis and Burt sat together on the flight from New York to Los Angeles. Chatting amicably, the Greek-American tried to convince Burt that everybody in Hollywood was a crook and a thief.

Burt later reflected, "It took me nearly four decades to realize that George was right."

In Los Angeles, at Paramount, Burt walked into a big Hollywood studio for the first time. He was impressed, but intimidated. "Everyone was running around hysterically," he said.

In the makeup department, prior to the beginning of his screen test, Burt was directed to sit down in a makeup chair next to an older actor, of whom he was only vaguely aware, not looking at his face. The makeup artist, an effeminate young man, asked him, "What kind of makeup do you want?"

Burt looked at the actor in the adjoining chair "I'll have whatever he's having." When that actor's makeup artist stepped back, Burt saw Clark Gable for the first time.

Burt couldn't believe it. "Here I was sitting next to Rhett Butler nearly twenty years later. Rhett hadn't held up too well. He was visibly shaking." Burt found out later that he was suffering from palsy.

"I was shaking more than Gable, out of pure nervousness," Burt said.

"To steady my nerves, Gable offered me a cup of what he was having: Coffee laced with gin."

Maharis was called in first for his screen test. Gable asked him, "Do you duck hunt?"

Clark Gable, once the King of Hollywood, shoots blanks in one of his last movies. Critics pointed out that "at least he acts his age," in scenes with Lilli Palmer.

"No way," Maharis answered. "I'm from New York."

When it came time for Burt to face the camera, Gable asked him the same question, to which Burt responded, "I used to go hunting in the Florida Everglades, but my mother took me to see *Bambi*. No more duck hunting."

When Coe was tested, Gable put the same question to a competitor Burt called "Pretty Boy."

Coe replied that at the Roosevelt Game Preserve, he had recently shot thirty-eight ducks and two geese.

It seemed that Gable wanted someone to go duck hunting with, and Coe got the role.

The next morning, Burt was on a plane flying back to New York. And although the

Both Burt and George Maharis (above) lost their chance to co-star with Clark Gable, but Maharis bounced back to travel *Route 66* on TV, his greatest hit.

other loser, Maharis, and he went their separate ways, the Greek was on the dawn of his biggest success when he was cast in the hit TV series *Route 66* as Buz Murdock, co-starring with Martin Miller.

In later years, both Burt and Maharis posed nude for magazines—Burt for *Cosmopolitan (in 1972)* and (fully dressed) for the cover of *Playgirl* (in 1981); Maharis for *Playgirl* (in 1973). Whereas Burt concealed his genitals, Maharis showed "the full monty." As Johnny Carson remarked on *The Tonight Show,* "It takes a daring man to pose nude next to a horse."

***

Back in New York again after his unsuccessful bid for a role in *But Not for Me,* Burt was cast in his last live television show, an episode broadcast on *Robert Montgomery Presents,* a hit TV series that NBC had launched in 1950. It often employed big-name stars such as Helen Hayes, Claudette Colbert, the Gish Sisters (Lillian and Dorothy), Charlton Heston, Grace Kelly, Angela Lansbury, Jack Lemmon, David Niven, and even his friend, Joanne Woodward.

Burt would appear with his newly minted friend, Lee Marvin, as well as veteran actor James Cagney, with whom Burt associated with all those gangster movies of the 1930s.

When he wasn't needed on camera, Cagney asked Burt to box with him, claiming, "It's the best kind of exercise."

"He was hard to hit," Burt said, "since he was such a bundle of energy, always bounding around with the skill of a dancer. He was very self-assured, cocky, and fast-talking, just like he was in his movies."

Cagney told Burt he was really a song-and-dance man, who got detoured in all those crime dramas. His favorite film was *Yankee Doodle Dandy* (1942), in which he played showman George M. Cohan. His performance brought Cagney an Oscar.

He asked Burt how he got started in show business, and Burt described some of his more hair-raising tales as stuntman. Cagney confessed that he got his start in show biz as a drag queen.

Burt laughed that off as a joke, until years later, he came across a picture of Cagney taken early in his career. Indeed, just as he had said, he had been a drag queen in vaudeville revues.

In his youth, Robert Montgomery romanced the leading ladies of Hollywood on screen, but later in life he hosted the long-running TV series, *Robert Montgomery Presents*.

Every day during the shoot, Burt lunched with Lee Marvin. But whereas Burt would actually consume some solid food (a burger with fries, for example), Marvin preferred a liquid midday meal. "It keeps me buzzed up for the afternoon," he said.

Marvin urged Burt "to give Hollywood another try," and promised to throw whatever he could in the way of acting jobs to Burt.

He knew he could not depend on Marvin, so he continued to

James Cagney, like many of the characters he played, was temperamental, arrogant, aggressive, and unpredictable.

As a psychotic gangster in *The Public Enemy* (1931) he behaves savagely by crushing a grapefruit into Mae Clark's face.

maintain his links to MCA. He contacted Monique James, a vice president of MCA who reported to Lew Wasserman, that company's president. She urged him to return to L.A. to update his records with them. MCA was the most influential talent agency in the entertainment industry, so based on that invitation, he flew to Los Angeles.

Money, however, was a problem. Before landing, he got in touch with Cookie Knomblach, an attractive nurse he'd dated in Manhattan. She was now employed as a nurse at UCLA.

She had a place to live—a modest apartment in Pasadena—and from what he gathered she was still unattached. She offered to let him live with her, temporarily, and to meet him at the airport in her new red MG.

As promised, she was there waving at him when he disembarked. She'd already prepared dinner, which only needed to be heated up. "We followed that with more heat between the sheets later that night," he confessed.

The next day, she gave him the use of her MG so he could make the rounds of the studios, looking for movie work. He decided to seek an acting job, since Tinseltown was overloaded with stunt men. "It was also top heavy with actors, but what the hell," he said.

The next day in Cookie's MG, he drove to MCA's Review Studios in the San Fernando Valley. He argued with the guard at the gate, telling him that he was Lee Marvin's best friend and wanted to see him. But the guard told him, "Get lost, kid!"

Dejected, he phoned his MCA contact, Monique James, who organized an on-site interview for him with members of her company's senior staff, with the understanding that he'd deliver a reading alongside whichever other actor he might persuade to accompany him.

For some unknown reason, he gravitated toward material from the film script of *All My Sons,* a World War II drama released in 1948. It had starred Edward G. Robinson and Burt Lancaster. Burt wanted to read lines from the Burt Lancaster part, and he needed another actor to read the lines portrayed in the film by Robinson, his father.

He headed toward the Lamplighter Bar, which he'd heard was patronized for the most part by out-of-work actors. There, he met a young man, Ed Thompson, who at first thought that Burt was trying to pick him up for sex.

But when Burt explained that he needed an acting partner for an upcoming reading already scheduled for senior agents at MCA, the actor became most agreeable. Burt invited him home to sample Cookie's cooking, and then they spent two or three hours going over the script together. After their first reading, Thompson wanted the Lancaster role, but Burt insisted that he take the Robinson part instead—that of the father.

The following afternoon, Burt, with Thompson, showed up at Monique's office. She was friendly and welcoming but told them they'd have to wait for two hours.

Her associate, Wally Hiller, had arranged the reading with MCA's president, the all-powerful Lew Wasserman. There, Burt met Jay Cantor, who—as it turned out—was also the booking agent for Marlon Brando.

"My God, boy, did anyone ever tell you that you look like my client, Marlon?"

"I never heard that one before," Burt answered. "Maybe Marlon looks a lot like me."

In the middle of Burt's big scene, Hiller's phone range and he picked it up. Remembering how Rip Torn had exploded midway through his reading at the Actors Studio, Burt imitated him. "I went ballistic and ripped the phone out of the wall. Then I stormed out toward the door. Just as I was leaving, I heard Ed Thompson tell the men, 'I can take over Burt's part. I'm real talented as an actor, and I'm not temperamental at all.'"

Burt turned in fury to confront the room. "Fuck you jerks. Fuck all of you!"

To cool down his rage, he walked two blocks to the aptly named Little Bar, a postage-stamp tavern that was patronized by actors, agents, and employees at MCA. He spent the rest of the afternoon there, drinking beer.

Although by 6PM, he was already completely intoxicated, he remained there and continued to drink until ten o'clock. Then he called Cookie, instructing her to take a taxi to the Little Bar, since he was incapable of driving her MG home without crashing it.

En route back to her apartment, she told him that her phone had been ringing all afternoon from someone named Monique at MCA.

"I made an ass of myself at MCA during the reading and behaved like a madman," he told Cookie.

Nonetheless, he returned Monique's call at around 11AM the next morning. Before he could apologize, she said, "Lew wants to sign you. Of course, he'll deduct the cost of a new phone installation from your first paycheck."

***

Back once again at MCA, after a long delay in the waiting area, Burt was ushered into the plush office of its chief executive, Lew Wasserman.

[Wasserman ("the last of the great Hollywood moguls") was the most powerful and influential player in the entertainment industry, remaining so for four decades in post-war Hollywood. Beginning his career as an usher in a movie house, he played a central role in persuading Hollywood to endorse the money-making potential of television, known at the time as "the little black box."]

When he entered Wasserman's office, Burt was both embarrassed and nervous, and filled with apologies for his outburst. He studied the man who sat behind the desk. Tall, gaunt, gray-haired, and wearing oversized black-rimmed glasses, he was known for building up actors' careers and for destroying them, too. He had once told Shirley Temple—an unimaginably profitable box office attraction during the 1930s—that she was washed up in Hollywood and unsuitable for adult roles.

"I'm famous for my temper tantrums," Wasserman told Burt. "But I'm the biggest fucker in town and can get away with them. You're nobody, so you don't have a right to throw a fit. Let that come later when you're a big Hollywood star. If you don't get control of yourself, your career will be destroyed before it even starts."

Lew Wasserman, one of Hollywood's most powerful moguls, told his staff to sign Burt.

"He's a real asshole, a prick, really, temperamental, arrogant, cocky, but I see talent hidden there."

"Yet I think that you have the potential to become a movie star," Wasserman continued. "You're raw, and it'll take work, but if you can control yourself, you've got a chance. Of course, I represent really big stars, those who come to me after they've already made it. But I also get a kick out of molding new talent, like yourself."

"Sometimes I can take a fading actor and steer him into a second act," Wasserman said. "Right now, I'm working on that has-been, Ronald Reagan. I installed him as President of the Screen Actors Guild, and then I made him a household name hosting the General Electric Theater on TV."

Now, I've got other plans for him. I'm going to make him either Senator from or Governor of California, and after that, President of the United States. Not bad for the man who co-starred with a chimp in *Bedtime for Bonzo* (1951)."

After fifteen minutes, Wasserman stood up, signaling the end of their meeting. "Monique has a contract for you to sign in her office. Welcome to MCA."

***

Even though Lee Marvin had told Burt to look him up when he hit Hollywood, he hadn't provided his address or phone number. When Burt had visited Review Studio to see him, he was turned away.

But when Burt, returned to the studio as a new protégé of MCA, he was on the arm of Monique James, one of its executives. Together, they were immediately ushered inside.

While strolling about, they encountered Lee Marvin, who warmly embraced him. His first question was, "How in hell is Rip Torn?"

James excused herself to take care of other business. "That's all right, lady," Marvin assured her. "I'll take Burt under my wing for the rest of the day."

Before lunch, he escorted Burt to the set where he was filming *M Squad.* *[Burt had once appeared in an episode of that series.]* He was introduced to the director, Don Medford, known as "Midnight Medford," because he was never satisfied with the first scenes an actor performed and always insisted on endless reshoots, many of them continuing on until after midnight.

The director looked at Burt like he was doing an inspection. "Did anyone ever tell you that you look a lot like Marlon Brando?"

"Never heard that one," Burt said.

After lunch with Marvin, Burt wandered around the studio, waiting for him to finish his day's shoot.

That night, they went bar hopping, marking the beginning of their enduring friendship.

Both men were hellraisers. For sport, they liked to ignite fights in seedy bars. "We got our ass licked a few times, but for the most part, Lee and I emerged as victors." Burt said. "Lee was full of surprises. You never knew what that guy was going to do next. At the age of four—yes, four—he ran away from home."

Marvin told Burt, "I didn't have to worry about where my next meal was coming from. I figured some child molester would pick me up."

"C'mon, Lee, you didn't know about child molesters at the age of four."

"So what?" Marvin said. "I never let truth get in the way of a good story."

Marvin had already described to Burt about how he got half of his ass blown off in the Battle of Saipan in June of 1944. What Burt didn't know was how horribly impacted his war experiences had left him.

"I learned to act in the Marines by pretending I wasn't afraid of combat," Marvin claimed. "I was so good I won the Purple Heart."

"He never recovered from 1944," Burt said. "He told me he took part in the invasion of twenty-

Noted for his utter lack of humor, here's Lee Marvin as the no-nonsense Lieutenant Ballinger in *M Squad*

one islands. His fellow soldiers were dying all around him. He remembered one eighteen-year-old kid from Idaho. 'He died in my arms with half his head blown off,' Marvin said to me. He also told me he had recurring nightmares and sometimes woke up screaming."

After the war, Marvin worked as a plumber's assistant. One assignment took him to a summer playhouse, where he had to unstop a clogged toilet. In the middle of a rehearsal, an actor took sick. The director spotted Marvin, handed him the script, and asked him to read the lines to the other actors.

"That was the day I was bitten by the acting bug."

According to Burt, "Lee suffered this awful guilt that he lived, while so many of his fellow soldiers had died violent deaths."

"During the year I spent in a hospital, I felt like a god damn coward," Marvin said. "Here I was between clean sheets, flirting with the nurses who brought me strawberry ice cream as I listened to Glenn Miller records. While I did that, other soldiers were dying on some god forsaken island in the Pacific."

Burt had seen two of Marvin's war movies and considered him a natural at portraying soldiers. Stanley Kramer had hired him to appear in *Eight Iron Men* (1952), portraying a character that Burt Lancaster had first played on Broadway.

Sometimes, Marvin assisted the director as an adviser about how to realistically portray troop movement or the use of firearms.

Marvin was also cast in Westerns, including *The Stranger Wore a Gun* (1953) with Randolph Scott.

As their friendship evolved, Marvin became more and more willing to gossip—and not always charitably—about the private lives of some of the tough-guy actors he'd worked with. Marvin asked Burt, for example, "Did you know Randolph Scott is a closeted gay—and not just with Cary Grant?"

In reference to *Gun Fury* (1953), in which he'd co-starred with Rock Hudson. Marvin asked Burt, "Did you know that Rock is ninety-five percent gay?"

On the set of *The Wild One* (1953), Marvin claimed that his co-star, Marlon Brando, had admitted to being bisexual—"and that he wasn't at all ashamed about it."

Marvin had co-starred with Spencer Tracy in *Bad Day at Black Rock* (1955). He asked Burt, "Did you know that Spencer Tracy is a closeted gay?"

"I didn't know that, and I find it hard to believe." Burt said.

Marvin had co-starred with Jack Palance in 1955 in *I Died a Thousand times.* "Did you know that Jack lives in the closet?" Marvin asked Burt.

The following year (1956), Marvin co-starred with Jeff Chandler in *Pillars of the Sky.* "Jeff is bisexual—and not only that, he's a cross-dresser. Ask Esther Williams about it."

That same year, Marvin co-starred with Paul Newman in *The Rack.* "Paul keeps it a secret, but he's bi," Marvin claimed.

Marvin also appeared in 1956 in *Raintree County* alongside Elizabeth Taylor and Montgomery Clift. "Monty is ninety-nine percent gay," Marvin claimed.

One drunken night, Marvin stared long and hard at Burt. "I've concluded that you're queer bait."

"I think I know what that means but tell me why you think so."

"You're a good-looking guy with a good physique," Marvin said. "Hollywood is crawling with gays. As you move up the ladder, rung by rung, you're going to be working with them every day. Get used to fending off their passes, 'cause kid, you're going to get a lot of them."

"I can handle myself," Burt said. "And you, of all people, know that I'm handy with my fists."

"So am I," Marvin said. "The biggest problem for a straight actor in Hollywood is that there's practically a stampede following behind him every time he goes to take a leak."

***

As the 1950s came to an end, Burt was signed to a seven-year contract at Universal, with the understanding that the studio reserved the right to cancel every six months if it so desired.

One of Burt's first gigs with his new contract was with a supporting role in a TV series, *Riverboat,* that ran for two seasons (1959 and 1960). Produced by Review Studios, it was set aboard a steam-powered Mississippi River paddleboat (*The Enterprise*) that its skipper had won in a poker game. An ongoing stream of

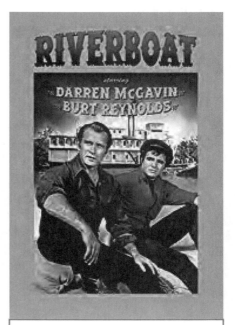

"Darren McGavin was a real shit," Burt claimed. "We starred in a series, *Riverboat,* one of the worst shows on television."

interesting characters (including a pre-presidential Abraham Lincoln) came aboard to interact and to gamble. Chronologically, *Riverboat* was positioned in the 1830s and '40s—a few decades earlier than most other "westerns" of its era.

Burt: "I played 'that dumb whistleblower' in *Riverboat*," opposite "that upstaging egomaniac," Darren McGavin.

Female characters were portrayed by many of the leading TV actresses of the late 1950s, They included Mary Tyler Moore, Elizabeth Montgomery, Anne Baxter, Vera Miles, Jeanne Crain, and Burt's former girlfriend, Jocelyn Brando.

Male guests making cameo appearances included Ricardo Montalban, Eddie Albert, Charles Bronson, Buddy Ebsen, John Ireland, and Richard Chamberlain. On the set, Burt also met Vincent Price, Cliff Robertson, and Robert Vaughn.

The star of *Riverboat*, and the character who, along with the paddle-wheeled steamer itself, bound the series together, was Darren McGavin. Portraying riverboat captain Grey Holden, he had studied acting at both the Actors Studio and the Neighborhood Playhouse in Manhattan. So had Burt.

Tall and ruggedly handsome, McGavin disliked playing in television, defining the medium as "purgatory for a working actor." He'd had one of the roughest childhoods of any actor in Hollywood. When he was sixteen, he'd run away from his home in the Pacific Northwest, living for a while beneath the wharves of San Francisco. One night, he was raped by four hobos.

Fourteen years older than Burt, he'd originally worked as a painter for Columbia Pictures. As an actor, he'd started out with bit parts before working himself to starring roles. In 1954, he was cast as the male lead in the Broadway production of *The Rainmaker. [To his regret, he lost that role in the 1956 movie adaptation to Burt Lancaster.]*

The following year, McGavin starred in the film *Summertime* (1955) with Katharine Hepburn, and he also played a drug pusher opposite Frank Sinatra in *The Man With the Golden Arm* (also 1955).

As for Burt, "I was stuck in this role of the Dumb-Dumb *Riverboat* pilot, Ben Frazer. I had to blow the boat whistle every now and then—and that was it. The cameraman shot close-ups of me, but they seemed to end up on the cutting room floor. They sure weren't aired, but there were lots of close-ups for McGavin."

"Frankly, the whole series was a piece of crap," Burt claimed. "I had such dialogue as 'Do you think the Indians are going to attack us?'"

Before he bolted, Burt co-starred in twenty episodes, including "Path of the Eagle," "Forbidden Island," "The Blowup," "Landlubbers," and "Tampico Road." When asked about which episode in the series had been his favorite, he answered, "None of the above."

In a 1963 interview, Burt recalled the trauma of co-starring with Mc-Gavin. "He did some little action to divert the eye of the viewer, thereby stealing every scene that featured me. During one of the few lines of dialogue I delivered during the course of the entire series, the fucker lit a cigar."

"We'd rehearse a scene three or four times, and I'd have my role down pat," Burt said. "But when the camera was turned on, he fed me entirely different lines to which I was supposed to react."

"Also, in my final rehearsal right before we went on, he always told me the same thing: "'You're not going to say it like *that*, are you?' Talk about building up an actor's confidence."

"Every day I wanted to bash McGavin in the face, but I had to make nice to him since he was the star," Burt said. "Since I couldn't work off steam by knocking him around, I devised another method."

"At the end of a day's shoot, I'd go to my dressing room after borrowing something from the Universal wardrobe department. Then I'd do something to my outfit that made me look like what homophobes call 'faggy.' It could be a pink scarf around my neck, a chartreuse shirt, red boots with elevated heels, and nearly always too-tight leather pants."

"Then I'd head out to some seedy bar in downtown

"In every scene with Darren McGavin, my co-star in *Riverboat*, he did everything in the book to divert attention away from me in any scene we had together," Burt said.

"He didn't unzip and pull out his dick, but he would stop at nothing to sabotage me."

Los Angeles. After a beer or two, it wouldn't be long before I was approached by some wiseass who'd call me a sissy, pansy, fag, whatever. I'd haul him outside in the alley, beat the shit out of him, and return to where I was living, feeling I could face another work day with McGavin."

"Of course, McGavin eventually found out how I really felt when I was interviewed by a reporter from *Variety*. I told him, "I will say this about McGavin: He's gonna be very disappointed on the first Easter after his death."

Riverboat continued to attract a large TV audience despite its bad reviews. *The New York Times* described its plots as "labored and dull." *The Los Angeles Times* claimed, "*Riverboat* is produced with the slick vacuity of a B movie with pleasantly inconsequential stories and an utter disregard for the color and background that the Riverboat *Enterprise* called for."

***

As the 1950s came to an end, there was much speculation about the identity of the mysterious woman who captivated Burt's romantic attention for almost a year. In his memoir, *My Life,* he identified her only by the pseudonym of "Sandi."

He claimed to have been charmed by her allure, especially her "free spirit and all-American prettiness that took my breath away." He also enjoyed going to a theater, buying a ticket, stocking up on popcorn at the food stand, and watching her on the screen.

Ever since the publication of his 1994 memoir—actually long before that—there was speculation that "Sandi" was actually the actress, Lori Nelson.

Our attempts to reach Nelson were unsuccessful. She was still alive in 2019, when she was around eighty-six years old.

When Burt was starring in *Riverboat* on TV, the studio's publicity department published a photo of him dining with Nelson and McGavin. The caption declared that Burt and Nelson were celebrating their engagement.

ROMANTIC HOLLYWOOD TRIVIA:
WHO WAS BURT'S MYSTERIOUS GIRLFRIEND DURING HIS GIG AS A RIVERBOAT PILOT?

Born Dixie Kay Nelson in Santa Fe in 1933, Lori Nelson was the great-grand niece of General John J. "Black Jack" Pershing (1860-1948), one of the most famous U.S. Army Commanders of World War I.

At the age of five, Nelson was designated as "Miss Little America" in a local talent contest. Two years later, she contracted rheumatic fever and was bedridden for four years. But she bounced back and won the title of "Miss Encino" at the age of seventeen.

In 1950, she signed a seven-year contract with Universal, after which makeup men and studio publicists defined her as "Hollywood's most beautiful blonde."

She was thrown into a lot of silly B-pictures opposite Francis "The Talking Mule" or in Ma and Pa Kettle films. In 1954 and 1955, she was a featured player in the remakes of two American classics. The first was Destry, *a recycling of* Destry Rides Again *(1939), which had co-starred Marlene Dietrich and James Stewart, who impregnated her off-screen. An abortion followed.*

The other was I Died a Thousand Times, *a remake of* High Sierra *(1941), which had starred Humphrey Bogart and Ida Lupino.*

In 1957, she reached a far greater audience when she was one of the three leads in the syndicated sitcom How to Marry a Millionaire. *Her co-stars included Merry Anders and Barbara Eden. The TV series was based on the 1953 film of the same title that had starred Marilyn Monroe, Lauren Bacall, and Betty Grable.*

Nelson received a lot of publicity in the early 1950s when she dated gay actor Tab Hunter. Columnist Sheilah Graham asked, "When Lori Nelson and Tab Hunter are photographed on a date, which one

Lori Nelson (left) appears in this publicity photo for Universal with Mamie Van Doren, snapped during their joint appearance in the B-list drive-in classic, *Untamed Youth* (1957).

What was it about? Two spirited but unlucky blondes work for crooks at a rock 'n' roll prison-farm.

103

is the most gorgeous.?"

Hunter admitted that he considered the possibility of marrying Nelson and *"taking her home to meet my mother." But he thought better of it. At the time that he was "officially" romancing Nelson, he was also involved in a torrid (secret) affair with figure skater Ronald Robertson.*

By 1960, Nelson married Johnny Mann, a union that lasted until their divorce in 1973.]

So the jury is still undecided: Was Lori Nelson the girlfriend who Burt identified only as "Sandi" in his memoir?"

***

In an interview with *Variety*, Burt recalled, "I wasn't happy doing the *Riverboat* series. Actually, I wasn't that good in it—in fact, I was quite bad. I really didn't know what I was doing since this was my first major role. My TV work in New York had mostly involved stunts."

"I wanted the damn writers to give me more to do, so I went to them and practically begged them to juice up my character and not let McGavin hog all the scenes. I even asked them to let me perform stunts, since I was good at that. So they wrote in a few for me. That's how I came to meet Hal Needham. At the time, he was one of the leading stuntmen in Hollywood."

"It's amazing that we became such good buddies, since we got off to a rocky start," Burt said. "When I learned he'd been assigned as my stunt double, I was very cocky and told him, 'Look, I don't want to keep you from earning a paycheck, but I want to do my own stunts.'"

Needham smiled at Burt. "Do you know how many actors have told me that over the years? I usually end up visiting them in the hospital."

"I offered to perform a stunt for Hal to show him how skilled I was. When I finished, he told me I was 'pretty good.'"

"What else can you do, kid?" he asked.

"Anything you can teach me," Burt answered.

"Okay, come over to my house in Thousand Oaks this weekend, and we'll have some stunt fun."

That weekend marked the beginning of Burt's long and durable friendship with Needham. *[Years later, it was further solidified when they worked together on the hit TV series, Gunsmoke (1955-1975).]*

When Burt arrived at his home in Thousand Oaks, Needham offered him a cold drink, and they chatted before he invited him to his backyard for some "high falls."

Burt didn't know what that meant. "Did his backyard open onto a ravine?"

In the yard stood a tall oak tree, actually sixty-two feet tall, according to Needham's measurement. There was a rope tied to a branch high in the tree and a safety net below, similar to that used by a trapeze artist.

"Now I want you to pretend you're Tarzan swinging from that vine on that rope. At some point, let go and fall into the net. And so that you don't break your neck, do a flip before you fall. That way, you'll land on your back."

Burt performed that stunt with ease, the first of many over the years with Needham. The following weekend, Burt returned for what he called "more punishment." On most Saturday afternoons, four or five other young stuntmen would be there, learning the business, too.

Hal Needham —once one of the highest-paid stuntmen in Hollywood—in 2011.

"Hal taught us how to 'tree fight,'" Burt said. "One other guy and I would battle while swinging from ropes until one of us knocked the other down, and he fell into the net. I rarely lost, [usually] emerging as 'King of the Jungle.'"

"I soon began hanging out at Hal's place every weekend," Burt said. "We were both lunatics risking our necks, but we had a hell of a lot of fun."

***

Every Monday, Burt reluctantly returned to the set of *Riverboat*, where he had to face Darren McGavin. When he wasn't needed, he wandered around the Universal lot, meeting and talking to movie stars.

"It was a thrill to meet and talk to the likes of Cary Grant and Kirk Douglas. Tony Curtis was a wild one, Ray Milland a bit too stiff for me. I made friends with young actors hoping to become big stars, guys like Robert Hutton, Robert Fuller, Doug McClure, even old pros like Ward Bond."

Burt learned new ways to relieve tension during his gig with *Riverboat*. In the boxing ring at Universal's gym, he sparred with Frankie Vann, a former professional boxer. "I was a southpaw," Burt said. "and I won all the amateur boxing matches I was in, perhaps around two dozen."

On several occasions, Audie Murphy came into the gym to exercise and to keep himself in shape. As he and Burt talked, a friendship developed. Murphy seemed to bask in Burt's flowing praise.

Burt had read a lot about Murphy, the highly publicized, most decorated American combat soldier of World War II. And like thousands of other Audie Murphy fans, Burt had seen the documentary, *To Hell and Back* (1955). It had focused on Murphy's heroic exploits during World War II. Now, Murphy, with the enthusiastic promotion of the studio's press and PR departments, had been reconfigured as a movie star, churning out westerns, despite Hedda Hopper's private belief that "He's the worst actor in Hollywood."

Burt was deeply impressed by Murphy's receipt of every combat award for valor that the U.S. Army could bestow. In January of 1945, when Murphy was nineteen and already wounded, he'd singlehandedly held off an entire company of Nazi soldiers for an hour at Colmar Pocket in France and then spearheaded a devastating counterattack.

In Texas, he'd dropped out of school in the fifth grade to pick cotton to support his family. His father had deserted them.

After the war, James Cagney had signed Murphy to a Hollywood contract and invited him to come and live with him."

Humphrey Bogart snidely said, "I think gun-toting Audie Murphy appeals to the gay streak in Cagney."

During their first week as friends, Murphy watched Burt in the ring, and he also lifted weights with him.

They even showered together after entering the steam room "bare-assed naked" (Burt's words).

Murphy gossiped about Sandra Dee during his co-starring performance with her in *The Wild and the Innocent* (1959). "I

Murphy poses for poster from movie, "Gunpoint" 1965

Audie Murphy, the poor son of Texas sharecroppers, went on to glory in World War II as America's most decorated soldier and Nazi killer. He couldn't act, but Hollywood made him a Western star.

When Burt scored a lucky punch and knocked him out in the boxing ring, the former war hero turned psychotic, chasing after Burt with a .45 to gun him down.

played Wild, and she played Innocent," he said.

"Instead of acting in silly movies, I'd rather be on the ranch breeding quarter horses," Murphy said.

One day after watching Burt boxing in the studio gym with Frankie Vann, Murphy asked if he could spar with him. Vann immediately signaled to Burt that it was a bad idea.

Burt didn't understand why and agreed to it anyway. "I'd feel like a real man beating the most decorated hero of World War II."

Back in the ring, wearing boxing trunks and with the gloves on, Murphy faced Burt.

"Audie and I danced around each other for a few minutes," Burt said, "and I decided I'd had enough of that. Then I delivered my ol' knockout punch, and the heroic soldier fell dead cold on his ass…zonked, the twilight zone, lights out."

"I went to the corner and came back with a pail of cold water, which I threw in his face," Burt said. "He slowly came to. I'll always remember his sitting up and looking at me. I was staring into the eyes of death."

Without saying a word, Murphy stumbled to his feet and headed in a rage back to the locker room. Then Vann turned to Burt. "Get the hell out of here."

"What's the problem?" Burt asked. "Audie and I are good buddies. We were just fooling around, and I scored a lucky punch. I'm sure there are no hard feelings!"

"Don't be a fool," Vann answered. "He takes winning very, very seriously. He'll kill you if you don't move your ass out of here."

Burt didn't believe him until he saw Murphy emerge from the locker room with a .45 in his hand.

"I did the hundred-yard dash like I was on a football field," Burt said. "I raced over to the next set, where Alfred Hitchcock was making *Psycho* with Anthony Perkins. The cast and crew were taking a break, and I hid in the set designed for the Bates Motel."

"When I thought that the coast was clear, I emerged from hiding and encountered Mr. Hitchcock himself. All was not lost. The pudgy director offered me a role in the next episode of his TV series, *Alfred Hitchcock Presents.*"

Burt contacted Vann later that night, and he advised him to "Get lost somewhere. Audie told me he's gonna hunt you down and shoot you."

Burt got into his car and drove south, stopping off for the weekend at a seedy motel north of Laguna. He let Vann know where he was, and a call then came through to him on Monday morning.

"Audie left for Pima County, Arizona," Vann said. "I guess it's safe for you to come out of hiding."

Later that day, Vann explained Murphy's mental state. Because of his horrendous experiences during the war, he on occasion was suffering from what was known at the time as "battle fatigue" or "shell shock."

"Audie can go for months, and he'll be sorta okay," Vann said. "Then, something will trigger him off and he goes ballistic. He's got into trouble before, but the government likes to keep it under cover because he's one of our great war heroes. This isn't the first time we've had to rescue Audie and pay to keep everyone quiet."

"Remind me not to get into the ring with him again," Burt said.

[On May 28, 1971, Brush Mountain, 20 miles west of Roanoke, Virginia, was covered in clouds, fog, and rain, with a visibility at zero. A private plane carrying Audie Murphy, four other passengers, and a pilot crashed, killing everyone aboard.]

***

One morning when Burt was filming yet another episode of *Riverboat*, it was decided that he wouldn't be needed on the set that afternoon. Instead of going home, he wandered around the studio lot. Since he was friendly with the guard at the door to the sound stage where *Inherit the Wind* (1960) was being filmed, he was allowed inside.

He stood out of sight in the background watching two of Hollywood's greatest stars enact a dramatic courtroom scene, the setting for the notorious Scope's "Monkey Trial," in which a schoolteacher had been charged with teaching Charles Darwin's controversial theory of evolution.

Spencer Tracy played a character based on the famous attorney who defended the (enlightened) teacher, and March was cast as the Bible-thumping, fundamentalist William Jennings Bryan. In Burt's view, March and Tracy were the two finest actors in Hollywood, and he felt he could learn much from them, especially Tracy, his favorite screen actor.

He'd seen as many of Tracy's films as he could, his favorite being *Adam's Rib* (1949), in which he'd co-starred with his longtime companion, Katharine Hepburn.

Burt had also seen, in a Los Angeles revival house, the two films for which Tracy had won back-to-back Best Actor Oscars: *Captains Courageous* (1937) and *Boys Town* (1938).

Burt showed up on the set of *Inherit the Wind* for the next three days in a row, hoping that Tracy might notice him. He didn't want

A courtroom encounter between Spencer Tracy (left) and Fredric March from *Inherit the Wind* (1960).

to barge up to him and introduce himself. On the final day, Tracy did take notice and stopped to ask him, "Are you an actor, kid?"

"The jury is still out on that, Mr. Tracy," Burt said.

"You sure have the looks for it," Tracy said. "You're a budding Clark Gable type, but you look like Marlon Brando, that jerk."

Burt was invited into Tracy's dressing room where the aging actor changed into his street clothes. Afterward, he invited Burt across the street for a drink, which lasted until closing time. "In a town of heavy boozers, he was the champ," Burt said. "He could go through a whole bottle of Scotch and keep talking, whereas I would be under the table."

Since Tracy was his favorite actor, Burt had already learned everything he could about him. Even though he was engaged in some sort of relationship with Hepburn, they didn't live together. A devout Roman Catholic, Tracy was unwilling to dissolve his unhappy marriage to Louise Treadwell, with whom he had produced a deaf son, John.

Tracy was known for his numerous affairs. When he'd made *A Man's Castle* (1933), he'd fallen in love with a 20-year-old Loretta Young, but his marriage survived.

He had been intimate with Ingrid Bergman when they made *Dr. Jekyll & Mr. Hyde* (1941), and he was said to have "deflowered" a very young Judy Garland.

Joan Crawford had seduced Tracy when they co-starred in *Mannequin* (1938), but it hadn't gone well. She later claimed, "He's a very disturbed man, a mean drunk and a bastard."

Other leading ladies and other stars also flowed through his life: Grace Kelly, Paulette Goddard, Myrna Loy, and a young starlet, Nancy Davis, who later married Ronald Reagan.

Burt had long heard stories, many of them scandalous, about Tracy's addiction to alcohol. He would have a sober period for a while, and then go on one of his infamous "binges." They'd last for a week, maybe two, during which time no one knew where he was. Sometimes, he'd check into a seedy hotel with a suitcase loaded with liquor and not leave until many days later, after drinking the contents of every bottle.

On occasion, during filming, and after drinking heavily, he'd throw fits, tearing up the set or the soundstage.

Tracy and Burt began to see a lot of each other, but rarely, if ever, within the cottage he occupied on the grounds of George Cukor's estate. Once, in a tavern, a reporter approached Tracy with questions. Burt heard him say, "Make up something. I don't care. Just promise me one thing: Make it a hell of a story."

One night, Tracy finally invited Burt to visit the cottage in which he was living alone. Hepburn had her own residence, but at this particular moment, she was in New York City, or perhaps Connecticut.

They brought back some potato salad and cold cuts, and they sat up eating, and—in Tracy's case—drinking, mostly Scotch.

Scotty Bowers, Hollywood's leading pimp, supplied young men returning from World War II battlefields to the leading homosexuals of Hollywood.

He slept with Spencer Tracy, and supplied an array of blemish-free girls to Katharine Hepburn.

It was well after midnight when Tracy suggested they get some sleep and invited Burt to share his bed. When Burt stripped down to his shorts, Tracy said, 'Off they come. Real men sleep bare-assed."

Burt fell into a deep slumber. At around three o'clock, he was awakened by Tracy getting out of bed. He muttered, "Gotta take a leak." He stumbled around but couldn't seem to find the light switch. Finally, giving up, he pissed in a corner of the bedroom.

Burt went back to sleep but was awakened about an hour and a half later with this strange sensation. Because he had not sobered up quite yet, it took him a moment to realize that Tracy was going down on him.

As he later told his friend, Hal Needham, "I eased out from under him as gently as I could. Without saying a word, I grabbed my clothes—at least some of them—and dressed in the front yard. I headed out as dawn was breaking."

"That was the end of my friendship with dear ol' Spence. He never met with me again, no more hanging out. It was sad. I still think he was the finest actor the movies ever saw."

[Spencer Tracy's closeted homosexuality and Katharine Hepburn's lesbianism had been widely known about in Hollywood for decades. Hollywood's press and PR machines hinted that they were lovers, but their closest friend, the director George Cukor, told his intimates that the relationship was platonic.

Tracy often complained to Cukor, "Katharine treats me like I'm dirt."]

In 2012, with the publication of the *Full Service,* the memoirs of Hollywood's leading pimp, Scotty Bowers, Tracy and Hepburn were outed as homosexuals. *The New York Times* published a review of his memoirs, and equivalent revelations about Tracy and Hepburn were published in newspapers from coast to coast.

***

"In the second season of *Riverboat,* I was no longer Mr. Nice Guy to Darren McGavin," Burt said. "In the first season, he had stolen every scene from me by upstaging me and trying to destroy my confidence."

"Now, after one of his scenes, I'd say something like, 'You're really losing it, boy. What a lousy job of acting that was. If you keep this up, *Riverboat* will be canceled.'"

"We didn't come to blows, but the crew knew that day was coming," Burt said. "We'd have to duke it out. It was just a matter of time."

Another reason Burt resented his co-star was the way he treated an array of actresses who appeared in various episodes. As Burt later revealed in a memoir, "He mistreated women and took a run at all of them, the opposite of suave. He'd back them up against the wall so they couldn't move. They'd call that sexual harassment today."

"I don't care who they were, McGavin went after them. I remember working with Arlene Dahl—what a beauty!, Pat Crowley, Stella Stevens, Gena Rowlands, Debra Paget, Mona Freeman. I'm not saying that McGavin went after all of them, because I wasn't around on all occasions. But I saw enough to label him a serial seducer."

Actually, as Burt related, it was not McGavin but the assistant director, Carter DeHaven, with whom he tangled. "At least McGavin was an attractive man that not all women wanted to resist, but DeHaven was an old, lusty coot, a fart born in 1886 when dinosaurs still roamed California. The only good thing he did was give the world Gloria DeHaven, that cute little musical star at MGM. Carter had broken into silents in 1915. Okay, so he worked with Charlie Chaplin. Big Deal."

"Carter was on my ass for every alleged infraction," Burt said. "If I was ten minutes late, he declared World War Three. If I didn't blow that damn boat whistle right, he tore into me like the Allied Invasion of Normandy. It was always something I did wrong. He hated my guts. In contrast, he always had this brown nose from having it up McGavin's ass. His boy could do no wrong. He even told me I could take acting lessons from McGavin."

"One day on the set of *Riverboat*, when the cast and crew had gone to lunch, I stayed behind—no appetite," Burt said. "I heard this racket coming from the far side of the boat, and I went to investigate. There was grandpa, Carter himself, in some struggle with this blonde actress—I don't remember which one. He was fondling her breasts, and she was struggling to get away."

"I exploded. It had been all I could do to hold back my temper with Carter, but I lost it that afternoon. I pulled Carter off the gal, who fled the scene, and picked the bastard up and tossed him into the studio lake. On tours of Universal today, guides still point out the scene of my violent attack."

"That afternoon marked the beginning of my 'bad boy' reputation in Hollywood," Burt claimed. "I knew that Lew Wasserman was disappointed in me for not taking his advice to control my temper. It was obvious that he was going to kick me out of MCA."

Carter DeHaven in his younger days.

According to Burt, "He was the assistant director on *Riverboat*, and he hounded my ass for the slightest infraction."

"When he wasn't shouting at me, the old fart tried to molest every beautiful woman on the set. What I did to him one day became the stuff of Hollywood legend."

"The word spread quickly through the Hollywood grapevine that I was unreliable. It was said that if someone looked at me cross-eyed, he'd get a fist in his face. I was called a hot head, even though I'd been a gallant knight saving a blonde from a fate worse than death. Wasserman would no longer take my calls, so I knew my days with that Universal contract were on life support."

"I needed a breather, so I returned to Riviera Beach for a reunion with my parents, who still loved me in their fashion. Soon after I got there, I encountered a reporter from *The Miami Herald*. He asked me what my biggest thrill had been. I knew he meant in Hollywood, but I told him, 'It was scoring a seventy-five yard touchdown on the first play of the game against Jacksonville Lee in 1953.'"

***

All on the same day, Universal did not renew the contracts of three young actors: Clint Eastwood, David Janssen, and Burt himself. "So what did this untalented trio do? We went out and got drunk."

In the days or years to come, Burt became friends with both Eastwood and Janssen. They did not see each other frequently, and didn't exactly hang out together, but a friendship flourished as all three of their careers in Hollywood ascended.

Burt had been fired because, "You're too disrupting, too unruly, and you have no talent whatsoever as an actor." The reason given for firing Eastwood was

Clint Eastwood—a publicity photo in 1961 for *Rawhide*.

"What a great friend he was," Burt said. "We were bonded at the hip for life through thick or thin, shit or gravy."

that his Adam's Apple was too prominent. Janssen was told that his ears were too big. He reminded them that the same thing had been said about Clark Gable, who had gone on to become the King of Hollywood.

"My friendship with Clint was a bit odd," Burt claimed. "He was six years older than me, and even more macho if such a thing was possible. He also had a red-hot temper, and I never once wanted to cross him. He could flare up at any minute."

"I remember one night in a bar when we were drinking, and I was talking a lot. He'd add five or six words every hour or so. This pushy woman came up to him and demanded an autograph. God, she was aggressive. We had a pitcher of beer in front of us. Clint took that pitcher and poured the beer over her head as she screamed for help. No man came to her aid. It seemed that no one wanted to take on 'Dirty Harry' that night."

"Clint liked to live privately, and for a long time I didn't even know his address," Burt said. "One night he invited me to dinner. Since it was right before Christmas, I gave him a present, a basset hound. That dog fell madly in love with Clint, and he took him everywhere, even during the making of films where the hound would sit beside the director, perhaps signaling Clint if he pulled off a scene or not."

"I thought of myself as a babe magnet, but when I went out with Clint, the girls flocked to him—not to me."

Eastwood told Burt, "I don't think I could ever be attracted to a girl unless she liked music. I can't even have lunch or a drink without girls crowding around, begging me to hand over my dirty plate or my empty beer bottle so they'd have a souvenir of me."

Over a period of time, Eastwood was known for seducing some notable women, none better known than Barbra Streisand, but also Bernadette Peters and the doomed Jean Seberg.

David Janssen in 1966 in the hit TV serial, *The Fugitive.*

"Although David Janssen and Clint were friends, that did not stop Clint from seducing Janssen's widow, Dani Crayne, after he died."

Eastwood told Burt, "Sex is only a small part of life. It's a good thing—great, really—but ninety percent of life is spent doing other things."

"He was my dear friend," Burt said. "On screen, he had this perpetual grimace, a gravelly voice, assorted mumblings, pained expressions, and a sleepy body language. His fans loved it—and so did I."

"Clint and I shared at least one thing in common," Burt said. "Both of us lost our virginity when we were fourteen."

Born in 1931 as the cold winds of March were blowing across the plains of Nebraska, Janssen was another handsome and very macho male who became both a television and film star. He was of Irish and Jewish descent. He faced desertion by his father when he was only five years old. At that time, his mother relocated to Los Angeles where young David assumed the name of his stepfather, Eugene Janssen.

He was awarded his first film role, and small it was, when he was just thirteen.

He landed his first television series, *Richard Diamond, Private Detective* (1957-1960), a CBS four-star hit that also introduced Mary Tyler Moore.

Janssen's greatest acclaim came when he starred in *The Fugitive* (1963-67), about a Midwest doctor wrongly convicted of murdering his wife. Seventy-five percent of American TV viewers tuned in for its final episode and finale.

Janssen's leading ladies in feature films included Angie Dickinson, Stefanie Powers, and Linda Evans. Some of his more notable films included *To Hell and Back* (1955), the autobiography of Audie Murphy; John Wayne's Vietnam War film, *The Green Berets* (1968), and Gregory Peck's *Marooned*

114

(1969) in which Janssen played an astronaut sent to rescue three stranded men in outer space.

"I liked being with David, but he was always tense," Burt recalled. "He was a very heavy drinker, and he smoked four packages of cigarettes a day."

"I saw all of his movies, at least three or four sitting beside him," Burt said. "He had great success, but like a lot of actors, he had to endure crap, such as appearing opposite Francis, the Talking Mule."

"He had two wives, but I think—in fact, I know—that he got a lot on the side. I remember one night how a drunken Shelley Winters came up to him and pinched his ear lobe. "What big ears you have, David," she said. "I hear that men with big ears have a big everything. How about it?"

"You're on, babe," he told her. "But I must warn you: I play rough."

Burt was saddened to hear of Janssen's death from a heart attack on the early morning of February 13, 1980 at his home in Malibu. He was only forty-eight years old.

***

Freed from his contract at Universal, Burt became a freelancer after his return to Hollywood. "Apparently, a lot of directors weren't afraid of my reputation, or hadn't heard about it. I got jobs, real minor stuff, some of them lasting only a day. I decided to behave myself and be a Southern gentleman, mainly because I had become fond of eating."

His first job after his return was a role in the hit TV "anthology" series, *Playhouse 90,* in which he appeared in two episodes aired on CBS late in 1959 and early in 1960.

Of all the competing series being broadcast at the time, *Playhouse 90* was the most artistically ambitious, hiring top-rated directors and actors. During its first season, it was filmed live at CBS Television City in Los Angeles.

Burt's first appearance, and a brief

How did Burt meet many of the old-time players in vintage Hollywood? By starring with them in episodes of TV series when they were past their big-screen heydays.

Top photo shows Burt's co-star, Bonita Granville, as she appeared in her biggest hit, the midwar propaganda film, *Hitler's Children* (1943)

115

one, was as "The Actor" in *The Velvet Alley*. Its star was Art Carney, who portrayed a struggling writer heading for the bigtime. Along the way, he meets human jackals, cutthroats, and rotters. Carney's role was based on the life and show-biz career of Rod Serling, the writer and developer of *The Twilight Zone*.

Burt was a supporting player to such actors as Leslie Nielsen, Katharine Bard, Jack Klugman, and Bonita Granville, the former sharp-nosed, brazen child star whom Burt had first seen in a film released during the darkest year of World War II, *Hitler's Children* (1943).

[One of the most financially successful films ever produced by RKO Studios, Hitler's Children *depicted some of the atrocities of the Hitler Youth movement. Although critics dismissed it as "a successful piece of propaganda trash," it earned RKO a profit of $1.21 million and evolved into the fourth-highest grossing film of 1943.]*

Burt returned to *Playhouse 90* for a second episode named "Alas, Babylon," based on Pat Frank's acclaimed book, the first apocalyptic novel of the nuclear age.

For his appearance in yet another TV series, Burt joined the cast of *Johnny Ringo,* a Western series that aired on CBS in October of 1959, fading into the sunset in June of the following year. The series was very loosely based on the notorious gunfighter and outlaw (Johnny Ringo), who tangled with Wyatt Earp and Doc Holliday and was found dead at thirty-two.

Whereas Don Durant was cast in the series' lead role, Burt appeared in a single episode entitled "The Stranger." The series was the creation of Aaron Spelling, who would go on to greater things and it was produced by Dick Powell's Four Star Television.

[Back then, it seemed that every cowpoke drama had to have a "gun gimmick." Equivalent examples from other actors included Steve McQueen's "saw-off" with a trick holster, or Richard Boone's hidden Derringer. In Johnny Ringo, *the hero (as portrayed by Don Durant) had a gun that fired an extra bullet instead of what could be loaded into a conventional six-shooter.]*

Television was awash at the time with Western series, a total of thirty in all. *Johnny Ringo* was competing at the time with ABC's *The Real McCoys* (1957-1963), starring Walter Brennan and broadcast during prime time every Thursday.

Burt had met Alfred Hitchcock accidentally,

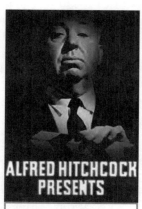

ALFRED HITCHCOCK PRESENTS

"Hitchcock told me he wished he'd been born a sex symbol like I was," Burt claimed.

"He lamented his bald pate, pear-shaped body, tiny cock, and lugubrious drawl."

back when Audie Murphy was threatening to kill him. Hitchcock asked him to join in one of his episodes on *Alfred Hitchcock Presents*. *[Time magazine had reviewed that series as "One of the 100 Best Shows of All Time."]*

The program was broadcast from 1955 to 1965, in episodes formatted as dramas, thrillers, or mysteries. When he signed to host the series, Hitchcock had already been directing full-length films, many of them classics, for three decades.

[When he filmed his episode, Burt was joining a parade of other stars who had worked for Hitchcock in one or more episodes of this famous series. They included Dick York, Mildred Dunnock, Vincent Price, Robert Vaughn, Robert Redford, Steve McQueen, Dennis Morgan, Joseph Cotten, Dean Stockwell, and Peter Lorre. At around the time Burt worked on his episodes, even Bette Davis had appeared. In Out There—Darkness *playing a self-involved, unattractively aging egomaniac. In the words of one online reviewer, "Through it all, Davis remains Davis, enunciating oh so precisely and doing a near-parody of the inimitable character that inspired a thousand and one campy mimics."]*

Burt's episode, "Escape from Sonoita," focuses on two criminals as they drive a car through the desert. When it breaks down, they steal a tanker from Bill Davis (the character played by Burt) and his friend, Andy. The thieves aren't aware that Bill and Andy know how to survive in the desert. The next day the police find the tanker and the dead bodies of the two thieves. The kidnappers had turned on each other when their water ran out, not realizing that the tanker they'd stolen was carrying plenty of water.

Burt's next role was in an episode of yet another TV series, *Lock Up*, in which Burt played Latchard Duncan in "The Case of Alexis George." Burt later said, "I don't recall what I had to do. I was in and out."

Lock Up (1959-1961) starred movie actor Macdonald Carey as a corporate attorney in Philadelphia who had devoted his life to saving innocent people arrested on circumstantial evidence. *[Each episode of* Lock Up *was based on case histories in actual police files.]*

United Artists Television usually hired big-name actors for episodes within the series.

This ad for a series in which Burt played a role in a single episode ran in 1960 in a local newspaper

117

They included Dyan Cannon, John Carradine, Jack Cassidy, Robert Conrad, Buddy Ebsen, Wandra Hendrix (the former wife of Audie Murphy), Mary Tyler Moore, and Stefanie Powers. When Burt was added to that list, he was virtually unknown.

Burt followed his gig on *Lock Up* with bigger roles on yet another TV series entitled, *The Blue Angels*.

[Broadcast on syndicated TV stations everywhere between 1960 and 1961 and produced in cooperation with the U.S. Department of Defense, it showcased the Blue Angels. Established in 1946, its mission focused (and still focuses) on state-of-the-art aircraft whose pilots are skilled at flying in synchronized formations above parades and rallies as part of morale-building demonstrations of the Navy's aerobatic skill.]

Blue Angels starred Dennis Cross as Commander Arthur Richards, the head of a four-man flight squadron touring the country for flight exhibitions and recruitment programs.

Burt starred in the series as Chuck Corman in "Fire Fight" (according to Burt, "the title gave away the plot") and later in "Powder Puff Pilot." *[In that episode, a female pilot discovers that her airplane's mechanic isn't performing proper maintenance because of his involvement in a gambling ring.]*

***

Burt was later assigned a role in *Michael Shayne*, a TV series broadcast from 1960-1961. It was based on a fictional detective whose crime adventures had already entertained millions of readers and movie goers. He was quickly brought up to date about who this publishing sensation was.

[The detective character of Michael Shayne was created by "Brett Holliday," a pseudonym for the writer Davis Dresser. He wrote his first suspense novel, Dividend on Death, *in 1939. An instant bestseller, it spawned fifty more paperback novels in the same genre, none of which was issued as hardcovers until 1958. After that, in the same context with many of the same characters, a series of ghost writers took over, producing twenty-seven additional paperback originals. This avalanche of books*

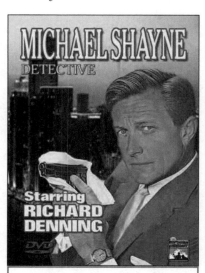

In 1960, once again, Burt was assigned a small role within someone else's TV series.

118

went on to spawn 300 short stories, a dozen film adaptations, radio and TV dramas, and even comic books.]

As World War II was raging in 1940, soon to engulf the United States, Americans often turned to escapist fare. Beginning with the film *Michael Shayne, Private Detective,* Lloyd Nolan would star in seven movies in the title role. Always predictable, Nolan was no-nonsense and reliable, certainly not in a sexy way except in the view of Truman Capote, who harbored a lifelong crush on him.

Once at a party, Capote told Burt, "I've had Errol Flynn, and I've had Marlon Brando, but the one man I desired above all others was Lloyd Nolan."

In 1942, 20th Century dropped the series. But in the first year after the war, the fictional character of Michael Shayne inspired the production of five low-budget movies, each released in 1946 with titles that included *Blonde for the Day* and *Murder Is My Business.* They starred Hugh Beaumont.

***

As the popularity of TV increased in the 1950s, there was an increasing demand for police dramas, and the character of Michael Shayne was resuscitated yet again. Beginning in 1960—the year John F. Kennedy ran for U.S. President—a TV series with thirty-two episodes, *Michael Shayne,* began broadcasting into prime time every Friday night at 10PM. Starring Richard Denning, it faced stiff competition, competing with Rod Serling's *The Twilight Zone* on CBS, and *The Detectives with Robert Taylor* on ABC.

In Burt's episode, broadcast in 1961, he portrayed Jerry Turner in a segment entitled *The Boat Caper.* Its plot centered on two business partners who detest each other. When one of them dies in an explosion at the Marina, the surviving partner emerges as a prime suspect and is arrested by the police and charged with murder. Sleuth Shayne isn't convinced that he's guilty and sets out to investigate and unearths clues that lead to an unexpected verdict.

[Half a century would pass before the Michael Shayne character would in-

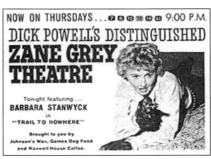

NOW ON THURSDAYS...☷☷☷☷☷☷ 9:00 P.M.

DICK POWELL'S DISTINGUISHED ZANE GREY THEATRE

Tonight featuring...
BARBARA STANWYCK
in
"TRAIL TO NOWHERE"

Brought to you by
Johnson's Wax, Gaines Dog Food
and Maxwell House Coffee.

Barbara Stanwyck was one of the most famous stars to appear on TV's *Zane Grey Theatre.*

She told Burt, "I'll agree to appear in a Western, providing the damn writers give me a macho role—not some damsel in a long cotton dress racing down the steps, asking 'Where have all the cattle gone?'"

119

spire yet another movie. It was Kiss Kiss Bang Bang *(2005) starring Robert Downey, Jr. and Val Kilmer. It was based on the novel,* Bodies Are Where You Find Them.*]*

***

Before Burt made his debut in a feature-length film, he appeared in an episode of yet another hit TV Western series, *Dick Powell's Zane Grey Theatre* (1956-1961).

[Although in its early years, its plots and themes were inspired by the novels and short stories of the fabled Western author Zane Grey, other writers, including Aaron Spelling, began submitting original material too. On a trivia note, although its producer, Golden-Age matinee star Dick Powell, hosted the entire run of 149 episodes, he starred as a character in only fifteen of them. The Zane Grey series was ground-breaking in that five of its episodes evolved into subsequent spin-off series that showcased stars who included Robert Culp, Chuck Connors, Brian Keith, and Steve McQueen.]

Broadcast in 1961 and entitled "Man from Everywhere," Burt's episode focused on the story of a man who is taunted into accepting a job as bodyguard for a gambler standing trial.

***

Burt's feature film debut, *Angel Baby*, a 1961 Allied Artists release, was viewed as a "knock-off" of *Elmer Gantry.* That film had starred Burt Lancaster and had won an Oscar for his performance as a fast-talking, silver-tongued evangelist, who liked to drink heavily when not womanizing and saving sinners from a fiery hell. The irony is that *Angel Baby* was filmed before *Elmer Gantry* but released after the award-winning movie.

Burt's first starring role in a feature film, *Angel Baby*, was called a rip-off of Burt Lancaster's more acclaimed *Elmer Gantry (1960).*

Actually, *Angel Baby* was in the can before filming began on *Elmer Gantry.*

Filming would be in Burt Reynolds' native Florida, with location shooting at the University of Miami in Coral Gables, in neighboring Coconut Grove, and in the Everglades, Burt's former teenage stamping ground.

Angel Baby was based on the novel, *Jenny Angel,* by Elsie Oaks Barber. Burt played a rapist in sixth billing after its stars, George Hamilton, Mercedes McCambridge, Salome Jens, Joan Blondell, and Henry Jones. Dudley Remus, Burt's friend, had the minor role of Otis Finch. He would later play a far larger role in Burt's future when he became production manager of the Burt Reynolds Dinner Theater in Jupiter, Florida.

The film (as well as the novel on which it was based) was set in the redneck South. It depicted Angel Baby (as played by Salome Jens), who has been mute since the age of eight. She is first seen enduring a possible date rape by Hoke Adams (as portrayed by Burt). The girl's mother chases Hoke away from her daughter, and they later attend a tent revival where Paul Strand (George Hamilton) is a hell-and-damnation preacher, thrilling a devoutly religious (and pumped-up) audience of Florida-based, Bible-thumping crackers. Although Paul is married to an older woman (Mercedes McCambridge), he becomes romantically inclined toward Angel Baby after he restores her ability to speak.

A native of Philadelphia, Paul Wendkos became Burt's first feature film director, although Burt initially wasn't impressed with his credentials. He'd just helmed a massive teenage box office hit, *Gidget* (1959), starring Sandra Dee. After the completion of *Angel Baby,* he'd churn out *Gidget Goes Hawaiian* (1961) and *Gidget Goes to Rome* (1963).

In his portrayal of Paul Strand, the preacher in *Angel Baby*, Hamilton is married to an older evangelist, as portrayed by McCambridge. He claims that his prayers have restored the speech of a former mute, Salome Jens, playing Angel Baby. His ministry gets complicated when he falls in love with this younger woman, who evolves into an evangelist, too.

As the plot unfolds, Paul (Hamilton) from within his revival tent produces a revival meeting that includes provocatively costumed array of "repentant sinners" inspired by famous characters of the Old Testament, including Delilah and Jezebel.

Angel becomes devoted to Paul, a relationship cemented when she is attacked by Hoke (Burt), but rescued by Paul. Angel Baby sets off on her own traveling ministry with the help of Ben

Burt Reynolds with Salome Jens in *Angel Baby* (1961). "I played a character who believes in ripping off a girl's clothes if she ignores my advances."

and Molly Hays, as portrayed by Henry Jones and Joan Blondell.

In their respective roles, Blondell and Jones played broken-down, alcoholic, over-the-hill wrecks, trying to collect donations from people too poor to contribute. She is reeling, spouting hell and damnation to the sinners. Henry Jones played the role that one viewer described as "a growling, spewing, scarlet-faced, spraying man of Jesus."

Joan Blondell with Henry Jones in *Angel Baby.*

"I was this sodden evangelist who finds Jesus in a whiskey bottle," Blondell recalled. "In our roles, we inhabit a world of seedy tent revivals, decaying trailer parks, rusty old cars

"We played alcohol-sodden preachers trying to take the hard-earned money of our white trash audiences," Blondell claimed.

with leaky roofs, and unreliable motors."

"The white trash audience reminded me of the 1947 film, *Nightmare Alley,* I made with Tyrone Power. The dialogue in *Angel Baby* was feverish enough to make Tennessee Williams blush. All of us were a bit guilty of overacting, maybe more than a bit."

"George Hamilton intrigued the hell out of me," Burt said. "Both of us had gone to Palm Beach High, and when each of us was only fourteen, we were seduced by the same older woman."

"When George hit Hollywood, every actor wanted to be the next James Dean or the next Marlon Brando," Burt said. "Not George." He wanted to be the next David Niven. He borrowed a Rolls Royce and parked it every afternoon in front of the gates to MGM. One day, he got lucky and was spotted by an executive, probably a gay one."

When Hamilton starred with Burt, he was an actor in demand, having already filmed *Crime and Punishment U.S.A.* (1959). The film was seen by Vincente Minnelli, who cast Hamilton as the younger son in *Home from the Hill* (1960), a Southern melodrama starring Robert Mitchum.

The movie was popular, and MGM signed him to a long-term contract. However, his next picture, *All the Fine Young Cannibals* (1960), with Natalie Wood and Robert Wagner, was a box office flop.

Hamilton bounced back, however, with a big hit, *Where the Boys Are* (1960). According to Burt, "When I said goodbye to George, he was off to co-star with Lana Turner in *By Love Possessed* (1961)."

"I always told people that if Paramount producer Robert Evans and

Tony Perkins ever had a baby boy, he would look like George," Burt said. He later altered his description, claiming, "This guy looks like the son of Tony Curtis."

"George indulged in some high profile seductions, including Lynda Bird Johnson, Imelda Marcos, the co-dictator of the Philippines, and even Elizabeth Taylor," Burt said. "Throw in the aging but still-beautiful Merle Oberon, Britt Ekland, Mary Wilson of the Supremes, Vanessa Redgrave, Julie Newmar, Susan Kohner, heiress Charlotte Ford, and even the Duchess of Bedford."

"He also dated enough Miss Worlds and Miss Universes to hold his own pageant," Burt said. "He even told me his secret: 'I always make a woman feel like a lady.'"

[ROMANTIC TRIVIA: When the then-popular jazz singer named Keely Smith migrated with her act to Miami Beach, she was on the verge of divorcing her husband, Louis Prima, a fellow performer. Burt began to date her, but according to Burt, when Hamilton arrived on the scene, "he snatched her out of my arms."]

"The director of Angel Baby forced me to appear in a fight scene with Hamilton, who beats me up," Burt said. "When I heard that, I told him, 'You've got to be kidding.' That boy is no fighter and hardly a match for me. In the dumbest fight scene ever to appear on the screen, he sort of lifted me up, and I made a big leap into the bushes, faking it like he'd tossed me there."

Burt looked on to watch Hamilton and

Mercedes McCambridge and George Hamilton in *Angel Baby*. "I got to show Burt Reynolds that I, too had a chest worthy of viewing," Hamilton said.

Angel Baby. The character portrayed by Salome Jens gets assaulted by "hot-to-trot" Burt

McCambridge during the filming of a fight scene. "After the first take, she made fun of me for being such a Southern gentleman," Hamilton said. "I just couldn't whack her like the script demanded. She told me not to hold back my punches, so I let her have it. The next day, she showed up with a neck brace, and my right arm was in a sling."

"Burt played the second banana to me in this one, but when we made

The Man Who Loved Cat Dancing, I was the second banana," Hamilton said.

McCambridge remembered Hamilton as "having been out in the sun too long and having too white teeth and patent leather hair. He is supposed to make love to me while I quote from the Old Testament about the evils of lust and fornication."

McCambridge recalled "a local Florida Boy in the cast, who was cute and cocky. He was always disappearing into the buses with a scantily clad dollie he'd picked up at the university. The crew called him 'hot pants.' The kid was girl crazy. I don't remember his name but someone told me after the picture wrapped that he was headed to Hollywood to try to break into the movies."

"Hot Pants turned out to be Burt Reynolds."

***

Born into a family who worked in vaudeville, Joan Blondell parlayed a beauty pageant into movie stardom.

At Warner Brothers, during Pre-Code Hollywood, she shot to stardom as a sexy, wise-cracking busty blonde beauty. Often cast as a gold-digger, she would appear in more than a hundred movies and TV episodes. She won a Best Supporting Actress Oscar nomination for *The Blue Veil* (1951) opposite Jane Wyman.

She told Burt, "Movie fans are always asking me what James Cagney and Humphrey Bogart were really like. I could tell them far sexier stories about Errol Flynn, Bing Crosby, Clark Gable, or John Wayne."

She had once been married to actor/producer Dick Powell and was later wed to Mike Todd before Elizabeth Taylor made off with him.

"Mike was a violent man, and we were often broke because of his gambling losses," Blondell told Burt. "In a fight, he once broke my arm. In another row, he held me out of an eighth-floor hotel window by my ankles. Elizabeth was welcome to him."

Blondell's husband in *Angel Baby*, Ben Hayes, was portrayed by Henry Jones, a familiar face to movie-goers at the time. He had starred in films that included *The Bad Seed* (1956). Over the course of his long career, he appeared in 180 films and TV shows, including *Butch Cassidy & the Sundance Kid* (1969).

"Mercedes McCambridge was one of the most talented actresses I ever worked with," Burt said. "I'd first seen her with James Dean in *Giant* (1956) and also in *Johnny Guitar* (1954), where Mercedes and Joan Crawford looked like a couple of dykes battling it out. Two tough old broads. I later had my own experience with Crawford and sorta agreed with Mercedes' appraisal. She called her 'a mean, tipsy, powerful, rotten egg lady.'"

McCambridge described the faithful who flocked to the tent revivals in *Angel Baby* as "raucously roaring, terrible people...dumb, red-necker crummy gospel nuts! It was an audience of Dixieland Christians whose minds had grown mushy from mildew."

Cast as Angel Baby and born in Milwaukee, Salome Jens was a contemporary of Burt's. She'd gotten into a lot of trouble when she'd told a reporter, "The only time I can imagine contemplating suicide would be if I were told that I had to go back there and live forever."

Shortly after working with Burt, she'd married Ralph Meeker, whom Burt had always considered a rival.

"People who knew Meeker better than me considered him brazenly macho and less-than-lovable," Burt said. "He was perfect to take over Marlon Brando's role in *A Streetcar Named Desire* after Brando left the cast in 1949."

Jens had achieved critical acclaim in New York, starring in the premiere of Jean Genet's *The Balcony*.

The climax of *Angel Baby* is reached when the faithful realize that they have been duped.

Most of the cast members thought the picture might have attracted a wider audience, but it was operating on a thin-ice budget, "with barely enough to develop the negative," in the words of its director, "much less advertise it."

For his debut movie role, Burt got almost no mention except for a line in *Daily Variety* that acknowledged that he lent "adequate featured support."

As advertisements for *Angel Baby*, its producers captioned posters with an image of Jens and the proclamation, "If she's good enough for Satan, she's good enough for me!"

Even though she was thirty years older than Burt, he found Joan Blondell "still alluring and quite sexy. It was not just her bosom, but her

Two views of pre-code Blondell, "the Ultimate Dame." Burt, savvy connoisseur of older women, was not immune to her charms.

125

saucer eyes, which had been described as 'martini olive green with a coffee bean perimeter.' Those eyes always sparkled at dawn or at midnight. They seemed to draw you in like moths to a flame."

One weekend, Blondell asked Burt to drive her to Palm Beach to attend a fund-raising gala at the Kennedy compound. Rose Kennedy was there, but JFK was on the campaign trail, running for President of the United States.

"I was eager to go," Blondell said, "even though I'm a secret Republican."

After the event, Burt and Blondell were too tired to drive back to Miami, so they stopped at a small motel to the north of Hollywood (Florida).

"I was surprised when he booked us into a double room," Blondell said.

She said, "He was so much younger and very handsome, a real man. As we undressed, he told me he had this thing for older women, but also liked 'em young."

"He delivered that night, and wanted more loving at four o'clock that morning," she claimed. "I'll tell you this: Burt Reynolds is welcome to put his shoes under my bed at any time of the day or night."

***

At the conclusion of *Angel Baby*, Burt wondered if he'd ever work again. Then one night, he received a call from director Byron Haskin.

"Reynolds," he said. "How would you like to go to Germany to make a war movie set in 1944?"

CHAPTER FOUR

WHAT EVER HAPPENED TO BABY JANE?

How the Young Horndog, Burt Reynolds,
Inaugurated and Sustained
Brief, Neurotically Charged Affairs with Both

BETTE DAVIS &
JOAN CRAWFORD

ARMORED COMMAND

Burt Plays a Soldier in a World War II Film that Even the
Studio's Highest-Octane Press and Publicity Couldn't Save.

MARLON BRANDO

Burt's Feud with, and How He Coped with
His Striking Resemblance to

GUNSMOKE

Burt, Bored with the Unrelieved Monotony of another Minor
Role, Plays a Half-breed Blacksmith Named Quentin

THE WAITING GAME: GETTING A GIG AS AN ACTOR
In the late 50s and early 60s, Burt developed his acting skills as a military hero under fire,
and as a frequently unemployed actor filling in with small parts on TV series
whenever possible

Burt's second feature film, *Armored Command*, set during World War II and released in 1961, was a low-budget B-film from Allied Artists. Its plot unfolds during the infamous Battle of the Bulge, Hitler's last attempt—with a Nazi Panzer attack— to invade France. Although filmed in southern Germany, the plot defined the setting as the Vosges Mountains of eastern France.

Burt was welcomed to Munich by the film's director, Bryon Haskin, who was born in 1899, the same year as Humphrey Bogart. Haskin was best known for helming *Treasure Island* (1950) for Walt Disney and also for *The War of the Worlds* (1953). He was also acclaimed for his special effects, for which in time he would receive three Oscar nominations.

Burt wasn't due to report to work until Monday morning, so he had the weekend to explore Munich on his own. He later wrote about German women, claiming they had "the greatest legs in the world." How he knew that remains a mystery, since he arrived in Munich in the dead of winter when its people were heavily clothed. He was particularly rhapsodic about the calves on these women, although admitting that he was not generally known as a "leg man."

Haskin eventually introduced Burt to the star of *Armored Command*, Howard Keel, who was better known for his rich bass-baritone singing voice, as demonstrated in such films as *Annie Get Your Gun* (1950). *[He had co-starred in that film with Betty Hutton after Judy Garland was fired.]* The following year he made one of his most famous movies, *Show Boat* (1951) opposite Kathryn Grayson and Ava Gardner.

Burt later said, "*Armored Command* was the one picture of his in which Howard did not sing, a terrible mistake."

That Saturday night, Burt visited the most famous beer hall in Germany, the mammoth Hofbräuhaus, a former haunt of Nazis before the war. On the night of his visit, the beerhall was filled with beer-drinking local men and women, but also with a lot of Allied American soldiers still stationed in Germany.

An infantryman signaled for Burt to take the one remaining chair, and he did, seating himself between the soldier from Chicago and a stunningly beautiful Bavarian girl whom he described as "a budding Marlene Dietrich in the making."

She knew only two words of English, "Hello, Yankee."

All he could learn from her was that her name was Hildegard Lerche. At one point in the evening, he felt a hand creeping up his pants' leg. He hoped it was the girl's—and not the infantryman's. It was Hildegard who "gave me the feel of a lifetime."

"Before midnight, she also gave me one of 'those long, overripe Kim Basinger I-want-you-bad-and-I want-you-right-now' looks. I thought cheese and crackers. I'm in love."

The evening ended in her dismal apartment that had survived the war, but only barely. It reminded him of the apartment in the film, *A Foreign Affair* (1948), that the character played by Marlene Dietrich had occupied.

"That night, among other things, I began to teach her vital words in Eng-

Filmed entirely in Germany, with the cooperation of the U.S. Army, this film depicts the Battle of the Bulge, the Nazi Panzer attack on the weakly defended Allied Line.

It was Hitler's last-ditch attempt at Western penetration.

lish—fuck, suck, penis, breasts."

"Hildegard turned out to be a real sexual athlete," Burt said. "By Monday morning, I staggered to the studio to report for work on the interior shots. Hildegard made it clear to me that she would have a wonderful dinner prepared for me if I gave her twenty bucks for food, as she was unemployed."

Burt later claimed that he never got around to seducing the beautiful co-star of *Armored Command*, Tina Louise. The former star of *God's Little Acre* (1958), she had been voted "The World's Most Beautiful Redhead" by the National Arts Council.

Burt with Tina Louise in *Armored Command*. He's unaware that she's a Nazi spy.

[Tina Louise's greatest fame came later on a TV sitcom in which she played the campy and vapid movie star, Ginger Grant, the character stranded on a tropical island in CBS's Gilligan's Island. *She claimed, "That damn role sabotaged a promising career."]*

Haskin called cast and crew together to discuss the script of *Armored Command*. Keel would play the cigar-smoking Colonel Devlin whose biggest challenge was to convince the Allied Command that the Nazis were planning to attack from the weakest point along the Western defenses.

In the movie, the character played by Tina Louise was deliberately shot in the arm by the *Wehrmacht* as part of a ruse to convince Allied soldiers that she's an innocent French victim of the Nazis. Unaware that she's a Nazi spy, a U.S. soldier named Mike, played by Earl Holliman, rescues her and falls desperately in love with her. Thus begins her character's successful run at gathering sensitive secrets about Allied defenses against Nazi penetration from the East.

According to Burt, "Once again, I was playing a rapist named Skee, like I did in my first movie. I hoped I wasn't getting typecast. In one scene, I strip down to my boxers and flex my muscles

Howard Keel in *Armored Command*, playing a ruggedly forceful tank comander who doesn't sing a note.

130

in front of the troops. It was my first big cheesecake appearance—or is it called beefcake?"

Holliman and Burt were adversaries on film but comrades in private. Born in Louisiana in abject poverty, Holliman, as a teenager, saved up a little money and hitchhiked to Hollywood, later joining the U.S. Navy after the outbreak of World War II.

After the war, he got roles as an actor, appearing in *The Rainmaker* (1956) with Katharine Hepburn and Burt Lancaster, and in *Gunfight at the O.K. Corral* (1957), with Kirk Douglas and (again) with Lancaster.

In the words of one critic, "Holliman is a schoolboy in love with the Nazi spy as played by Tina Louise. In contrast, Burt Reynolds is the confident Alpha male who will harm her whether she wants him or not."

Jonah M. Ruddy wrote in *Hollywood Diary:* "Burt Reynolds is the corrigible of the outfit. He pretends to have a twisted ankle he'd sustained in a night-scouting party, so that he can stay behind when the troops leave on another night-scouting party. He takes a bottle with him as he visits the bedroom of the Nazi spy. After a couple of slugs of cognac, he has his way with her."

Near the end of the film, Burt is killed during his attempt to hold a road with a heavy machine gun against the Nazi advance. One reviewer claimed that Burt handled his role "in a slimy and impactful way, giving the best performance in the movie."

Supporting roles were played by Warner Anderson as a lieutenant colonel; Carleton Young as a captain; and Martin Ingels as a Brooklyn-born comedian named "Pinhead."

The film opened to a lackluster audience, the Los Angeles Times calling it "a poor man's *Battleground*." The reference was to MGM's hit

When he wasn't filming, Burt was shacked up nightly with a beautiful German girl who spoke only German. She was a deadringer for a young Marlene Dietrich.

When he taught her some English and they began having conversations, "she turned out to be a Hitler-loving bitch," he claimed.

World War II drama starring Van Johnson.

The New York Times defined it as "an improbable little wartime melo-drama." The studio's strenuous press and publicity slogan ("THE BIG RIDE TO HELL AND BACK WITH THE JOLTING JOES OF THE HELL-ON-WHEELS 7TH ARMY') didn't seem to help ticket sales.

Burt's affair with Hildegard lasted until the end of filming. She was a fast-learning linguist. "I should never have taught her our language," he said, "and I sure regretted it. The bitch turned out to be a fascist. The shit coming from her mouth sounded like the daughter of Himmler. She loved the swastika. She also claimed that Hitler was still alive, was living in Argentina, and that he'd come back to lead the German people to victory."

"So I wouldn't be bringing Hildegard back to Riviera Beach as a Nazi war bride. It's just as well, because Big Burt still hated Germans because of the war."

***

After his return to Hollywood, in reference to the two films he'd recently completed, Burt quipped, "*Angel Baby* and *Armored Command* were the kind of flicks they show in prisons and on airplanes, since the audience can't escape."

Had his luck been different in the early 1960s, Burt might have appeared twice in major-league roles.

Before casting Natalie Wood as Maria in the hit musical, *West Side Story* (1961), co-director Robert Wise had considered other actresses who had in-

WHAT MIGHT HAVE BEEN: Burt was considered, but rejected, for the role of Tony in the 1961 screen version of Leonard Bernstein, Jerome Robbins, and Robert Wise's *West Side Story*.

Depicted above are Natalie Wood and Richard Beymer in the iconic, potentially career-building characters of Maria and Tony.

cluded Ann-Margret, Jane Fonda, Audrey Hepburn, and Pier Angeli.

For that blockbuster film's male lead, its executive producer Walter Mirisch had wanted Elvis Presley, but its choreographer, Jerome Robbins, convinced him that Elvis would be wrong for the part. Ironically, Burt Reynolds evolved as the next choice. Robbins, however, found him "too tough-looking, too much of a hoodlum." Ultimately, Richard Beymer ended up playing *West Side Story's* male lead, Tony.

For the role of Will Brocious in *The Broken Land* (1962), two actors were auditioned: Jack Nicholson and Burt. Producer Leonard Schwartz asked each man if he could ride a horse. Both Nicholson and Burt said they could.

As it turned out, however, Nicholson was better on a horse. After the "non-success" of *Armored Command,* Burt found the pickings for movie roles slim. "I finally got work playing heavies in every TV series aired. Those were depressing years for me."

His first gig during that era emerged in two episodes of *The Aquanauts,* an adventure drama that aired on CBS in the 1960-61 season. It co-starred Keith Larsen and Jeremy Slate.

In mid-season, Larsen dropped out and was replaced with Ron Ely, a 6'4" Texan with an athletic build.

Ely would go on to greater fame in 1966 when he won the role of Tarzan. Like Burt, he insisted on doing many of his own stunts. That decision led to him suffering a dozen major injuries, including two broken shoulders and various lion bites. Coincidentally, this "hunk of beefcake," as he was called, ended up dating Dinah Shore after Burt ended her affair with the singer and TV host.

In weekly installments, *The Aquanauts* focused on two Southern divers showing off their athletic builds and making their livings salvaging sunken wrecks. Burt played Jimmy in "The Big Swim" and Leo in "The Kidnap Adventure."

Even though it wasn't well-reviewed, the series often employed big-name stars who included Carroll O'Conner (later, Archie Bunker in *All in the Family)*, James Coburn, Dyan Cannon, Peter Falk, Joyce

As Burt became increasingly identified with a "genre" of the TV characters he ended up playing, he even nabbed a role in an episode of a sea-adventure TV series. For a while, one of its two male leads was Keith Larsen, who Burt in some way resembles.

Meadows, and Keenan Wynn.

It was during his appearance in *The Aquanauts* that Burt was first introduced to the doomed actress, Inger Stevens, with whom he would later be tragically involved.

Unable to compete with NBC's more highly rated *Wagon Train* (1957-1965), *The Aquanauts* was eventually canceled.

Around the same time, Burt also found work in the 39-episode TV crime drama *The Brothers Brannagan* (1960-61). Portrayed by Stephen Dunne and Mark Roberts, it focused on two fictional detectives operating out of a resort in Phoenix, Arizona.

The series never featured any big-name stars, but two out-of-work former child actors, Bobby Driscoll and Jackie Coogan, were included in its roster of players.

Cast as Abelard, Burt starred in only one episode ("Bordertown"). *[Ironically, it had the same name as a 1935 film noir that had co-starred Paul Muni and Bette Davis.]*

It was around this time that Burt encountered the real Bette Davis.

***

After bolting from the set of *Riverboat,* where he'd made such a violent exit, Burt returned to his former talent agency, MCA, hoping they'd sign him up again. To his chagrin, he couldn't get beyond the receptionist. She informed him that "We're representing only big stars—not wannabes." In spite of that insult, he gave her his card with his contact information "in case Mr. Wasserman changes his mind."

In the lobby, on his way out, he checked the names on the building's list of corporate occupants, hoping he knew someone who'd steer him toward another agent.

He turned as the elevator door opened again and from it emerged Bette Davis wearing a black suit. He hesitated, reluctant to approach her. Finally, mustering enough courage, he approached her and said, "Miss Davis, you are the greatest actress in the history of cinema. And Spencer Tracy agrees with me."

She looked him up and down with an experienced appraisal, the same she might, in days of yore, have

Bette Davis, as she appeared about a decade prior to her sexual encounters with Burt, in *All About Eve* (1950).

used to inspect George Brent, Franchot Tone, Howard Hughes, Henry Fonda, Barry Sullivan, Gig Young, or director William Wyler.

"And who might you be other than a good-looking devil with a mischievous twinkle in his eyes?" she asked.

"I'm Burt Reynolds, an actor, or at least a former football jock who imagines he can act."

"So, you know Spence?"

"We're intimate friends," he answered. "I met him when he was filming *Inherit the Wind.*"

Outside on the sidewalk, she asked him if he'd hail her a taxi.

"I could do that, but I'd much rather drive you home in my car. I must warn you, it's not a Rolls Royce."

"That would be nice since we have this mutual friend in Spencer Tracy."

En route to her home, she spoke of Tracy. "I idolize the man, a great performer, and he never lets you catch him acting. Regrettably, we made only one picture together, *20,000 Years in Sing Sing* (1932)."

"I wish I'd seen it," he said.

"I had a lot of fun playing a gun moll to Spence," she said. "I developed this powerful crush on him, but at the time, I was busy getting married and honeymooning with my first husband, Harmon Nelson. After getting to know Spence, I realized I'd married the wrong man."

"I wanted Spence for *Dark Victory* (1939)," she said, "but he had just made a movie with Joan Crawford and didn't want to work with such a strong woman so soon again after that."

[*She was referring to the 1938 film,* Mannequin.]

"I was at Warners and MGM had manly men such as Clark Gable or Spence," she said. "I often got weaker men as my lead: Gig Young, David Bryan, James Davis come to mind...even George Brent."

"Perhaps Warners figured that with you as the star, box office was assured, and they could save money by signing a lesser actor," Burt said.

When he arrived at her house, she invited him inside. "I'm all alone, no one but me. I trust you're not a serial killer."

"Not lately," he said. "Gave it up for Lent."

"Let me make you a drink."

"I'm not much of a drinker, but that's an invitation I can't turn down."

Burt and Bette sat in her living room and talked and drank until seven that evening. "She seemed very lonely," he said.

He noted that she was just coming down from her divorce (July 1960) from actor Gary Merrill. She'd met him when he was her leading man during her portrayal of Margo Channing in *All About Eve* (1950).

"I met Gary when we were both still married. It was love at first sight, if you believe in such things," she said. He was eight years younger than me."

"I, too, have an appreciation for more seasoned women," Burt said. "Ever since I was a teenager."

"You sound like you were once seduced by an older woman," she said.

"I was, for an entire year," he answered. "Age fourteen. I still have the fondest memories of it...my indoctrination into love."

Gary Merrill, cast as a playwright opposite actress Bette Davis, was her husband on screen in *All About Eve.*

Off screen, he became her lover, and eventually, she married him, finding he was "a real man—and hairy, too."

"Are you married, or were you ever married?" she asked.

"Never been married, and I don't plan to get married." He later recalled that "the liquor must have taken over. "Provocatively and flirtatiously, he said. "I would consider getting married if asked by a certain star of *Old Acquaintance* (1943), and I don't mean Miriam Hopkins. I never understood how Gig Young could leave Kit Marlowe (the character played by Bette) for that spoiled brat of a girl. Likewise, I never understood why Joe Gillis would leave the endlessly fascinating Norma Desmond for that pedestrian Nancy Olson."

[He was referring to Gloria Swanson and William Holden in Sunset Blvd. *(1950).]*

"All my marriages were failures," she said. "So were my love affairs. Right now, I'm working on my autobiography, *The Lonely Life.*"

"Can't wait to read it," he said.

"I think marriage is an overrated institution," she said. "The men I've married have been weak. Except for Gary Merrill. He is a real man. Most men can't handle powerful women, though. My fame is too much for the bastards. I like men, but I can't seem to stay married to them."

Bette had returned from Broadway, where she had starred in Tennessee Williams' *The Night of the Iguana* (1961). Since it was getting near dinnertime, she invited him to stay over for a meal she'd cook herself.

As he later wrote, "I found Bette in a strange way very sexy."

What he didn't reveal was that he became very nervous at the prospect of staying over and bedding her. After all, she was twenty-eight years older than him. But the age didn't matter to him. What did was that she was the formidable Bette Davis, known for "cutting the balls off her leading men"—and lovers, too.

"I felt something was going to happen between us," he later claimed.

"But that night didn't seem right. It was too soon. There had to be more time to make me feel comfortable around her, though I had been fascinated by her image since I was a little boy, never missing a single Bette Davis film when it came to our little movie house on Riviera Beach."

Sensing his apprehension, she told him to call her as soon as he returned from New York, *[He had told her he was leaving soon to appear in a play there.]* He promised he would.

"At the door, I was way up there, and she was way down there, very short," he recalled. "She loomed so large on the screen. Then I did the most impulsive thing. I grabbed her and kissed her, expecting a slap like the jaw-dislocating one she'd given to Errol Flynn when they'd co-starred in *The Private Lives of Elizabeth and Essex* (1939)."

"But instead of a slap, I got the flicker of her tongue, that same tongue that used to give blow-jobs to Howard Hughes," he said.

Her final words to him were, "Until we meet again. I will count the days."

***

In Manhattan, in the autumn of 1961, Burt rented a small room in a seedy hotel off Times Square. Rip Torn had tipped him off that the noted director, José Quintero, was auditioning actors for a new play, *Love, We've Come Through.*

Auditions were being staged in Greenwich Village at the Circle in the Square Theater, which theater historians sometimes define as the birthplace of Off-Broadway.

[A gay son of Panama, Quintero already was one of the most celebrated of New York City directors. He had famously staged Eugene O'Neill's The Iceman Cometh *at the Circle Theater in 1956. It had launched the stage career of Jason Robards, the future husband of Lauren Bacall.*

Quintero would go on to direct such major stars as Fredric March, Geraldine Page, Jane Fonda, Ben Gazzara, Ingrid Bergman, and Colleen Dewhurst. He would also direct plays by Tennessee Williams, Jean Cocteau, Thornton Wilder, Brendan Behan, and Truman Capote.

In Rome, he had just directed The Roman Spring of Mrs. Stone *(1961), based on a Tennessee Williams novella and starring Vivien Leigh and Warren*

Beatty.]

Burt read a copy of *Love, We've Come Through* and became convinced that he'd be ideal for the role of Skip, a trashy sailor who evoked Stanley Kowalski in *A Streetcar Named Desire.*

The plot by Hugh Wheeler was the story of an unattractive girl who is stood up by her date. In the aftermath, she encounters a gay man with whom she develops a close relationship.

Wheeler had a good track record as a playwright, novelist, and screenwriter. In time, he would win Tony Awards for the scripts he wrote for the hit musicals *A Little Night Music, Sweeney Todd,* and *Candide.* He would work with Leonard Bernstein, Harold Prince, and Stephen Sondheim.

José Quintero in 1958. "In the play, I unzip my pants to entice a gay boy," Burt said.

"The director had to decide how far I should go. Should I flop it out, onstage, or not?"

Without knowing it, the first work by Wheeler that Burt had ever seen was a movie, *Black Widow* (1954), starring Ginger Rogers, Van Heflin, George Raft, and Gene Tierney. Wheeler had written it under the pseudonym of Patrick Quentin.

Burt showed up for his audition on time. Although Quintero was nowhere in sight, he was told that he was seated in the theater's back row. Burt read the lines of Skip three times, altering the characterization each time. At the end of each reading, Quintero bellowed from the back, "READ IT AGAIN!"

Nothing seemed to please him as he directed Burt to repeat his reading again and again. Finally, Burt could take it no longer. He stepped to the front of the stage, shouting at the faraway Quintero, "JUST WHAT THE FUCK DO YOU WANT?"

"THAT'S IT!" Quintero shouted back. "YOU'VE GOT IT! YOU'RE OUR SKIP!"

***

Years later, in reference to his direction by Quintero, Burt recalled, "When I wasn't rehearsing," Burt said, "I was virtually ignored by Quintero and the other cast members, too. "They called me 'Mister Hollywood.' Stage actors always resented people in the movie industry taking over their roles. Quintero started his days by giving his actors a pat on the back, but he ignored me. During breaks, I wasn't invited to join them in their gossipy little circles. There was one exception, however."

He was referring to a young actress, Collin Wilcox of Cincinnati. "I didn't know if she were married or not, and I was too polite to ask, but I went after her," Burt said. "She told me she was living in Highlands, North Carolina, so we shared a Southern background. We hit it off and came on strong."

She had already worked with Elaine May and Mike Nichols with the Compass Players in Chicago. She'd been on Broadway in 1958 in a play by Maxwell Anderson, but it closed after only three performances.

Collin Willcox as she appeared as a fraudulent courtroom witness (Mayella Violet Ewell) in *To Kill A Mockingbird*.

The young actress was on the dawn of playing her biggest role when she was cast in the screen version of *To Kill a Mockingbird* (1962) as Mayella Violet Ewell, who falsely claimed that she'd been raped by a black man, Tom Robinson (Brock Peters).

"She was talented, but her film career didn't really take off," Burt said. "In 1997, Clint Eastwood, my buddy, invited me to a screening of his *Midnight in the Garden of Good and Evil*. Suddenly, I saw a much older Collin on the screen, cast as an uncredited extra, 'Woman at a party.'"

Zohra Lampert, a New Yorker born and bred, had been designated as the play's female lead. She had just finished her role in Elia Kazan's *Splendor in the Grass* (1961), starring Warren Beatty in his debut film and Natalie Wood. Although that film had not yet been released, it was getting rave reviews from those who had seen it.

"William Inge had promised the role to me," Burt claimed, whether it was true or not. "But along came Beatty, and the double-crosser got the hots for him, instead of me."

***

Running for only five performances in October of 1961, the most dramatic scene in Quintero's *Love, We've Come Through* involved Skip (Burt) enticing a young gay man (Ralph Williams) over to him. Once the boy approached Burt, he unzipped his fly as the audience gasped.

He later wrote: "I'm sure they thought I was going to flop something out. But I zipped up my pants and laughed at the boy."

"In rehearsal, Quintero seriously discussed the possibility that I might actually take out my dick and expose it to the audience. But there was fear that if I did, we might get shut down. Had this play been presented in 1971, instead of 1961, I'm sure we could have gotten away with it, since nudity became the rage both on and off Broadway."

Quintero had directed that as the curtain went up at the beginning of Act Two, Burt would be laughing. "As I started laughing, I looked at the lineup in the front row of the audience: Tennessee

Burt as he appeared in *Love, We've Come Through*. It closed after only five performances.

Williams with Warren Beatty and Natalie Wood holding hands."

"I had an opening line, but my brain froze at the sight of all those august people staring at me," Burt said. "I just kept laughing until my brain came unfrozen and I could deliver my lines. Until that happened, I viewed my stage laugh as a life preserver, and I was in the middle of the Atlantic at the sinking of the *Titanic.*"

After the show, Ben Gazzara was the first to climb a winding staircase that led to Burt's cubbyhole of a dressing room. "Ben was the hottest actor on Broadway. He congratulated me on holding that laugh for so long."

"I'd seen Ben in the film role of Jocko de Paris in the movie *The Strange One* (1957), a part I dreamed about playing myself. I also coveted his stage role of Brick in *Cat on a Hot Tin Roof.* Did you know that actors are sometimes envious of their fellow actors?"

Both of the audience's famous playwrights, William Inge and Tennessee Williams, also climbed those narrow stairs to congratulate Burt. "Once again, they made those bullshit promises to me that each would write a play in which I would star."

Sarcastically, Burt continued: "Yeah, right!" Both of them had put their money, or whatever, on that Beatty boy. I decided that very night that I'd make it on my own without any help from those old queens."

At a cast party, Burt flirted with Natalie Wood, "but she paid me no mind. She obviously preferred Beatty's dick to anything I had to offer."

Later that night, Burt read *The New York Times'* review of the short-run play on which he'd spilled so much blood, sweat, and tears. Its critic said, "Attention playwrights and directors: Please don't let the young actor Burt Reynolds go to Hollywood."

Despite the words of that reviewer, at 6AM on the morning after the production's fifth and final performance, Burt boarded a dawn flight to Los Angeles. At least Bette Davis might be waiting for him, but he didn't know who or what else.

***

There are eight million stories in the... NAKED CITY

With no feature film roles in sight in Hollywood, Burt called around and got cast in an uncredited role ("Young Man") in an episode ("Requiem for a Sunday Afternoon") of the TV series *Naked City*.

A police drama series from Screen Gems was aired intermittently on ABC from 1958 to 1963. Inspired by the 1948 feature film, *The Naked City*, starring Barry Fitzgerald and Howard Duff, it originally starred John McIntire and James Franciscus.

Each episode concluded with the narrator intoning the iconic line, "There are eight million stories in The Naked City. This has been one of them."

Highly rated, the series included cameo appearances from some of the major stars in Hollywood: Dustin Hoffman, Jon Voight (Burt's future co-star), Robert Redford, Claude Rains, and Mickey Rooney. Two of Burt's friends, Rip Torn and David Janssen, were also cast in it.

Burt played "Defenestrated Guy," (i.e., a man thrown out of a window). His co-star was Marisa Pavan, the Italian beauty and twin sister of Pier Angeli. *[Angeli had had a doomed affair with James Dean before marrying a wife-beater, the singer Vic Damone.]*

***

Burt's performance in *Naked City* was followed by a brief appearance in *Ripcord*, a TV series that ran for seventy-six episodes from 1961 to '63, highlighting the exploits of a sky-diving operation. The show starred Larry Pennell as the handsome, headstrong, and audacious skydiver.

Playing "The Assassin," Burt appeared in only one episode, "Crime Jump," which aired on October 5, 1961. Because of its limited budget, only minor actors were hired in lieu of major stars. Listed among its "pre-fame" cast members were Burt and the then relatively unknown James Coburn, his future co-star..

***

A few days after his return to Hollywood, Burt phoned Bette Davis, uncertain as he was about the status of his relationship with the great star. Before phoning her, he talked to his stuntman friend and confidant, Hal Needham.

"I'm not really sure if I want to see her again. She scares me, yet I'm attracted to her and have been since I saw all her movies as a boy in Florida."

"Go for it, kid," Needham said. "Bill Holden told me that when he hit Hollywood, he became a male whore, seducing the big female stars of the 1930s, or even some from the '20s—and not just Barbara Stanwyck."

Burt phoned Bette on her private line, and she seemed delighted to hear from him and invited him over that very night. She wanted him to arrive early, at around five o'clock.

He drove over to where she was living, expecting one of her home-cooked dinners. When she opened the door, she was beautifully dressed and coiffed and—in his view—had never looked more stunning. It was obvious that she expected to be taken out, and he was a bit alarmed because he had only thirty dollars in his wallet.

He was relived when she told him that she wanted to be taken to a movie house in Pasadena. It was showing Tennessee Williams' film interpretation of *Suddenly, Last Summer* (1959) with Montgomery Clift, Elizabeth Taylor, and Katharine Hepburn. "I've put off seeing it until now because I know it will break my heart."

En route to the theater, she explained what she meant. "I was slated to play Mrs. Venable, Elizabeth's rich, shady, and unhinged aunt, who's pressuring her to have a lobotomy to blot out the fact that her homosexual son was eaten by cannibals on the beach—a bit grotesque, I admit."

"I was in negotiation with the director, Joseph Mankiewicz, and I had two conversations about it with Tennessee Williams. He told me I'd be his dream choice, perfect for the role. But something happened along the way. He betrayed me. He met privately with Hepburn at her townhouse in Manhattan, and practically begged her to take the role. A complete double-cross."

After the movie, Bette and Burt went to a small hideaway restaurant in Pasadena. Over dinner, she discussed her admiration for Katharine Hepburn. "I always wanted to look like her, with her narrow face and high cheekbones, instead of my round, drawn face. I've also wanted to co-star

142

with her, especially in *The Night of the Iguana*, that play by Tennessee, but she turned it down. Two Yankee ladies… we would have been great together on the stage."

"Back when I won the Best Actress Oscar for *Dangerous* in 1935, I chastised the Academy for not awarding it instead to Hepburn for *Alice Adams*. She delivered a better performance in it than I did in *Dangerous*."

Katharine Hepburn as Violet Venable in *Suddenly, Last Summer* (1959). She's waiting for Elizabeth Taylor to undergo a lobotomy.

[Burt had never heard an actress be that generous to a rival. Bette also claimed that Hepburn should have won the Best Actress Oscar for Suddenly, Last Summer, *but it had gone instead to Simone Signoret for her role in* Room at the Top *instead.*

"She might have won, but Elizabeth Taylor demanded to be nominated for Best Actress instead of Best Supporting Actress, thus canceling each other out by splitting the votes cast by admirers of* Suddenly," *Bette said. "The same thing happened to me in 1950 when Anne Baxter insisted on being nominated for 'Best Actress' instead of 'Best Supporting.' That paved the way for Judy Holliday to win for* Born Yesterday, *although it was Gloria Swanson's only chance to win for* Sunset Blvd. *All of us were giving the greatest performances of our lives."*

Not surprisingly, probably because of the egos involved, her opinion of Hepburn had changed by 1964, when Bette was scheduled to co-star with Joan Crawford in Hush…Hush, Sweet Charlotte. *When Crawford dropped out, the director wanted to replace her with Hepburn. Bette adamantly refused to interact with her onscreen. Consequently, Olivia de Havilland was assigned the role instead.]*

As Burt drove Bette home after dinner, he suspected she'd invite him to spend the weekend with her. As he later told Hal Needham, "I wanted to, but was reluctant, a bit leery of my audition. Part of me wanted her, but another part of me was holding back. I wondered if she'd control the seduction, because she was overpowering as a woman."

He'd already heard much of the gossip associated with her long and outspoken career: When she'd opened the Hollywood Canteen during World War II, she was known for taking home a serviceman every night. Actor Jack Carson, who worked with her at the Canteen, said he'd heard that "she screws like a minx."

The Hungarian-born director, Michael Curtiz (who was known for mixing his metaphors and genders), called her "a sexless son of a bitch."

Humphrey Bogart was quoted as saying, "That dame is so damn uptight. What she needs is a good screw from a man who knows how to do it."

The following day, Burt boasted to Needham how the weekend and the sex had proceeded.

"Bette is a very passionate woman. She's not the tarantula she's reported to be. She had her tender moments when she covered my body with kisses—arms, chest, hips, stomach, before descending on the family jewels. I imaged it was Kit Marlowe from *Old Aquaintance* doing me."

"I hammered relentlessly, and her moans let me know I was hitting the spot. She made me feel like a real stud. Her only words to me were, 'Please tell me I'm beautiful.'"

After their intimacies, as Burt related, he and Bette took a shower together. Back in the bedroom, when the lights had been switched back on, he noted a picture of Howard Hughes on her dresser.

"Maybe I shouldn't ask but is this the man who got away?" he asked.

"It's okay, but marriage to him would never have worked out," she said. "He was very eccentric. I don't know why I still keep his picture. Right from the beginning, he confessed his homosexual leanings. He was also a premature ejaculator who, during fellatio, likes his partner to talk about feces. He asked me if, as I performed, it was okay if he closed his eyes and pretended I was a man."

"How romantic," Burt said. "Another Hollywood illusion shattered. I thought he was a real ladies' man. Before we go to sleep, I have one final request."

"It's granted. So what have I agreed to?"

"A repeat performance," he said. "I want more."

"Come on over here, you darling man," she said. "I adore a man who can't be satisfied with just one bout."

After Burt related that to Needham, he asked, "Are you going to keep seeing her?"

"Absolutely," Burt said. "Any time she calls for me. After all, she's Bette Davis. I'll answer her call and treat it like a royal command."

***

Commenting on his frequent appearances in TV dramas and television series, Burt said, "I learned more about my craft in those guest shots than

I did standing around looking virile in *Riverboat.*"

He was next signed to appear in two episodes of the TV series *The Ever-glades,* a crime and adventure series that ran in syndication for a single season (1961-62) and later in reruns. Burt's involvement would require a return to Florida, his teenage stamping ground, in a location only miles from where his parents were living. Their reunion was overdue.

The series starred actor Ron Hayes as Constable Lincoln Vail. As a law enforcement officer assigned to *[you guessed it]* the Everglades, his preferred means of transport in a fan-operated airboat with a shallow draft. Hayes was also an avid outdoorsman, a stuntman, and a conservationist.

Burt felt at home once again among the Seminoles, many of whom were hired on location as extras. When Burt wasn't needed, he rented a boat and made his way through this myriad of birds, reptiles, and mangrove estuaries.

In Burt's first episode, he portrayed Lew Johnson in "Greed of the Glades" (1961). His second appearance was as Trask in "Friday's Children," (1962). Nearly all the plots followed a basic theme that involved the patrol cop as he hunted down criminals, stopped poachers, and rounded up environmental bad guys.

Somewhere along the way, Burt formed a friendship with actor/singer Jack Cassidy, who would in time appear in episodes of both *The Everglades* and Burt's more long-running series, *Gunsmoke* (1955-75).

At the time Burt met him, Cassidy was married to actress/singer Shirley Jones. He was the father of two teen idols, David and Shaun Cassidy.

During the early stages of his relationship with Cassidy, Burt did not realize the extent of his mental disorder, which seemed to grow worse as he got older. At first, Burt merely considered him a heavy drinker.

David Cassidy, in his autobiography, *C'Mon, Get Happy,* claimed that his father suffered from bipolar disor-

Burt was assigned a role in two episodes of the TV series about crime-fighting on his home turf, the Florida 'Glades.

The charming and engaging Ron Hayes spearheaded the cast, even though some fans said that the airboat (propelling the shallow-draft boat through the swamps by means of a giant fan) was the real star of the series.

der and acute alcoholism.

He also wrote that his father was bisexual and had had a number of same-sex affairs, notably with composer Cole Porter. In her 2013 memoir, Shirley Jones confirmed that her former husband was bisexual.

"At the time, I figured that Jack was just mixed up—but so was I," Burt said. "However, the first time I drove over to see him on a hot Sunday afternoon, he was standing jaybird naked in his front yard, watering the grass."

Burt laughed it off. "What you doin', buddy, putting on a show for the neighbors?"

"As time went by, it became obvious to me that Jack wanted to see me naked, too," Burt said. "We showed our butts in the steam room and went skinny-dipping in a private pool at an estate in Beverly Hills when the owner, Jack's friend, was in New York. When we drove somewhere together, and I had to take a leak, he always followed me to see what was hanging."

"He was always checking me out," Burt said. "I didn't punch him out like some redneck—in fact, I was rather flattered. I was just beginning to get my first fan mail. It began as a trickle, but by the 1970s, it kept the post office working overtime. Nearly one of every four letters was from a gay man, and throughout most of my career, gays were among my most loyal fans. I appreciate these gentlemen for that."

"One night, Jack (Cassidy) and I shared a motel room in Mexico after driving to Tijuana to attend the bullfights," Burt said. "In bed together that night, he confessed to me that he was in love with me. "Well, I didn't go crazy and kick him out of the bed. But I had to make it clear to him that I was a hopeless straight. He could admire me, even sleep in the same bed with me, but no hanky-panky."

"If Jack taught me anything, it was a lesson in how to keep my gay admirers, or even my gay friends, without alienating them."

Shirley Jones, matriarch of *The Partridge Family*, with her husband, Jack Cassidy.

Cassidy had declared his love for Burt, who dismissed it as "a case of the hots."

"I once talked this over with Bette Davis, who was by then a gay icon," Burt said. "To my surprise, she told me she was always a bit uneasy around homosexuals, although adored by them—and often imitated by drag queens."

"I never could understand why anyone would be attracted to a person of the same sex," she said.

Burt claimed that she never endorsed any gay causes and in private often made flippant anti-gay remarks. "She made it clear that she believed in equal rights for all people, regardless of their sexual orientation."

"These people obviously have good taste," she told Burt. "A more appreciative, artistic group of people for the arts does not exist. Conceited as it may sound, a great deal of it has to do with their approval of my work. They are knowledgeable and loving of the arts, and they make the average male look stupid."

"My good friend, Clint Eastwood, cast Jack in his film, *The Eiger Sanction* (1975)," Burt said. "It was a sort of travesty of those James Bond thrillers. After working with Clint, Jack told me his greatest sexual fantasy was to have Clint and me in bed together."

When Cassidy informed Burt of that fantasy, Burt didn't know that the older actor had only a few months to live. On December 12, 1976, after a night of heavy drinking, Cassidy returned to the apartment where he'd been living alone.

He collapsed on his Naugahyde sofa and lit a cigarette, then dropped off to sleep after a few puffs. The cigarette ignited a blaze that quickly spread.

After extinguishing the fire, firemen discovered a charred corpse near the exit. Apparently, Cassidy had tried to escape.

His identity was established by his dental records and by a signet ring he wore with the Cassidy family crest.

***

In 1962, Burt signed to star in an episode ("Love Is a Skinny Kid") of the hit TV series, *Route 66*. Its stars were Martin Milner as Tod Stiles and George Maharis as Buz Murdock. Whereas Tod (as portrayed by Milner) is a clean-cut, decent, all-American young man, Buz (the character played by Maharis) is looser, hipper, and a sort of "beatnik."

[TV TRIVIA: Robert Redford had originally tested for, and lost, the role eventually awarded to Milner.]

Burt had not seen Maharis since they'd flown in adjoining seats from New York to Los Angeles, each competing for the same role in a Clark Gable movie. *[Each of them had lost to Barry Coe.]*

Before the series was named *Route 66*, it had been identified with the working title *The Searchers*. Each of the weekly episodes was set in a different location, with a different set of emotional entanglements, as the regulars drove along the famous highway in their Chevrolet Corvette.

[Stretching from Chicago to Santa Monica, California, U.S. Route 66 opened in 1926 and quickly became famous because of literary references that included John Steinbeck's The Grapes of Wrath (it passed directly through the ravages of the Dust Bowl), popular songs, and the above-mentioned TV series. Many of the business owners who had managed to support themselves during the peak years of traffic along the highway fought to keep Route 66 alive when it was bypassed by the Interstate Highway System, of which it was not a part.]

The Vintage 50s and its love affair with cars: Martin Milner and George Maharis in *Route 66*.

Maharis told Burt that the series was very loosely based on Jack Kerouac's 1957 "road trip" novel, *On the Road*. It had evolved into the Bible of the Beat Generation.

At one point, Kerouac had filed a lawsuit against the producer, charging that the series had "misappropriated the characters" of his iconic novel, but the lawsuit went nowhere.

Many big-name stars were featured in the series, including both up-and-coming actors and fading idols of yesteryear. The roster included Joan Crawford, Miriam Hopkins, Rip Torn, Lee Marvin, Ralph Meeker, Martin Sheen, Walter Matthau, Dorothy Malone, and—before his *Star Trek* fame—William Shatner. Arguably, the single most powerful performance in the series was delivered by Ethel Waters when she starred in an episode called "Goodnight, Sweet Blues."

Route 66 also featured performances from that unholy trio, Boris Karloff, Lon Chaney, Jr., and Peter Lorre. Chaney reprised his role of "The Wolfman," and Karloff donned his famous Frankenstein makeup for the first time in twenty-five years.

Later, Burt learned that Maharis had to drop out of the series because he had come down with infectious hepatitis. "I have to protect my future," he told the press. "The stress of changing locations every week got to me.

I'd be a fool to continue to ruin my health. Even if you have a cool four million in the bank, you can't buy another liver."

In July of 1973, Maharis posed frontally nude for *Playgirl*. A month later, a gay magazine claimed that he had "the most beautiful cock of any actor in Hollywood." *[That same magazine then named Jerry Lewis for having "the most pathetic."]* The editors did not reveal how they had gathered the information that allowed them to make comparisons.

***

In 1962, a gig emerged for Burt in an episode of the hit TV series, *Perry Mason*, a long-running legal drama first televised on CBS in September of 1957.

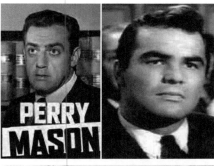

Its title character was played by Raymond Burr, a fictional Los Angeles criminal defense lawyer crafted by the novelist, Erle Stanley Gardner. Nearly all the series' TV episodes followed the same formula: They opened with one of Mason's clients facing a murder charge.

The same supporting actors appeared in every episode. They included Della Street (Barbara Hale), Mason's confidential secretary; Paul Drake (William Hopper), his private investigator who always turns up with last-minute evidence; Hamilton Burger (William Talman), the district attorney; and Lt. Arthur Tragg (Ray Collins), the police homicide detective.

On his first day, Burt met Burr, who told him that he'd had to drop sixty pounds to get the role. He still looked corpulent to Burt, who had seen him play a suspected murderer in Alfred Hitchcock's *Rear Window* (1945), starring James Stewart and Grace Kelly.

Top row, left: Raymond Burr in the title role of Perry Mason. Top right: Burt Reynolds as he appeared in one of its episodes.

Lower photo: Raymond Burr as Perry Mason with Barbara Hale as his long-time secretary, Della Street.

"I'd already heard that Burr was gay, and he held my hand a little too long," Burt said. "I think he was hot for me. I didn't feel he was deprived sexually, though. A few months before, or so I was informed, he'd taken a partner, Robert Benevides."

[That union lasted until Burr's death in 1993.]

Burt learned that in 1957, Burr had auditioned for the role of the district attorney, not for the male lead he was eventually assigned. But when the creator of the character (Erle Gardner) met him, he instantly defined him as "my fantasy of what Perry Mason looks like."

Then, Talman was assigned the role of the district attorney.

[Shortly after that, Talman was fired after being arrested, along with fifteen other men and women, at a private home in Beverly Hills. After they raided the house, the police charged that most of the party guests were nude or semi-nude and smoking marijuana. Later, after the allegations of lewd vagrancy were dropped, Talman was rehired to continue his involvement in the TV series.]

Veteran actor Ray Collins had made his film debut in Orson Welles' *Citizen Kane* (1941). In *Perry Mason,* even though he was past the age of retirement for a real-life police officer, he was assigned a role as the irascible police lieutenant.

Hedda Hopper's son, William Hopper, was assigned to portray Perry Mason's private investigator, Paul Drake, but only after he was rejected for the lead role of Perry Mason.

"Your mother has mentioned me once or twice in her gossip column, but it's always been a dig," Burt said.

"I have no control over what my mother writes," Hopper answered.

Burt had seen William Hopper in James Dean's *Rebel Without a Cause* (1955), in which he had played Natalie Wood's emotionally distant father.

In Burt's episode of *Perry Mason*, he played a minor role, that of the son of one of the episode's secretaries. The best lines went to Otto Kruger, a former leading man in the 1930s. Kruger played August Dalgran, an aging CEO with mental problems. His nephew moves in to wrest control of his company away from him and has him declared incompetent. When the nephew is murdered, the Dalgran character is suspected. Forgery eventually becomes the key to solving the murder.

The last film in which William Hopper ever appeared was *Myra Breckinridge* (1970), starring Mae West and Raquel Welch. *[Based on Gore Vidal's outrageous novel with the same name, it satirized transsexuality, deviant sexual practices, and feminism.]* According to Burt, "Fortunately, Bill died right before its release, and he didn't have to sit through this atrocity."

***

At the end of filming of the episode he was in, Burt was called into the office of Gail Patrick Jackson, the executive producer of the *Perry Mason* series.

[Using the stage name of "Gail Patrick," she'd been a minor movie star, usually playing "the other woman" or "bad girl." She'd co-starred in many notable films, including My Man Godfrey *(1936) with Carole Lombard;* Stage Door *(1937) with Katharine Hepburn and Ginger Rogers; and* My Favorite Wife *(1940) with Cary Grant and Irene Dunne.]*

Meeting with Jackson, Burt learned that she was aware of his friendship with Bette Davis. At the time, she was hawking a role for an episode of *Perry Mason* that she wanted to fill with Bette Davis as the star.

Burt agreed to present the script to Bette, but warned Jackson that he'd only be the errand boy, merely a "cog in the wheel" who wasn't responsible for Bette's often volatile response.

Charged with the task of delivering the script to her, Burt phoned Bette. She immediately invited him to the set where she was filming *What Ever Happened to Baby Jane?* (1962) at Producers Studio on Melrose Avenue.

When he got there, Bette had just finished a scene and was heading toward her dressing room. He was astonished at her costume and makeup: Her face was coated in a shade of ghastly white, and she wore a long platinum blonde wig and a sloppy dress.

In her dressing room, she told him that lunch would be served to them there. "Once," she said, "I tried to get lunch at the café across the street, but I caused a riot."

"Your makeup and outfit came as a big surprise to me," Burt told her.

"I'm playing an aging child star from the 1930s," Bette answered. "I'm living with, and tormenting, my sister, who was a movie star from that era and now partially paralyzed. My aim is to look like Mary Pickford during her decay."

"Sounds like fun," he said.

Then Bette spewed out how much she detested her co-star, Joan Crawford. "I'll say this for the bitch...No one in Hollywood plays Joan Crawford better than she does. She's slowed down a bit, but in the 1930s at MGM, she fucked everybody except Lassie."

"She's loaded every day on the set," Bette claimed. "She pretends she's drinking Pepsi, but it's mostly vodka. Every time we have a scene together, she straps on a new set of boobs. They get larger and larger every day, even though she's playing a frail woman wasting away. I keep running into those boobs—sometimes they're bigger than the Hollywood Hills."

Despite her hatred of Crawford, Bette predicted, "It's virtually certain that I'm going to win another Oscar with this one. Every time I'm called before the camera, I've got another scene to do where I virtually devour the scenery. Crawford is confined to bed, with little to say or do except to look distressed."

Then she snorted, blowing smoke out through her nostrils. "It's a strange business we're in. You and I are swimming in shark-filled seas. Are we sane? What person in his right mind wants to spend his life impersonating somebody else? Think about that." Then she puffed contemplatively on her cigarette.

"I'm hoping that Baby Jane is so successful it brings back women's pictures," she said. "You men have dominated the screen for too long. Crawford and I are both scrambling through the rubble of a studio system long gone."

Then Burt, prompted by the promises he'd made to the executive producer of the *Perry Mason* series, handed Bette the script for an upcoming episode entitled "The Case of Constant Doyle."

At first, she scoffed at the idea, telling him that in 1934, she'd rejected the role of Della Street, Perry Mason's secretary, in a feature-length film, *The Case of the Howling Dog.* It had starred Warren William, a leading man of the 1930s. It eventually evolved into the first of four legal dramas in which William played the defense attorney named Perry Mason.

Burt explained to her that for this episode being discussed, she would herself portray the episode's defense attorney, since Raymond Burr would be temporarily absent.

Bette agreed to read the script and communicate with the producer (Gail Patrick Jackson), whom she'd known in the 1940s. As an additional incentive designed to maneuver her into accepting the part, Burt told her that if she rejected it, the role would be offered to Joan Crawford.

As Bette removed the heavy layers of her makeup and dressed in conventional street clothes, Burt wandered around the set of *What Ever Happened to Baby Jane?*

There, he encountered a regal-looking Joan Crawford. No longer in character as a paralyzed invalid, she

Bette Davis with William Hopper (playing Paul Drake) in a 1963 episode of *Perry Mason.*

wore a tailored olive-green suit and towering platform shoes. *[Since the 1940s, when Crawford herself had made them popular, their retro style had jokingly identified as "Joan Crawford fuck-me shoes."]*

Crawford was a formidable presence even in the 1960s, the very definition itself of a movie star, an iconic and very tough beauty of dazzling confidence. Burt had heard that she was bisexual, and that her list of lovers would stretch out the door to the street. They had included Clark Gable, John Wayne, Barbara Stanwyck, Spencer Tracy…and Rock Hudson.

Burt was surprised that she knew who he was. When she saw him from afar, she walked over to him and introduced herself.

"I know who you are, Miss Crawford," he said. "The whole world knows who you are."

"I know you're here to see Miss Davis," Crawford said, "but I've been wanting to get in touch with you because I think you'd be ideal as the male lead, playing a young man in a script written especially for me. Could you call me about coming over this weekend and reading it with me?"

"Are you kidding?" he said. "I'd jump at the chance to be your leading man."

She handed him her private number. "You must promise me one thing…DON'T TELL BETTE! She'd cut off her left nipple to play a role like this. As for you, I think the part of the young man is powerful enough to propel you into stardom."

"An offer I cannot refuse," he said. "It'll be our secret. I'll call you late Saturday morning, after your beauty sleep."

"Dear heart, you're a divine-looking man, and I think I still have enough power to make you a star. Until then, goodbye."

"*Adios*, Miss Crawford."

He had to wait another forty-five minutes for Bette. When she did appear—in vivid contrast to her rival—she looked a bit dowdy.

***

When Burt arrived the following Saturday night at Joan Crawford's house, she greeted him in the foyer, where she asked him to remove his shoes before walking on her white carpets.

[He later quipped, "First, off came the shoes, later, the jockstrap."]

In a white evening gown, Crawford was elegant and artfully made up. ("She'd had a lot of practice") and beautifully coiffed. He'd assumed that on their first date, she'd want him to take her dinner at Chasen's and then perhaps to Cocoanut Grove. He'd borrowed a tuxedo and withdrawn $200 from his bank account, leaving a remainder of only $144.14.

153

As they sat in her living room, she said that she should have warned him that their dinner would be catered that night. "Until I finish *What Ever Happened to Baby Jane,* I don't want to make Bette Davis jealous. She might not even finish *Baby Jane* with me if I do. I have a percentage of the profits."

After a reasonable time had passed, Burt asked, "I've really been anxious to hear about this possible movie we might make together, with you getting star billing, of course."

She looked startled for a moment before answering, "Of course. And after we make our film together, I want you to be seen with me everywhere," she said. "Your picture will be plastered over all the newspapers. All the publicity will help turn you into a big star."

Then she described two or three of her most famous vintage films, seemingly to test his knowledge of her previous successes. "You probably know that I've already played some older women having romances with younger men."

She cited *Sudden Fear* (1952), a film in which she'd co-starred with Jack Palance. "He's out to get my fortune and conspiring with that cheap blonde, Gloria Grahame."

"Then, in *Female on the Beach* (1955), Jeff Chandler played a beach bum wanting to become my kept toy. And in *Autumn Leaves* (1956), I married a much younger Cliff Robertson, who turns out to be mentally ill."

"But in this newest script I've been offered, I'll play an older woman and you'll be a virile, hot, charming young man in ardent pursuit of me," she said. "But here the theme differs from the earlier versions: You won't be playing some dumb punk. You'll be, in fact, a high-minded young man who genuinely prefers making love to older women. You turn to them not only for sexual gratification, but for inspiration and guidance and wisdom, too. Of course, the script demands that you'll also have a young piece of fluff running after you too—it sounds ideal for Sandra Dee—but you'll

Two portraits of Joan Crawford from around 1964. She declared, "I like to be the first, and I'm not used to taking Bette Davis' sloppy seconds, but I'll make an exception for that divine Burt Reynolds."

154

reject her and prefer me."

"Not all men, you know, prefer teenagers," she continued. "I hear you're having a fling with Bette Davis. If you can go for her, surely you'll find me ravishing."

"As indeed I do," he answered. "I think a film like the one you projected could fill entire theaters with middle-aged women. It might fulfill their wildest dreams. I could do a role like that—and if I pull it off, it'll make me a star."

"I'm glad you agree," she said. "Normally, I'd have asked you to take me dancing or something. But tonight, I'm having dinner catered."

Burt would later tell Lee Marvin and a few others what happened after dinner that night. "I think she had her kids locked up or strapped down on an upper floor," he said. "Not a sound was coming from there. She lured me into a lower room, a sort of library with a sofa that converted into a bed. It already had white sheets on it. She slowly slipped out of her clothes and suggested I do the same. I did a striptease."

"As we made love, I felt like we were making a movie. She was both the star and director, telling me in detail what I was to do. She wanted a lot of love made to her breasts, which she claimed were more seductive than those of Marilyn Monroe. I'd already made love to Marilyn's breasts, and knew that hers were sexier than Crawford's, but outwardly, at least, I made it a point to agree with Crawford."

"You play a pool boy in our movie, so you'll get to show off your superb physique in the film. You'll get lots of fan mail, I predict."

"When my act with her was over, she said I'd sent her to heaven," Burt said. "Translated, that meant she'd been royally f—cked. She also referred to her breasts as 'ninny pies.'"

Then they lay in bed and talked for an hour or so. He admitted to his attraction for older women. As he confessed that when he was fourteen in Palm Beach, a woman in her forties had seduced him multiple times throughout the course of an entire year.

"I rose from Crawford's bed at four o'clock that morning," he said. "As I was getting dressed, she said something truly amazing. She told me that her long-ago lover, Clark Gable, and I had the exact same penis, both in shape and dimension. She saw that as a good sign that I would, one day—sooner than later—become the next Clark Gable on the screen."

In his memoirs, although Burt had high praise for Bette Davis, Crawford didn't fare as well. He claimed that she was known for "eating up her leading men and spitting them out." He cited a line delivered by Zachory Scott, her co-star in *Mildred Pierce* (1945), as an example. "She was such a phony, though, to be fair, she had her devotees."

After his "one-night stand" with her, he never returned any of her phone calls. That movie script she'd talked about never materialized.

Years later, in May of 1977, Burt escorted Bette Davis to a party in Hollywood. During the course of that party, where TV news broadcasts ran as background noise for chattering party guests, some late-breaking news surged out of Hollywood: "Screen legend Joan Crawford," the broadcast said, "has died."

In front of the other guests, most of whom had fallen into a hush, Bette reacted loudly and forcefully: "Well, at last the cunt is dead."

Burt was shocked by the harshness of her reaction and appraisal, especially because he was standing next to Arthur Knight, author of the monthly "Sex-in-Movies" column for Hugh Hefner's *Playboy.*

Then, as if taking a cue from Burt, Bette softened her tone. "I must say this for Crawford," Bette then announced to the room at large. "Unlike Marilyn, she showed up on time. Since Crawford is dead, and because you're supposed to say only good things about the dead, I'll say it now. 'Joan Crawford is dead. GOOD! A highlight for me was when I got to serve baked rat to Crawford in *What Ever Happened to Baby Jane,*" Bette said. "I only regret that I didn't get to slap her around more."

In reflection on all this, years later, Burt said, "Contrary to Jack Warner's prediction about box office poison, those two old broads (Burt's words) sure did have them lined up at the box office for *Baby Jane.*"

***

In reaction to a summons from Bette Davis, Burt visited the set of *Perry Mason,* where she was filming her episode, "The Case of Constant Doyle." By everyone's estimate, she was the biggest star to ever appear in an episode of that TV series.

Having (temporarily, as a TV oddity) commandeered the function of the defense attorney, a role usually played by Raymond Burr, Bette was smartly dressed in a tailored suit. Noting her striking appearance, he quipped, *"What Ever Happened to Baby Jane?"*

In addition to Gail Patrick Jackson, the series' executive producer and a long-time acquaintance, Bette also met Peggy Ann Garner, who had been a child actress and had received an Academy Juvenile Award for her contribution to film, notably for her role in *A Tree Grows in Brooklyn* (1945). Like so many child stars, she was experiencing difficulties moving on to adult film roles.

Bette told Burt, "I want to show the TV audience that as a lawyer, a woman can stand up against William Talman, the prosecuting attorney."

Her performance was reviewed as "restrained, warm-hearted, and sharp-tongued."

In the episode she was in, Bette defended a young man, played by Michael Parks, who is accused of murder. Parks had been hailed as "The New James Dean," even though that comparison had also been used for several other up-and-coming actors of his generation. The handsome young man made Burt jealous.

According to Burt, Bette was acting "somewhat the cougar. She often touches his broad shoulders and at one point even swats his buttocks."

Born in Corona, California, Parks was four years younger than Burt. Before becoming an actor and singer, he had picked fruit, dug ditches, driven a truck, and fought forest fires. He had been briefly married when he was sixteen, the union producing a daughter.

Michael Parks cast as Adam reaching for Eve in the 1966 Italian/American religious epic, *The Bible: In the Beginning.*

At twenty-four, he married again, this time to actress Jean Moriaty, but after a few months, she committed suicide.

After his gig with Bette, movie-goers would see a lot more of Parks—including many views of him nude after John Huston cast him into the role of Adam in *The Bible: In the Beginning* (1966).

Parks became even more famous in the 1980s when he starred in ABC's *Dynasty* and its spin-off series, *The Colbys.* In time, he'd work with such filmmakers as Quentin Tarantino.

"Bette didn't discard me and take up with Parks," Burt recalled, "but I think she was tempted. That Parks was not only good-looking, but, as it turned out, he was a damn good singer too. His song, 'Long Lonesome Highway,' became a big hit."

At the end of filming of her *Perry Mason* episode, Bette told the press, "Michael Parks is the finest young actor working in films today."

When Burt heard that, he said, "I wished she'd said that about me."

***

157

One night, Ben Gazzara phoned and invited Burt to dinner at Romanoff's. There was some vague possibility that they might co-star in a Broadway production together, and the dinner had been conceived as a "meet and greet." It was there and then that Burt first encountered (disastrously) Marlon Brando.

As they entered the restaurant, Gazzara spotted Brando sitting about twenty feet away with an attractive blonde starlet, Liz Renay, winner of a Marilyn Monroe lookalike contest.

Gazzara knew Brando from the New York stage. With Burt trailing him, he walked over to his table.

"Marlon," Gazzara said. "Great to see you. This guy with me is Burt Reynolds…you know, the one everybody says looks like you."

Brando did not look into Burt's face even as he extended a limp and wet handshake. *[Rightly or wrongly, Burt later told people that Brando's hand had just emerged from the vagina of Liz Renay. A long white tablecloth concealed any underground movement.]*

As a gesture of contempt for Burt, Brando rolled his eyes toward the ceiling, mumbled something, and immediately turned his attention back to Renay. "But Marlon," she said. "This guy does look like you. He could play your brother in a movie."

"Shut your face, bitch," Brando told her, harshly. "Who are you? Some fucking casting director?"

Burt walked away as Gazzara remained behind for a few additional words with Brando.

Over dinner, Burt could hardly concentrate on what Gazzara was saying, as his

Liz Renay, known as both an exhibitionist and a "star-fucker," was the most outrageous starlet in Hollywood. She claimed that over a period of 30 years, she had been sexually intimate with 200 male actors, each a marquee name.

Although Burt threatened to kill his arch-enemy, Marlon Brando, he settled for satirizing him on TV.

fury at Brando was "making my blood boil."

At the end of their time together that evening, Burt casually asked Gazzara for Brando's address. Gazzara had visited him there on several occasions.

"After leaving Romanoff's, I drove to Brando's house and parked across the street," Burt recalled. "Only a porch light was on. My fury had reached the boiling point. Okay, I was a bit mad. At the time I was known for beating the shit out of guys, and I thought I could take Brando on."

Ben Gazzara as prisoner in *Convicts 4* (1962). Burt envied the roles this tough, talented actor from Manhattan's Lower East Side won with his dark, sinister looks and compelling performances.

"As the night wore on, and until the early hours of morning, I wanted to kill him" he said. "Perhaps I could get him in a stranglehold and choke the fucker to death. He deserved to die. He had harmed my career. Haven't you ever wanted to kill someone?"

"When the sun came up, I had simmered down a bit, and my sanity was slowly returning," he said. "What good would killing Brando do for me? I'd be caught and would end up with a life sentence in jail."

"After mulling it over, I got control of my temper and drove home for some much-needed sleep."

When he woke up at two o'clock that afternoon, he decided that some other form of revenge was needed. But what?

In one of those weird coincidences that so often happen in life, he received a phone call from Rod Serling, famous for *The Twilight Zone,* a big hit as a TV series.

Serling had written a script for an episode of that series entitled "The Bard." Its plot focused on an inept screenwriter, Julius Moomer (Jack Weston).

After endless failures, he uses black magic to resuscitate William Shakespeare from the grave to write a play for him.

Serling wanted Burt to portray a Method actor named Rocky Rhodes. "It'll be a send-up of Method actors in general, and Marlon Brando in particular—his mumbles and his mannerisms—and whatever else you can come up with. David Butler will direct. He told me this morning that you'd be the best man in Hollywood to pull this off as a satire of Brando."

Burt later referred to this opportunity—in spite of the ridiculous plot—

as "heaven sent."

On his first day on the set, Burt met the episode's director (Butler) and its lead actor, John Williams, too. Cast as "The Bard," he wore a costume inspired by Shakespeare's Elizabethan heyday at London's Globe Theatre.

It was later reported that Brando was alerted to the satirical send-up after the episode's filming, and that when it was broadcast, he became so furious that "he threw something at his television set and broke it," Burt claimed.

Then yet another coincidence occurred. After the airing of that episode, Rita Moreno phoned Burt and invited him to a party she'd be attending at Brando's home. Burt had known the actress in New York when he'd been a struggling actor auditioning for parts on Broadway. Burt would later co-star with Moreno in a TV episode of *B.L. Stryker*.

"There is no other way to say it," he wrote in a memoir. "Rita is just a great broad."

[At the time of her invitation, Moreno was having a torrid affair with Brando. Perhaps she wanted to appear with Burt as a means of paying Brando back for his affair with the sleazy Renay. In 1974, as part of a publicity stunt, Renay became infamous for running totally nude down Hollywood Boulevard until she was arrested by the police.]

"In the living room of 'The Great One,' I encountered Brando for the second time," Burt claimed. "He was sitting like some potentate in a big armchair. This time, I didn't even get a handshake. He mumbled something and looked away, as if I bored hell out of him. I tried to make some small talk before he turned on me, looking into my face for the first time."

"You're trying to capitalize off your alleged resemblance to me, although I don't see it," Brando told him. "If you look like me, you're the dime-store version. I'm told

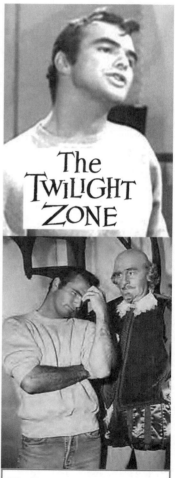

After Burt was evicted from Marlon Brando's home, he ended up on *The Twilight Zone*, mocking his own acting style to the "time traveler and playwright" William Shakespeare.

160

that you can't act."

"It seems the only thing you have going for you is a cheap imitation of the real thing—namely, Yours Truly."

"Fuck that!" Burt said, his voice rising in anger. "I'm not undergoing surgery to change the look I was born with. Frankly, I'm sexier and better-looking than you. If some director wants me for a so-called Brando role, at least he won't get the fat version."

Burt turned and walked away and was never to directly confront Brando again.

[Despite that confrontation, Burt, perhaps provocatively, opted to remain at the party for another hour. Standing not too far from Brando, at least within hearing distance, he confessed to three male party-goers, "I fucked Brando's sister, Jocelyn, when we worked together in a play."

He had heard that Brando and Glenn Ford had conflicted when they co-starred together in Teahouse of the August Moon *(1956).*

"Glenn Ford saved that picture," Burt said. "I thought he was terrific in it. Brando with those buck teeth, impersonating a Jap was an insulting stereotype."

Burt didn't stop there: Later that same evening, he told two separate party-goers, both of them male, a rumor that had spread about Brando:

"Truman Capote told me that he sucked off Brando in Japan during the filming of Sayonara *(1957)—and that he has a small dick."*

Still seated in his armchair, Brando signaled for his bartender and when he got there, Brando whispered something in his ear. The bartender then approached Burt, ordering him out of Brando's house immediately.

Without hesitation, Burt left at once. He'd work with Moreno in the future, but he would never see Brando again.

There's a footnote to the Brando/Reynolds feud. Brando had signed to play Don Vito Corleone in The Godfather *(1972). Its director, Francis Ford Coppola, offered the role of Michael Corleone to Jack Nicholson, who rejected it. It was then offered to Warren Beatty, who also rejected it.*

The director than turned to Burt, who accepted it. Burt's resemblance to Brando would coincide gracefully with the script, which had defined the character he'd play as a member of the Corleone family.

But when Brando heard what Coppola had done, he threatened to walk off the picture if he signed "that Reynolds fag."

Consequently, the role of Michael Corleone went to Al Pacino.]

Years later, Burt summed up his impression of Brando. "As an actor, he's a genius and even when he's dull, he's still much better than most actors who are at the top of their form. But he has preserved the mentality of an adolescent. It's a pity. When he doesn't try and someone is speaking to him, it's like a blank wall. In fact, it's even less interesting because behind a blank wall you can always suppose that there's something interesting there."

[Liz Renay, known as one of the leading "star fuckers" in Hollywood, made several attempts to hook up with Burt for seduction, but failed to reach him. However, among the 200 major or minor stars, she was sexually intimate with, she seemed to make extra efforts to review and evaluate Marlon Brando:

"Marlon was very proud of what he called, 'My noble tool'—perhaps more than he should have been. I heard that when he wasn't screwing Tallulah Bankhead or my rival, Marilyn Monroe, he liked to plug the boys, especially James Dean."

"Shelley Winters was crazy about him, and she slapped my face one night in a club when she saw me. (She'd heard that he was banging me.)"

"With me, Marlon was just great, and I knew him in his heyday back in the early 50s. He was fantastic, exciting, warm, and earthy, and I can almost understand why Rita Moreno practically committed suicide over him. During the filming of A Streetcar Named Desire, he told me he fucked both Vivien Leigh and her husband, his Highness (he had some title) Laurence Olivier."

"There was nothing phony about Marlon, He knew what most bastards in Hollywood were like. Phonies, the whole lot of them. He told me I should have been a bigger star than Marilyn. I know I could have been if it weren't for the phonies. He told me I was better in bed than Marilyn, too."]

***

In reference to one of the most profitable and longest-running TV series in entertainment history, Cecil Smith, a columnist for the Los Angeles Times, wrote: "Gunsmoke was the dramatization of the American epic legend of the West. It's our own Iliad and Odyssey, created from the standard elements of the dime novel and the pulp Western as romanticized by Ned Buntline, Bret Harte, and Mark Twain. It was even the stuff of legend."

Set in Dodge City, Kansas, it ran for 20 seasons from 1955 to 1975. It was the creation of director Norman Macdonnell and writer John Meston. The star of the series, Marshal Matt Dillon, was portrayed by James Arness, who stood 6'7".

[Mae West, who was offered a guest role on an episode of Gunsmoke, turned it down. But after she met Arness, she said, "Let's forget about the six feet. What I want to talk to you about are the seven inches."]

Robert Stack, Bill Conrad, and Raymond Burr were each considered for the character of Matt Dillon, but each was rejected. John Wayne was instrumental in the director's selection of Arness for the role to which he would devote much of his life and career. He would portray Dillon for decades.

[Twelve years after the series went off the air, Arness returned as Dillon in the movie, Gunsmoke: Return to Dodge *(1987). He appeared as the Marshal again in the 1990s in made-for-TV movies.]*

The actor had been severely wounded in the Battle of Anzio in Italy during World War II, and from his wounds, he was in pain for the rest of his life. Although he covered it well, it became intense every time he had to jump on a horse.

Supporting Arness was a cast of regulars. Among the most consistent was Dennis Weaver playing Chester Goode, Dillon's trusty, limping, hillbilly partner.

Cast as "Doc" (Dr. Glen Adams), Milburn Stone, like Arness, remained a member of the cast for the entirety of its twenty-year run. At the debut of the series, makeup artists tried to make Stone look older, but by the end of the run of the series, his advanced age fitted the role perfectly.

The leading lady of the series was Amanda Blake, who portrayed the red-haired Miss Kitty Russell, a saloon keeper/prostitute. Early in her career, she was billed as "The Young Greer Garson."

A devoted animal lover, she often showed up on the set with her pet lion, Kemo.

Three views of James Arness. top photo   In the opening credits of *Gunsmoke*; middle photo: With Miss Kitty (Amanda Blake); and (lower photo) with Burt Reynolds as Quint.

As a sideline to her acting career, she maintained a company dedicated to breeding cheetahs in captivity.

When Weaver (as Chester) announced that he was leaving the cast, a search was conducted for his replacement. In the script rewrites that followed Weaver's departure, it was determined that the new character—that of a "half-breed" blacksmith, Quint Asper—would be deliberately configured as a departure from the original.

Auditions for the role attracted 300 applicants, one of whom was Burt Reynolds. When Macdonnell met him, he told him, "Your face is too fat to be that of an Indian."

"If you want the real thing, head for Oklahoma," Burt told him.

On second thought, Macdonnell reconsidered and awarded the role to Burt, "fat face" and all.

Burt met Weaver on his last day on the set. "Has Shelley Winters fucked you yet?" Weaver asked.

"Not yet," Burt said.

"She'll get around to you, I predict. She did for me in 1952 and got me a contract with Universal."

When Burt met Milburn Stone, the older actor told him, "The audience will always forgive you for being wrong, but they will never forgive you for being boring and dull."

Some of Burt's best-known episodes on *Gunsmoke* included "Innocence" (1964), "Circus Trick," "Winner Take All," "Elibab's Aim," and "Bank Baby" (each of the latter four released in 1965).

Burt appraised his character of Quint as "being a guy who loves physical contact, has no prejudices, and is completely independent. He takes people at face value, and he could just as soon fight as he would eat."

Macdonnell said, "I have the feeling that if Burt Reynolds ever got the bit in his teeth, he'd run away with it. He's not afraid of man, beast, or God. He's really made an effort to fit in with us. That's not easy for a newcomer to a cast that's been working together like a family all these years."

The director also said: "Burt's a damn good actor. He's definitely leading man material. And that represents a problem for us: We can use only one leading man—and that's James Arness."

Most of Burt's scenes were dull, although they did attract some voyeuristic interest because he often appeared shirtless, pounding a horseshoe on an antique anvil. Regularly, he badgered Macdonnell for scenes that would build up Quint, the character he played.

"You're not standing out in the role," the director said. "James Arness, Amanda Blake, and even Dennis Weaver get fan mail. You've come up with the least."

"Fan mail?" Burt said. "Who in hell is going to write fan mail to an Indian half-breed?"

"After two and a half years, I decided not to pound any more horseshoes," Burt said. "Even though I was making $3,000 a week, real good pay back then, I was going nowhere as an actor. All my friends urged me to stay, since it was steady employment. I wanted to break away and go after stronger stuff or else I'd end up an old man, since *Gunsmoke* seemed it might run forever. About all I got to do as Quint was ask Marshal Dillon if I could go and get his horse."

One evening, long after Burt left the show, he encountered Arness at a party. "I now own the company that produces *Gunsmoke*," Arness told him. "In the first seven years of doing the show, I sold it to CBS, bought it back from them, sold it to them again, and then bought it back again. Duke Wayne got me the role. Ironically, I've made more money off *Gunsmoke* than Duke did from all the damn movies he's made over the decades."

***

In the 1960s, it was the custom of studios to charter a private plane and fly its stars in summer on nationwide tours to promote their fall lineup. Nine cities, including Chicago, New York, and Boston, were targeted.

Burt was included in the press and PR promotion after he was defined as the newest member of *Gunsmoke's* cast.

The tour was also a way for a studio to test-market a potential star. In Burt's case, some studio executives thought he might be marketed as a sex symbol, and they were eager to see whether women gravitated to him as fans, or whether they stayed away in droves.

Walter Brennan was also part of the tour. On its first leg, aboard the flight from Los Angeles to Chicago, he sat next to Burt on the airplane. He was already familiar with Brennan's *persona* and with many of his previous roles. He had often been cast as a curmudgeonly old codger, with or without his false teeth.

Onscreen, he'd appeared as a somewhat lovable character, but in person, he was different, a right-wing extremist, "a mile to the right of John Wayne," in Burt's estimation.

Brennan was very agitated about the emerging Civil Rights movement. "The Negroes were content with their station in life until all these communist troublemakers from the North headed South to cause riots. Most of them are on the payroll of the Soviet Union. I'm a member of the John Birch Society. My fellow members plan to protect the rights of white people."

On the next leg of their tour, Burt avoided sitting next to Brennan, preferring the company of cast member Richard Crenna, whom he likened as "a dead-ringer for George Hamilton."

Within minutes, Crenna, a Los Angeles born actor, had Burt laughing. He later claimed that Crenna was "the funniest human being I've ever met." At the time, he was playing Luke McCoy on the long-running (1957-63) hit TV series, *The Real McCoys*.

En route to the toilets at the tail end of the airplane, Burt spotted a young girl seated in the final row. Her flirtatious eyes met his.

Back in his seat, he pointed her out to Crenna. "See that girl with the short hair, bright smile, and cute body—too cute for her own good. Just who is she?"

"That's Judy Carne," he answered.

The English actress, Judy Carne, pictured here with "friend," was about to enter Burt's life. As he later said, "I would never recover from it."

CHAPTER FIVE

JUDY CARNE

BURT SEDUCES, & MARRIES THE BISEXUAL BRITISH COMEDIENNE.
THEIR UNION IS MARKED WITH VIOLENCE & INFIDELITIES

ROY ROGERS

BURT GOES BORDELLO-HOPPING WITH
THE KING OF THE COWBOYS
BURT ENTRENCHES HIS PUBLIC IMAGE AS A GOOD OL' BOY

GEORGE WALLACE

WHY THE FOUR-TERM ALABAMA GOVERNOR
WANTED BURT—A FAMOUS BUT GOOD OL' SOUTHERN BOY—
AS HIS VICE-PRESIDENTIAL RUNNING MATE IN THE
PRESIDENTIAL ELECTIONS OF 1968

CARY GRANT

BURT AROUSES HIS EROTIC LUST

MORE "GOLDEN AGE TV GIGS"

BRANDED! FLIPPER! RAWHIDE! 12 O'CLOCK HIGH!
WITH MORE TO COME AS BURT GETS PERMANENTLY ASSOCIATED
WITH "LIKABLE TOUGH GUY" TV ROLES

Only months before England declared war on Germany in 1939, Joyce Audrey Botterill (later, Judy Carne) was born in Northampton, which is in the Midlands of Central England, north of London. The world wouldn't come to know her until she starred in Rowan & Martin's *Laugh-in* as "The Sock-It-To-Me Girl."

Her parents were "greengrocers," but they managed to send her to the prestigious Bush-Davies Theatrical School in East Grinstead in 1948. It catered to upper-class girls ages eight to sixteen.

She later described the scene as "straight out of *Jane Eyre*." Her classmates mocked her lower-class accent and teachers dug their fingernails into her skin at the least infraction. At the time, she idolized Margot Fonteyn and wanted to be like Moira Shearer in ballet movie, *The Red Shoes* (1948). But even more than becoming a ballerina, she wanted to be an actress, a singer, and a tap dancer like Ann Miller in those MGM musicals.

After graduation, she made her way to London, where she found her first acting gig, appearing in the television musical *The First Day of Spring* at the Apollo Theatre.

It was during the run of the show that she later confessed that "an older man took my virginity. I expected fireworks, earthquakes, trumpets blaring, but ended up miserably disappointed."

She got her first break in television when she was cast in *Danger Man* (1961), playing a nightclub singer who becomes involved in a murder rap. She also recorded two songs from the show for MGM Records.

She began to get gigs, including a TV appearance on *The Dave King Show*, where she performed a song-and-dance number with a young Roger Moore before his fame as *The Saint* and as James Bond. She also appeared in an intimate review called *For Amusement Only* in which she sang and danced and performed in comedic sketches.

While performing in this show, she met Glen Mason, a young British pop star. "The attraction was immediate, and we had a brief fling," she recalled.

"His best friend was Sean Connery, who in time, of course, would be an even more famous James Bond than Moore," she said.

"I heard that in Scotland, he'd posed nude in a posing strap, or maybe none at all, for art classes. He could take off that posing strap for me any night."

Also in 1961, she appeared in the BBC sitcom, *The Rag Trade,* in which she played a wisecracking Cockney seamstress with a beehive hairdo.

London was Swinging in the 1960s, and Judy wanted to be hip, dressing in a Carnaby Street wardrobe and going to the Vidal Sassoon hairdressing salon on Bond Street. There, she got to see the young man soon to become the most famous hairdresser in the world. One of his assistants, a very effeminate young man from Liverpool, gave her the "geometric cut," which she described as "an angular space-age design."

She began to patronize The White Elephant, a chic private club in London, frequented by the likes of Princess Margaret. There, she finally met her idol, Sassoon himself. He was soon bedding her "with his inhibitions forgotten," she claimed.

Then one night, Stirling Moss, the best-known race car driver in Britain, walked into her life. From the moment she met him, she launched what she called "a comfortable romance." Everything was electronic in his household; even the toilet seat was electrically heated.

But she preferred the human warmth coming from his body, as he made love to her night after night.

One of his closest friends, the actor Steve McQueen, arrived in London, and he double-dated with Moss and Judy. McQueen waited until a subsequent visit before he, too, seduced Judy. In her words: "It happened magically and spontaneously."

Along the way, another high-profile performer entered her life. Anthony Newley was working on a musical called *Stop the World, I Want to Get Off,* and practicing its hit song, "What Kind of Fool Am I?".

Race car driver Stirling Moss in 1961. Judy Carne pondered her dilemma: "Who will win the race for my heart? Darling Stirling or dear Burt?"

"Tony was a little kinky," she said. "He lived with his mother and liked to have sex with me with the door open so she could hear us going at it."

Their affair continued until one day, after a show, she came backstage to his dressing room for their regular date.

"I opened the door and barged in. I found Tony in his jockey shorts seated at his dressing table. On his lap was the luscious Joan Collins. She glared at me, already looking like that venomous Alexis Carrington in her future TV role, *Dynasty*. Enter Joan. Exit Judy."

Her life was about to change when Cy Howard, the American producer, flew into London. He was casting a new TV series called *Fair Exchange*, the story of an American and an English couple who exchange their teenaged daughters for a year.

Judy's adventures as a Brit in Hollywood: Steve McQueen.

"He preferred sloppy seconds," Carne claimed. "That meant he brought along another bloke to do the honors first."

It was an awkward meeting at first. She barged in and said, *"Allo, govnor, I 'ear you're lookin' for an English bird to take back with you to 'ollywood."*

After some additional awkward exchanges, he awarded her the part.

Before flying to Los Angeles, Newley warned her, "Those vultures in Hollywood will eat you alive, girl."

The first week of shooting was at Desilu Studios on Hollywood Boulevard, owned by Lucille Ball and her divorced husband, Desi Arnaz. "I met Lucille the first week," Judy said. "With her bright red-dyed hair, she looked older than I had imagined. She warned me to stay away from Desi, or else I'd be finished in American television. I hadn't even met him yet."

The next day, Judy did meet Ball's ex-husband, and he welcomed her to Hollywood. She found him outgoing and friendly, and he invited her to a party he was hosting that night at his penthouse apartment in the Chateau Marmont.

Anthony Newley and his wife, Joan Collins, in 1963.

"When she decided she wanted him, she got him," Carne said. "I was shoved aside."

It was a lavish event, and she got to meet members of the Hollywood elite.

170

Arnaz asked her to stick around, which she did. But he'd been drinking heavily all night. She was the one who showed the last guest out. All of them were drunk. When she re-entered the living room, Arnaz was asleep on the sofa, snoring in a drunken stupor. She quietly let herself out.

The following week he invited her to enjoy the weekend at his ranch at Del Mar, south of Los Angeles. He spent the day showing off his ranch and its horses, including, in her words, "his prize stud majestically strutting about like a matador, his phallus growing immense." She watched as he mounted a mare.

"Later that night, I was introduced to Desi's Cuban salami," she confessed. "I found out that his father took him to a bordello in Havana when he was only fifteen. The man loved sex. He couldn't get enough of it—and of me."

"I was enjoying a slightly older Desi. When he was young, or so I was told, he could go more rounds than he did with me that weekend, taking on Betty Grable, Lorenz Hart, Cesar Romero, Lana Turner, and all the girls at Polly Adler's notorious whorehouse in Manhattan."

"I loved Lucy," Desi Arnaz told Judy Carne. "So did half the other men in Hollywood, from Milton Berle to Orson Welles."

As he drove her back to Hollywood that Monday morning, he told her, "Don't fall in love with me. A few peccadilloes mean nothing to me. As the owner of a studio, the world is my oyster. When I want a gal, I need only to say, 'Come here!'"

"Thanks for the warning," she said. "And I could easily go for a stud like you."

She later admitted, "I didn't mean a word of what I said. But I think he was flattered and believed me. Tell men what they want to hear—never the truth."

In her somewhat sanitized tell-all mem-

Arnaz and his studio (Desilu) worked hard to promote the Hollywood newcomer, Judy Carne, as a player in their TV series, *Fair Exchange*.

This press release, sent out to CBS affiliates nationwide, explained the image above like this:

"Eddie Foy, Jr. shows vivacious Judy Carne the results of American ingenuity in the form of an automatic coffee dispenser in a New York cafeteria in Desilu's new comedy series, *Fair Exchange*, seen Friday nights at 9:30PM (EDT) on CBS."

oir, she claimed she avoided Arnaz's sexual advances. Later, she explained to friends why she avoided mentioning any of them in print.

"I didn't want to infuriate Lucille Ball, fearing she would carry out her threat to remove me from American television. Even though they were divorced, she was still jealous of Desi whenever she was directly confronted with news about his affairs with younger women."

Judy's life in America was about to change when she became involved as a promoter in a press junket for *Fair Exchange*. On board, as part of the same promotion, was Burt Reynolds hyping *Gunsmoke*. They found themselves on their way to Florida, which to her meant alligators in the Everglades and oranges growing in one's frontyard.

At some point during their publicity tour, in Miami, a network executive introduced Judy to Burt.

"There was a mischievous twinkle in his eye as he took my hand," she said. "So you're Judy Carne. I would have thought you were Peter Pan."

"At first I thought you were Marlon Brando. I've heard of him. But I've never heard of Burt Reynolds. You excited about seeing Miami? Is it your first trip to Florida?"

"Hell, no," he answered. "I was raised here. I'm heading home and getting the studio to pay for my family reunion. Not bad."

***

Judy later claimed that while they were still on board the airplane to Miami, she and Burt might have "ravished each other" had they not been surrounded by studio representatives and other actors. "We might have become members of the Mile High Club," she said. "Perhaps even doing it while strapped to the wings of the jet."

Arriving at the airport, Judy, Burt, and the other stars and representatives were transferred in a fleet of limousines to the Fontainebleau Hotel on Miami Beach. Judy and Burt were each assigned suites on the same floor, each unit opening onto balconies overlooking the ocean.

As she was unpacking, her phone rang. She knew who was on the other end. Burt invited her for a drink and she accepted, think-

"It was not a match made in heaven," said Burt of his affair and later marriage to Judy Carne. "Our mating was conceived below heaven and in the lower depths."

172

ing it would be in the bar downstairs. Within fifteen minutes he was knocking on her door, proposing that they stay in and order drinks from room service.

She later claimed, "I wondered what sex with Burt would be like. Would I please him? More to the point, would he satisfy me? As actors go, would he be a better lover than Steve McQueen?"

Inside her suite, he didn't waste time. "I felt a rush," she said. "We fell into each other's arms like long-lost lovers."

As they were ripping off their clothes, the phone rang. It was from a representative, reminding them that they were due in the lobby in thirty minutes for a cocktail party and interviews.

"It's showtime!" Burt said, kissing her goodbye as he rushed back to his room to shower and dress.

The cocktails, the chit-chat, the interviews, and the subsequent banquet were followed by an after-dinner party and more cocktails.

By midnight, "giggling like kids" (Judy's words), they were seen entering the elevator to return to their suites—or at least her suite.

Later, in print, she reviewed his performance, claiming that he paid "scrupulous attention to my sexual desires." He seemed to hit her "hot spots" time and time again. Three o'clock in the morning found them standing nude on her balcony, looking over the ocean and smiling with satisfaction at the Man in the Moon.

The next day was filled with more scheduled activities, more interviews, more cocktail parties, more dinners.

During the press junket, Burt got to know Eddie Foy, Jr., Judy's co-star in the TV series, *Fair Exchange.* He was the son of the famous vaudevillian, Eddie Foy, and he was one of the "Seven Little Foys" immortalized in the 1955 movie of the same name.

A show biz veteran, he'd made his debut on the stage in Florenz Ziegfeld's 1929 extravaganza, *Show Girl,* starring Jimmy Durante and Ruby Keeler. Since he resembled his father more than the other children, he played him in four feature films, including *Lillian Russell* (1940) and *Yankee Doodle Dandy* (1942).

Judy and Burt each had the day off on Sunday, so Burt drove her north to Riviera Beach, where he introduced her to his parents, Big Burt and Fern. She also met his sister, Nancy, and other members of the Reynolds clan.

Later, in the kitchen, Fern approached her, saying, "It's time Burt settled down, and you look like the kind of gal he should marry—and give me more grandchildren."

Back in California, Judy found that Burt lived in a sparsely furnished bachelor pad in the center of Hollywood. At the time, she was sharing a small apartment with a girl named Susan Kroull.

Following a month of steady dating, they decided to live together. After much searching, they rented a wooden cottage on a cul-de-sac, Hermit's Glen, above Laurel Canyon, high in the Hollywood Hills.

She furnished it mainly with pieces she'd collected, and he brought in his football trophies, two saddles, and a collection of rifles, guns, and knives. One of the saddles had been used as a prop by Roy Rogers in *Rainbow Over Texas* (1946); the other by Gene Autry in *Cow Town* (1950).

Burt's wardrobe seemed to come directly from the costume department of *Gunsmoke*. He wore a cowboy shirt, a ten-gallon hat, a leather belt with a huge silver buckle, tight blue jeans, and what he called "my shit-kicking boots."

She appraised his outfit, suggesting it might be ideal for hustling gays along Santa Monica Boulevard.

"So that is the opinion of Peter Pan?" he asked mockingly. He suggested she wear a dress instead of pants, along with a bra and a pair of high heels—and also let her trademark bobbed hair grow long.

"I don't need a bra, as you well know," she said. "I'm the Audrey Hepburn type, not Jayne Mansfield."

"He hated my dress, but loved my home cooking," she said. "I was new to Hollywood and didn't have friends, but he did. Soon, I was cooking for the cast and crew of *Gunsmoke*. But I warned him that I'd never be turned into a little 'ol homebody, waiting for her man to return home from work. I let him know that I planned to pursue my career as avidly as he did his own."

Redbook reporter Claire Safran later wrote that Judy "was different from the type of woman to whom Burt Reynolds had been attracted in the past. She was more pixyish than pretty, with a slender, almost boyish body. She was also a free spirit who became a Flower Child in the 1960s. At first, Burt found these qualities terribly exciting, but his fascination would not last. After all, he became known for his short attention span."

On weekends, he liked to drive her to the horse ranch of stuntman Hal Needham in the San Fernando Valley, where his stables were air conditioned. He was making good money renting his horses to the producers of *Gunsmoke* as well as to many of the other Western series that were all the rage on television at that time, including *Bonanza* and *Wagon Train*. One of Burt's best friends, Clint Eastwood, was a big success in the long-running (1959-1965) TV series, *Rawhide*.

Hal would greet Judy by lifting her up in the air as if she were weightless. Perched on his broad shoulders, she would go into a dancer's pirouette while airborne before he sent her flying through the air back to the arms of her lover.

Later, Judy ended up hanging out with Hal's wife, Arlene. Burt practiced a stunt with the horse falling over, as Burt gets thrown from its back. "It looked to me like a great way for a bloke to be crippled for life," Judy said.

Burt and Judy got to know Needham very well, and he often spoke of his boyhood growing up during the Great Depression in Arkansas.

Deep in the Ozarks, the Needhams lived three miles from the nearest road. "We had all the luxuries of life in America's wilderness in 1830," he told Burt. "We shot a rabbit or squirrel for dinner."

Needham dropped out of school in the eighth grade and in time became a "tree topper." His first stunt was when, unplanned, he fell seventy feet from a tall pine. He landed in a pile of leaves, which saved his life.

In 1951, he joined the 82nd Airborne, and earned extra money on weekends by staging dangerous jumps out of an airplane. "My second stunt was a pure accident," he said. "My parachute didn't open but my reserve chute flew open right before I was to hit the ground."

During the week, Needham worked for Richard Boone on his hit TV series, *Have Gun—Will Travel* (1957-1963).

On two different weekends when Burt and Judy visited Needham, Boone was there. "When Burt was away with Hal, Boone flirted with me," Judy said. "He was no beauty, with his leathery skin and craggy-looking face, a grizzled sort of guy who had been a boxer and a roughneck in the Texas oil fields. During World War II, he'd been a Navy gunner. He wasn't my type, so I said no."

Over the course of Boone's career, he'd worked with such stars as Paul Newman, John Wayne, and Kirk Douglas, but his most famous gig remained *Have Gun—Will Travel*.

On some weekends, Burt and Judy visited Clint Eastwood and his wife, Maggie Johnson, whom he'd married in 1953. The couple lived in a rustic house in the hills near Encino, their grounds opening onto a panoramic view of the San Fernando Valley.

One afternoon, when Eastwood and Burt were outside, Maggie told Judy, "Did you know that Clint is in love with himself? He

Richard Boone in his hit TV series. Many fans found the title of the series had a phallic connotation.

175

goes after women who look like him—take me, for example: prominent nose, pronounced cheekbones, and a lean face."

Judy later recognized the same narcissistic streak in Burt. "Both actors over the years, at least when they were young, like to doff their clothes in front of the camera, and in some movies, they appeared in the buff—rear view only. Many times, they were photographed in their underwear. Clint even appeared in revealing jockey shorts, and he was fond of bathtub scenes. I heard he did his screen test nude—or maybe with just a jock-strap."

***

As Burt and Judy moved deeper into 1963, the subject of marriage came up. "I guess we became engaged," he said, "although I don't remember actually proposing to her."

There was the question of religion, one subject that had never been talked about, since neither of them had any religious affiliations. Their decision on which church they'd select as the site of their wedding hinged less on its religious affiliation and more on how much it would charge and which had the most convenient location.

The closest church to their home was the First Methodist Church on Tijunga Avenue in North Hollywood. The Rev. William Merwin was most gracious, assuring them that they did not have to be Methodist.

Burt sent airplane tickets to Big Burt and Fern in Florida, inviting them to fly on their first visit to Hollywood.

Judy's parents, Harold and Kathleen Botterill, flew in from London, meeting Burt for the first time. They greeted him with their thick Midlands accent. Burt later likened Harold to actor Wally Cox, the lover of Marlon Brando, and he compared Kathleen to Rosanne at her maximum poundage.

What shocked him were their long noses. "Each could compete with that *schnozzola* of Jimmy Durante."

He asked his bride-to-be, "With noses like your parents have, what happened to you?"

"Ask my plastic surgeon," she answered.

"With a big nose in your genes, if we have a kid, he'll look like Danny Thomas. When he grows up and comes through a door, his nose will precede him by thirty seconds."

The weeks before their wedding was a time for parties, dinners, and showers. Maggie Eastwood hosted Judy's bridal shower. "I ended up with enough kitchenware to open a restaurant," Judy said. "That included six toasters."

The morning after Burt's bachelor party, Judy quizzed him aggressively, even though he was reluctant to talk about it. "I hear that at these bachelor parties, American men hire strippers and have a big orgy."

"That didn't happen at my party," he said. "The host showed 'blue movies,' including two that Joan Crawford made in the '20s before she hit it big. Some of the guys jacked off—and that was all the action there was. I kept Junior zipped up."

A dress rehearsal was held shortly before the wedding. Moments before its scheduled beginning, Burt had still not left the set of *Gunsmoke*. Running late, he showed up at his wedding's dress rehearsal in his Western garb. The pastor asked, "Is this going to be a cowpoke wedding?"

That Saturday night, Hal Needham threw a lavish event at his ranch, Burt likening the atmosphere to Mardi Gras in New Orleans.

The night before the ceremony, Burt insisted on sleeping without Judy in a separate bedroom, even though he'd been lying at her side for months. "As we kissed good night, we went our separate ways," she said. "In bed alone, I could think only of how much I loved him and how much I wanted to feel his presence in bed beside me, and how much I wanted to be falling asleep right next to him—and what a wonderful life we would have together. Tomorrow was going to be a special day."

At the wedding (June 28, 1963), Burt felt that more members of the press showed up than friends. Amanda Blake and Milburn Stone came from the set of *Gunsmoke,* and Jimmie Rodgers, the popular country / western singer, provided the music. A friend of Burt's, Dudley Remus, flew in from Florida as Best Man. For her Maid of Honor, Judy asked Sharon DuBord, a friend she'd made at Desilu Studios.

Burt was twenty-six, Judy twenty-two.

The wedding dinner, a twelve-course affair, was held at Coolibar's, their favorite French bistro. Burt skipped the escargots. "When it comes to snails, that's something I crush with my boot after a heavy rain."

It was midnight when Burt and Judy kissed and hugged their friends and got into his '55 red Thunderbird and speeded along the Pacific Coast Highway. They finally arrived at the Highland Inn in Carmel-by-the-Sea where the bridal suite had been reserved for them.

"As soon as we came into the suite," she later wrote, "he tore off his clothes and mine, too, for a wild night of lovemaking. On top of me, he stared deeply into my eyes during the entire act. We'd made a supreme commitment—and that was to love each other until death do us part."

Back in Hollywood, when Ava Gardner saw the wedding pictures, she told the press, "I always suspected that Burt Reynolds was gay, and now I see that he's married a boy."

[She would say the same thing when her ex-husband, Frank Sinatra, married Mia Farrow.]

After their wedding ceremony, a pedestrian couldn't walk past a newsstand without seeing their pictures on the covers of fan magazines. There was speculation that Judy would give up her career just as it had started to blossom.

During the early part of their marriage, Burt was collecting a $3,000-a-week paycheck from *Gunsmoke,* and she was working, too. They decided to take out a $38,000 mortgage for a charming little house on Laurel Crest Drive in Studio City, overlooking a panoramic view of San Fernando Valley. They divided the cost of the down payment between them, as they did a $12,000 loan for renovations.

After they moved in, Burt set out to define himself as the man of the house, and every room from the bedroom to his den was decorated to suit his taste and convenience. "He let me have only the kitchen to myself," she said.

***

"As you Americans say, my marriage to Burt 'went south' just weeks after our wedding day," Judy claimed.

Burt told Hal Needham, "Sometimes the things that attract you when you're dating and romancing are the first things that drive you crazy in a marriage. If you come from the kind of background I do, you think of settling down, raising kids, and having a conventional marriage life. She wouldn't go for that. She's too...wild and crazy. She accused me of trying to recreate a scene or a style of life I saw on the TV sitcom, *Father Knows Best.*"

According to Needham, "I loved Burt dearly as a man's man. But I knew he wasn't the easiest person to get along with. He had a rotten temper and liked to settle arguments with his fists."

One night in their kitchen, during a bitter argument over her mode of dress, her unconventional friends, and her boyish look, Burt struck Judy hard, knocking her down.

She rose from the floor and stared at him with contempt. "God, you're boring."

Then she stormed out of the room and spent the weekend with a girlfriend, Jane Sheenhan. Burt had met her once and deplored her butch haircut, cowgirl outfit, and boots. "Who in hell does she think she is? Annie Oakley? Better watch yourself around that one."

After promising never to strike her again, he picked Judy up and brought her home.

But despite his promise, that fight in their kitchen marked the beginning of many others, some of them violent, that raged during the tumultuous duration of their ill-fated marriage.

"We never experienced that wedded bliss people talked about," Judy said. "Anything but. Tennessee Williams entitled one of his plays *Period of Adjustment* (1960). Burt and I experienced a Period of Maladjustment. I should never have married him. Day by day, we were destroying each other. We were two strong individuals, our egos the size of glaciers in Greenland. Neither of us was willing to give in during an argument. Both of us refused to surrender any parts of ourselves to accommodate the other's personality. He wanted me to be a conventional housewife. That I could never be—no way, no how."

"More and more, he kept striking me when he started to lose an argument," she claimed. "I went out and bought him a punching bag and installed it in his den. When he came home, I showed it to him. 'If you want to hit something, hit this,' I said to him."

During the early days of their marriage, with money still coming in for both of them, Burt took out a hefty mortgage and bought a 180-acre ranch in Jupiter, Florida.

He then proceeded to move Fern and Big Burt from Riviera Beach to look after his property, which they were glad to do. Big Burt had already retired as the police chief of Riviera Beach, and Fern was still the housewife that Burt wanted Judy to be.

The property in Jupiter had been the hideaway retreat of gangster Al Capone when the temperature got too hot in Chicago.

***

Burt and Judy managed to put up a good front whenever friends came to dinner. Such was the case when Clint and Maggie Eastwood arrived with a copy of a script they wanted to read out loud, mainly for Burt's opinion.

Entitled, *Per un Pugno Di Dollari* (*A Fistful of Dollars*), it was to be shot in Italy and directed by Sergio Leone. The director in Rome had seen two episodes of Eastwood's *Rawhide*, which had been translated into Italian. "I thought Clint's appearance on the screen was extraordinary. He has this lazy, laidback quality to him. He just appeared and stole every scene without saying very much. He's ruggedly handsome—an actor men can admire and women swoon over. "

Eastwood went to Italy for filming, and the "Spaghetti Western" was born, a genre that would soon envelop Burt, too.

Burt and Judy also developed a friendship with another married couple, Ryan O'Neal and Joanna Moore. They were married at around the same time as Burt and Judy.

In 1964, O'Neal was starring as Rodney Harrington on the ABC nighttime soap opera, *Peyton Place*. Fan mail was arriving in bags.

As Judy confessed years later, "Ryan was a knock-out. I realized I'd married the wrong man. He was a former boxer, and he and Burt often worked out together, and I enjoyed gaping at their half-naked bodies."

Burt had met O'Neal in 1962 when he was a regular on NBC's *Empire,* a modern-day Western. *[It ran for thirty-three episodes.]* "Both Burt and Ryan wanted to make feature films and graduate from TV series when the time was right," Judy said.

Ruggedly handsome and dangerous, Clint Eastwood.....and the Spaghetti Western, if not born, was reinforced.

According to Judy, she never made any moves toward seducing O'Neal, but admitted, "I sure was tempted."

One night, Joanna told her, "Ryan is an incredible lover, totally devoted to giving a woman pleasure." She didn't know it at the time, but some of the world's most beautiful and desirable women lay in O'Neal's future, as they also did for Burt in the years to come.

Judy then confessed something to Joanna: "Burt is good in bed, too, but, believe it or not, I don't think of him a sexy. Unlike your Ryan, I doubt if women fans will ever view Burt as a sex symbol. He seems trapped in some self-styled stereotype of himself—that of a virile, macho brute. Buried underneath that is a kinder, gentler man, which I try to reach but fail to do so. I know that person lurks somewhere beneath his image, but finding it is an awesome task."

During the early stages of their marriage, Judy admitted, "We felt like we owned Fort

Ryan O'Neal in 1968, at the peak of his beauty and sex appeal. "Half the women in America, maybe more, wanted to be seduced by him, especially me," said Judy Carne.

Knox, which until recently I had never heard of. We spent lavishly when he was still drawing a salary from *Gunsmoke,* and I was pulling in $200,000 a year—first from the TV series, *A Fair Exchange,* and later from *The Baileys of Balboa* (1964), where I played the daughter of a rich California yachtsman."

"In that series, I had to be an American, and Burt rehearsed me night after night until I got the accent right. The director never knew I was from England until the show had been on for some time. One day, a guy pissed me off, and my Midlands accent came out in full force."

"More and more fans were beginning to recognize me. Whenever we went out, they crowded around me, asking for my autograph. Burt was ignored. No one asked him for an autograph. He told me he felt like Norman Maine."

[She was referring to the role James Mason played in A Star is Born *(1954), where movie star Norman Maine's screen career fades as his wife's ascends.]*

Burt was about to enter what he defined as the worst part of his marriage. When he dropped out of the cast of *Gunsmoke,* hoping to find better roles in feature films, he entered a period of months with no money.

"I came from a family tradition where the man was the breadwinner, not the gal," he said. "It was hard for me having to live off Judy. I couldn't make my share of the mortgage payments on our home in California, or on my ranch in Florida, either. I had to turn to her. She was wearing the pants, and I didn't like that."

***

Looking for work one day, Burt encountered blonde-haired Tab Hunter, who enjoyed a brief reign as a screen heartthrob in the 1950s, appearing in such hits as *Damn Yankees* (1958). After he foolishly left Warner Brothers, where he'd been a contract player, roles were no longer plentiful.

In the 1950s, Hunter had been one of the "pretty boys" under contract to the gay talent agent, Henry Willson, who operated the busiest casting couch in Hollywood, not only laying Tab upon it, but Rock Hudson, Troy Donahue, Guy Madison, and Rory Calhoun, too, among many others.

Over lunch, both actors poured out their ca-

A Reluctant Sex Object

Tab Hunter romantically entangled, against his character's will, with Gwen Vernon in *Damn Yankees* (1958).

reer woes to each other. By the end of the meal, Hunter agreed to introduce Burt to his new agent, Dick Clayton, at the Famous Artists Agency.

True to his word, Hunter set up a meeting between Clayton and Burt that Tuesday afternoon in Clayton's office. The agent was already familiar with Burt's limited repertoire.

Clayton was an unknown to Burt but was set to become his personal manager and closest friend for the next two decades.

The two men bonded at once. "Dick was gay, but unlike Henry Willson, didn't have a casting couch in his office," Burt said.

Gay talent agent Dick Clayton with *starlette* Tuesday Weld in 1960, as they appeared in *Modern Screen* Magazine

A native of New Jersey, Clayton had arrived in Hollywood before World War II with hopes of becoming an actor. He did get some small parts in such films as *The Hunchback of Notre Dame* (1939) with Charles Laughton; *Knute Rockne, All American* (1940) with Ronald Reagan; and *High Sierra* (1941) with Humphrey Bogart.

During World War II, Clayton enlisted in the U.S. Army and later earned a Purple Heart for wounds suffered. Back in Hollywood, he tried once again to become an actor, but got only bit parts. One of them was in *Sailor Beware* (1951) in a brief screen appearance with another actor. He and James Dean became lovers.

Abandoning acting, Clayton became an agent and joined the staff of Famous Artists Agency.

During their first meeting, Clayton promised Burt he'd get him work, "but the parts will be low-budget at first." Then he invited Burt to Palm Desert to join Hunter and himself for a weekend at a small vacation retreat they'd built.

Burt eagerly accepted, taunting Judy by telling her, "I'm heading to the desert for a gay weekend."

[Unknown to Burt, Judy was planning her own gay weekend, having arranged to spend it with a female employee of Desilu who had become her lover. Although married to her, Burt did not know that she was bisexual.]

His weekend at Palm Desert was a big success, and Burt learned that Clayton was already negotiating for him to star in a picture set in war-torn

Vietnam, not the safest of places at the time for movie-making.

"I poured out my guts to Dick that weekend," Burt said. "Tab disappeared for most of the day with some good-looking golf caddy."

Burt talked openly and honestly with Clayton. "I know I got off to a bad start in Hollywood, throwing temper fits on the set of *Riverboat*," he admitted. "I came here dreaming of stardom, but that fantasy is fading day by day. "You're my last hope. Get me any role. I'll play any character, go anywhere in the world—and work for almost nothing. And by the way, I don't really want to have to suck cock like Marilyn or Rock when they got started."

"I hope you've realized that with me, that's not part of the deal," Clayton said. "That doesn't mean I don't find you sexy. I do...very sexy. You can put your shoes under my bed any night of the week, but that's not mandatory for me to become your agent."

"It's a deal," Burt said. "Let's shake on it, partner. If I can't pull off this final try, I'll be tossing in my jockstrap and heading back to Florida, where I might get a job as a coach at the University of Miami. If not that, painting boats. If not that, hunting and skinning alligators in the Everglades to make purses for women."

He told Clayton that he felt he didn't fit into the mold of one of Henry Willson's pretty boys of the 1950s: Tab or Robert Wagner. "I feel I'm a different kind of actor, a somewhat wild and crazy good ol' Southern boy who can play more manly roles."

"I agree," Clayton said. "Let's give it a try."

"And I can do my own stunts," Burt boasted.

Clayton had driven Burt to his desert retreat and had to return early Monday morning. So as a means of prolonging his time away, Burt called his close friend, Lee Marvin, who was in Palm Springs at the time with his new girlfriend. Marvin agreed to let Burt come and stay with them.

Marvin drove to Clayton's house to retrieve him. There, he was ushered inside by a Japanese caretaker and directed to the swimming pool. "Burt must have gotten on fine with Clayton and Hunter," Marvin said. "I found all three of these guys jaybird naked hanging out by the pool. I was asked to join them but had to turn them down. I'm a tits-and-ass kind of guy, with a hankering for the female anatomy."

[Marvin had wed Betty Ebeling in 1951, and they remained married for sixteen years, having four children. Their divorce would not come through until 1967. In the meantime, the actor had a new live-in girlfriend, Michelle Triola.

She was a former lounge singer and dancer, and in 1958, had appeared on Broadway in a production of Flower Drum Song *directed by Gene Kelly. She'd taken up with Marvin when she was a stand-in on the set of* Ship of Fools *(1965), starring, among others, Vivien Leigh.*

Later, at Marvin's villa, Burt asked him about Leigh. In Ship of Fools, *Marvin makes a drunken pass at the British star, who violently assaults him. Burt's question was, "Did you get to fuck Viv off-screen?"*

Marvin's big role that year had been in a Western comedy spoof, Cat Ballou *(1965), in which he played dual roles: the gunfighter (Kid Shelleen) and also the criminal (Tim Strawn).*

Burt had another question, too: "Did you get to fuck Jane Fonda?"

Later, Marvin won the Best Actor Oscar for Cat Ballou, *beating out Richard Burton for his performance in* The Spy Who Came in from the Cold *and Laurence Olivier for* Othello.*]*

Burt hoped that Marvin, with his new-found clout, would help him break into bigger roles. Marvin tried to get him cast in the World War II epic, *The Dirty Dozen* (1967), but its director, Robert Aldrich, preferred John Cassavetes instead. That was not the only role that Burt lost to Cassavetes. Burt also tested for *Rosemary's Baby* (1968), opposite Mia Farrow.

"Lee was one of the most outspoken friends I ever had, and he was not gun-shy about speaking out on issues. I admired his political courage."

[Marvin once told the press, "What transfers between two adults is their own damn business. If a girl likes to have a Coca-Cola bottle shoved in her ear, that's her choice. A third party, like a police officer, has no reason to get involved unless he's a voyeur."

"All voyeurs are deviates. Our archaic sex laws date back to the days of witch-burning. The first witch burned in America was a young girl set on fire because she refused to go down on the local parson."]

***

Judy Carne wondered where Burt got that saddle that Roy Rogers had worn on Trigger in a long-forgotten Western. One night, she found out.

Burt phoned her one afternoon and told her he was bringing home two friends, a married couple for dinner. He didn't want to tell her who the couple was. "It's a surprise."

She was surprised all right when Roy Rogers, the King of the Cowboys, showed up at their door with his wife, Dale Evans, the Queen of the Cowgirls.

Unlike a lot of American-born children growing up and attending Saturday afternoon Westerns at the local Bijou, Judy had never seen one of their movies. However, their reputation had preceded their visit.

Roy Rogers had come to personify the American Western hero, although he was born Leonard Franklin Slye in Cincinnati into a life of poverty. Eventually, he hitchhiked to Hollywood where he found a low-paying survival job as an itinerant fruit picker, working with Mexicans who crossed the border to harvest crops.

He disguised himself as a cowboy after joining a singing group, Sons of the Pioneers. Signed with Decca Records, they released a hit song in 1934, "Tumbling Tumbleweeds."

That led to Rogers getting cast in Westerns beginning in 1935. Billed as "America's Singing Cowboy," he became a rival of Gene Autry.

From 1939 to 1954, he was the all-time number one money-maker in Western films, second only to Walt Disney in merchandising items with his logo and label. He also lent his name to a string of franchised family-friendly restaurants across the nation.

Dale Evans was a "real Texas broad" (Judy's words), who was born there in 1912 under the name of Lucille Wood Smith. Roy was her fourth husband. At the age of fourteen, she'd eloped with her first husband, a big band singer, with whom she had a child. After her divorce from him, she married two more times before settling down with Rogers.

She'd met him when Republic Studios cast them together in a Western.

"I suffered through an evening with these two cornpones," Judy said. "At one point, Dale asked if I had been saved. I told the bitch I'd never been lost."

"The two of them were a bit too Christian for me," Judy said. "Burt kept his mouth shut and tolerated them, even though he was a most tolerant person. Both of them were bigots, hating black people, Jews, and reserving a particularly fiery furnace in hell for gay men. Roy looked at the world through squinty eyes."

"Instead of liking such music as 'Happy Trails,' Roy, it turns out, was a jazz devotee, preferring Duke Ellington's music despite the singer's color," Burt said. "In my time, I've been out with a lot of music stars, but never have I seen the adoration of fans when I went somewhere with Roy Rogers. He was mobbed and endlessly signed autographs as I impatiently looked on, perhaps with envy. One evening, he gave me a pair of Roy Rogers pajamas, but I told him I slept buck naked, with my pecker hanging

Campy TV Memorabilia & Americana:

Roy Rogers, Dale Evans, and Trigger in 1958.

down."

"Roy fancied himself a big-game hunter, but the cowpoke couldn't shoot straight," Burt said. "Once, we took a boat to this remote island. We were lying on the beach one day buck naked when this moose wandered out from the forest for a drink of water from the river. Roy jumped up, took his rifle, and fired once and missed, and then fired again and missed."

"I told him to give the moose a break and he did. Ignoring the shots, the moose finished gulping down the water and slowly wandered back to the forest, perhaps hunting for Mrs. Moose."

"I found out how he'd gotten Trigger," Burt said. "He acquired the wonder horse on the set of *The Adventures of Robin Hood* (1938), starring Errol Flynn. Trigger had been the horse ridden by Olivia de Havilland. Under Roy's ownership, it became the most famous horse in America."

Rogers quoted Flynn as telling him, "I fuck cowboys. How about it, sport?"

"Roy claimed that he socked the swashbuckler and made his escape," Burt said.

"Roy and I remained friends for years, even though Dale hated my guts," Burt said. "He told me that Dale was afraid that I would lead him astray. She also claimed that I was gay and trying to get in his pants. She was not right about that gay thing but was on target about leading Roy astray."

"That wasn't hard to do. He sure didn't need any persuasion when I invited him to this whorehouse in Los Angeles. His choirboy morality was confined to the movies. He liked to go after the gals, and once, he ordered a trio at the same time: One blonde, one redhead, and one brunette. He told me that Dale would do it only in the missionary position, and that he preferred more variety in his sex life."

"Eventually," Burt said, "Roy wandered off into the Western sunset, and I got involved with a very different crowd—namely Frank Sinatra and Duke Wayne."

***

In an attempt to snag film roles for Burt, his new agent, Dick Clayton at Famous Artists, gathered some fellow executives together and showed them film clips of Burt in various episodes of his TV series. He was shown running in and out of boats, down alleys, through crowded streets, dodging cars, and jumping over the roofs of ramshackle buildings.

"As you can see, he can do his own stunts," Clayton told the men.

"Okay," one of the vice presidents said. "So the guy knows how to run.

186

But can he act? I suggest that you confine your work to promoting the careers of Hugh O'Brian, Doug McClure, and Ray Danton. I predict those hot studs, not Burt, are going places bigtime."

Born to an English mother in Glendale, California, in 1935 (a year before Burt), McClure became a rival of Burt's, often competing for the same roles. In 1960, Burt had wanted to play the younger brother of Burt Lancaster in *The Unforgiven* but lost the part to McClure.

Burt also wanted the role of the cowboy Trampas in the long-running NBC-TV Western series *The Virginian*. "That damn series ran so long (1962-1971) that McClure got married and divorced twice during its run," Burt said.

In 1965, as his marriage to Judy Carne was crumbling, Burt urged Clayton to get him cast as James Stewart's son-in-law in *Shenandoah*, but the role went to McClure.

In 1971, Burt also wanted to co-star with his aging friend, Bette Davis, in a projected TV series. He would play an amateur detective, and she would appear as a retired, hypochondriacal judge. McClure got the role instead. *[Ironically, despite all the passion poured into it by both Burt and McClure, the project was eventually rejected as a TV series and released instead as a "telemovie" in 1972 entitled The Judge and Jake Wyler, still with Bette Davis and with McClure cast as one of the male leads.]*

COMPETITION: It was the role that Burt desperately wanted, that eventually was awarded to Doug McClure, who's depicted as Trampas in *The Virginian* (1962-1971).

Boasting a run of more than nine years, it was a career-builder for the actors cast into its principal parts. It was not the only role that Burt lost to McClure.

On December 2, 1972, Burt sat in front of his television set watching it and realizing that he would never get to co-star with Bette.

In spite of rejections from his colleagues about his promotions of Burt, Clayton persisted and came up with a leading role for Burt in one of the lowest budgets ever projected for a film to be shot abroad. For $75,000, the director, Christian Nyby, planned to film a spy thriller that was temporarily entitled *Last Message from Saigon*. The director agreed to sign Burt for the leading role, since he could do his own stunts. *[As director, Nyby would save money by not hiring a professional stuntman.]*

Burt would be cast as C.I.A. agent Mark Andrews, who arrives in Saigon to save the American ambassador from an assassination.

"Every day brought another disaster," Burt claimed. "I had to wrestle with a cobra, but its venom had not been removed, and it came close to giving me the kiss of death. The idiot prop man had not put blanks in this gun that the villain fires at me, and I was al-

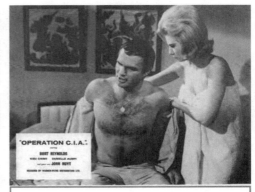

The photo above replicates a Lobby Card advertising Burt and his sex appeal as a key player in *Operation C.I.A.* (1965), a film Burt later described as "the worst movie I ever made."

On his right is Danielle Aubry. When Burt saw this shot, he said, "I look far sexier than her."

most killed. Thank God he was a rotten shot, and the bullet only grazed my arm. In this fight scene in the world's most polluted river, I swallowed some water that was to have life-threatening complications later. Remember, I no longer had a spleen to help purify my blood." *[EDITORIAL NOTE: As explained in an earlier chapter, Burt lost his spleen (and his potential career as a football star) in the medical aftermath of a near-fatal car accident during his formative years in Florida.]*

After only two weeks of shooting, the State Department asked the film crew to leave Saigon because it was too dangerous to go on filming there because of wartime conditions.

The remainder of the film was shot in Bangkok and Laos. Producer Peer J. Oppenheimer had hired two actresses as Burt's leading ladies. One of them was Danielle Aubry, who played a *femme fatale*. This slim, attractive, Canadian blonde had just completed a role in *Bikini Beach* (1964).

The other was Kieu Chinh. Burt's scenes with her included one in which their characters made a fast getaway in a slow boat.

Chinh, who was only a year younger than Burt, had been born in Hanoi, then part of French Indochina. In time, she became the best-known actress to emerge from Vietnam, with a career spanning sixty years. When Burt met her, she had just made *A Yank in Viet-Nam* (1964).

In 1975, she was filming in Singapore when she heard that the North Vietnamese communists had overrun her home in Saigon. She left for the United States, where she settled.

Two years later, she was seen in the hit TV series M*A*S*H in an episode entitled "In Love and War." Written by Alan Alda, it was based on her own story.

She later became a well-known philanthropist, co-founding the Vietnam Children's Fund.

One critic summed up the film. "It was good to see Burt Reynolds kicking back in the Orient and making it with cute Asian chicks."

When Burt saw the final cut back in Hollywood, he said, "It was the worst movie I ever made. If shown on a plane, the passengers would open the door and jump out without a parachute."

Movie posters promoted the film, now renamed *Operation C.I.A.* (1965), as "THE HOTTEST SPOT ON EARTH."

"It was," Burt said. "The movie wasn't."

***

Despite Burt's misgivings about *Operation C.I.A.*, its producer, Peer Oppenheimer, liked Burt's performance in it and signed him to co-star with the Australian actress Diane Cilento in *Deadly Contest*, set to be shot on location in Germany.

Burt was looking forward to working with her. At the time, she was married to Sean Connery. Burt had become entranced with her when she played Molly Seagrim, the lewd gamekeeper's wench in Tony Richardson's sprawling and bawdy 1963 film adaptation of Henry Fielding's *Tom Jones.*

Burt's film deal, and the movie itself, never materialized. Cilento went on to play Caterina de Medici, the love interest of Charlton Heston in *The Agony and the Ecstasy* (1965).

***

Instead of flying di-

WOMEN WE LOVE

Diane Cilento, Australia-born actress and long-suffering wife of Sean Connery, is depicted here with Albert Finney in the film adaptation of *Tom Jones*, the bawdy novel from the English Restoration.

Released to universal acclaim in 1963, it was considered the "breakout film" for Albert Finney.

Burt was thrilled with the chance to co-star with Cilento, but like many other hopes and dreams, it never came true.

rectly back to California, Burt opted to visit Selma, Alabama, instead. A re-union with Judy Carne did not seem among his top priorities.

He watched as other celebrities and movie stars had joined the protests there, advocating the civil rights of African Americans, and he felt guilty that he, too, had not joined them—hence, the decision to head for Alabama.

But moments after his arrival at the Birmingham airport, he collapsed in one of its lounges and had to be rushed to the local hospital in an ambu-lance with dome lights flashing.

After extensive medical tests, he was diagnosed with schistosomiasis, more popularly known as "snail fever." *[The disease is caused by parasitic flatworms which affect a patient's urinary tract and intestines.*

When informed of his affliction, he traced it back to the polluted water he'd swallowed in Saigon in a mock fight with an actor playing an assassin during the filming of Operation C.I.A.*]*

During his first week in the Birmingham hospital, he received an un-expected visitor, a Southern woman of grace and charm, despite her far-right political beliefs. Lurleen Wallace was the First Lady of Alabama, the wife of the racist governor, George Wallace.

Despite Burt's limited exposure in movies and television, he was sur-prised that she even knew who he was. She had, however, seen his feature film, *Angel Baby* (1961), set in the South, and she and her husband had been faithful followers of *Gunsmoke.*

Beside his hospital bed, she welcomed him to Alabama, claiming, "George and I aren't the monsters we're made out to be in the Yankee press."

Lurleen had high praise for him as "a good ol' Southern boy. Thank god you're not one of those agitators like Marlon Brando arriving in Ala-

George Wallace and his extraordinary, often tragic wife, Lurleen, welcomed Burt as a per-sonal friend and an image-builder for Alabama.

bama to stir up trouble."

He couldn't bring himself to spoil her illusion by confessing that he was on his way to Selma to join the protesters.

"You're most welcome in Alabama," Lurleen said. "But what brings you here?"

He had to think fast. "I have this script set in the rural South, and I stopped off to drive around your beautiful state scouting locations."

"That sounds wonderful," she said. "Movies are made in Florida, even Georgia, and Alabama should get in on that. It brings much-needed revenue to our state. Incidentally, what is this script about? Pray it's not another one of those 'racial justice' movies which George and I detest."

He had to think quickly and invent a plot. His facile mind came up with one rather quickly. "It's about a Scarlett O'Hara-like woman, and it takes place ten years after Rhett Butler left her. She's become a successful businesswoman and meets the true love of her life, a handsome young politician on the rise who hankers to become the next governor of Alabama. This is no Huey Long of Louisiana governor, but a builder who sets out to bring industry and jobs to his state and help its citizens escape poverty. He and the Scarlett character bond in a partnership that makes Alabama the most progressive Southern state in the Union."

"My, it sounds like a part I could play," Lurleen responded.

"You'd be great in it," he said. "A fabulous idea, but I have to warn you. You'd be called upon to enact love scenes with me."

She smiled flirtatiously. "That doesn't seem like much of a hardship. Of course, I'd have to get permission from George."

"We'll talk about it some more," he said.

"George wants you to come to dinner

Three views of Lurleen Wallace. Her personal and political lives intertwined, sometimes tragically, in ways never before or since repeated in American history.

191

when you're released from the hospital. I'll order the kitchen to roast a pig." Then she leaned over and placed a light kiss on his forehead. "Get ready for some true Southern hospitality."

"I'm counting the hours," he said, winking at her.

"Oh, you men…" she said before walking away. "We'll see you soon."

***

Not fully recovered, but at least mobile, Burt paid a visit to George and Lurleen Wallace at the Governor's Mansion in Montgomery, the state's capital, before returning to Hollywood to confront Judy Carne.

Both George and Lurleen came down from upstairs to welcome him to their home. He had been expecting a Southern barbecue with a lot of invited guests and was surprised that she had arranged an intimate dinner in their private quarters instead.

During the first hour of their talking and drinking, the conversation centered mainly on their joint Southern backgrounds. The governor asserted that his father had died in 1937, and that his mother had to surrender their farmland because she had no money to pay the mortgage.

In high school, when Burt had played football, George had spent time as a boxer and later went to study law at the University of Alabama.

The governor asked serious questions about Burt's snail fever before mentioning his own life-threatening illness. It had occurred in 1943 during his service in the U.S. Army Air Force.

"I came down with spinal meningitis. Sulfa drugs saved my life, but I suffered a partial hearing loss and permanent nerve damage. I hope you don't have any after-effects."

"I hope not, too," Burt responded. "Otherwise, half the women in Hollywood will be horribly disappointed."

Lurleen later said, "George and Burt had their good ol' boy laugh at that macho remark while I poured more wine to loosen their tongues."

On the nightly news, Burt had heard George give his inaugural address as governor, during which he roared that he stood for "SEGREGATION NOW, SEGREGATION TOMORROW, AND SEGREGATION FOREVER."

"George was called the most dangerous racist in America, supporting Jim Crow policies," Burt said. "But I felt reasonably comfortable talking to him, although politically, we were miles apart. While I was his guest, I didn't plan to let him know that."

"In many ways, it was almost like having dinner with Big Burt," Burt said. "He and George were on the same page politically. But over the years, Big Burt changed. He ended up hugging Sammy Davis, Jr. and hanging out with him. He used to consider so-called faggots the curse of the world, but in time, he grew to love entertaining my good friend, Charles Nelson Reilly, though he had once viewed him as a 'flamer.'"

The conversation inevitably turned to politics. "I first ran for governor in 1958," George said. "I was opposed by the state attorney, John Malcolm Patterson. He had the support of the KKK, and I was endorsed by the NAACP, and I lost the Democratic Party's Primary. I was outniggered by that shit. But you can ask Lurleen here. I vowed never to be outniggered again."

George claimed that he had planned to run against "that whoremonger," John F. Kennedy in 1964. "After he was assassinated, I was delighted when Lyndon took over the Oval Office. But the bastard is betraying us and sucking up to every nigger's ass. He's not standing up for his own folks."

Then Wallace astonished Burt by telling him that he had asked John Wayne to run as his vice-presidential running mate. "The Duke not only turned me down but spoke out against me. I had to turn to William Miller, a congressman in New York."

According to Wallace, "The Duke is nothing but a war-mongering hypocrite who never served in the military. He didn't see *The Sands of Iwo Jima*—only the sands of Malibu." Then he reiterated what Wayne had told the press:

Appearing before newsmen, Wayne had blamed white supremacists for all the unrest and protests over civil rights. "If blacks had been allowed to vote all along, we wouldn't have all this protesting and horseshit going on. George Wallace is part of the problem—not the solution."

"I had admired the Duke until he uttered that moronic opinion," George said. "I also heard that in his early days, he let that bisexual director, John Ford, suck him off."

"George, watch your language, dear," Lurleen said.

"I'm gonna run again in 1968, and this time I think I can win," George said. "I know that Tricky Dickie Nixon has his eye on the prize, as does that goat, Hubert Humphrey." I can divide the vote and slip through the cracks to victory by uniting blue-collar whites and stealing the law-and-order folks from that crook, Nixon."

"Lurleen here tells me you're heading for bigtime stardom and that you have the potential of becoming an even bigger star than Wayne," George said. "A biggie at the box office. I want you to consider letting me name you as my Veep running mate in '68. Two good 'ol Southern boys giving 'em hell!"

Astonished and at first hesitant, Burt managed to say, "I'll think about that and get back to you."

After that dinner with them in Alabama, Burt never heard from George and Lurleen again. Nor did he make any attempt to contact them.

[Alabama's State Constitution did not allow George Wallace to succeed himself in office, so Lurleen ran in his place, becoming the first woman governor of Alabama. She was viewed as a "caretaker" governor, with her husband as a "dollar-a-year" advisor, making all the major decisions. She remained in office for fifteen months, from January 1967 until her death from uterine cancer in May of 1968.]

Wallace (second from left) standing against desegregation at the University of Alabama in 1963, around the time he was courting Burt Reynold's political support and endorsements.

Facing Wallace, with his arms crossed, is Deputy U.S. Attorney General Nicholas Katzenbach, demanding that Wallace move out of the way and allow black students to enroll in classes, as instructed by his boss, Attorney General Robert F. Kennedy.

Burt, interpreting all this as bad for his longevity as a movie star, never contacted the Wallaces again after their initial invitations to join their campaign in his capacity as a white and Southern "Good Ol' Boy."

***

In her own memoir, Judy Carne described getting a phone call from the office of Governor George Wallace, informing her that her husband was desperately ill and being treated at the General Hospital in Birmingham.

She stated that she flew to Alabama at once, and that the governor's chauffeured limousine was waiting for her at Birmingham's airport. Then she described in vivid detail her ride to the hospital, and how she encountered protesting African Americans who attacked her vehicle after recognizing it as belonging to the governor.

The driver ordered her to get down onto the floor and threw his jacket over her, telling her that it would protect her from shards of glass if the car's windows were shattered. She remembered protesters dancing on the roof and pounding on the vehicle.

The car was rescued from protesters when a police guard arrived to escort her the rest of the way to the hospital. There, as she reported, she found Burt desperately ill. She claimed that a cot was hauled in, and she stated that she slept on it, attending to his needs throughout the night, with the guidance of an occasional nurse who popped in to check on him.

When Carne's memoir was published in 1985, Burt read the account. "I found it very dramatic. The only problem is that it never happened. I flew back to California alone."

In his own memoirs, he delivered a radically different account—one that involved his homecoming (alone) and his subsequent reunion with his errant wife.

He described, in writing, his return to his home, saving the raunchier details for oral transmission to Doug McClure, Dick Clayton, and others.

"At first, I thought I had been transplanted to Fire Island on a July 4th weekend," he claimed. "I'd come home to recuperate in peace and now I found myself in the midst of a nudist camp. Everybody was either naked or half-naked, and all of them were zombie-coked out, having long ago drifted from their marijuana pothead high."

Music was blaring as boys danced with boys, girls with girls. "Many of Judy's guests looked transgendered, and there was a wide range from the most effeminate of young boys to the butchest of gals. A couple of guys were on my sofa in the living room getting sucked off by persons of unknown sex."

Burt said, "As I headed down the hall in a search for Judy, a young blonde boy, about sixteen, extended a sexual invitation and told me that he'd been trained in an array of sexual delights. I told him, 'Stop, you're giving me a hard-on,' before turning down his invitation and moving on. But his description of what his tongue could do to my rosebud was mighty tempting."

He called out to Burt with "I like to make it with a Daddy."

"I decided to get the hell out of there, and look for Judy on another day," Burt said. "Heading out the door, I met two bikers, real Hell's Angels. They looked at me like they had gang-rape on the brain."

"I located my keys in the hall drawer. Judy had her own set. I headed to the garage, where we kept three cars, but not a one of them was there. I was enraged as I stormed back into the house."

"The only room I hadn't searched was the small guest room. I opened the door and there, before my eyes, was Judy in bed with two other naked girls. They were having a daisy chain of cunnilingus. Seeing me, she raised her head from her work."

"Oh, Burt, welcome home!" she said. "Come and join us—plenty of quim to go around."

"And so that is how I found out my Peter Pan wife was a bisexual," he recalled.

"You dirty little lez," he told her. "Where in the fuck is my car?"

"I don't know, honey," she answered. "I lent two of them to these wonderful people—I don't remember their names. They wanted to drive down to Tijuana. The other one, your favorite, is being driven by Stirling Moss. You must know who he is...the world's greatest racing driver."

"Yes, I know who Moss is," he said. "But more to the point, do I put on my gorilla suit and drive all these jerks from the house—or do you?"

"OK, I'll do it. God, you're so fucking square," she said.

Near the phone in the hallway, Burt shoved aside a guy who was placing a call to Europe. He phoned Doug McClure to come and pick him up.

Although McClure had been his rival for certain roles, he had never let him become aware of that. On the surface, at least, "Doug was one of my best buddies."

Soon, McClure pulled into the driveway, and Burt got into his car. He wondered if he'd divorced his present wife and found another while Burt was abroad. "That Doug," he said, "was the marrying kind."

***

When Burt finally came back home, he found the house empty of "all those depraved jerks" he'd encountered at his initial homecoming. Although the living room was empty, he heard voices coming from the kitchen.

When he walked in, he found Stirling Moss sitting at the kitchen table, drinking a beer while Judy stood at the stove cooking his dinner. "I hope I'm not intruding on this cozy domestic scene," Burt said, sarcastically.

Moss rose and greeted him, extending his hand with a smile. Burt talked to him in a restrained way. He respected the Brit's achievements as a race-car driver but resented the fact that he'd had a previous passionate affair with his wife.

In the seven-year span between 1955 and 1961, Moss finished as a championship runner-up four times and came in third in three other races. The press described him as "the greatest driver never to win the World Championship."

He spoke of the crash of his Lotus during a run competing for the Glover Trophy in 1962. He told Burt that the accident had put him in a coma for a month and that for the next six months, the left side of his body had been partially paralyzed. "Judy came to see me at least every other day in the hospital, and her visits meant a hell of a lot."

"The doctors flawlessly reconstructed his face, and he came out of that coma with his memory intact," she said.

She later recalled, "Burt pouted through dinner and was rude to Stirling. After the meal, which he hardly sampled, he got up and without saying goodbye retreated to the bedroom. I walked Stirling to his car, apologizing for Burt's rude behavior."

"Don't worry about me, kid," he told her. "You're the one I'm worried about. I hope you can handle him."

After that horrible homecoming, and for the next few weeks, Burt and Judy settled down together. Both of them were out of work and looking for gigs. Money was running low, and bills were arriving daily with no means of paying for them.

She got a brief role as an Irish nun on a TV episode of *Bonanza*. She was also given a tiny role in *The Americanization of Emily* (1965) starring Julie Andrews.

"When I heard the title, I thought it was the story of my own life," Judy said.

When Burt learned that she had to appear in a semi-nude scene with James Garner and James Coburn, he flew into a rage.

She was given a guest shot on another TV series, *Twelve O'Clock High*, in which she had several romantic scenes with a good-looking young actor, Andrew Prine. That caused Burt to explode into yet another jealous fury, during which he accused her of having an affair. He slapped her hard several times before knocking her down onto the floor.

Several days after Burt's return, he confronted Judy with her lesbianism. He chastised her for not revealing her bisexuality to him before they were married.

"He was furious with me for having had numerous affairs with men, but when I revealed my girl-on-girl action, he seemed to get excited. I hear many straight men get off on watching lesbian porn."

"One night he suggested to me that he might like to join me in bed if I brought him a beautiful woman," she claimed. "In fact, after a few days, he insisted on it. I finally gave in to his demands because I knew many girls who were bi, and some of them had seen Burt on TV and wanted to make it with him."

She provided no further details about any

Judy Carne, famous as the "Sock-It-To-Me" Girl, cast as a well-intentioned Irish nun on her husband's TV-land "Turf," an episode of *Bonanza*.

197

three-ways going on in their bedroom, revealing only one more tantalizing detail. She suggested that she might bring home this handsome young man she'd met at the studio. "He has a really beautiful body," she told him.

Burt exploded, throwing yet another temper tantrum, and he attacked her, another beating leaving her bruised. "I didn't have any film work, and I had time for my black and blue bruises to heal."

One night, he told her about what had happened to a friend of his in Saigon during the filming of *Operation C.I.A.*

"I knew this so-called friend was actually Burt himself," she said.

At the time of his visit to Saigon, that city was filled with massage parlors/houses of prostitution catering mostly to U.S. servicemen.

"These beautiful geishas were trained to fulfill every man's sexual fantasies," he told her. "My friend told me he was worked over by three nude girls who brought him time and time again almost to the brink of orgasm. Then they left the room. Suspended overhead was this lovely Eurasian girl who looked no more than fifteen. She was suspended in a basket with a big hole in its bottom, with direct access to her genitals. A cable lowered her, in the basket, until she was on top of my friend. When he penetrated her, the basket began spinning until he blasted off with a ferocious orgasm. My friend claimed it was the best he'd ever had."

"Sounds like your friend had a hell of a time," she said.

Judy went on to assert that that evening of exotic revelations from a brothel in Saigon was a conversational exception, and that as their mutual search for acting jobs proved fruitless, they talked to one another less and less.

"He was not only out of work but was suffering from a loss of his hair. He was already wearing a hairpiece. "I told him he'd get all those roles intended for Yul Brynner, and that he'd look far better than him. I was rewarded for that with a slap in the face."

Many nights when she came in, she'd find him unshaven and alone in his den. "His moods were as black as the room with its heavy draperies drawn."

"My slightest remark would piss him off," she said. "I was often rewarded with a fist in my face if I asked him how his day had gone. The only thing he seemed to enjoy was a football game on TV. The sport bored me."

Finally, what she called "the last day of my marriage" arrived. It was one of the longest, hottest days of the year, a dry, parched July. "Burt had been gone for most of the day in some fruitless job search, and he came into the house hot, sweaty, angry, and coming toward me to commit violence," she said.

"Someone told me about you and Ryan O'Neal," he said.

She denied having an affair with their mutual friend.

He ripped off her cotton dress and then smashed his fist into her face, bloodying her nose.

"I fell against the fireplace in the living room and hit my head on the iron grate. I was knocked out for a while. I could have been dead for all he cared. When I came to, he was gone. My head was causing me the greatest pain, and I called our neighbors, the Parhams, and they rushed me to the hospital, where the doctor told me I had suffered a concussion."

"The marriage was no longer working," Burt said. "I knew she was heading down the road to drug addiction, and I could not save her. I went to the home of my friend, John Mitchum, whose brother Robert (Mitchum) was a big star. John and I bonded for months and often hung out together. He told me that if things ever got too rough with Judy, I could come and stay with him."

Doug McClure was sent to retrieve Burt's possessions from his house, including his Western saddles, his private papers, and his football trophies.

A week later, Burt phoned Judy and told her she could file for divorce. "You can have the house, but you'll have to take over the mortgage payments."

"Even though we're divorcing, let's be friends," she said. "You're always welcome to come over and jump on my bones any night."

"Hearing those tender words, I put down the receiver. My marriage had been one dismal failure."

"Burt used to tell me that every person has only one true love in life," Judy said. "Was Burt that one true love for me? I don't really know. In my future loomed so many other men…and women, too."

"After my divorce, many of Burt's cronies phoned me," she said. "They were eager to jump into his barely cold bed with me. It seemed that every man in Hollywood wanted a little romp with Burt Reynold's old lady."

Ryan O'Neal was the first man to arrive on her doorstep, with Warren Beatty waiting around the corner.

***

After leaving Judy Carne and his home, Burt moved in temporarily with the actor John Mitchum, the younger brother of Robert Mitchum. Burt had first met John on the set of *Riverboat*. He played the cook.

"John was usually dismissed as just the brother of a bigger, more famous star, but he was also an actor, and a pretty good one. He was also a singer, guitarist, and a poet of sorts, but no Byron…not even Walt Whitman," Burt said.

Moving into the guest room of John Mitchum's house, Burt was introduced to his host's wife, Nancy Monro, whom he'd married in 1952. "Hers was a tragic story," Burt said. "She suffered from Grave's disease, and bone surgery made it hard for her to keep her eyes from falling out of their sockets."

"I'm not making that up," Burt said later. "She suffered day and night from this disease, and John was a loyal husband, standing by her until the end, which came in 1976."

[Graves' disease is an autoimmune disorder that causes hyperthyroidism (an overactive thyroid), and potentially, serious complications affecting the circulation and nervous systems. It can also cause retracted eyelids, swollen eyes that seem to bulge out from their sockets, and double vision.]

Sometimes, John discussed his boyhood growing up with his eventually much more famous brother Robert. During the Depression, they "rode the rails" together, getting off at some unknown settlement to grub for food. "We usually found some lonely widow to take us in and feed us in return for stud duty."

"When Bob and I hit Hollywood, we wore tight jeans and hung out on Hollywood Boulevard, hustling queers," John said. "One night, we picked up prissy Clifton Webb, and he became our best customer."

John was a heavy drinker, and during the filming of *Riverboat*, Burt always knew where to find him. He had his favorite perch at a seedy tavern, The Keys, which stood across from the entrance to Universal Studios. "At five o'clock, he sat there drinking for two or three hours before heading home for supper, and I often joined him," Burt said.

John amused Burt by telling him how he broke into the movies. "An agent picked me up one afternoon as I was walking along Santa Monica Boulevard. At first, I thought he wanted to pay me for a blow-job, but he told me I should be in the movies. I can't tell you how many times I've heard that line. But this guy really was legit."

"I found myself cast into this small part in a nothing movie called *The Prairie* (1947), starring Alan Baxter, whoever in the hell he was. In this scene, I was to fist-fight him. The director didn't tell me to 'pull' my punches. My left fist pounded into Baxter's face, coming home right above his left eye. Blood spurted across the set, and that poor guy needed six stiches to close up the wound."

John admitted that he couldn't help but be jealous of his older brother's success.

"After the war, I came back to Hollywood and was finding it hard to break into the movies. As an ex-G.I., I was barely making a living on the ninety dollars a month government stipend I got. During the war, I had never gone into battle, except in barroom brawls from Florida to Honolulu. I spent some time in the brig after one drunken night in a bar when I beat the shit out of a colonel."

"My brother, Bob, became a star after the release of *The Story of G.I. Joe* (1945). He came over and was bitching one night about all the tax the government was taking from his paycheck at RKO," John said. "He went on and on until I told him to shut the fuck up. I reminded him that guys were coming home from the war with their legs or arms missing. Bob slugged me, and I tore into him. We wrecked his living room until his wife, Dorothy, intervened. If she hadn't, we'd probably have destroyed her house."

Robert sometimes got his brother, John, cast in some of his movies. Eventually, John became recognized by movie audiences as Frank DiGiorgio, the overweight cop who trailed behind Harry in Clint Eastwood's *Dirty Harry* movies.

Burt lived with John during his gig as Trooper Hoffenmueller in eleven episodes of *F Troop*, the TV series (1965-67) starring Forrest Tucker. "I like Forrest a lot," John said. "But he has this annoying habit of unzipping to show everybody how big his dick is."

Months after Burt moved out, he went late one afternoon to join John at his favorite hangout, The Keys. There, Burt was introduced to Robert.

He told Burt that he was currently appearing as John Wayne's "leading lady" in *El Dorado* (1967).

"I just saw the first rushes," Robert said. "I look like a shark with a broken nose."

One by one, several women in the bar drifted over, making flirtatious overtures to Robert. He whispered to Burt, "I tried to become a sex fiend, but I couldn't pass the physical. I get drunk, follow some broad out of the bar, make a fool of myself, then stagger home to Dorothy, who puts me to bed."

"Bob is just being modest," John said. "Ask Lucille Ball, Ava Gardner, Rita Hayworth, Shirley MacLaine, Jane Russell, Jean Simmons, or Marilyn Monroe."

"Yeah, just ask Marilyn," Robert said. "Dig up her grave and ask her. She reviewed me when we made *River of No*

SIBLING RIVALRY: Robert Mitchum, with his less well-known younger brother, John Mitchum (left) in the 1967 Western movie, *El Dorado*.

Return (1954). She said I had bad breath and was a lousy kisser."

"I'm not really an actor," Robert said, "but it beats having to work for a living. When I made *Undercurrent* (1946) with that dyke, Katharine Hepburn, she told me, 'You know you can't act. If you hadn't been good looking, you would never have broken into the movies.'"

He also quoted something that its director, Mervyn LeRoy, had said about Mitchum's performance in that film. He told him, "You're either the lousiest actor in the world or the best. I can't make up my mind which."

Years later, after Burt had emerged as a box office champion, Robert was asked what he thought of him as an actor: "Without a car crash in his movies, Reynolds can't act worth shit."

***

Cary Grant was the actor Burt most admired, even positioning him before Henry Fonda, James Stewart, Spencer Tracy, John Wayne, and Gary Cooper.

During Burt's gig at Universal, filming *Riverboat,* which he loathed, his tiny dressing room stood across from the much larger quarters assigned to Cary Grant.

Gossip had it that the English-born actor was tight-fisted and frugal. Every day at noon, Burt watched as the mailman delivered letters. Whereas Burt got almost no mail, Grant would get bundles of it.

Burt watched as Grant stood on his stoop, holding the letters up to the sun, checking to see if they contained any money. *[In those days, fans mailed cash to the objects of their admiration, anywhere from one to ten dollars, and requested an autographed photograph. Grant tore open the letters that contained money and pocketed it before tossing the letters, unanswered, into a garbage can.]*

Watching him, Burt vowed that if he became a star, he would answer every fan letter personally and individually, like Joan Crawford did.

Almost faithfully, Burt stared at Grant during his mail ritual until one day, the older actor called out to him, "Hey, kid, what you looking at? Don't just stare, come over and introduce yourself."

As he approached Grant to tell him who he was, Grant beat him to it. "You're Burt Reynolds! I've inquired about you. I even saw one episode of *Riverboat.* Wretched crap! All you do is blow that boat whistle."

"Don't rub it in," Burt said. "I've been staring at you because I was intimidated by the idea of approaching you. I don't want to be another love-struck fan you toss into the garbage. I worship you. As a kid in Florida, I'd stay in the movie house and sit through your films two or three times."

"A boy after my own heart," Grant said. "And a good-looking one at that. Did anyone ever tell you you look like Marlon Brando?"

"I hear that every day," Burt said. "I hate Brando."

"I don't think much of his style of acting—too mannered, too stylistic for me. I like natural actors like Spencer Tracy."

"So do I," Burt said. "You inhabit a role. It's not like you're caught acting."

Cary Grant as he appeared in 1963 with Audrey Hepburn in *Charade*, a suave comedy-mystery in the Hitchcock vein.

"I sure try," he answered. "I have an idea. If you're not booked up tonight, come by my dressing room at five and we'll go out."

"You mean, I can be your date?" Burt said flirtatiously.

"Exactly. You catch on quick, kid."

At five o'clock, Burt was right on time. Grant opened the door and let him in. He was changing into his street clothes. Burt was mildly surprised to see that he wore women's nylon panties.

When he spotted Burt checking him out, he said, "I prefer them. They're easy to wash and dry, which comes in handy for me since I move around so much, always on the plane to New York."

Burt had been in Hollywood long enough to have heard a lot of rumors, especially about the actor's homosexuality. He'd been married a number of times, most famously to the Woolworth heiress Barbara Hutton.

Grant's roster of sexual conquests was the talk of the town. They had included Gary Cooper, Howard Hughes, Noël Coward, the tobacco heiress Doris Duke, Grace Kelly, Sophia Loren, and Ginger Rogers. It was common knowledge that the love of his life had been Randolph Scott, with whom he had lived in the 1930s.

Over dinner, Grant did not talk just about himself, as so many superstars do, but seemed genuinely interested in Burt and his career aspirations. He even gave him some advice.

"You've got to create an image and stick to it. With your looks, you could be a romantic matinee idol. You come on strong and that's good."

"I invented Cary Grant," he said. "I'm actually Archibald Leach, born in England with a thick accent. I wanted to be suave and debonair, and I used Noël Coward, Cole Porter, and a character actor named Jack Buchanan as my role models. Presto! I became Cary Grant."

"Who do you suggest I model myself after?" Burt asked.

"Take a little from several matinee idols: Clark Gable, Errol Flynn, Tyrone Power, Robert Taylor."

"That's an awesome challenge," Burt said.

"Maybe you can even learn something from me," he said. "I'm a star. You could hang out with me and see how a star moves through his public."

"I'd like that, I mean, I'd really go for that. I can't believe this is happening to me. Burt Reynolds and Cary Grant."

"You got the billing wrong, kid," Grant said. "Let's begin with me taking you to the races Saturday afternoon," he said.

"I'd love to go," Burt said. "I'll be your date."

"At least I'll know what sex you are," Grant said. "When I was sixteen in Manhattan, I lost my virginity to a female impersonator, Francis Renault. At least I think she (he) was a female impersonator. I was never sure if he (or she) were male or female—and I was too shy to ask."

The next day, Burt discussed his encounters with Grant with John Mitchum. "Do you think I'm setting myself up for something I can't get out of?"

"Don't worry," Mitchum advised. "Are you kidding?" He's Cary Grant. You'd be a fool not to hang out with him."

"But what if he wants to carry it to the next stage?" Burt asked.

"Don't be naïve," Mitchum said. "He's Cary Grant. "I hear he'll settle for giving you a quick blow-job. Is that too much to ask?"

"I guess not, but I'm not gay."

"You don't have to be gay to get a blow job. Just follow in the footsteps of Gary Cooper and Clark Gable. Imagine it's coming from your favorite screen goddess."

Burt went to the races with Cary Grant, who had invited six other male friends, too. He collected two dollars from each of them for a betting pool. Burt thought that was ridiculously low, so he slipped the runner a hundred-dollar bill. When their horse won the race, Grant split the winnings equally among every member of his party. Each member of the betting pool collected ten times what he should have.

Grant didn't ask any questions about why the payoff was so large, since every member of the pool had (supposedly) contributed only two dollars, and Burt received the same share as the other gamers.

After the sixth race, Burt whispered to Grant, "I've got to take a piss."

"I do, too," Grant said. "C'mon. I'll show you the way."

Although everyone at the racetrack seemed to recognize Grant, no one accosted him for an autograph. Politely, everyone stood back, making way for them to pass.

As Burt would later relay to his gay agent, Dick Clayton, "There was a line of fifteen urinals. Cary took the one next to mine. He didn't conceal that he was checking me out."

"At first, I was intimidated and had a hard time peeing, but nature won out in the end. Cary must have liked what he saw."

"We were alone in the men's room, and he invited me into one of the stalls. I didn't know what to say. I followed him in, and he gave me a blow job, a very skilled one at that. Then, without making any mention of it, we returned to his friends in the stands."

"I couldn't believe he did that to me, and in a men's toilet, too," Burt said. "This suave, sophisticated man in a stinking, smelly toilet."

"I'm not surprised," Clayton said. "Cary is known in Hollywood for sex with men in dangerous places. Once, he was arrested in the men's room of a department store in Los Angeles. He was going down on a teenage stock boy. He bribed his way out of it. It was hushed up."

"There have been other incidents, too, including an arrest in a men's room at Griffith Park. He always manages to escape a booking at the police station."

"What should I do?" Burt asked. "He might want to make this a regular thing."

"Oh, you poor dear," Clayton said. "Having to suffer a blow job from Cary Grant. I think every wannabe actor in Hollywood would go for it. Just close your eyes and enjoy it. When he isn't actually doing you, he might teach you some class."

A few days later, Grant phoned Burt: "I've talked to Mae West. As you know, she got me started in the movies. I was telling her about you, and she wants to meet you. She's going to be at this big party Saturday night, and she suggests I bring you. I think she wants to look you over."

"I can't believe this is happening," Burt said. "First, Cary Grant. Now, Mae West. A long time ago in New York, when I was just getting started in the business, I turned down Greta Garbo. I vowed that if a legend approached me for sex ever again, I'd be there, ready, willing, and able."

"I'm going to hold you to that promise, kid," Grant said.

***

At the party, Burt was introduced to the reigning sex goddess of the 1930s. Her first words to him had already been repeated many times: "When I'm good, I'm very good. When I'm bad, I'm better. Tonight, I'm bad. Call me the Statue of Libido."

For the party, she had dressed like Diamond Lil in glitzy 'gay 1890s' drag. She paid no attention to the fashion of the decade. Under a blonde wig, she was heavily accessorized with eyelashes that were obviously false and exaggerated. She wore a diamond necklace and a diamond bracelet.

"I adored her and she began to flirt with me," Burt said. "She was my kind of gal—every zinger from her mouth was suggestive. It was all an exaggeration: She managed to exude the impression of a drag queen. She was never boring. No wonder Depression-era audiences gravitated to her movies for pure escapism."

Mae told Burt, "I hear you're on the road to thirty, which to me is the finest age of a man. A man of thirty has more character in his face since he's suffered so much more than when he was a green twenty-year-old."

"How do I describe her?" Burt later said. "Just as she was on the screen—big, blowsy, blonde, and bosomy. In World War II, the Royal Air Force named their inflatable life-vest a *Mae West.*"

"Miss West, the screen has had its Crawford, its Garbo, its Dietrich, but with just a flicker of an eyelash, you've got all those dames beat," Burt told her.

"You're a man after my heart, though I'm prepared to give you something lower down, too. Dearie, if there's some music at this party, I'll dance the shimmy with you. If you don't know how, I can teach it to you…among other things."

As she spoke to him, she sashayed around a bit in her sequins and pink feathers. "I like men, dearie," she said. "Just ask Cary here. Of course, the only thing I like better than men are dia-monds."

The hostess of the party that night, Rosalind Russell, came over, welcoming Burt with a kiss and giving her former co-star, Cary, a big hug.

Seated with Burt and Cary in a room away from the rest of the party, West seemed delighted to be seeing Grant again, as several years had passed since their last meeting. "Cary calls on me at my apartment from time to time, always finding me dressed from head to toe in virginal white."

She spent most of the evening talking about her favorite subject: herself. "I got Cary here cast in a career-making picture, *She Done Him Wrong* in 1933 where I played Lady Lou, who was no lady. That picture really established Cary as a leading man, and it broke box

Overblown, oversized, over-sexed, and over-the-top: Mae West, a few decades before her inaugural flirtations with Burt.

office records. In fact, it saved Paramount from bankruptcy."

"I'm sure Cary won't mind if I explode that myth about seeing him on the lot of Paramount one afternoon and casting him as my leading man," she said.

"Oh, Mae, must you tell that story?" Grant protested. "I was young and naïve at the time. If Burt buys it, I hope he won't spread it around."

"Cary and I were working on Broadway at the time," she said. "As a sideline, I was running a male escort service. I hired Cary, and he became my most requested boy."

"Mae, please don't go on," Grant pleaded.

"No, dearie, the boy here must learn the inside secrets of show business. I hooked Cary up with Noël Coward and Cole Porter, and Clifton Webb went ape-shit over him, as did Fred Astaire—all those gay darlings."

"You also hooked me up with that dreadful flamer, Orry-Kelly," Grant said.

She turned to Burt. "He was a leading costume designer, and Cary went to live with him. Cary was once known as Archibald Leach. When Cary moved on to greener pastures, Orry said that Cary was aptly named, accusing him of being a leech. I was the one who told Cary to take what he could get from those queens."

"The studio objected, but I demanded that Cary also be my leading man in my next picture, *I'm No Angel* (1933), in which I played a lady lion tamer. The studio gave in to my demands. I became the highest paid woman in America."

"Jean Harlow and I certainly made blondes fashionable. In the 1950s, we got all those untalented bitches like Jayne Mansfield and Mamie Van Doren. That Marilyn Monroe may have had something, although I don't know what it was. I think she stole that whispery voice from Jacqueline Kennedy. I heard that Monroe had a hygiene problem.

"Beginning with *She Done Him Wrong*, Mae did me right," Cary said, "and I'll always be grateful to her. At the time, I didn't fare as well with my other leading ladies."

Proof of Cary Grant's durability as an actor who grew into the roles he was assigned is this view of him interacting with Mae West as a Flapper-Age younger swain, smitten with her charms, in *She Did Him Wrong* (1933).

207

[Grant was referring to Tallulah Bankhead, Marlene Dietrich, and Carole Lombard.

When he'd starred with Dietrich in Blonde Venus *(1932), she told a newspaper reporter, "There is no romance between Grant and me because he is a homosexual. In the love department, I'd give him an F for fag."*

Of course, that revelation would not be printed at the time.

In The Devil and the Deep *(1932), Cary Grant was a supporting player in a picture that starred Tallulah Bankhead, Gary Cooper, and Charles Laughton. Drunk one night, Bankhead loudly proclaimed to the room at large, "Fortunately, I had the Montana Mule (a reference to Cooper) to take care of my sexual needs. I think Laughton got Grant."*

Even Carole Lombard gave Grant a failing grade when they co-starred in Sinners in the Sun *(1932). "For the life of me, I could not raise a hard-on in Grant," she announced.]*

"What those ladies didn't know was that Cary had made *Hot Saturday* (1932) with Randolph Scott, and it was love at first sight," West said. "He didn't need those devouring tarantulas."

"I, too, made a picture with Cary's boy called *Go West, Young Man* (1936). I nicknamed Scott 'Randy,' and he certainly lived up to that reputation—not with me, of course, but with Cary. I thought Randy was an American guy next door. Of course, you'd be lucky if you lived next door to him. He was very handsome...I never got to audition him, as he was saving it all for Cary."

Burt enjoyed hearing all this, although he noticed that Grant squirmed a bit.

"I've made it with a few actors in my time," West said. "but for the most part, I prefer manly men, especially boxers. I like them either black or white—just like my pictures. I prefer a man who spends time in my bed, not an actor staring at himself in the mirror to see if his makeup is on right."

Beginning that night, Burt's relationships with Grant and West would extend for many decades.

Lovers, when being lovers was not okay:

Cary Grant (left) and Randolph Scott in pre-Code Hollywood.

When the party was over, Burt and Grant walked West to her limousine, where a chauffeur was asleep at the wheel, waiting for her. Burt had told her that he was headed for New York. "When you're back in town, come up and see me sometime," she said.

"That I'll do," he said, a promise that he would keep.

After she drove away with the chauffeur, Grant asked Burt if he'd accompany him to the hideaway apartment in West Hollywood that he and Scott maintained to escape from prying eyes.

Burt was aware of what was coming next, and he was prepared to go through with it, although there were other bed partners he would have preferred.

Grant made it easy for him. As Burt later told Dick Clayton, "Cary did all the work. All I had to do was lie back."

***

"Finally, my pal and agent, Dick Clayton, came through with gigs in episodes of already-running TV series," Burt said. "I was still living with John Mitchum, and until better roles came along, I could afford hamburgers, blue jeans from Sears & Roebuck, and gas for my red '55 Thunderbird."

The first role arranged by Clayton was an appearance in an episode ("Now Join the Human Race") of the TV series *Branded* (1965), where Burt, once again, played an Indian.

Sponsored by Proctor & Gamble and set in the Old West in the aftermath of the Civil War, the series aired on Sunday night. Its star was Chuck Connors cast as Jason McCord, a U.S. Cavalry captain who had been drummed out of the service on an unjust charge of cowardice.

Connors, formerly a star athlete, welcomed Burt to the set. He'd made his film debut in *Pat and Mike* (1952), co-starring Spencer Tracy and Katharine Hepburn. Originally a professional baseball player, Connors had a reputation for carrying a "big bat" between his legs, and many women—and men, including Tracy and the director, George Cukor—had pursued him.

Over lunch, Connors and Burt "talked shop." In 1953, Connors had starred with yet another bisexual actor, Burt Lancaster, in *South Sea Woman*, but by the time Connors began his five-year stint on TV as *The Rifleman*, he was too big a star to have to "drop trou" again.

In the plot of his episode of *Branded*, Burt, playing "Red Hand," is helped by Jason McCord (Connors) to escape death in a town filled with prejudice and hate for his being an Indian.

Another 1965 gig for Burt followed with two appearances in the TV series *Flipper* aired on NBC. It was the saga of a bottlenose dolphin, Flipper, sometimes dubbed "an aquatic version of Lassie."

A lot of the filming took place at the John Pennecamp Coral Reef State Park in Key Largo, Florida. As part of his contract, Burt got another free trip to Florida, where he reunited with his parents at his ranch in Jupiter.

In the *Flipper* series, Burt appeared in a two-part episode ("Dolphin in Pursuit"), interacting on screen with Brian Kelly (the star, playing a widowed father looking after his sons) and the Swedish actress, Ulla Norstrand, cast as an oceanographer.

Burt portrayed a villainous escaped convict. Al Bardeman, who threatens the Ricks as they share a family vacation on an otherwise deserted island. His character also endangers Ulla's submarine, trapping her inside and underwater. Flipper, of course, saves the day.

***

During the course of Burt's marriage to Judy Carne, she had appeared in an episode of the TV series *12 O'Clock High*. In 1965, Burt, too, was cast in that series, appearing as Technical Sergeant Vern Chapman in two separate episodes: *The Jones Boys* and *Show Me a Hero, and I'll Show You a Bum*.

Chuck Connors in publicity photos for his Western drama/action-adventure TV series, *Branded*.

Upper photo shows Connors with Anne Morrell portraying an Indian maiden, and

Lower photo depicts Connors with Burt Reynolds portraying an Indian brave named "Red Hand."

The World War II drama was based on a 1949 movie with the same name starring Gregory Peck. The TV series followed the missions of the fictious 918th Bombardment Group of the U.S. Army Air Force. Stationed in England, it was equipped with B-17 Flying Fortress Heavy bombers.

As a flight engineer, Burt's character is exposed for his illegal weapons trades on the black market.

***

Both Clint Eastwood and Burt's agent, Dick Clayton, were instrumental in getting Burt the starring role in his first "spaghetti Western." It was produced by the Italian director Dino de Laurentiis.

Eastwood had recently returned to Hollywood after completing *A Fistful of Dollars*, directed by Sergio Leone. He invited Burt to a private screening.

At first, he wasn't impressed with either the opening or the music until Eastwood appeared onscreen with a cowboy hat, a Spanish poncho, a cigar, black Levis, boots, spurs, guns, and holsters left over from his days as a player on *Rawhide*.

Burt sat mesmerized until the end.

"So what do you think?" Eastwood asked.

"I think it's one hell of a picture," Burt said. "Both you and Leone are guys with big *cojones*."

Eastwood would soon be returning to Italy to make another film, *For a Few Dollars More* (1967), and he promised Burt he'd hook him up with either De Laurentiis or with Leone.

He urged Burt to consider the genre of the spaghetti Western, telling him it was well-suited to his look, skills, and talent.

The next day, Burt flew to New York, where he had dinner at Sardi's with Clayton, who was also in town on business. In one of those coincidences that happen in life, Clayton was shopping the next day on Fifth Avenue

Was it indeed, the Golden Age of Television:

For Burt, one series segued into another as he snagged jobs on everything from *Flipper* to *12 O'Clock High*.

According to Burt, "A job is a gig is a paycheck. And I need a job."

when he had a chance encounter with De Laurentiis, whom he had previously met in California.

The two men went together to P.J. Clarke's for some drinks. De Laurentiis had met with Marlon Brando the day before. "I wanted to fly him to star, in Europe, in the latest picture I'm producing, a Western called *A*

211

Dollar a Head. Brando found the script laughable and refused it."

"You're in luck," Clayton said. "I represent an actor who's a dead ringer for Brando. He's had experience in the Western TV series, *Gunsmoke*, and he can do his own stunts, which can save you a lot of money and time."

The following evening, Clayton and Burt dined together with De Laurentiis, and a deal was struck even before Burt read the script.

There was a problem, however: Shooting would begin in a month, and the director wanted Burt to drop twenty-five pounds, since his chest and arms would be prominently on display.

After signing a contract, Burt flew to Jupiter for a reunion with his parents. He later claimed, "Fern locked me in my bedroom and fed me meals of only 300 calories a day. By the time I was ready to travel abroad, I'd dropped that extra poundage."

During his time in Florida, he was sent a copy of the script with its revised title, *Navajo Joe*. Before he read it, Burt had envisioned it as a role similar to Eastwood's in *A Fistful of Dollars*. "I had visions of me coming on like Duke Wayne or Gary Cooper. But to my horror, I learned that I'd been cast once again as a god damn Indian."

From *The North American Indian, by Edward Curtis, published in 1906 as commissioned by the NYC financier, J.P. Morgan.* "I played so many Indians on TV, I should have been made a member of some tribe," Burt said.

CHAPTER SIX

LA DOLCE VITA
Playing a Navajo in an Italian Spaghetti Western,
Burt Introduces His Tomahawk to
INGRID BERGMAN & ANITA EKBERG

MAE WEST TELLS BURT
"Come Up & See Me Sometime."
His Immersion into her Unique Brand of Camp

HAWK
Burt Stars Simultaneously as an Iroquois and as a
New York City Police Detective

FADE IN FADE OUT
Burt Plays His First Romantic Lead
But Paramount's CEO Demands that the Film Be Buried

SHARK
As a Self-Styled "Homoerotic"in Tight Pants,
Burt Tangles with "Jaws" and a Femme Fatale.

LA DOLCE VITA
& Burt's Spaghetti Westerns

NAVAJO JOE

After his arrival in Rome for the filming of *Navajo Joe [eventually released in 1966]*, the first person to greet Burt was the film's producer, Dino De Laurentiis, who had installed him in a suite at the deluxe Excelsior Hotel on the Via Veneto.

De Laurentiis (1919-2010) had helped bring Italian cinema to the attention of moviegoers around the world after World War II. During the eventful course of his career, he produced or co-produced more than 500 films, winning an amazing thirty-eight Oscar nominations.

Burt defined him as "a mogul with eyes like a cobra...all crystal green, the most dangerous eyes you ever saw. He could charm you into doing anything. And if that didn't work, he'd break your legs." De Laurentiis had begun his life on the streets of Naples, selling spaghetti from his father's pasta factory.

Burt had seen two of his films, including *Riso Amaro (Bitter Rice;* 1949)

214

which starred his wife, Silvana Mangano, and *La Strada* (1954).

The next day, Burt met his director, Sergio Corbucci. He had been told that the director was to be Sergio Leone, but there had been a last-minute switch. Burt had never heard of Corbucci.

[A Roman born and bred, Corbucci was best known for his spaghetti Westerns and his bloodless Bud Spencer and Terence Hill action comedies. He'd launched himself by turning out "sword-and-sandal" films. His first big commercial success had been the cult spaghetti Western Django *(1966), starring Franco Nero. It set a new level of violence in Westerns.*

Corbucci Westerns were dark and brutal, with characters playing sadistic anti-heroes. A viewer could count on high body counts and scenes of mutilation. Despite blasts from critics, the director developed a loyal cult following.]

The flamboyant director assured Burt that there would be more killings in *Navajo Joe* than Clint Eastwood had managed in *A Fistful of Dollars.* "More brutal deaths, bigger box office."

[The final 116-page script of Navajo Joe *called for 115 deaths, three dozen of them to be executed by Navajo Joe himself. According to Burt, "In one scene, I massacre eleven men within minutes of fighting. I also performed every stunt I'd ever learned—and invented a few more."]*

Corbucci introduced Burt to the Italian actress, Nicoletta Machiavelli, cast as Estella, a beautiful Mestizo girl.

After meeting her, Burt insisted that some torrid love scenes be written in, including one depicting them naked in a tent together. Corbucci adamantly refused, claiming, "No messy love shit, very little talk, lots of killing. Make for great success."

But within days, Burt learned that De Laurentiis had rejected the first draft of the violent script. "That was followed by the producer rejecting the second, third, fourth, and fifth versions of *Navajo Joe* before agreeing to go ahead with the sixth," Burt said.

He later wrote that while waiting five weeks for the script to be rewritten, he spent a lot of time at sidewalk cafes—his favorites were on the Piazza Navona—drinking *molto vino* (lots of wine) and reflecting on the ironies of casting in the movie business. "Since I had Cherokee blood in me, and that became well known, di-

Nicoletta Machiavelli in one of the many broodingly violent scenes within *Navajo Joe.*

215

rectors cast me as a Native American in every role except that of Pocahontas," Burt said.

Sitting in a café, he wrote Big Burt and Fern at the Jupiter ranch. "I love Italy and I love the Italians. All of them are mad, but, as you know so well, so am I."

Burt was called to the studio for a costume fitting as an American Indian. "There, I met this 150-year-old wardrobe designer who had been born in Sardinia, where he tracked dinosaur mud into his home. He didn't have the faintest clue as to what an Indian looked like but had some ancient drawing. It looked like an Indian who greeted Columbus."

"His costume for me was all in feathers with the world's tiniest jockstrap. I tried to explain to this great-great-grandfather that no actor dreaming of matinee idol worship wanted to be seen on the screen in a jockstrap more suited for a five-year-old."

"This hairdresser came in with a black wig that made me look like Natalie Wood," Burt said. "I ended up wearing this fright wig and a Japanese slingshot. I had to look stoic—and have a deep voice. Apparently, there's no such thing as an Indian with a high-pitched voice sounding like Truman Capote. And even if you're playing a half-breed, you have to shave your arms. It was easy for me to get the left one, but the right one was a pisser to reach."

Despite Burt's strenuous objections, Corbucci approved the costume. The director told him, "I'm the boss, and I reserve the right to change my mind at the last minute about dialogue, costume, and stunts—and about how to slaughter all these extras we've hired."

After a long delay, De Laurentiis allowed the much-rewritten script of Burt's first and final spaghetti Western to be shot. It was scheduled for a release in Italy in November of 1966, with an American showing by United Artists early in 1967.

The plot called for Burt, as a Navajo Indian, to oppose ragamuffin varmints who have been scalping members of his tribe, selling the bloody scalps for a dollar apiece. They're led by "Vee" Duncan, played by Italian actor, Aldo Sambrell.

After waging a guerilla war against the cutthroats, he's hired by the residents of the small town of Esperanza—none of whom are armed, believe it or not—to save them.

Fighting off surprise attacks from Navajo Joe,

Egomaniac: Director Sergio Corbucci. Intent on (cinematically) killing most of the extras.

Duncan and his hoodlums hijack a train with a horde of cash. Joe's assignment is to bring it back to Esperanza.

Navajo Joe was one of Burt's most athletic performances. He slashes, burns, ravages, kills, jumps, bounds, and leaps before being strung up by his heels. Ultimately, he prevails. Expect violence, buckets of blood, and a high body count.

For filming of the desert scenes, cast and crew were transported to a location in southeastern Spain, the coastal Mediterranean city of Almería.

At the time, film directors flocked to Almería because of cheap prices and the arid, dramatic, almost Biblical-looking scenery nearby. North of the city was the desert wasteland of Tabernas, where David Lean had filmed scenes from *Lawrence of Arabia* (1962), starring Peter O'Toole. During his shoot in the region, Burt claimed that one day he survived temperatures of 122° F. *[Perhaps he exaggerated a bit, but temperatures in and around Almería are known to reach 112°F.]*

During the shooting of *Navajo Joe*, Burt fell in love with his horse, Destaphanado, whom he described as "an old, swaybacked thing that looked like Don Quixote's horse. His ears were bent down, and he didn't have a mane or tail." Nevertheless, Burt bonded with him, and the horse obeyed his every command.

It was so violent, with so much carnage, that some critics cited it, off the record, as a voyeuristic thrill for sadists.

In this poster, Burt, as a form of torture, is depicted hanging upside down, presumably in agony.

He called in the makeup men to disguise him as a pinto. They applied water-based paint to hide the imperfections of his skin, and attached a thick mane and a long, silky-looking tail. "They made Destaphanado look like Ricardo Montalban."

"My beloved horse was fearless, and even let me ride him by the side of a moving train, which most horses won't do," Burt said.

On the final day of the shoot, he was in tears when he told the horse goodbye. He kissed his forehead and departed.

Before the shooting ended in Spain, Dick Clayton placed a transatlantic call to Burt to inform him that he was due in New York right away. He'd just closed a deal with ABC-TV for Burt to star as a detective in a new series called *Hawk.*

Burt met at once with Corbucci, telling him he had a wrap the picture earlier than planned because of his other commitment.

"But there are more men for you to kill," Corbucci protested. Burt came up with a solution. "We'll dynamite the bastards."

De Laurentiis okayed the change in the script and thought it would be more dramatic.

He gave Burt a hug that rivaled the Heimlich maneuver and a sloppy wet kiss on the mouth.

Eastwood had told Burt to expect $350,000 in U.S. currency placed in an envelope at the end of filming. This was the first time he'd heard what his actual salary would be.

Although *Navajo Joe* found an audience, it did not come anywhere near the success of Eastwood's spaghetti Westerns. It survives today as Burt's only venture into this genre.

Writing in *The New York Times,* Bosley Crowther dismissed the movie as "colorless, another of the super bloody Westerns made by Italians and Spaniards abroad with an international cast."

Ken Tucker in *Entertainment Weekly* rated the film a "D," claiming it was a "dubbed Italian botch which was inferior to most Westerns in this genre, a pale imitation of a Clint Eastwood spaghetti Western."

***

"When Burt returned to New York, he told me about his romantic entanglements in Rome," said Dick Clayton. "It's understandable that he opted not to include them in his memoirs. Too many jealous lovers or husbands would be gunning for him."

During his first week in Rome, Dino De Laurentiis had invited Burt to a lavish dinner at his home outside Rome. "It was the biggest house I'd ever seen were people actually lived—a castle, really."

In the foyer of the mansion, De Laurentiis introduced Burt to his beautiful and charming wife, the actress Silvana Mangano. Ever since he'd seen her in *Bitter Rice* (*Riso Amaro,* 1949), he'd been entranced by her appeal.

Even though almost two decades had passed since her cinematic heyday, she still had her allure. She wore very high heels and a low-cut velvet gown with a ruby-and-diamond necklace around her shapely neck.

His admiration of her was reciprocated as he later wrote, "She told her secretary that she thought I was 'very sexy, very very sexy.'"

Before the night was over, and when her husband was saying goodbye to guests in the hallway, Mangano slipped him a phone number. "It's the apartment of a friend of mine named Anna. I'll be in her apartment Sunday afternoon at two o'clock. Call me there. We'll get to know each other better."

"I'll count the hours, little darling," he whispered to her.

Most of the other guests at the party were Italians, and he had never heard of them until that night. An exception was the stunningly beautiful Claudia Cardinale, an Italian-Tunisian film actress and sex symbol.

Many of her movies were popular in the United States, including the box office hit, *The Pink Panther* (1963), co-starring Peter Sellers and David Niven. Niven had raved about her, claiming, "After spaghetti, Claudia is Italy's greatest invention."

She was at the party with the co-stars—Anthony Quinn,

Giants of Vintage Italian Films

Upper photo: A rear view of Silvana Mangano in *Bitter Rice* (1949)

Lower photo, Mangano with her co-star, a young Vittorio Gassman in his acting days, before his evolution into a director.

George Segal, and Alain Delon—of her latest picture, *Lost Command* (1966).

Later, he got to spend some time with Cardinale, but not very much. "She wasn't quite comparable to those two divas, Gina Lollobrigida or Sophia Loren, but *Paris Match* hailed her as Italy's answer to Brigitte Bardot," Burt said.

Up close to her, he found that Cardinale had "the most alluring eyes and a husky voice."

She told him, "I hope Dino *[De Laurentiis]* might cast us as co-stars in a film together. I think we'd have great chemistry on the screen."

"Perhaps off screen, too," he interjected.

"We'll see about that," she said. When he asked her about her recent roles, she revealed that her latest film was playing at a small cinema in Rome. "It's called *Circus World* (1965). In it, I play the daughter (a trapeze artist) of Rita Hayworth."

"I wish I had Rita Hayworth as my mother," Burt said. "Talk about incest."

"Oh, an American Indian with humor," she said. "Dino said you're a full-blooded Indian. You're wearing boots. I was told that Indians wore moccasins."

"Not always, but we have great big tomahawks."

"I don't know what that is," she said.

"If we could meet privately, I could show you," he said.

"My English may not be good enough, but I think you said something naughty." She turned and walked away.

Then he struck up a conversation with one of his favorite actors, Anthony Quinn. The Mexican actor could also play an Indian convincingly, as demonstrated by his performance in *They Died With Their Boots On* (1941), in which he was cast as Crazy Horse opposite Errol Flynn.

Quinn told him, "I adore both Sophia Loren and Claudia. Sophia creates an impression of something unobtainable. I relate better to Claudia—she's not easy, but still within reach."

The actor told him that in a few days, after her return to Rome, he'd be entertaining Ingrid Bergman. Burt had not seen their recent film, *The Visit* (1964) "I want you to come and meet her."

Anthony Quinn told Burt, "I want to impregnate every girl in the world."

"I'd be honored," Burt said.

"It's a bit more complicated than that," Quinn continued, "because my date book is full. I can't fit her in for boudoir duty, and I'd like you to take her off my hands."

"Ingrid Bergman?" Burt said. "You've got to be kidding! I'd love to meet her. She's a goddess to me."

After exchanging their phone numbers, Quinn rushed off with an attractive but unknown young Italian woman.

Burt's final chat at the dinner party was with Joseph Mankiewicz, the film director, screenwriter, and producer. He had helmed one of Burt's favorite movies, *All About Eve* (1950). It had starred Burt's friend, Bette Davis, cast as the temperamental stage actress, Margo Channing.

Claudia Cardinale in 1960, giving Sophia Loren competition.

"I always wanted to co-star with Bette," Burt said. "If you come up with a plot about a man in love with an older woman, think of me. I adore older women."

"Actually, such a film once crossed my mind," Mankiewicz answered. "It was inspired by some tabloid's coverage of Barbara Hutton, the Woolworth heiress. She was involved with a beautiful young man at the time. He looked like a kid in college. I thought of filming it in Madrid, perhaps casting the younger man as one of those matadors that Ava Gardner seems to specialize in. You look like a Spaniard. If Robert Evans could be convincing as a matador in Hemingway's *The Sun Also Rises* (1957), you could beat him. We'd dress you up in one of those 'suits of light.' Ernesto himself told me that many of those bullfighters who wear them stuff their crotches."

"Sounds like a fabulous role," Burt said. "We could call it *The Man Who Loved Older Women.*" *[Years later, Burt starred in* The Man Who Loved Women *(1983), a film with an almost equivalent name.]*

Mankiewicz found a receptive ear when he described the horrors he'd experienced during his helming of *Cleopatra* (1963), co-starring Elizabeth Taylor and Richard Burton in Rome. "I regret making that film to this day. I wasted two years of my life. And it almost sent Fox into bankruptcy."

"Miss Taylor is a formidable dame who can explode at any minute," he said. "If you continue to rise in Hollywood, I'm sure that at some point, you'll be summoned to her bed. Joan Crawford, too, specializes in seducing new boys in town."

"Been there, done that," Burt said.

Before Mankiewicz left the party, he promised they'd get together to discuss their projected idea of a love story between a young matador and an aging heiress.

But Mankiewicz never called, and the concept devolved into just an idea that never materialized.

***

Sunday afternoon in Rome found Burt—wearing a red shirt unbuttoned to the waist, too-tight blue jeans, and leather cowboy boots—climbing to the fourth floor of an apartment building in a historic neighborhood. Silvana Mangano was there to greet him and usher him out onto a terrace for a view of the magnificence of the Spanish Steps in the distance.

The owner of the apartment was gone for the day. Mangano assured Burt that they would not be disturbed. She offered a choice of tea or red Tuscan wine, and he chose the latter, saying, "I'm not much of a tea-drinker."

Each of them described their early days. He delivered tales about battles with alligators in the Florida Everglades. She had grown up in abject poverty during World War II. She moved with athletic grace, reflecting the seven years she studied dance while earning a living as a model.

In 1946, at the age of sixteen, she was crowned "Miss Rome" after entering a beauty contest, the first since the end of the war. The following year she and Gina Lollobrigida, among others, competed for the title of "Miss Italy." Although each of them lost to Lucia Bosé, the losers ended up becoming movie stars.

Along the way, Mangano fell in love with a rising young actor, Marcello Mastroianni. He opened doors for her that led to a movie career.

Then came *Riso Amaro (Bitter Rice;* 1949) and a marriage to director Dino de Laurentiis. During their turbulent marriage, neither of them was known for being faithful to each other.

Soft music was playing in the apartment, as she helped him remove his already unbuttoned shirt. All these details Burt would later relay to Dick Clayton.

"I was tense at first, but she relaxed me. Her eyes met mine. The kiss was passionate. I buried my nose and tongue between her cleavage. I know this reads like a paperback romance, but that's what happened."

"It was a delightful afternoon that stretched into early evening," Burt said. "We ended with a long walk through the darkening streets of Rome, stopping first for Campari and then for espresso. Dino was never mentioned."

"I told her that if I stuck around Rome much longer, I'd make her my squaw. I'm sure she didn't know what the fuck I was talking about. I never saw her again."

***

Soon after that, Anthony Quinn phoned Burt and invited him, late one afternoon, to an apartment a few blocks from the Via Veneto. He told him that Ingrid Bergman was due there in a few hours, and that he wanted him to arrive early "so that we can hang out a bit, chew the fat, and talk about the glories of *poontang.*"

Inside the apartment, Burt's host seemed to morph into something larger than life. Film historian David Thomson put it best: "With an Irish father and a Mexican mother, Quinn worked twenty years as a Hollywood exotic—redskin, dago, wop, greaser. His mixed origins swallowed every variation."

Burt had seen many of his films and envied Quinn's skill as an actor, complimenting him on his performance in *Zorba the Greek* (1964). "I have Cherokee blood in me, but Tony plays a better Indian than I do. He also could play Mafia dons, Hawaiian chiefs, Filipino freedom fighters, Chinese guerillas, and an Arab sheik in *Lawrence of Arabia* (1962). And he was completely at home as a Mexican in *Viva Zapata!* (1952).

During their get-acquainted session, Quinn told Burt that as a teenager, he'd wanted to be a priest. "But as my dick got bigger, I changed my mind."

Years later, his co-star, Inger Stevens, said, "Women can understand why it's so easy to fall in love with Tony. He's the perfect embodiment of the virile male that all women subconsciously seek."

Quinn and Burt shared memories of their first seduction. Each had been fourteen at the time. According to Quinn, "I had passed out drinking beer on Seal Beach. When I woke up, I was getting a blow job from this beauty on the beach. I pretended to be asleep until I climaxed in her mouth."

Quinn had known Bergman for years, even before her love affair and subsequent marriage to the Italian director, Roberto Rossellini, in 1950. "She fell in love with him, and he made her pregnant while she was still married to Petter Lindstrom," Quinn said. "She was even denounced on the floor of the U.S. Congress. For a while, at least, the scandal destroyed her Hollywood career."

She'd played a nun in *Bells of St. Mary's* (1945), and a virginal saint in *Joan of Arc* (1948). She told the press at the time, "My fans see me as a saint. I'm not. I'm just a woman."

"What man wouldn't fall in love with Ingrid Bergman?" Quinn asked. "She was radiant, the most beautiful woman in the world...and the nicest. She was a warm Swede married to a cold Italian."

With churlishness and an utter lack of charity, her former director, Alfred Hitchcock, said, "Ingrid would do it with a doorknob."

She once told Lindstrom, "I have to be in love

"I fell in love with Ingrid Bergman as Ilsa (left photo, above) when I saw *Casablanca* ten years after it was made."

Years later, Burt found a more mature "Ilsa" in Rome (right photo above), "as alluring and enchanting as ever."

either with my leading man or with my director." Her affairs included the likes of Gregory Peck, Yul Brynner, director Victor Fleming, Gary Cooper, Bing Crosby, Spencer Tracy, Leslie Howard, David O. Selznick, and Joseph Cotten.

Quinn admitted that he'd fallen desperately in love with her during their filming of *The Visit* (1964) outside Rome.

"We fought during the day over how the picture should be shot, but made love at night," Quinn confessed. "When you love too much, it's like a horse riding you, not you riding the horse. I almost lost my own identity in her arms. She's too strong for the average male. If I had fallen too deeply in love with her, it would have been the tragedy of my life. Not being able to control a woman, or at least having equal dominance, is an impossible situation."

When Bergman finally arrived, she was elegantly dressed in a sky-blue suit with pink accessories. Although Burt instantly noticed that significant time had passed since her 1940s heyday in Hollywood, she was still supremely beautiful, almost more gracious and charming than before.

Although nervous with the reason for their introduction and his purpose for being there, Burt soon fell under her spell and relaxed.

After Quinn bid farewell and left for adventures of his own, a short Italian matron emerged from the kitchen to announce that dinner was ready. Bergman took Burt by the hand and led him into a small, candlelit dining room.

He didn't expect her to, but Bergman raised the subject of her marriage to the Swedish producer, Lars Schmidt. "I love him dearly, but we are not often together for long periods of time. His work as a producer and my work as an actress send us to different parts of the world. We have a very modern marriage. Both of us feel we should not be denied sex during our long separations. Sex is permitted as part of our agreement but falling in love is *verboten.*"

"I'm so pleased you wanted to spend quality time with me in a romantic setting," she continued. "As an older woman, it's important to my well-being to feel that handsome younger men are still attracted to me. Most of today's movie-goers seem to regard me as a relic of Hollywood's past, the actress who played Ilsa to Bogie's Rick in *Casablanca* (1942)."

As Burt would later admit to Dick Clayton, "I waited for her to make the first move. I felt awkward, like the fourteen-year-old Buddy in Palm Beach seduced by that antique dealer. After dinner, over espresso, our affair unfolded gradually. She made it easy for me."

"One moment, we were kissing, and I spent a lot of time making love to her lovely neck. A soft embrace, gentle kisses, led to more passion, even grand passion. We frolicked playfully until it grew more serious. I satisfied her, and I satisfied myself. I must have done a good job because she invited me to spend the weekend with her. It turned out to be one of the most memorable of my life."

Years later, he recalled, "None of my former or future ladies quite matched being in the arms of the Swedish goddess, Miss Ingrid Bergman."

***

During his final days in Rome, it was "party, party, party every night," Burt said. "I felt that Rome was the party town of the world. Its days as Hollywood on the Tiber were over, but the partying had continued."

"It seemed inevitable that I'd encounter Anita Ekberg," he said. "Like Bergman, she, too, had been born in Sweden. But they were as different as Grace Kelly from Jayne Mansfield."

Movie fans became familiar with Anita's bosom after her performance in Federico Fellini's *La Dolce Vita* (1960). In one of cinema's most iconic scenes, she played Sylvia Rank, the unobtainable "dream woman" of the character portrayed by Marcello Mastroianni. The highlight of the film unfolded in the streaming waters of Rome's Trevi Fountain.

La Dolce Vita became an international sensation. Ekberg fell in love with Italy, becoming a permanent resident in 1964.

"I first saw Anita across a crowded room," Burt said. "Wearing a green stain gown with plunging décolletage, she was chatting with Roberto Rossellini, Ingrid Bergman's ex. Well, at least she was chatting. He was mainly staring down into her ample bosom."

"When Rossellini went to take a piss, I moved in on her," Burt claimed. "Immediately, I told her

Two views of Mastroianni and Ekberg in *La Dolce Vita*.

Each of them emerged from Fellini's classic as among the most potent avatars of the power of Postwar Italian style, even though Ekberg had been born in Sweden.

225

how much she'd turned me on in *La Dolce Vita*."

She pretended surprise at hearing that same praise she'd heard from so many other men. "Surely, you've seen some of my other movies, too? You're one handsome devil. I saw your picture in the paper the other day. You're playing an Indian for Dino *[De Laurentiis]*."

"I'm part Cherokee," he said.

"I find that thrilling," she said. "I've never made it with an Indian before."

"You don't know what you're missing," he said. "We have heap big tomahawk. I'll make you my squaw."

"Stop!" she protested. "You're turning me on. If you're free tomorrow night, I'd like to invite you for a Swedish dinner."

"I'd love to sample whatever you're serving," he said.

"I'd run off with you tonight, but I promised that old goat, Rossellini, that I'd make it with him tonight. I'm hoping he'll cast me in one of his films."

She gave him her phone number, and he left the party quickly, not wanting to encounter the Italian director. For some reason, he felt a sense of guilt for having seduced his ex-wife *[Ingrid Bergman]*.

The following evening, during dinner, Ekberg lived up to her reputation. In the Italian tabloids, she'd been candid, even blunt, about the film directors and actors who had seduced her. If she disliked one of these men, she never hesitated to point out their deficiencies and flaws.

She provocatively held up a Swedish meatball. "What does that remind you of?" she asked.

"One of my balls," he said with a smirk.

"I can't wait to taste them," she said.

As he relayed later to Clayton, "Anita Ekberg was not the shy, demure type. I never knew from moment to moment what outrageous remark she'd make next. She seemed to say whatever came into her head."

"She never once asked about me or how I was doing with my work in Italy," he said. "Everything was about her career or her former lovers."

"I've also worked with Dino," she said. "He cast me as Helen in *War and Peace* (1956). He throws every hot dame onto the casting couch. I hope he didn't put you on it."

"I missed out," Burt said. "I don't appear to be his type."

"I was no poor and innocent little thing when I lay on that couch," she said. "In Hollywood, I auditioned the stars. John Wayne once put me under contract for $75 a week. He's a big man on the screen, but off screen, he's afraid of women."

"Paramount billed me as its answer to Marilyn Monroe, but I never made it like that whore."

"My biggest thrill," Ekberg graphically continued, "was working with Victor Mature in *Zarak* (1956) and again in *Interpol* (1957). And I'm certainly not alone. Lana *[Turner]* and Betty *[Grable]* and Rita *[Hayworth]* and Elizabeth *[Taylor]* have all praised this glorious specimen of male flesh."

"In Hollywood, I always kept my sheets warmed: Frank Sinatra, Lex Barker, Yul Brynner, Rod Taylor, Errol Flynn, Tyrone Power. Bob Hope fucked me in Greenland when we were entertaining the troops. I did *Artists and Models* (1955) with Dean Martin and Jerry Lewis. Dean's Italian salami is just fine, but when Lewis takes off his clothes, it's pathetic."

"I've had my disappointments, not just in men, but in roles I missed."

"So have I," he said.

"Cubby Broccoli once offered me the role of the Bond Girl in *Dr. No* (1962), but the bastard double-crossed me and gave it to Ursula Andress. There went my opportunity to fuck Sean Connery."

"Broccoli was a fool," Burt said. "You're far sexier than Andress."

"I think so, too," she said. "We're in full agreement on that."

"Say, it's getting late, and I've got an early call," he said.

"You sound like you're raring to go," she said. "I promise you, you will think you've arrived on the doorstep to heaven."

"I hope to get beyond the doorstep," he said.

"You will, dear boy, you will."

As Burt later reported to Clayton, "Anita wanted me to make love more to her tits than to her nether regions. But she showed me a good time. My only fear involved what she might tell the tabloids the next day. And if she did, how would she rate my performance?"

***

Burt had very little to say about Marcello Mastroianni, Italy's major male movie star, in his memoirs, but the two of them made a connection during Burt's filming of *Navajo Joe.*

Once, when Burt entered the commissary of Cinecittà, Marcello spotted him and signaled for him to join him at table, where he was dining alone. Eventually, they formed an amicable but passing friendship. Before the end of his sojourn in Rome, Marcello invited him to four parties and had two private dinners with him.

Burt had admired Mastroianni's work. Certainly, he'd made an impression on Burt when he'd co-starred in *La Dolce Vita* (1962) with Anita Ekberg. He had played a disillusioned and self-loathing tabloid columnist, who spends his nights exploring the high society of Rome. He'd followed that in 1963 when Federico Fellini cast him in *8½*. In it, he played a film director filled with self-doubt and drowning in troubled love affairs.

Burt considered Marcello's acting style every bit as good as Cary Grant's—and that was high praise, indeed.

According to Burt, "Marcello wanted me to play this role in a film he was contemplating. I was very flattered, since I didn't think it possible that he'd seen any of my meager work. He told me he thought we'd be good together on film. He'd be cast as a struggling Neapolitan dockworker whose beautiful Italian wife is lured away from him by a rich American tourist (me) heading for a summer holiday in Capri. I wanted very much to take such a role, but it never happened—it was only something we dreamed."

Film historian David Thomson wrote, "Melancholy and post-coital disenchantment shone in Marcello's eyes. Is it possible that he appeals to women because he is partly gelded by satiation? Or is his inertia a goad to women to provoke their amorousness?"

Alexander Walker analyzed Mastroianni's "mixture of advertised sex appeal and actual apathy as verging on impotence."

"Wherever we went in Rome, Marcello was idolized by women," Burt said. "But in talks with me, he downplayed his sex appeal."

"To tell you the truth," Marcello told Burt, "I'm not a good fucker. Acting is a pleasure to me like love-making. No, wait a minute…not always. Love-making is often an ordeal."

"I liked working with Fellini," he said. "I knew him back in college. He gave me a sexual tip which I practice to this day: 'When making love to a woman, a man should always wear a pair of black socks and keep them on during intercourse.'"

One night at a party, Marcello introduced Burt to the luscious Sophia Loren. He'd seen topless pictures of her and knew how voluptuous she was. In front of Marcello, she said, "Marcello is a man who thinks like a man, talks like a man—is a man! He has so much magnetism, he brings out the very soul of a woman."

She quickly moved on as Burt whispered to Marcello, "Sounds like an easy conquest."

"Don't go there," Marcello cautioned.

Later that night, Marcello confessed, "I don't win over all my leading ladies." Then he described the filming of the award-winning drama, *Il bell'Antonio* (1960). "I fell in love with Claudia Cardinale, but she rejected me. She did not take my love seriously, considering me one of those actors who can't help falling in love with their leading ladies. But my love was genuine."

Burt was asked how he'd handle his leading ladies if and when he ever became a big movie star. He answered, "I'll pursue every one of them. Even if I can't seduce them, I'll demand that the director shoot a nude scene of us between the sheets."

One night, Burt asked Marcello, "How did you know who I was when I walked into the commissary that day for lunch? *Navajo Joe* hasn't been released. In fact, we haven't even finished shooting it."

"Anita Ekberg told me all about you," Mastroianni responded. "I mean everything—even a description of the hair under your armpits."

***

[In the years that followed, Marcello indulged in some high-profile affairs, beginning with Faye Dunaway when they co-starred in A Place for Lovers *(1968), and with Catharine Deneuve in* It Only Happens to Others *(1972). Deneuve's affair with Mastroianni would last from 1971 to 1975. In the year her affair with Mastroianni ended, she co-starred with Burt in* Hustle *(1975).*

Dunaway said, "I wanted a child by Marcello, but he gave one to Deneuve instead."

According to People magazine, Mastroianni also had affairs with Anouk Aimée, his co-star in 8½, *Ursula Andress, and Lauren Hutton, who later became Burt's co-star, too.]*

***

"After *Navajo Joe*, I swore off Indian roles for life," Burt said. "So what was I offered next? An Indian role in a TV detective series. I needed work and I needed money, and $6,000 a week wasn't bad pay in those days."

He signed to star in a crime drama, *Hawk*, in which he would play John Hawk, a full-blooded Iroquois working for New York City's district attorney as a special detective. The series aired on ABC from September 1966 to December of that same year.

Hawk marked Burt's first starring role in a TV series since *Gunsmoke*. As scripted, his partner and fellow detective in the series was "Dan Carter," an African American portrayed by Wayne Grice. As a team, they dealt with murder, organized crime, and arson. Because of Hawk's Native American heritage, the character he played would often be subjected to discrimination and racism.

Each of the episodes would be filmed at night on the streets and sidewalks of New York city. Producer Paul Bogart said, "We wanted to show the city after dark because that's when people come out of hiding, a pack of fascinating weirdos."

About a decade later, Bogart became known for his direction of some of the final episodes (1976-1979) of the long-running TV sitcom *All in the Family*.

"Hawk is quite a character," Burt said. "He's very hostile. I'm hostile, too, although I don't know why. My performance was inspired by Kirk Douglas' *Detective Story*. I played Hawk as a tough, hard-boiled detective. If Hawk doesn't go over with the public, it's their fault—not mine."

"Thanks to Bogart, I didn't have to run around in moccasins and a feather headdress while playing an Indian," Burt said. "However, in the pilot I was asked to hide knives up my sleeve, but I refused to go along with that. I didn't plan to scalp anybody on the streets of New York."

"I saw what Bill Cosby had done for blacks on *I Spy* (1965-68). He played an undercover black detective without racial stereotype. I wanted to portray an Indian in the same manner."

Renée Valente, a production consultant for the *Hawk* series, was responsible for casting Burt. "The man was special," she said. "He had charm, and he projected both strength and vulnerability. Combine that with compassion, humor, and animal magnetism. Add a dash of antagonism, a few grains of insecurity, and a cup of 'down home' ol' Southern boy—and you have quite a stew. If you believe, as I do, that the eyes are the mirror of the soul, then look into his."

Right before the series' premiere, Burt granted an interview to the *Chicago Daily News*. "I'm happier than I've ever

HAWK

Full-blooded Indian, cold-blooded job. New York after dark is his beat.

New Show

abc **9:00 In Color**

"We shot *Hawk* under the blanket of night on the most dangerous streets of New York," Burt said. "Eyewitnesses thought we were real and called the cops to report on shootouts, car chases, and cold-blooded murders. But it was all make-believe."

been in my life. I'm not prepared for a flop, but I'm not prepared for a hit, either. The director goes into a panic when I insist on doing my own stunts."

"The other day, I slid down about seventy-five feet of rope, flipping into the water from a boat. Stunts mean I don't feel like a chess pawn. I also help direct, cast, and write the scripts for *Hawk*. I'm falling in love with the production side of the business and realize that directing is my ultimate aim. Clint Eastwood told me he feels the same way I do, and one day he may direct behind the camera instead of appearing in front of it."

As a recently divorced man, Burt was targeted by many young women with seduction on their minds. During September and into October of 1966 he averaged, according to his estimate, three or four different sexual adventures a week.

He often took his dates to the elegant bar of Manhattan's very posh Carlyle Hotel, where Bobby Short was a regular performer.

It was here that he met the Canada-born Peter Jennings, a high school dropout who evolved into a newscaster, who was soon to become his friend. Burt advised him that if he wanted to go over on TV, he'd have to get rid of his lisp.

[Their close relationship endured for many years. Jennings eventually became the sole anchor of ABC World News Tonight. That gig lasted from 1983 until his death from lung cancer in 2005.

Jennings moderated several presidential debates and covered major news events that included the Gulf War in 1991. During that international crisis, he spearheaded a marathon news-anchoring stint, spending twenty of the unfolding crisis's first forty-eight hours on the air, spearheading a surge in ABC's ratings to one of its all-time highs.

Burt would also remember Jennings' coverage of the September 11 attacks in Manhattan, when he was on the air for seventeen virtually uninterrupted hours. At the time, his broadcasting stamina was defined as Herculean.]

"Peter Jennings showed the world just how far a high school dropout could go," Burt said.

Hawk was assigned an unlucky time slot, appearing on Thursday nights in competition with the formidably popular *Dean Martin Show* and simultaneously with CBS's *Thursday Night Movie*. Its unfavorable scheduling contributed to the network's cancellation of the show after seventeen of its episodes had been filmed.

Notable guest stars appearing on *Hawk* with Burt included Gene Hackman, Martin Sheen,

Robert Duvall, Diane Baker, Elizabeth Ashley, Kim Hunter, and James Best, an actor who had remained one of Burt's best friends.

Hawk's Episode #17, in which Burt appeared with Best, was unusual in that it had Hawk on a hunt for a murderer with unusual targets: All his victims were cab drivers with seven-year-old daughters.

Charles Durning sometimes appeared in *Hawk* in the background and wearing a police uniform. He had long maintained a friendship with Burt and was his co-star on occasion.

Hawk developed a small, loyal following and received a lot of critical acclaim. *The New York Times* said, "It is too shrill and intense to be entirely winning, but it does have enough virtues to suggest the series may find a niche for itself."

"It was a good show," Burt said, "but we never found that niche *The Times* suggested."

It was during the shooting of *Hawk* in Manhattan that Burt first met Jon Voight, his future co-star in *Deliverance.* One night, Voight offered him tickets to an off-Broadway play in Greenwich Village in which he was performing.

It was Arthur Miller's *A View from the Bridge,* set in 1950s America in an Italian-American neighborhood near the Brooklyn Bridge. Voight co-starred in it with Richie Castellano, Robert Duvall, and—doubling as its assistant director and stage manager—Dustin Hoffman. [*Voight and Hoffman would soon be filming* Midnight Cowboy *together. A movie based on a then avant-garde, shocking concept focused on a male, 'pay for play" hustler, it would win the Best Picture Oscar in 1969, the first X-rated movie to win such an award.]*

The play's director, Ulm Grosbard, suggested to the play's author, Arthur Miller, that Hoffman would one day make a great Willy Loman in *The Death of a Salesman.* Miller later wrote, "My estimate of Grosbard all but collapsed as, observing Hoffman's awkwardness and his big nose that never seemed to get unstuffy, I wondered how the poor fellow could imagine himself a candidate for any kind of acting career."

After the show, Burt enjoyed a friendly camaraderie with his fellow actors, and was particularly impressed with Duvall. In his six-decade career, Duvall would be nominated for seven Academy Awards, winning for *Tender Mercies* (1983) in which he played a country western singer and did his own singing.

Burt called Castellano, "the ugliest man I've ever met but a damn good actor. This Bronx native was related to the Gambino crime family. Later, he had a memorable role in *The Godfather* (1972).

***

During the shooting of *Hawk* in New York City, its director included so many dangerous fight scenes that he eventually ran out of stuntmen. One morning he told Burt that he had hired the boxer, Emile Griffith, for a scene in which Burt would fight as part of that episode's drama. "Count Me Out," Burt said. "Like hell I'm doing a fight scene with that killer."

Burt had been at ringside in Madison Square Garden on March 24, 1962 when Griffith had battered "Benny the Kid" Paret, a Cuban boxer, almost to death. Paret died in a hospital on April 3, about a week later.

"But Emile and I became friends," Burt said. "He was not the ferocious killer I had imagined. Actually, I found him a sweet man, very sensitive, almost childlike."

"After the shoot, I asked him to work out with me at the gym, and he gave me many pointers," Burt said. "I knew he was gay, and when we showered together, he always checked me out, but he never made any inappropriate move toward me."

"He spoke about his past life. As a teenager, he'd been sent to the reformatory where he was gang-raped every night," Burt said. "He also told me that he wanted to be an actor more than a boxer. Actually, he was also a hairdresser and had once designed women's hats."

Burt may have been wrong about Griffith being gay. He preferred to identify himself as a bisexual. The boxer once told *Sports Illustrated:* "I like men and women both. If you ask me which is better, I'd say women. But I don't like the words homosexual, gay, or faggot. I love men and women the same."

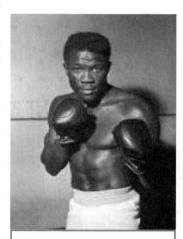

Born in St. Thomas in the U.S. Virgin Islands, Griffith had trained for years as a boxer, becoming a world champion in the welterweight, junior middleweight, and mediumweight classes. In 1963 and '64, he'd been voted "Fighter of the Year" by *Ring Magazine.*

As Burt came to know Griffith, he described what had happened that notorious night at Madison Square Garden.

The two African-Americans were vying for the Welterweight Championship. "The Kid" had a lifetime record of thirty-five wins and ten knockouts.

Burt's friend, sparring partner, and stuntfighter, boxing champion Emile Griffith, who self-identified as a bisexual.

In 1962, he took on a homophobic opponent in the ring, and killed him.

233

Millions had tuned in that night to watch *ABC's Fight of the Week*.

Before the fight, at the "weigh-in," Paret ("The Kid") had patted Griffith's buttocks and called him a *maricon [Spanish slang for "faggot']*. That had infuriated Griffith so much, he'd attacked Paret on the spot, but was restrained.

In the 12th round, after a relatively tame fight, Griffith backed Paret into a corner and unleashed a massive flurry of punches to the champion's head. Dazed by the onslaught, Paret seemed unable to fight back other than holding up his hand in a vain attempt to stop the deadly punches. The very controversial referee, Ruby Goldstein, allowed the fight to continue, and Griffith delivered twenty-nine powerful and consecutive punches, knocking Paret through the ropes.

He was hauled out of the arena on a stretcher and rushed to Roosevelt Hospital, where—as noted above—he died from a massive brain hemorrhage.

Governor Nelson Rockefeller established a seven-man commission to investigate the fatal fight. Fans of Paret accused Griffith of murder, and he on occasion was attacked on the streets.

"Emile continued to fight in the ring for another decade or so, but not very well," Burt said. "He was always holding back, afraid of killing somebody."

Griffith died in the summer of 2013 at an adult care facility in Hempstead, New York. At the time of his death, he was suffering from *dementia pugilistica*.

***

When Burt was filming *Hawk*, he formed two romantic relationships, each a brief fling. "Actually," as he recalled, "I changed my appraisal from romantic to purely sexual."

He had met actor Robert Webber, whom he characterized as "crazier sexually than anyone I had met up until then."

Webber was one of those actors the public knew when they saw him. He'd star in dozens of films and in TV series, including a role as Juror #12 in the classic *Twelve Angry Men* (1957).

In World War II, he'd been a Marine fighting in Guam and in Okinawa. When Burt met him, he'd just finished a role in *The Sandpiper* (1954) with Elizabeth Taylor and Richard Burton.

"Wild babes" seemed to gravitate to Webber, and one night, Burt managed to insert himself into one of Webber's three-ways with a pair of attractive young women. The party (now comprised of four) retreated to

Webber's apartment, where the host offered Burt a drink before disappearing into the shower.

While Webber was in the bathroom, the two women stripped and performed a sex show for Burt. Impulsively, after about ten minutes of that, he grabbed one of them—"the prettiest one with the best legs"—and helped her get dressed. "We fled out the door before Webber exited from his shower. Being a generous person, I left the more unattractive one for him."

Robert Webber exended an invitation to Burt for an orgy.

The young woman stayed with Burt for most of the autumn. "Then one day, she dumped me," he said. "The last I heard, she ran off with Mick Jagger and was seducing all the members of The Rolling Stones."

Before *Hawk* ended its run, Burt got involved with yet another young woman, a would-be actress. "She was even wilder than the first one." He did not name her, but she appeared in an episode of *Hawk* in which, as a detective, Burt rescues her from a rape attempt by a leather-clad motorcycle rider. The episode depicted a motorcycle race roaring around and through Times Square.

In her evaluation of the scene they'd filmed, the actress surprised him by saying, "I wish the guy had gone through with the rape. I was disappointed that you rescued me before I was satisfied. I believe that if a man wants to rape you, lie back and enjoy it. Don't put up a fight."

He invited her to a German restaurant on West 46th Street near the Hudson Theater. Even before the appetizer was served, she was wildly groping him under the table. She surprised him by unbuttoning her blouse and exposing her breasts in the crowded restaurant.

"I like to do that in public places," she said. "It gives me an extra thrill."

After dinner that night, he took her home to his apartment. "There, she fulfilled every one of my sexual fantasies, including three or four I didn't know I had. But she couldn't spend the night."

As it turned out, she was living with Robert Evans, who in the year that followed (1967) would become the head of Paramount Pictures. There, he was the force behind the success of *Romemary's Baby* (1968) which Burt auditioned for, as well as *Love Story* (1970), which starred his friend, Ryan O'Neill. It also featured Ali MacGraw, one of Evans' seven wives, whom he married in 1969.

Burt had seen him on the screen after Darryl F. Zanuck cast him as

Pedro Romero, a matador, in the 1957 adaptation of Ernest Hemingway's *The Sun Also Rises*, much against the wishes of its co-star, Ava Gardner, and Ernesto himself.

Burt remained fascinated by the life of Evans and always said, "If a movie is made of the life of this guy, I want to play him."

Joe Eszterhas in his book, *Hollywood Animal*, claimed that "all the lies told anywhere about Robert Evans are true."

Without Robert Evans knowing it, Burt was seducing his girlfriend.

***

When *Hawk* was canceled, protest letters poured in from across the country, including one with 250 signatures. Al Salerno in the *New York World Telegram* wrote: "The letter writers raged against the network holding on to so much of what it considers pap while cutting off a strong adult drama with a forceful central character well acted by Burt Reynolds."

"After Hawk failed, I left with a pocket filled with some good reviews, but a mouth full of dust," Burt said. "I appeared in a few more TV series, but my career was going nowhere, and I wasn't getting any younger. I set about to make a series of feature films, ones that had been rejected either by Steve McQueen or Robert Redford."

Dick Clayton, Burt's agent, lined up a series of TV episodes in which he would appear for the 1967-68 season.

Burt agreed to be a guest star in the TV series, *Gentle Ben* (1967-69), starring as the co-pilot of a small aircraft in an episode entitled *Voice from the Wilderness*.

Gentle Ben was a bear in a bestselling children's novel authored by Walt Morey and introduced to the public in 1965. It was the story his ongoing encounters in the wild with Mark Anderson, a teenager living in Alaska. The lonely bear bonds with the lonely boy.

The plot formed the basis of the 1967 film, *Gentle Giant*, starring Clint Howard as the boy, along with Dennis Weaver, Vera Miles, and Ralph Meeker.

What intrigued Burt was the script's change of location from Alaska to the Florida Everglades, his stamping ground as a teenager. Instead of a brown bear, the animal was changed to an American black bear, a native species of Florida.

The CBS-TV series premiered in September of 1967, with Clint Howard (the brother of Ron Howard) repeating his movie role

"The role of the pilot flying over the Everglades did nothing for my career," Burt said, "but got me a free ticket to visit with Big Burt and Fern."

***

Depicted here are the two stars of a TV series (*Gentle Ben*, 1967-69) in which Burt Reynolds made some appearances.

Left to right in the photo above, are child star Clint Howard and a congenial black bear in the Florida Everglades named Ben. During the series' heyday, each became TV celebrities

"Relegated to a bit part, I was upstaged by an eight-year-old and an animal," Burt said.

More work followed when Burt was a guest star on the long-running hit TV series, *The F.B.I.* (1965-1974). Burt was cast in two different episodes, playing different characters.

Sponsored by the Ford Motor Company, it ran for 241 episodes and starred Ephrem Zimbalist, Jr., Philip Abbott, and William Reynolds.

J. Edgar Hoover, the notorious, scandal-soaked Director of the F.B.I. served as a consultant for the series until his death in 1972.

During his first appearance on the show, Burt played Michael Murtaugh in an episode entitled "All the Streets Are Silent."

In it, two deaths, 3,000 miles apart, put Inspector Erskine (Zimbalist) and Colby (William Reynolds) on the trail of Cosa Nostra boss Duquesne (Burt). The mob believes that Duquesne needs to eliminate his ex-wife, since she has information that implicates him in the first murder.

In a later episode, aired in 1968, Burt played John Duquesne in "Act of Violence."

***

Premiere was an American TV anthology series that aired briefly on CBS from July till September of 1968. They were summer replacements for *The Carol Burnett Show.* All the presentations were pilots, none of which would be purchased by any of the networks for a series.

Burt was directed by Sam Wanamaker as Pete Lassiter in a series called *Lassiter,* the story of a magazine journalist who goes undercover for his stories. The pilot was shot in Reno, Nevada, in November of 1966.

Another offer came in which Burt refused. William Dozier, the executive producer of what eventually evolved into the hugely profitable *Batman* TV series, wanted Burt for the title role. Burt, partly because of its endless emphasis on campy (sometimes unfunny) themes, had serious doubts if he could pull it off and rejected it before anyone knew how popular it would become.

He heard that Lyle Waggoner would be the new Batman until he read in *Variety* that Adam West, who was about eight years older than Burt, had signed for the role. Bard Ward played Robin.

"I'm not sure that playing Batman did a lot for West's future film career," Burt said.

LIFE — MAD NEW WORLD of Batman, Superman and the Marquis de Sade

MARCH 11 · 1966 · 35¢

***

Back in Hollywood, and with money in the bank, Burt moved into the newly constructed "Bird House." Named after the architect who had designed it, it was a wood-and-brick house on Miller Drive in the Hollywood Hills.

At night, he'd stand on its terrace, taking in a glitzy panorama that included the neon lights of Sunset Strip and stretching all the way to the movie star mansions of Beverly Hills.

He called it "my ultimate bachelor pad. It came with hot and cold running dames. The hot ones were invited back, the others told to go and chill out. I was thirty-two years old but looked twenty-two."

What he didn't have were the acting roles he coveted. Regardless of how hard he tried, bigtime stardom eluded him. "Every director in Tinseltown viewed me as a macho Southern redneck, an Indian, or a brutish Marlon Brando type. Brando, incidentally, was moving on in years and had a weight problem. Maybe I could have been cast in roles no longer suited for him. He'd also priced himself out of the market. I worked cheap."

"Since I had bills to pay, I took almost any role offered, bad script or not," he said. "I wanted to appear in comedic roles that Cary Grant or David Niven used to do, sophisticated comedies."

Years later, looking back over the course of his career, he said, "I coveted *Blume in Love*, *Where's Poppa?*, *The Owl and the Pussycat*, and *A Touch of Class*. I also wanted to do *Barefoot in the Park* opposite Jane Fonda, and also to co-star with Paul Newman in *Butch Cassidy & the Sundance Kid*. But I was told that I wasn't refined enough for a Robert Redford role. I campaigned for a co-starring role in *All the President's Men* but lost to Redford again."

"What followed for me was a series of pictures of which I'm not proud," he said. "If you watch any of them, I suggest you tank up first with a quart of Carolina moonshine to get in the mood."

With some newly acquired money, Burt made improvements on his 180-acre ranch at Jupiter, Florida. Its main house had been built by Al Capone in 1923 as a hideout, and it needed a lot of work.

He added a swimming pool, a guest house, and a gym. "After all, I had to keep my body trim and gorgeous. Many of my female fans, and some of the guys, came to see my movies just to see how many clothes I was going to take off."

He added a tree house in a grove of pines. "It was a great place to seduce the Florida wenches." Accessible via a spiral staircase with red outdoor carpeting, it resembled an oversized mushroom. A swinging bridge led to a nearby gazebo.

Burt commissioned the dredging of a circular canal that curved around the main house, giving the impression that it stood on an island.

"I filled the little lake on the grounds with my pet alligator and stocked it with fish," Burt said. "Fred, my pet, had plenty to eat. He loved it when I came and fed him ice cubes."

As money came in from film work, he purchased a property in Arkansas, too. There, in years to come and according to local legend, he hung out with Bill and Hillary Clinton. "Bill was mainly an Elvis fan, but I think he liked my good ol' Southern boy movies too."

Burt's long-ago football injuries and car accidents were the source of increasing degress of arthritic pain, and to alleviate it, he opted for some corrective surgery. "I got the same doctor who treated my friend, Joe Namath."

It took him three months to recover before he could pick up the thread of his acting career.

***

After his surgery and his subsequent return to Hollywood, the first call he made on a lady involved a visit to the lavish apartment of Mae West, as he had promised.

As part of a phone conversation she gave him her address at the Ravenswood apartment complex, a sprawling pseudo-Gothic pile in the suburbs south of Hollywood.

He walked down a long corridor and rang her doorbell. A peephole opened, and a male voice asked him to identify himself.

"I'm Burt Reynolds. Miss West didn't invite me just to come up and see her sometime but extended a precise invitation to me for two o'clock today."

The peephole closed and about thirty seconds went by before the door was opened by Paul Novak, a bodybuilder who had been West's "companion" for many years. "Come this way," he said, leading Burt into a gaudily decorated living room where he was directed toward an armchair across from a long sofa.

During his fifteen-minute wait, he surveyed the room, which was unlike any he'd ever seen before. It looked like a small, tacky version of a reception area for France's Sun King, Louis XIV.

Above the sofa was a large painting of a nude Mae West in a silver frame. In a corner was a nude statue of West on a marble pedestal. In another was a grand piano draped with a white shawl. Scattered everywhere were bowls of white plastic flowers.

Suddenly, West made one of her famous entrances, emerging as a white goddess in a low-cut gown and laden with diamonds.

"My goodness," he said, standing up to greet her.

"I want you to know that goodness had nothing to do with all these diamonds. Sit down, dearie." Then she anchored herself across from him and began to chat.

The eyes that took in his measure as a man were smoky blue. She spoke with certain intonations that evoked a slight Brooklynese accent.

"If you're wondering about the décor of this room, I'll tell you: When I came to work for Paramount, they sent a decorator over. The furnishings are from the set of Rudolph Valentino's film, *Monsieur Beaucaire* (1924). I never changed the décor except for new carpeting and upholsteries. The press seems to think I live at Ravenswood all the time, but I have this beach house and also a ranch in San Fernando Valley."

She asked him nothing about himself, explaining to him, "I don't care where a man's been before meeting me. I only care about what's being written when he comes face to face with Miss Mae West. Well, I didn't mean face to face. Perhaps with another part of the anatomy."

"Those boys in the press accuse me of exploiting sex, when I am merely doing what comes naturally. When I opened *SEX* (1926) on Broadway, only eighty people showed up the first night. I guess the name of the play scared everyone off. But word got out and soon, theater-goers were lined up around the block. It ran for 375 performances."

"*SEX* opened in a brothel. At one point, the play was raided by the police, and I spent a night in lockup at the Jefferson Market Women's Prison. At the trial, I was sentenced to a fine of $500 or ten days in the women's workhouse. I chose prison because I wanted to see what the conditions were like. But I refused to surrender my red silk panties."

"When I was forced to strip completely naked, everybody wanted to see what I looked like in the nude. They got an eyeful."

"I followed with a play called *Drag* in 1927," she said. "No one had dared do a play about homosexuals. I paraded out forty men, each dressed as a woman."

"The plot centered on two men in love. A shock went through the audience. During the first act, some bluenoses stormed out of the theater. The gays over the years have become my best friends, and drag queens are always impersonating me. They know I'm the genuine article."

"I have no prejudice against gays," she said, "or blacks. Duke Ellington, along with a lot of black boxers, have paraded in and out of my boudoir. Of course, I don't confine myself just to black boxers. Jack Dempsey has come and gone, if you don't mind the *double entendre.*"

"I don't mind," Burt said.

"The whole world knows I dig weightlifters, muscle boys like Paul Novak. Sometimes I go in for movie stars, ever since I made pictures for Paramount. Gary Cooper was the king of 'em all, but I've sampled all the boys from David Niven to Anthony Quinn. George Raft called his thing 'black snake.' It was aptly named. I take off my clothes for men in a dimly lit room. I didn't have to take off my clothes in any of my pictures. Men imagined what was underneath."

"I always say, it's not the men in your life, but the life in your men," she said.

"Speaking of men, we get around to you. For some time, I've been thinking of a return to pictures. When I first saw a photo of you, I thought you'd be ideal as my leading man. The two of us have enough sexual chemistry on screen to ignite an explosion."

"I'm honored," he said.

"Of course, there will have to be an audition. With all my leading men, except W.C. Fields, I needed to know what's in the bread box."

"A full loaf, I assure you," he said.

"That's reassuring."

She said she would have returned to pictures sooner had it not been for Elvis Presley's punitive and very difficult manager, Col. Tom Parker.

"Elvis wanted me to co-star in several of his movies, but Parker always interfered. Elvis has a sex personality. The first time I went to see him, he was performing in a tent. I sat in the first row, and he came out shaking his hillbilly pecker in my face. He really dug me."

"But Col. Parker was afraid of me," she said. "He thought I was too showy and that I would dominate the screen and steal the picture away from Elvis."

"Another choice I considered as a leading man was Tom Jones," she said. "When I first caught his act, his pants were so tight you could tell he was uncut."

That afternoon marked the beginning of several visits Burt made to Ravenswood. It is not known for certain if they had sexual relations, but a clue came from Dick Clayton, Burt's business manager and confidant.

"Burt told me that all those rumors about Mae being a drag queen were totally false."

"Mae's a real woman with a real woman's plumbing. Perhaps it got a little rusty over the centuries, but it's still functioning fine," Burt said.

"Those famous bosoms are not altogether fallen."

***

Burt's next film, *Fade In* (1968) had one of the oddest histories of any of his movies. "It should have been called *Fade Out,*" he said, "since it was suppressed for years, gathering dust in some vault at Paramount."

It would be Burt's first full-scale love story, the kind of tender, romantic film he'd wanted to interpret for years. "It was the best movie I'd ever done, an American version of *A Man and a Woman (Un homme et une femme),* released in 1966."

[Un homme et une femme, fondly remembered during la nouvelle vague as groundbreaking and avant-garde at the time by millions of French movie-goers, had been written by Pierre Uytterhoeven and Claude Lelouch. Directed by Lelouche, with many wonderful scenes shot in Deauville, it had starred Anouk Aimée and Jean-Louis Trintignant. Its plot focused on the inhibitions and romantic abandon of a widow and widower whose carnal outpourings are complicated by (and tormented by) memories of their deceased spouses.

Burt liked that film so much that when he made Hustle *(1975) with Catharine Deneuve, he persuaded the director to insert a clip from it into that movie. He and Deneuve are seen in a movie house watching the iconic closing scene of that film. They are also depicted exiting from the theater together, with a marquee displaying the name of the film visible overhead.]*

Filming of *Fade In* started in July of 1967. Simultaneously, and in the same location (Moab, Utah), and with murky financial and administrative interconnections, a different cast and crew also filmed a Western movie entitled *Blue*. As predicted by Judd Bernard, the producer of both films, "These two movies are either going to be great or else a duo of disasters. There will be no middle ground for either of them."

[Blue *was later reviewed by* Leonard Maltin's Movie Guide *as "an undistinguished, poorly written Western." Movie critic Rex Reed said, "I don't know what is worse—a bad cowboy movie or bad art cowboy movies. Blue is both."]*

On location in Utah, Burt was reunited with his close friend, Ricardo Montalban, the star of *Blue*, backed up by Terence Stamp, Joanna Pettet, and Karl Malden.

The roster of actors in Burt's *Fade In* included the beautiful blonde, Barbara Loden, wife of director Elia Kazan; and James Hampton, who would appear in several more of Burt's future films. Its director was Jud Taylor.

A native New Yorker, Taylor (who had sometimes used the pseudonym "Alan Smithee"), was best known for his 1960s TV classics such as *Star Trek* and *The Man from U.N.C.L.E.* In time, he would helm the final screen appearances of Susan Hayward in *Say Goodbye, Maggie Cole* (1972) and David Janssen in *City in Fear* (1980).

In the plot of *Fade In,* Jean (Loden) arrives in Mexico to work as an editor for a movie entitled *Blue*. [*Confusingly and iron-*

un homme
et une femme

anouk aimée
jean-louis trintignant
pierre barouh

un film de
claude lelouch

Depicted above is the French film on which Burt's less successful film, *Fade In* was based.

FADE IN

Fade In was never shown in movie houses. "Too bad," Burt said. "It was my first full-scale romantic love story in which I got to go under the sheets with the blonde goddess, Barbara Loden. She insisted I take off my jockey shorts for the scene."

243

ically, that was the Western being shot nearby and at the same time with Montalban.]

Loden's character soon falls in love with a handsome and charismatic ranch hand, named Rob (as portrayed by Burt), who is working as a driver on the production crew of *Blue*. Thus evolved another murky example of how *Fade In* got combined with the shooting of *Blue*.

Burt and Loden were housed next door to each other at a seedy motel in Moab, which made their connections with each other convenient after dark.

"Barbara was an enigma to me, even though I made love to her at night," Burt said. "Actually, love is the wrong word. I had sex with her, but it was merely a physical act. At no point did we even kiss. She told me that sex relieved the tension that had built up during the day. I performed my stud duties without emotion. Our lack of sexual chemistry was also on the screen and was noted by the few critics who actually saw the movie."

The celebrity director, Elia Kazan, visited the set in Utah for a one-week reunion with his wife. "I don't think he found out about Barbara and me," Burt said. "Kazan, of course, was a director of Marlon Brando. I had breakfast with him and Barbara. Do you know what the fucker said to me? He asked me if looking like Brando had been a hindrance—or a blessing—to my career."

Some critics hailed Loden as "The Female John Cassavetes." She had gravitated to New York—where she found work as a model and chorus line dancer— from "the sticks of the Blue Ridge Mountains,". She'd joined the Actors Studio, where she met Kazan, who cast her in *Splendor in the Grass* (1961), co-starring Natalie Wood and Warren Beatty. Loden played Beatty's sister.

Burt had first met Loden in New York when she'd performed in the Broadway production (1964) of *After the Fall,* which earned her a Tony Award for Best Featured Actress.

Years after its release, *Fade In* was given a new title, *Iron Cowboy*, in the vain hope that it would find an audience. What did generate a buzz was this sexy picture of Burt.

A gay underground paper sold on Hollywood Boulevard did some alterations to it. Called "photo-shopping" today, it depicted Burt with a long, thick penis hanging out of his tight white pants.

Burt heard that "the rag" with his altered image sold like hot cakes.

After the death of his wife, Marilyn Monroe, playwright Arthur Miller had written this controversial play, which was clearly based on his late wife. Reviews had hailed Loden as "The New Jean Harlow" and as a 'blonde bombshell."

Kazan compared Loden's style of acting to that of Brando. "Like Marlon, there was always an element of improvisation, a surprise, in what she was doing. You never knew exactly how she would play a scene."

"In private," Kazan continued, Barbara was 'anti-respectable.' She observed none of the conventional middle-class boundaries. She was a roulette wheel that never stopped spinning. She was fearless on the streets, of dubious ethical principles, wild as a river, a hillbilly from the backwoods, setting out to conquer New York and its men."

Burt never saw Loden after starring with her on location in Utah. In 1978, she was diagnosed with breast cancer. She and Kazan were estranged at the time, and planning to divorce, but her illness precluded their separation. She died in September of 1980.

After sitting through a screening of *Fade In*, Robert Evans, who then headed Paramount, ordered the film to be "buried." Eventually, Paramount sold it to CBS-TV for a showing on *The Late Show*.

One critic who happened to see it wrote, "It was the first movie to fully showcase the charm and charisma that would become Burt Reynolds' trademark a decade later. Loden is awful throughout the picture."

Another critic claimed, "Burt

What's a high-class actress like you doing in a "dog shark" like this?

BARBARA LODEN

To the theatrical arts crowd, Loden was even more famous than Burt

In 1964, she poses for publicity for *After the Fall*. On the left is Arthur Miller, the play's author, and on the right is Jason Robards, Loden's co-star.

It's been suggested that Loden's greatest artistic triumph was her directorship and production of *Wanda* (1970). It focuses on a woman with limited options who goes on the run with a bank robber. Loden is depicted above with her husband, superstar director Elia Kazan,

Kazan claimed to have written the initial script and then "[Loden] rewrote it many times, and it became hers."

Reynolds is something of a cowboy here, but not quite the good ol' Southern boy he later developed in *Smokey and the Bandit* during his 1970s heyday."

***

Dick Clayton came through with a starring role for Burt in yet another low-budget film. Whereas it was originally entitled *Caine,* its title was later changed to *Man-Eater* and then to *Shark!* before its release in 1969.

In it, Burt's co-stars included Arthur Kennedy, Barry Sullivan, and Silvia Pinal, a blonde-haired actress previously unknown to Burt.

She had been a legendary performer in her native Mexico. Her popularity had soared during "the Golden Age of Mexican cinema," an era generally acknowledged as 1933-1964, with special emphasis on the 1940s.

[Before working with Burt, Pinal had achieved international recognition by starring in a famous film trilogy by director Luís Buñuel: Viridiana *(1961),* El ángel exterminador *(1962), and* Simón del desierto *(1965).* Shark! *represented a disappointing comedown for her.]*

As Burt's backup team, Sullivan and Kennedy—each of them enormously talented— deserved better roles. Solid and reliable as a leading man, Sullivan had never quite obtained star status. He had delivered a memorable performance in *The Bad and the Beautiful* (1952) opposite Kirk Douglas and Lana Turner.

Kennedy, a five-time Academy Award nominee, was a versatile supporting player. Based on confusion with the politician, he had opted to change his original name from John Kennedy. Some of his best work included a role in *Champion* (1949) with Kirk Douglas; and *Some Came Running* (1958) with Frank Sinatra. Arguably his best performance was in *Bright Victory* (1951).

The filmscript of *Shark!* was based on a novel, *Bones are Coral* by Victor Canning. Originally, it was to be filmed with George Montgomery, the former husband of Dinah Shore, Burt's future girlfriend. That film, entitled *Twist of the Knife,* was later abandoned.

The director of *Shark!*, Samuel Fuller, hadn't made a movie since the in-your-face drama, *The Naked*

Steamy Silvia Pinal with Burt. Famous in her native Mexico , she played a mysteriously scheming multinational *femme fatale.*

Shark—Some said that as it struggled to keep abreast of its many changes in scripts and visions, its marketing campaign was better than the movie itself.

Kiss (1964) starring Constance Towers as a prostitute trying to change her live by working in a pediatric ward. In time, the French New Wave would cite Fuller as a major stylistic influence on their avant-garde "revolution."

Fuller was known for his low-budget genre movies (especially Westerns and wartime thrillers) with controversial themes.

He set about rewriting the script. "I liked the idea of making a story where, for once, the hero is really heavy, the heavy is the girl, and there's another heavy—and you find out in the end that they're all heavies."

[Editor's note: What is "a heavy" as it applies to a character in a film script? Depending on the context, it's a mirthless character without gaiety, a baddie, a beast, a brute, an evildoer, a fiend, a hound, a miscreant, a monster, a rogue, a reprobate, a scalawag, a villain, or a scoundrel.]

After reading the director's much-revised script, Burt said, "All the characters, including me, are amoral. Caine (read that 'me') doesn't get the girl at the end. She's a villain who doesn't go to jail. Instead, I let her be eaten by sharks."

The setting was to be coastal Sudan, but on Fuller's budget, he had to send cast and crew to Manzanillo, Mexico, which had to be subbed because it was cheaper. Shooting took nine weeks in 1967.

During its filming, a tragedy occurred when stuntman José Marco was attacked and killed on camera by a white shark which

Burt and Arthur Kennedy get confidential and boozy in Shark.

broke through the protective netting. This fatal shark attack stirred up a lot of publicity, including a photo spread in *Life* magazine. That's when Fuller changed the film's title to *Shark!* as a means of taking advantage of the buzz.

Burt's role was that of a gun smuggler who finds himself stranded and broke in a small Sudanese town. He is hired by Silvia Pinal, cast as the treacherous Anna, who commissions him to recover gold bullion from a shipwreck in the shark-infested waters of the Red Sea.

There was a romantic scene between Pinal and Burt on a beach. Fuller told them, "Think Burt Lancaster and Deborah Kerr in *From Here to Eternity* (1953).

Barry Sullivan, as Professor Dan Mallare, played Burt's grumpy collaborator.

The only touching scene in the entire movie involved Burt's relationship with a scroungy street kid named "Runt" (Charles Berriochoa), who smokes cigarillos like a seasoned pro.

According to Burt, "I played Caine as homoerotic, in tight white pants. I was real cocky, showing off the hair on my chest."

George Kennedy delivers an over-the-top performance as "Doc," a failed medical professional who, it's revealed, has hit the bottle far too many times.

The producers didn't like Fuller's final cut and aggressively reedited it. "The bastards ruined it," he claimed. "It was terrible, and I demanded that they restore my original version, but they refused. I then demanded that they remove my name from the credits. They refused to do that, too."

One critic described the film as "typical Reynoldsian action-infested dumbness with plenty of thrills, brawls, and violent confrontations."

The *Los Angeles Times* defined the plot as "threadbare."

Six years after its 1969 release, *Shark!* was re-released as *Man Eater* in 1975 as a means of cashing in on the success of *Jaws* (also 1975).

***

It was during the filming of his next movie, *Impasse,* a United Artists release for 1969, that Burt met a beautiful Japanese actress, Miko Mayame. He would begin a long affair with her, eventually moving her into his Hollywood home.

CHAPTER SEVEN

MIKO MAYAME

In Tokyo, Burt Falls for a Kabuki Dancer
And Flies Her Back to Hollywood as His

PRIVATE GEISHA

IMPASSE

Burt's Heist Adventure Evokes Memories of
Corregidor, one of World War II's Bloodiest Battles

MORE B MOVIES & SILLY SITCOMS

Sam Whiskey, 100 Rifles, & Love, American Style.
Burt's Nude Scene with Angie Dickinson

"Angie was the only woman I ever loved."
—JFK

MYRA BRECKINRIDGE

Plotting and Scheming Her Comeback
Mae West Wants to Co-Star with Burt and

ELIZABETH TAYLOR

Cast as a Transgendered Person

"Elizabeth Is No Trannie."
—Burt Reynolds

INGER STEVENS

Burt is Implicated in the Death of Hollywood's
"Replacement" for Grace Kelly

Kabuki Theater, "B" Movies, and Silly Sitcoms

Burt viewed 1969 as the year that solidified him as a motion picture star—"at least in B movies." He made one film after another, leading a nomadic life from location to location, traveling with only one suitcase. "I liked to keep my wardrobe simple."

Sicily-born Richard Benedict, an actor and influential director with many dozens of screen credits, got Burt involved in his next film. Burt had seen him in two feature films: Billy Wilder's *Ace in the Hole* (1951), starring Kirk Douglas, and *Ocean's 11* (1960), with Frank Sinatra and the Rat Pack. Benedict sent Burt the script of *Golden Bullet* (later released in 1969 as *Impasse)*, to be shot in the Philippines, and lobbied hard to get him involved.

Burt found the script intriguing and was especially enticed to learn that his co-star would be Ann-Margret, whom he considered the sexiest actress in Hollywood.

He phoned Benedict and told him, "Sign me up." Before heading for the Philippines, he received a call from the director, informing him that Ann-Margret had dropped out, and that Diana Hyland had been signed in her place.

Then, only days before Benedict left California for location shooting, he phoned once again to tell Burt that Hyland had been replaced with Anne Francis.

***

Three weeks before the beginning of filming in the Philippines, Burt flew to Tokyo for some time off. "I wanted to see a lot of Kabuki Theater.

250

Believe it or not, it fascinated me for years."

One night at a Kabuki Theater on the fringes of Tokyo, he spotted a young Japanese actress named Miko Mayama, who entranced him with her stunning beauty and charm.

"I'd never seen any woman like her," he said. "She had hair halfway down to her rear, a rear that you could deliver drinks on. Unlike most Asian women, she had gigantic breasts and was gorgeous. She also had the most beautiful, shapely, athletic legs I'd ever seen, and I'd seen some of the best in Hollywood. In addition to her figure, she had a sultry voice. I later found out that she was four years younger than me, but she looked sixteen."

As an actress, she'd been cast in the TV series, *I Spy*, and had also appeared as Yeoman Tamula in a *Star Trek* episode. While playing a supporting role in *The War Wagon* (1967), she'd captured the eyes of both of its co-stars, John Wayne and Kirk Douglas.

After the show, Burt went backstage to meet her. He made his intentions very clear, even after discovering that she didn't speak one word of English. Beginning that very night, she went to his hotel and was there every evening for a week.

He had fallen in love. Determined to take her back to the United States, he had to get permission from her parents, a task he dreaded.

By train, they arrived in Osaka for a meeting. Burt found them "gentle souls" who at first opposed the "kidnapping" of their daughter. Her brother spoke broken English. With him as translator, he won them over by promising that through his connections in Hollywood, he would make her a big movie star.

Almost from the beginning, he lived up to his promise by persuading Benedict to give her a supporting role in *Impasse*.

Top Photo: A traditional Kabuki actress

Lower photo: Miko on *Star Trek* with William Shatner. Burt had promised her super stardom in Hollywood.

Resigning from the Kabuki Theater, Miko flew to Manila with Burt.

***

Before he met Miko, Burt's plans had involved shacking up with his co-star, Anne Francis, a beautiful blonde with captivating blue eyes. He'd faithfully watched her in her TV series, *Honey West* (1965-66), in which she played a detective who drove a Cobra and had a pet ocelet.

He found her as beautiful as she was on the screen but was disappointed by her topics of conversation. "She was full of all this spiritual claptrap, talking about the essence of her being, the inner workings of her mind and spirit, whatever in hell that meant. She lost me. Thank god I had Miko."

"My buddy, James Best, did far better with Anne than I did," Burt said. "They co-starred in an episode of *The Twilight Zone* (1963) in a segment called 'Jess-Belle.'"

Impasse was written by the hard-boiled *film noir* scriptwriter, John C. Higgins, who had penned such films as *Raw Deal* (1948) and *He Walked by Night* (also 1948).

In *Impasse*, Burt was cast as Pat Morrison, a shady salvage operator in Manila. He wants $3 million in gold bullion hidden by the U.S. military during World War II, just before the Allied evacuation of the Philippines.

"By now, such a testosterone, sweaty role was familiar fare for me. It called for me to leap and jump all over the place, which was also familiar turf for the characters I played. I'd become a master of the chase."

For romantic interest, Anne Francis was cast as Bobby Jones, a tennis champ. One critic later claimed that she was too old to be a tennis pro, but she photographed young and beautiful. Actually, she was six years older than Burt.

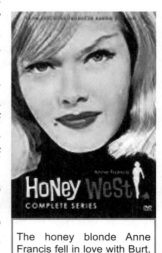

Morrison (Burt) rescues the only person capable of locating the gold, a sickly veteran played by Clark Gordon, who had been part of the original wartime operation to conceal it. Together, they uncover the cache in a labyrinth of concrete tunnels on the island of Corregidor.

As a subplot, Morrison falls in love with his guide's daughter, Bobby Jones (Anne Francis). Complicating matters, Burt's character is also sexually involved with the wife (as portrayed by Burt's new girlfriend, Miko Mayama) of one

The honey blonde Anne Francis fell in love with Burt, but only on screen.

of his business associates.

As a means of actually retrieving the gold, Burt has to assemble a team of cohorts. To that effect, he enrolls an Apache Indian (Draco, as portrayed by Rodolfo Acosta), living in the U.S. on an Indian reservation. A telegram from Burt sends him packing off to Manila.

Rounding out Burt's team is Carl Hansen, a bigoted World War II veteran played by Lyle Bettger. A racist, he has self-destructively lived among the kind of people he hates. Before he can join Burt's team, he has to be broken out of jail. *[A long-established character actor, Bettger was best known for his role as the wrathfully jealous elephant handler in Cecil B. DeMille's Oscar-winning* The Greatest Show on Earth *(1952), starring Betty Hutton.]*

"*Impasse*, the title of this film, described the status of my career at that time," Burt said. "It was a rough period for me."

It seemed almost mandatory for every Burt film to include a chase scene either by car or on foot. In this case, it was on foot through a gritty, seedy, and dangerous part of Manila.

"I told the guy I was chasing in the film to knock down anything that stood in his way," Burt said. "Some of the streets were blocked off. Everything was caught on a zoom lens. At the last minute, he ran into a busy marketplace which had not been blocked off. It was filled with fruit, meat, and vegetable vendors."

"He knocked down old ladies, everybody. This angered a group of Filipino bastards who went after me and beat hell out of me, all of it captured on film but not part of the script."

"Me, Mr. Tough Guy, limped around for days, but Miko gave me foot massages and other wonderful curative procedures, restoring me to my fighting weight."

The climax of *Impasse* is striking, grim, and violent. The unholy band stealthily zeros in on Corregidor's Malinta Hill and its infamous tunnels, the site *[according to the plot]* of the buried gold.

[The blood-soaked Malinta Tunnels were built on Corregidor ("the Gibraltar of the East") between 1922 and 1933 by the U.S. Army Corps of Engineers as a fortress and military stronghold for the defense of Manila. Conceived as a bomb-proof storage bunker for personnel and ammunition, it was later expanded into a military hospital. Key moments in the U.S. abandonment (in 1942), and reconquest (in 1945) of Corregidor transpired here, and U.S. veterans of the Pacific the-

ater of World War II remember it with something approaching reverence.

Locals insist that its interior is haunted with the ghosts of the American sol- diers and medical personnel who died or were enslaved here, and with the spirits of the Japanese soldiers who committed ritual suicide during the site's reconquest by Allied Forces in the final months of World War II.]

Impasse ends after Burt's gang confronts the Filipino police. Hansen dies, Draco is wounded, Jesus is captured, Bobby is seen boarding a plane to the United States, and Burt in handcuffs is hauled away by the police.

The film had only a limited release and was often the second movie shown in houses presenting double features. It also suffered from a release date that was simultaneous with that of bigger-budgeted action films, in- cluding *Where Eagles Dare* and *On Her Majesty's Secret Service.*

Howard Thompson of *The New York Times* said that *Impasse* was "a good one that may get away all too soon. There are glaring plot holes, but I give it high praise for its exotic setting, good performances by its star, Burt Reynolds, and fine direction by Richard Benedict."

***

After his return from the Philippines, Burt set up housekeeping with Miko Mayama, who was learning English by watching Bugs Bunny car- toons. Her favorite expression was, "What's up, Doc?"

As her English improved, she found gigs on television series that in- cluded *The Flying Nun,* starring Sally Field, Burt's future girlfriend. Among other shows, she was also a guest on episodes of *The Beverly Hillbillies.*

Throughout the 1970s, Miko got cast in a series of acting gigs, mostly on television. However, she did join the cast of a feature film, *The Hawai- ians,* (1970), starring Charlton Heston.

Her romantic relationship with Burt would last for more than three years, but he was never faithful to her. Dick Clayton was a frequent visitor. "I loved Burt dearly, but he wasn't really husband material. I was his confidant back in those days, and I knew he played the field. He treated Miko like a geisha. After dinner, she took off his shoes to massage his feet."

"She seemed to cater to his every whim," he said. "I think she was truly in love with him. I just

Miko with Burt in *Impasse.* "She gave a great foot massage."

hoped he would not break her heart. She never challenged him, even when he staggered into the house at 4AM. Never once did she ask where he'd been."

There were many romantic moments, as he relayed to Clayton over the upcoming months. "She was all wet little kisses with a tongue like a flame," Burt confided. "I returned her lovemaking, and in my way, loved her yet I wasn't in love with her, if that makes sense."

"I knew that the day will come when I leave Miko," he said to Clayton. "Given my nature, it's inevitable. In the future, I would meet some woman who would lure me away. Bur right now, she convinces me every night that I'm the man for her. I know that I satisfy her, but at times, I want something else, even though I'm bathed in perfection right at home. Oh, tame my fickle heart."

"Did you make up that line or steal it from some poet? It doesn't sound like Burt Reynolds," Clayton said.

"Miko is like a pink Japanese cherry tree in blossom. She's all flower petals in the morning, clean and refreshing. She calls me a beautiful man, but she is the beauty, soft and firm, a delectable combination."

Burt and Miko were regularly photographed attending parties, premieres, and social events. To photographers and to the outside world, they looked very much in love. Many tabloids hinted that marriage would soon be forthcoming, though no date had been set.

He tried to dispel such rumors. "We're just good friends," he said. "Marriage is the last thing on my mind. You forget. I tried wedding bliss once and it was hell. From now on, put me down as not the marrying kind."

***

"My next picture, *Sam Whiskey,* was a comedy Western way ahead of its time," Burt claimed. "I was playing light comedy, and nobody seemed to care, damn it all and to hell and back. I'd wanted it to be a big hit."

Its screenplay was by William W. Norton, who would go on to write other scripts for Burt, notably *White Lightning* (1973) and *Gator* (1976). Arnold Laven was hired to direct.

During the course of his career, Laven would be known mainly for his long-running Western series, *The Rifleman* (1958-63), starring Chuck Connors, and *The Big Valley* (1965-69) featuring Barbara Stanwyck.

In World War II, he'd worked with the U.S. Army Air Force's First Motion Picture Unit, headed by Army Captain Ronald Reagan. The films it produced had included morale-boosting appearances by such stars as

William Holden, Alan Ladd, Arthur Kennedy, and George Montgomery. As Laven told Burt, "For me, turning out Army films was the best film school in the world."

When Burt first worked with him, he'd just finished *Rough Night in Jericho* (1967), a Western starring Dean Martin, Jean Simmons, and George Peppard. Laven also produced Elvis Presley's *Clambake* (1967) and *The Scalphunters* (1968) with Burt Lancaster and Ossie Davis.

Burt's co-stars in *Sam Whiskey* were Clint Walker, Ossie Davis, and the "luscious" Angie Dickinson.

Set in the post-Civil War era, Burt, as Sam Whiskey, is a poker-playing, womanizing, hard-fighting rogue and adventurer. He's persuaded by a widow, Laura Breckenridge (Dickinson), into setting out on a dangerous mission to retrieve a quarter of a million dollars in gold bars resting in a riverboat that sank into Colorado's Plattle River. Sam enlisted the help of Jeddiah Hooker (Ossie Davis) and a local blacksmith, O.W. Bandy (Clint Walker), who is also an eccentric inventor.

Burt with Angie Dickinson in *Sam Whiskey*. She taught Burt how to appear nude.

Georgia-born Davis was one of the most talented African American actors working at the time in feature films, TV, or on the stage. Married to performer Ruby Dee, he was also a director, poet, and author.

"Clint Walker was the biggest bruiser I ever worked with," Burt said. "At the time, he was best-known for his TV western series, *Cheyenne.*

Walker was a client of the notorious gay agent, Henry Willson, who had put a series of handsome young actors on the casting couch before launching them into stardom: Guy Madison, Rock Hudson, and Tab Hunter, among others.

Walker had an impressive physique, standing 6'6" with a 48-inch chest and a 32-inch

Burt with Clint Walker in *Sam Whiskey*. Burt claimed Clint's shoulders rivaled those of King Kong.

waist. "That's not all about Clint that's big," said Willson.

Directors liked to cast him bare-chested, as they did Burt himself. Film critic Howard Thompson wrote: "Cline Walker was the biggest, finest-looking Western star ever to sag a horse."

Burt and Walker bonded and hung out together during the shoot, telling each other tall tales about their lives. The gigantic actor had just played a meek convict, Samson Posey, in the war drama *The Dirty Dozen* (1967).

He related an incident that occurred when he'd made *None But the Brave* (1965) with Frank Sinatra. "Frankie and I were standing side by side at a public urinal. Frankie seemed to be comparing my thing to his. He said, 'Oh, if only Liberace were here today.'"

A hot-to-trot beauty from the cold winds of North Dakota, Angie Dickinson was married at the time to Burt Bacharach, so he interpreted her as off-limits, "but mighty tempting."

Burt praised her for her appearance in her first big screen role, Howard Hawks' *Rio Brava* (1959), in which she played a flirtatious gambler named "Feathers." Her co-stars included John Wayne, Dean Martin, Ricky Nelson, and Walter Brennan.

She was quoted as saying, "I dress for women, but undress for men." Her beaux reportedly included Frank Sinatra, Dean Martin, David Janssen, and Johnny Carson. It was said, but not confirmed, that she had an affair with President John F. Kennedy, which she denied.

However, she kept an autographed photo of the former president. The inscription he added said, "To the only woman I ever loved."

The director told Burt that he was going to shoot a nude love scene between Burt and Angie. "Oh, how I suffer for my art," Burt jokingly said.

He later admitted to Angie, "I'm petrified, even though I'm known for my ego, *braggadocio*, boldness, and derring-do. The director told me I won't be completely nude. Under the covers, I'll wear a Japanese slingshot."

She told him it was nothing to worry about. "You just emerge from your dressing room nude and act normal, greeting the director and camera crew. You'll soon get used to wearing no clothes."

The next morning, he peered outside his dressing room door as she emerged stark naked, heading for the set.

"She caused a meltdown—equal to the atomic bomb that dropped on Hiroshima—among the crew. Unlike Angie, I emerged wearing a terrycloth robe and made a hundred-yard dash to the bed. I took off my robe under the sheets as Angie joined me."

"I looked up at the rafters—known in movie parlance as the grid—and I saw 150 Peeping Toms, many of them from the set of Westerns being shot, especially *Laramie* and *Wagon Train*. They'd all come to take in the view."

Later, to avoid an "R" rating, Laven cut the scene of Angie nude from the waist up and subbed a tighter shot showing her torso only from the shoulders up.

Burt took a still from the original and had it blown up. He hung it over the bar in his home under the caption, "AN ACTOR'S LIFE IS PURE HELL!".

Vincent Canby of *The New York Times* wrote, "Comedy Westerns are not my favorite form of entertainment, and *Sam Whiskey* is not one of the best of the breed. But its pleasures are unexpected, and they deserve some modest appreciation. The film has a kind of clumsy charm contributed by Reynolds, who bears a creepy resemblance to Marlon Brando."

Film critic Dennis Schwartz came down harder: "An amiable Western, it has a tagline—"Don't mix with Sam Whiskey—it's risky!" The film nevertheless proves tiresome. The cornball antics, the uninspired acting, and the weary plot so slackly handled—it all adds up to leaving this dull Western in a state of mediocrity. This one might appeal only to die-hard fans of Reynolds."

John Mahoney at the *Hollywood Reporter* wrote, "Reynolds' *Sam Whiskey* character has more guts than staying power. But he can handle a greater share of the rough stuff than most of his contemporaries."

Although it wasn't a commercial success, *Sam Whiskey* did establish Burt's on-screen persona of a 'cocky hero.'"

***

Burt told his agent and friend, Dick Clayton, that he wanted to play a role like John Garfield did opposite Lana Turner in *The Postman Always Rings Twice* (1946). No such parts were offered. "Instead, a producer hands me a script and says, 'I know it's not there now, kid, but we can make it work."

Clayton called and told him he'd been offered a leading role in the original black comedy feature film M*A*S*H (1970), that eventually spawned the long-running (1972-1983) TV series. but Burt turned it down. "The producer said the other two leads would be assigned to Barbra Streisand's husband [*Elliott Gould*] and to that tall, skinny guy who was in *The Dirty Dozen*," Burt said. "Tom Skerritt played the role I turned down."

Finally, needing work, Burt accepted the third lead in another Western, *100 Rifles*, a Marvin Schwartz film to be shot in Almería (Spain), where he'd previously filmed some of the scenes from *Navajo Joe*.

The stars would include the reigning sex symbol of the '60s, Raquel

Welch, with Jim Brown as the male lead.

[Brown was a former professional American football player hailed as one of the finest athletes of all time. He'd been a running back for the Cleveland Browns in the NFL from 1957 to 1965, when he retired to become an actor. Right after working with Burt, he would star in Shaft (1971), the film that led to the rise of "blaxploitation" movies, a genre specifically targeted to inner-city black audiences.]

That fading Latin Lover of the 1950s screen, Fernando Lamas, would get fourth billing.

Based on Robert MacLeod's novel, *Californio,* the movie was directed by Tom Gries. He had just completed his masterpiece, *Will Penny* (1968), starring

This poster shows the carnage and gun-toting feminism associated with Raquel Welch's role in *100 Rifles.*

Charlton Heston, a Western which the star later proclaimed as "my favorite film."

Gries told the press, "Jim Brown is a great actor with a lot of appeal, and Raquel Welch in some situations is just a piece of arm candy, but I think she will prove in this film that she can act as well." He was asked about Burt Reynolds. "Yes, he's also in the film."

Shortly after his arrival in Almería, Gries lasted three days in the scalding heat before he came down with typhus. He had to be hospitalized while the cast and crew waited for him to recover.

"I was playing Yaqui Joe, an Indian with a mustache," Burt said. "Raquel had a Spanish accent that sounded like a cross between Carmen Miranda and ZaSu Pitts. Brown was afraid of only two things in the entire world: One was heights, the other was horses. There was a scene on horseback where he fights me on a cliff. It just didn't work."

One of its most controversial scenes would depict Brown and Welch making love, a pairing that, in the 1960s, was interpreted as rare and (to some) deeply shocking. It would generate massive publicity.

Brown told the press, "I'd like to bring a style to the screen that means something to the cats on the street. It's an image I want to portray of a strong black man breaking down social taboos. In *100 Rifles,* it's a different thing for a black man to portray a lawman, get the woman, and ride away into the sunset."

The setting for *100 Rifles* was Sonora, Mexico, in 1912. Yaqui Joe (Burt)

who is half Yaqui Indian and half "Yankee and white," is a bank robber who has stolen $6,000 from an Arizona lawman named Lyedecker (as portrayed by Brown), who chases him into Mexico where both the lawman and his prey are captured by a Mexican army officer, General Verdugo (as portrayed by Fernando Lamas).

Yaqui Joe tells Lyedecker that he stole the money to buy rifles for his people, who were being repressed by the U.S. government he represents. In collaboration, the lawman and the bandit he's chasing escape from a Mexican firing squad and flee together into the hills. There, they're joined by Sarita (Welch), a lovely Indian revolutionary who is harboring a vendetta against the Mexican soldiers for having murdered her father. The unlikely trio bond together as allies.

Where's the beef? It's here, in the person of Jim Brown. Despite their cozy stance in this publicity photo, Welch and her co-star grew to hate each other.

A native of Chicago, and four years younger than Burt, Welch had only recently generated press for her role in *Fantastic Voyage* (1966). Burt had first seen her image when she'd posed in a doeskin bikini. The poster sold thousands of copies, and Burt hung a copy of it in his garage.

Critics noted Welch as a sex symbol with an independent, non-submissive streak.

One of them, noting the beauty of both her face and figure, wrote, "The era of the blonde bombshells of the '50s, as exemplified by Marilyn Monroe and Jayne Mansfield, has ended."

Born in 1915, Fernando Lamas had been the Argentine heartthrob of the 1950s, and had been broken in by Evita Perón in Buenos Aires. "He was past his peak when I met him," Burt said, "and married to the star of *Neptune's Daughter* (1949), Esther Williams."

"He told me that he was a handsome Latin and a great lover," Burt said. "Not exactly modest. We lunched together. He said that on Broadway, he'd co-starred with Ethel Merman in *Happy Hunting* (1956)."

"In one scene, I had to kiss her," he said. "It was somewhere between kissing your uncle and a Sherman tank."

Lamas' son, Lorenzo, was cast as an Indian boy in *100 Rifles*. The big moment in his career would come much later when he was cast as Lance Cumson, the son of Angela Channing, played by Jane Wyman, in TV's *Falcon Crest* (1981-1990).

"I never told the kid that I thought his mother, Arlene Dahl, was the hottest thing that ever emerged from the screens of the 1950s," Burt said. "A dazzling, radiant redhead, she was the stuff of which wet dreams are made."

"Even though I played a half-breed," Burt said, "I made it seem like the other half of me was this Southern guy from Alabama. I played my character as nasty and funky, and I looked like a Christmas tree—wristbands, armbands, and even these jangling spurs. When I walked I couldn't hear the dialogue."

"When I wasn't before the camera, I was the referee in fights between Jim and Raquel."

"I think that in the beginning, our stars were sort of attracted to each other," Burt said. "Both of them had tempers. Later, the critics would murder them—after all, they're not Alfred Lunt and Lynn Fontanne."

According to Brown, "Raquel resented me, telling everyone that I was trying to steal the picture from her. She got hung up on who was being favored in the closeups...shit like that. Burt was a stabilizing influence. He's a heck of a cat. He tried to assure her that nothing was being stolen from her."

She later said, "I was the balcony in a cheesecake factory. I'm sorry that Tom Gries wanted to get all the sex scenes with Brown wrapped up on the first day. There was no time for icing—and that made it difficult for me. Brown was very forceful and I was feisty and uncomfortable with his aggression."

According to Burt, "Jim is the most honest man I know, and Raquel is a gutsy broad. She did her own stunts. There's a performance in there somewhere."

"Miko, my Japanese girlfriend, joined me on location, so my sexual needs were satisfied. However, one day when I was alone with Raquel, she asked me why I hadn't made a pass at her."

"I'm positive that if I'd pulled up your dress and pulled down your panties, I'd find an eight-by-ten glossy of your cunt," he told her.

He later described her in a memoir, confessing that at that moment and during others, too, he had been "an asshole. She had every right not to speak to me again."

"I'm glad I never became her lover because she was once quoted as saying that she'd never found a man who could satisfy her and fulfill her

Raquel Welch in *100 Rifles*. She indulged in an off-screen feud with Burt.

261

needs. I guess that includes Richard Burton, her co-star in *Bluebeard* (1972)."

Near the end of *100 Rifles*, there's gunfire, stabbings, hangings, explosions, strangulations, and dismemberments. Raquel's character is killed in combat.

The noted film critic, Roger Ebert, said, "*100 Rifles* is pretty dreary. Brown and Reynolds are good together. Brown has a cool, humorous charm, and Reynolds plays it like the other half of a vaudeville team. The celebrated love scene between Brown and Raquel is a big fizzle."

Burt got better reviews than either Welch or Brown. "Yaqui Joe is played with real style," claimed the *Newark Star-Ledger.* The *Hollywood Reporter* proclaimed, "Gutsy Burt Reynolds has stardust all over him."

"If the character of Yaqui Joe had been more carefully scripted, Burt Reynolds would have easily stolen the picture," wrote the critic for the *Los Angeles Herald Examiner.*

"Of the trio of co-stars, Reynolds is the only one who knows how to act," according to the *Cleveland Press.*

"Reynolds plays this half-breed with a full-blooded eye twitch, milking the most from the obvious chuckle-bait and finding the laughs," wrote the critic for the *Chicago Tribune.*

Even though super stardom still eluded Burt, he became a popular guest on the talk show circuit, most notably beginning with his appearances on *The Merv Griffith Show.* But called himself "America's most well-known unknown. When they show one of my movies, theater ushers bolt the doors so no one can escape."

"Beginning with Merv and later growing even more popular on Johnny Carson's *Tonight Show,* Burt became a household word. "These appearances on talk shows changed everything for me. I'd spent ten years looking virile, often as an Indian, and telling some actor on camera to 'put up your hands.' After Merv, and most definitely after Carson, I appeared with other hosts, including David Frost and ultimately, Dinah Shore, which changed my life. I suddenly had a personality to peddle."

"I realized that people out there in TV land liked me, that I was somebody of interest. My goal became to transfer that character on TV—the irreverent, self-deprecating side of me, my favorite side, in fact—onto the big screen. I felt if I could do so, I could have a big career."

Griffith had begun his career as a radio and big band singer, going on to appear in films and on Broadway. He'd gone on the air with *The Merv Griffin Show* in 1965, attracting twenty million viewers.

He booked the most eclectic mix of entertainers on TV. Ranging from authors to politicians, they even included a bodybuilder who became the 38th governor of California. Fresh from Austria, Arnold Schwarzenegger made his talk show debut on Merv's show in 1974.

Griffith was not afraid of controversy, booking such hell-raising performers as Richard Pryor, Dick Gregory, and George Carlin. The talkative, always provocative Zsa Zsa Gabor was a frequent guest, too.

Burt appeared on a show that was devoted to bachelors, featuring Hugh O'Brian (TV's Wyatt Earp) and Cesar Romero. "Merv knew that Romero was gay, but he put up a good front," Burt said. "I sat through their mush where they seemed to love everything and everybody...pure bullshit."

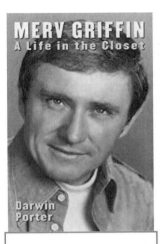

"When my turn came, I criticized every stinking movie I'd been in, and I think I did so with humor. At first, the audience was shocked but then applauded my honesty. I even talked about love affairs gone wrong. I got some laughs, but also sympathy. We've all had love affairs that went south."

"Merv thought I was hot, and he asked me to return the following day for a show that featured Sophia Loren and Gina Lollobrigida.

"That was one hot show," Burt said. "The whole world knew that Gina and Sophia were rivals. There was no love lost between those bombshells. In fact, Sophia had been quoted as saying, 'Gina's screen presence is limited. She is good playing a peasant but she's incapable of playing a lady.'"

WANNA KNOW MORE ABOUT MERV?

Produced and published by Blood Moon Productions in 2009, this is the first post-mortem, unauthorized insight into Merv Griffin, a failed singer and unsuccessful actor who unexpectedly rewrote the rules of America's broadcasting industry.

He became the richest man in TV, befriended everyone in media who mattered, bought a casino, and maintained a secret life as America's most famously closeted homosexual.

Gina was known for affairs with men who included Fidel Castro, Dr. Christiaan Barnard, and Yul Brynner, her co-star in *Solomon & Sheba* (1959).

"My whole life has been a big, long battle to tell men I don't wish to take off my clothes," Gina said. "I cannot help the way I look. Sex appeal I do not do on purpose. I do it sincerely, I am always dressed in my pictures. I get very irritated when people think I must be the same person I portray on the screen."

Sophia, too, discussed her sex appeal, claiming, "I am not just another cheesecake pot. Everything you see I owe to spaghetti. Sex appeal is fifty percent what you've got, and fifty percent what people think you've got."

Griffith had been given comments about what people had said about this Neapolitan beauty. Alan Ladd, her co-star in *Boy on a Dolphin* (1957), claimed, "It's like being bombed by watermelons."

Noël Coward claimed, "She should have been sculpted in chocolate truffles, so that the world could devour her."

This episode—which also included Burt—became one of the most widely viewed in the series. At the end of the broadcast, Sophia placed a big kiss on his lips.

Merv asked me back show after show, twelve in a row, which must have been some sort of a record," Burt said. "He asked me to share his dressing room, and I admit I did a striptease for him as I changed my clothes. But he didn't grab me, keeping his distance. I knew he wanted to. Through him, I was revealing to America that I had a sense of humor. The joke going around Hollywood was that I had had a personality transplant."

Film critic Nancy Streebeck wrote, "Burt Reynolds unashamedly utilized his own personality as an investment in himself, and his unexpected candor, wit, and frankness were delightfully refreshing and entertaining. Audiences positively adored him."

***

Dick Clayton lined up one of Burt's busiest years for 1970, leading off with a guest appearance on the TV series, *Love, American Style*. The series, part of ABC's Friday night primetime lineup, aired between 1969 and 1974,

"That was one hot show," Burt said, in reference to his appearance on the Merv Griffin show as the male counterpart to the explosive competition that day between Italian uber-divas Sophia Loren (left) and Gina Lollobrigida (right).

Burt, in the center photo, a publicity shot for *Sam Whiskey*, proves that he has mastered the fine art of smoking a cigar in a bathtub.

each week featuring unrelated stories, most often with a comedic touch.

In one of the episodes, "Love and the Banned Book," Burt was cast as Stanley Dunbar, A G.I. who returns home from overseas to find that his wife, played by Elizabeth Ashley, has become a literary sensation.

[It was part of a trilogy that featured two other episodes — "Love and the First-Nighters" and "Love and the King."]

Then a more tempting offer to appear in a feature film came from Mae West. She had been offered a script in which she wanted to make her come-back in this 1970 release of Gore Vidal's *Myra Breckinridge*. She hadn't made a film since the 1943 disaster, *The Heat's On*. In *Myra*, she would get star billing, but her role was actually the third lead in the plot. For the leading man and woman, she wanted Burt to co-star with Elizabeth Taylor.

Using her star power, she had already gotten a then-unknown, Tom Selleck, cast as one of the "studs." Farrah Fawcett, Burt's future co-star and lover, was relatively unknown when she was also cast.

When Burt agreed to visit West in her lavish apartment at Ravenswood, she asked him to bring Elizabeth Taylor along with him.

Burt was eager to be introduced to Elizabeth, picking her up like a man on a date. He'd followed her life in one tabloid exposé after another. Her own self-assessment was music to his ears, especially when she told a reporter, "All I can say is that I dig sex." On another occasion, she claimed, "I guess the world thinks of me as a scarlet woman. Actually, I'm almost purple."

Howard Hughes had said, "Every man should have the opportunity of sleeping with Elizabeth Taylor—and at the rate she's going, every man will."

Her late husband, producer Mike Todd, said, "Lemme tell ya—any minute that this little dame spends out of bed is totally wasted."

Her then-husband Richard Burton weighed in with his ap-praisal. "Elizabeth's breasts are apocalyptic. Before they wither, they will topple empires."

Published in 1968, the novel (*Myra Breckinridge*) on which the film was based was Gore Vidal's most controversial. Its plot focuses on the exploits of a transgendered

Burt with Elizabeth Ashley in an episode of *Love, American Style*. According to the plot, he wonders where his wife learned all that raunchy sex stuff she put into her red-hot best-seller.

male who undergoes a sex-change operation.

Defining herself as the widow of the man she had once been, she manipulates her uncle, Buck Loner, an over-the-hill "singin' cowboy" into granting her a position at his Hollywood acting school. As a teacher, Myra introduces "femdom" into the curriculum.

The plot also introduces one controversial theme after another, including a provocative female-on-male rape.

West didn't call it her "comeback" picture, but a return to the big screen that she'd once dominated in the 1930s. In *Myra,* she had signed for $350,000 to be cast as Leticia Van Allen, an octogenarian casting agent who was supremely skilled in the politics of Hollywood's casting couch rituals, systematically seducing young men who come in for auditions.

Raquel Welch as *Myra Breckinridge* decides to "pull down my bloomers and show studio executives what I've got. They might as well see what a real woman looks like," Myra boasts.

What the men saw was not a real woman at all.

***

In his new Mercedes, and in one of his new custom-made suits, Burt drove to Elizabeth Taylor's home in anticipation of their rendezvous with Mae West.

When Elizabeth greeted him, she was a vision in lavender, which accented her violet eyes. Everything about her was lavender, from her makeup to her gown to her high heels. She was four years older than him but looked much younger. Some critics suggested that her once-fabled beauty had faded, but he disagreed. He also suspected her diamonds might surpass those of West herself.

Elizabeth surprised him by giving him a kiss on the mouth. Her first words to him were, "I'm cheap and available, and I have so much money, I can give it away for free these days—no charge."

Her candor amused him, and he assumed she was joking, but she left

266

open the possibility that she wasn't.

"So now I learn you're no longer that prostitute you played so brilliantly in *BUtterfield 8*. Why haven't you gotten around to making me your leading man?" he asked.

"Every actor in Hollywood wonders that," she answered. "I can't do them all. But I'm trying. You're next in line if Mae has anything to say about casting."

When West had informed both of them that she wanted the director to cast them together in *Myra*, each of them had quickly read the short novel.

En route to Ravenswood, Elizabeth said, "As you know, Mae wants me to play Myra, but would anyone in the world ever believe me as a trannie?"

"Only those with the most vivid imaginations," he answered.

Mae West wanted Elizabeth Taylor to be her co-star in *Myra Breckinridge*.

"Think of Myra as a Barbie Doll on steroids," West told Taylor. "A wonderfully cheesy sex goddess, a radical departure for you."

Both of them already knew West, Burt far more intimately than Elizabeth. She told him of her first meeting with West. It had transpired at the Broadway Theatre in Manhattan in September of 1951.

Attired in elaborate Gay Nineties finery, West evoked her earlier success as the vamp ("the most wicked woman in the world") on Broadway in 1928, *Diamond Lil.*

At their meeting, Elizabeth congratulated her on her zany one-liners, comparing her favorably to Charlie Chaplin and W.C. Fields.

"Don't mention that drunkard, Fields, to me," West said. "Once, he stuck his filthy paw up my gown to see if I were a real woman. He'd heard all those rumors I was a drag queen. The jerk found out I was all woman— and then some!"

"She gave me some career advice," Elizabeth said, years later. "She told me I should always insist that a redheaded man be cast in my films,"

"Redheads bring a performer good luck," West told Taylor. "I always insist that one be cast in any of my performances. Before going on stage, I run my fingers through the guy's hair. A star should always surround herself with a real swish, maybe two. A woman looks more feminine when she's got a swish hovering over her, doing her hair, her nails, or tightening her gown."

West greeted both Burt and Elizabeth warmly. "Hello, dearie," she said to Elizabeth. "Welcome to my humble abode. It seems that you and I are the only love goddesses left. As for you, Burt, I'd kiss you but I just washed my hair."

[She had borrowed that famous line from Bette Davis in the movie, Cabin in the Cotton *(1932).]*

"It's definite," West said. "I'm returning to the screen to bring back glamour. Burt, I want you in the picture not only on screen, but off screen as well. I think before a woman goes on camera, she needs to have an orgasm. That also pertains to her stage work."

Then she turned to Elizabeth. "When your late husband, Mike Todd, produced my *Catherine Was Great* in 1944, he would always give me the quickest orgasm before I went on."

"Not so with me," Elizabeth said. "He delayed my orgasms for two hours before he brought me a release."

"After an orgasm, a woman looks more beautiful than ever," West said.

"My goodness, how you ladies talk before a bashful ol' southern boy like me," Burt said.

Then West began touting the role of Myra to Elizabeth. "You play a ballsy bitch of a gal, a real man-eater. It'd be your way of getting back at all those macho creeps who fucked you during the 1940s and 50s."

"My role of Leticia Van Allen calls for a powerful, dynamic, horny, and middle-aged foxy chick," she said. "Naturally, Fox thought of me. Who else in Hollywood can pull off such a role but me?"

"At first, when Fox called, I thought they wanted me to play Myra," West said. "Up to now, I've refused to play any gal over twenty-six. But they convinced me my role of Leticia was the last *femme fatale* of the Golden Age of Hollywood. Myra, of course, is a fantasy, a by-product of silicone, surgery, and hormone injections, and in contrast, I'll be the real deal."

"Are you saying that's when you thought of me as Myra?" Elizabeth asked, as she cupped her breasts. "I'm the real deal too…these jugs are genuine."

"I didn't say it right, dearie," West said. "Forgive me. I just thought your portrayal as Myra would restore some of the glamour you lost after that harridan you played so brilliantly in *Who's Afraid of Virginia Woolf?*"

"Okay, girlie," Elizabeth said. "You're off the hook."

"I thought of you because Myra is a completely liberated woman, a formidable opponent of any mere man who stands in her way," West said. "No man ever possesses Myra Breckinridge. She allows men to seduce her in her own good time and in ways convenient to her tyrannous lust."

"Fuck! That would be the story of my life," Elizabeth said.

Late the next morning, Burt placed a phone call to his agent, Dick Clayton, to talk over his possible involvement in the filming of *Myra Breckinridge*.

Dick said, "Your getting cast in that isn't going to happen, I predict. But besides that, how did your evening with Elizabeth end?"

"I promised her that if she'd come home with me, I'd feed her chili which I had ordered from Chasen's, since I'd read it was her favorite dish. Mike was out of town. That freed me to offer 'me' to Elizabeth."

"Did she get 'me?'" Clayton asked.

"Yes!" he answered, but then refused to supply any further details.

Mae West as the sexually voracious Leticia Van Allen

***

As it turned out, West's concept of a rewrite for Buck Loner was rejected by the director, Michael Sarne. Instead, he cast John Huston into the role of the old codger, yesterday's screen cowpoke..."fat and gross, with breasts larger than Myra's."

Elizabeth rejected the role of Myra, the part going to Raquel Welch.

Although it developed its own kind of cult following, *Myra Breckinridge* was a dud at the box office, a spectacular, much-ridiculed flop, generating some of the most lacerating reviews of the 1970s.

Time called it "as funny as a child molester." The *Miami News* nominated it as "the worst movie ever made," and Gore Vidal, author of the novel on which it had been based, denied any links to it.

West herself bore the brunt of the attacks. Critics labeled her everything from "an aging drag queen" to "a reanimated walking corpse." One of them noted that, "She lusts after men young enough to be her great-grandsons."

Many predicted that *Myra Breckinridge* would be West's last farewell to her legend. Not so. She had one final farewell picture in her, and once again, she'd call on Burt.

Mae was not the only campy element in *Myra Breckinridge*.

The photo above shows Rex Reed and Raquel Welch displaying opposite sides of the gender gap, before-and-after incarnations of Myra's sex change.

Against Dick Clayton's advice, Burt had rejected one of the lead roles in the original film version (1970) of *M*A*S*H*.

Instead, he accepted star billing in *Skullduggery* (1970). It would be filmed in Jamaica, a substitute for Papua New Guinea, the setting for the novel on which the film was based.

Produced by Saul David and directed by Gordon Douglas, *Skullduggery* was a sci-fi adventure movie based on a favorably reviewed French novel published in 1952, *Les Animaux dénaturés* by Jean Bruller, who wrote under the pseudonym of "Vercors." The novel became a bestseller in the United States when it was published as *You Shall Know Them* in 1953, *The New York Times* reviewing it as "a humanly sardonic story."

Originally, Otto Preminger plotted to adapt the novel into a movie, but he was lured away by other film projects.

The plot involves a group of adventurers who travel to New Guinea to discover a tribe of apelike creatures, the Tropis, who are being exploited as slaves by humans.

As Douglas Temple, Burt is the leader of this expedition, and many fans thought he'd never looked sexier as the film's macho hero, wearing a cap and smoking a cigar.

The Canadian actress, Susan Clark, was cast as the prim scientist, Dr. Sybil Greame. She and Burt, as expected, get involved romantically, one critic referring to their on-screen lovemaking as "kitchy-kooing."

In some respects, the movie seems to spoof adventure dramas like *King Kong*. When the expedition comes upon the Tropis, the scientist wonders if she has discovered "the missing link" between man and the apes.

In the unlikely role of Topazia, Pat Suzuki is the leader of this tribe of ape-like, intelligent creatures portrayed by diminutive students from the University of Djakarta wearing hairy suits. One critic suggested that Suzuki resembled "a simian version of Myrna Loy."

The financial backers of the expedition suggest that the Tropis be bred like animals for slave labor.

Toward the end, Burt flees with Suziki, who is pregnant. Her baby is stillborn, but Burt pretends he killed it, deliberately wanting to provoke an international trial whose high-profile results, he hopes, will legally define Tropis as humans rather than animals.

The courtroom scene attempts to answer that question. To some viewers, they suggested the famous Scopes trial in which the lawyer, Clarence Darrow, matched wits with William Jennings Bryan in what came to be known as "The Monkey Trial," debating the theory of evolution.

Burt found working with Suzuki, a second generation Japanese American, a delight. Her nickname was "Chibi," meaning "short person."During World War II, she and her family had been rounded up and sent to an American concentration camp in Colorado.

An accomplished singer, she was discovered by Bing Crosby and later appeared on Broadway as one of the leads in the Rodgers and Hammerstein musical, *Flower Drum Song* (1958). Her rendition of "I Enjoy Being a Girl" became famous.

When Burt met her, she was divorced from Mark Shaw, the photographer for John F. Kennedy. She had been one of the performers at the President's 1961 inaugural.

Susan Clark as the lady scientist later married the football star, Alex Karras, with whom she co-starred in the TV sitcom, *Webster* (1980). When Burt met her, she had recently appeared onscreen with his friend, Clint Eastwood, in *Coogan's Bluff* (1968). She had just completed *Tell Them Willie Boy Is Here* (1969), with Robert Redford.

Skullduggery, an ethno-biological conflict ending in a courtyard drama about evolution. Lower photo shows Burt as a humanitarian hero.

Burt was surprised by the February 1973 issue of *Playboy*. In it, he discovered that Clark had posed topless.

A Londoner, Edward Fox, had recently distinguished himself in such British films as *Oh! What a Lovely War* (1969) and *Battle of Britain* (also 1969). His greatest success would come when he beat out Roger Moore and Michael Caine for the starring role in *The Day of the Jackal* (1973), playing a professional assassin hired to kill General Charles de Gaulle.

At the conclusion of filming, Buck said, "Nobody knew how to sell the picture. When you have Pat Suzuki dressed as a small ape, you're in trouble. I should have accepted the lead in M*A*S*H instead."

***

Director Bernard Girard offered Burt the lead role (once again he'd play an Indian) in a made-for-TV movie, *The Return,* scheduled for airing on CBS in March of 1970. The title was considered too dull, so it was changed to the more provocative *Hunters Are for Killing*.

After reading the script by Charles Kuenstle, Burt demanded a rewrite that removed any mention of his character as a Native American, since the plot was thick enough without it. Surprisingly, although he lacked star power at the time, his wish was granted. He flew to Tucson to begin shooting the movie.

The plot follows a man who returns home after serving time in prison to claim his share of his deceased mother's estate. However, his stepfather, who holds him responsible for his own son's death, intends to fight him every step of the way.

Burt's co-star was Melvyn Douglas, that suave leading man of the 1930s. Burt had never seen the films of his heyday, although he knew he'd been Garbo's leading man in her 1939 romantic comedy, *Ninotchka*. [He'd *also been her co-star in 1941* Two-Faced Woman *(1941), her adieu to the screen.*]

Douglas was born in 1901, and by the late 1950s, he had visibly aged, and had reverted to playing older man or fatherly types. Burt had seen him in *Hud* (1963), in which he'd appeared opposite Paul Newman and had won a Best Supporting Actor Oscar. The year Burt worked with him he'd been nominated for a Best Actor Oscar for his portrayal as a vindictive patriarch in *I Never Sang for My Father* (1970).

The female lead of *Hunters Are for Killing* went to Suzanne Pleshette, whom he'd seen in Alfred Hitchcock's suspense thriller, *The Birds* (1963).

She'd appeared with heartthrob Troy Donahue in *Rome Adventure* in 1962 and had married him in 1964. But, as she told Burt, the marriage lasted only a few months. She came home early from the studio one afternoon and caught him in bed with Rock Hudson. "I knew his interests lay elsewhere," she said.

Although she'd been Steve McQueen's co-star in *Nevada Smith* (1964), she was finding jobs hard to come by. Burt recommended that for greater exposure, she appear on *The Tonight Show*. She went over big on the show and had a real chemistry with the show's host. TV producers saw her and cast her as the wife on *The Bob Newhardt Show*, which ran from 1972 to 1978.

Burt would last see her when she played Manhattan hotelier Leona Helmsley in the made-for-TV movie, *The Queen of Mean*, in

Burt with Suzanne Pleshette in this 1970s publicity photo for *Hunters Are For Killing*.

1990.

"When I heard she had lung cancer, I went to visit her in the hospital," Burt said. "This Brooklyn-born dame was one hell of a gal, but major stardom eluded her."

At the age of seventy, she died in January of 2008.

***

"The next gig Dick Clayton came up with for me was another damn Indian role," Burt said. "To sweeten the deal, I asked that James Best, still one of my best buddies, be cast as the villain whom I kill at the end."

"What made me take the role was when I learned that my co-star would be Inger Stevens, the Swedish blonde, sometimes called a wannabe Grace Kelly. What I could not have known at the time were the tragic events that would occur after I met her."

Originally entitled *The Tradition of Simon Zuniga*, the made-for-TV film was scheduled to be aired on ABC's *Movie of the Week*. Before Burt flew to Arizona to shoot the film, producer Aaron Spelling phoned to tell him that the title had been changed to *Run, Simon, Run*. Burt flew first to Tucson, where James Best met him and drove him to the Papago Indian Reservation.

There, Best took him to a small motel, where they would share a room, as they had so often in the past. The handsome actor had often been a weekend guest at Burt's home and, whenever both of them were free, they shared road adventures together, first discovering the glories of California and later, of Utah and Colorado.

Other actors in key roles include Rudolfo Acosta, Ken Lynch, Royal Dano, and Don Dubbis. Burt and Acosta had recently starred together in the film *Impasse*.

Cast as a Papago Indian, Burt appears on the screen as he is being released from a long-term prison confinement for a killing he did not commit. His heart is filled with vengeance. His secret aim is to hunt down the real killer (Best) and fatally shoot him for the slaying of his brother.

As Burt is running along a deserted desert road, he is accidentally struck by a motorist (Inger Stevens), cast as a rich socialite who does charity work, helping tribal members who live on the reservation.

After seeing that he's all right, she asks him to get into her car for the final drive to the reservation, where a shack has been set aside for him. In his brown makeup and black wig, he looks exceedingly handsome. It's obvious that Inger is going to fall in love with him.

As the film moves along, and her affair on-screen with Burt deepens, she foolishly agrees to help him track down Best, who is living somewhere in Arizona under an assumed name.

When Burt was introduced to Inger, he found his attraction for her was reciprocated. She was as beautiful as she was photographed in her movies. In the heat of the desert, she smelled as sweet as if she'd just emerged from a perfumed bath.

Her lips looked soft, moist, and warm, and he longed to kiss her instead of shaking the graceful hand she extended. He held it far too long, but she didn't seem to mind. That was all the signal he needed to move ahead with his ultimate aim of seducing her during location shooting. Fortunately, she occupied the motel room immediately adjacent to the one he was sharing with Best.

Born in Stockholm in 1934, she was two years older than Burt.

Reporter Gary Brumburgh described her like this in his article, *Wounded Butterfly:*

"One of the most radiant of blondes in the late 1950s and '60s Hollywood, Inger Stevens seemed to have the whole world in her corner. Bright and breathtaking, she possessed the cool, classic glamour of a Grace Kelly on screen, yet came off more approachable and inviting. Her warm smile and honey-glazed vocal tones could melt an iceberg. She was a paradoxical beauty, a study in contrasts — tender yet elusive, welcoming and guarded, stunningly attractive yet modest — and this kept audiences intrigued."

As gossip columnist Hedda Hopper wrote, "When Inger Stevens turns those questioning blue eyes on an audience, they've had it."

During his filming of *Run, Simon, Run,*

"Not another god damn Indian role," Burt said. But, eager to work, and to his later regret, he signed on to star in *Run, Simon, Run*

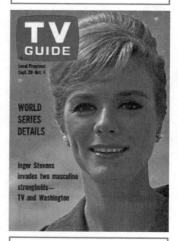

The Farmer's Daughter

Inger Stevens on the cover of TV Guide's edition of Sept 28, 1963, just weeks before the assassination of JFK.

It was an era when a lot of good-looking Hollywood blondes were getting implicated in a lot of scary stuff..

Burt was seeking a new adventure in his life. He'd grown a bit tired of his Japanese-American mistress, Miko Mayana, and was looking elsewhere for sexual liaisons. He still admired and respected Miko, but the candle was burning on a low flame. At the time, Miko was busy with her own career, appearing in such TV series as *Matt Lincoln* and *To Rome with Love*.

In bed, Inger lived up to her reputation of having seduced most of her leading men—and now Burt, too. Her passion matched her beauty. Their first night together marked the beginning of an affair that would last even after their film was shot, at least for a few weeks more.

"Out here in the loneliness of the Arizona desert, we turned to each other for love and understanding," Burt said. "Without meaning to, I got serious about her. I got her on the rebound from a sting of broken hearts, and she caught me in one of my restless moods when I was looking for love and reassurance outside home and hearth. She was also going through a secret and disastrous marriage to the black actor, Ike Jones, the news of her wedding to him carrying a certain shock value for me."

Considering her past record of broken romances, he didn't expect her infatuation with him to last very long—or his for her. Somehow over the course of his time with her, he learned of her previous involvements with her leading men: perhaps she confided them to him herself.

According to reports, she had a chronic case of "leading man-itis," meaning that she tended to fall in love with her male counterpart in any picture she appeared in. In instance after instance, she'd then leave him at the end of filming. Either that or he'd leave her, returning home, in many cases, to his wife.

One reporter wrote, "The druggy vacuity of *Valley of the Dolls* seems campy to us today when we see it on the screen, but it is the harsh reality in the life of Inger Stevens."

After emigrating from Sweden to New York, Inger first worked as a model and attended the Actors Studio with James Dean, Marlon Brando, and Carroll Baker. At night, she danced in the chorus line at Latin Quarter for $75 a week.

There was an early marriage in 1955 to her agent, Tony Soglio, but it was doomed from the beginning because of his excessive jealousy and physical abuse.

She drifted to Hollywood, where

Working with Inger Stevens in *Run, Simon, Run*, Burt had high expectations. The blonde star was known for seducing her leading men.

she signed a seven-year contract with Paramount. She appeared in a family drama, *Man on Fire* (1957), opposite Bing Crosby. Although he was thirty years older than her, she began an affair with him.

She thought he was serious about her, and there was talk of marriage. He'd been married before to the singer-starlet Dixie Lee. Inger was the latest in the line-up of stars he'd seduced, i.e., Joan Bennett, Joan Blondell, Ingrid Bergman, Frances Farmer, Betty Hutton, Mary Martin, Jane Wyman, and Grace Kelly.

In reference to Crosby, Inger later said, "I became sick with all the stress that man caused me."

She had begun decorating a house Crosby owned, overseeing—at his request—the placement of ermine-covered toilet seats in all the bathrooms. He promised her he'd live in that house with her after their marriage. One afternoon she had the radio on when an announcement came on the air: Crosby had married his second wife, the actress, Kathryn Grant.

She followed her breakup with Crosby with sexual relations with her latest co-star, James Mason, when they appeared together in *Cry Terror* (1958).

"James has his ups and downs, mostly downs," she said. "Behind his icy smile, he seemed afraid of life and avoided all confrontations. I never got to know him because he seemed to carry some dark secret deep within his soul. He told me that he was a virgin until he was twenty-six and married his first wife. At the end of our picture, he bolted from my bed."

Inger's next movie was *The Buccaneer* (1958), the story of the swashbuckling pirate, Jean Lafitte. She faced a difficult choice: Which of her leading men would she seduce? Charlton Heston or Yul Brynner? She chose neither, settling on Anthony Quinn. *[Best known as an actor, he was directing* The Buccaneer.*]*

"Tony deflowered me the second night after he'd met me. He even asked me if I would have his child, but I wasn't ready for that."

"He was such a bullshitter, telling me he couldn't live without me. He then dumped me at the end of the picture, but we resumed our affair when we co-starred in *Dream of Kings* (1969)."

In the immediate aftermath of her breakup with Crosby, Inger suffered a series of career setbacks. Potential movie roles evaporated. She lost the role of the female lead in Alfred Hitchcock's *Vertigo* (1958) to the lavender blonde, Kim Novak.

That was followed in 1961 with the loss of two more choice roles she'd coveted and for which she had been considered. The female lead in *The Misfits* (1961), whose script had been written by Arthur Miller, went to his estranged wife, Marilyn Monroe, her last picture. Inger had lobbied hard to portray Holly Golightly in Truman Capote's *Breakfast at Tiffanys* but lost the role to Audrey Hepburn.

For her next movie, MGM's end-of-the-world drama, *The World, the Flesh, and the Devil* (1959), Inger co-starred with the singer/actor Harry Belafonte. When she'd been a model in New York, she was alleged to have had affairs with several African American actors. During the shooting of her latest movie, tabloid gossip linked her to an affair with Belafonte.

One reporter wrote, "Her addiction to on-set affairs, and her involvement in a number of secret affairs with black performers, have been extremely destructive to her mental stability. She is promiscuous, but apparently has never had a love affair that was nurturing."

Inger's life changed drastically in September of 1960 when she met Ike Jones at a party in the home of a Hollywood publicist. Each of them had arrived at the gathering with different escorts. At the time, Jones was producing a show for Nat King Cole.

During the party, Inger had huddled with Jones and set up a contact with him for later that same evening—which meant the early hours of dawn.

Month after month, their affair continued, but they made no public appearances together. Both of them were aware of what Mai Britt's marriage to Sammy Davis, Jr., had done to derail her career as a movie actress. If Inger or Jones had to attend a public event, each went with a person of their own race.

By November of 1961, they were secretly married in Tijuana.

A career highlight came for Inger when she was cast in the TV series, *The Farmer's Daughter* (1963-'64). It was loosely based on the 1947 RKO movie that had earned an Oscar for its female lead, Loretta Young.

From the beginning, Inger's marriage to Jones was rocky, characterized by brutal arguments that often ended in violence. Because of different work schedules, they were frequently separated for weeks, or, on occasion, months. During those periods away from each other, they each reportedly engaged in adulterous affairs.

Sammy Davis, Jr. entered their lives when Jones became the first African American to produce a major feature film. *A Man Called Adam* (1966). He played a self-destructive jazz musician dealing with race and identity during the turbulent civil rights era.

The film co-starred Cicely Tyson, with Lola Falana having a brief "cheesecake walk-on." Peter Lawford, the former brother-in-law of the late John F. Kennedy, also had a role, with guest appearances by Frank Sinatra, Jr., Mel Tormé, and Louis Armstrong.

Unknown to their friends, especially secret from Jones, Davis and Inger began a secret affair when Jones was on the road. That on-again, off-again affair with Davis continued until 1970.

As her marriage raced to its doom, Inger had more affairs with her leading men. Burt's friend, Clint Eastwood, starred in *Hang 'Em High* (1968) with Inger, and the tabloids linked them romantically.

Burt said, "I heard he was banging her, but Clint was my good friend. He's not the kind of guy you ask such questions."

In *5 Card Stud* (also 1958) Inger became involved with Dean Martin, who played a gambler. The director, Henry Hathaway, claimed that "Inger and Deano were making it—often in his dressing room. She also shared her Norse Goddess favors with their co-star, Robert Mitchum. She was a busy gal."

After Martin and Mitchum, Burt became the last of her leading men to seduce Inger. At the end of filming their latest picture, *Run, Simon, Run,* they flew for two weeks to his ranch in Jupiter.

This led to an angry dispute between Best and Burt, because Burt had promised him that he—and not Inger—would return to Florida with him.

Burt would later confess to Dick Clayton that while in Florida, "I made love to her twice a day—around three in the afternoon and shortly before midnight. She was always ready and willing for a toss in the hay."

"In the beginning, we had not planned to fall in love, but in Jupiter, we confessed to each other that I was Mr. Right for her, and she was Miss Right. Actually, she wanted to become Mrs. Right, and I proposed marriage. That meant breaking up with Miko and Inger divorcing Ike Jones. That was our intention when we flew back to Los Angeles."

After Inger's return to California, she discovered that Ike had come back home after their latest estrangement, their longest so far. He'd found out that she'd spent time with Burt in Florida. He'd beaten her severely, and she postponed seeing Burt until her bruises healed. She did not tell him that Ike had returned and that he wanted a reconciliation.

On April 27, 1970, Inger and Burt were seen dining with Producer Aaron Spelling and his wife, Candy, at La Scala restaurant in Los Angeles.

Spelling had been so pleased with Inger's role in *Run, Simon, Run* that he told her he was casting her in a new TV series, *The Mostly Deadly Game,* which would be shot at various locations around the world. Her co-star would be George Maharis, Burt's former rival for movie roles and the star of the TV series, *Route 66.*

The next afternoon, a very troubled and near-hysterical Inger had a long session with Dr. Ralph Greenson, who, coincidentally, had been the psychiatrist of Marilyn Monroe during her final days. He later reported, "Inger was extremely distraught."

The details of Inger's final days are murky. What is known is that Burt accompanied her to the memorial for her friend, Gypsy Rose Lee, America's most famous stripper, who had died of lung cancer. The memorial service was held on April 29 at 10AM at Pierce Brothers in Beverly Hills. Before she became ill, Burt and Inger had visited her in her 17-room house in Beverly Hills, where she lived alone. From time to time, she issued admonitory statements about theatrical nudity, of which she strongly disapproved. "Bare flesh bores men," Gypsy said. "In burlesque, you've got to leave 'em hungry for more. You don't dump the whole roast on the platter, only a slice or two of it handed out."

Death had come to her at the U.C.L.A Medical Center. She was only fifty-six years old.

On Inger's last full day on earth, the last person she was known to have seen was Burt. He went to dinner at her home. It was not known where Jones was that evening, but he must have been out of town. Otherwise, she would not have dared invite Burt to dinner. She had purchased three bottles of vintage wine and had roasted a lamb.

At first, the evening had started out romantically by candlelight. But after they finished off those bottles of wine, the night turned sour.

They got into a fight about other lovers. He confronted her with her fascination for African American men. "You not only married one, but I found out you've slept with a lot of others. I know all about your affair with Sammy Davis. He even brags about it."

"While you're exposing revelations about me, there's one I found out about you," she said. "While making our little film, I learned one of your secrets. You and James Best have been lovers for years. In the movie you want to kill him. Off screen, you prefer to make love to him. My god, Burt, you're a fag! I never knew that. I have nothing against gays, but you, Burt? Who would have thought it? Better keep it a secret."

He later told Dick Clayton what had happened that night. He admitted, "I struck her, and she fell down on the floor, bleeding at the chin. You know what a violent temper I have. I stormed out of her house and swore I'd never return."

The next day, on April 30, 1970, Lola McNally, Inger's housekeeper, arrived at her home and discovered Inger unconscious on the floor. She called

Gypsy Rose Lee was a stripper who always kept enough apparel on "to keep them guessing." Burt and Inger Stevens were seen at he funeral.

an ambulance. Inger was dead on arrival at the hospital.

The police, suspecting murder, investigated and discovered no forced entry, deciding she must have known her attacker and let him in—or else he had a key, which pointed to Jones.

In her bedroom, police discovered two 8" xc 10" photos of Burt concealed under the carpet. He was brought in for questioning. He confessed to having that final dinner with her and that he had struck her.

Both Jones and Burt became prime suspects in her possible murder. Pills were strewn across the kitchen floor and around her body. An odd piece of evidence rested on the kitchen counter. She appeared to have been in the process of making a ham and tomato sandwich. It was half assembled, its ingredients resting beside an open jar of mayonnaise. If a suicide, it seemed odd that moments before, she was making something to eat.

One theory was that her murderer had forced her to overdose on sleeping pills, causing her to die of barbiturate intoxication, which was what the autopsy report maintained.

Questions remain: Had Burt returned to her house after their fight, perhaps for a reconciliation with her—or perhaps to murder her?

Or had Ike Jones come back from his trip to Las Vegas a day earlier than expected?

Various people were called in to testify. Lola McNally said that Inger told her that she was madly in love with Burt and that she planned to marry him.

However, her psychiatrist, Dr. Greenson, claimed that during his last session with her, Inger told him that she was going to break up with Burt as she found him "obnoxious and egotistical."

As long as he lived, Burt never escaped lurid speculation that he was somehow responsible for the death of Inger Stevens.

When William T. Patterson in 2000 was compiling her biography, *The Farmer's Daughter Remembered,* he went to the Los Angeles Police and asked to review her file.

He was told that the records of her death had been destroyed.

In ways that eerily evoked the mysterious, unresolved death of another blonde, equally tragic actress, Marilyn Monroe, the case left many dozens of unresolved answers.

INGER STEVENS:
MURDER OR SUICIDE?
CASE CLOSED

CHAPTER EIGHT

LATE-NIGHT TV
BEGINNING IN 1971, OOZING HUMOR & MACHO CHARM, BURT BECOMES A HOUSEHOLD NAME ON
JOHNNY CARSON'S TONIGHT SHOW

BURT AS 007
AN OFFER FOR BURT TO REPLACE SEAN CONNERY AS JAMES BOND FIZZLES AND DIES

FUZZ
BURT'S FEUD WITH RAQUEL WELCH

DINAH SHORE
THE G.I. SWEETHEART OF WORLD WAR II—A CLASSY DAME WHO JUST CAN'T SAY NO—BECOMES BURT'S "MRS. ROBINSON"

CENTERFOLDED BURT
BURT POSES, SEMI-NUDE AND WITH A LOT OF NEGATIVE IMPACT, FOR COSMO

DELIVERANCE
A GEORGIA-BASED SAGA ABOUT MANHOOD, SELF-KNOWLEDGE, BRUTALITY AND ACCORDING TO SOME, "THE BEST FILM EVER MADE." IT SKYROCKETS BURT INTO HIS LIFETIME DREAM OF SUPER STARDOM

JAMES BEST
BURT DEFINES HIM AS "MY LIFETIME BUDDYBOY."

PLUS: *EVERYTHING YOU WANTED TO KNOW ABOUT SEX* *BURT GETS CAST AS A SPERM IN A SILLY FILM FROM WOODY ALLEN*

The death of Inger Stevens has never been resolved, and her close friends and Hollywood reporters speculated for decades about whether it was a suicide or murder. Burt's involvement in her final hours was often the source of much lurid speculation.

Celebrity psychic John Cohan was a close friend and adviser to the doomed actress and had met and talked with her during the final weeks of her life.

He was known as the "Celebrity Psychic to the Stars," and for decades his predictions were published annually at the end of every year by Cindy Adams in the *New York Post*.

Over the years, many stars turned to him for insights during some crisis they might be having and for guidance for their futures. His clients included Elvis Presley, Elizabeth Taylor, Merv Griffin, Lana Turner, Rock Hudson, Natalie Wood, Joan Crawford, and Nicole Brown Simpson. Cohan also played a special role in the life of Sandra Dee, whom he defined as having been "The Love of My Life."

"John is a great man to know during one's darkest hours," said publisher Danforth Prince, President of Blood Moon Productions. "He's kind, he's generous, he's deeply spiritual, he has valuable insights into the agonies of 'the celebrity experience,' and he's an emotionally intelligent and very positive guiding force for anyone barging a path through the insecurities and doubts of a career in show-biz."

In a memoir, Cohan wrote: "My gift is something that has been with me since I was born. Most of my adolescence, I spent time and energy ignoring or suppressing my psychic ability, because I didn't know what it was that possessed me. Finally, I grasped hold of it and actually embraced my talent."

Many of Cohan's insights and revelations have been published in *Catch a Falling Star,* an overview of his life as a psychic.

Cohan warned Inger to expect disappointment but not disillusionment in marriage or love relationships. "I've been disappointed but never pessimistic. True love is the one infallible shield against all the ugly and harsh things in the world. Once you find it, hold onto it and cherish it carefully, forever."

But in her final days, Inger was still searching for that elusive love. She confessed to Cohan that her marriage to her African American husband, Ike Jones, was a disaster.

"She told me that she and Ike were very unhappy in their marriage, and he often took out his frustration on her. Many of their arguments ended violently. "The men in my life have hurt me," she said. "It started with my father and ended with Ike."

She admitted that she and Burt were talking about her divorcing Ike and marrying him, but she feared it would not work out, and he agreed.

"Inger was the sweetest and most sensitive lady," Cohan said. "While working in Arizona with Burt and his best friend, actor James Best, she came to realize that Burt was bisexual."

"He and James had the room next to mine, and the walls of this little motel where we stayed were paper thin. I became aware of what was going on. James was very jealous of me."

When Cohan wrote his memoir, he revealed that Burt was bisexual.

Elizabeth Taylor, his former client, once said, "most Hollywood actors are homosexual or -bi, particularly in their younger days."

Ever since the publication of the Kinsey report in the late 1940s, it was revealed how prevalent homosexuality was among millions of American males, even if at relatively infrequent intervals.

In spite of her marital troubles with Ike and her apparently doomed relationship with Burt, Cohan did not think that Inger committed suicide.

"Suicide was something she wouldn't do at that point in time," he claimed. "Her career was never better, with a new TV series looming. As

Celebrity psychic John Cohan wrote, "My purpose has always been to use my gift to bring love, understanding, happiness, and insight into the futures of all my clients."

she'd matured, she looked exquisitely beautiful."

In *Catch a Falling Star*, Cohan reported on a strange vision he had when news reached him that his friend and client Inger was found dead by her housekeeper under mysterious circumstances.

"This most charming and vital lady had so much to live for in spite of her mishaps in love, as she'd drifted from one affair after another with men such as Bing Crosby," Cohan said.

When Cohan learned of Inger's death, he was visiting relatives who lived in the mountains near Dos Rios, California. He'd gone for a walk in the mountains before mist shrouded the trail and rain began to fall.

He relayed this experience in a memoir and reinforced it later in interviews with the authors of this book:

"Everywhere I walked, the dirt became muddy, and I started to slip on the side of the mountain. I ran a bit, hoping my feet would grip the ground. I knew I would be in trouble wherever I landed. Just then, toward the bottom of the mountain, I saw a vision of Inger, holding out her hands. I remembered thinking, "Is this a sign that I would be joining her?"

Still on my feet, but slipping down the muddy path, toward huge rocks, I couldn't seem to slow down. Since she seemed to be welcoming me, I managed to steer the direction of my slide toward her outstretched hands.

"I fell onto wet dirt, avoiding crashing into the rocks on my left that would have killed me instantly. On the right were cliffs and an instant drop."

"As if by a miracle, I'd landed safely. I knew it was that vision of Inger that had saved me."

Inger Stevens, "The Farmer's Daughter," in a rough approximation of how she appeared a few days after her death to celebrity psychic John Cohan in a moment of crisis.

Later, he sought medical attention, his doctor telling him that if he'd landed on the rocks or fallen off the cliff, he would have been killed. "It's a miracle you're alive," he told Cohan.

Cohan agreed.

***

Burt had met James Best, the Kentucky-born actor, when they both had appeared on the TV series, *Pony Express*, in 1959. He was ten years older than Burt and, like Burt himself, he would have a career that spanned more than sixty years.

In time, Burt would refer to him as "my Renaissance buddyboy," a reference to the fact that he was a star of TV, film, and stage, as well as a writer, artist, acting coach, director, college professor, and musician.

In spite of those other accomplishments, Best is remembered by his fans as the bumbling Sheriff Rosco P. Coltrane in the TV series, *The Dukes of Hazzard*, which aired on CBS from 1979 and 1985. Burt would appear in a feature film adaptation of that series in 2005 as "Boss Hogg."

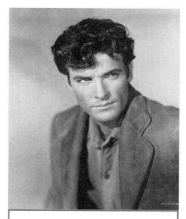

James Best during the early years of his friendship with Burt. "Being a male model was not my thing. But it paid the bills."

Burt called his new best friend "a good ol' Southern boy." His mother had died of tuberculosis in 1929 when he was three years old. He was sent to an orphanage and later adopted, growing up in Indiana.

During World War II, he joined the U.S. Army and trained as a gunner aboard a bomber in Biloxi, Mississippi. After the war, he traveled through Germany as part of an acting troupe entertaining American soldiers who remained stationed there.

After that, he drifted to Hollywood. By 1949, he had a contract at Universal Studios, where he joined players who included Rock Hudson, "who became my first best buddy." He also hung out with Julie

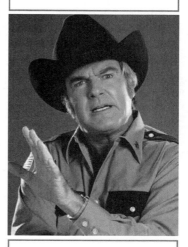

James Best in the TV role that made him famous, Sheriff Coltrane in *The Dukes of Hazzard*.

Adams, Tony Curtis, and Piper Laurie, among other hopefuls, each dreaming of stardom.

Best and Burt did not really bond until they were featured together on *Gunsmoke*, into which Burt was cast as Quint Asper, the half-Comanche town blacksmith. "It was on the set of *Gunsmoke* that Burt and I became bonded at the hip," according to Best. If they didn't see each other every day, they talked on the phone, since both actors were often away on location.

Their friendship would last—interrupted only by an occasional alienation—until Best died in 2015.

"A man can't have a better friend than Burt, even though he sometimes pisses me off," Best said. "He's such a devil."

"Burt was responsible for getting me jobs," Best wrote in his 2009 autobiography, *The Good, the Bad, and the Beautiful.* "You cannot help but love Burt Reynolds. I will never forget his generosity and true act of friendship at a time I was in dire need. Once, when I was going down with financial burdens, he offered me five-thousand dollars, which was all the money he had in his bank account."

Although Best would never make it as a major-league movie star, he was one of the most employed actors in the entertainment industry throughout the course of his long career, guest starring in at least 280 episodes of TV shows.

Along the way, he married a woman he called "Mattie," and the union produced a son, Gary. By 1959, when Burt met him, he had married his second wife, Jobee Ayers.

Best and Burt often toured through the West together, camping out, climbing mountains, and attending rodeos. "The guy was crazy about fishing and I indulged him," Burt said.

Best had earned a black belt in karate and tried to teach the technique to Burt. "I was no good at it. I've seen Japanese men do it, and they are the world's experts. I'll leave it for James and the Japs."

It is not known when Burt's relationship with Best turned sexual, perhaps during one of their long trips through Colorado or Utah.

Burt already knew that Rock Hudson had seduced his friend when they'd starred together in *Seminole* on location in 1953. In time, Best would make six movies with Rock, who pressed sex onto him, and, as Best confessed to Burt, "I went along with it. I liked Rock a lot in *Seminole.* I played a soldier who was drowning. Rock had to swim down and rescue me. He deserved a reward."

"Underwater, the first thing he

After filming of *Seminole* ended for the day, Rock Hudson introduced Best to his "tomahawk."

286

grabbed were my private parts. He must have liked what he felt, because he later paid homage to them."

As Burt confessed to his agent, Dick Clayton, "James and I are best buddies. We share secrets together, leave nothing out. The tabloids would love to hear what we say to each other."

As a team, Burt and Best often spent weekends together with Clayton and his friend, Tab Hunter, who shared ownership of a vacation home near Palm Springs.

"Burt often called me to work with him on a job, and I never thought he paid me enough," Best said. "But then he would promise to take me fishing in Florida, so I said okay."

By his bedside, Best always kept an autographed photo of Burt. He'd signed it, "To Jim. Love always, Burt."

"Like my friend, Rock Hudson, Burt preferred straight men for his occasional seductions," Best said. "He got along with gay men and had no prejudice. But for his 'buddy-buddying,' he liked 'em straight. Finding such men sexier than the gay ones. Also, messing around with straight guys didn't threaten his macho image of himself."

"Actually, I knew little of the private world inhabited by James Best and Burt Reynolds," Clayton said. "I knew they cared for each other very much. Once, they got into an argument about some picture deal, and they even struck each other. But in the middle of their fight, they started laughing, fell into each other's arms, and headed for the bedroom, where they remained for the rest of the night, staggering out nude the next morning at around 10AM for a swim."

"Girlfriends and an occasional wife will come and go," Burt told Clayton. "But Jewel is here to stay for the long haul."

"Why do you call him Jewel?" Clayton asked. "Do you mean that he's a gem?"

"His original name is Jewel, compliments of his mother."

***

The next gig Dick Clayton got for Burt was as a detective, *Dan August*, the title character in a crime series that aired on ABC in September of 1970.

As a police lieutenant, he would investigate homicide cases in the upscale but fictional town of Santa Luisa, California. Inspired by Santa Barbara, it was filmed in Oxnard in Ventura County.

At first, Burt was reluctant to play another detective. "I don't wanna get typecast as Dick Tracy."

He had such little regard for the role that he almost decided "to price myself out of the market." His demands were transmitted to the executive producer, Quinn Martin. *[Martin, "the last of the great acts on television," had produced both The Untouchables and The Fugitive, the latter starring Burt's friend, David Janssen.]*

Burt wanted a guarantee of twenty-six episodes of *Dan August*, as well as script approval and to be allowed to direct some "second unit stuff."

He met with Martin to discuss salary. Although he didn't really have very much star power at the time, he asked for the highest-ever salary for any actor starring on TV.

1h | Crime, Drama | TV Series (1970–1971)

Martin checked and found that that distinction had been awarded to Michael Landon for his starring role in *Bonanza*, for which he'd been paid $25,000 a week.

"I'll give you $26,000 a week," Martin told Burt.

"My resistance is over," Burt said. "I'm your friggin' cop."

"I was thirty-five years old at the time, and I knew I had to make it big—or else I'd soon be reduced to character roles," Burt said. "I still had sex appeal and my good looks, and I was in need of one great breakthrough role."

His two co-stars would include Norman Fell and Richard Anderson.

[Fell was cast as Burt's partner, Police Sergeant Charles Wilentz. Fell would later become more famous for his performance as the landlord, Mr. Roper, in Three's Company *(1977-84), a comedy sitcom starring John Ritter. An actor from Pennsylvania, Fell would also have the dubious distinction of starring in Ronald Reagan's last feature film,* The Killers *(1964).*

Anderson played Police Chief Untermeyer, with whom Dan August often tangled. "Always a chief," he jokingly said to

DAN AUGUST

Rough cops, rough streets, rough stunts: Burt as a visual centerpiece for this TV police drama series.

288

Burt. "Never an Indian like you."

Anderson usually portrayed authority figures as he did in various episodes of Perry Mason, The Six Million Dollar Man, *and* The Bionic Woman.]

In *Dan August,* an arsenal of big-name actors made guest appearances with Burt. They included Mickey Rooney, Harrison Ford, Billy Dee Williams, Larry Hagman, Martin Sheen, Janice Rule, Joan Hackett, Vera Miles, Carolyn Jones, and Diana Hyland. Even Burt's close friend, Ricardo Montalban crafted an episode with Burt. Other actors who made appearances alongside him included Sal Mineo, Fernando Lamas, Bradford Dillman, Richard Basehart, and Jan-Michael Vincent. *[Burt would eventually co-star with Vincent in other projects.]*

With the money coming in from *Dan August,* Burt bought a new Mercedes, a Cape Cod-style residence in the Hollywood Hills, and additional real estate in Florida and Georgia.

He insisted on doing his own stunts, one of which required him to race into a burning building and rescue an infant. During its filming, a plastic "prop baby" replaced a human child. The fire was so hot it melted in his arms and burned him. Adding to his physical agony, but as mandated by the script, he jumped out a window to escape from the flames. The stunt went badly, leading to a shoulder injury that caused him pain for the rest of his life.

Regrettably, *Dan August,* as a TV series, faced stiff competition from two other popular detective series: *Hawaii Five-O* starring Jack Lord on CBS and *McCloud* with Dennis Weaver on NBC.

Burt was notified that *Dan August,* after the completion of 26 episodes, would be canceled after its first season.

***

Next, Dick Clayton came up with offers for Burt to star in two made-for-TV pilots, each a detective series following the same lines as *Dan August.* He rejected both roles.

Instead, he returned to the stage, starring in *The Tender Trap* at the Arlington Park Theatre in Arlington Heights, an affluent suburb of Chicago close to Evanston.

It usually booked top stars such as the Gabor sisters (Eva and Zsa Zsa), John Carradine, Don Knotts, Art Carney, and Richard Chamberlain. "Even though Burt Reynolds was not as famous as he later became, he had every horny woman in town clamoring for tickets," a former usher remembered. "There was a rumor going around that he'd appear shirtless and in his underwear."

Written by Max Schulman, *The Tender Trap* had opened on Broadway in 1954 and starred Robert Preston and Kim Hunter. In 1955, Frank Sinatra and Debbie Reynolds made a film adaptation.

In the play, Burt played Charlie Y. Reader, a 35-year-old theatrical agent who is leading an idyllic life as a womanizing bachelor. Then a bright, charming, singer-actress comes into his orbit.

***

Burt was a guest on *The Merv Griffin Show* after the cancellation of his TV series, *Dan August*. There, he revealed that he treated his appearance there "like a joke. I told the audience how happy I was. I'd just purchased this fabulous manse with a gated driveway on Carolwood in Holmby Hills, and I'd also bought a Mercedes large enough to fit in two bedrooms."

He went on to tell Merv's audience that movie offers were rolling in. "Only this afternoon, Cubby Broccoli offered me to take over for Sean Connery and play James Bond."

[Cubby Broccoli, the producer, was the architect of the James Bond/007 movie franchise. In time, Bond films generated more than two billion dollars in gross revenue, becoming the most fiscally successful movies in motion picture history.

A New Yorker, Broccoli, born in 1909, had lowly beginnings, including such odd jobs as a casket maker. Once, he worked as a "gofer" for Howard Hughes on the set of The Outlaw (1941). "Accidentally—or perhaps not so accidentally—I walked in on Jane Russell as she was changing clothes. Hughes and I agreed on one thing: Jane has the best tits in the history of Hollywood."]

Sean Connery, as the deadly secret agent with a license to kill, had immortalized himself in *Dr. No* (1962). International cash registers rang again when he reprised his version of James

This photo of Sean Connery was snapped in Amsterdam in 1971 by a historian for the Dutch National Archives during the filming of *Diamonds Are Forever*, a film franchise staple that, for a brief shining moment, was offered to Burt Reynolds.

Bond in *From Russia With Love* (1963).

Now, after getting cast as Bond once again in *You Only Live Twice* (1967), Connery was ready to move on to other roles.

"This is my last time as Bond," he told the press. "I do not want to spend the rest of my life as 007. I existed before Bond, and I will exist after him, too. Playing Bond has been both a blessing and a curse."

In a post-Connery era, Broccoli had no intention of ending the Bond franchise. He set out to interview and test some actors in Britain. Although he tested dozens of them, none of them seemed suitable—perhaps Richard Burton, but he wasn't interested.

Then he began considering some American actors. Of course, it would be up to the scriptwriters to explain why an American was working as a British secret agent.

"For an international franchise, an American actor wasn't as dumb as it sounded," Broccoli said. "The Beatles had broken up, and the sun was setting on the British Empire, as well as England's cultural sway. American actors dominated world cinema and international grosses."

Several actors surfaced as a possibility to replace Connery, although United Artists persisted with their hope that Connery might change his mind.

Steve McQueen was suggested, and Broccoli met with him. "He was smaller than I thought, and he didn't seem to have the elegant presence of Bond. He looked more like he belonged on a motorcycle."

Clint Eastwood was suggested, so Broccoli met with him, later telling colleagues, "He laughed at me."

"There's no way in hell I'd play Bond," Eastwood said. "For one thing, I'm an American. For another, I would never follow in the footsteps of Sean Connery. There's no actor in the world who can replace him without getting his performance trashed. No matter how much money you offer me, I'll never be your James Bond."

Finally, someone proposed Burt Reynolds, and Broccoli agreed that he might be a possibility. He'd been impressed when Burt had played Hawk on the TV series with that name.

"I wanted someone who had sexual assurance, and Burt seemed to have that. He wasn't the big star then that he became, and I heard that women were hot for him. I'm not saying he was a great actor, but I knew the difference between an actor and a film star. Didn't they find Gary Cooper when he was working as an electrician?"

"Burt was a bit short, but he had the physique for Bond, and he had the walk. He oozed masculinity on the screen, and he had the *cojones* to play love scenes with some of the world's most desirable women."

Broccoli met with Burt, who was startled by the idea.

At first, he had the same response as Eastwood: "I can't be Bond. I'm an American and part Cherokee at that."

When money was discussed, he became more intrigued. He asked Broccoli to give him a week to mull it over.

In the meantime, Broccoli was shown a screen test of John Gavin, whom he'd seen play Julius Caesar in *Spartacus* (1960), starring Kirk Douglas. Gavin was tall, remarkably handsome, and he was a good athlete. Forgetting about Burt, he signed Gavin as the star of the next 007 flick, *Diamonds Are Forever* (1971).

Two days later, Burt phoned Broccoli, telling him he'd thought it over and that he wanted to play Bond.

"You'll save tons of money because I can perform my own stunts. How about $300,000 for my playing Bond?"

"You're too late making up your damn mind," Broccoli said. "I've signed John Gavin." Then he put down the phone.

In the meantime, behind Broccoli's back, David Picker, the chief honcho at United Artists, had been in secret negotiations with Connery. Knowing that he was shrewd about money, Picker offered him a deal he could not afford to reject.

For his return to the screen as Bond in *Diamonds Are Forever*, Picker had offered him an astonishing $1.25 million, plus 12.5 percent of the international gross. At the time, that was the best financial deal ever offered an actor in motion picture history.

Connery agreed to the terms: "Sign me up." Of course, that meant that Broccoli would have to pay off Gavin for canceling his contract.

Months later, after Burt read about the international grosses of *Diamonds Are Forever*, he told his agent, Dick Clayton, "I made the biggest career mistake of my life. If I had signed to play Bond in one picture after another, I could one day be the richest actor on the planet."

***

After all that exposure on *The Merv Griffin Show*, it seemed inevitable that Merv's competitor, Johnny Carson, would invite him for a guest appearance, too. His casual, conversational approach and extensive interaction with his guest stars had already made him an American icon.

Burt watched Carson whenever he could. Quite by chance, Burt had tuned in to the series' history-making first show, on October 1, 1962, when a spectacular lineup of guests had included Joan Crawford, Skitch Henderson, Groucho Marx, Tony Bennett, and yesterday's crooner, Rudy Vallée.

"I'd heard a lot about Carson, and I admired him," Burt said. "Johnny and I each had an appreciation of female flesh."

Like Burt, Carson didn't always get good reviews from women. "He's not a sophisticated man," said Alicia Bond, the Israeli actress. "I wouldn't want to wake up with him and sit across from him at the breakfast table."

Director Billy Wilder said, "Johnny is the Valium and the Nembutal of a nation. No matter what kind of dead-asses are on the show, he has to make them exciting. He has to be either nurse or surgeon. Every night in front of millions, he had to do the *salto mortale [circus parlance for an aerial somersault performed on a tightrope)*. What's more, he does it without a net."

When Carson met Burt, each had already been married and divorced. Carson had wed Jody Morrill Wolcott in 1949, divorcing her in 1963 to marry Joanne Copeland, which would also end in divorce. Two more wives awaited him in his future.

"As I got to know him, Johnny never wanted to talk about his wives," Burt said. "He told me that giving advice about marriage would be like the captain of the *Titanic* giving lessons in navigation."

Monte Markham, a friend of Burt's, said that Merv Griffin had been the first talk show host to capitalize on Burt's fascinating personality. "But it was on the Johnny Carson show that millions came to realize what an easy-going guy Burt was, a guy who could laugh his way through a scene better than many who play it moment to moment. That's just the way he is."

Burt's life changed considerably on the night of April 7, 1971, when he first appeared on *The Tonight Show,* which was taped in Manhattan. As the cameras rolled, the TV host and the actor immediately established a friendly rapport, bantering and joking. At times, laughter drowned out a few of Burt's comments.

Burt was such a success that

Burt brought a can of whipped cream onto the set of *The Tonight Show.* Host Johnny Carson was surprised, even shocked, when Burt suddenly pulled open Carson's leather belt and squirted a great glob of cream into his jockey shorts.

293

during a commercial break, Carson leaned over and asked him if he'd like to host the show on May 31 so that Carson could take a night off. This was just one of the many surprises awaiting Burt in 1971.

***

Burt compared Carson's invitation to host *The Tonight Show* to Richard M. Nixon, asking him to preside in the Oval Office for one day. "After all, Johnny was the High Lama of all talk show hosts. Almost from the beginning of our long relationship, Johnny viewed me as his alter ego."

One night on air, Carson asked him, "Where are you going after the show?"

"I'll walk along Broadway to see if anyone recognizes me," Burt said.

"On my frequent appearances on his show, I established a character for myself," Burt said. "Without actually referring to it, I suggested I had this enormous cock. I was subtle, but the audience got it. I was Mr. Wise Cracker, Mr. Carefree, Mr. Daredevil, an inveterate womanizer deflowering every petunia in the flowerbed."

TV critics later noted that it was on *The Tonight Show* that Burt created the characters he would play in his future films, including *Smokey and the Bandit, White Lightning,* and *Hooper.* "He found his first legs and learned to walk on Johnny's show," claimed Ed McMahon.

"Was the character Burt played with Johnny a reflection of the real man?" one reporter wanted to know. Burt surprised him by saying, "Before I go on the air, I sneak into a phone booth and change into my Burt Reynolds costume like that guy in the comic strip."

"Thanks to Johnny and some other lucky breaks, my career really took off in 1971," Burt said. "The country began to wake up to the fact that Burt Reynolds had arrived. I could forget that decade of playing Heap Big Injun and looking virile, mad, and dumb. The talk shows, not just Johnny's, but others, including Merv Griffin and Dinah Shore, even Mike Douglas, made me a household word."

"Many millions of my new fans around the world had never seen any of my early duds on the screen."

"Johnny gave any number of young performers—including me—exposure on the air that launched their careers," Burt said. "In fact, my appearance led to me getting cast in my greatest and most acclaimed picture."

One critic cited Burt's "cheek, his bravado, his self-mockery, his cocky arrogance...and, lest we forget, his incredible sex appeal—yet, he could be modest."

One night, Burt said, "I was walking down Hollywood Boulevard last week, and I saw this pack of horny females coming my way. I didn't know which of them to seduce first. As it turned out, they ran past me, heading for Warren Beatty, for him to figure out which of them to seduce first."

He felt free to joke about his career. "You should meet my dad, Big Burt. He's addicted to TV, watches everything he can on it, except when I come on the screen. Then he heads for the kitchen for a few beers until I go off the air."

"One time, he sat through an entire episode of *Gunsmoke*," Burt told the audience. "He gave me a review, telling me I just stood around looking like this dummy blacksmith. He asked, 'Couldn't you do something, like throw an anvil at Jim Arness?'"

"In the South, a boy is not a man until his dad tells him he is," Burt said. "I'm still waiting for Big Burt to anoint me."

"I was a constipated actor until I'd made a few appearances on Johnny's show," Burt said. "I started to loosen up, touching people, saying outrageous things, squirting a can of whipped cream into Johnny's fly, shit like that. If somebody didn't like me, screw 'em."

"I have short legs," he confessed. "Some other dude is walking around with my legs. I should be six feet, five inches tall. As it is, I only feel that tall."

"Around Hollywood, I'm thought of as redneck heaven. I drive a red sports car. My house is painted barnyard red. My living room is red, even the upholstery. And naturally, so is my bedroom. I don't have an ego yet my license plate for some reason is EGO 22. That was the number on my jersey when I played football in college."

After knowing Burt for a month, Carson invited him to his apartment for late night drinks. When he arrived, Carson was there, drinking with Ed McMahon.

"As much as I loved Johnny was how much I detested McMahon," Burt said. "He was a real shit, constantly coasting on Johnny's shirttails."

"As the night wore on, all three of us had too much to drink," Burt said. "Ed insisted on busting my chops. He knew I was getting a lot of fan mail after every appearance on the show, and he was getting none. He kept putting down my image as a sex symbol."

"You suggest you're the biggest stud in Hollywood," McMahon said. "But I heard from one gal who went to bed with

Ed McMahon pumping Budweiser sales in this print ad from 1966. "It's a living, and it's show-biz."

you that you're known as Princess Tiny Meat."

That insult proved too much for Carson, and he tossed McMahon out of his apartment.

"Sometimes after the show, Johnny and I made the late-night rounds in Manhattan, stopping off at Danny's Hideaway. P.J. Clarke's, even Sardi's. I remember the first night we dined at Jilly's, and Frank Sinatra came in. It was his favorite hangout. As he passed by our table, Johnny looked up at him and yelled, "God damn it, Frank! I told you 12:30 sharp. It's two in the morning."

"Fortunately, Ol' Blue Eyes took that as a joke," Burt said. "Otherwise, the mob might have mowed down Johnny and me before dawn."

"A lot of people didn't know this, but Johnny was a secret astronomer," Burt said. "In his apartment, he had a telescope at every window. One night, he told me he had discovered a hidden planet filled with millions of creatures colored purple, with long tails. I think both of us had had one too many that night."

On another night, Carson and Burt talked about "the first time," Burt relating that he was inducted into sex by a woman in her forties in Palm Beach when he was only fourteen.

Carson claimed that he waited until he was seventeen. "It was with this gal called Francine, known in high school as a lady of easy virtue. The act took place in the back seat of my dad's 1939 green Chrysler Royal in Norfolk, Nebraska. The whole thing was a disaster."

One night, they discussed that when the day came for them to retire, each of them would write an autobiography of their adventures. "I've already got the title for mine," Burt said. "I'm gonna call it *My Life*."

"How dull," Carson said. "You won't sell many copies with that title. I'm going to entitle mine *Toads & Tarantulas*."

***

When Raquel Welch learned she was to co-star with Burt in her next picture, a United Artists' crime drama called *Fuzz* (1972), she protested. "I will not work with Burt Reynolds, and I will not appear in even one scene with him."

The producer, George Edwards, and its director, Richard A. Colla, solved that problem like this: Welch's role in the movie was not large. She played a woman detective, known as "McHenry." Colla shot scenes with Burt, using a double for Welch, and then he left the set. Welch was then summoned, and her scenes were also shot with a double who stood in for Burt. At no point in the movie are they seen in the same frame.

"This was a first for me and my leading lady," Burt said. "As in many of my pictures, I'm between the sheets with my leading lady both on and off the screen."

In an interview with a reporter, Welch said, "People have accused me of being tough. They want me to be more vulnerable. I want to be vulnerable, too, but only for the good and happy things. I want nothing to do with meanness and self-pity." She also said, "Men either want to take me to bed, or else they feel threatened by me. I don't think the world had ever seen a more discreet sex symbol than me...My god, I'm practically prudish."

For nine days' work, Welch drew a salary of $100,000. Even for that price, she refused to appear in one scene set in a men's room where she was to be filmed wearing only her bra and panties. United Artists had been promised this scene, but she continued to refuse to do it.

When Burt heard that, he said, "I'll double for her."

Burt was cast in *Fuzz* as Detective Steve Carella. His co-stars included Yul Brynner as the villain, and Jack Weston and Tom Skerritt as fellow detectives.

Evan Hunter wrote the screenplay based on his novel. It had been published as one of the 87th Precinct detective tales he churned out under the pseudonym of Ed McBain. Although most of his stories were set in New York, Boston was chosen as the location for filming.

The script called for Burt to investigate a murder-extortion racket run by the mysterious "Deaf Man" (Yul Brynner). The police are trying to prevent the murders of several high-ranking city officials.

One fan wrote, "The best thing in the movie was the voice of Dinah Shore, Burt's real-life girlfriend, singing 'I'll Be Seeing You.'"

The funniest scene is when Burt and Weston go undercover disguised as nuns. Burt didn't shave his mus-

It was a first for Burt, a co-starring role with an actress who refused to be present on the same sound stage with him. Thus, even the upper tier of the promotional material displayed above show portraits of Burt and Raquel which were photoshopped to create the illusion that they were actually getting along and in the same room together.

297

tache, so he's not very convincing as a sister.

Although Yul Brynner's career was in decline when Burt knew him, in 1957 and 1958, he'd been one of the top ten box office stars in the world, forever remembered for his performance as the King of Siam in *The King and I* (1956) with his friend, Deborah Kerr.

According to Brynner, "I've played everything from an Egyptian pharaoh to a Western gunfighter. When I go on location, I demand that every suite I occupy be painted this particular shade of tan. I also refuse to eat white eggs, only brown ones. No one knows my real self. I wish to be identified only as a nice, clean-cut Mongolian boy—or else the King of Siam."

"Yul's list of lovers was far more distinguished than mine, very impressive," Burt said, "and I don't just mean Marlene Dietrich or Nancy Davis."

An Exotic with a Past

Yul Brynner, as Pharaoh Ramses II, looking highly sexed and over-indulged in Cecil B. DeMille's erotic overview of the Bible, *The Ten Commandments* (1956).

["Nancy Davis" was a reference to Mrs. Ronald Reagan back when she was a Hollywood starlet.]

Brynner's other "star fucks" (as Burt called them) included Tallulah Bankhead, Anne Baxter, Ingrid Bergman, Claire Bloom, Joan Crawford, Yvonne De Carlo, Judy Garland, Maria Schell, and Marilyn Monroe.

"When Yul wasn't on camera, he was lighting up one cigarette after another, cancer be damned," Burt said.

Burt told the press, "*Fuzz* was a bit fuzzy, made by one of those hotshot TV directors. I liked working with Jack Weston, Raquel Welch was my leading lady, but I didn't work with her—you figure. I liked Evan Hunter's script and one day would like to direct a movie made from one of his novels."

Fuzz did not end well. One critic wrote, "Had it not been for those two sex symbols, Burt Reynolds and Raquel Welch, I don't think anyone would have gone to see it."

***

298

The mating of Burt Reynolds with the famous singer and television host, Dinah Shore, became one of the most defining moments of his life.

After watching Burt's appearances on the TV shows of both Merv Griffin and Johnny Carson, Dinah wrote to him, inviting him as a guest on her own afternoon TV show. It was devoted to cooking and celebrity chitchat.

He rejected her invitation. "Why me?" he asked. "I don't cook."

"Maybe she has something else in mind," Dick Clayton suggested.

It's almost impossible to overstate how famous Dinah Shore was as an American Icon. Everyone adored her.

Displayed here are her musical hits from an era when her morale-building helped win World War II.

As her invitations kept coming, he ignored them. Then she turned up the heat by morphing his refusals into a running gag on her show. "Another turndown from Burt Reynolds arrived today," she announced.

Her producers then warned that Burt might one day unexpectedly emerge onto her set as her guest of the day, but the guests who appeared were never Burt..perhaps Dick Martin, but not Burt. Three months went by without him.

One day, Burt was a guest on an (unrelated) game show with actors Earl Holliman and Roddy McDowall. *[Roddy privately confessed to Burt that he had a crush on him.]*

Backstage, Burt was introduced to Dinah's producer, who urged him to appear on her show. "We've carried on enough with this campy gag about your failure to show up. Let's surprise her…The gal thinks you hung the moon."

It was agreed that Burt would hide in a closet on the TV set, waiting for her to open it. "She'll probably faint," the producer said, "when she sees you."

Minutes into the show, as the cameras rolled, Dinah opened the door and out popped Burt. She burst into laughter and so did he. He took her in his arms and gave her a big hug.

"Oh, my God!" she said. "It's really you." Then she turned to the audience, a look of disbelief on her face. "Ladies and gentlemen, it's Burt Reynolds. THE Burt Reynolds."

"Zing, went the strings of my heart with Dinah in my arms," he later said.

At one point, he propositioned her on the air, asking her to run away with him to Palm Springs for the weekend.

"You're crazy," she said. "NO."

A few minutes later, he came back with the same question, and each time she politely refused.

"OK, have it your way." Then he stood up and threatened to walk off the set, claiming, "I'm going to kill myself."

Then, changing his mind, he ran back onto the set [it was arranged like a kitchen] and hoisted himself up onto one of the countertops. It collapsed, sending pots and pans and fully prepped bowls of camera-ready ingredients crashing to the floor.

The producer cut to a commercial. "What a mess," she said. Then she bent down to see if he'd injured himself.

After the show, she didn't immediately accept that invitation to run away with him, but they talked for hours in a process of getting to know each other.

As for the 120 minutes of footage that emerged from the taping that day, only fifteen minutes of it could be salvaged and broadcast. According to the director that day, "The rest was X-rated."

After the taping, Burt claimed "I was rattlesnake-bit, blissfully charmed, scratched behind the ears, my tummy rubbed. It was like my first love."

Her romance with Burt was featured as front-page news stories in tabloids throughout the English-speaking world. Older women identified with her success, as an older woman, to attract and keep an amorous (and rich and famous) younger man in her orbit.

"We didn't hit the sack the first night or for many evenings to come," he said, "although we did some heavy necking. I followed her around from city to city when I could. She was going on promotional tours."

He was only vaguely aware of the details of her personal life but collected most of her albums. Rivaled only by Doris Day, she was his favorite vocalist.

Eventually, he persuaded her to discuss her private life.

Named Fanny Rose Shore, she was born to Jewish parents on February 29, 1916 in Winchester, Tennessee. She'd been stricken with polio when she was eighteen months old. Her parents provided intensive care for her, doctor after doctor, and at times feared she'd never walk again. How-

Dinah Shore was an icon as American as Chevrolet itself. She was featured on the cover of *Life* (February 1, 1960), long before she ever met Burt.

ever, after years of painful and rigorous exercise and rehabilitation, she eventually walked, albeit with a deformed foot and a slight limp.

When she was sixteen, her mother died of a heart attack. Her father enrolled her into Vanderbilt University in Nashville, Tennessee, where she pursued a singing career. After her rendition of the popular song, "Dinah," disc jockey Martin Block couldn't remember her name and introduced her as "Dinah." In part because she had never liked her name [*Frances*], she changed it to Dinah, which in time became famous throughout America.

At the time of her graduation from Vanderbilt, Burt was two years old. Against her father's wishes, she gravitated to New York, where she was hired as a vocalist on radio station WNEW. There, she sang alongside a skinny Italian boy [*Sinatra*] from Hoboken, New Jersey. He didn't like her at first, but in time, they become lovers and later, close friends for life. By 1940, a year before America entered World War II, she signed a contract with RCA Victor Records.

Early in her career, false rumors were rampant that she was biracial and that she'd given birth to a child fathered by an African American.

Dinah's fame grew, especially in 1940 and '41, when her marketers directed her songs at pony-tailed bobbysoxers and zoot-suited Sinatra wannabes.

Although Jo Stafford had a better voice, Dinah evolved into a "jukebox darling" and a G.I. favorite during World War II. Eddie Cantor made her a regular on his   Monday night radio show (1940-41) *It's Time to Smile*.

Dinah later credited Cantor for teaching her self-confidence, comedic timing, and ways of connecting with an audience.

Her first major hit recording was "Yes, My Darling Daughter," selling half a million copies. By 1943, she starred in her first film, *Thank Your Lucky Stars,* with Cantor. She also appeared with Glenn Miller and recorded hit songs that included "You'd Be So Nice to Come Home To," "I'll Walk Alone," and "Blues in the Night," the latter selling a million copies.

Her success as a singer continued during the Postwar Era, particularly with her big hit, "Shoo Fly Pie and Apple Pan Dandy," peaking with "Buttons and Bows."

Before appearing in films, she had her teeth capped, her nose bobbed, and her hair dyed blonde.

Her brief screen roles never pleased her. She knew she was not a good actress and didn't like the way she photographed. *[In 1944, she co-starred with Danny Kaye in* Up in Arms, *and also filmed* Follow the Boys *(also 1944) with Marlene Dietrich and George Raft, along with W.C. Fields and Sophie Tucker. That same year she also appeared in* Belle of the Yukon *with Randolph Scott and the Stripper, Gypsy Rose Lee.*

She made it clear that she was so embarrassed by her appearance in Aaron Slick from Punkin Crick *(1952) that she threatened to leave Burt if he stayed up to watch it on late-night TV.]*

Late in 1942 at the Hollywood Canteen, Dinah met the heartthrob movie star, George Montgomery, then a G.I. He was eating a ham and cheese sandwich as she approached him. "I'm your biggest fan," she gushed.

"What a coincidence," he responded. "I'm YOUR biggest fan."

In reference to Montgomery, Bing Crosby later said, "Poor George. Dinah might give the appearance that cotton candy wouldn't melt in her mouth, but she knew what she wanted. She was hard as flint. My God, when she met George, he was engaged to Hedy Lamarr, and Dinah took him away from her."

Their romance and later marriage flourished, lasting until their divorce in 1963. She later said, "When I saw him in *The Cowboy and the Blonde* (1941), I thought George was the handsomest

Although Dinah didn't get top billing for her appearance in this corny vintage film, it was her face that appeared front and center in this poster advertising its charms.

302

man God ever placed on the planet."

As the 1940s came to an end, she had another big musical hit, "Baby, It's Cold Outside." Doris Day and Patti Page emerged as her stiffest competition.

Her singing career remained strong in the 1950s, as she returned to RCA to record 100 sides for a million dollars (about $10 million in today's currency). Her biggest hits included "My Heart Cries for You," "Sweet Violets," and "Love and Marriage."

In 1959, she went over to Capitol Records, but her popularity was declining, and they dropped her in 1962. Over the next twenty years, her output diminished as she recorded only a handful of albums.

She renewed her career on TV, however, and came back big in 1956 when she starred on NBC's *The Chevy Show,* sponsored by Chevrolet. "See the USA in a Chevrolet" became her signature song, and Americans were soon humming it. The sponsors decided that she was going over so big that it was time to reconfigure the program into *The Dinah Shore Show,* a weekly event marked by her *mmm-wah* kissoff at the close.

From 1970 to 1980, she hosted two daytime programs, including *Dinah's Place* (1970-74) on NBC and *Dinah!* (later *Dinah and Friends*). Guests included Frank Sinatra sharing his recipe for spaghetti sauce and Spiro Agnew demonstrating his skill at the piano. Many guests were old friends, such as Bob Hope, Lucille Ball, and James Stewart.

A latter-day critic summed up her appeal as "a little bit of Oprah, a little bit of Martha Stewart."

When they fell in love, Dinah was a well preserved fifty-one, Burt thirty-five. "I was a lucky man to have encountered her at the crossroads of her life. It might not have worked a decade earlier. Frankly, I wasn't mature enough back then to appreciate her."

"She is one dedicated woman who knows exactly what she wants—and sets out to get it—and usually succeeds. I'm very lucky she decided she wanted me."

"Many of those tabloid jerks claimed I'm just using her for career advancement," he said. "That's pure bullshit! I'm not a superstar, but I made a million dollars last year."

At first, she was slow to give her heart away, as she was still sad at the failure of her wartime marriage and later divorce from Montgomery. Burt was also distressed by his ill-fated marriage to Judy Carne.

"I found Dinah very attractive and also very sexy in a ladylike way," Burt said. "She got my jokes and could match me with some razor-sharp comebacks."

"It took quite a while to get her to go to bed with me," Burt told Dick Clayton.

Helen Gurley Brown reigned as editor-in-chief of *Cosmopolitan* magazine for thirty-two years. Born in the bowels of Arkansas in 1922, she eventually made her way to Manhattan, where she advanced rapidly to become one of the nation's highest paid copywriters. In 1954, she was put in charge of *Cosmopolitan* (sometimes known simply as "Cosmo"), and in 1959, she'd married the noted film producer, David Brown.

The Cosmo Girl, Helen Gurley Brown, in 1996.

"A woman is never too old to desire sex."

In 1962, she'd published her biggest hit, a "how-to" lifestyle guide entitled *Sex and the Single Girl*, which became a best-seller in almost thirty countries. Two years later, it was adapted into a hit movie starring Natalie Wood.

Brown is credited today with the transformation of *Cosmo* from a literary magazine into a publication aimed at the modern (and single) career woman. As an advocate of women's sexual freedom, she claimed, "Girls, you CAN have it all—love, sex, and money."

From the pages of her magazine, the "Cosmo Girl" was invented—glamourous, fashion-focused, and often man-hungry—who did not believe in maintaining her virginity until her wedding night.

She read every issue of *Playboy* with a certain undisguised contempt, and often ridiculed its publisher, Hugh Hefner. One day, she decided to "send him up" by running a nude male centerfold.

She could find any number of male models willing to pose nude, but she wanted someone who was famous, deciding it should be a celebrity. Football star Joe Namath seemed ideal, as he had already posed for some provocative ads, but he turned her down.

She got in touch with Steve McQueen, as she'd seen an underground picture of him frontally nude. He, too, rejected her. Another macho star, Clint Eastwood, told her "I only show my dick in private."

Warren Beatty was her next choice, until she learned that his movie contracts stipulated that he would not be photographed without his shirt. Paul Newman didn't seem averse to posing shirtless, however, so she contacted him, only to be rejected.

Brown was very close to abandoning her vision for a nude male centerfold in her magazine until she found herself in the wings of Johnny Carson's *Tonight* Show, bantering with Burt Reynolds.

"I realized I'd found the Perfect Man," she said later. "He was macho, very good looking, and from what I'd heard, straight."

She wanted a male nude centerfold for her April 1972 edition, and during the next commercial break, she asked him if he'd pose for it. To her surprise, he accepted.

The next day, he checked with his press agent to see if he felt that it was wise. David Gershonson told him, "Go for it. It'd be high camp. Get you noticed."

What happened next would make publishing history.

Burt had misunderstood Brown's offer, thinking he'd pose with a beautiful girl, perhaps Angie Dickinson. But he soon learned that the camera would be trained only on his nude body. From the beginning, however, it was clearly understood that his genitals would not be exposed or visible.

An internationally renowned fashion photographer, Francesco Scavullo, was hired for the shot.

Burt brought a quart of vodka to the photographer's studio. When he got there, he found it very cold—"too cold to show off a man at his best," he said. He was told to lie nude on a bearskin rug, and for some shots, a St. Bernard was included as part of the visuals. The photographer was assisted by two young men "both of them looking so gay their hair was on fire."

As he drank more vodka, his poses became more provocative, but he wasn't worried, since Brown had given him final approval of the photo that would eventually be published. He was also promised that he'd be given all the negatives—or that they'd be destroyed.

In the aftermath, he said, "I expected to make a splash by posing nude, not a tidal wave. Overnight, I made my reputation as an *homme fatale.*"

When *Cosmo* hit the stands, ninety-eight percent of the copies were sold within two days. Brown immediately ordered the printing of an additional 700,000 copies. Some "cheapies" didn't actually buy a copy of the magazine but used razorblades to cut out the centerfold without being detected by the vendor.

On the day of its publication, Burt

Cover art for the April 1972 edition in which Burt appeared, to the avid attention of millions, nude except for one appendage.

was booked on the *Tonight* Show. On the air, he lampooned his own decision to pose for the centerfold, self-satirizing himself in a style perhaps inspired by Don Rickles. "I told every joke I could about it, beating other comics to the punch."

"At one point," he said, "I got on a plane, and this guy calls out to me, 'thanks for the lovely flowers.' I'm getting more wolf calls from men than from women. It seems that all of America wants to bed me. That Dinah Shore must be one lucky gal!"

Don Rickles, the inspiration for Burt's humor in this instance, watched Burt's routine on television. Later, he said, "Burt Reynolds in that centerfold looked like a cigar-smoking, hairy-chested kewpie doll."

"If I were trying to prove something, why would I cover it with my hands?" Burt asked Johnny Carson's audience. "I have small hands."

In the weeks ahead, Burt received hundreds of Polaroids of women in the nude. Many males also sent him naked pictures of themselves. Months later, during promotions of his next film, *Deliverance,* in Denmark, he flipped through a porn magazine and discovered a print of himself "dry humping" that bearskin rug. He'd been told that all negatives had been destroyed.

At first, he rejected all offers for interviews, although editors from *Time, Newsweek,* and *The Associated Press* wanted to quiz him. Brown, however, talked to AP, telling a reporter, "Burt's got a beautiful body, and he's adorable."

One reporter reached his mother in Jupiter. Fern said, "I'm proud of my boy. I'm also proud of his centerfold. After all, Buddy was my creation. I bought a copy of the magazine, but someone stole it from my living room. Buddy is a good boy."

Finally, Burt broke down and granted an interview. "I agreed to pose for *Cosmo* for free. I did it because it was fun and funky and a good sendup for *Playboy.* Hugh Hefner's male chauvinism is nonsense. I don't take this sex symbol crap seriously. I doubt if the chicks at the roller derby are going to paste up my centerfold in their lockers. I ex-

"Peek-a-boo. It's me, tanked up on vodka when I posed for the photographer from *Cosmo.* His assistants wanted me to pose with an erection for their private collection. Did I do It? I don't remember, as I was too drunk."

pect a lot of gals will be turned off by it, especially those who don't like body hair on a man."

Dinah Shore was asked what she thought about it: "I think the whole thing is a hoot. I'll have it enlarged and placed as the centerpiece of my living room. I've got no more to say, as I have to rush home to fry hush puppies and catfish for my man."

Bags of mail poured in from around the world, as many women proclaimed, "You were the sexiest thing since Clark Gable appeared on the screen in the 1930s."

Dick Clayton told Burt that he should have retained the licensing rights to the centerfold. "You'd have already made at least five million dollars if you had."

His nude appeared on license plates, key chains, bedspreads, and ironing boards. Once, when he checked into a hotel in New York City, he found that the bedsheets had his centerfold printed on them.

He said, "Every day I had to face the same old cliché: 'I didn't recognize you with your clothes on.'"

The major change in his film career was that he was now getting first refusal on any number of scripts. "No longer did a script sent to me have the fingerprints of Warren Beatty, Paul Newman, Steve McQueen, or Robert Redford."

Dozens of offers poured in for frontal nude shots of him. He was told that a nude calendar might earn him as much as three million dollars. He did accept one offer: Posing without his shirt for *Esquire*.

In November of 1972, he considered suing *Cosmo* for printing one million nude posters of his centerfold. "I was outselling the posters of Raquel Welch."

The executives of Jockey underwear wanted him to model their line, wearing skimpy briefs, showcasing his genitals.

He rejected the offer, but baseball great Jim Palmer of the Baltimore Orioles went for it instead, finding it very lucrative.

The controversy of his posing for the centerfold raged for years to come, some critics claiming that the pose launched him into superstardom. In 1985, he said, "I'd like to think it was my performance in *Deliverance* that put me over the top—rather than

Celebrity strips: It started a trend. Jim Palmer for Jockey

THE JOCKEY FASHION STATEMENT IS BOLD.

JIM PALMER, STAR PITCHER FOR THE BALTIMORE ORIOLES, WEARS ELANCE™ BRIEFS.

JOCKEY
The first name in underwear

élance

me showing my delectable tits."

Twenty years later, he confessed, "I'm sorry I posed for *Cosmo*. It was one of the greatest publicity stunts of all time, but also my biggest mistake. After that, I don't think anybody took me seriously as an actor."

***

His first stage appearance after the *Cosmo* spread was in a theater in Arlington Heights, Illinois, a suburb of Chicago. when he co-starred with Lois Nettleton in *The Rainmaker*.

"It was obvious that the audience, mostly women, were more interested in my pubes than in the play. I think they wanted a male burlesque show. In one scene, when I'm removing a hairpiece from Lois' head, as a prelude to a love scene, someone in the audience rose and shouted, 'Burt, take it off! Take it all off!' Soon, thirty people were standing up shouting for me to take off my pants."

Dinah flew into Chicago, where he met her at the airport and drove her to Arlington Park, where she discovered that he'd booked her into a suite with himself at the Arlington Park Towers.

During her visit, she watched his performance in *The Rainmaker* as a charming Depression-era trickster named Starbuck, who, for a fee, promises to bring rain to a drought-ridden farm community in the West.

After his performance, they returned to their suite, where champagne was chilling

Dinah Shore flew to Chicago and was driven to the Arlington district to see Burt perform on the stage with Lois Nettleton in *The Rainmaker*. Burt Lancaster and Katharine Hepburn had previously starred in the movie version (above).

"That was the night, later in our suite, that Dinah got to see what readers of *Cosmo* didn't get to see."

and supper had been prepared. He headed for the shower and when he emerged, as he later relayed to Dick Clayton, "I came out wrapped in a towel. Dinah was lying on the bed in a flimsy black *négligée*."

"I dropped the towel and told her, 'Take a look at what readers of *Cosmo* didn't get to see.'"

As he later recalled, "That night showed me how different sex can be when your heart is full of real love, and your body aches for life to be full."

As Burt told Dick Clayton, "We have passion between us, and Dinah's very vivacious. I think I fulfill her sexually and she does satisfy my lusty self. The difference in our ages doesn't matter to me. As you know, I've long had this thing for older women, without overlooking the young ones, too. She's my ideal Southern belle. We're both athletic, especially in golf and tennis."

"I called my father, Big Burt, to tell him I was going steady with a jock. He said, 'I knew Hollywood would turn you into a queer.' I had to explain to him that this jock was Dinah Shore, who, as it happens, is his favorite singer."

Once Dinah started dating Burt—more than dating, actually—the duo became tabloid fodder, the press calling them a May-December romance. According to Dinah, "Those guys could have been more flattering to me, labeling it May-September. After all, I'm hardly in the winter of my life."

Burt did not collaborate with any of the publicity whirling around them. "Our bond is too precious to exploit. We spend most of our evenings in private, with me enjoying her great cooking. We talk, we listen to music, and we have a lot of friends. Chief among them is Frank Sinatra."

"Dinah cooked not only on her show, but for our guests. She was the best and tempted me with all these Southern dishes—especially my favorite dessert: pecan pie. We entertained Jack and Mary Benny, George Burns (who didn't like me at first) and Gracie Allen—even Mel Tormé and Groucho Marx."

"Ella Fitzgerald often came to visit when she was in town, and she and Dinah stayed up one night singing until dawn broke, a private concert just for yours truly."

George Montgomery was asked for his opinion about his ex-wife's new love. "I'm very happy she's found a wonderful man. If Burt makes her happy, then I'm happy for her." Then he went on to claim that he had recently been invited to pose for a nude centerfold in *Playgirl*, and that he had turned it down.

George Montgomery in *Riders of the Purple Sage* (1941).

Before Burt, Dinah Shore set out to snare this ruggedly handsome bundle of macho charm, although she had to eliminate Hedy Lamarr.

According to Dinah, "I'm aware of what Burt expects of me as a woman, and my Southern heritage helps me in that regard. We're both bundles of energy during the day but prefer quiet evenings. We're not part of the party circuit, although we're showered with invitations."

"Burt is a bundle of macho charm, but when the sun sets, he's actually a vulnerable, sensitive man."

As for Burt, when he spoke about Dinah, he said, "She and I have made a pact. We're going to make the most of our relationship while it lasts. Perhaps it won't go on forever. Who knows? If forever is in the cards, how terrific that would be for me."

As she confessed, Dinah was never a women's libber: "It's a man's world and may always be that way. Right now, there is a very special man in my life, and his name is Burt Reynolds. He makes my decisions for me. I say to myself, 'Dinah, you're one lucky girl.'"

Jokingly, when they started going together, she told friends, "We were computer-mated. The attraction was immediate when he came onto my show. He's Aquarius, I'm Pisces."

She even went so far as to add another room to her mansion, painting it in earth colors and allowing him to move "all his cowboy junk" into it.

Not only that, but after her first visit to Jupiter, in Florida, she told him, "Burt, you've got to add a tennis court"—and he did.

She admitted to being mildly shocked by the nude *Cosmo* layout. "I don't believe in exhibitionism, and I was worried that such exposure would damage his career as a serious actor. I even feared damage to my own career, since he was my boyfriend. Over my objections, he went ahead and posed anyway. But when he showed me the proofs, I laughed. It was not distasteful. It was just one big put-on, a send-up to Hugh Hefner at *Playboy*."

When Burt was asked if he planned to marry Dinah, he said, "I believe in marriage as much as I believe in the tooth fairy."

***

When Burt opted to move in with Dinah, he knew that the time had come to end his relationship with Miko Mayama. She's been living alone in his home. Occasionally, he'd drop in, and no mention was made of his affair with Dinah. She told a friend or two, "He'll get it out of his system and come back to me—I just know it."

He'd cheated on her before, and he figured that she must have known about it, but she had never confronted him about his outside liaisons.

He'd even bragged about his womanizing on the *Tonight* Show. "I fool around, I chase girls, I chase life. I pick up all the options. That's what it's all about, isn't it?"

He would always remember his final hour with Miko, as relayed through Dick Clayton. He'd been fairly content living with her as "an unmarried man and wife" [*his words*]. When he arrived for his farewell to her, he was slightly embarrassed to see that she'd prepared a rather elaborate Japanese dinner for him. He had absolutely no appetite, and he didn't want to prolong his time with her.

At his invitation, she sat across from him in the living room. "The look on her face told me that she knew some bad news was coming."

"We've got to end it," he said. "I've fallen deeply in love with another woman. I can't go on without her. It can't be kept secret. She's famous and I'm sure that the tabloid vultures will get onto it."

He had anticipated that she might become hysterical, denouncing him with all sorts of accusations. But, as he later said, "Miko handled it with her customary Asian grace—that was the kind of woman she was. There wasn't one trace of emotion in her face as I fed her the news. She said nothing at first, just looking at me with sad eyes. No tears. No arguments. She didn't make any last minute attempt to hold onto me, and she didn't show the slightest bit of jealousy about this other woman."

In the early 1970s, palimony suits were virtually unknown. Although she got an occasional gig in a film or on TV, Burt knew that Miko would need extra cash. At first, he offered to pay her fare back to Tokyo, but she wanted to remain in California.

He asked her what he could do to help her and was rather shocked at how quickly she answered: "I want an apartment on the beach, a Cadillac convertible, and five-hundred dollars a week for two years."

He mulled that over, deciding that he could afford it, though it might be a strain on his budget, especially because of his expenses in Jupiter. But after a brief delay, he agreed to her terms.

He rose to his feet, telling her that one of Dick Clayton's assistants would come for his personal possessions. He allowed her to continue living in his house until he found her an apartment on the beach, perhaps in Malibu.

"She cashed every one of those $500 weekly checks, even the final one that came two years later. The following day, when the money spigot ran dry, I heard that she'd married Barbra Streisand's business manager."

From time to time, he heard about her, including news that she'd given birth to a son.

Her marriage didn't last, and she filed for divorce, reportedly receiving a lot of money in its aftermath.

One afternoon, years later in Los Angeles, Burt, in his Mercedes and Miko in a Rolls-Royce, stopped side by side on a double lane for a traffic light. He remembered her as elegantly dressed and with wraparound sunglasses.

"We eyed each other for a moment and waved weakly," he said.

Then she called out to him, "What's up, Doc?"

When the light changed, she stepped on the accelerator and sped off heading north along Sunset Boulevard.

That was the last time he ever saw her.

***

Two weeks before Burt was scheduled to host the *Tonight* Show, he met with its producer, Fred de Cordova, who wanted to know which guests Burt wanted to interview. De Cordova was surprised when Burt came up with the name of his divorced wife, Judy Carne, who he hadn't seen in the six years since their divorce.

During that time, Carne had become famous for her appearances on *Rowan & Martin's Laugh-In* (1968-70). Her most popular (and oft-repeated) routines ended with her saying "Sock it to me!" and then being almost instantly drenched with water or assaulted in some way.

Eventually, she decided that the show was "one big, bloody bore," and dropped out, except for an occasional guest appearance.

When Burt reunited with her on *Tonight*, she had already starred on Broadway in a 1970 revival of the musical, *The Boy Friend.* [*Earlier productions had been hugely successful in London in 1953 and on Broadway (starring Julie Andrews) in 1954.*]

Carne had married producer Robert Bergman the same year (1970), but their union by now was disintegrating.

She later reported that she was shocked that Burt wanted her to be a guest on his show. De Cordova instructed that her former husband did not want to see her before the show, preferring instead to stage their reunion in front of million of viewers. "I was terrified and excited at the same time," she said.

On the evening of her appearance, she strode out, admitting, "I was mesmerized by the sight of Burt. He looked more attractive than when I was married to him."

He warmly embraced her before she took her seat. As she sat down, she said, "God, you look good."

"I'm sorry to say, so do you."

"What are you doing now?" she asked.

"Oh, nothing much," he answered. "Just selling old Burt & Judy towels on the street corner. They're hard to move."

As he recalled, "Our show was like watching a high school football captain at a reunion with his former girlfriend, the lead cheerleader."

[*To understand the other questions and answers that followed (they're laid out below), one must know that at the time of their reunion, Burt had already posed*] *nude for* Cosmo *and was engrossed in his affair with Dinah Shore.]*

"Have you seen my centerfold?" he asked.

"Of course," she said. "Who hasn't?"

"I think it's terrific, but it's missing your best feature." Then she paused as a hush came over the audience. The crowd was obviously thinking that this was a reference to his penis.

After a pause, she blurted out in a Cockney accent, "YOUR ARSE!"

The audience burst into laughter. "It's true," she said. "This guy has the most divine little arse. In fact, Burt, I've been getting all these calls from people who want to know what's underneath your hand in that nude layout."

"Arm!" he said, correcting her.

"Hand!" she countered.

"ARM!" he said, more defiantly.

Finally concluding the debate, she said, "HAND!"

[Based on this exchange, De Cordova was getting nervous, so he quickly signaled for a commercial.]

Back on the air, with the cameras rolling again, Burt asked Carne, "Are you seeing anyone?"

"That I am," she said.

"A younger guy, I suppose," he said.

"Well, yes. Actually, I hear you've gone older," making an obvious reference to his affair with Dinah Shore.

Her reference to Dinah's age drew boos from the audience. Burt moved quickly to rescue her. "Not older, classier."

The audience applauded him, and Carne later admitted, "I knew I had made a boo-boo. "I'm sorry," she said. "That wasn't nice. I really admire her. I was just going for the joke."

"Some things are sacred," he later claimed. "Mom, apple pie, the American flag, Dinah Shore."

"You love Dinah, don't you?" he asked.

"Yes, I love her," Carne replied.

"You own all her records, don't you?" he asked.

"Yes," she answered.

"You're lying. But that's okay. The crowd still loves you too."

Then he turned to the audience, its members applauding.

He later described the show in an interview he delivered to *Playboy's* Hugh Hefner and a reporter:

"Judy and I were on for more than half an hour together, and it was explosive, frightening, and beautiful. She cried, and laughed and made me *laugh, and it was just fabulous.*

The audience loved her and wanted us to get back together…A lot had happened to me in the six years since we'd been divorced. I'd grown up. I'd gotten a lot of confidence, and I'd become an adult, so I told her all that, and said, 'You know, whatever problems we had, the divorce was my fault.'"

"She said, 'No, it was my fault.' And all of a sudden, we were going back and forth about whose fault our divorce was. We forgot where we were, and it was very funny."

After the show, Burt, De Cordova, and some of the crew gathered at Sardi's. Judy's parents, Harold and Kathy Botterill, were in New York at the time, and Burt greeted them warmly.

He told Carne, "Dinah's been great for me, and I love her dearly. We have quiet evenings with friends like Jimmy Stewart and his wife. Frank Sinatra drops in regularly. I know you and I lead different lives and follow different career paths, but I still feel we have a special bond."

He bid her parents goodbye, saying, "I'd better go before I fall in love with your daughter all over again."

After a farewell kiss, he then walked out of Carne's life forever.

In the years ahead, and still from a distance, he watched as Judy's life deteriorated. He read that in 1978, she was found guilty of heroin possession and was involved in a car accident that broke her neck. She continued her addiction to heroin and was arrested once again.

In 1985, Burt read her autobiography, *Laughing on the Outside, Crying on the Inside, the Bittersweet Saga of the Sock-It-To-Me Girl.* In her confessional, she wrote about her struggles as a druggie, her failed marriage to Burt, and her bisexuality.

In the 1980s, she left the United States, returning to England where she settled in the little village of Pitsford in Northamptonshire. There, she lived quietly and mod-

MEMORIES, PERHAPS WITH REGRETS

Judy Carne and Burt Reynolds in 1964, shortly after their wedding.

This cozy, intimate portrait of two young people in love was featured in Judy's autobiography.

314

estly until September of 2015, when she died at the age of seventy-six.

***

After his first stint as a guest host on Johnny Carson's *Tonight* Show, Burt flew back to Los Angeles, where an urgent message was waiting for him. It was from director John Boorman, who wanted to set up an appointment with him the following day in his office at Warner Brothers.

Burt thought he knew why Boorman wanted to meet with him. He'd read in *Variety* that the director had acquired the rights to the James Dickey novel, *Deliverance*. Burt had already read it and also some of Dickey's poetry. Born in Georgia, Dickey had been named Poet Laureate of the United States in 1966, and wrote *Deliverance* in 1970.

An unusual departure from his usual style, it's the tragic saga of four mild, middle-class men from suburban Atlanta who embark on a dangerous canoe trip through the isolated northeastern corner of Georgia. Wild and savage, the river itself will soon disappear beneath the waters of a newly formed lake, the by-product of a recently installed hydro-electric dam. As it turns out, it isn't just the unexplored backwoods they'll have to conquer, but a cabal of sinister mountain men, who will menace their lives.

As critic Dwight Garner wrote, "Before the story is over, the carnage is nearly complete: Three men have been crudely buried, one has been raped, and the survivors have had the bark peeled from their modern sensibilities."

Put another way, the Atlanta men in the movie meet real monsters and recognize their ability to become, in Dickey's phrase, "counter-monsters."

The novel became a bestseller in 1970 as Americans were also reading *Love Story, The Godfather,* and *The French Lieutenant's Woman.*

Burt was fully aware that he wasn't the first choice as the film's focal point. Months before, *Variety* had announced casting that was spearheaded by Burt's nemesis, Marlon Brando, and supplemented with James Stewart and Henry Fonda. But Stewart and Fonda each dropped out after realizing how strenuous the action would be.

Then, when Brando also dropped out, Lee Marvin was offered the male lead, but had another commitment. Then Boorman thought of

"I was enthralled by the James Dickey novel, *Deliverance,*" Burt said. "But when I met the author, I found him to be a braggart and a total shit."

315

Jack Nicholson and Robert Redford, but they weren't available. Then Gene Hackman and Charlton Heston phoned, each offering their services, but Boorman didn't think they were right for the part.

Burt found it odd that an English director like Boorman would feel at home directing an adventure set in the bowels of redneck Georgia. Most of what he knew about Boorman came from his close friend, Lee Marvin, who told him that the director had gravitated to Hollywood to make films with larger budgets. He'd already helmed Marvin in *Point Blank* (1967), based on the Richard Stark novel. It brought a stranger's vision to the decaying fortress of Alcatraz and the proto-hippy world of the West Coast. Marvin had nothing but praise for Boorman, which he shared with Burt.

[Boorman had also worked with Lee Marvin during the filming of Hell in the Pacific *(1968), a fable of two soldiers stranded together on an island. Burt had not seen it but had read that Boorman had received a Best Director Award at Cannes for his latest film,* Leo the Lost *(1970), which had displayed some influence from Fellini. It had starred Marcello Mastroianni, who had befriended Burt in Rome.]*

MIDNIGHT COWBOY

Meeting with Boorman, Burt pointedly asked him which of his previous films led him to cast him in the lead of *Deliverance.*

He was surprised when Boorman told him that he hadn't seen any of his movies. "But I decided you'd be ideal as Lewis after watching you host *The Tonight Show.* There were six guests, and you were in firm control all night, maneuvering your way through them. This kind of control is needed for the character of Lewis, who takes command of his party, finding a strength of character he didn't know he possessed."

"But there may be just one problem," Boorman continued. "Can you imitate a Southern accent?"

Burt laughed before switching into his good ol' boy drawl. "I grew up in Florida wrestling alligators in the Ever-

Brenda Vaccaro (a "client") with Jon Voight (her gigolo) in *Midnight Cowboy* (1969).

According to Voight, "Hustling ain't fun, and hustling ain't easy."

glades and hot-roddin' it down country roads. Have you made your choice of the actor who'll play my best friend, Ed?" Burt asked.

"Indeed, I have," Boorman answered, rising to his feet and opening the door leading into the next room. "Meet Jon Voight."

Voight had only recently completed his own breakthrough performance in *Midnight Cowboy* (1969) playing Joe Buck, a hustler from Texas who arrives in Times Square to sell his body to the sexually deprived women of New York City.

[After the release of that movie, both Voight and his co-star, Dustin Hoffman [as Ratso], had been nominated for Oscars, although they'd lost to John Wayne for True Grit. Midnight Cowboy, *however, would win as Best Picture of the Year, the first X-rated film to ever do so.]*

"Talk about becoming the best of friends," Burt said. "In no time at all, Jon and I were jabbering like old pals. We did an improvisation for Boorman's inspection and we clicked. The chemistry between us was obvious. When we finished, Boorman told both of us that we had the roles."

"At first, I feared that a talented guy like Jon would blow me right off the screen, but I dug him," Burt said, "especially after he assured me that *Deliverance* would do for me what *Midnight Cowboy* had done for him. I felt, rightly or wrongly, that this picture was *it* for me, the one I'd waited for for so long."

Dinah wanted to clear her busy schedule and fly to Atlanta with Burt and then motor to Georgia's northeast corridor. But he didn't think that was wise. Burt also let Carson know that if he needed him to host his show, that he'd return to Manhattan for a taping.

With Burt already cast as Lewis, and Voight as Ed Gentry, there remained the problem of who would play Bobby and Drew, their mild-mannered, placid friends from Atlanta, who would go on the river adventure with them.

Boorman, with Burt and Voight, flew to Washington, D.C. to see Ned Beatty and Ronny Cox perform in *Pueblo Incident*. Later, the director and his two already committed stars went backstage, and the trio raved about the performance of the two less famous actors. Boorman then offered them the supporting roles.

Much of the action in *Deliverance* would take place along Georgia's Chattooga River, fifty miles of treacherous white water that turns and twists as it hurdles down the southern tier of the Great Smoky Mountains.

The cast and crew were transported in vans to the small backwater town of Clayton, Georgia (population, 1,000).

Voight and Burt were relieved to find that they would be living luxuriously in cottages on the grounds of the exclusive Kingwood Country Club, with its manicured grounds and golf course.

The setting was in Rabun County, known as "the home of the nine-fingered people." That name derived from its unfortunate record, over many generations, of farming accidents, industrial accidents, hunting accidents, and poor medical facilities to treat them.

Burt, in the role of Lewis Medlock, proclaims, "This is man's last chance to see an untamed, unpolluted, and un-fucked river in the South before it becomes a dam and a tranquil lake."

According to Burt, "The character of Lewis held a certain fascination for me. I got off killing a guy to save another man. It was orgasmic. I also felt at its root core that my relationship with Jon was essentially homosexual. Let's face it: Many macho men are secretly attracted to other virile men, even if they don't do anything about it sexually other than hang together."

Burt learned that Warners didn't have high hopes for the movie and had allocated only $1.8 million to film it. He was usually paid more for his work, but the budget called for him to make only $50,000 for three month's work.

He learned that Voight—because of his Oscar nomination—would get top billing and that he'd be paid more, too. Much of the budget would be spent on U.S. Navy rafts, ropes, pulleys, and waterproof camera equipment, plus various other filmmaking aids and props.

The actors had to undergo advanced training in firing a bow and arrow and shooting whitewater rapids. Voight had to learn to scale a cliff that towered two-hundred feet, and at one point, he nearly fell to his death when his footing slipped.

Ned Beatty, a native of Kentucky, made his film debut in *Deliverance*. He'd go on to appear in some 160 other movies. He'd eventually get nominated for an Oscar for his performance in *Network* (1976), where he portrayed a TV network's bombastic but shrewd chairman.

In *Deliverance*, Beatty would perform one of the most controversial movie scenes of the 1970s. As Bobby Trippe, his character is forced to strip at gunpoint by mountain men who humiliate him by raping him and forcing him to squeal like a hog.

[That same year, Beatty also starred in The Life and Times of Judge Roy Bean (1972), a Western with Paul Newman.]

Also making his film debut as the fourth man from Atlanta was Ronny Cox, a singer/songwriter whose output he described as "folk, western, jazzy-bluesy, and just plain cornball stuff." Cox would go on to co-star in two TV movie and TV series franchises, *Beverly Hills Cop* and *RoboCop*.

Cox later described his involvement in *Deliverance* in his autobiography, *Adventures of a Suburban Boy*. In it, he said, "When you look at the film today, you see the incredible artistic choices that John Boorman made—the way in which it was shot is both naturalistic and surrealistic. You under-

318

stand the metaphor of the rape of Bobby and the raping of the land and river."

In an unusual but effective casting decision, Boorman cast James Dickey [author of the novel on which the film was based] as the sheriff who appears at the end of the movie.

When Burt met him, the writer was astonished to learn that a Hollywood actor had actually read some of his poetry.

Burt described him as "a kind of down-home Hemingway. After a few drinks, I wanted to drop a grenade down the throat of this blowhard. The guy was a big, wild-eyed bear. He made up tall tales about his background, all of which were lies."

Voight had attracted a new, much-expanded fan base since the release of *Midnight Cowboy*. News of his arrival with Burt in Georgia spread throughout the state, and many women drove to Clayton to try to get their hands on them, erotically. Although word had spread that Burt had posed nude for *Cosmo*, when he filmed *Deliverance*, his centerfold had not yet been published.

"Many women, and a lot of gay men, heard that I was showing the world the family jewels" [Burt's words.] Women hung out in front of Burt's dressing room, and parked their cars in the driveway of his cottage, waiting for him to come out. One woman [an alleged winner of the Miss Georgia contest three to five years previously] pounded on his door yelling, "C'mon out and get it, honey!"

During a phone call from Georgia, Burt told Dinah, "Maybe you should have come down here to fight all these horny Southern magnolias who want a piece of me."

The roles of the two hillbilly rapists required special casting. Burt remembered a beat-up actor who might be suitable, someone he'd met and performed stunts with years before. He was Herbert ("Cowboy") Coward, who was now working at a battered Wild West-themed amusement park (Ghost Town) in Maggie Valley, North Carolina, near Asheville.

Boorman sent for him. The moment he arrived for his interview the director knew he'd be ideal as a toothless, psychotic hillbilly.

Boorman had to ask

Though it shocked and horrified almost everyone who saw it, the rape scene was later justified by the film's producers as a device that engaged men into thinking about the after-effects of sexual assault.

him, "Are you okay performing in a scene where you have to rape another man?"

"Shit, yes!" Cowboy answered. "I've done far worse things than that."

The other hillbilly role went to Bill McKinney, a redneck from Chattanooga. *Deliverance* would be his breakthrough role. His reckless screen persona and villainy would in time attract such A-list directors as John Huston and Stanley Kubrick. Burt later brought him to the attention of Clint Eastwood, who employed him in several of his films, too.

Herbert "Cowboy" Coward played the dentally challenged rapist-degenerate.

Burt remembered him as a risk-taking Hollywood stuntman with a death wish.

"Bill was a little bit bent...more than a little," Burt said. "One day I rose early and looked out the window of my cottage, watching him run nude on the golf course when the sprinklers were turned on."

"On the day of the rape scene, I saw him eying Ned with lust in his eyes. He'd studied Method acting, but I feared he was carrying the Method too far."

Bill invented and improvised the now-famous line, "Squeal, piggy, piggy," during the rape scene.

Burt said, "I swear to God, but Bill actually produced an erection on camera and tried to penetrate Ned. It was all up and raging at full mast. I ran into the scene and pulled Bill off helpless Ned, who was crying from rage and fear. Ned grabbed a big stick and started beating Bill on the head for violating his maidenhead. The crew separated the two guys."

"The die was cast for Bill. In the years ahead, he became the leading sicko in movies. I had a nickname for him: Butt Plugger."

During the shoot, at least three members of the crew came close to losing their lives, performing reckless stunts on camera. Actually, the most hazardous scene was performed by Burt himself. The script called for his character of Lewis to be propelled down the raging whitewater and over the most treacherous waterfall in Georgia. Burt arrived at the set to watch Boorman film it with a dummy, nicknamed "No Balls" by the crew.

"It looked like shit, so I persuaded Boorman to let me perform it, although I had a fear I might drown and my part might have to be reshot with James Caan."

During the shoot, Burt almost died after the raging waters swept him down a vertical drop of ninety feet.

In one of his most vivid descriptions, he recalled what happened: "I heard this terrifying sound, as a hydroelectric dam about four miles upriver released its water. I looked up as an ocean was coming down on my head, slamming me against a boulder that cracked my tailbone."

This is the weekend they didn't play golf.

Deliverance

He surfaced once and literally filled his lungs before making the plunge again. "I did an involuntary triple axel, landing on my head, which gave me a concussion."

He was swallowed up by an underwater whirlpool that, in his words, "spun me around like a cement mixer."

He remembered stuntman Hal Needham's advice years before, so he swam to the bottom of the whirlpool and then launched himself upward like a torpedo from a ship. He surfaced about one-hundred yards downstream, where he staggered out of the river completely naked. The whirlpool had ripped off all of his clothing.

He was immediately rushed to a hospital in the little town's only ambulance. Boorman visited him later that night. "How did it look?" Burt asked.

"Like a dummy going over the falls," the director answered.

***

After *Deliverance* was released, many daredevils headed for Rabun County to attempt a replica of Burt's underwater achievements as filmed in the movie. It was reported that over the course of several months, some twenty men lost their lives.

Although the film was wildly popular in other parts of Georgia, it offended locals because of its depiction of "hillbillies inbred to the point of idiocy."

When the reviews came in, nearly all of them were favorable. *Time* magazine asserted, "The movie is Burt Reynold's personal deliverance, as overnight he has zoomed up to become the Frog and Prince of Hollywood."

"Burt Reynolds is a hidden iceberg that breaks out like gangbusters," proclaimed *After Dark*.

The Boston Herald stated, "Reynolds displays the proper balance of muscle and overstated courage."

The Shreveport Times called his performance as Lewis "unflinchingly portrayed."

Cosmopolitan proclaimed, "Burt Reynolds has that old Clark Gable sardonic quality, and is superb in this outing as a machine-ridden jock who thinks life is a game."

Arthur Knight of *Saturday Review* wrote: "Even before the opening titles have cleared the screen, while we are still watching two cars, canoes atop, penetrating unpaved mountain roads through dark, foreboding forests, the film starts to take effect. The bulldozers are already at work, readying ground for a dam that will transform this forest primeval into a placid lake."

Of all the major critics, Roger Ebert cast the most sour note: "The scenes of violence and rape work, although in a disgusting way. The appeal to latent sadism is so crudely made that the audience is embarrassed. Reynolds and Voight are fine-tuned and very good. What the movie totally fails at, however, is its attempt to make some kind of significant statement about the action."

"James Dickey has given us a fantasy about violence, not a realistic consideration of it. It's possible to consider civilized men in a confrontation with the wilderness without throwing in rapes, cowboy-and-Indian stunts, and pure exploitative sensationalism."

Burt's centerfold in *Cosmo* had still not been published. He felt that word of his posing nude would work against his being taken seriously as an actor. In reviews of the movie, many critics brought up the nude *Cosmo* spread.

"After my long climb, rung by rung, up the latter of stardom, I felt I was being knocked down a few rungs. But I wasn't giving up. I vowed I'd keep trying and come up with a picture in which I would take home the gold. I had the determination of a prizefighter who got whooped but agrees to get back in the ring on another day and slug it out."

His only fear was that he was on the road to forty. "My god," he said. "That's middle age, isn't it?"

Burt had hoped he'd be nominated for a Best Actor Oscar that year and was disappointed that he was not. "*Deliverance* was my best role and my best alltime performance. It's a picture that picks you up and crashes you against one of those Georgia boulders. You feel everything and just crawl out of the theater. It was beautifully cast and fabulously directed. Vilmos Zsigmond, the cinematographer, wasn't nominated for an Oscar— a great example of how stupid the Academy of Motion Picture Arts and Sciences can be."

Although both Burt and Voight were ignored at Oscar time, *Deliverance* was nominated for three Academy Awards. Boorman was cited for Best Director, losing to Bob Fosse for *Cabaret*. Tom Priestly was nominated for Best Film Editing, losing to David Bretherton, also for *Cabaret*. For the biggest prize of all, Best Picture of the Year, *Deliverance* competed with *The Godfather,* but lost.

During the making of the movie, Boorman was never disappointed with Burt in his performances. He became upset with him only after the movie was wrapped and he approached Burt with a proposal to cast him as the lead of his next film.

He visited Burt at his home and read to hm the script of *Zardoz,* a post-apocalypic sci-fi film set in the 23rd Century and eventually released in 1973. Burt rejected the role, but Sean Connery went for it.

***

After *Deliverance,* Burt wanted to wind down from all the tension, danger, and exhaustion it had caused him.

He accepted an offer from Woody Allen to appear in an episode of his latest film, *Everything You Wanted to Know About Sex (*But were Afraid to Ask).* Scheduled for a 1972 release, it consisted of seven short sequences inspired by Dr. David Reuben's bestseller with the same title.

Among the questions one might be afraid to ask were issues associated with sodomy, cross-dressing, bestiality (with a sheep), perversions, sexual experiments, and the functioning of the body during intercourse.

The episodes depicted such mini-dramas as "What Is Sodomy?", "Are Transvestites Homosexuals?", and "Do Some Women Have Trouble Reaching Orgasm?"

"Woody cast Tony Randall and me as sperm in a sequence entitled 'What Happens During Ejaculation?'" Burt said. "At no point during filming did Woody even speak to us. Tony and I had to wing it."

Burt was filmed as a switchboard operator, and he and Randall run an arms control room governing a man's body as he has sex with a date.

At the climax, white-uniformed "sperm," one of whom is portrayed by Allen himself, are dispatched, paratrooper-style, into Outer Space.

The movie was successful, in spite of many critical assaults. It generated some $25 million, having been made for a budget of only $2 million. Critic Christopher Null cited it as "a minor classic and Woody Allen's most absurd film."

***

323

Decades later, in his evaluation of key moments and the pivotal decades of his life, Burt consistently recognized *Deliverance* as a watershed, and so did many of his fans.

Jon Voight later wrote, "The extent of Burt's talent has not been recognized before *Deliverance*. My recognition had already come with *Midnight Cowboy*. His performance in the plum role of Lewis Medlock would expose his enormous talent to the world and change his career forever."

Scenes from *Deliverance* which Burt considered "My alltime greatest role, even if the dummies who award Oscars didn't get it right that year."

In the lower right-hand photo, Jon Voight, Burt on crutches, and Ned Beatty look on as a corpse is exposed. On that photo's far right is John Dickey himself, the author of *Deliverance*, who also played Sheriff Bullard in the epic drama.

CHAPTER NINE

DYAN CANNON
IN *SHAMUS*, SHE TRIES TO RECREATE, WITH BURT, THE GLORY DAYS OF
BOGIE AND BACALL

MAMIE VAN DOREN
"I ALWAYS THOUGHT OF MYSELF AS THE MALE VERSION OF YOU"
—*Burt to the blonde wannabe clone of Marilyn Monroe
before their mutual seduction*

JOHN WAYNE
ULTRA-CONSERVATIVE AND UNFUNNY, THE VINTAGE FILMSTER
"HYPERVENTILATES" ABOUT SEX, THE MOVIES,
WOMEN AS "VULGARITIES," AND "FAG-DOM."

THE MAN WHO LOVED CAT DANCING
SARAH MILES IS IMPLICATED WITH BURT IN A SUSPICIOUS DEATH.
WAS IT MURDER?

FAN MAIL
AFTER POSING BARE-ASSED FOR THOUSANDS OF HORNY FANS
OUR HERO PUBLISHES THEIR MOST INDISCREET LETTERS

WHITE LIGHTNING
CHASING CARS IN THE COON DOG SOUTH,
IT'S THE FIRST OF BURT'S "MOONSHINE MELODRAMAS"

*GOOD OL' BOYS AND DIXIE DARLINGS IN CUTOFF JEANS
SPAWN A RASH OF SPIN-OFFS*

SOMEONE'S IN THE KITCHEN WITH DINAH
BURT DENIES HE'S HER GIGOLO

LOVE & FORTUNE

Burt's Celebrity Everything

After *Deliverance*, Burt entered filmdom's Hall of Glory, reigning as a box office champion. In 1973, he became number four on the list of the top ten movie stars of the United States.

Basking in the adoration of his die-hard fans, he would remain among American's top ten contenders until 1984, when his box office began to fade.

Regrettably, he followed *Deliverance* with films that were less memorable, with fewer acting challenges, less dramatic meat, and a higher risk of typecasting him into the same "good ol boy" character roles.

White Lightning (1973) set the theme for a series, many with sequels, of "redneck flicks"—lampoons of the Deep South and good ol' Southern boys. Most of them featured car chases. These were exploited "to the max" in such hits as *W.W. and the Dixie Dancekings* (1975) and *Hooper* (1978).

As phrased by Turner Classic Movies, their themes "traded on some of the most blatant stereotypes of the South, filled with corrupt sheriffs, endless car chases, irascible outlaws, moonshine, and sexy Daisy Duke-class young beauties. Their popularity lay in their comic tone, playing *clichéd* elements cartoonishly—and with Burt's self-mocking machismo."

***

Set for a 1973 release by Columbia, *Shamus* was Burt's biggest film offer since *Deliverance*. Once again, he would be cast as a detective, this time as Shamus McCoy.

His leading lady would be the luscious Dyan Cannon, known for her curly blonde tresses and her marriage to the bisexual actor, Cary Grant (1965-'68).

Burt had recently seen her in *Bob & Carol & Ted & Alice* (1969).

326

"With Burt and Dyan, I hope to bring back the glory days of Bogie and Bacall," said producer Robert M. Weitman. Years before, in the 1960s, he'd offered Burt a key role in a TV series, *The Lieutenant*, but Burt had rejected it.

"I liked Burt's screen persona," Weitman claimed. "He's funny. Throws away lines like Kleenex. He is like a hidden iceberg moving toward the *Titanic*."

In the 1960s, Weitman had been a top executive at MGM before becoming independent. He'd worked with Cannon before, casting her opposite Sean Connery in *The Anderson Tapes*.

The director, Buzz Kulik, had wanted Steve McQueen for the role, but had to settle on Burt. [*Coincidentally, Kulik would eventually helm McQueen in his last movie, The Hunters (1980). Decades before, Kulik had been known for his direction of the hit TV series, Playhouse 90 (1956-60).*]

He ordered his scriptwriters to feature at least one scene of Burt in his boxer shorts. "Because the women and gays will want to see him at least semi-nude."

Cannon had seen Burt perform on stage in *The Rainmaker* and was eager to work with him. She'd been in semi-retirement since her divorce from Cary Grant and the failure of Otto Preminger's *Such Good Friends* (1971).

Burt and Cannon bonded during the making of *Shamus*. One of their love scenes depicted her with her tongue hanging out. According to Kulik, "I don't know if they made it with each other or not, but I suspect they did. Even though Dinah Shore was waiting for him at home, Burt had not lost his roving eye."

One afternoon between takes, Cannon told Burt that she had been talked twice into taking LSD with her husband, Cary Grant. "He thought it had some psychological value, but it made me violently ill."

Burt concealed from Dyan that he had known her husband quite well. As he told Kulik, "I didn't want her to know that Cary would have preferred me over her."

Columbia hoped that *Shamus* would bring back the glory days of the private eye depicted in all those films of the 1930s and '40s with Humphrey Bogart or Dick Powell, among others.

FOREPLAY: Dyan Cannon affectionately licks Burt in this publicity photo for *Shamus.*

[In one scene, Shamus evokes The Big Sleep *(1946) starring Bogie with his wife, Lauren Bacall. In that movie, he enters a bookstore to find an attractive blonde, Dorothy Malone, behind the counter. Burt, too, enters a bookstore to find the attractive Kay Frye peddling books.]*

Burt, as Shamus, lives in a bleak walk-up apartment, with his bed resting atop a pool table. His roommate is the famous Morris the Cat, who was known across America for his *9 Lives* commercials. Many fans found that Morris was "the best actor in *Shamus.*"

The movie opens violently as Vincent Pappas and his girlfriend are set on fire with a flame thrower. Aimed at them through a skylight from above, it also sets their building ablaze. Thieves make off with a fortune in diamonds, jumping out the window in flame-proof suits.

As a private eye, Shamus is hired by an icy millionaire, Hume (Ron Weyland), to recover the gems. The plot grows convoluted when he stumbles upon a group of crooks who traffic in stolen government arms.

The film was shot in New York, using locations that included remote dockyards never depicted in films before. One of the most thrilling, though implausible, scenes shows Burt driving an Army vehicle at breakneck speeds through the streets of Manhattan without police interference.

"*Shamus* was not a bad film," Burt claimed. "If the picture had been as good as the title sequence, it would have made big millions. As it turned out, it made five million."

Roger Greenspan in *The New York Times* defined the film as "workmanlike, well-paced, modest, sometimes scary, and sometimes genuinely funny. Reynolds plays it for bemused embarrassment."

A fan said, "*Shamus* is full of violence, sex, and thrills. Reynolds is the Philip Marlowe of the chewing-gum generation."

Alan R. Howard in the *Hollywood Reporter* claimed that "Burt Reynolds and Buzz Kulik turned cartwheels and backflips to give *Shamus* substance and locomotion. Reynolds is no James Bond; he's a real human being who even feels fear. The force of his personality has never been better used in a movie."

***

Mamie Van Doren was one of the trio of blonde goddesses of the 1950s along with the Queen herself, Marilyn Monroe and her clone, Jayne Mansfield. All of them briefly enjoyed their time in the sun.

But whereas Marilyn and Jayne each died prematurely, Mamie endured, even after she faded from the drive-in screens of the 1950s.

The bosomy, hot-to-trot platinum blonde cutie emerged from the wilds of South Dakota to dazzle Hollywood. She drifted from one campy picture after another; *Francis Joins the WACS* (1950); *Running Wild* (1955); *Untamed Youth* (1957), and *Sex Kittens Go to College* (1960).

In 1987, she wrote her autobiography, *Playing the Field*. Coming (no pun intended) and going from her boudoir were a string of famous men: Steve McQueen; the football great, Joe Namath; bandleader Ray Anthony (whom she'd marry); Rock Hudson (premature ejaculation); baseball star Bo Belinsky; and even Johnny Carson.

She attracted the roving eyes of her former co-star, Clark Gable, as well as Warren Beatty, Frank Sinatra, and the aviator/film producer Howard Hughes. To that list, if a one-night fling counts, can be added Burt Reynolds.

COWGIRLS WEAR WHITE

Mamie Van Doren in *Born Reckless* (1958).

In 1971, Mamie was performing in *Will Success Spoil Rock Hunter?* at the Arlington Dinner Theater in Arlington Heights, Illinois. *[Near Chicago, Burt had previously starred there in* The Rainmaker.*]* Van Doren had been reluctant to accept the part because her rival, Jayne Mansfield, had previously made her implant on the role in its 1957 film version.

Her co-star in the dinner theater's production was the actor, James Hampton, one of Burt's closest friends. They had met and bonded on the set of *Gunsmoke* in 1963. *[Hampton would also co-star with Burt in three of his upcoming films during the 1970s.]*

"I talked to Burt the other night," Hampton told Mamie. "He's in New York shooting his latest film, *Shamus*. He's dying to meet you."

"Burt Reynolds," she said. "Count me in. I saw his nude layout in *Cosmo*."

That night, Burt phoned her, and they joked and laughed together. Since the din-

Mamie Van Doren a decade later in *Voyage to the Planet of Prehistoric Women* (1968).

A B-list flick popular in drive-in theaters during the Vietnam War, it was about American astronauts on Venus who encounter dangerous monsters and women who sunbathe in seashell brassieres. It's the kind of movie that goes well with marijuana.

329

ner theater's production of *Rock Hunter* was almost over, he asked her to fly to New York to meet with him.

In Manhattan, she checked into the Pierre and phoned his dressing room at the designated time. He agreed to send a studio car to retrieve her at her hotel. It would transport her to Brooklyn, where he was slated to perform a stunt.

She accepted, and within the hour was crossing the Brooklyn Bridge. *[They had agreed, after the completion of his stunt, to have an early dinner together…"and then whatever."]*

When she arrived at the set of *Shamus*, she met Burt for the first time, and they warmly embraced. He had arranged a seat for her with a clear view of the location of his stunt. He told her he'd broken into show-biz as a stuntman.

She waited and waited, growing impatient at how long it took to set up the action scene. "That's the movie business," she sighed. "It's more about waiting around than acting."

She noticed that many members of the crew were ogling her, as she'd worn a very tight-fitting white dress with plunging *décolletage*.

Many of her lovers had already told her that her breasts were "far more delectable" than those of either Jayne or Marilyn Monroe in their heydays.

Reportedly, Mamie responded to that assessment with this: "Both of the breasts of those two have withered in their early graves."

Through a megaphone, the assistant director called for quiet. As silence blanketed the set, Burt could be seen running toward a window of easily breakable glass. As he hit the ground, he bounced up immediately, seemingly unharmed.

The director approved the scene and the crew applauded his daring. Then he rushed over to ask Mamie, "What do you think?"

"Fantastic!" she said, not meaning a word of it.

"That was some real excitement," he said. "I think *Shamus* is going to be a big hit."

"With you starring in it, its success is guaranteed," she said. "You're a big star now. Your love-sick fans will go to see any picture you're in."

After he'd changed into street clothes, they set out for dinner. They were driven to an Italian trattoria in Greenwich Village, where every item on the main course plate seemed covered in a canned tomato sauce.

"I'll say this for Burt," she later said.

One of the dozens of stunts Burt performed in *Shamus*, similar to what so collossally bored Mamie Van Doren in the events leading up to their bizarre one-night stand.

"He has one sense of humor, which he revealed so well on Johnny Carson's *Tonight* Show. I knew Johnny very well, so we talked a lot about him before the conversation switched to both of us being born under the sign of Aquarius."

She later confessed, "He came on real strong. Perhaps it was the third bottle of champagne, but he made an outlandish claim, predicting that our little dinner marked the beginning of a glorious affair."

"Our chance meeting just happens once in a lifetime," he told her.

She found that startling, because he'd only recently said the same thing in a statement given to a magazine reporter. She later labeled much of his talk as bullshit.

After dinner, she accepted his invitation to go with him to the apartment of actress Candice Bergen, where he was staying during his time in New York. He and the actress had become friends long before they would co-star in a picture together.

Like Bergen herself, the apartment was a class act, everything tastefully furnished, as befitted its Park Avenue location.

Burt had held her hand on the elevator and paused with a key at Bergen's door. "He was still cracking jokes like he did on Johnny's show."

Turning the key in its lock, he said, "I have a hunch this is gonna be one of the most memorable nights of both of our lives."

In a "champagne fog," she wandered into the apartment, feeling both tipsy and sleepy.

At this point, in her eyes, he was still Mr. Macho, Mr. Cool. Once seated together on Bergen's sofa, he made a strange confession. "I've never told anybody this, but I have long considered myself the Male Mamie Van Doren."

Van Doren: "He sees himself as me? Whatever was Burt talking about?"

As she later told friends, "What on earth made him think of himself with an image like mine? I tried to picture him in a blonde wig as a drag queen but couldn't stop giggling."

"I've certainly never thought of you that way," she said. "In that *Cosmo* centerfold, no one would mistake you for me. You've got too much body hair."

"You're overlooking some comparisons," he said. "First, you're acclaimed for that quality as I am in the male department. I'm very handsome, and you're very beautiful. I've seen you photographed from the rear. Great ass! As Judy Carne revealed to million on Johnny's show, I, too, have a 'great arse.' We've both posed virtually nude. You've got great tits, and so have I, the male equivalent, of course. Shall I go on?"

"No, stop!" she said. "You've convinced me. But I can never see my image as the female Burt Reynolds."

In the bedroom, as described in detail in Van Doren's very specific memoirs, both of the stars began to undress in front of each other like a slow striptease performed on stage.

"I've seen nearly every bit of your body in *Cosmo*," she said, "except for one vital part." When she said that, he removed his white boxer shorts, letting them fall onto the carpet as her pink panties cascaded to the floor, too. She later said, "A penis should never be judged when it's soft."

Both of them piled into bed together, and he kissed her passionately, nuzzling her neck and fondling her breasts.

As she later wrote, "He began to thrash wildly. Soon his sound and movements betrayed an immediacy. I hoped he wasn't getting ready to blast off so soon. He began to moan, saying '*ohhhhh!*' *Ohhhhh! Juuuuuuud-dddddyyyyyyy!*"

She later assumed that Judy was a reference to Judy Carne.

"At least he didn't say 'Dinah.'"

He lifted himself off her and collapsed onto the mattress beside her, seemingly exhausted after the long day of shooting and the sex.

"Burt…" she said softly. Then, all she heard was the sound of soft snoring.

She waited fifteen minutes and then quietly slid out of bed, gathering up her clothing and dressing in the bathroom. She tiptoed out of the apartment and hailed a taxi on the street for transit back to the Pierre.

Back in Hollywood, she was asked what she thought of Burt's centerfold in *Cosmo*.

"It was an exaggeration," she said. "He didn't need to cover it up with a hat. A cigar would have done nicely."

[*Although it was never printed in* Cosmo, *Burt admitted on* The Tonight Show *that for one photograph, he'd used a hat to cover his genitals.*]

***

In 1973, Burt signed to perform in four specials on TV: *Burt Reynolds at Leavenworth Prison; Burt Reynolds in London; Burt Reynolds in Nashville;* and *Burt Reynolds and the Girls.*

The first show was launched at Leavenworth. Burt invited Dinah as a guest. He came on first, and with every joke the prisoners cheered wildly, as they seemed starved for entertainment. When he brought Dinah out, she got a standing ovation before singing to them. She complimented them on how well the grounds were maintained but said, "I wouldn't want to live here."

Burt and Dinah were supported by Jonathan Winters and the country musician icon, Merle Haggart. The singer told the audience that he'd once been arrested for robbery and that he'd served time in San Quentin.

Burt found Winters "the funniest comedian I've ever encountered, even though he suffered from bipolar disorder."

***

Burt met John ("Duke") Wayne through his long-time friend, stuntman Hal Needham. He had taught Duke how to throw a more realistic punch in *The Undefeated* (1969), and after that, Wayne wanted him to work with him on all his future pictures. Needham suggested that Duke perform what's known as a "roundhouse," which makes a punch look real, although it doesn't actually smash a fist into an opponent.

Burt had stayed overnight at Needham's ranch, and had already had breakfast when Duke pulled up in his latest model Cadillac. A bumper sticker on his car read: "They can have my guns when they pry them loose from my cold dead fingers."

Even though he was around sixty-five years old, he had recently been given a big boost to his career when he won the Oscar for *True Grit* in 1969.

Burt recalled Wayne as "a force of nature. He'd been fairly good-looking when he was younger, but now appeared craggy. He'd lived a tough life, and it showed in his grizzled face."

Even so, Wayne looked fit, as Burt was told by Needham that he had recovered from lung cancer in 1964, beating all odds.

A month before, Burt had met and talked with Kirk Douglas at a party. The actor worked with Duke in 1964 on a picture called *In Harm's Way*, a drama set against the bombing of Pearl Harbor in World War II.

"Duke is the kind of star that really is gone with the wind," Douglas said. "Of course, he's still around, but from an America of long ago. He has the image of tough guy to protect, and he acts the part. He developed this character on the screen, and he

John Wayne (aka The Lonesome Cowboy, aka The Duke) was already a deeply entrenched cult icon by the time he began his dialogues with Burt. Streets had been named in his honor throughout California, and the Alt-Right had already enrolled him as a spokesman for some of their cultural platforms.

has to live up to it."

Ironically, that same appraisal would be expressed about Burt as it related to many of his own screen appearances, especially in the 1970s (i.e., his immediate future).

"I hear you're a red-blooded Cherokee, so why aren't you afraid of me?" Wayne asked Burt. "If you've seen any of my movies, you know I kill Indians."

Wayne and Burt sat and talked for at least four hours as Needham and his wife prepared a late afternoon barbecue. Burt later gave a blow-by-blow report to Dick Clayton on what had transpired that afternoon. He called his introduction to Duke "historic."

"I've been hearing a lot of gay rumors about you, Reynolds," Wayne said. "I'll be blunt: The word is out that you and Jon Voight fucked each other down there in those backwoods of Georgia while you were making *Deliverance*. Is that true? Are you a fag?"

"I'm a red-blooded, all-American heterosexual male," Burt answered, defensively. "I've got a lot of satisfied women who will testify to that."

"Don't be so defensive," Duke said. "I believe you. The fact that you're shacked up with Dinah Shore proves you're straight...Of course, one can never be sure. My main competitor on the screen, Gary Cooper, had a lot of gay experiences in his younger days."

"Don't get me wrong," Duke said. "I have nothing against fags. But I don't find their existence something to jump up in joy about. I can't help but feel it's abnormal. I don't think God put us on this earth to be fags. At least God created women with a purpose—that is, to give us men some pleasure in the sack and to have our children. The one thing I can't forgive God for is making people black. Being colored makes it so much harder for them to get ahead. God could have solved the problem by making them white, and then we wouldn't have all these marches and riots."

"If you work in Hollywood, you've got to get used to fags," Wayne said. "I'd say that on any film crew I work on, half of the guys are gay. They flock to Hollywood, land of make-believe, in droves. In *The Undefeated*, Rock Hudson was my 'leading lady,' so to speak."

"When I made *The Alamo* (1960), Laurence Harvey was my leading lady. Day after day, he begged me. He'd say, 'Duke, please go to bed with me tonight, just this once. I'll be the queen, and you can be my king.' I passed on that damn offer."

"I prefer fucking my leading ladies when they're real women," he said. "I mean like Claire Trevor in *Stagecoach* (1939). The best lay I ever had was Marlene Dietrich when we co-starred in *Pittsburgh* in 1942. What a piece of ass! Have you fucked Joan Crawford yet? There are very few men she's missed."

334

"I seduced her," Burt confessed. "Or rather, she seduced me."

"The same year I fucked Marlene, I made *Reunion in France* with Joan Crawford. I plowed her time and time again in her dressing room. Then the bitch goes and tells the press, 'Take Duke out of the saddle—and you've got nothing.' You can't trust any of these hussies."

"I call all women 'vulgarities…it's my special word for them."

"There was a war going on in 1942, and I was getting plenty. That same year, I made it with Paulette Goddard, Chaplin's former gold-digger, when we made *Reap the Wild Wind.* Like Crawford, the whore had had every man: Clark Gable, Spencer Tracy, Gary Cooper."

"Goddard gave me the weirdest compliment I ever got in my life. She told me I was better in bed than her acting coach, that old dyke, Constance Collier."

***

After the barbecue, Wayne discussed his future projects. At no point during their long day together had the Duke even asked about how Burt's career was going, and he had not seen *Deliverance.* "I'm not going to go see any fucking movie where a man is raped by another man."

He said he'd brought along three copies of a novel he'd read. "Don't look so startled, guys. I read on occasion. But mostly, I hire this guy, Tom Kane, to pour through dozens of manuscripts."

Wayne had presented Needham with a copy of the novel, which, co-incidentally, Burt, the reader of the trio, had already devoured, *The Man Who Loved Cat Dancing,* a Western by Marilyn Durham.

"I can't believe this violent tale was actually written by a woman," the Duke said.

Unknown to Wayne, his story editor, Kane, was already in negotiation for him to star in *Cat Dancing.* In 1972, MGM had acquired the rights, and the Western was being adapted by Eleanor Perry into a screenplay.

Kane read the novel and felt that even though Wayne was aging, it would be a good vehicle for him. Especially since—according to the novel—his character had just been released from a twenty-year prison sentence. He'd killed the man who had raped and murdered his wife, an Indian squaw known as "Cat Dancing."

But when Kane contacted an executive at MGM and hyped Wayne as the star, he was told, "The Duke is too old. We're thinking of casting it with Steve McQueen and Ali McGraw. *[At that time, the couple were married and had recently starred together in The Getaway (1972).]*

"The role calls for a young Humphrey Bogart opposite a young Katharine Hepburn," said producer Richard C. Sarafin. "But Bogie's dead and Hepburn is a dinosaur."

Sarafin finally settled on Burt, accepting him as the right age with the right look for the part. Burt eagerly accepted, but phoned Needham. "I can never face Duke again. He'll think he tipped me off about the novel and that I stole it from him, which is *not* what happened. Do you think he'll come gunning for me?"

"My advice," Needham said facetiously, "is to get out of Dodge. Lay low for a while before daring to show your face in this town again."

Burt was excited to learn that Jane Fonda might be his leading lady. Then he was told that his friend, Candice Bergen, was being considered. *[Although that didn't work out, Bergen would become his leading lady later on.]*

Carol Lynley also wanted the role. She said, "There are two roles every actress in Hollywood wants—that of Daisy in *The Great Gatsby* and that of Catherine Crocker in *The Man Who Loved Cat Dancing*."

A week before the beginning of shooting, Burt was told that Sarah Miles would be his leading lady. Of course, he had no inkling of the scandal that awaited both of them.

*[A few years later, Burt and Wayne would each be considered for the same role in a film—*Beyond the Poseidon Adventure *(1979). Burt received a copy of the script, but rejected it, as did his friend, Clint Eastwood, who called it "a piece of shit."*

Warners was surprised to receive a call from Wayne, who said he wanted the role. But once he read the script and learned that an upside-down wreck of a ship rested on top of a volcano, he turned it down. "All this drama is just too, too much."

Burt finally concluded, "Although I'm sure Duke didn't give a damn for me, he is an inspiration to me, an actor who continued to find roles until his dying day. That's exactly what I plan to do, too."]

***

Marilyn Durham, a housewife from Evansville, Indiana, seemed an unlikely prospect to write a Western novel, *The Man Who Loved Cat Dancing*. She knew little about the West except for what she'd seen of spaghetti Westerns starring Clint Eastwood.

She needed money to pay off the mortgage of her widowed mother's house. In 1970, she sat down at her typewriter and began to churn out what she described as "a big, juicy, and dirty bestseller." Amazingly, it did become a bestseller, *The New York Times* describing it as "beautifully executed."

Before the novel was even published, MGM paid $50,000 for the screen rights, the exact amount they'd shelled out for *Gone With the Wind*.

Eleanor Perry was assigned by producer Martin Poll to write a screenplay. She later called it "the first women's lib Western. I admit my script is female fantasizing. But what else was *Wuthering Heights?*"

That inveterate reader, Burt himself, had read the book because he was immediately drawn to the title. Coincidentally, he had previously named one of his race horses "Cat Dancing" before he'd ever heard of the novel.

Sarafin, the director, and producer Martin Poll lined up a cast of supporting players. They included Lee J. Cobb, George Hamilton, Jack Warden, and Bo Hopkins. The plan was to finish location shooting and have the film ready for a release later in 1973.

As Burt had done before, and would do in the future, he managed to get James Hampton in the film, interpreting the minor role of Jimmy. "Bedding chicks is one thing," Burt said. "But, as we say in the South, a guy needs some asshole buddies to hang out with, too. Jim is that for me. We'd soon be working together again and again."

Burt was eager to work with the English actress, Sarah Miles, whom he'd recently seen in *Ryan's Daughter* (1971), for which she received an Oscar nomination. She was also known for *The Servant* (1960) and *Blowup* (1966).

They met at the Beverly Hills Hotel and were introduced by their director, Sarafan, whom she described as "a fat, sloppy puppy dog of a cigar-smoking cowboy villain."

At the time, Miles was married to the British playwright, Robert Bolt. Burt seemed more impressed with her than she was with him. He described her speaking style as "cut-glass and aristo English."

"Burt had huge lifts on his shoes and an obvious *toupée*," she said. "He was bald as a coot. He was a total nightmare. I don't even want to speak about his dodgy character."

Burt had a very different reaction to her: "She had slept with some of her leading men," he said, "including Laurence Olivier. I was attracted to her. There was sexual chemistry, but I wanted to be faithful to Dinah. I loved Sarah's craziness. The attraction was real basic."

She told him that Robert Mitchum, her co-star in *Ryan's Daughter*, had warned her about him. "Watch your step," he'd said. "It's highly

Lower photo: Sarah Miles with Burt. Their greatest drama would take place off-screen.

337

likely you'll fall in love with the son of a bitch. He's funnier than hell, sweet, and he's gallant with women. But you must know he wears a hairpiece. While making love to him, don't accidentally rip it off. That pisses him off."

"Did Bob tell you about his false teeth?" Burt countered.

***

In *Cat Dancing*, Burt was cast as Jay Grobart, an outlaw once married to Cat Dancing, an Indian squaw who is raped and murdered. Grobart kills the rapist who committed the crime. For that, he serves time in prison. When he's freed, he joins a trio of desperadoes played by Jack Warden, Jay Varela, and Bob Hopkins.

The men rob a train and capture Catherine (Sarah Miles), who's fleeing from her sadistic rancher husband (George Hamilton). He wants her back even though he's aware that she doesn't love him.

One of Burt's favorite character actors, the very talented Lee J. Cobb, was cast as Harvey Lapchance, who leads a posse to hunt down the train robbers.

Despite the fact that she's being held as a captive, Catherine (Miles) in time falls for Burt's character of Jay. A ton of complications are woven into the intricate plot. Jay and Catherine continue their perilous journey, but a desperado named Dawes hunts them down. He rapes Catherine and plans to kill Jay and escape with the train loot. Before he can do that, Jay (Burt) kills him.

Although the novel had included a brutal rape scene, it did not appear in Perry's first film script. The producer (Poll), however, demanded that it be reinstated.

"As I saw it, Catherine Crocker (Miles) was an 1880s heroine, an independent sort of woman, and I thought she could defend herself against being raped," Perry said. "But Poll got his wish, telling me that scenes of rape turn some men on, and that a 'good' rape will stimulate box office."

Most of the film would be shot on location in Gila Bend, Arizona. Midway between Yuma and Phoenix, it was founded in 1872 in Maricopa County, near a bend in the Gila River. A desert trading post, it was

Sarah Miles as an English *equestrienne*, new to the wide open spaces of Britain's former colonies, and new to the charms of American men like Burt.

home to about 1,000 people, most of them "wranglers" (cowboys).

Other locations included Bryce Canyon National Park and sites near the Virgin River and Silver Reef in Utah.

During their first lunch together in Gila Bend, Sarah shocked Burt by telling him that she regularly drank her own urine as a means of fighting the aging process and advised him to do the same. "You're an Indian, and surely you must know that your fellow tribesmen drink their own pee. That's what Gandhi did, and that's what Nero did. That's what everybody does who wants to look fantastic in their old age. It tastes like good beer. You should drink it every evening and in the morning, taking it from the middle part (not the beginning, and not the end) of your urine stream. You just swig it down and watch the wrinkles fade."

During the shoot, the crew faced flash floods, heavy rains, dust storms, and hailstorms. Burt and Sarah would each be injured. Burt was still insisting on performing his own stunts, even though a stand-in had been hired. He had to be rushed to the hospital after a fist fight with actor Jack Warden, cast as Dawes. They had to tumble down the stairs, punching each other on top of a bar, twisting across the floor in a killer embrace, and smashing through a glass window. Burt's hernia burst.

In another scene, Sarah had to fall off a horse. She fell on a rock with a sharp point, and it dug so deep into her knee that it opened the flesh to a view of the bone. She was rushed at once to the hospital for immediate surgery. Regrettably, she had to shoot the scene over again, and the wound on her kneecap split open, ripping out the stiches and forcing another rush to the hospital to have "my wretched knee sewed up again."

During *Cat Dancing*, Burt caught up with George Hamilton, whose exploits he'd been following in the press. They shared memories of Burt's first film, *Angel Baby*, shot in Florida.

Hamilton had a record of being cast as an All-American, oh-so-handsome boy next door. But in *Cat Dancing*, he played an unattractive villain.

He told Burt, "Early in my career, I tried to put value on male characters with manners, breeding, and elegance. Then Brando and James Dean commercialized the appeal of hostile young men in torn shirts and 'upstaged' me." [*Burt noted that when Hamilton's film career diminished in the early 1970s, he revived it by playing—against type—the title role in the 1972 biopic of daredevil Evel Knievel.*]

On the set, Sarah introduced Burt to David Whiting, a writer for *Time* magazine with whom she was having an affair. Neither of them tried to hide their jealousy of the other.

Whiting showed up every day on the set. In marked contrast to everyone else on the set, who wore dusty jeans and sweaty T-shirts, he was immaculate in pin-striped, three-piece suits from London's Savile Row.

Everyone—cast, crew, directors, and stars with their lovers and entourages—stayed at the Travelodge Motel. With Sarah was her five-year-old son, Tom, and his nanny, Jane Evans.

For Burt's 37th birthday celebration, Merv Griffin and some of his crew flew in to tape a segment about the filming of *Cat Dancing*, and to film part of the party being hosted in Burt's honor. At the time, everyone thought it would be a promotional boost for the eventual release of the movie.

George Hamilton: "I like to make my women feel like ladies."

The shindig was held at the Palamino Bar & Restaurant in the neighboring copper-mining town of Ajo. Burt asked Sarah to be his date, and pointedly did not invite Whiting.

Sarah found the party boring—"All they did was gorge on Southwestern cuisine."

Cobb was leaving early, and she asked him to take her back in his new Maserati Citroën, which he drove at 130 miles an hour along the lonely desert highway.

Back at the Travelodge, she was invited by Bob Hopkins to dance with him in the bar. As time went by, he told her that Burt had already returned to his room, and that perhaps she might want to go there and apologize for abandoning him at the party, since she had been his date.

HEEEERE's MERV!

Burt claimed, 'He had the hots for me."

She knocked on Burt's door and found that he was getting a massage from Letsogo, a Japanese-American masseur. Sarah sat and watched, eating an orange as Letsogo "trampled back and forth across Burt's impressive physique while he moaned and grunted."

It's generally assumed that Burt seduced Sarah after the departure of his masseur, since she did not return to her own quarters until 3:15 AM. First, she checked on her son and his nanny, who were lodged in separate quarters, before entering her own bedroom.

Whiting was there, and immediately, he demanded to know where she'd been all night. "If you don't tell the truth, I'll kill you," he threatened. She later reported that he began to pick her up and throw her around the room. The occupants of the room next door heard her screams. As they grew louder, the nanny rushed in from next door to pull him off Sarah. He fled from the motel room. Sarah ended up with one of her fingers broken, a split lip, and two lumps on her head. She later described Whiting's fury as so great, "It made Olivier's *Othello* pale in comparison."

She begged the nanny to call Burt to come and rescue her, which he did within minutes appearing at the door in his boxer shorts. By then, Whiting had disappeared.

After ensuring that her son and the nanny were all right, Burt took Sarah back to his bedroom, and she didn't emerge until eleven the following morning. With trepidation, she returned to her own quarters, not knowing if "David were still lurking there and might cause me harm."

The date was February 11, 1973, a crucial moment in one of the most mysterious deaths in Hollywood history.

In her son's room, she found Tom playing on the carpet and the nanny getting ready to take him outside with her.

But when she entered the bathroom of her own quarters, she almost stumbled over Whiting's body as it lay on the floor. She fled immediately, rescued Tom, and went to find Burt. When he opened the door and discovered her with Tom in her arms, she blurted out, "David's dead!"

Burt rushed to her quarters, where the front door had been left open. He later testified, "Whiting was in a very strange, very awkward position, his arm bent up behind him. There was a plastic pill container in his hand, and red pills were scattered all over the bathroom."

"I don't know why, unless it was something I learned by watching movies, but I felt his pulse, finding it ice cold. I took the pill container out of his hand, like a dummy."

When asked where the container was now, he said, "I didn't read the label. I don't know where it is. I must have lost it somewhere."

The chief of police found Whiting lying in a two-foot-wide pool of blood. It was discovered that he had an inch-wide, star-shaped laceration on the back of his head, as if hit by a blunt object. An examination discovered other cuts and bruises on his body, including his stomach. The indication was that he had been in a violent physical confrontation before swallowing pills. His body was hauled off in an ambulance for an autopsy.

Word spread quickly to Merv Griffin and his crew. Within the hour, the wire services picked up the story. There was wild speculation that Whiting had walked in on Burt and Sarah making love, and that he and Burt had engaged in a fight so violent that he was killed.

That legend still persists to this day.

***

At Gila Bend, reporters claimed that Burt was a prisoner in his own room. He had to hire off-duty policemen as 24-hour-a-day guards to keep people away. It was noted that the telephone at the main desk at the motel rang night and day.

Some members of the press wrote that this was the second suspicious death in which Burt had been implicated, citing the mysterious murder or suicide of Inger Stevens.

There was a certain irony here: At one time, Whiting had also dated Stevens.

To lessen the hysteria, Lee J. Cobb advised Burt to "Get the hell out of town."

Griffin was flying with his crew on to Flagstaff, and he invited Burt to depart with him.

Months before, in Las Vegas, Burt had formed a friendship with singer Wayne Newton. Burt phoned him and asked if he would pick him up at Flagstaff's airport (a drive of about four hours) and haul him back to Las Vegas.

Wayne retrieved him at Flagstaff's airport, then drove with him to Casa de Shenandoah, his 52-acre ranch near Las Vegas, where he bred Arabian horses. Burt could hide out there for as long as he needed. Even Dinah didn't know where he was, although he phoned her daily.

Impulsively, Burt decided he wanted to go to Utah, where Big Burt had grown up as a boy. In his private plane, Newton flew Burt to St. Cloud, where he, in disguise, checked into a remote motel, registering under the name of his business manager, Dick Clayton.

He later claimed that he spent the rest of the day and night in bed, weeping.

MGM lawyers fought hard to keep Sarah and Burt from having to appear at an inquest but lost the battle. Burt had to return to Gila Bend where the judge postponed the inquest for a month to allow the cast and crew to finish filming *Cat Dancing*.

Attorney John Flynn was dispatched by MGM to represent Burt. When he arrived at Gila Bend, he denounced all the "rumors, innuendos, speculation, and false statements."

With Burt, he drafted a statement issued on March 3. "I do not like that I have been put in the position of defending myself when there isn't one single logical reason in the whole world for me to be defensive or to give an explanation. My only personal involvement in the entire situation was the fact that I sheltered for one night a woman who had been badly beaten up by a man, who later took an overdose of pills and killed himself. That is the total extent of my personal involvement."

A day later, MGM released its own statement: "It is terribly sad that a human being's life has ended prematurely. It is equally sad that two people who are alive are having their names and reputations dragged through the mud simply because they happen to be celebrities. MGM has not suppressed any facts and does not know of any facts that have been suppressed."

In the meantime, the local medical examiner of Gila Bend, Dr. Heinz Karnitschnig, claimed that the wounds on Whiting's body had no bearing on his death. No reason was given for the extraordinary amount of blood found at the scene.

Whiting's mother, Mrs. Louise Campbell of New York, flew in, announcing to the press that the investigation by local authorities was too perfunctory because the celebrities involved had been given preferential treatment.

Campbell hired her own pharmacologist, who reported that the drugs in Whiting's bloodstream weren't concentrated enough to have been fatal.

She also demanded to know why her son's pillowcase was bloody, tissues were bloody, and his towel was red with blood. The washbasin was also bloody, as was his pale blue sweater.

Sarah Miles would later compare the inquest at which she appeared to a "bad B movie." The courtroom was overflowing as she entered, having made her way through a horde of reporters, sightseers, and photographers "waiting in ambush outside."

She was wearing clog shoes and a clinging white jersey blouse with a long patchwork skirt. She made the Justice of the Peace, Mulford Winsor, disconcerted. He administered the wrong oath and had to correct himself and restate it. "You're so pretty, you shook me up," he told her.

She, too, found his appearance disconcerting, as he was dressed in a Christmas inspired red suit. When not presiding over the court proceedings of his township, Winsor was the town plumber.

Sarah claimed, "Dear David was half-mad and subject to fits of depression and mania. On three different occasions, I prevented him from committing suicide."

No mention was ever made of her 48-year-old husband, the British playwright Robert Bolt.

[Bolt divorced Sarah two years later, in 1975. He had a stroke in 1987, and the couple reunited, getting remarried in 1988. "I would be dead without her," he said. "When she's away, my life takes a nosedive. When she returns, my life soars." He died in 1995.]

Dr. Frederick Meyers, a professor of pharmacology at the University of California Medical Center in San Francisco, said, "My conclusion is that no cause of death has been found," thereby disputing the finding of the Maricopa County Medical Examiner, Heinz Karnitschnig. The examiner had testified that the body contained enough sleeping pills to have caused death. Contradicting that, Meyers said that the residue of drugs found in

Whiting's stomach was "little more than a single tablet."

Dinah had flown to Arizona "to stand by my man," echoing the Tammy Wynette song. "If I were in trouble, I know that Burt would have my back," she told reporters. "It was natural for Sarah Miles to have called Burt when she desperately needed help."

When Burt appeared at the inquest, Mrs. Campbell stood up and yelled "murderer!" at him. He was dashing and handsome in a chocolate brown suit, brown boots, and a black shirt open to the waist, showing off his manly chest.

Two women on the six-person jury seemed "in a state of fluttering," as later described by a reporter.

Both Burt and Sarah repeated the carefully rehearsed testimony they had already given.

"If I'd seen Whiting beating Sarah up, then, being the male chauvinist pig I am, I'd have fought with him. But he wouldn't have had that so-called gash, probably a result of his fall. If I'd seen him, he'd be alive today. He would have been too battered to get to his feet to take all those pills. I know the penalty for perjury. I stand on my oath that I did not see, or physically touch, Whiting. I will also under oath say that I did not have an affair with Sarah Miles."

That day, one reporter suggested that Whiting committed suicide and that he'd artfully arranged the discovery of his body to make it appear as if Burt had murdered him.

At the end of testimony, Judge Winsor said, "There is a lot of things left unanswered. There's been a lot of contradictions."

Then the chief of police, J. T. Cromwell, stated that the case of the death of David Whiting was officially closed.

***

During Burt's next appearance on Johnny Carson's *Tonight* Show, he told the audience that all those scandalous stories spread about David Whiting's death were "just a bunch of hockey puck."

Sarah, however, soon realized that her involvement in the death of Whiting had seriously damaged her chances for an acting career in America.

She had been slated to appear at a theater in Los Angeles performing G. B. Shaw's *St. Joan*. Katharine Hepburn sat on the theater's board of directors and told her fellow members, "We'll have to drop Miles. We can't have a whore playing a saint."

After the completion of *Cat Dancing*, Burt never saw Sarah again. Years went by, and one day he received a note from her. "I'm an old woman now, and you still look fairly young to judge from your pictures. You'll always have a place in my heart. Love, Sarah."

Once, in London, he had tried but failed to reach her. "I wanted to tell her that I loved her, too. Our relationship was one of those unresolved things between friends."

Putting up a brave front and faced with a hostile press, Burt, with Dinah, attended the gala premiere of *Cat Dancing* at United Artists Theater in Westwood.

He was horrified to see how MGM was promoting the movie. Billboards announced "BURT AND SARAH IN LOVE STORY THAT SHOCKED THE COUNTRY."

Film critic Roger Ebert rarely seemed to miss reviewing a Burt Reynolds movie: "By his own admission, Burt Reynolds has appeared in mostly junk until *The Man Who Loved Cat Dancing* came along. Even his performance in *Deliverance* emphasized only one aspect of his character. Here, he's given a very difficult dramatic role, and he's fine in it. He finally goes over the top."

Roger Greenspun, writing in *The New York Times*, said, "The film's poetry is as numbing as its violence. It is, indeed, a festival of incompetence. Each performance is uncertain, like something in an early rehearsal."

Charles Champlin, in the *Los Angeles Times,* said the movie "boasts gorgeous widescreen location photography, an interesting spin on traditional Western formula. The film proves, once and for all, that Burt Reynolds is capable of handling a straight dramatic role as well as a lightweight comic one."

According to Burt, "Our movie was not as good as the book, and I was disappointed."

The Man Who Loved Cat Dancing cost $3 million to make and generated only $3.6 million at the box office. Burt felt that the bad publicity surrounding the making of the film and David Whiting's death greatly harmed box office receipts.

Months later, when Burt was escorting Dinah to a party, a reporter cornered him, asking questions about the death of Whiting. "There is nothing to say about the filming of *Cat Dancing,*" he said, "except that it gives me pain. I'd rather not talk about it."

Burt became furious at the author, Bruce Jay Friedman, who wrote an article for *Playboy* entitled "The Dirty Little Deed in Gila Bend, or Burt Reynolds Puts on His Pants One Leg at a Time."

Months later, Burt confronted him in Manhattan's Russian Tea Room for writing "such a filthy, lying story."

Friedman replied, "I'm sorry. Looking back, I'm not proud that I did that."

The rumors would never die and followed Burt for the rest of his life. It also led to the breakup of many friendships, including his relationship with TV talk show host Merv Griffin.

Burt attended a party at the home of Johnny Carson in Malibu. Guests included Merv with his "arm candy," Eva Gabor, and also Sidney Poitier and his wife, Joanna.

Griffin had had too much to drink and confronted Burt with: "Everybody knows you killed David Whiting."

Burt rose and threateningly headed toward Griffin until restrained by Carson. "If you'd been this amusing on your show, you'd still be on the air," Burt said. "Now shut up or get out!"

After Griffin fled with Gabor, Burt told his friends, "He's still pissed at me because I wouldn't let him go down on me."

***

Burt resented all the loot pouring into the coffers of *Cosmo*, the magazine for which he'd posed nude and for free. "I couldn't go the beach and rent a towel without seeing a reproduction of my nude layout emblazoned on it."

He wanted to get in on the gold dust trail, and in 1972, he made a deal

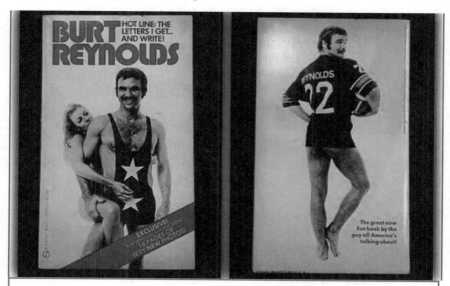

In a sleazy paperback, Burt published provocative letters he'd gotten from horny women and his gay admirers. On the front cover was a beautiful woman reaching for his crotch.

"On the back cover, I posed bare-assed," he said. "My first wife, Judy Carne, told TV audiences I had a 'great arse,' so now, I was showing it to the world."

346

with New American Library. An anthology of fan letters he'd received with his short, saucy answers were published under the title of *Burt Reynolds: The Letters I Get…and Write.*

A paperback, it was hyped on the market as "the great fun book by the guy all America is talking about!"

As advertising copy, an editor wrote, "What letters the endless stream of fans write—raunchy, desperate, funny, frantic, sassy, weird, and whacky—Burt takes 'em all in stride, never blowing his fantastic cool as he answers some pretty way-out queries."

What made the book successful was not necessarily the letters, but sixteen pages of Burt as the centerpiece of sexy photos, many of them posed with beautiful women. Like the layout in *Cosmo*, he didn't show the Full Monty, but there were several bare butt shots.

In one of the more provocative photos, a beauty reaches inside his bathing suit, her hand resting above his pubic hair. In another, wearing a hat and smoking a cigar, he sits naked in a chair, his genitals concealed by the back of the chair. In yet another, a girl's hand rests at the bottom of his zipper.

Some of his fan letters—in fact, many of them—were judged as too pornographic to publish and therefore omitted from the text.

One of the editors, however, leaked some of the hottest mail to one of the underground tabloids that flourished briefly in the 1970s.

Here's a sampling from horny fans of letters to Burt considered too lurid to print but leaked to tabloids.

★ *"Dear Burt, I'll massage your broad, hairy chest until your prick rises up for me in heated desire. I'll stroke and placate it before plunging down on the monster."*

★ *"Dear Burt, I want you to cover my swan neck with bites and kisses, then make your way down to my voluptuous Marilyn Monroe breasts. I want you to chew on my nipples before your mouth plunges down on my Delta of Venus—first your tongue, replaced by man's greatest gift to women."*

It was estimated that at least a quarter of Burt's fan mail came in from men.

★ *"Hi Stud, I bet you've got at least eight inches, maybe more. I want to suck you dry."*

✶ *"Dear Burt, That wicked look on your face had my balls rising up to meet my body. More, more of you—I can't get enough. Please, next time you pose, show your rosebud. My tongue is waiting."*

✶ *"Dear Burt, Please screw me."*

Economically, at least, the book was a success.

***

One of Burt's favorite women in show business was Carol Burnett, the most talented performer ever to emerge from the bowels of poverty-stricken San Antonio, Texas. Both of her parents were alcoholics and deserted her. She later moved to the poorest section of Hollywood with her grandmother. She attended Hollywood High, where she was an avid movie-goer, never missing a Tarzan picture. She perfected the famous Tarzan yell as a little girl. Years later, Burt recalled, "I always knew it was Carol on the other end of the phone. She started out with that damn Tarzan yell."

At UCLA, she studied theater and musical comedy, marrying her college sweetheart, Don Saroyan, in 1955, divorcing him in 1962. When Burt met her, she was married to TV producer Joe Hamilton, the divorced father of eight.

Whenever he could, Burt watched her on her ground-breaking *The Carol Burnett Show,* the first of its kind to be hosted by a woman. It debuted on CBS in 1967 with such regulars as Harvey Korman, Lyle Waggoner, Tim Conway, and later, the teenaged Vicki Lawrence. At first, CBS was reluctant to let her host her own show, claiming, "Only men like Bob Hope or Ed Sullivan can do variety."

How wrong they were.

A reporter once asked Burt which woman would he select if he were stranded on a desert island.

"Carol Burnett," he answered, jokingly. A few days later, she sent him a picture of herself in a bathing suit. On its back, she'd written, "When?"

That led to his appearance on her show in 1972, performing in a skit called "The Lavender Pimpernel." On that same episode, Burt sang "As Time Goes By," forever linked to his favorite movie, *Casablanca* (1942). The other guest of honor that night was Nanette Fabray.

[The Scarlet Pimpernel *had been spoofed on TV before in 1957 when then comedy team of "Wayne & Schuster" did a skit called "The Brown Pumpernickel." Instead of a red flower, the hero's calling card, he leaves behind a loaf of pumper-*

348

nickel.]

Burt and Carol formed a friendship that lasted until his death. They pulled frequent tricks on each other. He sent her a box of chocolates for her birthday, and she returned them, having bitten a piece from each candy.

Once, he sent her flowers. She kept them for two weeks and mailed them back with the note: "Your flowers died."

It was speculated that Carol could not make up her mind which of two actors was more handsome: Rock Hudson or Burt Reynolds. She later appeared in stage performances with each of them. *[She eventually starred opposite Rock in a regional theater performance of* I Do! I Do!.*]*

In time, Carol would travel to Jupiter for an appearance at Burt's theater there. Dom DeLuise directed them in the play *Same Time, Next Year.* It had opened on Broadway in 1975, written by Bernard Slade, starring Charles Grodin and Ellen Burstyn.

[Its plot describes the bittersweet story of a man and woman who meet once a year for a romantic tryst which they'd begun twenty-five years ago. They are each married to other partners. It was reviewed as the funniest piece ever written about adultery.

A New York critic vacationing in Palm Beach went to see it and compared Burt's performance unfavorably to Grodin's. Carol, however, got a rave.]

Two views of one of the most poignantly funny comediennes of her era, Carol Burnett..

Burt always purchased a copy of *The National Examiner* "to see what filth they're writing about me now." One day in 1976, he was horrified to read an exposé of Carol Burnett, falsely asserting that she was seen drunk and disorderly in a Washington restaurant with Henry Kissinger, then the U.S. Secretary of State.

The story was particularly upsetting to her because both of her parents had been alcoholics, and she didn't want the public to think she was following in their footsteps. She sued for libel, and a jury initially awarded her $1.6 million. The case dragged on through appeals until a final award of $200,000, and even that was affected by an out-of-court settlement, with an eventual payout of perhaps $150,000, according to Burt.

Even though she had to pay out "ghastly" legal fees over the course of many years, her win over the tabloid was viewed as a victory for libel victims.

Burt read one so-called exposé after another about his own life, and he sought his revenge, but not in the courts. The headquarters of the *Enquirer* was in Lantana, Florida, about twenty-five miles from Jupiter. He owned a black helicopter at the time and also a stable for horses. He gathered up a large tub of horse manure, put it in his helicopter, and headed for Lantana.

Every year, the *Enquirer* erected and decorated what it defined as the tallest Christmas tree in America. Tourists came from all over the state to photograph it.

From his helicopter, Burt dumped the entire tub of manure onto the tree. "The *Enquirer* writes crap about me, and I throw crap back at them."

***

"We didn't know it at the time, but my 1973 film, *White Lightning*, released by United Artists, marked the beginning of a whole series of movies set in the redneck South," Burt said. "It was about the South and basically targeted at Southerners. No one seemed to care if it were distributed in New York or San Francisco, because the producers could make back the cost of the negative just from theater attendance in Little Rock. It was shot in Arkansas, Bubba Country. Box office anywhere else was gravy. As it turned out, our film payed from East to West, even in Yankee Land—and was a big hit."

In these movies, the rural South and its "good ol' boys" came alive as cameras and scripts focused on seedy pool halls; car chases along dirt roads; gritty, sweaty hillbillies wearing jockey shorts with brown stains; murky swamps; whiskey stills; sounds of screeching tires; packs of coon dogs; backwoods intrigue; fat, corrupt police gorging on ham hocks and grits; plenty of guns; and Dixie darlings in cut-off jeans "right up to their cooze." At least that's how Burt saw *White Lightning*. "If you're not from the South," he continued, "you need to know our title translates as 'illegal moonshine or *likker*.'"

[In its early stages, when its working title was McKlusky, White Lightning was conceived as the directorial debut of Steven Spielberg, who worked on its pre-production for two months. He met Burt once.

According to Spielberg, "I found the locations in Arkansas and had even begun to cast it. But one night I decided that this was not the kind of film in which

350

I wanted to make my debut as a hard-hat journeyman director. I desired something more personal. So I dropped out. Instead, I made Sugarland Express *(1974), a slickly made "road picture."]*

Burt was cast into the lead of *White Lightning* as Gator McKlusky, a bootlegger who'd been arrested by "revenooers' and sent to prison. It marked his first appearance as Gator. *[There would be a sequel.]*

Some scenes of *White Lightning* were shot at Tucker Penitentiary in Tucker, Arkansas, with a few correctional officers appearing as extras. Burt was photographed in the barracks during his pre-mustache era. "I was a good ol' Southern boy as much as overly sugared iced tea is on a hot afternoon in Georgia."

In prison, he gets word of the death of his kid brother, whose corpse has been discovered in a nearby swamp after his arrest by the police.

He learns that a corrupt and paunchy sheriff, J. C. Connors (Ned Beatty), is responsible for the boy's death. "I had to fight like hell to get Ned in the film," Burt said. "In case you don't know who Ned is, he's the guy who endured rape by a hillbilly pecker in *Deliverance.*"

Burt credited the director, Joseph Sargent, for "bringing out the best in all of us. Even though he was born in New Jersey, he seemed to understand Southern degenerates."

Gator knows that the crooked sheriff is taking money from moonshiners, so he reluctantly agrees—as an act of revenge for the death of his brother— to become an underground informer for a Federal agency that wants to expose the sheriff. Gator gets a job running (delivering) moonshine with "Rebel Boy" Boone (Bo Hopkins). *[That actor had previously worked with Burt on the ill-fated* The Man Who Loved Cat Dancing.]*

Rebel Boy has a sluttish girlfriend, Lou (Jennifer Billingsley), who eventually ends up in Gator's arms. This would mark her only role as Gator's girlfriend. She would be replaced in

SLAM! BANG! CARS IN MIDAIR! And Thank You, Ma'am!

follow-ups and sequels by Sally Field, who eventually morphed into Burt's on- and off-the-screen lover.

White Lightning marked the early appearance of Diane Ladd, who would soon go on to greater roles, including *Chinatown* (1975), with Jack Nicholson. That same year, she was also nominated for an Oscar for her role in *Alice Doesn't Live Here Anymore.*

Moonshining drama in the Deep South. Formulaic! You bet. His fans loved it.

Although it earned mixed reviews, *White Lightning* was a hit at the box office.

The *Monthly Film Bulletin* defined it as "a moonshine melodrama with a veneer of serious intent, which is rapidly paned away by Burt Reynolds' frivolous acting and Joseph Sargent's weakness for car chases."

Roger Greenspun of *The New York Times* posted the harshest critique, labeling it "a fairly awful movie with endless car chases, a crushing bore."

Gene Siskel of the *Chicago Tribune* wrote, "What sets *White Lightning* apart from a demolition derby is special work of the entire cast in creating a totally believable world out of characters that we've seen countless times before. Only an abrupt ending keeps the film from achieving some level of greatness."

Gary Arnold of the *Washington Post* wrote that the film "begins straight and then starts messing around at random. The inevitable result is an expendable movie, neither a straightforward crime drama nor a consistent shaggy-dog comedy."

Charles Champlin of the *Los Angeles Times* wrote: "Burt Reynolds, abetted by William Norton's sharp, accurate dialogue, creates a vivid character—tough, earnest, sardonic, crafty, and also sensitive. He carries his weight in the brawlings, but he also lets you know the shame he feels at being a stool pigeon, even in a good cause. William Faulkner it was never intended to be, but Reynolds lends unexpected dimensions to a straight-out melodramatic role."

Burt claimed that the movie was "a breakthrough in that area of blending comedy and action. It made a lot of money, so other producers wanted to try the same thing. We smashed up some sixty cars, so they tried to top us by wrecking a hundred. In my opinion, all those crashes had nothing to do with the success of *White Lightning*. I think our movie is an excellent example of a picture that is everything it tries to be—no more, no less. I liked it a lot."

Before and after Dinah's marriage to actor George Montgomery and her affair with Burt Reynolds, she had been known to date other men, none more notable than Frank Sinatra.

She was seen out with Ron Ely, often hailed as "the sexiest screen Tarzan of them all."

Other escorts, perhaps lovers, included singer Andy Williams and Eddie Fisher; actors Rod Taylor and Wayne Rogers; and comedian Dick Martin.

Dinah once said, "Other men have come and gone, but no one occupied that special place in my heart more than George (Montgomery) and later, Burt."

At Romanoff's in Hollywood, Burt and Dinah had a quiet dinner to celebrate the first anniversary of their love affair. He had long tired of reporters asking him about the difference in their ages. "I don't know how old Dinah is, and I've never bothered to ask."

On some occasions, his violent temper resurfaced, and he was known to slug a few reporters until he mellowed out a bit. He became particularly enraged if he suspected, rightly or wrongly, that a reporter was from the *National Enquirer.*

He maintained a different tone with Doug Weston of the *Hollywood Reporter.* "Okay, go on and ask me: 'What's a hot macho stud like me doing dating an older woman?' I'm one lucky man. I'll tell you the secret of how she holds on to me. She makes the world's best chicken noodle soup. Any red-blooded male would give his left nut to live with Dinah. On second thought, don't print that. Make it his right arm."

"Dinah and I are great together, loving, supportive, and kind. She's one bright, classy lady. The only time she pisses me off is when she beats me in a game of tennis, which she always does. But I get my revenge. I pick her up and carry her to the bedroom and fuck the daylights out of her. On second thought, don't print that last remark. She wouldn't think it was tasteful, and the one thing she has is taste."

"I'm going to beat the shit out of the next reporter who calls me a gigolo," Burt said. "I'm thirty-eight years old and earning my own living. Contrary to the press, I don't like women who are swingers, screwing a different man every night. I find such gals

Long before Burt entered her life, Dinah developed a deep friendship with Frank Sinatra. They appear onstage together in this photo from 1962.

353

disgusting. On most evenings with Dinah, we spend it alone, just talking, listening to music, watching movies. Both of us are devotees of black-and-white films. We eat the world's best pizza, made fresh by Dinah herself. We act silly, giggling a lot, playing like kids. In spite of my reputation, you might call me a Hollywood Square."

"As far as the age thing goes, women don't get their act together until they're thirty-five," he said. "When I'm depressed, which is more often than I like, I retreat into a womb, locking myself away. Young bitches can't understand that and would feel neglected. Not Dinah. She gives me my space. Besides, she's busier than I am, often loaded down with obligations with her show."

"Actually, she and I have the most fun when we retreat to my ranch in Florida," he said. "She's a good painter, and she's got me painting, too. Of course, I'm no Van Gogh. But in Jupiter, we often retreat to my meadow where sheep are grazing. Both of us take our paint and easels with us and can spend an afternoon there."

Dinah herself gave an occasional interview about Burt, telling a reporter from *Variety*, "A sensuous man is one who doesn't try to seduce every woman he meets. A sensuous man to me is one who is sure of himself and secure in who he is. Burt is that kind of man. He's also the kind of man you could study for ages and, just when you think you know him, he'll turn around and do something that will completely confuse you. He is the most unpredictable man I've ever met, and that's one of the reasons I find him so attractive, a surprise every night. Life with him is never boring."

In New York, columnist Earl Wilson commented: "Dinah Shore is more vivacious, scintillating, and attractive and all those other adjectives than she's been in years, undoubtedly due to her friendship with Burt Reynolds. According to her Hollywood friends, seeing them together, one thinks only of her youthful appearance."

On her TV show, Barbara Walters became rather intrusive. At the time, she was separated from her husband. In July of 1973, she got Burt to admit that he was in love with Dinah. "Why don't you two get married?"

He shot back, "Why don't you get divorced?"

Dinah was rather shy in talking about her love affairs, and she never provided any details of her secret liaison with Frank Sinatra.

She also deplored the new films coming out that where sexually explicit. "Directors want to strip Burt down in every film and depict him in bed with his leading lady. Such graphic portrayals take the mystery out of sex for me, as I am not a voyeur. I enjoy sex by doing it, not by watching it on the screen. A blue movie would turn me off."

"I believe in marriage, and certainly would consider marrying again," she said. "George Montgomery and I had many happy years together. Marriage is the ultimate fulfillment. Don't get me wrong. I have no intention of marrying Burt. We're happy with our present arrangement. Why spoil a good thing?"

"Everything between us is nice and easy. We don't have arguments, and we've never had a fight. Both of us have successful careers, and our lives are going along nicely." She paused in the interview, quickly adding, "As long as it lasts."

"The world I've created with Burt is something we've built together," she said. "We have something great, and I feel so very lucky. There is no substitute for Burt Reynolds."

"When we first got together, the press practically accused me of cradle snatching, although Burt will soon be forty," she said. "But lately, most reporters seem to have concluded, 'what the hell.' We make a perfect couple."

When Sinatra was asked what he thought of the Reynolds/Shore liaison, he said, "Whatever makes my gal happy is just fine with me. She's a big success, and she's in love. What more does a girl need?"

As Burt's film career soared, and Dinah's television variety show was receiving high ratings, she got some good news and some bad news all at once.

In May of 1974, her TV show won an Emmy as the best daytime variety show.

She was delivered a telegram of congratulations from Larry White, the network vice president of NBC. After congratulations, he delivered the blow: "I'm sorry the exigencies of the business require us to drop your show. We hope we can work together again."

She showed Burt the telegram, and he at first thought White was joking. "He's just pulling your leg. You're the biggest thing on afternoon TV. There's no way in hell they're firing you."

"It was a terrible, terrible ordeal for me," she said. "But Burt was there to comfort me."

Dinah was a survivor, and within two weeks, in October of 1974, she'd closed a deal with CBS to launch a new shop entitled simply *Dinah!*

"She came back bigger and better than ever," Burt said.

***

Living with Dinah meant that Burt would also get involved on some level with her friends, particularly Frank Sinatra.

Ol' Blue Eyes from Hoboken had first met her when she was what he called "this teenage hillbilly singer from redneck Tennessee."

He was not impressed when comedian Eddie Cantor introduced the singer to him, claiming "her voice is wrapped in silk."

Sinatra and Dinah came together when he was appearing on a fifteen-minute radio spot in New York, getting paid only seventy cents a week, which he called "paltry pennies," but he took the gig for recognition and experience. When not on radio, he was working nights at a restaurant in New Jersey for $15 a week, plus tips.

As Dinah relayed to Burt, "It took a while for Frank to come on to me, but I won him over."

World War II was on the horizon, and both of these singers with their different styles were headed for super stardom, Sinatra finding it with bobbysoxers and Dinah with military men going off to war.

Soon, she was recording on the same label as Sinatra, along with such stars as Pearl Bailey and Rosemary Clooney.

Dinah introduced Burt to Sinatra in Hollwood, and soon, Burt was invited to join him in poker games. He also became a regular visitor to Dinah's home.

"I often sat in the living room watching TV," he told Dick Clayton. "They were together in the kitchen, cooking. I was a bit jealous of Frank. She never confessed it to me, but everybody in the business knew that Dinah and Frank had been lovers in the 1940s."

"The list of that guy's seductions would stretch along Times Square," Burt said. "You name 'em: Lana Turner, Jacqueline Kennedy, Zsa Zsa Gabor, Judy Garland, Grace Kelly, Elizabeth Taylor, Natalie Wood, Nancy Davis Reagan—and the list goes on."

"He was a skinny little guy, but everybody in Hollywood talked about his endowment," Burt said. "Ava Gardner said, 'There's only ten pounds of Frank, but there's 110 pounds of cock.'"

Sinatra told Burt, "Every time I sing a song, I'm making love to a woman. I'm a boudoir singer."

"Of course, he didn't get total approval," Burt said. "I met Lauren Bacall one night at a party. She'd fallen from Frank after Bogie died. She was very blunt: 'The guy's a complete shit,' she told me."

"I once met Marlene Dietrich," Burt said. "She told me that she considered Sinatra 'Mais oui...the Mercedes-Benz of men.'"

"What man wouldn't be jealous of a guy like that...and he could sing, too," Burt said. "Well, I mean he could sorta carry a tune...sorta."

"I liked him a little bit," Burt said, "although we were always trying to out-macho the other. I overlooked the fact he was a child molester, marrying that little girl, Mia Farrow."

"You've got to love livin', baby," he told Burt, "because dying is a pain in the ass."

Burt said, "Years later, people used to ask me, 'What was Frank Sinatra really like?'"

"I had some words for him: Horndog, brawler, tuxedo-clad rat packer, king of cool, heavy boozer, cavorter, hellraiser. He was a guy who ruled the world, overpowering we mere mortals. To get along with him, you had to accept him on his own terms."

"When Dinah told me Frank was coming over, I always ordered extra bottles of Jack Daniels," Burt said. "Sometimes, he arrived with his fellow Rat Packers, Sammy Davis, Jr. and Dean Martin. I loved Dean. What a guy, so damn funny and likable. It was party time when Deano was around. He could drink us all under the table."

"I'd met Sammy before in clubs in New York, and over time, we developed a real friendship," Burt said. "we became so close, I invited him to come and stay with me in Jupiter. I didn't know what Big Burt would think of me showing up with a black man. My father was not a great advocate of civil rights. But after the first day, Big Burt and Sammy became the best of friends. I took a picture of them with my father's arm around Sammy. I think he liked him more than he did me."

Burt was far more impressed with Sinatra's Rat Packers than he was with his children. "I knew the guys who kidnapped Frank Jr.," Burt said. "Ryan O'Neal introduced me to these losers. And once or twice I played softball with them. But I think both of them didn't have an elevator that ran to their top floor. Imagine having the nerve to kidnap Frank's son in Reno. The cops caught up with them, and Sinatra got his son back."

"I met the boy on two occasions," Burt said. "He was polite, but a big bore. The kid was the dullest guy you would ever meet. Of course, in no way could he match his father in anything, especially his singing."

"I also met his daughters, Nancy and Tina," Burt said. "I didn't like them, either. They were little princesses who thought they were entitled, as the daughters of Frank Sinatra. I guess they were."

Burt's friend, actor Doug McClure, dated Tina for a while. "He was terrified of Frank," Burt said.

Sinatra one night warned McClure, "You mess up Tina, and I know these boys who'll take you for a ride in the desert. When they bring you home and dump you at your door, you'll be missing your pecker."

***

As the first half of the 1970s unfolded, Burt was still in love with Dinah. But, as he confessed to Dick Clayton, "I can't always control my hormones. Every corner I turn I run into temptation. It's thrown into my lap, and I mean that literally. Does every beautiful woman in Hollywood want to screw Burt Reynolds?"

Two women loved him.
One died for him.
One killed for him.

THE
MAN WHO
LOVED
CAT DANCING

BURT REYNOLDS   SARAH MILES

His fans found him staggeringly appealing, both as whatever character he was portraying on the screen, and as a real-life adult male. In the photo above, he appears in the TV police drama, *Hawk.*

BURT
REYNOLDS
IS ALL
YOURS!

BURT
REYNOLDS
THE MAN BEHIND
THE 'GOOD OLD BOY'

To give you a hint of all the great articles and color photos of Burt, check out this dynamic contents:

TEEN BEAT
2 Park Ave., Dept TB59

Commercializing his sex appeal: *Teen Scream* Fan Magazines celebrated "The Man Behind the 'Good Old Boy.'"

358

CHAPTER TEN

THE LONGEST YARD
Mauled by Inmates Itching to Take Down a Movie Star
Burt Scores Touchdowns in Prison

W.W. & THE DIXIE DANCEKINGS
Cornpone, Rebel Yells, Hot Rods, & Country Music
Applauded as an Archive of the Postmodern Deep South

This film "comes at a time when my curiosity about Southern roads, motels, soft-drink brands, idioms, and Good Ole Boys is pretty much exhausted"
—Film Critic Roger Ebert

ADRIENNE BARBEAU
Men Are Pigs: A Hard-Working Starlette Comes and Goes and Records Most of It in Her Memoir.

Black and White in Color
AT LONG LAST LOVE
Burt Disastrously Shakes a Leg with Cybill Shepherd in a Cole Porter Musical

"He can't sing, and he can't dance, but he's good for box office!"
—Fox Executives demanding more scenes
with Burt in Peter Bogdanovich's tribute
to romantic comedies of the 1930s

BURT DUMPS DINAH
"It was the hardest thing I ever did"
—Burt Reynolds

LUCKY LADY LIZA!
Burt's Rumored Affair with Ms. Minnelli
and His "Real McCoy" Affair With Her Sister, Lorna Luft.

CATHERINE DENEUVE
Burt Romances the Renowned French Actress While She's
Cast Opposite Him as a Prostitute

SILENT MOVIE
Beauty and the Beast: Mel Brooks & Anne Bancroft

BIG BAD BURT
After he sticks you up, you'll be sorry to see him go.

The Longest Yard

Minnelli!

PETER BOGDANOVICH'S
At Long Last Love

In his autobiography, Burt added an unusual entry: "In 1974, less than a year after imagining myself in prison for manslaughter, I was actually in one of the toughest lock-up facilities in the country."

He was referring to escaping charges associated with the death of David Whiting, the boyfriend of Sarah Miles on the set of *The Man Who Loved Cat Dancing* in Arizona. He was also referencing the Georgia State Prison where most of the scenes of his latest movie, *The Longest Yard* (1974), were filmed.

Albert S. Ruddy was the producer, and Robert Aldrich was the director.

Burt called his friend, Bette Davis, and had dinner and a long conversation with her about Aldrich. He had helmed her in *What Ever Happened to Baby Jane?* (1964).

Davis told Burt, "I owe a debt to Aldrich for single-handedly reviving my career and my pocketbook. But he can have a strange lapse in taste. In *Charlotte,* he had this head rolling down the stairs. That was a bit much."

Later, Aldrich told the press that he felt like an umpire directing Bette Davis and Joan Crawford in *Baby Jane.* "I directed them like they were two men."

Burt had seen Aldrich's *The Dirty Dozen* (1967), starring his friend, Lee Marvin. He called Marvin, who convinced him that the director would be ideal to pull off a gritty football prison drama with dozens of violent scenes. He also met with the producer, Albert S. Ruddy. Burt promised Ruddy that he'd make "the greatest football picture in film history."

A Canadian, Ruddy had co-created the hit TV sitcom, *Hogan's Heroes* (1965-71), and he'd won a Best Picture Oscar for *The Godfather.* [*That award had been presented to him onstage by Burt's friend, Clint Eastwood.*]

Inspired by a short story written by the producer himself, the script for *The Longest Yard* was by Tracy Keenan Wynn, the son of the character actor Keenan Wynn and the stepson of the gay actor, Van Johnson, a screen heartthrob from the 1940s. Tracy was selected as screenwriter because of the success of scripts he'd written for a made-for-TV drama about prison life, *The Glass House* (1972).

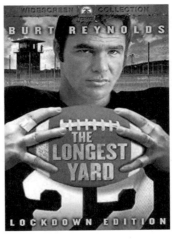

When Burt, a former football player himself, was given a copy of the script, he said to Tracy, "It's obvious that the title of *The Longest Yard* was inspired by the length of my dick."

"Surely you exaggerate," the writer answered.

Originally, the film was to be shot in Oklahoma State Prison. Burt went there with Aldrich and Ruddy. "The conditions there were horrific, you wouldn't believe how bad," Burt said. However, when the trio returned to Los Angeles, they learned that shortly after their visit, the inmates there had rioted and burned the facility to the ground.

In their scouting for a new location, Burt and Aldrich flew to Atlanta, where they met with Georgia's governor, Jimmy Carter. The film location they wanted was Georgia State Prison at Riedsville. Its most famous prisoner had been Martin Luther King, Jr. He'd been jailed there in 1960 until pressure from the Kennedy family secured his release.

Burt found Carter "personable, smiling, and gracious."

He warned Burt and Aldrich, "This facility is a maximum security prison, one tough place. The inmates are the most dangerous in the state, many of them vicious killers. However, if you're taken hostage, I'll go there and replace you."

Jokingly, Burt turned to Aldrich and, in front of the governor, said, "This politician lies so well I bet he'll be president one day."

All the men laughed, but sometimes jokes come true.

By the time cast and crew were ready to fly to Georgia, the key roles had been assigned. Burt would play the lead, supported by Eddie Albert, Ed Lauter, Michael Conrad, James Hampton (one of Burt's best friends), Harry Caesar, and Bernadette Peters, with the voice of Michael

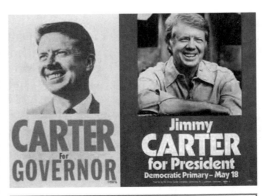

Georgia Governor Jimmy Carter met with Burt in his office. He offered Burt some peanuts he'd grown himself. He also warned him that he'd be shooting at "the most dangerous prison in the South."

J. Fox as the announcer.

A number of the actors had previously played pro football. They included Ray Nitschke, a middle linebacker for the Green Bay Packers, who, in 1978, would be inducted into the Pro Football Hall of Fame; Mike Henry, who played with the Pittsburgh Steelers, later for the Los Angeles Rams; and Joe Kapp, quarterback for the Minnesota Vikings.

Eddie Albert (right) in an uncharacteristically mean role, and Ed Lauter cast as a sadistic guard who abuses prisoners.

The movie was the brutal saga of a disgraced former NFL player, Paul ("Wrecking") Crewe, who recruits a motley band of inmates to play football against the guards, most of whom have brutalized them. The convicts have no respect for Crewe because he was kicked out of the NFL for "point shaving."

Eddie Albert, as the most vicious character he ever portrayed, was cast as Warden Rudolph Hazen, defined by one critic as a "despicable, oily, warden type." As a gridiron freak, he believes in winning at all costs.

Albert was better known for the TV sitcom, *Green Acres* (1965-71), in which he co-starred with his urbanite screen wife, Eva Gabor, who sets out with him to lead a rural life in a farm community. "Give me Park Avenue," she chants. Albert was Oscar-nominated for his 1972 role in *Heartbreak Kid*.

"Eddie was the sweetest, nicest, guy," Burt said. "But the role—at least on camera—brought out the vicious side of him. After one scene, Aldrich got so angry he called Albert 'a candy ass son of a bitch.'"

Burt was surprised when he didn't take offense. In response, Albert answered, in reference to Aldrich: "I love the guy. We've made five pictures together."

Ed Lauter was cast as Captain Wilhelm Knauer, head guard and coach. A bitter, hateful, convict-abusing sadist, the character seemed to represent all that was wrong with the American prison system.

In a career spanning forty years, Lauter would appear in some 200 movies and was known for his 6'2" height and his bald head. "A lot of people come up to me," Lauter said, "and say, 'I know you from somewhere. You're in the movies. I don't know your name."

[*Lauter would also have a minor role in the 2005 remake of* The Longest Yard.]

Michael Conrad was cast as Nate Scarboro, a bruised and aging ex-football player. He helps Crewe's seemingly hopeless team on the slim change that its players might win.

James Hampton played the doomed "Caretaker," James Farrell, a likable prisoner who brings the team together and pushes Crewe and his players ahead to win the game.

Charles Tyner was the psychotic "Unger," who plots to kill Crewe. He wants Crewe dead, and he fashions a homemade bomb from a light bulb filled with combustible fluid set to detonate when he switches on a light. Instead of Crewe, Caretaker (Hampton) enters the cell and switches on the light. He's set on fire, and Unger locks the cell so he'll be burned to death before he can be rescued.

The singer, Harry Caesar, billed as "Little Caesar," was cast in the role of "Granny" Granville, the first black inmate willing to play on Crewe's team. After watching Granny keep his cool when harassed by prison guards, other black inmates join the team, perhaps in retaliation for the treatment of Granny by the guards.

The "campiest" role of the film is the warden's horny secretary, "Miss Toot," played with subdued humor by Bernadette Peters. She wears cinema's tallest beehive hairdo, and is known for sexually harassing the male prisoners, demanding sex. Crewe (that is, Burt) has to put out for her, and has only fifteen minutes to perform. As his reward, Crewe is given a newsreel of the guards playing football, so that he can "fingerprint" their "weak points" as players.

As *The Longest Yard* opens, Crewe is shown as the kept boy of a rich socialite, Melissa, played by a minor actress, Anitra Ford. She became better known as the model on Bob Barker's game show, *The Price is Right* (1972–80 and 1985–86).

Tired of stud duties, Crewe kicks her out of bed and assaults her. He then hot-rods away in her Maserati-engined Citroën. Vengefully, she calls the police, who chase after Crewe until he jumps out of the vehicle before it runs off a bridge into deep water. He later said, "I sure earned that car," referring to all the sex he'd given Melissa.

When Burt, cast, and crew arrived at the Georgia prison compound, they saw some of the inmates. In Burt's words, "They were murderers, mass shooters, gay rapists, bank robbers, pedophiles, and some fey-looking boys used for sex, often having to take on as many as twenty convicts a night, especially if they were pretty and young."

Bernadette Peters abusing a prisoner.... in this case, Burt

"The guys looked like they had eaten steroids for breakfast all their lives," he said. "It must have been the worst coven of badasses in the nation."

"Me and my buddies huddled together, as none of us was ready for a *Deliverance*-style rape. Some of the hands on these inmates looked like ham hocks from a giant sow."

The actual warden of the real-life prison assigned Burt a personal bodyguard named "Ringo." He was considered one of the most brutal inmates in Georgia, serving a ninety-year sentence for mass murder and decapitation.

"Throughout the shoot, Ringo had my back, saving me from physical assault, even rape, when not a camera."

"On the day I left prison, I slipped Ringo a thousand-dollar bill, and thanked him profusely. I later heard he killed one of the inmates for accusing him of 'brown-nosing' me."

On location, before the beginning of filming, Aldrich, the director, delivered an insulting and demoralizing speech to the cast and crew. "I know that at least one of you is a fucking asshole. I'm sure enough I'll find out which one of you it is. Just rear your ugly god damn head, and I'll chop it off. Now get to work and make a picture. If some of you are injured, and there will be a few casualties, don't expect any sympathy from me."

According to Burt, "Aldrich reminded me of Ernest Borgnine taunting poor skinny Frank Sinatra in *From Here to Eternity* (1953)."

The hardest scenes to shoot were the bone-crunching football plays, often hailed as the most violent ever depicted on screen. "It was like a slaughterhouse," Burt said. The game between the prison guards and the inmates took up one-quarter of the final cut.

Some of the more severe injuries resulted in lifetime after-effects for those fallen on the field.

Not every scene depicted horror, at least when the camera cuts to the all-black team of cheerleaders, perhaps the campiest cheerleading squad ever shown on film. Perceptive viewers quickly realized that everyone on the squad was a cross-dresser.

"The movie was vicious, sexist, homophobic, racist, and misogynist," Burt said. "African Americans called whites honkies, and the guards labeled the inmates as niggers."

Aldrich would first shoot a scene as written in the script. Then he would film a "schtick take" with Burt, allowing him to clown around. The completed film included 65% of Burt's schtick takes.

Burt had to tangle with "Bogdanski," as portrayed by Ray Nitschke, the confrontational and fiercely competitive pro footballer with the NFL. *[Known for his fearsome and sometimes violent temper, he was defined early in his career as the best linebacker in college football.]*

According to Burt, "The game he played was 'kill the movie star' and I was the victim. I've never been hit so hard in my life. He wanted to see my head rolling across the field."

The script called for Burt's character to tell Nitschke's character what a particular play was. "It's a drop kick, you son of a bitch."

After delivering that (scripted) line, Nitschke grabbed Burt and told him, "You say that line to me again, and you're mince pie." He didn't care if that were in the script or not.

Burt asked Aldrich what he should do.

Aldrich advised, "During the scene, read the line as written—and then run like a bat out of hell."

That's exactly what Burt did. Eventually after several laps around the field, an exhausted Nitschke collapsed.

As the visiting movie star, Burt faced other violence from a semi-pro football team brought in from Augusta as extras to fill out the corps of on-screen players. "Those guys loved hitting me. I don't think anything could satisfy them until they saw me hauled off the field on a stretcher."

On the last day of filming, Aldrich told Burt, "You're probably three inches shorter from all the beatings you took."

Ray Nitschke, legendary pro with the Green Bay Packers, playing a barely-under-control sadist, seen here with Burt in *The Longest Yard*. He wasn't acting.

He later evaluated his male star to the press: "Burt on occasion is a much better actor than he's given credit for. Not always, though. Sometimes, he acts like a caricature of himself. I thought he scored a touchdown in *The Longest Yard*."

Years later, Burt agreed with film critic John Patterson's appraisal of Aldrich: "He was a paunchy, caustic, macho, and pessimistic director who depicted corruption and evil unflinchingly, and who pushed the limits of violence throughout his career. His aggressive and pugnacious film-making style, often crass and crude, but never less than utterly vital and alive, warrants your immediate attention."

Most reviews of *The Longest Yard* were positive, with the occasional brickbat. *Variety* wrote: "It became obvious more than a year ago that Burt Reynolds has finally reached stardom." The critic for the *Los Angeles Times* called it "an outstanding action drama, combining the brutish excitements of football with the brutalities of modern prison life."

The New York Times stated, "*The Longest Yard* is a terrible picture with prison guards behaving like leering sci-fi monsters, and Reynolds doing a bad imitation of Marlon Brando in *On the Waterfront*."

Pauline Kael of *The New Yorker* wrote that Burt "was perfect in his brutal comic fantasy about a football game between crazily ruthless convicts and crazily ruthless guards. For all these bone-crunching collisions, the picture is almost irresistibly good-natured and funny."

Tom Shales of the *Washington Post* claimed, "It might seem morally imperative at this point to condemn with indignation what this movie is trying to do—stir up gut-level reactions at a mob-baiting level. And yet, however one may feel about that goal, it would be hard to deny that the movie achieves it."

Charles Champlin of the *Los Angeles Times* stated, "The story is both clever and unsubtle, the action riot-gun fast from start to satisfying finish, the characters vivid and boldly drawn, the jokers set up and paid off with old-pro efficiency. The bone-snapping, billy-club violence is by Aldrich's standards restrained and by any standards allowable."

Burt later said, "I wanted Ronald Reagan to see it. After all, I won one for the Gipper."

***

In the 2005 remake of *The Longest Yard,* an aging Burt was offered (and accepted) the role of Nate Scarborough. For this reprise of Burt's 1974 original, Adam Sandler took over Burt's role as Paul Crewe, the disgraced professional quarterback for the Pittsburgh Steelers.

As in the original, he's forced to form a team comprised of prison inmates for a football showdown against the vicious guards.

Chris Rock, the African-American comedian, actor, writer, producer, and director, took the role of "Caretaker," Crewe's friend.

A New Yorker, Sandler had gained attention as a cast member of *Saturday Night Live* and went on to become a major star in his own right.

The director of the remake, Peter Segal, would helm three of Sandler's movies, beginning with *Anger Management* (2003) which also starred Jack Nicholson.

The remake was shot at the New Mexico State Penitentiary outside Santa Fe. In spite of getting a lot of negative reviews, many of them unfavorable comparisons to the original, it did well at the box office, generating nearly $50 million during its opening weekend. It went on to become the second-highest grossing sports comedy in film history.

Chris Rock won a BET Comedy Award for Outstanding Supporting Actor in a theatrical film. For his effort (or lack thereof), Burt won a Golden Raspberry Award for Worst Supporting Actor of the Year.

***

Burt had only bad memories of his starring role in *W.W. and the Dixie Dancekings,* a 1975 release from 20th Century Fox. "The director, John G. Avildsen, and I fought over every scene. He was a son of a bitch, a real asshole. He kept trying to tell me how to play a good 'ol Southern boy, and he was from Illinois. What did he

The Longest Yard
If You Can't Get Out, Get Even!

THE LONGEST YARD

Adam Sandler starred in *The Longest Yard's* 2005 remake. Burt, with a cameo appearance in the remake, appears to the right of Sandler in this publicity poster

366

know?"

When Burt first read the script by Thomas Rickman, he felt it was tailor-made for him. The time frame was 1957, and Burt's role as W.W. was that of an easy-going bandit with "aw-shucks" charm. To make a living, he robs gas stations, but only those owned by the fictional SOS (Southland Oil System). Before driving off with the contents of the cash register, he always hands over a twenty to the underpaid gas station attendant to give a little assist to his forty-a-week salary.

Livin' can be easy in the Deep South.....an autographed promotional pic of Burt in *Dancekings*.

W.W. has a grudge against SOS, a company taking in a million dollars a day, and its chairman, Elton Bird (Sherman G. Lloyd), a character modeled on the American billionaire, H.L. Hunt.

W.W. drives a souped-up gold-and-black 1955 Oldsmobile, custom-built and altered from the (then twenty-year old) standard issue. Everything about it was fascinating to classic car buffs.

During one of his flights from the police, Burt encounters, charms, and then hides out with a country-western singing group, the Dixie Dancekings. Disguising himself as a music promoter, Burt convinces the singers that he has powerful connections in Nashville, which he doesn't.

The 1955 Oldsmobile--a vintage marvel by any car aficionado's standards--that starred alongside Burt in *W.W. and the Dixie Dancekings*.

Although Burt wanted Dolly Parton for the role, the lead singer was played by Conny Van Dyke. Back-up singers included James Hampton (Burt's close friend), Don Williams, Richard Hurst, and singer Jerry Reed, making his feature film acting debut. Burt liked working with Reed so much, he got him cast a year later in his upcoming film, *Gator* (1976).

Before signing with Avildsen, Burt called Jack Lemmon for advice. Lemmon had been helmed by that director in *Save the Tiger* (1973) and had carried home a Best Actor Oscar for his performance in it.

[Ironically, Sylvester Stallone had applied for one of the supporting roles in Dancekings *and was rejected. He would, however, join forces with Avildsen to produce the blockbuster* Rocky *(1976), which became the highest-grossing picture of the year, winning Best Picture and Best Director Academy Awards.]*

Conny Van Dyke, a singer and actress born in Virginia at the close of World War II, had been one of the first white women signed by Motown.

She recorded "Oh Freddy," written by Sonny Robinson. When she worked with Burt, she was readying a new album, *Conny Van Dyke Sings For You.* Burt suggested she change her name "to something more country—your last name sounds like a lesbian Dutch painter."

Art Carney plays a fundamentalist former sheriff, Deacon Gore, who is assigned to hunt down W.W. and bring him to justice. Many of his fans didn't recognize him, as he was much more familiar during his portrayal of Ed Norton on the classic TV sitcom, *The Honeymooners* (1955-56).

Dancekings. Burt with Ned Beatty--perhaps with memories of Beatty's contribution to *Deliverance.*

Just recently, in 1974, Carney had won a Best Actor Oscar for his role in *Harry and Tonto.* He told Burt he'd sobered up for the role, as he had long been an alcoholic.

Burt's friend, Ned Beatty, was cast as "Country Bull," a successful singer and songwriter, who agrees, as laid out in the plot, to write the Dixie Dancekings a song for a thousand dollars.

Singer Mell Tillis has the small role of "Golden Cowboy." He and Burt bonded, sharing memories of having grown up in the same area of Florida. As a result of a childhood bout with malaria, he had a speech impediment that affected his speaking patterns but not his singing voice. Tillis would later appear with Burt in *Smokey and the Bandit* (1977) and *Cannonball Run* (1981).

The movie was shot in Nashville and its environs. "It turned out wrong, but it made a lot of money," Burt said. "It was important to me that we not make fun of the people of Nashville. It was a bouquet to them."

Vincent Canby of *The New York Times* called the movie "an unexpectedly pleasant surprise. One of the charms of the film is the casual way it seems to discover its story while it wanders from one minor crisis to the next."

Roger Ebert wrote, "If it were not an anatomical impossibility, I'd say I have road movies coming out of my ears. The pain, in any event, is elsewhere. After the fine *Payday* and the dismal *Aloha, Bobby and Rose* comes Burt Reynolds in *W.W. and the Dixie Dancekings.* It's not really a bad movie, but it's not very interesting, and it comes at a time when my curiosity about Southern roads, motels, soft-drink brands, idioms, and Good Ole Boys is pretty much exhausted."

He continued: "Reynolds moves through the movie with his usual ease, relaxed and ingratiating, with a con man's smile. He's an engaging actor, especially when he has an attractive actress to work with (there seems to be something chemical involved), and he makes a passable W.W., but the movie just doesn't supply the Good Ole Boy with enough to do or a plausible world to inhabit."

The writer, Thomas Rickman, later reported that he was "disgusted" at the liberties Avildsen had taken with his script and wrote a novelization that was truer to his intentions.

Filmmaker Quentin Tarantino later credited that novelization with interesting him in the art of writing. "I read the book before I saw the movie. After watching Burt Reynolds and the gang, I asked myself, 'What in hell is

Gettin' rednecky and gun-happy with Burt in *Dancekings*. Here, he is seen robbing a gas station at gunpoint.

this?' I was offended. The novelization was pure. But Burt's movie was Hollywood garbage. So that's why I started writing screenplays. I was that outraged!"

***

Actress and singer Adrienne Barbeau entered show business as a sex symbol whether she liked that label or not. A native of California, she moved to New York in the late 1960s, getting a gig as a go-go dancer in clubs catering to the mob.

She made her Broadway debut in the chorus of *Fiddler on the Roof*. Leaving the show in 1971, she took the lead role of Cookie Kovac in the off-Broadway nudie, *Stag Movie*. Among her routines, she had to sing and dance in the buff in thirteen numbers, including one in which she had to sing upside down in a handstand on a raked platform "with my unfettered breasts hitting me in the chin."

That launched her into more that two dozen musicals, including roles in *Grease* and *The Best Little Whorehouse in Texas*, which would later be turned into a movie with Burt as the lead.

Adrienne gained her greatest exposure when she starred as Carol Traynor, the daughter of Bea Arthur, the title character in the hit TV sitcom *Maude* (1972-78).

Adrienne's life was about to change when she was asked to fly to Nashville to be a guest star on a charity telethon for Easter Seals. The host of the show was Burt Reynolds, whom she'd seen exposed in *Cosmo* and during a number of appearances on Johnny Carson's *The Tonight Show*.

He was in Nashville with actor James Hampton, nearing the end of the filming for *W.W. and the Dixie Dancekings*. The charity event went over well, and he asked her to visit him and Hampton at their rented modern home, where the studio had arranged for them to live, on the outskirts of Nashville. For the occasion, Hampton had ordered a Cajun dinner for them.

After the meal, Hampton disappeared, and she and Burt "talked and talked," finding a certain sexual chemistry. She had an early flight to Jacksonville and could not stay, so Hampton was summoned to drive her back to her hotel.

Burt asked her to return after her commitment was over in Florida, and three days later, she showed up on his doorstep once again. That night, she discovered he was a "romantic." She went on to say that he was the first man in her life who had ever fitted that bill. He took her to bed, and she later wrote in a memoir (*There Are Worse Things I Could Do*) that she found him "incredibly seductive."

Even though he was still involved in his ongoing affair with Dinah Shore, he confessed to her, "I've never had such powerful feelings for any woman before until I met you."

Before Adrienne flew out of Tennessee, he left the suggestion open that he might break it off with Dinah and commit to her.

Two weeks later, as she watched the televised Academy Award Oscar presentations, she saw Burt's stunningly handsome appearance with Dinah. They looked radiant and in love.

Adrienne dialed the phone number he'd given her in Los Angeles and after several attempts to reach him, he finally came on the line. He assured her, "I miss you terribly. Think of you all the time."

From that point on, their relationship seemed to be one of "phone tag," as each of them migrated through different parts of the country. He would go for a week or more without any attempt to call her. At long last, she rejoined him in Nashville, where he was filming the final scenes for *Dixie Dancekings*. Regrettably, she found him complaining of various aches which he attempted to relieve by swallowing large numbers of "little red pills."

At one point he gave her a Quaalude, which had a dire effect on her body, as she was not used to either pills or alcohol. They slept in the same bed, and, when he was in the mood, they had sexual encounters.

Two views of Adrienne Barbeau, upper photo where she's "kncoking about" and lower photo as she appeared with Ernest Borgnine in the sci-fi horror flick, *Escape from New York* (1981)

Their first public outing, at which time they were photographed together, came when he invited cast and crew of *Dixie Dancekings* to a screening of *White*

Lightning.

Then Burt, with Adrienne, returned to his rented home. She stayed there until she had to fly to Michigan.

After wrapping *Dancekings*, he flew back to Florida. In a Detroit paper, she read an item stating that Dinah had flown to Jupiter and was staying with Burt on his ranch. He had assured her that he and Dinah were no longer lovers, but that didn't seem to be the case.

Adrienne flew to San Diego to begin rehearsals for William Inge's play, *Bus Stop*, which Marilyn Monroe had famously brought to the screen.

Burt had returned to Los Angeles, and she expected him to call and drive south to see her. But he didn't. She tried to reach him on the phone but got Hampton instead. He told her, "Burt is really, really tired, completely drained."

When she managed to visit him in his home, she ended up sitting in the kitchen as he and director Robert Aldrich spent most of the evening discussing script revisions in his living room.

Burt finally agreed to take time off to drive to San Diego to see her in *Bus Stop*, telling her he would have been ideal cast as the cowboy.

During his brief time in San Diego, there was no love making as he'd been "stabbed" by a splinter, which she worked to remove from his sore finger. He went to see her performance in *Bus Stop* that night, but could not stay the night, as he had to return immediately for an early appointment in Los Angeles.

He did remember to honor her birthday by taking out a full-page ad in *Variety* which reproduced some of the rave reviews critics had generated for her performance in *Bus Stop*.

When her show closed, she headed back to Los Angeles, where she hoped to have a rendezvous with him. He accepted an invitation to visit her one night at her home at 8:30PM. She waited and waited, but he didn't appear, nor did he call. At 3:30AM, she went to bed.

As she left the following morning for an appointment, she discovered a large blue envelope under the wiper blade of her car's windshield. It was addressed "SWEETHEART," and it contained nearly twenty hand-written pages from him.

In it, he confessed he was finding it difficult "to pull the plug" with Dinah. He assured her that he loved her deeply but didn't plan to phone her again until he was free. Of course, he didn't expect her to wait, and he assured her that he loved her "and always will."

Their affair was over, and she realized at once she'd joined the parade of women Burt had seduced and deserted.

"Burt loved me, or so he said," she claimed. "My only problem with that was he didn't plan to see me again."

***

"In a moment of insanity, I decided I wanted to star in a musical," Burt said. "So I went from a violent football and prison drama and foolishly maneuvered myself into a Cole Porter romantic musical called *At Long Last Love.*"

The musical, released by 20th Century Fox in 1975, was mostly written, directed, and produced by Peter Bogdanovich as a vehicle for his lover, actress/model Cybill Shepherd, with whom he had been conducting a love affair since 1971.

In pre-production, long before Burt was cast as the male lead, the musical had been cast with other actors. Bogdanovich had planned it as a tribute to those great Hollywood musicals of the 1930s, films such as *Top Hat* (1935) with Fred Astaire and Ginger Rogers. Bogdanovich purchased the rights to sixteen Cole Porter songs (including "It's De Lovely," "Well, Did You Evah?," and "Just One of Those Things") which Porter wrote while waiting for medical technicians to arrive on the scene of the accident that would cripple him for life.

Cybill had recently recorded an album, *Cybill Does It…to Cole Porter.*

"I liked it," Bogdanovich said. "The lyrics conveyed a frivolous era. Porter's lyrics were less sentimental than those of Gershwin, who was the better musician, but Porter was a better lyricist. I was more interested in the lyrics than the music."

Bogdanovich also asserted that he'd been inspired by the movies of Ernest Lubitsch, including *The Merry Widow* (1934), starring Jeanette MacDonald and Maurice Chevalier. "All those stars did everything live in the 1930s with the orchestra right off the camera. Even today, you can still feel the spontaneity. I wanted to recreate that same feeling that imbued those early musicals, some made at the dawn of the talkies."

Bogdanovich had previously directed Cybill in *Daisy Miller* (1974),

Originally entitled *Quadrille, At Long Last Love* was to have starred Cybill, Madeline Kahn, Ryan O'Neal, and Bogdanovich himself. Eventually, however, he dropped out, offering his role to Elliott Gould. But a few weeks later, both O'Neal and Gould, too, departed (some said "fled") from the scene.

Financing the movie was 20th Century Fox, and the executives there more or less "forced" the director to cast Burt as the male lead, thinking he would be the best choice for box office appeal. Bogdanovich was reluctant but had to go along with this odd choice for a musical.

Cybill Shepherd and Burt emote in the musical *At Long Last Love*. Trouble was, neither of them could sing or dance.

The casting of Cybill and Madeline remained unchanged, but the new male actors included not only Burt but Duilio Del Prete, an Italian singer and songwriter.

The plot centers around four socialites. Burt was cast as a handsome, dashing millionaire playboy, Michael Oliver Pritchard III, who meets a second-rate Broadway star, Kitty O'Kelly (Madeline Kahn). The heiress Brooke Carter (Cybill) falls for a penniless Italian lothario, Johnny Spanish (Del Prete) at the racetrack. Romantic complications flourish.

Others in the cast included Eileen Brennan playing Cybill's companion, who throws herself at Burt's butler and chauffeur, as portrayed by John Hillerman.

Bogdanovich also hired the marvelous character actress, Mildred Natwick. She had recently won an Emmy for her role in the TV miniseries, *The Snoop Sisters* (1972), co-starring Helen Hayes.

At first, it was decided to shoot the film in black and white, like those old musicals, but it ended up being art-directed in what was called "Black and White in Color."

Ruefully, Bogdanovich evaluated the musical talents of his cast: "In the 1930s, both Jeanette MacDonald and Maurice Chevalier were accomplished singers, but that certainly wasn't true about Burt. He held us up in the shooting because he was not a natural—in fact, he screwed up a lot. At times, he became so nervous and upset he hyperventilated into a paper bag."

Although Burt had been eager to work with Bogdanovich because of his past success, he became disillusioned after the first week. "He had the hots for Cybill, so his entire focus seemed to be on her. If I fell on my ass, shit my pants, or whatever, and she came out looking good, he would print it. That pissed me off."

According to Burt, "The songs were recorded live like they used to be in those old movies. Also, as Dinah told me, Cole Porter numbers are the toughest to sing—and she should know."

"We had little receivers in our ears and wires running down our legs to pick up the musical accompaniments," he said. That was Bogdanovich's

Cybill Shepherd, Burt, Madeline Kahn, and Duilio Del Prete in *At Long Last Love*. "Peter (Bogdanovich) had his little darling, Cybill," Burt said. "As for me, I'm a Madeline kind of guy."

tribute to the past. I begged him to insert subtitles—'that's live, folks.' It was tough because all of us had to do a song in one take, both the singing and the dancing.

"My receiver picked up strange messages, once hooking me into a radio broadcast from Tijuana. Right in the middle of one take I heard a loud voice calling 'BREAKER! BREAKER!'"

When Fox executives saw the rough cut, they demanded "more scenes with Burt." He can't sing or dance, but he's good for box office!"

When Burt met his co-star Madeline Kahn, he claimed, "I developed this terrible crush on her. She was a sexy doll, and she was real funny, a great dame. We gravitated to each other at once. She helped me get through the bad days when I wasn't performing like I wanted to. When my ego had been battered during a shoot, she restored my manhood in her dressing room, if you get my drift."

[Actually, Burt had been attracted to her when he's seen her recent pictures. As an inveterate movie-goer, he'd gone to see her feature film debut as Ryan O'Neal's hysterical fiancée in Bogdanovich's screwball comedy, What's Up Doc? *starring Barbra Streisand.*

Bogdanovich had also directed her in Paper Moon *(1973), for which she'd received an Oscar nod as Best Supporting Actress. The film had starred Ryan O'Neal and his daughter, Tatum, both of whom would be future co-stars of Burt.*

Mel Brooks had also directed Madeline in Blazing Saddles *and* Young Frankenstein, *both released in 1974.]*

Cast and crew became aware of the affair of Burt and Madeleine. "I was afraid word would get back to Dinah, and I didn't want to upset her," Burt said. "But Madeline was a hard woman to resist. With all those blabbermouths on the set, I feared someone might spill the beans to Dinah."

Over dinner one night with Dinah, Burt brought up what he called "rumors" of an affair with Madeline. "They're just gossip, not a word of truth in what they're alleging. Madeline and I are just good friends, and she's helping me survive this musical. I wish you could have been my leading lady."

Later, he said, "I don't think Dinah believed a word of what I was saying, but she's not the type to confront me like a jealous fishwife."

Years later, reflecting on *At Long Last Love*, Bogdanovich said, "Nobody seems to understand what I was trying to do. Maybe I didn't know what I really wanted. I set out to shoot a film about people who couldn't talk to each other. Since they couldn't communicate with each other, they spoke in greeting cards. These so-called cards took the form of song. I didn't care so much about the musical part of the film. I wanted to come off depicting people talking, only they were singing. Sounds confusing, doesn't it?"

"Perhaps I was very arrogant during the making of the film. That arrogance masked my insecurity. I knew it was possible that some of my ideas were wrong. But I always insisted they were right. Burt claimed I gave him a hard time, and perhaps I did."

The film previewed in San Jose, and Burt drove Dinah there. They sneaked into the theater after the lights were turned off and left before the final credits flashed across the screen.

"It was a disaster," Burt said, "but Dinah did her best to bolster my ego, telling me I was a combo of Frank Sinatra and Cary Grant."

Bogdanovich was horrified. As a culmination of months of lacerating artistic struggles, Fox showcased their pre-approved, studio-crafted version and not his own final cut.

At Long Last Love received the worst reviews of any film to this point in Burt's moviemaking history. Frank Rich in *The New York Times* wrote: "It's the most perverse musical ever made, a colossal, over-extravagant in-joke. Every time Bogdanovich's stars open their mouths or shake their legs, they trample on Cole Porter's grave. As for Shepherd's dancing, the best to be said is that it may not be recognizable as such: When this horsey ex-model starts prancing around she tends to look as if she's fighting off a case of the trots."

Gene Siskel in the *Chicago Tribune* joined in the condemnation. "The musical numbers are a mess. Nobody knows how to dance; nobody knows how to sing. Shepherd tries to hit the high notes and ends up sounding like a choir girl with a changing voice. Reynolds maintains good cheer, but too often slides into a Dean Martin accent that has nothing to do with the 1930s."

Also in Chicago, a differing opinion was expressed by Roger Ebert of the *Chicago Sun-Times*. "It's impossible not to feel affection for *At Long Last Love*. The stars sip champagne almost without respite, dance the night away, run through a series of wrecked limousines and tour cars, trade partners, and try never, ever to be bored."

Ebert continued: "Burt Reynolds isn't really expected to sing and dance well. The fun is watching him try to have fun in a low key without making a fool of himself, and he generally succeeds. His Clark Gable-styled mustache and his overall bearing remind us of Gable grinning foolishly during absurd production numbers and having a ball."

[The producers of an upcoming biopic, Gable and Lombard *(1976), agreed with Ebert, and offered Burt a crack at the male lead. But after reading the script, Burt wisely rejected the offer, the part eventually picked up by James Brolin. Reviews were mostly unfavorable.]*

In reference to *At Long Last Love*, Molly Haskel, writing in *Viva* magazine wrote: "Peter Bogdanovich has fashioned a beautiful casket in which to bury Cybill Shepherd, whom he brought to the brink in *Daisy Miller*. The Art Deco silvers and blacks, the Hollywood Grecian palace, the black-and-white scheme carried through in costumes and plush, barren sets, convey an air of expensive embalming that would propel only an undertaker into song."

Gene Shalit on the *Today* show said, "Cybill Shepherd cannot walk or talk, much less sing."

Vincent Canby of *The New York Times* said, "casting Cybill in a musical comedy is like entering a horse in a cat show." He also said, "The film's most pleasant surprise is Burt Reynolds, a performance that doesn't invite comparisons with any except earlier ones by Reynolds. He sings reasonably well. He dances. He plays the comedy lightly and earnestly, with low-key good humor of the kind that everyone else (except Miss Kahn) lacks."

Jay Cocks of *Time* magazine stated, "This Cole Porter coloring book, mounted with great expense and no taste, is one of those grand catastrophes, that makes audiences either hoot in derisive surprise or look away in embarrassment. When dancing, the stars look like they're extinguishing a campfire."

The *Los Angeles Times* said, "Burt Reynolds sings like Dean Martin with adenoids and dances like a drunk killing cockroaches." Pauline Kael in *The New Yorker* called it "a stillborn musical comedy, a relentlessly vapid pastiche." John Barbour, film critic, wrote, "If this fiasco were any more of a dog, it would shed."

John Simon in *The National Review* wrote, "*At Long Last Love* may be the worst musical of this or any other decade. Miss Shepherd is like a kid from an orphanage trying to play Noël Coward."

In *The Worst Films of All Time*, published in 1978, *At Long Last Love* was headlined as "The Worst Musical Extravaganza of All Time." In the Hollywood Wall of Shame, it was listed as a major financial disaster, too. The film earned $2.5 million and cost $5 million to make.

Burt learned that his musical was one of the last to be shown at Manhattan's Radio City Music Hall before it closed down for several years. Orson Welles at a Hollywood party chastised Burt for "shutting down the Rockettes."

Burt himself said that the film was "not as bad as it was reviewed. What was reviewed was Cybill and Peter's relationship. You see, Peter Bogdanovich has done something that all critics will never forgive him for doing. That is, stop being a critic, go make a film, and have that film be enormously successful." *[Burt was referring to Bogdanovich's early success with* Paper Moon *(1973).]* "What he did then was to go on talk shows and be rather arrogant and talk about how bad critics are. That was the final straw. So they were waiting with their knives and whatever. And along came Peter who finally gave them something they could kill him with. Unfortunately, there I was, between Cybill's broad shoulders and Peter's ego. And I got killed along with the rest of them."

***

After Liza Minnelli's great success as Sally Bowles in *Cabaret* (1972), she said, "I was sent 400 scripts before I found one I wanted to do." It was *Lucky Lady*, a 1975 20th Century Fox release, a saga about bootleggers during Prohibition, boating their illegal cargoes from the Pacific Coast of Mexico into San Diego. Liza (as Claire) romances her two male counterparts and smuggles liquor.

The film's producer, Michael Gruskoff, was all too aware that there were only two "bankable" female stars who might portray Claire: Liza and Barbra (Streisand). Streisand rejected the part, but Liza went for it after reading the script by Willard Huyck and Gloria Katz, who had scored big with their authorship of the script for *American Graffitti* (1973) directed by George Lukas. They were paid $450,000 for the script, which at the time was a record for an original screenplay.

Steven Spielberg had been offered a chance to direct *Lucky Lady*, and the writers wanted him to accept, but he was already committed to pre-production of what eventually morphed into *Jaws* (1975).

Alan Ladd, Jr., son of the famous actor of the 1940s and '50s, and CEO of Fox, turned instead to Stanley Donen and hired him as the director for $600,000.

Liza was thrilled when she learned that Donen had signed on as the film's director, and that both Paul Newman and Warren Beatty had been offered the male leads. "I could fall for either of those guys," she said."

As the daughter of Judy Garland and director Vincente Minnelli, Liza had grown up appreciating the musicals of Donen, who had once had an affair with her friend, Elizabeth Taylor. Donen had helmed Fred Astaire dancing on the ceiling, and Gene Kelly *Singin' in the Rain*. He directed some of her favorite movies, including *Charade* (1963) with Cary Grant and Audrey Hepburn. He said that in the old days, *Lucky Lady* would have been cast with Jean Harlow, Spencer Tracy, and Clark Gable.

Hackman, Minnelli, and Burt—the unholy trio, and each smoking a cigar— in *Lucky Lady*.

Liza Minnelli and Burt Reynolds in Lucky Lady

Vaguely reminiscent (or at least it tried to be) of Zelda and F. Scott Fitzgerald.

Liza was disappointed when both Newman and Beatty turned down the script and were replaced by Burt, for $500,000, and George Segal for $750,000. Segal later bowed out, his role going to Gene Hackman, who at first was reluctant to accept. However, when he was offered $1.2 million, he said, "It would have been obscene for me to refuse that figure."

For the shoot, which would last a hundred days, cast and crew were flown to Guaymas in Mexico, a site defined by the location agent for Fox as "a sleepy seaport on the Gulf of California." It was thought at the time that Guaymas would be ideal because of the calmness of its waters. But production was delayed on several occasions when harsh winds swept down from the north, threatening nearly a hundred vessels moored nearby.

Burt said, "All this rock 'n rolling saved me millions of dollars. At that point, I had been seriously considering investing in a yacht. I hung in there because my last two or three movies had gone down the tubes, and I felt it was vital to make *Lucky Lady* a hit."

"I was left only with a memory of choppy waters," Liza said. "Lots and lots of water and a rocky boat that made me seasick. I will never make another film on water."

Hackman said "I was going bananas with all the delays. I did not find my role satisfying."

Depending on which accountant you listened to, production delays cost *Lucky Lady* anywhere from $13 to $22 million.

Burt and Liza worked happily with the very talented Hackman, who had gained notice when he'd starred with Beatty in *Bonnie and Clyde* (1967). For his portrayal of Buck Barrow, he received an Oscar nod for Best Supporting Actor. He'd also received an Academy Award for *I Never Sang for My Father* (1970). A year later, he won the Best Actor Oscar for his performance as the New York detective "Popeye" Doyle in *The French Connection* (1971).

[*Ironically, years before, at the Pasadena Playhouse, Hackman and his friend, Dustin Hoffman, were voted "Least Likely to Succeed."*]

Hackman told Burt, "Ever since I was ten, I liked action guys in the movies, none better than James Cagney. I envy you for having worked with him. [*As a young actor in New York, Burt had co-starred with Cagney and Lee Marvin on the TV series,* Robert Montgomery Presents.]

Robby Benson was cast as Billy, the cabin boy. In time, this talented young man would also emerge as a singer, musician, director, producer, educator, and composer. He and Burt became friends. At the time, it was thought that Benson would be cast as Luke Skywalker in *Star Wars,* but he lost the part to Mark Hamill.

Benson, in a film he wrote, directed, and produced, would appear again with Burt in *Modern Love* (1990).

As a sign of Burt's expanding popularity with women, he was literally mobbed when he showed up at a drunken wedding party. "The women were very aggressive," Donen said. "Once or twice, Burt got his crotch felt, and one woman exposed her breasts to him."

Soon, Burt and Liza were generating tabloid headlines that heralded their "torrid affair." That brought Jack Haley, Jr., her husband, to the scene. To help calm things down, Dinah took time out from her busy schedule to fly in on weekends.

As Liza reportedly said, "Burt was not screwing me, but he *was* bedding my sister, Lorna Luft."

In the original script of *Lucky Lady*, the characters portrayed by Burt and Hackman were slain by G-men. But Ladd, the head honcho at Fox, wanted a happier ending and demanded that it be reshot. Regrettably, Liza, at that point, had already migrated to Rome for the filming of *A Matter of Time* (1976) with Ingrid Bergman and directed by her father, Vincente Minnelli.

The revised ending was scripted to occur a decade after the previous scene and featured Liza, Hackman, and Burt together in bed as a *ménage à trois*.

Fox, of course, deemed that as unsuitable, so a third conclusion to the film was scripted and filmed, and their scene as an amicable threesome at bedtime was cut from the final version.

Liza later criticized Donen "for taking out the part that made you feel like the three of us are in peril. I saw the finished picture, and I was never once afraid for us. Most of our serious moments were removed. *Lucky Lady* was not the film that Burt, Gene, and I set out to make. What was released to the public could have been another *Road* picture with Hope, Crosby, and Dorothy Lamour in a sarong."

For her criticism, Donen publicly accused Liza of being "an emotional child."

Burt defended Liza, accusing Donen "of ruining our picture. It is now an abomination, destined to fail at the box office. It could have been a classic, garnering another Oscar for Liza."

Burt later expressed a different assessment: "I'm in the minority, mind you, but I don't think it was a bad film. I don't even think I turned in a bad performance."

Jay Cocks of *Time* said, "Liza Minnelli is better than she has ever been, sweet and raffish, while Burt Reynolds cuts up with infectious bemusement. Much of the heavy acting falls to Gene Hackman." Roger Ebert called the movie, "A big, expensive, good-looking flop." Vincent Canby of *The New York Times* found it "ridiculous without the compensation of being funny or fun. This is difficult to understand, considering the talent involved."

Gene Siskel of the *Chicago Tribune* stated, "There's an arrogance to this project I don't like. Apparently, the filmmakers believed that the public would be sufficiently impressed with the antics of Gene, Liza, and Burt, and that it wouldn't care if the story made sense."

Arthur D. Murphy of *Variety* claimed that "the film is strident, forced hokum. Donen's film caroms from one sequence to another with pointless abandon, a major disappointment."

Gary Arnold of *The Washington Post* wrote, "If you were looking forward to an entertainment with a little class, *Lucky Lady* is likely to prove a resounding letdown."

Charles Champlin of the *Los Angeles Times* stated, "By squinting hard in the mind's eye, you can almost make out what it was that made *Lucky*

Lady seem worth doing. The movie we actually see is cynical, vulgar, contrived, mismatched, violent, uneven, and an uninteresting disaster."

Burt later recalled, "I loved Liza Minnelli and Gene Hackman, and I loved the Jack Lemmon kind of character I played, but there were times when I felt Stanley Donen was petrified and lost. Scared of the boats, scared of the explosions, of the gunshots. I'd look at him between takes and he'd be like this *[crouching with hands over his head]*. But the bedroom scene with the three of us was so beautifully done. I remember going to rushes and saying, 'This is going to be a winner—it really works!' It was a beautifully mounted picture, but the last forty minutes, the battle, was not his kind of film. Nobody knew what was happening, and you didn't care for the characters."

***

All of Hollywood and fans across America were shocked when gossip columnist Joyce Haber announced on April 17, 1975 that Dinah and Burt were breaking up their affair. Weeks before, news about it had traveled along the Hollywood grapevine, and now reports were moving across the wire services.

Friends sided with one party or the other. Farrah Fawcett denounced Burt in the press. "I think Reynolds revealed the news to reporters because he was too much of a coward to face Dinah himself. Don't expect her to give any interviews about the breakup. She's too busy crying."

Burt's press agent, David Gershonson, rushed to his defense. "They were never married, so it's not like they're getting a divorce. They also have no kids to worry about, so it's a much easier break. There are hundreds of couples in Hollywood who hook up with each other, and then later go their separate ways. It's no big deal. Burt and Dinah were just going together. There will be other women for Burt, and, I'm sure, other men for Dinah, who is most attractive and charming. Of course, for Burt now, the world is his oyster, as he is just entering his glory days as a movie star."

In the years leading up to their breakup, Dinah had flown to Mexico where Burt was shooting *Lucky Lady* with Liza Minnelli. "She lit up the place whenever she was around," Liza said, "especially Burt's eyes. He seemed to adore her. She'd fly back on Sunday night, often with Burt's dirty laundry."

During the last weeks of the shoot, Burt was out of touch, and she could not get through to him on the phone, thinking first that the phone wires were down. He finally sent word to her that he would see her when he got back, but "I'll be staying at my own place."

To Dick Clayton, he confessed, "Thanks in part to you, my career is soaring. Women are literally throwing themselves at me. I want to enjoy the fruits of my fame. I've worked so hard to get where I am, and I hope to take advantage before I'm too old to enjoy the reward that comes with being a box office champ."

"More than that, I also want a kid of my own, and Dinah can't give me that. I still love her, and I guess I always will."

The following night he phoned Dinah, telling her that he had returned from Mexico and was coming over. "I'll remember it always. She was sitting in her living room listening to an album by Frank Sinatra. She had a hanky in her hand as if she was prepared for what I was about to tell her. I never sat down but stood before her. I wanted to make it quick before she could melt my resolve."

"When I told her I was leaving her, she was very composed. She took the news with all the dignity I had come to expect of her. I knew I had to be striking a blow to her heart, but I had to go through with it. I was the second fella who'd walked out on her. The first was the love of her life, George Montgomery, her longtime husband. George broke her heart, just what I was doing. But I also knew that heart of hers would mend—the lady, after all, is a survivor."

"In my own heart, I began to miss her the moment I walked out the door. For weeks, I could think of nothing else but Dinah. I had promised I'd be her friend forever—and meant it. But that wasn't the same as turning over in the bed at night and finding her by my side."

Throughout their relationship, Dinah had always tried to be accommodating, rearranging her schedule to fit his needs and wants. She would come home from the studio after enduring a heavy work schedule and prepare him a gourmet dinner.

"I'm sure Burt came to miss Dinah, but I didn't feel that sorry for him," Clayton said. "He was having an affair with Lorna Luft but didn't seem to want to talk about it."

[As much of America knew, Lorna had been born in 1952, the daughter of Judy Garland and Sidney Luft, and the half-sister of Liza Minnelli. An actress and singer, she was unmarried at the time. By 1977, she'd wed Jake Hooker, the lead guitar player of "The Arrows."

When confronted by the press, Lorna said, "Burt and I like each other very much. We go out together and have a lot of fun. He has a great sense of humor. Don't blame me for his breakup with Dinah. When he started going out with me, he had already decided to split with Dinah. If it hadn't been me, it would have been some other girl."]

"The press came down hard on me." Burt said. "Leaving Dinah was like breaking up with the Stars and Stripes. First in any relationship comes the fireworks. Then you ease into the next stage. Passion can die, and you settle in together leading a more subdued life. By then, it's a different kind of love. The final curtain can be that you grow old together, sitting around watching television."

"Dinah once told me she didn't want to grow old in my arms, and I understood that. I guess I wanted to put that first stage passion back into my life. I wasn't ready to settle down into domestic bliss, at least not now."

"The breakup was awfully hard on Dinah," said Jane Brolin, wife of Jim Brolin, the *Marcus Welby* star. "Dinah gives, gives, and gives some more. She's low right now, but I feel she'll bounce back. That's what she does."

Peter Marshall, of TV's *Hollywood Squares*, was a friend of Dinah's. "She puts up a good front, even though her heart is breaking. Of course, that good ol' Southern boy has upset her a lot. Many people like Esther Williams told me she thinks Dinah is getting too old to start another passionate relationship with a man."

Lorna Luft in 2010.

[Actually, Dinah was seen going out on a number of dates, notably with Ron Ely, best known for portraying Tarzan on the 1966 NBC TV series. This was one tall Texan, standing 6'4" with an athletic build. He was even younger than Burt by two years.

He was the same age as Frank Langella, who also was spotted going out with Dinah. A stage and film actor, this Italian American from New Jersey would win four Tony Awards.

He had not yet married Ruth Weil, which he did in 1977. After his divorce from her, he became

Burt claimed, "I had to face a rough choice: Which of Judy Garland's daughters, Liza or Lorna, should I get involved with?"

Lorna drew the lucky number.

the partner of Whoopi Goldberg. When he published his memoirs in 2012, The New York Times claimed, "The book celebrates sluttiness as a worthy—even noble—way of life."

Dinah was also seen out with Frank Gifford, the American football player, actor, and TV sports commentator. For twelve years, he'd been a halfback and flanker for the New York Giants.

For a while, Dinah also dated Wayne Rogers, the film and TV actor known for playing the role of Captain "Trapper" John McIntyre in the CBS TV series, M*A*S*H.

An incongruous beau was Iggy Pop. Burt had been born in 1936, but the "Godfather of Punk" entered the world in 1947. Often appearing on stage barechested with long hair, he was the vocalist of the proto-punk band, "The Stooges."

Dinah also dated Joseph A. Iacovetta, a tennis pro who taught the game to many children of Hollywood legends, becoming a figure in the Hollywood jet set. He and Dinah put on many charity tennis tournaments in Palm Springs.]

At a party, Dinah talked with Dean Martin and two other friends. "I'm going to do what I've always done, and that is throw myself into my work, the best medicine to overcome life's disappointments. I don't want people to feel sorry for me. What's done is done. In the words of our beloved Frankie, love often fades with the summer wind. It's today and tomorrow that counts, not yesterday."

Ticker Freeman, who once accompanied her on the piano, said, "Dinah will never grow old. She's the only one in our crowd who doesn't age. I think she takes a drink every morning from Ponce de Leon's Fountain of

Youth."

One afternoon in October, a mass of flowers was delivered to Dinah's door without a card. At around midnight, she got a call from Burt. Without asking for an invitation, or even inquiring to see if she were with some "gentleman caller," he announced he was coming over. An hour later, he arrived with a suitcase. "I brought my toothbrush," he said as an indication that he planned to spend the night.

Actually, he was moving back in.

The following morning over breakfast, he told her, "I'm back for good. This time, it's forever."

To celebrate his return, she leased a beach house for $300,000, the height of luxury, in Malibu. While they were living there, Dinah was having her elegant Beverly Hills home redecorated, more to his taste than hers. Occasionally, they went out together, but never to a gala or premiere, preferring an intimate dinner at their favorite restaurant, The Saloon, in Beverly Hills. When a reporter asked Burt if he had reconciled with Dinah, he answered, "We're just good friends."

Their romance continued even when he went to Valdosta, Georgia, to shoot his latest movie, *Gator*, released in 1976.

When friends asked him about Dinah, he said, "She's my very best friend. I see her often. I visit her place in Malibu." He left out mention of the fact that he was living there, too. "I see her on occasion when we have something to talk over."

"Dinah's in a kind of limbo," said Sinatra. "I talked to her about Burt. He's back, but she can't count on him staying."

Before the end of December, Burt moved back into her redecorated Beverly Hills home. When asked by the press, he said, "My relationship with Dinah is better and more romantic than ever. She has the body of a 25-year-old and the mind of a mature woman."

But in a few weeks, without warning, he didn't come back to her beautiful home—and didn't even call.

Disillusioned for being "dumped" a second time, Dinah said, "There's one thing I've learned about men. You can't trust them, no woman can. They're adorable creatures, but more gamesmanship than trustmanship."

As time went by, their friendship remained, but the love affair was over.

Burt had fallen in love with another singer: Tammy Wynette.

[In the spring of 1993, word leaked that Dinah had been diagnosed with ovarian cancer. Burt phoned her and wanted to come by. She told him, "Those reports are exaggerated. I'm feeling fine, nothing wrong with me. I'm playing golf, exercising. I may start dating some new guys, perhaps Tom Cruise or Brad Pitt."

On February 24, 1994, Dinah died at her home in Beverly Hills, only five days before she turned 78. Her first husband, George Montgomery, was at her side, along with her two children.

When Burt heard the news, he broke down in uncontrollable weeping. "A part of me, a large slice of my life, is gone forever."]

***

While Burt was in Nashville filming *W. W. and the Dixie Danceckings,* he got a call from director Milos Forman, who urgently wanted to see him about something he didn't want to discuss over the phone. Burt invited him to fly to Tennessee.

Even though Forman didn't tell him the reason for the confab, Burt knew why he was winging in. *Variety* had reported that Forman had been assigned to direct *One Flew Over the Cuckoo's Nest,* based on the brilliant novel by Ken Kesey.

Unlike Clark Gable, who never read *Gone With the Wind,* Burt sometimes read three books a week, and he had been enthralled by the Kesey novel. He considered this son of Colorado a link between the Beat Generation of the '50s and the hippies of the '60s.

In a nutshell, *Cuckoo's Nest* was the story of a supposedly sane man, Randle McMurphy, who gets himself committed to a mental institution as an escape from criminal prosecution. Burt had seen Kirk Douglas perform the role on Broadway, and he coveted the part for himself. He told Dick Clayton, "The character has Burt Reynolds tattooed on his forehead."

When Burt learned that Michael Douglas would be co-producer, he assumed he'd assign the choice role to his father, Kirk. But then he read that the son had to tell his movie star dad that he was too old to star in the film. Kirk had already performed the role on Broadway.

Burt had also heard that his longtime rival, Marlon Brando, had rejected the role, as had Gene Hackman and James Caan.

Burt was at the airport to greet Forman. Since he wasn't due on the set until that afternoon, he invited the director to a breakfast whose discussions about *One Flew Over the Cuckoo's Nest* filled most of the rest of the morning.

"I'm perfect for the part," Burt said. "I know that character to my toenails."

"I think so, too," Forman answered. "Otherwise, I'd wouldn't have flown to Nashville."

As Burt recalled, "His next statement hit me like a sledgehammer to my forehead."

"The choice of the lead has narrowed down to two actors, you and another guy."

"I think I can guess who this other guy is: Jack Nicholson?"

"Yes," Forman answered. "Actually, I think either of you would be perfect. But the final choice will probably be made by Michael Douglas. If he were gay, I'd suggest you fly to Los Angeles and seduce him, but he's a straight arrow."

Before flying back to California, and after a long talk about how to play the role, Burt drove Forman back to the airport. Before boarding, his final words were, "I'll be in there pitching for you, kid."

Burt never heard from him again. Later, he read in *Variety* that Nicholson had been signed. "I bet he'll walk away with the gold."

He was right. Some film historians consider *One Flew Over the Cuckoo's Nest*, released in 1975, as one of the best movies ever made.

Burt later wrote, "One of my biggest mistakes was rejecting the lead role in *Cuckoo's Nest.*

That statement wasn't true. He should have written, "One of my biggest disappointments was not getting the lead in *Cuckoo's Nest.*"

***

"Instead of the lead I wanted in *Cuckoo's Nest*, I starred in a movie called *Hustle*," Burt said. [*In it, a 1975 release from Paramount, he would once again be directed by Robert Aldrich.*] "And instead of an Oscar, I got Catherine Deneuve. Other men have experienced worse fates."

It all started when the screenwriter, Steve Shagan, sent Burt a screenplay called *Hustle*, based on his novel. Burt took out an option on the property. At the time, he was being directed by Aldrich on the set of *The Longest Yard.*

Then Aldrich made an unusual demand: He agreed to direct and produce *Hustle*, but only if Catherine Deneuve played the female lead. It was understood that Paramount would pay Burt for his option and would put up the financing. And whereas Burt would not be designated as one of the producers or investors, he would be paid for his performance as the film's star.

Aldrich later explained why he demanded the inclusion of Deneuve in the cast:

"I thought American middle-class mores would not believe that a policeman would have a love relationship with a prostitute. Because of some strange quirk in the American background, a mass audience wouldn't buy that. But they would believe a seductive French woman in such a part— hence my choice of Catherine Deneuve."

Burt and Aldrich flew to Paris to persuade her to accept the role. At that time, the project's working title was *City of Angels*. Later, it was changed again to *Home Free*, until some executive at Paramount retitled it *Hustle*.

In suites at the swanky George V in Paris, Deneuve kept them waiting for a week. As Burt later confessed to Dick Clayton, "I prepared for my role of the whore-loving cop by arranging to seduce a trio of the most ex-

385

pensive prostitutes in Paris, each of whom charged me $1,000 a night."

"At long last, Catherine agreed to meet with us in the elegant bar of our hotel. The lobby, incidentally, was filled with some of Europe's most high-priced hookers, who catered to the libidos of the rich international businessmen who frequented the place."

Before actually meeting Deneuve, Burt had read a lot about her. Apparently, she'd lost her virginity when she was seventeen to director Roger Vadim, who also became the husband of Brigitte Bardot and later, Jane Fonda.

Vadim perhaps provided the best description of Deneuve: "You know Catherine with her long, chestnut hair, her sensitive but severe face, her rather stiffly held figure, her impeccable makeup. She is the elegant romantic of French cinema, used to good effect by [the French New Wave director] Jacques Demy."

"Her figure is slender," Vadim continued, "the shy and discreetly perverse adolescent figure of a Colette heroine. She liked to laugh but goes through life with an air of gloom. A fay cat in an ermine coat. She views love with the intransigent eyes of Lamartine's heroes. A walking paradox, modern and out-of-date. She is a mixture of Columbine [a stock theatrical character that first appeared in the early 1500s in Italian commedia dell'arte as a clever and saucy servant girl]; and Boadaceia [the Celtic Queen of the Iceni tribe who led a revolt against Roman occupation of what is now East Anglia, England.]"

Seated with Aldrich, Burt rose to greet Deneuve as she made her entrance into the chic and very glamorous bar of the George V.

Before Vadim had entered her life, she'd made an international reputation for herself working with such directors as Luis Buñuel, François Truffaut, and Roman Polanski. She'd risen to prominence in Demy's musical *The Umbrellas of Cherbourg* (1964), later starring in Polanski's *Repulsion* (1965) and Buñuel's *Belle du Jour* (1967).

When Burt met her, she'd just ended her relationship with Marcello Mastroianni, with whom she'd had a child.

Many high-profile men had commented on her allure, Polanski saying, "She looks like a professional virgin, but sexy." Vadim claimed, "I've never seen such beautiful breasts." Steve McQueen found her "gorgeous, but an iceberg."

As she sat down at the table with Aldrich and Burt, she said, "Welcome to Paris. All men are Arabs."

She did not hesitate in saying, "I have read the script, and I will do your picture. I desperately want to please both of you, but if give everything to a film or to a man, I will have nothing left for myself. The mystery of who I am and what I want would be lost. Something would have flown out of me."

"You have my guarantee that we will demand a lot but leave your soul intact," Aldrich promised.

"A woman is old the moment she is no longer desirable," Deneuve answered.

"To me, the French actress, Catherine Deneuve, was the world's most beautiful woman," Burt said.

"As a detective in *Hustle*, where she played a prostitute, I didn't have to pay. That was true off screen, too."

"I can assure you, Miss Deneuve, you are not only desirable, but in fact, most desirable," Burt said. "I also agree with the polls. You are the most beautiful woman in the world, replacing the lofty position once occupied by Hedy Lamarr."

"How very flattering," she said. "and that coming from a man who, according to gossip, has known some of the world's most beautiful women." She smiled at him flirtatiously. "You seem to be undressing me with your eyes."

"Perhaps that was because I'm seeing you for the first time in the flesh," he answered. "Before tonight, I had only your two nude *Playboy* pictorials [*published in 1963 and 1965, respectively*] pinned to my wall, inspiring many a midnight fantasy."

"So you're a reader," she said.

"And a devotee of fine art," he answered.

Aldrich and Burt flew back to Los Angeles, where most of the scenes of *Hustle* were shot. Deneuve joined the cast, which included Paul Winfield, Ben Johnson, and Eddie Albert, with whom Burt had co-starred in *The Longest Yard*. Ernest Borgnine and Eileen Brennan, with whom Burt had recently worked in the disastrously reviewed *At Long Last Love*, were also included.

In *Hustle*, Burt played the smug, hard-nosed police lieutenant, Phil Gaines, in love with Deneuve's character of Nicole. Seemingly, he's tolerant of sharing her favors with other men who meet her price.

"Catherine and I were a case of one and one makes three," he said, "so that brought some interest to the film." He did not explain either the math or the meaning of that statement.

His favorite line in the film was "Sometimes you can't tell the Christians from the lions."

Deneuve was convincing as a high-price hooker, and Burt threw himself into the role of the hard-edged, disillusioned detective. Despite his dreams of escaping from a sleazy world, he moves inexorably toward his death.

One long-ago boozy night, John Wayne had warned him, "Don't die at the end. The public will stay away. You and I aren't supposed to die at the end of our movies but survive to go on to another day."

"I think that the Duke was right," Burt said.

"Catherine took my breath away," he said. "She's a fantastic woman, setting styles and conducting herself with true elegance and class. We got along beautifully. There was nothing not to love about her. She brought out the boy in me."

"I went to this trendy French bistro in L.A., Ma Maison, and got the makings of an elegant picnic. I drove her high into the Hollywood Hills, and the day was ours."

"It was the most romantic picnic of my life. We were truly smitten with each other. I told her of a dream I'd had only the night before. It involved going to live with her in Paris."

"At the end of the shoot, Catherine kissed me goodbye and flew back to France. It was just as well. She was much too much woman for me."

Before saying *adieu* to Aldrich, Deneuve told him, "Any time you're ready to make a picture devoted to the life of Madame de Pompadour, call on me." Then she paused. "Most definitely Catherine de Medici. I'd also be brilliant as Marie Antoinette."

Back in Paris, she told the press, "The only American actor I'm dreaming about is Robert Redford. Two blondes. Perfect for a movie together, as he is as pretty as me."

She also mentioned Burt: "There is a rumor going around that he likes only older women or very young ones. Not true. He likes all women. He is a friend of women."

"He is one of the most charming men in American movies," she said. "He's very funny and sometimes obscene, but always delightful to work with. Many actors resent actresses because we are prettier than they are. Not Burt. He is genuinely interested in his female co-stars and doesn't' spend all day looking at himself in the mirror."

"I'm glad I didn't have to work with an Italian leading man. Except for Marcello, I find all Italian men try to seduce me to beef up their image of masculinity. Such men have their brains—you know—between their legs."

Hustle, on a budget of $3 million, generated box office revenues of $10 million.

Roger Ebert said that it was "about characters primarily. It cares more about getting inside these people than it does about solving its crime. The two lead characters become unexpectedly interesting because they're made into such individuals as Burt Reynolds and Catherine Deneuve."

A.H. Weiler of *The New York Times* wrote, "If this apparent tribute to the Raymond Chandler-Dashiell Hammett detective genre is slightly manipulated for effects, and if it strains a mite too much and too long for its cynicism, it still emerges as a realistic inspection of flawed men's efforts to cope with an obviously flawed society."

Gary Arnold of *The Washington Post* stated, "Screenwriter Steve Shagan persists in fogging up his scripts with a dense layer of Hollywood *Weltschmerz* that makes in impossible for the interesting or entertaining possibilities in his material to break through. *Hustle* would be easier to consume if it were an unpretentious slice of low-life, but Shagan's sensibility turns it into stale baloney."

Kevin Thomas of the *Los Angeles Times* said, "While this is a wonderfully flexible genre, it does not accommodate comfortably a self-conscious nostalgia that quickly become soggily and cloyingly sentimental because it seems out of place."

Arthur Murphy of *Variety* stated, "Because of some over-contrivances in plot, excess crassness and distended length, *Hustle* misses being the excellent contemporary Bogart-Chandler-Hawks-Warner Brothers cynical urban crime-and-corruption melodrama it obviously emulates."

Gene Siskel of the *Chicago Tribune* claimed that "violence takes a back seat to character development and storytelling techniques that are classical. *Hustle* is the kind of picture you don't want to see end. It's going to be a cult favorite."

***

What Burt knew about tennis was what Dinah Shore had taught him during their long love affair. But in 1976, Johnny Carson phoned and invited Burt to fly with him to London for a brief vacation, at which time they would attend Wimbledon to watch Chris Evert in the semi-finals.

He wasn't that interested in tennis but went anyway because Carson had invited him.

Before meeting Evert, who had been "born in my part of the world," *[Fort Lauderdale]*, he read up on her:

[One of the most famous athletes in the world at the time, Chris Evert would eventually win a total of 157 singles championships and 32 doubles titles. As a tennis pro, she won eighteen Grand Slam singles championships and three doubles titles. When Burt met her, she was the year-ending World number 1 singles player in 1974, 1975, and 1976. That would be followed with other major wins in 1977, 1978, 1980, and 1981.]

Because some of Burt's films had been popular in Britain, he was recognized wherever he and Carson went. Carson, however, was relatively unknown, as his *Tonight* Show had failed to find an audience in the U.K and was canceled. "My humor didn't cross the Atlantic," Carson told Burt. "It went down like the *Titanic*."

After her championship win, Evert accepted Carson's invitation to dine with Burt and himself at Claridges for a late night supper, followed by dancing at Annabel's, a chic nightclub then at the top of every trendsetter's wish list in London.

"I liked Chris a lot," Burt said. "I found her sexy. I told Johnny that in some way she reminded me of Dinah Shore. It was the tennis thing."

"Johnny, my fellow horndog, had booked the two of us with some very special entertainment during our stay in London. The less said about that, the better. One night we shared the same hooker imported from Paris. She wasn't Catherine Deneuve, but what woman is?"

Three months later, Burt was dining with Dick Clayton at Manhattan's deluxe "21" restaurant when he spotted Evert across a crowded room, dining with another young woman. He waved at her, and she wrote a note, sending it over by the waiter. It read, "I've learned we're both staying at the Plaza. Why not give me a call?"

He phoned her before midnight and set up a date for the following evening. For the next few days, they were seen out together at chic hot spots in Manhattan.

She was said to have expressed her admiration for Dinah and praised her for her promotion of tennis in California. "Do you have this thing for women tennis players?" she asked.

"I guess I do," he said jokingly. "I find them sexier than male football jocks."

As he later told Clayton, who had returned to Los Angeles, "It was a brief fling, not madly romantic, but diverting. She's a great gal, lots of fun."

In 2015, he remembered her fondly in his last memoir, writing about his playing tennis with her. "She beat me every time—in fact, she could beat me with her right hand tied behind her back. She's right-handed, incidentally. Chris is a real champ."

Evert would also appear in memoirs of other lovers, which Burt avidly read. Before he met her, she'd been involved in a rather public romance with the top men's tennis player, Jimmy Connors. They had each won the 1974 singles titles at Wimbledon.

She was nineteen when they became engaged, but there would be no wedding bells. In 2013, Connors wrote his autobiography, claiming that Evert was pregnant with their child, and that she had unilaterally decided to terminate the pregnancy. She told the press that she was "extremely disappointed in him for misrepresenting a very private matter."

In 1979, Evert married John Lloyd, the British tennis player. However, they later separated when he learned of her affair with Adam Faith, the British singer and actor. Later, they reconciled, only to divorce in 1987. A year later, she wed Andy

Chris Evert, a World No. 1 tennis player, around the time she was dating Burt.

Mill, the two-time Olympic downhill skier and had three sons with him. At the time of their divorce in 2006, she had to settle $7 million on him.

"The last I heard, she married the Aussie golf pro and sports franchiser, Greg Norman," Burt said. The union lasted about a year. Perhaps Chris and I should know by now that we're not the marrying kind. Getting hitched can cost you millions, especially if you marry Loni Anderson."

***

With no movie work in sight for the summer of 1976, Burt decided to return to regional theater and the stage. He accepted an intriguing offer from the Ohio-based impresario John Kenley on the "straw-hat circuit," for performances with the Kenley Players in cities that included Dayton, Akron, Columbus, Toledo, Cleveland, and Warren, Ohio.

To star in familiar Broadway plays such as *West Side Story* or *Camelot*, Kenley hired some of the biggest names in show business, including Tallulah Bankhead, Mae West, Mickey Rooney, Ethel Merman, Gloria Swanson, Jayne Mansfield, Marlene Dietrich, and Rock Hudson.

Kenley's theaters could seat 5,000, and he never charged more than $1.50 a ticket, so it was always standing room only at any of his regionally famous shows.

When Burt met the founder, he found Kenley rather on the effeminate side, but friendly, quick witted, and a genius for promotion.

During the first week Kenley worked with Burt, he self-identified as "John." But a week later, Burt spotted a woman coming into the theater and thought she was John's sister because she looked like his twin. But, as it turned out, "John" had transformed himself or herself into "Joan," a look he/she retained throughout the duration of the second week.

As Joan, Kenley told Burt, "I'd like to extend an invitation for you to put your bedroom slippers under my bed any night of the week."

"Thanks," Burt said, "but I'll pass on that."

On another occasion, he told Burt, "Androgyny is overrated."

Burt asked one of his best friends, actor James Hampton, who'd co-starred with him in movies such as *The Man Who Loved Cat Dancing* and *The Longest Yard,* to join him on the circuit in Ohio that summer.

In a memoir, Burt wrote about that

Ann Miller (as Dolly Levi) with John Kenley, backstage at his theater in Warren, Ohio, during the summer stock heyday of Ohio's greatest regional theater company, the Kenley Players.

memorable summer touring through Ohio. It was almost obligatory for stars to meet their fans after the final curtain call of every performance to sign autographs. Burt was mobbed by hordes of fans. He described them as "mostly housewives, sweet ladies out to tear up the town, but wilder than cats in a jungle." He praised Hampton for his skill at detecting which of them were true "party animals."

Often, the two actors disappeared into their suite with as many as eight women. "There was more laughter than sex," Burt claimed, "but there was plenty of crazy sex, too."

***

Burt received an unexpected call from Mel Brooks, the Brooklyn-born producer, filmmaker, actor, comedian, and composer. He'd met Burt before, telling him, "God, you're funny!"

"To have my humor appreciated by Mel Brooks was praise indeed," Burt said.

At the time that Brooks contacted Burt, the filmmaker was at the peak of his career, his movies among the top ten box office hits of the late '60s. and '70s. They included *The Producers* (1968), *Blazing Saddles* (1973), and *Young Frankenstein* (1974).

Burt had seen several of his movies, laughing at the antics on the screen. They had "a satiric touch with farcical styling." Of course, Brooks had his critics, some of whom defined him variously as "too manic, too Jewish, too slapstick, too derivative of the Borscht Belt, and too much."

Brooks wanted to cast Burt in a cameo in his latest film, *Silent Movie*, set for a 1976 release from 20th Century Fox. Brooks told him that he would be the star, playing Mel Funn, a once-talented director whose career had faded because of his alcoholism. He hopes to revive his career by convincing Hollywood's biggest stars to make a silent movie, an homage to Charlie Chaplin, Mack Sennett, and Buster Keaton.

The leading players would include Dom DeLuise, who had remained one of Burt's best friends, along with Marty Feldman. Burt would also be reunited with Bernadette Peters, with whom he'd made love in *The Longest Yard*.

TV's Sid Caesar, who had helped launch Brooks into show business, would be cast as the studio chief, a "braying donkey."

Guest cameos like Burt's would be performed by Brooks' wife, actress Anne Bancroft, as well as Burt's former co-star, Liza Minnelli, Paul Newman, and James Caan. The only word spoken throughout the entire duration of this "silent film" was the French '*non*' uttered once (and only once) by Marcel Marceau, the world's greatest mime.

Two weeks later, Burt met with Brooks to complain about the way his cameo was written. It depicted him as a man in a wheelchair who performs a number of wacky stunts. In contrast, Burt wanted to play a self-enchanted movie star, more or less a send-up of himself. To his surprise, Brooks endorsed the rewrite.

"My character in the movie has this big house on the hill. I have a big "R" stolen from Republic Studios on my gate. My home is decorated in Early Gauche. I had my initials everywhere—BR on the rugs, the ashtrays, everything. I can't pass a mirror without looking in it to admire my male beauty."

In a memoir, Burt revealed that before Brooks ordered the cameras to roll, he checked out his groin. "Jesus, look at the size of that swansticker. Are you going to want separate billing for that?"

One of the film's funnier bits of schtick was a shower scene where everyone in it was shot from the waist up. Burt is joined under the running water by Dom DeLuise and Marty Feldman. "The guys pulled a joke on me," Burt said. "At one point there are eight hands on my body, including my own, soaping me. I don't know who it belonged to, but one of those hands grabbed my crotch. Of course, that didn't make the final cut."

Burt got along beautifully with Anne Bancroft. They were seen talking and laughing together. She was oddly but glamorously cast as a flamenco dancer in a flame-red satin gown with a feather boa.

"Mel was clever but cruel," Burt said. "He has a nasty sense of humor that's hysterical if you're not the brunt of it."

Beauty and the Beast: Brooks with Anne Bancroft in 1991 at the Cannes Film Festival.

Silent Movie was made for $4 million and generated $36 million at the box office.

Gene Shalit in the *Ladies' Home Journal* said, "Burt Reynolds proves what I have been saying for years: that given the right roles, he could be the most sophisticated Cary Grant-like comedian on the screen today."

Vincent Canby of *The New York Times* wrote, "The film can be enjoyed as a virtually uninterrupted series of smiles but doesn't contain a single element moment that ever seriously threatens to split the sides."

Variety claimed, "Considering the pitfalls, the brisk pic works exceedingly well."

Charles Champlin of the *Los Angeles Times* found, "Some of the bits and pieces work better than others, but so many work so clownishly, zanily, idiotically well that *Silent Movie* is certain to have the year's noisiest audiences."

Gary Arnold of the *Washington Post* found the movie "a misbegotten but tolerably amusing novelty item." Roger Ebert noted that "*Movie* isn't all silent. It's filled with wall-to-wall music, sound effects, explosions from a Coke machine, whistles, crashes, and, yes, one spoken word."

One evening, Brooks invited Burt to his home for a dinner with Bancroft and himself. During the course of the evening, he suggested that Burt and Bancroft might search for a property in which they could co-star. All three of them agreed that would be a splendid idea.

"You can bring them into the theater," Brooks said to Burt, "and Anne here can keep them there."

"That damn remark cut me to the quick," Burt later claimed. "It'll be a cold day in hell before I spoke to Brooks again."

But is he speaking French, too? In this scene from *Hustle*, Burt interrupts one of his exchanges with Catherine Deneuve.

"I was gang-raped in that shower scene in *Silent Movie*," Burt claimed.

CHAPTER ELEVEN

BURT'S PEAK
As a Box Office Champion and Sex Symbol

Burt's Affair with
TAMMY WYNETTE
The Queen of Country Music
Say Bye-Bye to Your Man?

GATOR
That Business with Lauren Hutton
"How lucky can a guy get?"

NICKEOLODEN
Boring, Misconceived, and Schmaltzy
Bogdanovich Bombs Again

LUCIE ARNAZ
"Is Loving Lucie the same as Loving Lucy?"

SMOKEY & THE BANDIT: REDNECK CHIC
Hot Rods, Shorty-Shorts, & Box Office Receipts

HEADLINES WITH SALLY FIELD
She Doesn't Fly, and She's Not a Nun,
But Everybody Seems Obsessed with Their Affair

A SUICIDE-THEMED COMEDY
The End

HOOPER
Stuntsmanship, Scathing Reviews, and BIG Box Office

Smokin' Gators, Hot Fast Cars, & Fast Hot Women

Around the time Burt reached the peak of his box office appeal, he was quoted as saying, "I come across as Henry VIII in the tabloids, but I'm just a swinging bachelor who loves women—at least most of them. Some of them love me back. I'm not trying to become another Don Juan, or even Errol Flynn."

[Flynn, one of the most promiscuous movie stars in the history of the 20th Century, claimed to have seduced 7,000 women of all types and races around the world.]

"I like all sorts of women," Burt continued, "from my little Japanese darling, Miko Mayama to Dinah Shore, my beautiful, classy, and talented Tennessee Belle."

"And I don't necessarily dream about only Jayne Mansfield or Marilyn Monroe types. After all, I married Judy Carne, a Peter Pan with absolutely no tits."

"Many women have passed in and out of my life, most of them one-night stands that I forgot about the next day. I have something in common with Peter Lawford: We sometimes encounter girls at parties and can't remember if we ever plugged them or not."

Sometimes, on television, Burt mocked his own image. "*Time* magazine described me as a 'honcho macho,' whatever in hell that is. I'm generally considered a walking streak of sex, but at times, I enjoy blowing this sex symbol image crap right out of the water."

"I can't help myself," he said. "Whenever I meet a woman, regardless of her age, I try to impress her with my easy-going charm. I flirt with her and flatter her whether it's deserved or not."

"As a live-in lover, I have a fatal flaw," he admitted. "Even dark glasses don't blind my roving eye. I might have a world-class looker waiting for me at home, but that doesn't prevent me from checking out the latest babe with her tits bouncing. Remember Lana Turner ("The Sweater Girl") in that movie *They Won't Forget* (1937)?"

"If pressed, I refuse to lie. I tell the truth that I fool around. Of course, I hate it when one of my steady girlfriends throws a jealous fit—it means she has no class."

"Dinah, at least, has too much class to bring up my indiscretions."

After finishing *Gator,* Burt flew to Nashville in September of 1975 to tape a syndicated TV talk show. The singer/songwriter, Tammy Wynette, had also agreed to appear on the show.

[Wynette, whose income-generating power on the country-western music circuit was rivaled only by Dolly Parton and Loretta Lynn, was called the "First Lady of Country Music." Her hits addressed the prevalence of loneliness, the pain of divorce, and the difficulties of friendship, loyalties, and love. During the late 1960s and early 1970s, twenty of Wynette's songs rose to the top of the charts.]

Burt had traveled to Nashville with the country singer, Jerry Reed *[he had just played the villain in* Gator*]* and with his best friend, actor James Best

The day before the taping of the talk show in Nashville, Reed called Tammy and told her that Burt, the following night, would like to have dinner with her after the taping. "Would you be able to make it?" he asked.

"Yes, of course I would," she answered. "I've been watching him on the *Tonight* Show, and I'm a fan of *Dan August* on TV. I'm dying to meet him."

Burt had long been one of Tammy's fans. The story of her

Burt with C&W singer Jerry Reed and Fred, the Bassett Hound in *Smokey and the Bandit*.

Fred was chosen for the part by Burt, "to some degree because he steadfastly refused to obey commands."

road to glory had impressed him deeply.

[In Mississippi, nourishing her dream of one day of becoming a singer, Tammy picked cotton and lived in a tarpaper shack, After running away from home, and desperate for an audition at the Grand Old Opry, she'd arrived penniless in Nashville. Before her breakthrough as a widely admired singer, she'd worked in a shoe factory and as a barmaid and waitress, and attended a beauty school in Tupelo, Mississippi. Even after her emergence as a major C&W star, she renewed her cosmetology license every year for the rest of her life — just in case she ever had to go back to a conventional day job.

Although her path was paved with heartbreak and setbacks, she climbed — rung by painful rung — the ladder to success. In 1969, she married a fellow country music singer, George Jones, with whom she produced many successful recordings as a C&W team. Their tumultuous marriage ended in divorce before she met Burt. Her detractors pointed out that she rarely followed the lyrics of her most famous song "Stand by Your Man," even though it became one of the best-selling hit singles by a woman in the history of country music.]

The recordings encased in album covers above were Burt's favorites, and he played them over and over.

"Tammy and I have been rich and we've been poor, and often miserable both times. But rich and miserable is better."

In reference to Burt, Wynette admitted, "I found his voice huskier and sexier than in his films. When I met him, I thought he was even more handsome than he was on the screen."

Everything went smoothly and as planned during the taping of their talk show in Nashville. When it ended, an entourage that included Burt, Tammy, James Best, and a few others, arrived at a local restaurant, Mario's, for a long evening of eating and drinking. ("Lots and lots of champagne," she recalled.)

"Hanging out with Burt showed me what it was like to be out with a movie star," she said. "And I saw he put up with a lot of shit. People were

398

always pestering him for something. Some obviously gay men followed him into the men's room whenever he went to take a leak."

At the end of the evening, Tammy invited Burt to her home, where she introduced him to her children. They even visited her mother's bedroom, where Burt found her reading a copy of the *National Enquirer.*

Later, according to Tammy, they sat in her living room "talking until the wee hours. I felt a strong physical attraction for him, but at some point, he had to leave because he had an early morning flight back to the West Coast. Before he left, I could have invited him to my bedroom because the rest of my household had gone to sleep, but I didn't want it to be a one-night stand. I later regretted sending him away into the night, because I knew I might never see him again. I should have abandoned my pride and taken his hand, leading the big lug toward my bed. But I didn't."

A month passed, and he never called, although he had promised that he would.

The next month she was invited to Los Angeles for an appearance and singing gig on *The Dinah Shore Show.*

Usually she stayed at either the Beverly Hills Hotel or the Beverly Wilshire, but this time she and her band booked themselves into a Holiday Inn.

Knowing she was in town, Burt tracked her down. He finally got her phone number from one of the staff members of Dinah's show. He told her he wanted to see her, but her schedule was full, and she had to be on board the first plane leaving LAX for Nashville the next morning.

The unfounded rumors circulating about an affair with Burt had made Tammy nervous, but as a TV host, Dinah was gracious and welcoming, giving Tammy a big hug.

After her return to Nashville, the first person who called was Burt. "We began a love affair over the phone, since we were always in different cities. I welcomed his calls from the road, and sometimes we talked for hours. That's how we got to know each other."

The next time she was in Hollywood, she checked into the Beverly Wilshire and phoned him. At the time, he was shooting his latest movie, *Nickelodeon.* She arranged for a catered Southern meal that night in her hotel suite, with the understanding that he'd arrive there at 8:30PM.

He never showed up but called to tell her the director had ordered him to stay for retakes. At three o'clock in the morning, he arrived. "I was sleepy, and he was dead tired," she said.

The warmed-over meal was served, but he didn't have much appetite. She was in the kitchen of her suite when she heard a crash in her living room. She rushed in to find him on the floor. Her first reaction was that he had had a heart attack.

"Paper bag," he muttered. She realized he was hyperventilating.

Rushing into the hallway, she encountered a maid, who found a paper bag in her linen closet. Still on the floor, Burt held it to his mouth and breathed in and out.

[When someone takes in more oxygen than his or her body needs because it's "hyperventilating," the result can be what doctors sometimes diagnose as respiratory alkalosis (high pH). The point of exhaling and inhaling into a bag is for someone to "re-breathe" exhaled carbon dioxide (CO_2) in the hopes of restoring a normal pH level. Although in theory, breathing into a paper bag might correct an attack of hyperventilation, it isn't always effective.]

He confessed that he'd been passing out a lot lately. "The doctors tell me it's from stress, exhaustion, overwork, and high anxiety."

The next morning, he was feeling better, but did not make love to her. Then he said that he had to go over to Dinah's home to discuss some business, but that he'd return to her suite in time for dinner.

Feeling embarrassed and awkward after he left, she made an impulsive decision. Hastily, she packed, checked out, and took a taxi to LAX. By 1PM she was back in Nashville.

He phoned her from L.A. that night, suggesting that she might have left a note.

They survived that embarrassment and continued their phone dialogues in the weeks ahead. Eventually, he invited her to Jupiter, where their affair began. She fell in love with the area and eventually bought a second home there.

For their first Christmas together, Tammy presented Burt with something he'd searched for but failed to find: a classic 1955 Lincoln Continental in mint condition. She had located it in Tennessee.

"I was knocked off my ass on Christmas morning when I looked out the window at what was sitting in my driveway. This was a fabulous gift from a fabulous lady. Her generosity was incredible. If she didn't stop this, I might even fall in love with her. But, no, I didn't want to get too carried away."

In the New Year, Burt would go for weeks without calling her. In the meantime, she began dating Michael Tomlin, a real estate agent who wore expensive suits and drove a Mercedes. Although he appeared to be rich, she was told by friends to be careful because he was a "fortune hunter."

Late in life portrait of the late, the great, Tammy Wynette.

400

She paid that no attention. After only four dates, she married him on July 18, 1976.

"He seemed to enjoy spending my money," she said.

Fewer than two months later, in September, she filed for divorce, calling it "my expensive 44-day marriage."

After her divorce, Burt and Tammy continued their affair, hooking up in Dallas, Atlanta, Miami, Los Angeles, and Jupiter (Florida). They maintained a mutual understanding that they'd made no commitments of fidelity to each other. She defined their relationship as simply "a loving friendship."

Thus began an on-again, off-again affair that would last for years. Neither was in the best of health, and they often met not for sex—"but to nurse each other," she said.

"One night, he collapsed in my bathtub, and nearly drowned before I pulled him out and summoned an ambulance to take him to the hospital," she said. As it turned out, he was suffering from hypoglycemia.

As the years went by, their sexual chemistry cooled, replaced by an abiding, loving, supportive friendship.

On April 6, 1998, after a litany of medical problems which resulted in frequent hospitalizations, at least a dozen major surgeries, and an addiction to painkillers, Wynette, while asleep on her couch, died at the age of 55. Although its cause was later disputed by three of her surviving children—with enormous legal complications that included the exhumation of her body more than a year after her death—Wynette's doctor said she died of a blood clot in her lung. She had continued to perform almost until the end of her tragedy-stricken life.

According to Burt, "I lost a dear friend, one who can never be replaced in my heart."

***

Burt made his directorial debut in *Gator* (1976). Based on a script written by William W. Norton, it was a sequel to *White Lightning*. He was cast as a "Moonshiner Swamp Rat" named Gator McKlusky.

"I waited twenty years to direct, and I enjoyed it more than anything I've done so far in the business," he said. "I think it's what I do best."

"In *Gator*, I wanted to turn out a movie that would find an audience beyond those who were brought up on gravy, grits, and possum."

"Of course, my most loyal fans expected some hair-raising car chases, and I aimed to satisfy. There was one chase that featured speedboats, helicopters, and alligator-infested mangrove swamps. In another scene, the *PO*-lice get their squad car stolen."

In ways that some critics described as baffling, violent action in *Gator* alternated with in-jokes, smooching, down-home wit, pathos, slapstick comedy, desperation, arson, intrigue, tears, and eventually, retribution.

Burt was delighted when the producers, Jules V. Levy and Arthur Gardner, cast Lauren Hutton, one of America's top models, as his leading lady. "How lucky can a guy get?" he asked. She played Aggie Maybank, a nosy TV reporter who places her career above Burt's romantic overtures.

According to Burt, "Hutton was more than a mannequin and wasn't just taking up space before the camera. She threw herself into the role of Aggie, and especially into those love scenes with me." As he later told one of the film's character actors, Jack Weston: "Her acting was so good, she even convinced me she was in love with me."

Burt related to Hutton, who had been born in Charleston, as a daughter of the Old South. Initially, when she gravitated to New York looking for work as a model, she was often rejected by agents because of her signature gap between her two front teeth. Eventually, a dentist managed

The studio decided to promote the sexual chemistry in *Gator* of its two co-stars, Burt and top model Lauren Hutton.

According to Burt, "I had a difficult time posed crotch to crotch with Lauren. It was hard to keep junior from getting hard. As for that gap between her front teeth, it was ideal for a man's tongue."

to fill it in, but as the years went by, some of her fashion layouts revealed the gap as clearly evident. Eventually, she launched herself as a model, earning only fifty dollars a week for Christian Dior.

In 1968, Hutton made her film debut in *Paper Lion* with Alan Alda. Five years later, in 1973, with Revlon, she signed the most lucrative contract in the history of modeling.

In conversations with Burt, she claimed, "I never spent much time worrying about the stuff most women do: Getting married, having kids… things like that. Growing up, I was a bit of a tomboy. I liked to go fishing."

Like Burt himself, she had grown up in Florida, later attending the University of South Florida.

Sometimes, her statements startled him, especially when Hutton claimed she wanted to go to Africa and live with the bushmen. She told him that she liked modeling because it was one profession where she could not be replaced by a man, and she adored acting because it allowed her to get inside some other woman's personality.

When Burt met her, she'd been involved in a love affair with her business manager, Robert Williamson, a liaison which would last until his death in 1997, even though he squandered some $13 million of her money. When asked during the shoot if she were having an affair with Burt, she answered, "I'm not a kiss-and-tell type girl."

The country/western singer, Jerry Reed, had worked with Burt before. In *Gator*, he played a villain, Bama McCall, the leader of an extortion ring. As one critic wrote, "He looks mean enough to chew up Waylon Jennings and spit him out."

Reed, a Georgia boy, was better known as a singer and songwriter than as an actor. One of his best songs was "Guitar Man." As sung by Elvis Presley, it became a "chart topper." Another of his hits was "When You're Hot, You're Hot." He told Burt, "No one can play a redneck crazy like me, with the exception of yourself."

The very talented character actor, Jack Weston, was cast as Irving Greenfield, an overweight, bumbling Federal agent on the trail of moonshiners.

As Gator, Burt is compelled to hook up with Weston to bring down Bama McCall. That will keep Gator's "pappy" from going to jail for moonshining. It will also prevent Gator's nine-year-old daughter from being sent to a foster home.

With humor and charm, Mike Douglas played the glib, fast-talking governor of the state. A rival of Merv Griffin, he was best known for his afternoon TV talk show.

Alice Ghostley, who played an engagingly shrewish clerk at the county's courthouse, is at first thrilled with the macho presence of Burt "until he goes too far."

Ghostley was better known for her appearances on TV's *Bewitched*, playing the Stevens' family maid, a well-intentioned but inept and bungling witch named Esmeralda. *[Ghostley had also played the town gossip in* To Kill a Mockingbird *(1962).]*

Opening in Savannah, Georgia, *Gator* drew mixed reactions but took in $12 million at the box office.

Richard Eder of *The New York Times* wrote, "It is not a terrible picture, and it has some good things in it. but it proceeds like a sleepwalker, perpetually wondering what it is doing—and falling asleep and doing it some more."

Gene Siskal of the *Chicago Tribune* claimed, "Unfortunately, the makers of the sequel, namely Burt Reynolds himself, forgot to include the very elements that made *White Lightning* a hit: a good story and a fine romance."

The *Monthly Film Bulletin* weighed in, too: "Elaborately gauche in all its parts as it is, however, *Gator* acquires a certain shaggy-dog charm overall, perhaps because of the exemplary lack of seriousness with which everyone takes it."

Arthur D. Murphy of *Variety* wrote, "There's nothing wrong with an unabashed popcorn movie, but there's no reason for *Gator* to be as uneven, contrived, and untidy as it is. It never takes itself seriously, veering as it does through many incompatible dramatic and violent moods for nearly two hours."

Charles Champlin of the *Los Angeles Times* stated, "*Gator* looks exactly like what it is, a commercial concoction assembled for an undemanding mass market. On those terms, it will probably work well enough. It is fast and splashy pulp stuff." Gary Arnold of the *Washington Post* called the film "peculiarly ambivalent and dismaying, which derives directly from Reynolds. One can see it in his glum, detached performance, as well as feel it in the aimless, miscalculated turns the story takes."

Jerry Renninger of the *Palm Beach Post* claimed, "What keeps *Gator* out of the swamps is unconventional acting by all hands and remarkably good direction by Reynolds. This is the first film he has directed, but it's plain that his many years as an actor have taught him how the job should be done."

Burt himself gave his own review. "*Gator* was like Chinese food—not a great picture, but great entertainment. You might want to go back for more two hours later."

***

Peter Bogdanovich needed a big hit, and he hoped that his latest movie, *Stardust Memories*, co-written by him, would be a box office triumph. Bogdanovich envisioned it as a love letter to early silent films—especially to those of D.W. Griffith—in which the actors would be dressed in the style of 1910.

During pre-production, he cast the lead roles with Jeff Bridges, John Ritter, Orson Welles, and his current girlfriend, Cybill Shepherd, who had co-starred with Burt in their recent flop, *At Long Last Love*, also directed by Bogdanovich.

The head of Columbia, David Begelman, thwarted Bogdanovich's vision, demanding instead that Ryan O'Neal and Burt Reynolds be cast as the two male leads. *[It was agreed that Ryan would have star billing over Burt]* and rejecting outright Bogdanovich's inclusion of his girlfriend, Cybill Shepherd.

Tatum O'Neal, Ryan's then 13-year-old daughter, was hired too.

Columbia also demanded that the movie's title be changed from *Stardust Memories* to *Nickelodeon,* and defined 1976 as its release date.

Both Burt and Ryan O'Neal wanted one million dollars each for their performances. *[They each eventually settled for $500,000.]* Tatum O'Neal took home $250,000; Bogdanovich got $700,000 to helm it. Columbia provided $8 million, and British Lion shelled out another $2 million. "It didn't have to cost so much," Bogdanovich said, "but the producers insisted on it getting bigger and bigger and costlier."

The plot revolves around Ryan's task of shooting silent films in a small desert town. Much of the film was shot in the foothills of Modesto, a region of California that Burt admitted he hated.

Ryan had already made two pictures with Bogdanovich. He described the filming of *Nickelodeon* as "a terrible experience. Peter took a tough little script about early Hollywood and turned it into a farcical series of precious little jokes. I tried to drop out, but it was too late."

In the second lead after Ryan, Burt was cast as Buck Greenway, a genial wrangler-turned-stuntman. His character was said to have been based on the fabled director, Raoul Walsh, the film pioneer with a black patch over one eye.

"The part I played was a sort of Gary Cooper type, with a little of Buster Keaton thrown in. "I do a lot of pratfalls and fall into things. I'm sorta sweet and likeable like I am in real life. The role I might have normally played was assigned to Ryan, a fast-talking guy who craves bigtime success."

Cast as Alice, Tatum played what she defined as "a crew member/odd-job helper/bit actor. I even learned to sing and tap dance for the film. It was supposed to be a comedy, but there was little humor on the set. After two weeks in the hot sun, most of the cast members weren't even speaking to each other. When he wasn't on the

Burt, Jane Hitchcock, and Ryan O'Neal in *Nickelodeon.* "I should have been cast in Ryan's role," Burt said.

405

set, my father (Ryan) was locked away in his trailer. I was horrified at how brutally the horses were treated."

Burt admired Tatum, and he was surprised at how indifferent Ryan seemed toward his daughter. She admitted to Burt that her father's womanizing had become compulsive within their "erotically charged" house.

According to Tatum, "Strange women are always coming and going from our house. I've seen him French kissing women in our living room, and I can hear them making love in his bedroom. He's often cruel to them, kicking them out when he's finished with them, even putting them in a cab in the middle of the night. Sometimes, he literally kicks them out the door."

The dysfunctional O'Neals, *en famille:* Tatum, Ryan, and Griffin. Their home was "erotically charged."

"My father practically ignored me throughout the shoot, and he was always angry and belittling me. I was defenseless. He made fun of me. Peter [Bogdanovich] also yelled at me, calling me fat. I cried a lot."

As Tatum later relayed privately, "Burt, too, was difficult. He did a lot of stunts and was always injuring himself, messing up scenes. Once, I was depicted sitting on his shoulders, and we had to do take after take. Finally, he shouted, 'I've had it with damn movie!'"

"Actually, I developed a crush on Burt—that is until John Ritter came along. I really loved him."

Tatum was the youngest actress to win an Oscar, which she did for her performance in Bogdanovich's *Paper Moon* (1973). She played a tough orphan who teams up with a charming con man portrayed by her father.

As detailed in her memoir, Tatum had been molested at the age of six. She always had to deal with her father's volatile temper. When he moved in with actress Farrah Fawcett, he abandoned her and her brother, Griffin, letting them live alone as teenagers. As time went by, she became painfully aware of her brother's drug addiction.

In 1986, Tatum married another temperamental man, tennis champion John McEnroe.

Cast into a minor role, Stella Stevens—a Southern belle from Yazoo, Mississippi—in the words of one critic, looked "juicy." Burt had already seen a lot of her in a trio of *Playboy* layouts, including when she was Playmate of the Month (January 1960). She was said to be one of the most photographed women in the world, and Elvis Presley took notice when she appeared with him in *Girls! Girls! Girls!* (1962).

An Alabama beauty, Jane Hitchcock as Kathleen Cooke didn't have a lot to do but look fragile and gorgeous as a silent screen heroine. The script called for her to be fought over by Burt and Ryan. She told the press that she preferred her life as a model instead of being an actress. The "ageless beauty," as she came to be known in the modeling world, was employed by such companies as Calvin Klein and Maybelline.

Many critics cited her "distracting" surname. She was said to have the same bone structure as Cybill Shepherd, who had been rejected for the role.

Burt and Jane Hitchcock in *Nickelodeon*.

Which man will make off—or make out—with this sexy flapper? Burt or Ryan O'Neal?

Actor John Ritter, son of the singing cowboy, Tex Ritter, was cast as "Franklin Frank," the seventh lead. His first TV acting experience had come when he worked with Burt on the *Dan August* TV series.

Ritter was cast as a campus revolutionary. He would go on to his greatest fame as Jack Tripper in the ABC hit sitcom *Three's Company* (1977-84).

Whenever he could, Burt got a job for his dear friend, James Best, who appeared in *Nickelodeon* as a character called "Jim."

Harry Carey, Jr. was cast as "Dobie," his actual nickname from childhood. Dobie was short for "Adobe," the color of his hair as a boy. He was the son of the famous actor, Harry Carey, Sr., born in 1878.

During World War II, Carey Junior worked with director John Ford making naval training films. He later appeared in some of Ford's most renowned movies, including *Red River* (1948) and *She Wore a Yellow Ribbon* (1948), both starring John Wayne.

Carey cited as his biggest failure his inability to seduce Marilyn Monroe during the making of *Gentlemen Prefer Blondes* (1953). One of his last films would be *The Whales of August* (1987), starring Burt's friend, Bette Davis.

Brian Keith was assigned the Orson Welles' role after the corpulent actor left after only one week on the set. Welles gave no reason for his hasty departure.

Nickelodeon was just one of the dozens of films in which Keith was cast, including key roles in such movies as *Reflections in a Golden Eye* (1967), co-starring

John Ritter in 1988.

Tatum's crush on Burt faded the moment she met this male charmer.

Marlon Brando and Elizabeth Taylor, and *With Six You Get Eggroll* (1968) with Doris Day. He would later appear with Burt in *Hooper* (1978).

Three weeks into filming, Burt collapsed, appearing to be in a rundown condition and overly stressed. He had to drop out for two weeks until he regained his strength. "I felt like shit during the entire shoot, and it showed in my lackluster performance. I felt this flop was going to put Peter *[Bogdanovich]* on the road to obscurity, maybe taking me with him."

When co-producer Irwin Winkler sat through the final cut of *Nickelodeon*, he delivered the first review. "The movie is atrocious, and I blame Bogdanovich for a failure in casting it. He simply screwed up a terrific little script by himself and W.D. Richter."

At the premiere, guests paid a nickel to get in, the price of a movie ticket in 1910 at the dawn of the talkies.

Roger Ebert wrote, "The actors are lifeless except for Burt Reynolds in this curiously flat movie. It does an abrupt turnabout from comedy to elegy about two-thirds of the way through. Bogdanovich's escaping hot-air balloons, elaborately staged pratfalls, and period sets aren't exploited—they're just there."

Kathleen Carroll of the *New York Daily News* wrote: "Reynolds shelves the sarcasm and acts the role of a country bumpkin who stumbles into the leading man league and grows disillusioned with the silly demands that come with the job."

It was noted by critics that Tatum's character had a sole function of looking owlish and wise beyond her years...and cute. It was also noted that none of the spirit she displayed in Bogdanovich's *Paper Moon* was evident in *Nickelodeon*.

The release of *Nickelodeon* marked one of the lowest points in Bogdanovich's career. It was the third of a trio of disasters, the others being *Daisy Miller* (1974) and *At Long Last Love* (1975). The director's credibility was severely damaged in the aftermath, when most of Hollywood turned against him. Bogdanovich himself admitted his contribution to his own demise as a filmmaker: "I was dumb and made a lot of mistakes."

***

Burt confessed one night to James Best, "I still have this thing for older women. For years, I thought I might seduce Lucille Ball. I think she could go for me bigtime. But instead of turning my macho charm onto Lucille, I've directed it at her daughter, Lucie Arnaz. That's Lucie with an '—ie' at the end. She goes ballistic when she sees her name misspelled in the paper as 'Luci.'"

The daughter of Ball and Desi Arnaz, Sr., Lucie was born in 1951. Her brother was Desi Arnaz, Jr.

Burt began his affair with Arnaz in 1976, near the end of her marriage to actor Phil Vandervort, whom she divorced in 1977.

Burt had first seen Lucie when she'd appeared briefly in walk-ons on her mother's TV series, *The Lucy Show.* She appeared again with her mother in *Here's Lucy* (1968-1974). In 1975, she played a murder victim in the NBC telefilm, *Who Is the Black Dahlia?*

"First, I dated the daughter of Judy Garland, Lorna Luft, before turning my attention to Lucie Arnaz (above) the daughter of Lucille Ball," Burt said.

"I'm realistic about show-biz," Lucie said. "Being the daughter of Lucille Ball is like being the son of Frank Sinatra. Sinatra Junior and I know we'll never come within miles of equaling the fame of our parents."

One night she told Burt, "Thank you for not asking what it's like to have super famous parents. Everybody I meet asks me that same question. I don't know how to answer it, because that's the only life I've known. When my parents used to take me out, they were mobbed by autograph seekers. In spite of her fame, Lucille was never a flamboyant movie star like Joan Crawford. She was a wife and mother first and second, and a star in third place."

"As a kid, I got used to walking into our living room and seeing Elizabeth Taylor, Richard Burton, Bob Hope, or Milton Berle. Henry Fonda might drop in or Katharine Hepburn."

"I was devastated when my parents divorced, and now, I'm getting my first divorce. I know I might marry again someday to someone."

"Why not me?" Burt asked flirtatiously.

"Just make that a serious proposal, and you'll see me walking down the aisle," she said. "It seems

Lucie Arnaz (left) with her famous mother and her brother, Desi Arnaz, Jr., in an episode of *Here's Lucy* in 1968.

you get off dating the daughters of famous stars. Take Lorna Luft, for instance. The daughter of Judy Garland and now the daughter of Lucille Ball."

"Yeah," he said, jokingly. "That's true. Actually, instead of the daughters, I would have preferred the mothers."

"Well, there may be some truth in that. After Dinah Shore, I wouldn't be surprised."

"I was glad when you agreed to go out with me," Burt said. "But at first, I was afraid I'd have to show up in a dress."

"Please don't kid me about that," she protested. "I've taken enough ribbing."

She was referring to her affair, beginning in 1971, with Jim Bailey, a cross-dressing "illusionist" known for his stage appearances as Judy Garland and Barbra Streisand.

"I adore Jim, and although we broke up, we've remained best friends," she said. "Lucille didn't understand it. She told me she was shocked when I started dating a man who prefers dresses to pants. Jim impersonates women on stage. The rest of the time, he wears pants. He likes women."

"Too bad," Burt said. "I was hoping you might hook me up with him.

"Are you always joking?" she asked.

"It seems I have something in common with your brother, Desi, Jr." Burt said. "He's involved in a serious affair with my recent co-star, Liza Minnelli. He's dating the daughter of Judy

WHO LOVES LUCIE?

Jim Bailey imitating Phyllis Diller. "The only thing wrong with my doing Phyllis was that my legs are more shapely than hers," Bailey claimed.

FIRST TIME IN NEW YORK!

"INCREDIBLE!"

JIM BAILEY

AS GARLAND!   AS STREISAND!

AS JIM BAILEY!

Tickets: $7.50, 6.50, 5.50, 4.50

Saturday Eve., FEBRUARY 5th at 8 pm

MAIL ORDERS FILLED. Please include stamped self-addressed envelope with your remittance.

CARNEGIE HALL
7th Ave. & 57th St., New York, N.Y. 10019
Information call: CI 7-7459

Posters from his 1971 appearance at Carnegie Hall advertised Jim Bailey doing his Garland and Streisand impersonations. "I did a better Judy than Judy herself. Ditto for Barbra."

Garland, and I'm going for the daughter of Lucille Ball. Junior and I should get together and chew the fat."

"It's hot and new with Liza, but it won't work," she said. "My brother learned from a psychic that he and Liza, in former lives, were Louis XVI of France and Marie Antoinette. For them to get married, they might be doomed as they were in their previous lives."

"Do you know who I was in a previous life?"

"Haven't a clue...Perhaps Bluebeard."

"Not at all. Henry VIII. Of course, I had put on more weight back then."

"As I said, always joking. At least you amuse me."

"To Judge from last night, I did more than that," he said.

On another night, she told him, "It's marvelous we get on so well, since we come from totally different backgrounds. I'm a true daughter of Beverly Hills, having known a life of luxury. My mother, my dad, and my brother are all in show business in one sense or another. Lucille prefers television while dad likes to work more in the background. Junior is breaking into the business of movies and television, too. But I prefer the stage. If I succeed there and become famous, it will be something totally different from my mother."

When queried by the press, Lucie said, "Burt is a lot of fun, and I enjoy being with him. There is no talk of marriage. He's endlessly repeated that he's not the marrying kind, and I'm in the throes of divorce and not anxious to rush into another bondage. Burt has a roving eye. For all I know, he'll fall in love with his next co-star."

As it turned out, she was right.

As Lucie later revealed, her love affair with Burt ended right before he met and fell in love with Sally Field, the co-star of his next film, *Smokey and the Bandit* (1977). "When it ended, I really cared for the big guy. Sally's a lovely girl. If he dropped me and ran off with some dummy, I might have cut my throat. As it is, I accept it. He got a gem in Sally."

"Of course, Burt will be missed. But he's not completely gone. We've vowed to become friends. He could have done worse than marrying me. But I can't live in the past when there's today and tomorrow to worry about. Didn't Judy say it all in that song about the man who got away?"

***

Burt's close friend, stuntman Hal Needham, made his directorial debut in *Smokey and the Bandit* (1977). At the time that Needham presented the script to Burt, he was living in the cottage behind his house. "Burt was constantly plagued with horny girls, often teenagers invading his property.

They'd hang out hoping to get a glimpse of him like they did with Elvis. Of course, most of them wanted something more than a glimpse. As he pulled out, they'd jump on his car, forcing him to stop to prevent an accident. They'd scream and yell for him. I couldn't believe some of the things they did, like exposing their breasts to him. I'm a gentleman, so I can't tell you."

The first version of the script for *Smokey and the Bandit* was formatted in Needham's handwriting on yellow legal pads. After Burt's first reading, he told Needham, "You cheap bastard. You didn't even pay to have it typed. This is the worst script I've ever read. I'll star in it, but I'll have to improvise like hell."

"When my friends heard I was doing Needham's script, they practically got down on their knees, begging me not to do it," Burt said. "But later, when the movie became such a big hit, all of them remembered urging me to make it."

Originally, Needham thought he could raise a million dollars to shoot the film, but when Universal came aboard, the studio committed $5 million to the project.

However, right before the beginning of filming, a corporate "hatchet man" flew to Georgia and shaved a million dollars off the budget. That decision led to Needham having to make drastic revisions to the script.

At first, Universal didn't want Burt to star in *Smokey*, but in a movie called *Convoy* instead. [*Released in 1978 and directed by Sam Peckinpah, it was about a trucker who leads protesting colleagues on a trek through the Southwest as he avoids the traps and pitfalls of a vengeful traffic cop. After Burt rejected the role, it was awarded to Kris Kristofferson, who teamed with Ali MacGraw.*]

Smokey was the first movie ever produced by Mort Engelberg. "It's certainly not *Citizen Kane*," he told Burt. "But we struck a chord with the public." He would go on to make more than a dozen other pictures, including *The Hunter* (1980), starring Steve McQueen.

In 1992, Engelberg branched out into Democratic Party politics, becoming the "advance man" for Bill Clinton in his successful race for the White House.

"When I started promoting Bill," Engelberg said, "no one had heard of him outside of Arkansas."

Burt had sent the script to Sally Field, with the assurance that the female role of Carrie was hers if she wanted it. When he phoned her, she told him she thought it was the worst film script she'd ever read.

"Don't worry," he assured her. "We'll improvise."

In *Smokey and the Bandit*, she plays a runaway bride fleeing from an idiot Southerner, Junior (Mike Henry), the son of a redneck sheriff portrayed by Jackie Gleason. She escapes from the church by hitching a ride with Burt, and they're pursued by the jilted groom and his father across the country. En route, they fall in love.

Carrie, according to the script, is a dancer and singer. The Bandit (Burt) nicknames her "The Frog," because she was "always hopping around, kinda cute like a frog."

[Another, less gallant reason he named her Frog, Burt said, "Was because I wanted to jump her."]

Cast as a "saddle tramp" known as "The Bandit," Burt falls for a runaway bride, a chorine he nicknames "Frog."

Before ending one of his phone calls to Sally, Burt said, "There's another good reason you might want to take the role,"

"And what might that be?" she asked.

"Because you might—just might—get me as part of the deal." Then he put down the receiver.

The brass at Universal opposed the casting of Sally, claiming, "She's not sexy, and the role calls for a Hot Pants type of bitch. My God, Reynolds, think Jane Fonda, even Faye Dunaway. Not *Gidget* or *The Flying Nun!*"

Sally later told *Entertainment Weekly,* "I found out Burt had been smitten with me ever since he's seen me on TV in *Gidget.* I decided to do the part of Carrie because it allowed me to be light and pretty, a big departure from my previous TV role as *Sybil* (1976), a young woman suffering from multiple personality disorders."

When Burt met her, he said, "I was taken with her at once. She was strong and funny and spectacular in a cold reading. The sexual tension between us was bouncing off the wall. I knew this could be the start of something big."

Originally, Richard Boone was preferred as the sheriff, but Burt wanted Jackie Gleason. He claimed that Boone "is a fine actor, but I want someone a little crazier, a little more dangerous, and a hell of a lot funnier."

Burt was a great admirer of Gleason's talent. "I have always prided myself for making chicken salad out of chicken shit, but Jackie can make it Cordon Bleu."

Gleason played Burford T. Justice, an apoplectic, arrogant, and bone-dumb Southern sheriff, a stereotypical image of bureaucratic redneck bumbling. "I played it like a pompous blowhard," Gleason said.

The pants he wore as sheriff required a 64" waistband. Throughout the shoot, Gleason kept demanding that his assistant bring him "a hamburger," a code word for bourbon. "Jackie was drunk throughout filming, but it didn't seem to affect his performance," Burt said.

One of Gleason's most memorable lines from the movie came after his son, Junior, had done something genuinely stupid. "There's no way that you come from my loins. Soon as I get home, the first thing I'm gonna do is punch your mamma in da mouth!"

Jackie Gleason as Sheriff Burford T. Justice pursues Burt the Bandit from Texarkana to Atlanta. His brawny dumbell son (left) was played by Mike Henry.

Gleason would forever be immortalized for his role as Ralph Kramden, the bus driver in the 1955-56 TV series, *The Honeymooners.* He'd also developed *The Jackie Gleason Show* (1949-57). *[Reruns of both of these series continued for many years after their final episodes were completed.]*

Ever since Burt had seen him play Minnesota Fats in *The Hustler* (1961) alongside Paul Newman, Burt was fully aware of how good an actor Gleason was.

"When bourbon-soggy Jackie and I hung out together, he told me fabulous stories about UFO's he'd seen." Burt said.

"He claimed that one night, he was abducted aboard a UFO and met creatures who looked like giant caterpillars but with incredible brain power."

"Gleason also told me that once, during a meeting with Richard Nixon, the president shared some of the secret information the government had collected about UFOs."

After seeing himself in the first rushes of *Smokey and the Bandit,* Gleason said, "I'm going to get a facelift. My eyelids are puffy and sagging, and no Basset Hound has jowls as droopy as mine."

Gleason hated to memorize dialogue, so he improvised frequently and made many suggestions for dialogue changes. In a diner where the Sheriff (Gleason) unknowingly encounters the Bandit (Burt), the corpulent actor devised a name for the redneck café, calling it "Choke & Puke."

Throughout the film, he frequently says *"sumbitch"* a moniker frequently used by Big Burt (Burt's father) during his tenure as Chief of Police in Riviera Beach.

A former linebacker for the Pittsburgh Steelers and the L.A. Rams, Mike Henry was cast as Junior, the doofus son of the sheriff. He wants to marry Carrie (Sally Field) but she bolts from their wedding and escapes by hitching a ride out of town with The Bandit. The sheriff and his jilted son take off in hot pursuit, hot-rodding after them throughout the South.

After the casting of Gleason and Field, Needham hired Jerry Reed, Pat McCormick, and Paul Williams in supporting roles.

Jerry Reed, the country music star, had worked with Burt before and would do so again. Originally, he had been cast as the Bandit until Burt took over the role. Reed was then assigned the less visible role of Cledus ("The Snowman"). In the film, whereas Reed would be driving the 18-wheeler, Burt "ran interference" in a souped-up Pontiac Trans Am as a "blocker" and advance vehicle that diverted police attention away from "Snowman's" illegal cargo.

After a drunken and "wasted" night, Jerry Reed had to write what emerged as *Smokey and the Bandit's* theme song, "East Bound and Down."

When Reed first sang it to Needham, there was a long silence. "I can rewrite it if you want me to," Reed said.

"If you change one word of it, I'll kill you," Needham responded.

After the release of *Smokey*, the song became Reed's biggest hit—in fact, in time it became his signature song.

The "partner" who accompanied Reed in the driver's compartment of his 18-wheel rig was a Basset hound named Fred. With his droopy ears and sad face, the Basset had beat out 2,000 other dogs in a canine beauty contest in Atlanta.

At the beginning of *Smokey*, in matching suits, Pat McCormick appears as "Big Enos" alongside Paul Williams as his son, "Little Enos." McCormick, with a walrus mustache, stood 6'7" and weighed 250 pounds. In contrast, Williams looked like a midget. Burt, as The Bandit, says, "It must have been a bitch finding matching suits for a 68 fat and a 12 dwarf."

Burt had known McCormick during his stint as a writer for Johnny Carson's *Tonight* Show. He'd also written for Red Skelton, Phyllis Diller, and for such TV sitcoms as *Get Smart.*

Songwriter Williams is known for such hits as "An Old Fashioned Love Song," and "We've Only Just Begun."

Burt called him "The talented Kid from Omaha." At the time of their first meeting, Williams had already written both the music and lyrics for *A Star Is Born* (1976) starring Barbra Streisand. "Evergreen," a love ballad he'd written for that film, eventually won an Oscar for Best Original Song in a Feature Film.

What ballooned into the script of *Smokey and the Bandit* was a distribution quirk associated with Coors beer. When the film was made, Coors (which was not pasteurized and therefore needed constant refrigeration) was not available for distribution east of the Mississippi.

Legally for sale only within eleven Western and southwestern states, it was already firmly entrenched in America's beer-drinking lore and legend. President Dwight Eisenhower had arranged for a steady supply of the beer, his favorite, flown in and delivered by special unmarked truck to the White House. Later, then Vice President Gerald Ford was known to have concealed some Coors in his luggage after a trip to Colorado. It therefore dawned on Needham that "bootlegging Coors would make a good plotline for a movie."

The script of *Smokey* reveals the intentions of two bigshots from Texas who want to hire a driver to illegally haul a truckload of Coors in his rig for an upcoming celebration in Georgia. They offer The Bandit (Burt) $80,000 to pick up 400 cases of Coors in Texarkana (where it can be legally sold) and haul it back to Atlanta within a time frame of only 28 hours. En route, they'll have to meander across territory crawling with state troopers hell-bent on stopping contraband cargoes, especially if they're speeding. Thus begins an elaborate, and very amusing, race—as Burt puts the pedal to the metal—across the redneck South. As Burt's "war chariot," Needham chose a soon-to-be-released 1977 Pontiac Trans Am.

For the most part, *Smokey* was filmed in Georgia, with a lot of the chase scenes filmed on Highway 54 between Fayetteville and Jonesboro, not far from Atlanta's southern tier.

One of the most dramatic scenes that only two daredevils like Burt and Needham would attempt was to send a Pontiac Trans Am, as a movie prop, roaring up and off a ramp, through the air, and landing on the opposite side of a river. Although it actually made it to the other side, the car was utterly destroyed.

Wearing tight, bell-bottom jeans and a 1970s-era mustache, Burt was called "the heartthrob for all white-trash trailer dwellers." Decades later, the movie evokes a bygone era of rebels, long sideburns, plaid western shirts, and a black Pontiac Trans Am with screaming chicken decals on its hood.

With verve, Burt portrayed a speed-demon outlaw in ways that would never be replicated in the same way again.

One morning, Burt did not show up on the set. Needham went to his dressing room trailer and discovered him looking ghostly white and having a hard time breathing. "He looked like death warmed over."

"The makeup men had a hard time working me over that morning, but I emerged with a George Hamilton suntan," Burt quipped. "If I had died that day, I'd have made a good-looking corpse."

A week later, Burt collapsed on the set, and Needham feared he'd suffered a stroke. He was rushed in an ambulance, its dome light flashing, to the local hospital.

He'd passed out. When he recovered, he had an intravenous needle with a tube attached to his arm. He told Needham, "I fear I won't be able to complete the film." The director did not conceal his acute disappointment.

Sally Field was his first visitor. "Burt was ill and no one, especially his doctors, knew what was the matter with him. Everyone was taking chunks out of him—eating him alive."

Burt's ill health had been obvious even during the filming of *Nickelodeon*. It took weeks for doctors to discover what was wrong with him.

During the filming of *Smokey*, particularly the more athletic scenes, he would suddenly pass out. Sally saw him hyperventilating on occasion, and his blood pressure would mysteriously drop. On occasion, he would lose his eyesight for a moment.

He went to at least three doctors, who each pronounced his heart in good shape. "They were quacks," he said. "I knew I might die at any moment."

In the press, *Smokey* got generally bad reviews, film critic Leonard Maltin claiming, "It's about as subtle as the Three Stooges."

The most favorable reviews came from fans, including, of all people, Alfred Hitchcock, who called it "a guilty pleasure." One Burt Reynolds movie buff claimed to have seen it 300 times.

Gary Arnold in the *Washington Post* called it a "live-action adaptation of a Roadrunner cartoon. It's the kind of super-charged comedy of manners that exploits down-home regional working-class American stereotypes."

Another fan, movie star Kirk Douglas, saw the film five times and phoned Burt to congratulate him.

One reviewer defined *Smokey and the Bandit* as "the king of redneck comedies, a real cornball entertainment that calls for extra butter on the popcorn."

One critic wrote, "*Smokey* is as fun as a dose of clap."

But Burt's fans adored it, citing him as "the ultimate phallic representation of male dominance. He emerges as a mythical, almost Quixotesque figure, racing along the Southern tier of the United States in his black Pontiac firebird."

Another critic called it, "The best hick film of the year."

Billy Bob Thornton weighed in, too: "Down South, we consider *Smokey and the Bandit* a documentary."

The film took in more than $300 million, the highest grossing movie of Burt's career before or after. He'd never again hit that high water mark financially, taking home $5 million.

In contrast, Gleason told Burt, "I made the biggest mistake of my life. I opted for a higher salary, turning down a percentage of the gross."

Smokey was the second-highest grossing movie released that year, second only to *Star Wars*.

It had a dismal opening, however, having its premiere in the wrong venue, Manhattan's Radio City Music Hall. "It didn't make enough money to pay the Rockettes!" Burt lamented. But when it played Southern cities such as Atlanta, movie houses were overflowing. By the time it was sent back to New York and opened in other theaters, it did land office business, drawing crowds from Chicago to Boston.

"At long last, I was the box office champ, beating out Steve McQueen, Paul Newman, and Robert Redford," Burt gleefully proclaimed.

With his newly made millions, Burt sold his bachelor's pad. *[Needham had been living in its guest cottage, moving out before the sale was finalized]* and bought a hacienda-style gated estate in the upmarket Holmby Hills neighborhood of Los Angeles. It had high vaulted ceilings, dark wood beams and paneling, and terra-cotta tiled floors.

In Florida, he also broke ground on a $20 million dinner theater a short drive from his ranch in Jupiter.

"As a fallout from *Smokey,* I got sandtrapped into a certain type of good ol' boy picture when I wanted to be starring in such movies as *All the President's Men* or *California Suite.* After *Smokey* became such a big hit, I was inundated with scripts riddled with car chases, each set in Redneck Country."

"It works like this in Hollywood. If I had played a pink flamingo, and it made millions, I would be swamped with pink flamingo roles."

"When audiences went to see Sally and me falling in love on the screen, they were actually witnessing a man and a woman falling in love off the screen, too."

***

Somewhere, sometime, somehow, during the making of *Smokey and the Bandit,* Burt Reynolds and Sally Field began an affair that would inspire lurid exposés in the tabloids and capture the imagination of their fans.

Slowly, the two of them got to know each other, although he admitted it was a "limited hangout. I'd done a lot of things I was ashamed of, and I didn't want to dig up all my dirt. Best leave it buried."

When the filming of *Smokey* ended in Georgia, both Burt and Sally returned to L.A. Neither of them had permanent lodgings at the time. Whereas the renovations he'd commissioned for his Holmby Hills house hadn't yet been completed, she had sold her house and was still in the process of converting another residence for occupancy by herself and her two sons. Yet because of her children and for other reasons, too, Burt and Sally wouldn't actually live together. Each maintained a separate household.

It was obvious to their friends that they had fallen in love—"or heavily in lust," as he more colorfully reported it. "Nothing seemed to matter but the tiny insular world both of us occupied when we were together."

"It was hard to say why he was attracted to me," she said. "He admired my search for truth in all situations, and I also think he was drawn to my never-say-die spirit. I was so determined that I never planned to buckle under to anything."

Both of them, enjoying quiet evenings, set out to get better acquainted, although their conversations were often interrupted by retreats to a bedroom.

Born in Pasadena in 1946, Sally was a decade younger than Burt. Her mother was the minor actress, Margaret Field, who had appeared in a string of low-budget "B" pictures, including *The Man from Planet X.*

Her father, Richard Dryden Field, had been a U.S. Army Officer. Her parents divorced when she was a little girl, and Margaret took a second husband, Jock Mahoney, one of the best known stuntmen in Hollywood and very briefly, a screen Tarzan.

Sally had begun her acting career in that frothy little TV sitcom, *Gidget* (1965-66), and went on to become even better known in the much-mocked *The Flying Nun* (1967-70), which one TV critic called "one of the most noxious sitcoms to ever come down the pike."

As sweethearts "BURT & SALLY," became a romantic mantra that tabloids promoted frantically.

But right before she became romantically involved with Burt, she'd starred in a serious TV drama, *Sybil* (1976), the sad saga of a young woman with multiple personalities. Her co-star was Joanne Woodward, who, more than two decades before, had played a similar role in her award-winning *The Three Faces of Eve* (1957).

At the age of seventeen, Sally's boyfriend had gotten her pregnant, which—according to her memoirs—led to an abortion in Tijuana. She married her first husband, Craig Stevens, in 1968, the union producing two sons, Peter and Eli. When the couple divorced in 1975, Sally retained custody of her boys. Her justification for divorcing Craig was, "I did not want to turn into an alcoholic housewife."

When Sally first met Burt before the filming of *Smokey* in Georgia, she was surprised that he was so much shorter than he appeared on the screen. Not put off by that, she found him "incredibly charming. He might be small in stature, but he loomed large on the screen, having worked for years to become the biggest box office movie star in America, as well as its most sought-after sex symbol. He seemed a bit floored by all his success."

Much of the world, especially women, viewed him as the quintessential definition of masculine pulchritude. "He seemed to be trying to fulfill everyone's expectations of him," she said.

Whereas their first date had transpired in the company of others, during the course of their second date, they were alone together in his hotel suite.

"As we talked, I began to get the feeling that Burt preferred his version of what he thought I was instead of who I actually was. Could that mean trouble ahead? However, I was glad that he saw beyond that all-American syrupy image he'd seen of me in those TV sitcoms, where I was the meaningless girl next door with no belly button."

Sally yearned to be viewed as a serious actress, and she had hoped that *Sybil* would inspire critical acclaim and better dramatic roles. In fact, she feared the reviews that *Smokey* would generate, afraid that both she and Burt would be ridiculed. The scripted dialogue in that film had constantly changed, and both Burt and Jackie Gleason seemed at times to portray caricatures. "I hoped that all of us would not come off like cartoons," she said.

Reportedly, she also worried about moving deeper and deeper into a relationship with him. In Georgia, the filming of *Smokey* had frequently been interrupted by flocks of young women who showed up for glimpses of Hollywood's sex symbol and "babe magnet." Sometimes, when crowds got out of control, Burt would grab Sally's hand and flee to his camper.

"Often, the door slammed without me *[being able to escape]* inside, and I had to flee to my own camper until Burt finally realized I was missing and sent someone for me."

Many of their evenings in Georgia passed smoothly, romantically, and without incident. That is, except for when a doctor arrived from Atlanta carrying a black leather bag. From it, he removed a needle. Sally always looked away except for one night when she saw the doctor inject the contents of that needle directly into Burt's chest.

Burt always insisted that she keep a cache of small brown paper bags into which he could hyperventilate. He seemed to thrive on Valium and Percodan.

Thinking he had some sort of heart disease, Sally convinced him to travel south to the Miami Heart Institute for an extensive examination of his coronary arteries. She slept one night on a cot wheeled into his room at the hospital. The following morning, his doctor told him he had a strong, healthy heart—"no problem at all."

But later, back in Georgia, he would still wake up in the middle of the night, gasping for air. She began to feel that his condition was brought on by stress and anxiety. She urged him to see a psychiatrist, but he dismissed that idea as "Shrink Poppycock." Yet even after dreadful nights, he'd rally before morning, at which time he was once again called up to "put the pedal to the metal."

After *Smokey* was wrapped, and after a final night in his arms, Sally flew back to California for a reunion with her sons. He drove south to Jupiter for recuperation at his ranch with Big Burt and Fern.

After three weeks, he flew back to California and a brief reunion with Sally before her departure on a publicity tour for the promotion of *Sybil*. He escorted her to its premiere, a three-hour event where she and Burt were seated beside Paul Newman. His wife, Joanne Woodward, had not accompanied him to the premiere of her film because, as Newman told them, "Joanne can't stand to see herself on the screen."

Later that evening, Burt admitted to Sally that he'd once briefly dated Woodward during their regional summer stock days in New York State "before Ol' Blue Eyes [*in this case, Paul Newman*] arrived to rescue his damsel."

With Sally away on her publicity tour for *Sybil*, Burt met with Clint Eastwood who told him that he, too, often hyperventilated.

One night in L.A., when Burt was socializing informally and discussing business with Hal Needham, he collapsed. Fearing that Burt had had a stroke, the stuntman/director raced with him in his car to Cedars-Sinai Hospital.

The next morning, Burt told Needham, "I felt my number had come up. It was the final curtain, I just knew it, and I had only started to live. Last night, as I was dying, two nurses asked for my autograph."

He remained in the hospital for days. After a battery of tests, he decided to fly back to Florida, where he remained at his ranch until shooting began on his next picture. He had lost twenty pounds. "There was something definitely wrong with me...but what?"

In seclusion in Jupiter, his condition worsened. Big Burt insisted that "those fag doctors," in Los Angeles were incompetent, and drove his son to a specialist in West Palm Beach.

There, Burt underwent six hours of tests. They revealed that he was suffering from hypoglycemia. He'd been plagued by this condition for so long that his adrenal glands had collapsed. That had played a factor in his passing out on occasion and being temporarily blinded.

He was given B-12 shots and put on a rigid diet of healthy foods. "Every thirty minutes or so, I had to eat something healthy like a raw carrot. No more Hostess pie for breakfast. I had been driving wide open for too long, and now I was running on empty."

"Forget the shit going on inside me. All I had to do was look in the mirror. If a director needed to cast a character to play a major asshole, I'd advise him to look at pictures of me from that period."

"I began to recover for my next film, *Semi-Tough*, in which I'd play another football hero."

***

As Burt and Sally settled into a relationship, she became increasingly aware of what a dominant male he was. "With a most assertive personality…a real Alpha male." He demanded she take his advice, even if it were contrary to her own wishes.

"If I wanted to give him an aspirin for a headache, he demanded Percodan," she said. "He often got impatient with me. For better or worse, we have begun a kind of married life together without a license. It would be a rocky road with a lot of bumps and twisting curves, but it could be smooth riding at times—and it was those moments I looked forward to."

As the days and weeks passed, he became more and more assertive, more in control. Sometimes, he would belittle or trivialize her, demanding that she give priority to his own exploding career at the expense of her own desires and dreams as an actress.

As Burt later claimed, "Sally and I talked about getting married, but never at the same time. When I was hot to take her in front of a preacher, she didn't want to walk down the aisle. When she tried to get me to marry her, I just wasn't in the mood. I remembered how disastrous my marriage to Judy Carne had been, and I didn't want to make the same mistake."

"Frankly, and I don't want to tell Sally this, but I think that if we'd taken the vows together, it would ultimately have led to a second divorce for the both of us."

"Even though we loved each other, at least for a time in the late 1970s, I feared that as man and wife, we were a mismatch. In case you haven't heard, fire and gasoline don't always go together like a horse and carriage."

"Yet in spite of it all, I felt I could be a good father to her two boys," he claimed. "I really dug those kids, and both of them responded to me. We had a lot of fun together, as they brought out the boy in me, a pair of great kids."

According to Sally, "I've always viewed myself as an independent woman, but Burt almost from the beginning tried to 'housebreak' me, dictating to me what was allowed and what was *verboten*. There was a lot of the latter."

"I learned soon enough not to mention men who had passed through my life. He'd heard a rumor that I'd had an affair with his friend, Johnny Carson, and that really infuriated him."

Burt once said, "I'm not going to get into a pissing contest with Sally, because I think I'd lose."

She'd once told the press, "America has a very adolescent attitude toward sexuality. Its men are like fifteen-year-old boys with a hard-on twenty-four hours a day."

Speaking of her own youth at the time, she said, "I was not wise, and people around me wanted me to stay the little darling, adorable Gidget forever."

"My relationship with Burt remained confused and complicated."

As Burt told Hal Needham, "I don't know if Sally suspected I had a number of quickie involvements with other beautiful women during the time we had together, but I suspect she did."

In an interview with Dave Itzkoff for *The New York Times*, Sally claimed that Burt was "swaggering and charismatic, their connection immediate and intense." But as she noted, they were hardly a blissful, well-matched pair. "He accepted only certain aspects of my life and personality while uninterested in or disapproving of others."

In Itzkoff's article, Sally shocked readers by suggesting that her romance with Burt was perhaps an attempt to "recreate a version of her incestuous relationship with her stepfather, Jock Mahoney, the famous stuntman and screen Tarzan who had married her mother. "I was somehow exorcising something that needed to be exorcised. I was trying to make it work this time."

Burt once told a reporter that what had most attracted Sally to him "was her cheerleader face evocative of my days on the football field as Saturday's hero."

She was once quoted as saying, "Sexuality isn't physical to me. I mean, a man doesn't have to look like Arnold Schwarzenegger. It just so happens that Burt looks like Burt. He could look like Truman Capote, and I think I could still be crazy about him."

"In some respects, Burt and I are very much alike. We understand each other, whereas somebody else might not. We have our fears. We both have the feeling we're not good enough. We're always fighting the feeling of 'you can't possibly

Sally Field's paternal nightmare: Jock Mahoney as the romantic lead in *Tarzan Goes to India* (1962). He molested his stepdaughter.

love me.'"

"I know that at times, he is insecure. It's like he's saying, 'I don't deserve you. I don't deserve your feelings for me. I'm gonna lose you.'"

"I had never felt a jealous moment in my life until I met Burt. Now I'm not Greta Gracious with the women in Burt's past. I want to claw their faces. He's very jealous, too…very jealous. Sometimes he wants so much reassurance from me that I have to kiss him thirty-thousand times a day."

"Although he likes to dominate me, I think he also admires my independent streak. That's one of the things he likes about me, but it also scares him. He knows I will always be willing to walk away if something isn't right between us. I want my life to be right, even if it means leaving him."

As time went by, and as Sally moved deeper into her relationship with Burt, she admitted, "Before him, I was just this little actress. My whole life changed when I began to be with him. My way of dressing changed. I usually dressed very casually. I upgraded my wardrobe, so that he was proud to be seen with me when we went out together in public. In a sense, I guess, I was representing him by his choice of a woman."

In an interview with *Playgirl* magazine, a reporter said, "Sometimes, you seem to live through Burt."

She admitted, "In some ways, I do. But I don't know if that's bad. I think it's how a real relationship works. You fit like puzzle pieces. I help him bring out his emotions, and I keep knocking, pounding on his door until he does. He can get up in front of a crowd and be charming. I get a thrill out of watching him, but crowd-pleasing is not for me. I sit and watch and it thrills me when the people laugh. I'm so proud I want to stand up in the audience and say, 'He likes me. See that man up there? He likes me.'"

She surprised one reporter who asked her, "What is your greatest dream?"

She answered, "To appear as Jon Voight's leading lady."

Deep into his affair with Sally, Burt, on occasion, could be rather candid. "Sally Field is the love of my life. But what you sometimes learn, and indeed I have learned, is that the person you love most may not be the one with whom you should spend the rest of your life."

***

According to Burt, "The 1970s was an astonishing time for me, and I've often said to people, 'If I met you between 1973 and '78, I'm sorry—I don't remember three or four of those years. I was on such a fast track, and Sally Field had entered my life. The air was heady, and I was having trouble breathing. How in hell are you going to smell the flowers if you can't breathe?"

"I vaguely remembered that friends in Hollywood came in herds and left in herds. Hollywood loves you when you're on top of the game. Once you're no longer a top draw at the box office, they don't know you."

"What I do remember is making *Semi-Tough,* and what man could forget Jill Clayburgh?"

Semi-Tough, a 1977 release from United Artists, starred Burt, Kris Kristofferson, and Jill Clayburgh in a romantic *ménage à trois.* Based on the novel by Dan Jenkins, Burt played Billy Clyde Puckett, with Kris cast as Marvin ("Shake") Tiller. These two football stars both fall for the same woman, Jill Clayburgh, cast as Barbara Jean Bookman.

Kris Kristofferson (left), Burt, and Jill Clayburgh in *Semi-Tough,* where they were cast as football heroes and fan.

To which of the two lugs would she surrender her heart?

As described by one critic, "She is a version of that most delicious of Hemingway's conceits—the intelligent and entirely feminine woman who is capable of being a man's man when the occasion warrants it."

Another critic noted that Clayburgh evoked screen memories of both Jean Harlow and Carole Lombard.

In supporting roles, *Semi-Tough* featured Robert Preston, Lotte Lenya, and Bert Convy.

Burt, Jill, and Kris appeared on screen as lost children of the 1960s, wandering into the '70s looking for new meaning in life. The movie is an evocation of that turbulent decade itself, a time of leisure suits, disco music, gas lines, disaster flicks, and *Happy Days.*

It came as a surprise that the legendary Broadway producer, David Merrick, was producing *Semi-Tough.* Burt knew very little about him, except for his fabulous reputation and his keen ability to create publicity stunts. Burt would know a lot more after the publication of Merrick's unauthorized biography, *The Abominable Showman,* by Howard Kissel.

Merrick showed up during the shoot and had lunch with Burt. He told Merrick, "I'd rather direct than act. I'd rather do that than anything. It's the second best sensation I've ever had. The first was fucking Marilyn Monroe."

By the time coffee was served, Merrick had offered to produce two films which Burt would direct without having to act in them.

Like so many luncheon deals in Hollywood, that promise went the way of Burt's first marriage.

Semi-Tough's director, Michael Ritchie, had scored some commercial success in helming sports movies such as *Downhill Racer* (1969) and *The Bad News Bears* (1976), and he also became known for his satirical scripts such as *The Candidate* (1972) starring Robert Redford. *Entertainment Weekly* wrote, "It's difficult to think of any director, ever, who had a more consistently uneven career."

Robert Preston in *Semi-Tough*, cast as the foul-mouthed owner of a football team.

Burt was not overly impressed, thinking that he knew more about how to direct a football movie than Ritchie did.

[In 1995, Burt phoned Ritchie at his apartment in New York City, and asked if he could spend the night alone at 12305 Fifth Helena Drive, the hacienda-inspired home in Brentwood where Marilyn Monroe was found dead in August of 1962. The year before, Ritchie had paid a million dollars for the building.

Burt had known Marilyn very briefly and had seduced her in Manhattan after hooking up with her at the Actors Studio. So far as it's known, he never revealed why he wanted to spend the night at the scene of her death, or what happened when he did.

He had obviously heard rumors that Marilyn's ghost still haunted the place.]

A Texan, Kristofferson was both an actor and a singer-songwriter known for such hits as "Me and Bobby McGee," and "Help Me Make It Through the Night." The son of a U.S. Army officer, he'd been reared as a "military brat," moving from place to place. He earned a Rhodes scholarship to Oxford University, where he also became an amateur boxer and played football when not writing songs.

Eventually, he made his way to Hollywood, where he had just co-starred with Barbra Streisand in a remake of *A Star Is Born* (1976). He had yet to appear in the notorious *Heaven's Gate* (1980), the overblown, overcooked extravaganza that bankrupted United Artists.

A stage and film actor, Robert Preston was best remembered for his performance as Professor Harold Hill in *The Music Man*, a 1962 film adaptation of the famous Broadway musical that first opened in 1957. His song, "76 Trombones," became legendary.

Nearing the final decade of an eventful career, Preston had once co-starred with such names as Barbara Stanwyck and Susan Hayward. In *Semi-Tough*, he was cast as "Big Ed" Bookman, the owner of a football team and the father of the character portrayed by Jill Clayburgh.

A subplot within *Semi-Tough* involves a parody of self-help guru Werner Erhard's "Erhard Seminar Training," nicknamed "est." *[Spelled out in lower-case letters, est is disguised in the movie as an organization called B.E.A.T.]* Burt Convy was cast as Friedrich Bismark, a take-off on Erhard, and he does so with marvelous malice.

In one segment, he doesn't allow his followers to go to the bathroom over long stretches of time. One attendee wets her pants, and he instructs her to "experience the warmth." Convy's character is known for his "sadistic abuse, pious drivel, and sheer double talk."

Convy was an actor, singer, and game host on TV series that included *Password*. In the 1980s, he joined with Burt in the establishment of their own movie-making company, "Burt and Bert Productions," turning out game

Left photo: Lifestyle guru Werner Erhard, as he appeared in 1974. His brilliant lifestyle seminars for EST were ridiculed, many said unfairly, in *Semi-Tough*, in ways that trivialized his messaging.

Right photo, game show host Bert Convy, the actor who portrayed (and lampooned) Erhard in *Semi-Tough*. Erhard's fans believed Convy's performance fell flat, bombing unfunnily and with an utter lack of accuracy to the visionary's legacy.

Happiness is a function of accepting **what is. Love is a function of** communication. Health is a function of participation. Self expression is a **function of responsibility.**

A core belief of EST, as advanced by Werner Erhard. *Semi-Tough* would have been a better movie without the misstated lampoons of Werner Erhard.

shows such as *Win, Lose, or Draw*. It debuted in 1987 as part of NBC's daytime TV lineup.

Many Dallas Cowboys and cheerleaders were hired as extras on *Semi-Tough*. Burt claimed he based his character on Don ("Dandy") Meredith, the legendary Dallas Cowboy quarterback celebrated for his "off-the-field" exploits.

Even though he had only recently gotten involved with Sally Field, Burt never controlled his roving eye. "I developed the hots for one of those gorgeous cheerleaders," he confided to Ritchie. The director warned him that the Dallas football players were forbidden to seduce the cheerleaders. Burt countered, "But I'm not one of the Cowboys."

He later said, "I had Sally waiting for me back at her home, but temptation is hard to resist. One day I knew I had to get my act together. But not now."

Before Kris and Burt shot scenes on the football field with the rugged Dallas Cowboys, Burt warned Kris not to tell them he had played football during the years he had attended Pomona College. Operating with the belief that they'd trivialize and go easy on him if they thought he'd never been on a football field before, Burt advised Kristofferson, "Tell the guys you studied drama in college—and do so with a lisp and a limp wrist."

Kris did not follow his advice and talked like a pro about the intricacies of football.

"I'd learned my lesson making *The Longest Yard* when those pro football players tried to kill the movie star. During the first scene on the field, those guys went after Kris like a massacre. The next thing I knew, he was being carried off the field on a stretcher. I found out later that his wrist was broken, and he had three broken ribs. As he passed by me, looking up at me in pain and anguish, I told him, 'For a Rhodes scholar, you are really dumb.'"

One of the great ultra-avant garde divas of the Viennese theater, Lotte Lenya, is shown with a semi-undressed Burt in this press and PR photo for *Semi-Tough*.

Presumably, the masseuse she depicted has been sadistically "working him over" as part of a satire of the then-innovative self-help techniques roaring through the pop consciousness at the time.

After he recovered, he was able to play the rest of his scenes reasonably well, but off the football field.

As for Lotte Lenya's role in *Semi-Tough,* fans asked her, "What in hell are you doing in a Burt Reynolds movie?"

The ultra-avant-garde Viennese actress, singer, and *diseuse* was best remembered for her vocal renditions of songs written by her husband, Kurt Weill. In English language cinema, she had been nominated for a Best Supporting Actress Oscar for her performance as the jaded aristocrat in *The Roman Spring of Mrs. Stone* (1961), co-starring Vivien Leigh and Warren Beatty, and also as the murderous, sadistic Rosa Klemm in the James Bond movie, *From Russia with Love* (1963), starring Sean Connery.

In *Semi-Tough,* Lenya was cast as Clara Pelf, a masseuse who practices a sadistic, very muscular therapy called "Pelfing," a send-up of the "rolfing" technique, a name inspired by its originator, masseuse Ida Rolfe.

Lotte later claimed, "As an aging masseuse, I was to dig into Burt's body. I took the day's work for five thousand dollars without reading the script. I just hoped I didn't have to work him over below the waistline or maul his balls—or something as vulgar as that."

When he lies down on her therapy table, she asks him, "You have sexual problems?"

Even though his character denies it, she says, "All American men have sexual problems."

He shrieks in pain as she attacks his body. Her probing fingers dig into his ribs. "You hate your mother, *non?*" she asks. "Then it's your father!"

At the end of her massage/therapeutic mauling of Burt, and after the cameras stopped rolling, Lenya hugged and kissed him, saying "You're a darling. I'm sure my massage cured all those sexual problems. I found you sexier than working with Sean Connery."

In its review of *Semi-Tough, The Wall Street Journal* criticized the direction of its satire, writing, "*Semi-Tough* isn't much—an erratic ramble—but it has some pleasant moments, and a delicious send-up of the self-improvement guru Werner Erhard."

Magill's Survey of Cinema described *Semi-Tough* as a "chiding of American religious fads and philosophies." The *Grove Book of Hollywood* called it "a cheeky film that pokes fun at the 'est craze' and other human potential fads."

Time cited *Semi-Tough* as "one of 1977's best comedies, and it is without a doubt the year's most socially useful film." *Allmovie* claimed, "Burt Reynolds works his charm overtime." *In Search of Stupidity* characterized the film as "Possibly one of the best movies ever made by Burt Reynolds."

In contrast, one critic defined Burt's performance as "merely a walk-through." Fans of the novel on which the movie had been based claimed that the movie adaptation "trashed it. If you'd read the novel and then went to see the movie you probably ran screaming from the theater, vowing revenge on the @$$hole writers, director, and producer who ruined one of the funniest sports books ever written."

***

When Burt was introduced to Jill Clayburgh, his leading lady, on the set of *Semi-Tough,* his first words to her were, "We almost became lovers."

"I must have been on something and missed out on that," she said.

"I was offered the role of Clark Gable to your Carole Lombard but turned it down." He was referring to the picture, *Gable and Lombard* (1976), which she'd just completed.

"Why didn't you do it?" she asked. "I think you could have evoked Gable on the screen. There's some resemblance."

"I didn't think Lombard and Gable are really dead," he answered. "Their images live on the screen."

"Too bad we didn't get to work together," she answered. "Gable was the All-American sex symbol, and you seemed to have taken his place."

"The question is, are you America's madcap playgirl like Lombard?"

"That's for me to know, and you to find out."

As Burt later told director Michael Ritchie, "I view that as a real challenge. She's throwing down the gauntlet. There's a problem: I'm already committed to Sally Field, and I'm having hot sex with this gorgeous Dallas Cowboy cheerleader. How many blast-offs am I supposed to have in a 24-hour period? My god, at times I feel like a phallic symbol to the world."

Finding Jill sexy and attractive, though not in the typical way, he set about learning what he could about her.

[Born into a well-to-do family in Manhattan, Jill Clayburgh, according to Burt, "understood me, in spite of our different backgrounds."

Jill, who spent a good slice of her life in therapy, was certain of what she wanted from life: Success as an actress, independence, good health, true love, and great sex. She asked Burt, "Which of those things can you give me?"

"The latter," he shot back.

As he got to know her better, he found she had a colorful way of expressing her outlook on life. "When one is leaping for the moon, expect to end up with an occasional fractured kneecap—like you got on the football field."

Jill found herself an outcast, separated from the other well-to-do girls in private schools growing up. "They were snooty, dreaming of growing up to marry a rich husband, and spending the rest of their days at parties and charity events. Not me. I wanted something more daunting."

At Sarah Lawrence, she made the decision to become an actress, and appeared in many of that college's theatrical productions. She made friends with two men who each wanted to act or direct, notably Robert De Niro and Brian De Palma.

Summer stock led to her joining the Charles Street Repertory in Boston. There, she met "the most intense young actor I'd ever seen." He was Al Pacino.

When they returned together to New York, they lived in a dreary little apartment in the East Village of Manhattan. A stipend from her father kept them fed and paid the rent.

Their affair lasted for five years, but when he got his breakthrough role as Michael Corleone in The Godfather *(1972), he had moved on.*

Her big break came when she starred in Hustling *(1975), based on Gail Sheehy's book on prostitution and its implications.*

Jill told Burt it was probably just as well that he'd rejected any involvement in Gable and Lombard. "Most critics found it about as exciting as a TV dinner."

She confessed that he and Clint Eastwood were her movie idols. "I can't decide which of you is more macho. I'm really confused."

"Why don't you answer that question by doing some experimenting?"

"I'm still not liberated enough to make the first move. It's your call."

"How about tonight?"

"You're on, Big Boy," she said. "I prefer my deflowering to take place in a sleazy motel. I find that venue more sensual."

She never provided any real details of her brief fling with Burt, other than saying, "He has an endless sense of humor. He can make fun of anything, and I love that about him. Physically, his legs are too short, but he makes up for it with other body parts."

"Burt was never serious about me," she said. "After Semi-Tough, *he dropped me. But when we co-starred in* Starting Over, *our friendship—let's call it that—started all over again."]*

***

Before starring in their next movie, *The End*, Burt and Sally flew to Atlanta for a roast of him at a banquet. When Sally addressed the audience, she looked down at Burt, seated in the audience. "The truth is that this man is a sex maniac. The hotel here installed a take-a-number machine outside his room. I got number eighty-eight but the line moves fast."

When Burt took the podium, he looked down at her: "Sally, you and I have a wonderful relationship. You were privileged tonight to see it end."

***

In Atlanta, on May 10, 1977, as *Semi-Tough* was playing in theaters across America, Burt attended the gala opening of Burt's Place, a bar and disco in which he'd invested a million dollars. Each of the many rooms had a different movie theme, examples of which ranged from *A Streetcar Named Desire* to the MGM musical, *Show Boat*.

Based on dietary restrictions from his doctors, he could not drink any liquor, so he settled on Perrier for the duration of the evening.

He was feeling his star power, presiding over a movie career whose "standard" salary had reached two million dollars per picture plus a percentage of the gross. "Today, I can get what I want even if it's Glenda Jackson as my co-star. Let George Segal drive the fucking car."

He and Sally flew together back to Los Angeles, and she kissed him goodbye as she headed for her own home and her sons. At long last, Burt's elegant home in Holmby Hills had been completed and he moved in. "My movies were grossing in the millions, and I wanted to live the good life of a movie star in posh surroundings."

Burt became a host, inviting friends like Carol Burnett, Dom DeLuise, Mel Brooks and Anne Bancroft, Norman Fell, Orson Welles, Lee Marvin,

Clint Eastwood and Betty White…and also Dinah Shore.

He escorted guests upstairs to show them "the largest bedroom in the state of California," telling them, "I needed a room big enough for roller skating in the middle of the night."

***

The End, a film scripted by Jerry Belson and eventually released in 1978, had been shopped from studio to studio for more than six years. No producer wanted to touch it, since it was a black comedy about death. The script had even been returned with the notation, "Death is no laughing matter."

Belson had originally written it for Woody Allen, who rejected it. Finally, producer Lawrence Gordon picked up the option and sent it to Burt, who read it three times before calling Gordon with, "I think it's outrageous. I not only want to direct it, but to star in it, too, and use Sally Field as my girlfriend."

"I'd read dozens of scripts, all of them comedies, and none were as particularly funny, until I read this one by Belson," Burt said. "It struck my strange sense of humor. There are a lot of minefields in the topic of death. You can deal with death on a totally Mel Brooks level, but when you try to make a film with parts that are really real amidst comedy, that's a big risk. Gordon didn't want me to wear a beard. Instead of playing a realtor, he preferred me to be a stock car racer. I won out."

It'll blow your mind!

BURT REYNOLDS
"THE END"

Burt admitted, "It's a big departure for me. Death is something even Howard Hughes and Onassis couldn't buy their way out of. I was daring enough to take on the plot. What the hell! I only enjoy skating if the ice is thin. When you're twenty-five or thirty, you're immortal. But after forty, you start reading the obits to see if you made it."

It wasn't easy turning a suicide attempt into a comedy, but as this movie poster shows, Dom DeLuise did his best to make the suicidal yearnings of the character portrayed by Burt into something of slapstick-ish appeal.

"In directing *The End*, I wanted to grow as an actor. I wanted a break from being the good ol' Southern boy fleeing from sheriffs and cops along Alabama roads. I haven't taken a chance in a long time, partly because the scripts that land on my desk are not Al Pacino material."

"Before directing *The End*, I asked other directors for advice. Robert Aldrich told me to always listen to everybody, and Mel Brooks advised me to remember to fire someone the first day."

Burt signed to co-produce, direct, and star in *The End*. At the opening, his doctor, played by Norman Fell, tells him he has only a short time to live because he is suffering from a fatal blood disease. Burt is portraying an unscrupulous real estate developer, Wendell ("Sonny") Larson. He decides he prefers suicide to being bedridden and suffering during his final weeks of life.

He sets out to meet with family and friends to bid them *adieu*. He calls on his aging parents, as played by Myrna Loy and Pat O'Brien. They were, of course, major stars in the films of the 1930s. Sonny also visits his ballet-dancing daughter, Julie, played by teen actress Kristy McNichol.

Loy said that Burt was the most impressive director she'd known in fifteen years. O'Brien countered with "I've been directed by better."

"It is Burt's tremendous wit that just keeps coming across," Loy said. "There's no acting style. Most people just play themselves. Spencer

1977 in the photo posted above, Pat O'Brien and Myrna Loy are smiling at the goings-on at the wrap party for *The End*.

During the course of their respective careers in golden-age Hollywood, each had been almost unbelievably famous, but dealt gracefully with their status as cameo players in this new and perhaps bizarre manifestation of modern moviemaking.

THE IRONIES OF AGING: Burt Reynolds' *The End* was not the only movie in which Pat O'Brien had co-starred with Myrna Loy. Depicted above is a scene from the 1931 potboiler, *Consolation Marriage* 1931) in which John Halliday (right) helps Myrna with her coat, as Pat O'Brien (left) looks on in mournful resignation.

Tracy used to say to me after a scene, 'Did I ham that one up?' If I said 'yes,' he'd say, 'O.K., let's do it again.' There's that same honesty in Burt Reynolds. He's a throwback to the old school."

After several failed suicide attempts, Sonny (Burt) is committed to a mental institution. There, he meets a fellow patient, a deranged schizophrenic—as portrayed by Dom DeLuise—whom Sonny enlists to help him commit suicide.

Burt was delighted to be working with his longtime friend, whom he'd always found amusing. He was also glad to be working with Norman Fell, who had, years before, played his police partner in the TV detective series, *Dan August.*

"Some people think the guy I play in *The End* is as far away from me as anybody could be, but people who really know me realize that the character is very close to my own personality," Burt said. "The guy crying in his doctor's office—that's me. The guy is totally nude."

"The original script called for DeLuise to kill me, but we changed it because we want to leave my character alive. Even though facing eminent death, we wanted the audience to feel that there's some faint hope that a cure will be found for me at the last minute, and that I'll be saved to face my tomorrow."

Burt's friend from long ago, Joanne Woodward, was cast as his character's ex-wife. She loathes him, with good reason. Over lunch with Woodward one day, Burt told her, "If you ever decide to dump that Newman guy, give me a ring and I'll give you a ring."

Sonny's best friend, as played by the Canadian comedian, David Steinberg, agrees with him that suicide is the best way out of his dilemma. Steinberg would appear on the Johnny Carson show 130 times, second only to Bob Hope.

Once again, Sally Field was cast as Burt's girlfriend in *The End.* "Burt, thanks to the series of movies I made with him, kept me from starving."

Her character was defined as "a sweet slob who lives in a clutter of cats and unwashed dishes." After a session of lovemaking, she admits to him that he has never given her an orgasm. She's just been faking it. His character asks her, "Is that true every time I take you to bed?"

Sally claimed that "Burt drew me out as an actress as no director had before."

Robby Benson, who would be the star of a future movie with Burt, was cast as a Catholic priest, Father Dave Benson, so young and naïve that he responds with "WOW" every time Sonny confesses to him.

Carl Reiner, the comedian, had starred with Sid Caesar in TV. He had a brief scene as a "death therapist."

Whenever he could, Burt cast James Best in his movies. This time he's seen as a pacemaker patient. Anytime Burt had a hand in casting he always recommended friends and acquaintances. Best said, "Burt can be a horse's butt, or he can be the nicest guy in the world. Even though he can be a horse's patoot, he has shown me time and time again that he has a heart of gold."

In addition to the small role Burt assigned Best in *The End*, he also designated him as the film's associate producer.

DeLuise claimed, "Burt is marvelous, very spontaneous, He's known as a superstar sex symbol, a real stud, but he is gentle and understanding, very talented."

Speaking for himself, Burt said, "It's fun to be in the director's seat. In the past, I've had movie directors who would have done better, perhaps, directing traffic."

As Burt neared middle age, he began to contemplate a possible future as a director, although he felt he hadn't really proved himself as an actor. "Time was running out. I knew I couldn't go on forever jumping out of a window, off a cliff, or pushing the pedal to the metal and hurling my car over bridges. I could walk away from the adulation I get as an actor and never miss it."

On the set of *The End*, Jock Mahoney appears briefly as "Old Man." He had once been acclaimed as the best stuntman in Hollywood, and he had also been the husband of Margaret Field, Sally's mother, in a marriage that lasted from 1962 to 1968.

This former U.S. Marine had doubled for Randolph Scott, Errol Flynn, John Wayne, and Gregory Peck, among others. He had auditioned to play Tarzan after the departure of Johnny Weissmuller, but the role went to Lex Barker instead. In time, however, Jock became the 13th actor to play Tarzan on the screen in *Tarzan Goes to India* (1962), shot on location in that country.

Burt always suspected, based on dialogues with Sally, that Jock had subjected Sally to sexual abuse as a young girl, but he was never certain, and never pressed her for details.

"Burt died shortly before the publication of Sally's memoir, *In Pieces*, and never learned the full story she presented to her readers. In it, she described how Jock would emerge from the shower fully erect. "I don't know how he ever got that thing in his pants, since I never saw him in any other condition." He tried to kiss her and enter her mouth with his tongue, but she kept her teeth closed. "He would set his penis, as muscular as the rest of him, between my legs and pull my littleness toward him…and it."

She claimed in her memoir, however, that he never invaded her.

Before *The End* was distributed into theaters, Burt said, "I expected to be eaten alive by the critics, and I was devoured. The mixture of suicide and comedy is a fatal combination for most people."

Vincent Canby of *The New York Times* went negative, as he often did with Burt's films. "This is half-heartedly satiric material that's been directed by Reynolds as if it were a broad, knock-about comedy sometimes and at other times, as if it were meant to evoke pathos, which it never does."

In a private remark, Canby said, "One sometimes gets the feeling that Burt Reynolds is not really acting in a film but visiting it as he would on the Johnny Carson show. He's gotten there. But he's got a lot to live down."

Variety called the movie "a tasteless and overripe comedy that disintegrates very early into hysterical, undisciplined hamming. DeLuise is absolutely dreadful, and Joanne Woodward poorly utilized."

Burt's favorite review was by John Barbour in *Los Angeles* magazine. "*The End* is the best thing Reynolds has ever done, either as an actor or director. There are some individual scenes in it, written by Jerry Belson, that are as bright and sharp and funny as those of any comedy to come out of Hollywood since Reynolds told Darren McGavin where he could shove *Riverboat*."

In spite of the many brickbats thrown at it, *The End* took in domestic box office sales of $45 million.

***

"My next picture, *Hooper*, was my tribute to the testosterone-fueled Hollywood stuntmen, each a daredevil shouting 'to hell with tomorrow,'" Burt said. "I launched my career trying to break my neck in TV dramas in New York, and our director, Hal Needham, was one of the best stuntmen in the business. He taught me much of what I know today."

Warner Brothers acquired the rights to *Hooper*, a 1978 action comedy with Burt cast in the leading role, a veteran stuntman [*"Achilles with a mustache"*] named Sonny Hooper, who's at the end of a dangerous career where he defied death every day.

Burt was supported in his role by his girlfriend, Sally Field, her third movie as his leading lady, and by Jan-Michael Vincent, an ambitious stuntman-in-the-making who's pitted against the far more experienced Sonny.

Its producers included Lawrence Gordon and Hank Moonjean. Each of them had held equivalent positions in Burt's previous film, *The End*. In 2008, when Moonjean published his memoir, *Bring in the Peacocks*, he asserted that *Hooper* had been the most financially lucrative film he had ever produced.

[He also relayed a story that unfolded on the Warner lot during pre-production talks:

Burt and Moonjean were in a huddle when Clint Eastwood entered their office. His conversation with Burt led to the promise that one day—soon, they hoped—they'd co-star in a film together.

Then, there was a sudden pounding on the door. Burt opened it to encounter Oscar-winning Jane Wyman, the ex-wife of Ronald Reagan. She was shouting profanities, yelling "Where in the fuck is my dressing room?" She was on the lot as one of the stars of the TV soap opera, Falcon Crest.

At the same meeting, Moonjean told Burt that the role of his character's former wife had been written out of the script, thereby radically altering the plot from how it had first been presented. Moonjean claimed that he had approached Angie Dickinson and offered her the part, but she had turned it down. "In the new script, she will only be mentioned," Moonjean said.]

***

Sally discussed Burt with the press. "You can't play a personality for as long as Burt has and not start playing yourself a little. He is changing. He is opening up, letting his emotions out. He's doing it publicly, as if asking, 'Is this all right?' I'm afraid that might hurt him. It's gotten so bad that he's begun to see his public as a person, someone to talk to, one-on-one directly. He goes to interviews, like he did for Barbara Walters, the way you go to see a friend to talk and to tell them something. And he comes back horribly depressed because there is no feedback."

"When I first met him on *Smokey and the Bandit,* all he wanted was to be Number One. There was none of this *ac*-tor stuff. Well he *is* Number One, and he still hears only criticism, not the love. Sometimes, I want to scream at him, 'STOP! We love you!'"

Francesca challenges Angela for Falcon Crest! Guest star: Gina Lollobrigida

FALCON CREST 10PM CBS ⊙3,6,9,11,2

ONLY IN AMERICA, and ONLY IN HOLLYWOOD might an actress who almost became First Lady barge into one of Burt's meetings in a rage, screaming profanities.

That's what happened when Jane Wyman, star of *Falcon Crest* and ex-wife of the future president, Ronald Reagan, couldn't find her dressing room.

In *Hooper,* Sally was cast as Gwen Doyle, the winsome, perky "gal pal" of Burt. She didn't think much of the role, claiming that her part as Burt's leading lady was "getting smaller and smaller, a cookie-cutter character. But nothing else was coming my way, so I was glad to be working."

One observer noted, "Sally echoes Reynolds' good looks and bad morals by running around in a tight shirt with her nipples showing and a pair of shorty shorts with her butt sticking out."

When she wasn't needed, Sally flew back to Los Angeles where she negotiated terms to star in her most famous role, *Norma Rae* (1979), which brought her a Best Actress Oscar. Whether she knew it or not, the role had been first offered to Jill Clayburgh, Burt's recent co-star. To her everlasting regret, she rejected it.

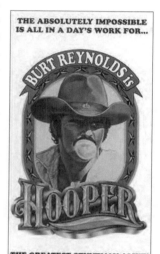

THE ABSOLUTELY IMPOSSIBLE IS ALL IN A DAY'S WORK FOR...

BURT REYNOLDS IS

HOOPER

THE GREATEST STUNTMAN ALIVE!

Another veteran stuntman of yesterday, Jock Mahoney had a brief cameo role ("Old Man") in *Hooper.*

"Jock must have brought back painful memories to Sally," Burt said. "There were those charges that he had sexually abused her as a young girl when he was married to her mother."

"Burt and Vincent became very close during the shoot, a case of male-on-male bonding," Needham said. "You might call it a father-son thing. They always had their arms around each other. Of course, there was gossip. One stuntman told me he accidentally walked in on Burt as Vincent was performing fellatio on him. I didn't believe that at all and fired the jerk."

"Burt was staying close to Vincent because he wanted to protect him," Needham said. "The kid had for years struggled with alcoholism and drug addic-

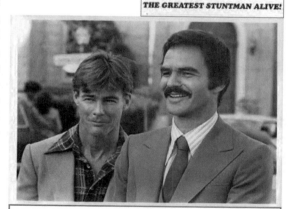

Jan-Michael Vincent and Burt Reynolds, each playing a death-defying stuntman, in this publicity photo for *Hooper* (1978).

Off screen, was it a father-son relationship, or something else? The gossipy crew of *Hooper* spread rumors believed to be false.

438

tion, and Burt wanted to keep him sober for our film."

Vincent was descended from a notorious family of bank robbers and counterfeiters who flourished in the 1920s and '30s. Before hooking up with Burt, he had worked as an actor for Universal in various TV series. A staring role had emerged in 1969 in the prime time soap, *The Survivors*, in which he co-starred with luscious Lana Turner and George Hamilton, but the series bombed. Vincent later starred with John Wayne and Rock Hudson in *The Undefeated* (1969) and opposite Robert Mitchum in *Going Home* (1971).

During the filming of *Hooper*, Burt's best friend, James Best, who was also in the movie, told Needham, "It seems I've been replaced as Burt's best buddy. That druggie really pisses me off. I don't know what Burt sees in him."

Burt had seen Vincent's most daring performance in *Buster and Billie* (1974), a romance where he stunned audiences by appearing frontally nude. "Jan was far more daring than I was when I posed for *Cosmo*. So he wasn't the best-endowed actor in Hollywood, but he had guts. He showed the world what he had..or didn't have. It was like he was saying, 'This is how I was made, and if you don't like it, go fuck yourself.'"

"In the late 1970s, Vincent's drug use got him into trouble with the police. During the filming of *Hooper*, he was arrested for possession of cocaine, but Burt got him a lawyer and posted bail.

Again in 1978 and '79, Vincent was arrested again on charges of possession of cocaine.

He achieved his greatest fame when he played the pilot Stringfellow Hawke in the CBS TV series *Airwolf*. The show was built around a cutting-edge helicopter that made its commercial debut in 1984. He made $200,000 per episode.

An arrest for drunk driving in 1988 got him committed to rehab. In 2000, his troubles escalated when a former girlfriend won a $374,000 judgment against him for charging that his physical assault on her led to her miscarriage.

As the 1990s rolled around, Vincent was involved in three car crashes, and there were more charges of drunk driving. In the summer of 1996, he broke three vertebrae in his neck and permanently injured his vocal cords. In most cases, he was sentenced to probation, but when he violated it, he was sent to the Orange County jail for sixty days. Reports surfaced that he was brutally raped by some of the inmates.

He later revealed that his right leg had been amputated below the knee in 2012 after he contracted an infection. He walked with a prosthetic limb and was sometimes confined to a wheelchair.

At the time of his death in February of 2019, Burt had not seen him in some time. "My efforts to save him proved futile," he said. "I never knew what demons possessed the poor kid."

In addition to Vincent and Sally, the supporting cast of *Hooper* also included Brian Keith, who played Sally's father, Jocko Doyle. He had worked with Burt on *Nickelodeon*. In *Hooper,* his role was that of a retired stuntman.

James Best, Burt's ever-faithful friend, was cast as Cully, the assistant to Burt's character of Sonny. "Burt sorta screwed me on the picture," Best said. "He gave a lot of my lines to Keith. He owed him one because Keith, on occasion, let him use his vacation home in Hawaii. Burt wanted to pay him back. I was a bit pissed off at first but was glad when Burt gave me the job. Keith sure ended up badly."

Best was referring to the tragic end of Keith's life. Suffering financial losses and lung cancer, he fatally shot himself in 1997, two months after his daughter also committed suicide.

Hooper was really "a movie within a movie." Burt played the stuntman working for Robert Keith, cast as Roger Deal, a director shooting a James Bond-type thriller, *The Spy Who Laughed at Danger.* Robert and Brian had the same last name but were not related. Burt later revealed that Robert Keith's character was actually a send-up of director Peter Bogdanovich, who had recently helmed Burt in two commercially disastrous films.

Adam West, cast as himself, was the star of the *Spy* movie. Burt reminded him that he had gotten his most famous TV role of Batman because Burt had rejected the role for himself. *[That did not endear him to West.]*

Klein's character is willing to risk the life of any stuntman, both Vincent and Burt, to "create the greatest action sequence ever filmed."

Needham and Moonjean flew to Tuscaloosa, Alabama, where most of *Hooper* would be shot. The University of Alabama planned to destroy their married student's quarters, which had been hastily erected after World War II to accommodate returning servicemen. The university planned to erect more modern buildings to replace them.

Needham offered to destroy the buildings for the university as part of his action/adventure film. "Only in Alabama could they allow a film company to demolish nine acres for the filming of a movie," he said.

"We also had to stage an earthquake. I located a collapsed bridge where a gasoline truck had exploded. I decided that Burt's red rocket car would attempt a leap across the bridge and over the river."

Before retirement, Burt, as Sonny, decides to perform one last stunt—a death-defying and record-breaking 456-foot leap across a river gorge in a rocket-propelled red sports car. His hope is that this Evel Knievel-type stunt will earn him a place in Hollywood legend. Of course, during the filming of the car's high-velocity trajectory through the air, dummies would have replace Burt and Vincent.

The director wanted a dramatic climax—an earthquake with explosions, fires, and car crashes. Before that, the viewers had sat through fisticuffs, gunfights, leaps, high falls, a chariot race, motorcycle spills, a runaway stagecoach, and leaps with parachutes from aircraft.

Burt's latest film inspired "the usual mixed reviews, but it grossed $78 million domestically, some forty percent less than *Smokey and the Bandit.*

Upon its release, *Hooper* in the main was recommended for popcorn munchers who liked "brash, brainless, and brawny action."

Arthur Knight of the *Hollywood Reporter* wrote, "Like the equally macho Clint Eastwood, beetle-browed Burt Reynolds seems to have carved up a profitable niche for himself by doing just one thing and doing it very well. Less dour and intense than Eastwood, but no less self-assured, Reynolds works with a quick humor, as if never taking his screen persona quite seriously."

David Ansen in *Newsweek* said, "*Hooper* doesn't dig deep into its Hollywood subject, but it's a good example of a decent, no-frills filmmaking that lets a surprising amount of feeling seep through the cracks of its all-action formula."

Gene Siskel of the *Chicago Tribune* wrote, "None of this makes very much sense. But sense is not the point in Reynolds-Needham films. Just thrills, spills, and Reynolds' leer. That's proving to be one of the most potent combinations in today's film industry."

Gary Arnold of *The Washington Post* defined *Hooper* as "a rousing and sweet-tempered sentimental comedy that should fully secure Reynolds a pre-eminent position in the affections of contemporary moviegoers." Penelope Gilliatt of *The New Yorker* labeled the film, "trite, containing frolicsome humor that is not contagious."

Charles Schreger of *Variety* said, "Reynolds continues to be one of maybe a half dozen dependable box office actors working today. His fans will flock to this one and not be disappointed."

The Tampa Tribune referred to Needham as "the Michelangelo of Mayhem, the Fellini of Falls, and the Sartre of Stunts."

***

Burt was certainly at the peak of his long career in 1978. A star bearing his name was embedded on the Walk of Fame along Hollywood Boulevard. That September, *Photoplay* magazine gave him two Gold Medal Awards, one as the Favorite Male Sex Symbol, and another as Favorite Male Star.

He was also recognized as the National Top Male Star of 1978 by the

National Association of Theater Goers. The Women's Press club nominated him for the Golden Apple Star of the Year, but he lost that prize, the award going to John Travolta instead.

"I've climbed to the top," Burt told Hal Needham, "and we've got a lot of biggies ahead of us, at least for a few more years. But then what? You know the answer to that. It'll be down the Hollywood ladder, rung by rung."

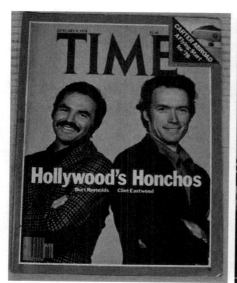

In January of 1978, Burt's image appeared on the cover of *Time* magazine alongside his friend and rival, Clint Eastwood. In September of that same year, dressed as *Hooper*, he appeared alone on the cover of a special edition of *The Saturday Evening Post*.

Tongues wagged, jealousies were awakened, and sleeping dragons bent on diminishing his reputation and allure were aroused. But the income that came in that year and the floods of publicity generated might, indeed, have represented the height of Burt's long-enduring career as a public figure before, as he stated it,

"It all began to come crashing down."

CHAPTER TWELVE

SUE MENGERS
BURT'S NEW AGENT, "A BULLDOG WITH CHARM"
ARRANGES A RENDEZVOUS WITH

HOLLYWOOD'S MOST FAMOUS HUNGARIAN
"It's Zsa Zsa, dahlink!"

BURT'S CHEATING HEART
MORE ABOUT SALLY FIELD

SEXTETTE &
THE OCTOGENARIAN LOVE GODDESS
MORE ABOUT MAE.

STARTING OVER
JILL CLAYBURGH & CANDICE BERGEN

ROUGH CUT
INSPIRED BY *TO CATCH A THIEF,* BURT PLAYS A MASTER THIEF
PLANNING A GENTLEMANLY JEWELRY HEIST

QUESTION: Could Burt Have Evolved Into a Cary Grant for the 1980?
ANSWER: Could Anyone?

THERE'S NO BUSINESS LIKE SHOW BUSINESS
BURT'S DINNER THEATER IN FLORIDA
"Serve drinks, keep them laughing, and keep them fed."

GAY BLADE
CHARLES NELSON REILLY

FARRAH FAWCETT & CANNONBALL RUN
BURT AND CHARLIE'S ANGEL CRASH-LAND BACK TO EARTH

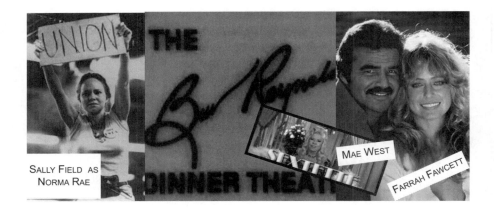

SALLY FIELD AS
NORMA RAE

MAE WEST

FARRAH FAWCETT

With money pouring into his coffers

—Burt made $5 million from *Smokey and the Bandit*—he spent lavishly and ostentatiously.

Part of his money went toward renovations on his recently acquired home on four landscaped acres in Holmby Hills. He also acquired yet another home in California, three homes in Florida, and an antebellum mansion in Georgia that evoked Tara in *Gone With the Wind*. He also purchased land in Tennessee near where Dolly Parton, his future co-star, had launched Dollywood, her amusement and theme park.

He also bought a private jet and a helicopter and hired two fulltime pilots to stand by if needed. He paid each of them a yearly salary of $100,000.

The day after Burt decided to leave his longtime agent, Dick Clayton, he signed with the formidable Sue Mengers.

"Sue was the toughest bitch in Hollywood," Burt said. "Just what I needed. She was brilliant, very schmoozy, and had more

Burt told his new agent, Sue Mengers, "Getting to the top is a hell of a lot more fun than staying there. I've got Tom Selleck crawling up my back. I'm moving on through my forties. I realize I have four or five more good years where I can play certain kinds of parts and get away with it. I don't want to be stumbling around town doing Gabby Hayes parts a few years from now. See to it that I don't."

444

of a sense of humor than I did. But in a second, her vicious tongue could shoot out toxic one-liners. She was small in stature, but large in life, acting like a man, whatever in hell that means."

Born in in 1932 in Hamburg, Germany, to Jewish parents, Sue was a small child when she landed in New York with her parents. Within a few years, her father committed suicide in a Times Square Hotel, and Sue and her mother moved to the Bronx, where her mother began working as an accountant.

In 1955, Sue gravitated to Los Angeles, where she got a job as a receptionist for MCA. That was followed by a tenure with the William Morris Agency before she, in time, branched out as a full-time agent with a list of some of the hottest stars in Hollywood.

Those included not only Burt but Steve McQueen, Barbra Streisand (who was her maid of honor at her wedding), Cybill Shepherd, Faye Dunaway, Gene Hackman, Candice Bergen, Peter Bogdanovich, Joan Collins, Dyan Cannon, Robert Redford, Ali MacGraw, and Michael Caine.

The first time Burt attended a lavish party at Mengers' home, he found himself talking to Sidney Poitier, Julie Harris, Paul Newman, and Warren Beatty.

"She didn't just represent stars," Burt said. "On other occasions, I met some of the greatest *auteurs* of the age, guys such as Arthur Penn and Mike Nichols. Sue was dynamite and was known for putting together winning combinations of authors, directors, and stars."

"Her home was extravagant like a French château once owned by Zsa Zsa Gabor," Burt said. "One night at Sue's home I met Zsa Zsa herself, and she flirted outrageously with me. She asked me to escort her home, and I decided to go for it."

"I knew I'd be following in the dust of Sean Connery, Prince Aly Khan, Richard Burton, Frank Sinatra, her stepson Nicky Hilton, and JFK. My only fear was that I was no match for her former lover, Porfirio Rubirosa, the playboy of the western world. In those days, when men in a restaurant called for a 'Rubirosa,' a very

Those Glamorous Gabors

Bombshells from Budapest

Great Courtesans of the 20th Century

DARWIN PORTER

In 2013, Blood Moon produced the most comprehensive overview of Zsa Zsa and her sisters ever published. The author is a die-hard fan of the trio of Hungarian sisters who redefined the links between the Hapsburgs and postwar Hollywood.

large peppermill was brought to the table."

Although Burt left Zsa Zsa's home at 10AM the following morning, he provided few details about the night he spent with her.

Finally, when Mengers cornered him, demanding details, all he had to say was, "Zsa Zsa wanted to know if she were as good—or better—than Dinah Shore."

"And thus began my association with Sue, a bulldog with charm."

***

"Sally Field knew how to be both a movie star and a hard-working mom to her two sons," Burt said. "She always went shopping for groceries without makeup, disobeying Joan Crawford's mandate that no star should ever emerge from her home without full makeup and a stunning dress."

"To me, Sally seemed like a wonder woman to her boys, tending to them while reading scripts and preparing for her next role. She was a truly amazing woman. And although she succeeded at all that, she didn't neglect my needs as her boyfriend."

"As for me, I still clung to my bachelor ways, not wanting to settle down into domestic bliss. I kept hopping from place to place."

When he described that to Hal Needham, he changed his statement slightly, claiming, "I hopped from bed to bed whenever opportunity arose—usually 'rising' to the occasion, which was frequent, even at an age (42) when a lot of men begin to slow down."

"But my relationship with Sally moved on," Burt said. "One night she bluntly told me, 'I want to get married.'"

"I was a smart-ass, telling her, 'I hope you find the right guy.'"

As her sons grew older, they resented Burt for "stealing" their mother away. Sometimes, at Burt's, they tugged at her arm and protested with: "Mommy, we want to go home!"

So-called friends and members of Sally's family called to alert her to *exposés* in the *National Enquirer* linking Burt to other women, frequently co-stars in his movies.

"I felt that I was being made a fool of," Sally said, "but I never confronted him with these accusations. In a way, I didn't really want to know."

Burt and Sally had one of their biggest arguments after she was interviewed by a reporter for *People* magazine for a cover story published on April 25, 1977. Burt became enraged. "Don't you dare try to capitalize off our love affair, and why didn't you get my permission before talking to *People*?"

One night, Sally cooked dinner for her two boys and a different meal for Burt. After she tucked her boys in for the night, she began packing Burt's dinner for delivery to his home in Holmby Hills.

Then her phone rang. It was Burt, "disinviting" her, and instructing her not to come over, as he had to meet outside his house with a star about a possible film role. He failed to mention the name of the star but promised to call her when he woke up in the morning.

***

Burt drove to Ravenswood, the apartment complex owned by Mae West, wondering what was on her mind. After only a fifteen-minute wait, Mae made her entrance. Wrapped in white fox, she wore black lace with gold trim as designed by Edith Head. Burt stood up to kiss her on both cheeks.

"So, the Bandit heeded my summons tonight, as I knew you would. I hear you left Dinah and are shacked up with the Flying Nun, a major change in your life. So sit down, dearie, and tell me how it's hanging."

"Just seeing you is causing a rise in my too-tight pants," he said. "That reminds me of my favorite of your very quotable lines, 'Is that a gun in your pocket or are you just glad to see me?'"

As she settled back on her sofa, she said, "I've got a million of them, dozens of golden oldies, plus some new ones, too. They're all being incorporated into this script I've turned out, with some contributions from this guy Herbert Baker. We've been greenlighted to release a new musical comedy, *Sextette*."

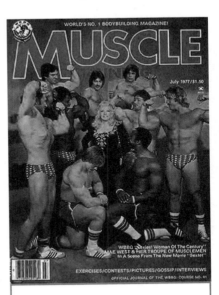

"I've named it that because the film opens as I'm on my honeymoon in London with my sixth husband. I play a legendary American movie star and international sex symbol, Marlo Manners."

"Sounds like type casting," he quipped. "How do I fit into this?"

"I want you to play my sixth husband, Sir Michael Barrington to my Lady Barrington. We've already signed your close buddy, Dom DeLuise. He only provides comic re-

July, 1977 cover of *Muscle* magazine, celebrating Mae's affinity for weightlifters and her "camp quotient" in *Sextette*.

447

lief—a guy that fat would never be one of my husbands."

"You'll play a knight," Mae continued, "So you've got to come up with a British accent. I think it would be funnier for you to fake a British accent than have a British actor in the role. Richard Burton would jump at the chance, but I want to work with you. I know it didn't work out for you to co-star with me in *Myra Breckinridge*, but perhaps you can arrange if for *Sextette*. I can see the marquee now: MAE WEST AND BURT REYNOLDS IN *SEXTETTE*. We'll have your fans and my fans lined up around the block."

Burt later admitted to Hal Needham, producer Hank Moonjean, and others, that he indulged Mae for the evening. He feared that even though she looked "divine," for an 84-year-old, he knew that the critics would ridicule her.

[Even Rex Reed, a critic who had been cast in Myra Breckinridge, *eventually denounced Mae in* Sextette *as "looking like something discovered in the basement of a pyramid."]*

Burt indulged Mae by patiently listening to her rundown of the plot. Eventually, he became horrified by her self-deceptions: "I'll photograph like a twenty-six year old sex goddess. Even at my age, I'll look ten years younger than Marilyn Monroe when she was knocked off."

"I'm bringing back the way I played Diamond Lil on Broadway in 1928, that wise-cracking, jewelry-loving Jezebel of the Bowery. Time, dearie, can turn you into a hag, but not if you let the bitch know who's the boss. I dress and look like a lady, but, of course, with my legendary cooch sway."

"I plan to rewrite some of my lines: As the men, including the U.S. Olympic Team, each of them wearing a satin bikini, crowd around me, I'll deliver one of my favorite zingers: 'My advice is to avoid temptation unless you can't resist it.'"

"That's advice I always followed." Burt said. "Other than this picture, is there anything you wanted to do in life but didn't?"

"Thanks for asking. When I was a little girl in Brooklyn, I wanted to be a lion tamer. Then I got to play one in *I'm No Angel* (1933). I don't know, I seem to get off cracking the whip."

She had her lover and assistant, Paul Novak, bring in an autographed photo of the President of the United States. On it was written, "To Mae West, from her favorite fan, Jimmy Carter."

"He invited me to dinner at the White House, but that's too far to go for just a meal."

"Will *Sextette* be shot abroad?" Burt asked.

"It'll be shot right here in Hollywood. In England, they go around quoting Shakespeare, but here in Hollywood, the favorite person to quote is Mae West herself. By the way, there's one of my zinger lines I want to slip into the script."

"What is it?" he asked.

"An orgasm a day keeps the doctor away."

"I'm so glad Edith Head is designing my clothes," Mae continued. "She was always my favorite. She did all my fittings directly from my nude body, and she shot down all those rumors that I was a female impersonator."

"In the 1930s, a rumor went around that one of Hollywood's three biggest stars was a drag queen. I was cited—so were Dietrich and Greta Garbo. Let's face it: Marlene had given birth to a child, so it wasn't her. That points the finger at Garbo. Imagine, maybe when she dies, we'll learn that Garbo was a man."

Burt later confessed to Moonjean, "I was a real bastard. From the beginning, I never had any intention of co-starring with her, and I never saw her again. It felt like a betrayal of our friendship, but I just couldn't do what she wanted."

The director of *Sextette*, Ken Hughes, eventually hired Timothy Dalton as Sir Barrington, and Tony Curtis, Ringo Starr, and George Hamilton played three of her character's former husbands. And a well-seasoned roster of character actors was assembled for the remaining roles. They included Walter Pidgeon and the notoriously self-destructive drummer for *The Who*, Keith Moon (his last appearance on the screen). George Raft, Regis Philbin, and Hollywood columnist Rona Barrett played themselves. Alice Cooper *["The Godfather of 'Shock Rock'"]* appeared as a waiter.

Dalton later told the press, "I admire the nerve of Miss West and enjoyed working with her. I was even interviewed on screen by Rona Barrett. It was a real stretch for me, and, frankly, after making love to a woman in her mid-80s, I knew I could handle my assignment."

His performance in *Sextette* assured Dalton his place in camp history. He'd go on to portray James Bond in the 007 movie series. Later, in the TV miniseries *Scarlett* (1994), he was cast as Rhett Butler, the role that originated with Clark Gable's performance in *Gone With the Wind* (1939).

Burt, slightly disguised, sneaked into a movie theater for a viewing of *Sextette* during its limited release. He later called it "a cartoon for grownups." He knew that Mae would be devastated by the reviews, some of the most poisonous of any movie made in the 1970s. The critic for *The New York Times* wrote, "Granny should have her mouth washed out with soap, along with her teeth."

Sextette was one of the worst movie flops ever made. It was shot for a budget that ranged from $4 million to $8 million, depending on who you asked. Over the years, it has gained a cult following and referred to as "the high camp movie of the decade."

On August 10, 1980, Mae fell out of bed, hitting her head. She was rushed to a hospital where it was determined that she had suffered a concussion. After news of it leaked to the press, Paul Novak claimed that she'd fallen out of bed "while dreaming of Burt Reynolds."

On the morning of Saturday, November 22, 1980, Mae's doctor told Novak that his goddess could not survive the remainder of the day.

Within minutes, she was gone. her still-loyal fans around the world, especially her gay ones, mourning her loss.

When Burt heard the news, he burst into tears, feeling guilty that after their first conversation about *Sextette,* he hadn't returned her calls.

Timothy Dalton, the future James Bond, with Mae West in *Sextette.*

"She broke barriers for what you could get away with on the screen," Burt said. "She made the movies grow a little bit, and she did it her way. The sex wasn't what it was all about, although there was plenty of that. I think film historians will recognize her one day as the 20th Century's greatest *comedienne.*"

***

Burt had already read Dane Wakefield's novel, *Starting Over,* twice, and eventually got his hands on a copy of its screenplay (also by Wakefield) too.

He became enthralled with the character of Phil Porter, a recently divorced man who is torn between the love he maintains for his ex-wife (she lives in New York) and a new girlfriend he encountered in Boston.

Burt thought he'd be ideal in the role. As he relayed to Hal Needham, "Don't get me wrong. I'm not jealous of Sally winning her Oscar for *Norma Rae,* but I want to walk off with some gold, too. *Starting Over* might do it for me. It could become *my Norma Rae.*"

According to Needham, "Burt desperately wanted to be taken more seriously by his peers and critics, and he wanted more than anything to earn the respect of those who praised the talents of Robert De Niro, Dustin Hoffman, and Al Pacino. This role of a sensitive unmarried man, befuddled and trying to begin a new life, might mean losing his drive-in faithful—you know, the guys who show up in pickup trucks. *Starting Over* (1979) might make him, in their eyes, 'Just another Hollywood fag.'"

Burt took the script to his agent, Sue Mengers, who read it overnight. She phoned him the next morning. "C'mon, Burt, are you crazy? You must be on something. Who in hell will believe a dude like you can't get a woman to date him?"

As he told Mengers, "Some actors are clones, remaining the same for twenty years. But I'm getting better than that."

Because he persisted, she used her influence to get through to the director, Alan J. Pakula, associated with the fast-evolving project.

Pakula was at the peak of his stellar career, having been nominated for a Best Picture Academy Award for *To Kill a Mockingbird* (1962) and a Best Director Oscar for *All the President's Men* (1976). He'd also directed Jane Fonda for her portrayal of a prostitute in *Klute* (1971), for which she earned an Oscar.

"Burt Reynolds?" Pakula said to Mengers. "Is this some kind of joke? There's not one car chase in the whole movie. I wanted a New York actor, maybe one trained by Lee Strasberg. Maybe Robert Redford, who'd be perfect."

But based on Burt's box office power, Pakula agreed to have lunch with him

"The role of Phil Potter is closer to the real me than that posturing good ol' Southern boy I often play. For *Starting Over*, I'd shave off my mustache. Goodbye, Bandit. Hello Sensitive Man."

Pakula was still unconvinced and instructed Burt to submit to a screen test, thinking that he'd bolt at the idea. He was surprised when Burt acquiesced.

"Here I was, a box office cham-

Burt shaved off his mustache to stand between two women, Candice Bergen (left) and Jill Clayburgh. Which one to choose?

"I wanted to be appealingly vulnerable," he said.

pion, my last two movies having grossed $400 million, and Pakula wants a god damn screen test."

Burt not only did a screen test but was called back for three more tests before Pakula reluctantly awarded him the role.

"There was something special that I liked about the story," Burt said. "The Swinging Sixties were over, and a lot of people like the character I was playing were dealing with the lingering hangover left over from the decade that had gone by."

Burt told a reporter, "By the time I'm fifty, I plan to retire from acting and devote my career to directing. At that time, I hope to be married with kids. A bare shirt guy like me can only hold in his stomach for so long, so my beefcake days are coming to an end. So are my bare-assed shots. I'm gonna be just great growing old behind the camera."

When Burt flew to New York, Sally remained in Hollywood, finishing her latest movie, *Beyond the Poseidon Adventure* (1979).

Burt was delighted with his supporting players: Candice Bergen would play his ex-wife, Jessica. She wants to divorce him, write songs, and pursue a singing career. [*It seems she can write, but not sing.*]

Jill Clayburgh, Burt's co-star and off-screen girlfriend from *Semi-Tough*, had been cast as Marilyn Holmberg. Burt's character meets her on a blind date after his move from New York to Boston. Burt's friend, actor Charles Durning, was cast as his brother Mickey. Burt's sister-in-law, Marva, was played by Frances Sternhagen.

The film opens with Bergen (as Jessica) demanding a divorce. Having accepted a teaching job and aiming for a clean start and a new life, Burt heads to Boston. There, he joins a therapy group for divorced men at weekly meetings in the basement of a local church.

Burt's brother, Mickey, fixes him up on a blind date with Marilyn, and he gradually falls in love with her—that is, until his ex-wife, Jessica, reappears and asks for a reconciliation. The audience already knows that the second try won't work, and that Burt will remain in Boston for a new life with Marilyn.

On location in Boston, Burt was disappointed by his reunion with Jill Clayburgh. Her romantic attentions were now focused on David Rube, a screenwriter and playwright. Clayburgh would marry him in 1979.

During their filming together, tongues wagged and tabloids gossiped when Burt was seen with Candice Bergen at elegant hangouts in Manhattan. Stories appeared about a breakup with Sally. But when Sally found the time, she joined Burt for a brief sojourn in Manhattan, returning soon after her arrival to get back to her sons.

Sally remained in Los Angeles for Christmas, and Burt stayed on location in Manhattan. So did Candice, who, during intimate moments, told Burt that she'd been miscast. *[Actually, she had wanted the Clayburgh role.]* "My character was so silly, so shallow, so self-absorbed. As Burt's wife, I was vain and venal. I didn't identify with such a person at all."

A decade younger than Burt, Candice was born into a life of privilege in Beverly Hills, the daughter of the famed ventriloquist, Edgar Bergen. As a child, she grew irritated at being called "Charlie McCarthy's *[a reference to the dummy her father used as part of his stage act]* younger sister."

By 1966, Candice had turned to acting, starring in a lesbian romp entitled *The Group* directed by Sidney Lumet. Her big hit, *The Sand Pebbles* (1966) co-starred her on the screen with Steve McQueen.

Later, Bergen generated rave reviews for her performance in *Carnal Knowledge* (1971), directed by Mike Nichols. According to tabloid gossip, during its filming, she had an affair with her co-star, Jack Nicholson.

Before working with Burt, she had also co-starred with Sean Connery in *The Wind and the Lion* (1975).

Almost a decade after *Starting Over*, beginning in 1988, Bergen became a household name when she played the lead in the hit TV sitcom, *Murphy Brown*, cast as a tough TV reporter. From 1980 to 1995, she was married to the French film director, Louis Malle.

[Long before that, Candice had lived with Terry Melcher, the son of Doris Day, at 10050 Cielo Drive in Los Angeles. After they moved out, Sharon Tate, and her husband, Roman Polanski, moved in. As the world knows, on August 9, 1969, fanatical followers of cult leader Charles Manson broke into the house, murdering the guests and repeatedly stabbing Tate in her pregnant stomach.]

Truman Capote claimed, "Candice is real pretty but with an appalling taste in men." *[It was unclear if he were referencing Burt Reynolds, Jack Nicholson, Warren Beatty, or all three of them.]* "There's something spinsterish about her," he continued.

Bergen's provocative comments were sometimes picked up by the press:

"Hollywood is like Picasso's bedroom."

"I always thought 'actress' was synonymous with 'fool.'"

"Most men are jerks about beautiful women… It's hard not to despise them."

Burt told Pakula, "Candice and I at first kept our distance from each other. We were friends, but not intimate friends. She had a reputation as an 'Ice Queen.' And she thought I only made car chase movies with cops on my ass. But we got to know each other by simply being ourselves."

"Before we went to Boston for filming, we went horseback riding together in Central Park. We started dating, and we introduced each other to our friends."

Soon, gossips like Dorothy Kilgallen and Walter Winchell were reporting on their romance. According to Burt, "The urge was there on my part, a very strong urge." Word eventually got back to Sally.

One night Bergen told him, "I'm the best actress in Hollywood for faking an orgasm. Ten seconds of heavy breathing, then roll your head from side to side, simulate a sigh like an asthma attack—and just die a little."

The sexual tension eventually led to a seduction. After Bergen rang his doorbell, Burt answered it half-dressed. "We're going to end up doing it, aren't we?" she asked.

"Dear God, I hope so," he answered, admitting her inside. As she stood before him, he said, "Let's get it over with." Later, he confessed, "I thought about what a prick I was being to Sally."

When the act was over, their passion cooled. In time, they evolved into "platonic friends."

Candice later said that Burt's sensitivity and generosity were responsible for her Oscar nomination (Best Actress in a Supporting Role) for her performance in *Starting Over*.

Barney Cohen, in his evaluation of *Starting Over* that appeared in *The New York Times*, credited Pakula for guiding Burt through his best performance.

Pakula said, "Burt turned out to really be a thinking man's actor, working his tail off to make the role look simple. Sure, he plays himself, but there's a technique to that. He's got it! And he's got that comic timing that really sparkled in drama—the deadpan reaction. You can cut to a take of him anytime, and he'll look like he's doing nothing, but it's riotously funny or meaningful, or whatever."

"Sure, Burt uses the Method," said Sally. "He's not a serious student, but he uses it. When he talks negatively about it, he's not really talking about the Method as a technique. He's talking about some of the guys who use it, actors like Marlon Brando whom he doesn't care for very much."

Starting Over was moderately successful at the box office, earning $36 million on a movie that cost $10 million to shoot.

Charles Champlin of the *Los Angeles Times* declared, "It is classy entertainment which, now and in years to come, will remind us quite accurately how things were between middle-class men and women, circa 1980."

Jack Kroll of *Newsweek* stated that the movie "starts out swell and continues well for about two-thirds of the way before succumbing to the creeping virus of cutesies."

Frank Rich in *Time* magazine said, "Though the film has a funny and potentially explosive story, it rarely generates any emotion beyond bland good cheer. Right up to the moment *Starting Over* is over, we're still waiting for the fireworks to start."

Gary Arnold in the *Washington Post* wrote one of Burt's favorite reviews: "As the newly divorced hero in *Starting Over*—a delightful romantic comedy destined for enormous well-deserved popularity—Burt Reynolds reaches a breathtaking new plateau of screen acting dexterity."

Roger Ebert wrote, "*Starting Over* actually feels sort of embarrassed at times, maybe because characters are placed in silly sitcom situations and then forced to say lines that are supposed to be revealing and real. When the gags do work, and occasionally they do, it's more a matter of acute social observation than good writing, as when a guy in a department store screams at a bunch of shoppers, 'Anybody got some Valium?'—and of course, everybody does."

Dave Pollock in *Variety* wrote: "Without his ever-present mustache, Reynolds is appealingly vulnerable, and in *Starting Over,* he no longer has to prove anything. With unfailing comic timing, and a superb sense of reaction, he is the core of the film, and underplays marvelously. It's a performance that should get the critics off his back once and for all."

***

During the U.S. Presidency (1953-1961) of Dwight D. Eisenhower, Alfred Hitchcock had conceived and directed a stylish movie about a retired jewel thief, a role played by Cary Grant, as supported by Grace Kelly as his romantic interest. Set against the backdrop of the French Riviera, released in 1956, and entitled *To Catch a Thief*, it was well-reviewed by the contemporary press. Since then, it's frequently cited as a good example of the suave elegance and acting maturity of then middle-aged Cary Grant.

According to Burt, "*Rough Cut* (1980), my next picture about a sophisticated jewelry heist, was my failed attempt to become a sort of unsophisticated Cary Grant of the 1980s." In it, he was cast as a jewel thief, Jack Rhodes, known in the underworld as "Jack of Diamonds." Parts of his performance were inspired as a kind of insider's joke by Grant's performance in *To Catch a Thief. Rough Cut* was about Burt's masterminding of a heist of $30 million worth of uncut diamonds.

Burt was not the first actor to evoke Cary Grant. Others had included Tony Curtis in the 1960s. In the 70s, George Segal, Ryan O'Neal and Gene Wilder gave it a try, too. None of them even came close to capturing Grant's nuances.

In an opening sequence of *Rough Cut,* as an insider joke that many viewers didn't consider clever or funny, Burt impersonates the voice of Cary Grant during a conversation with his leading lady, Lesley-Anne

Down.

"That is the worst Cary Grant I've ever heard," Down's character responds.

Burt shoots back, "I wasn't doing Cary Grant. I was doing Tony Curtis doing Cary Grant."

Thus began the flawed opening scenes of a film that Burt might have chosen for the wrong reasons—his hope of becoming recognized for a broader range than what had been showcased in his earlier films.

[Sue Mengers, Burt's new agent, evaluated Burt's frustrated ambitions as an actor like this: "Every morning, Burt rises with the ambition that he wants to be an Oscar-winning actor known for his dramatic roles and not for Smokey and the Bandit. Burt fears he's not able to reach that goal. Jon Voight is his good friend. But Burt told me that he really wanted to play the hustler, Joe Buck, in Midnight Cowboy (1969), partly because it brought Jon an Oscar nomination.

"I would have worn the tightest jeans on Times Square," Burt told her.]

Surprisingly, the producer of *Rough Cut* was David Merrick, a man usually associated with blockbusters (*Gypsy*, 1959; *Oliver*, 1963; *Hello Dolly*, 1964; *Breakfast at Tiffany's*, 1966) from the Broadway stage.

Merrick collaborated smoothly (at least at the beginning) with *Rough Cut*'s director, Donald Siegel, a veteran best known for his science fiction cult classic, *Invasion of the Body Snatchers* (1956).

[Siegel had already helmed five films with Burt's friend, Clint Eastwood, including the police thriller, Dirty Harry (1971). Siegel had also directed John Wayne's adieu to the screen, The Shootist (1976).]

Some of the cast and crew of *Rough Cut* were flown to London, where Siegel hired a lot of local talent.

Lesley-Anne Down, a Londoner born and bred, had worked as a fash-

It's hard to replicate a classic, and Burt's attempts to reprise (upper photo) Cary Grant and Grace Kelly's lighthearted banter and casual heat, as displayed in *To Catch a Thief* (1955), wasn't convincing to either the critics or the public.

The lower photo shows Burt with Lesley-Anne Down following something akin to the earlier film's premises in *Rough Cut*.

ion model before morphing into a singer and actress. She was widely recognized as Georgina Worsley in the TV drama series, *Upstairs, Downstairs* (1973-75). She had also appeared in *The Pink Panther Strikes Again* (1977); and *The First Great Train Robbery* (1979), with Sean Connery. Her leading men had included Kirk Douglas, Anthony Hopkins, Donald Sutherland, and Laurence Olivier.

When Burt met Down, she was just coming down from her decade-long relationship with actor-writer Bruce Robinson and had yet to marry Enrique Gabriel, a union that would endure for less than two years.

Down had been the second choice for the film's leading lady, Siegel having previously offered the role to Jacqueline Bisset.

Burt had demanded that Larry Gelbart be hired as the screenwriter for *Rough Cut.* [*The source material was a novel,* Touch the Lion's Paw, *by Derek Lambert.*]

"Gelbart was among my favorite writers," Burt said. "The writers whose work I adapt best to usually have backgrounds writing for TV. They don't usually have ego problems, and they're used to working under the gun."

Honor among thieves? Scenes of love & duplicity in *Rough Cut.* Lesley-Anne Down vs. Burt as a master jewel thief and safecracker,

Gelbart was fired, then re-hired.

In reference to *Rough Cut,* according to Siegel, "I was tired of action films, and wanted a change of pace. The novel it was based on was poor. In time, seven writers worked on its script, but in the end, it wasn't nearly as good as it should have been. A great deal of work was needed to shore it up. Frankly, I don't know why Burt, then at the peak of his stardom, took the role."

During Burt's first meeting with Siegel, the director told him, "This is the worst-prepared movie I've ever directed. It'll take a miracle to bring it off."

"I don't agree," Burt said. "Of course, you haven't made as many bad films as I have. I'd had experiences that make this one look worse than the shooting of *Gone With the Wind."*

Almost from the beginning, Merrick (as producer) and Siegel (as director) clashed and feuded. Siegel wanted to have *Rough Cut* renamed as *Jack of Diamonds,* saying "Critics will joke that our final release is a 'rough cut.'"

Siegel was eventually fired. Peter R. Hunt, the British filmmaker, was hired to replace him, but Merrick didn't like him, either.

Then Blake Edwards was invited onto the set. His vision about radically rewriting the script and starting over was rejected.

Eventually, Burt persuaded Merrick to rehire Siegel. Exhausted in the aftermath of those negotiations, he said, "I've done more in three days than Henry Kissinger did in three years at the State Department. I'll never get myself in a situation like this again."

David Niven played the third lead in *Rough Cut* as Chief Inspector Cyril Willis of Scotland Yard. Bristling with an English style he'd already displayed in dozens of classic films, Niven projected a dry, urbane, upper-middle class Londoner. One critic noted that Niven's "furrowed brown and quizzical look are treasures worthy of the British Museum."

[Niven had a history of seduction that Burt envied. Over the course of his film career he had charmed and in most cases become intimate with the A-list: Grace Kelly, Mae West, Loretta Young, Ann Sheridan, Norma Shearer, Ginger Rogers, Merle Oberton, Ida Lupino, Carole Lombard, Evelyn Keyes, Hedy Lamarr, Woolworth heiress Barbara Hutton, tobacco heiress Doris Duke, Ava Gardner, Paulette Goddard, Alice Faye, and Rita Hayworth.

"If you want sophistication, go have lunch with David Niven," Burt said.]

Rough Cut opens at an elegant party, where master jewel thief Jack Rhodes (Burt) meets a lovely, sexy woman who, as he soon learns, is a rival jewel thief. The couple fall in love, although the object of Burt's affection, Gillian Bromley (Down) is a kleptomaniac who's being blackmailed by Scotland Yard's retiring inspector (Niven). The audience is misled into believing that Niven wants to arrest Rhodes as a resounding climax to his career as a member of the cynical and world-weary "police establishment."

Burt interpreted Down's personal life as "a bad dream. She was surrounded by really bad people. She was good inside and so very sweet."

Sally Field flew to London to check up on

Survivor of a LONG history of golden-age moviemaking: David Niven in *Rough Cut.*

458

Burt. "She'd heard rumors," Siegel said.

Burt later wrote that after one day on the set, "Sally caught on immediately."

That night, she accused Burt of "screwing Down."

As he confessed in a memoir, "Sally could walk on the set and say, 'You're screwing the service girl.' She was very close to right every time."

After watching only a scene with Burt and Down, Sally gave Burt one of "those *Norma Rae* looks of 'I'll kick your ass.'" That night they had one of their biggest arguments.

Reasons that seemed important eventually compelled Sally to return earlier than planned to L.A. At the London Airport, she seemed angry when he told her goodbye.

Years later, Down would discuss how hard her life as an actress had been. "The casting couch was in full swing, and young women both expected it and dreaded it. My teen years were intense, a lot of pressure and a lot of horrible old men out there. I was promised lots of lovely big film roles by producers if I went to bed with them. Believe me, the casting couch was no myth."

"My life was rough because of all the lecherous men, studio executives, producers, and directors." She charged that in Hollywood, she suffered sexual harassment from producer Sam Spiegel and "a legendary Hollywood actor" whom she did not name. Could she have been referring to Burt?

Before the release of *Rough Cut*, Niven sued Merrick for $1,791,000, claiming that his likeness had not, as contractually agreed, been used in ads and publicity for the film. He also claimed that Merrick owed him another $91,000, too. According to Niven, "In my forty-six years as an actor in eighty films, this is the first time I have ever been involved in a lawsuit. I have always lived up to my contractual obligations and have always paid my debts. Merrick and Paramount have neither lived up to their contract with me or honored their debt to me."

During the early stages of his involvement with *Rough Cut,* one of its many scriptwriters Gelbart had been told that "All you've got to do on a Burt Reynolds picture was to keep it in focus, and it was bound to make you $50 million." That didn't happen. The film was budgeted at $10 million but took in only sixteen and a half million in domestic box office.

When Burt saw the final cut of *Rough Cut,* he said, "What I wanted to do was pay homage to Cary Grant. I tried hard, but it didn't work. Had I succeeded in that film, I could have thrown away my Levis and cowboy hat and would wear some decent clothes for a change."

George Anderson at the *Pittsburgh Post-Gazette* interpreted *Rough Cut* as "irresistibly mellow. The film is a stylishly done caper-comedy in which even the criminals have a touch of class. It's a clever, carefree switch for Reynolds, who proved last year in *Starting Over* that he's capable of much more than playing rednecks."

Charles Champlin of the *Los Angeles Times* stated, "At its least, *Rough Cut* is a sleek and featherweight care-lifter. At its best, it almost works as a caper to compare with the best of the genre." Larry Kart of the *Chicago Tribune* called it "one of the most quirkily fascinating films to come along in some time." Gary Arnold of *The Washington Post* found the film "all too aptly titled. The principal flaws are Don Siegel's stiff-jointed direction and lackluster plot."

Roger Ebert wrote, "Reynolds can mix subtle eroticism and sly wit in ways that do sometimes remind us of (Cary) Grant, but the movie itself doesn't make it. It's fun, it's slick, and it's carefully put together, but it's more of an exercise than an accomplishment. Everybody does their *schtick*, the plot complications unfold like clockwork, but we find ourselves not really caring. That was the thing with Alfred Hitchcock. He often reached technical perfection, but rarely at the cost of involving us on a gut level."

Variety asserted, "Miraculously, all of the production's difficulty does not result in a disjointed feeling in this picture. Problem instead seems to lie in much of the dialogue, which comes across as wooden and contrived. Reynolds and Down do what they can to keep things going, but their attempts at witty banter never appear natural."

Vincent Canby of *The New York Times* claimed, "Once the movie gets into the caper itself, which occupies the last quarter of the picture, *Rough Cut* suddenly acquires its identity as an action film, but it is nearly too late. By then, we're on the point of losing interest. It's all that dreadful dialogue."

Burt weighed in with his own review: "I felt the picture was meant to be a parody, but I don't think it's broad enough. It went for something subtle that might have been too subtle. I really don't think it's clear enough, and it could have been a lot better. Compared to *At Long Last Love*, it's a masterpiece. You have to look at these things in perspective, after all. Cary Grant and Grace Kelly pulled it off better in *To Catch a Thief*.

***

After the wrap of *Rough Cut*, Burt flew to Palm Beach, Florida, and from there, drove to Jupiter for the gala opening (February 1979) of the Burt Reynolds Dinner Theatre. For him, at least, it was a dream come true.

On the afternoon of the first day of his inspection tour, he told the staff,

"It was worth the two million of the hard-earned bucks I dumped into it."

The theater was his answer to what he called "the snooty" Palm Beach Playhouse. "My ticket prices were affordable, and you didn't need to be a rich Kennedy to get in to see a show."

He'd invited Sally Field to launch his theater's first season with an appearance in *Vanities*. Written by Jack Heifner, it focuses on the competitive and abrasive friendship of three cheerleaders from Texas as each of them grows more sophisticated and cynical during the tumultuous 1960s and early 70s.

Sally and Burt selected Tyne Daly—a much-awarded veteran who would eventually win six Emmy Awards and a Tony— as the second female lead. Sally invited Gail Strickland to play the third lead. Strickland, an Alabama-born actress, had previously co-starred with Sally in *Norma Rae* (1979).

Burt would always remember a volunteer at his dinner theater named Barbara. He didn't know her last name. "She was willing to do anything to help out, even cleaning the toilets if the janitor took sick. A marvelous lady. One day, she told me, 'I have a son who once made a movie with you.'"

"What film was that??" Burt asked, thinking it was some extra or minor actor.

"*Deliverance*. I'm the mother of Jon Voight."

"I nearly fainted."

Unknown to many of his fans, Burt's first-ever direction of a play starring Sally happened before his theater opened. It was presented in a rundown, tin-roofed relic of a building beside a railroad track, with seating for only seventy-five people. It was the stage play, *Bus Stop* by William Inge. [*Its film adaptation, released in 1956, had famously starred Marilyn Monroe.*"]

Sally was challenged but frightened by the role. What closed the deal for her was when Burt agreed to cast her mother, ex-actress Margaret Field, into the role of the owner of the café, where Cherie meets the outrageous cowboy who pursues her.

"Sometimes, our dialogue was drowned out by the roar of a nearby train passing by," Sally said. "When a storm came, the thunderous roar of rain hitting the tin roof almost drowned out our lines."

Sally and her mother were housed in a condo recently acquired by Burt.

When Burt's theater was up and running, Burt and Sally starred together in *The Rainmaker*, a drama he'd performed onstage before with another actress. Both Sally and Burt had been enthralled by the performances of Katharine Hepburn and Burt Lancaster in the movie version released in 1956.

The Rainmaker was a soppy old tale of a silver-tongued devil and con man named Starbuck, who swears he can bring rain to a drought-parched community in the western plains.

While appearing with Burt, Sally gave an interview to *Playgirl,* telling a reporter, "Before I met Burt, I used to go around trying to look sexy. I mean, if I could have, I would have worn see-through clothes so you could see I was a girl. When I was doing this act, I met Burt. Right away, he was on to me. I no longer had to pretend, as he made me feel sexy."

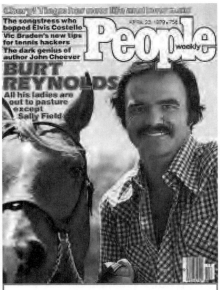

April 1979. The secondary banner on this cover of *People* says about Burt, "All his ladies are out to pasture except Sally Field."

Oy vey!.....

Burt admitted he was a nervous wreck before making his first appearance in his own theater. He was renewed when the audience gave him a standing ovation. Of course, he hadn't expected to top Burt Lancaster, but the next morning, Palm Beach critics were unkind. Sally offered him comfort, assuring him that his performance had been right on target.

The Rainmaker played to a sold-out house for most of the duration of its run. When it was over, Burt and Sally flew together for a romantic vacation to Bora-Bora, part of the Leeward group of Society Islands, northwest of Tahiti.

There, they made frequent love in a vacation bungalow opening onto a beach. Burt later remembered it as the most romantic interlude of his life.

Back in America, *Norma Rae* (1979) had opened to rave reviews. Sally experienced acclaim as an actress—something she had long been struggling to achieve.

A few days after their return from the South Pacific, she left Burt to care for her sons, Peter, nine, and Eli, six, so that she could attend the Film Festival at Cannes. There, she walked off with the Best Actress of the Year prize.

During her absence from America, there was much speculation in the press that a Reynolds/Field marriage would be imminent, perhaps immediately after her return from France.

At times, Sally's sons had resented Burt for "stealing" their mother on weekends. But when they were in his care, he planned daily activities to keep them amused—ball games, beach picnics, and slumber parties for their friends from school.

"I love Peter and Eli , he told his friends. "But marriage? I don't know. I do know one thing, however, and that is, I don't want to screw up the lives of those two fine boys by being their stepfather."

"I was sorta at the crossroads of my life, passing into middle age. Any time I went by a mirror and stopped to take a look at myself, I asked, 'Where did yesterday go? It passed so very, very fast.'"

"For years, I was forced to wear a hairpiece. I was getting tired of that. So I spent eight-thousand dollars on hair transplants. Every morning, I checked my gut in a full-length mirror. There was a thing known as middle-aged spread. I didn't want that to happen to me. My favorite dish was linguini with clam sauce. I gorged on it only one day a month."

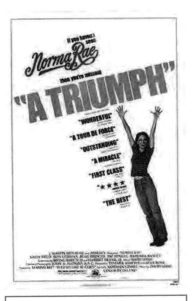

Like the character she portrayed in *Norma Rae*, Sally was smart, strong, and resourceful.

As Burt's critical reviews languished, Sally's performance as a downtrodden but courageous mill worker won her a "Best Actress of the Year" Academy Award.

When Sally returned from Cannes, a $40,000 mink coat was waiting for her. But around the same time, she learned that Burt had given Candice Bergen a $15,000 diamond bracelet, a gift reported in the press.

Sally was asked about it from a staff member at the *Hollywood Reporter*. "Did you hear about your boyfriend's gift to Candice Bergen?"

"I guess I caught Burt with his hand in the cookie jar," she answered. "I know what our relationship is, and I trust that. I never want to be the kind of woman who tells her man that he can't be friends with other women. When god passed out jealousy, he skipped me."

***

Burt had little time to perform as an actor in any of the plays he presented at his theater in Jupiter, but he directed plays there whenever he was available.

Its first winter season had been a sell-out. Based on that success, Burt was able to import TV and movie actors, some of whom had never appeared on a stage before, for their theatrical debuts. Sometimes, he got to work with his friends, as in the case of Carol Burnett, when they co-starred in *Same Time, Next Year.*

Farrah Fawcett made her stage debut at Burt's theater in *Butterflies Are Free.* Written by Leonard Gershe, it's a play about a blind boy's romance with his eccentric next-door neighbor, and her inevitable showdown with the boy's over-possessive mother. *[Back in 1972, Burt had seen the film version, starring Goldie Hawn, his future co-star.]*

Burt had formed a friendship with Martin Sheen, who eventually agreed to appear in five different theatrical productions at Jupiter, including *Mister Roberts. [Coincidentally, this was the play in which Burt had first appeared on Broadway in a minor role.]*

He considered Sheen one of the best actors in America, ever since he'd seen him in *The Subject Was Roses* (1968) and in *Apocalypse Now* (1979), for which he'd received wide recognition.

Once, Burt directed Sheen himself. "I sure had balls to do that, as I was following in the footsteps of such great directors as Oliver Stone, Francis Ford Coppola, Steven Spielberg, Mike Nichols, and Martin Scorsese."

Hal Holbrook took time off from the TV series, *Evening Shade,* to perform in *King Lear* onstage at Jupiter. Other actors who agreed to work for Burt included Ned Beatty, his co-star in *Deliverance,* along with Vincent Gardenia, Elliott Gould, and Sarah Jessica Parker.

One of Burt's favorite actors, Charles Durning, came to Jupiter for a reunion with Big Burt, his wartime Army buddy. In time, Durning would star in five plays for Burt at his theater. Durning won the Florida Drama Award for his performance in one of them, *Mass Appeal.*

The distinguished actress, Julie Harris, would also win the same award for Best Actress for her star role in Arthur Miller's *Death of a Salesman.*

Harris had become famous on Broadway for two back-to-back successes, first as young Frankie in Carson McCullers' *The Member of the Wedding,* and then as the unconventional Sally Bowles in *I Am a Camera* (1951). Burt was too young to have caught either of those stage triumphs, but he'd been Harris' ardent fan since her film performance with James Dean in *East of Eden* (1955).

Burt had long been impressed with the drama, *The Hasty Heart,* since he'd attended a screening of the 1949 film starring Ronald Reagan, Patricia Neal, and Richard Todd. The story by John Patrick was about a group of wounded soldiers in a makeshift British military hospital during World

War II.

For the production of *The Hasty Heart* at his dinner theater in Jupiter, Burt selected Robert Urich as the male lead. Ten years younger than Burt, Urich would appear in a record-breaking fifteen TV series over the course of his 30-year career. When he met Burt, he was taking time off from the hit TV series Vega$ (1978-81). His appearance in that series eventually earned him two Golden Globe Award nominations.

Burt and Urich later took their production of *The Hasty Heart* to Washington, D.C., where Burt had dinner at the White House with Ronald Reagan and First Lady Nancy. The President shared memories of his 1949 film with the same name. "I was recovering from my failed marriage to Jane Wyman and Patricia was recovering from her doomed affair with Gary Cooper."

Later, Urich revealed, "When the President was otherwise engaged, Burt flirted outrageously with Mrs. Reagan, and she seemed to enjoy it. What a daredevil that guy was."

Back in Jupiter, Burt became deeply impressed with the acting talent of the unknown John Goodman. "The guy's really talented," Burt said, "but he should watch his weight."

Goodman appeared on Burt's stage in Jupiter before achieving fame as the husband of *Rosanne* in the hit TV series.

Burt hired Kirstie Alley and Parker Stevenson as co-stars in *Answers,* an inter-connected trio of one-act plays. Alley would become a household name when she co-starred in NBC's hit sitcom, *Cheers* 1987-93). Stevenson had first come to Burt's attention when he played Frank Hardy in the

Burt had seen the movie version of *The Hasty Heart* starring Ronald Reagan, and wanted to bring the play to Jupiter.

In the movie, Ronald Reagan, after his divorce from Jane Wyman, found off-screen comfort in the arms of Patricia Neal, who was recovering from her heart-breaking romance with Gary Cooper.

Burt's version starred Robert Urich, "the handsome hunk" depicted below.

465

1970s hit TV series, *The Hardy Boys*. In 1983, he would co-star with Burt in the race car film, *Stroker Ace*.

Burt had first met the African American actor, Ossie Davis, when he was studying acting in the 1950s in Manhattan, and they had become good friends. Since then, Davis had made a number of movies, including *The Hill* (1965) starring Sean Connery.

Davis was a true native of Georgia, and he asked Burt, "Why do you pretend to be born in Waycross, Georgia, and I know you weren't?"

"I sorta liked the sound of the name," Burt said.

"I guess that's reason enough," Davis said.

As a boy growing up in Georgia, Davis had experienced the horror of the KKK threatening to hang his father.

According to Burt, "Ossie used to tell me that I was the only actor in America who was liked by both the KKK and the African American community."

Wanna know more about Ronald Reagan, his two Hollywood marriages, and his numerous affairs?

In 2014. Blood Moon published the definiive account, replete with ALL the marital and political gossip that Nancy spent decades trying to clean up and forget.

Burt admitted that he had long had a crush on Davis' wife, actress Ruby Dee, with whom he would eventually co-star. The pair would stay married for sixty years. .

At Burt's theater in Jupiter, Davis starred in *I'm Not Rappaport*. He told Burt he'd often rejected roles where he'd be cast as a downtrodden black stereotype like Stepin' Fetchit. "I preferred to follow the trail blazed by Sidney Poitier."

***

Around the time he opened the theater in Jupiter, Burt launched the nonprofit Burt Reynolds Institute for Film & Theatre, an educational organization for aspirant actors, both male and female, using $600,000 from his own bank account plus another $400,000 of charitable donations from other sources.

It offered him a rare moment to spread some of the information he'd gathered—both tech-centered and emotional—to avid, sometimes neo-phyte, sometimes star-struck students of varying degrees of skill and ambition. If Burt were unavailable, he sometimes brought in celebrity substitutes. The most famous included Liza Minnelli, Martin Sheen, Dom DeLuise, and Charles Nelson Reilly.

"I wanted a drama school for kids who couldn't afford professional training," Burt said. "The pupils weren't always high school or college students. On one occasion, for example, a policeman from Palm Beach signed on. Another was a teacher of Spanish from a local high school."

Not every class was conducted on the premises of his Jupiter Theater. Depending on the venue, some of them transpired in the Mirror Ballroom at Lake Park, in Palm Beach County, Florida, where he, as a student, had made his first stage appearance in *Outward Bound* in 1956.

In his classroom, Burt cited Spencer Tracy as master of his craft and an actor who didn't let you know he was acting. As part of his lesson plan, Burt sometimes screened the MGM classic, *Father of the Bride* (1950), in which Tracy played against the soon-to-be-wed Elizabeth Taylor. "This was a perfect demonstration of screen acting."

Burt rather provocatively discussed kissing on the screen, instructing his sometimes embarrassed students: "Don't insert your tongue into an actress's mouth unless you obtain her permission first. I always feel that if an actress sucks my tongue, it makes the scene more believable and passionate, but some actresses don't go for it. When Debbie Reynolds made *The Tender Trap* (1955) with Frank Sinatra, she was horrified when he fed her a foot of Hoboken tongue."

He told his students that every actor goes through three stages: young, old, and "you're looking good."

"In the Golden Age of Hollywood, some actors, if they had a big enough name, were stuck in romantic parts past their prime and sometimes appeared opposite young women who could have been their granddaughters."

He cited Gary Cooper opposite Grace Kelly in *High*

We're laying the foundation for the future one brick at a time!

BURT REYNOLDS INSTITUTE FOR FILM AND THEATRE

SEND YOUR DONATION TO:
PO BOX 264
JUPITER, FLORIDA 33468

THE BURT REYNOLDS INSTITUTE FOR FILM AND THEATRE, HOME OF THE BURT REYNOLDS MUSEUM, IS COMMITTED TO EDUCATING THE COMMUNITY IN ALL ASPECTS OF FILM, TELEVISION, THEATER, LIVE PERFORMANCES, AND EXHIBITIONS, AS WELL AS PRESERVING MR. REYNOLDS' MEMORABILIA AND THE HISTORY OF THE FILM INDUSTRY.

Noon (1952), and Clark Gable with Marilyn Monroe in *The Misfits* (1961). "Those guys tried to hang on in roles better suited to younger actors. You can't hold in that stomach forever."

He cited Clint Eastwood as a perfect example of a young actor who had successfully transitioned from the parts calling for a young stud into roles more appropriate for older character actors.

"It's even worse for actresses, who often fade from the screen even before turning forty—take marquee names from the '50s like Arlene Dahl. Actors get older, actresses just get old."

[Many fans of the Burt the world knew in his heyday thought that some of his later roles were unworthy of him—that is, if they even saw the string of lackluster movies he churned out in his later years.

Burt followed the advice he delivered frequently in his workshops and classroom lectures, working almost until the day he died. "No part should be beneath an actor, no part too small. I believe in working instead of retiring to a golf course, waiting to be hauled away in a casket to Forest Lawn, or to wherever else you chose to spend eternity. I looked like shit on the screen in my fading years, but what the hell. I was still a working actor."

With irony and humor, he once cited an example of what happened to him one afternoon when a former fan confronted him with: "Didn't you use to be Burt Reynolds?"

"I still am. At least what's left of me."]

***

Before a young Burt had left for Hollywood in the 1950s, Big Burt had warned him that he'd heard "the place was crawling with fags. If you ever bring one of those sissy boys around here, I'll shoot him and make a rug out of him for your mother."

In 1957 in New York, Burt had begun a longtime friendship with the very gay Charles Nelson Reilly, a comedian, actor, director, and drama coach at the Herbert Berghof (HB) Studio, where his pupils included Lily Tomlin and Bette Midler.

Reynolds and Reilly were seen together so frequently that gossips falsely defined them as lovers. "I was very close to this Bronx-born guy, but not at bedtime," Burt said. "I preferred women, and he liked studly guys. Our friends called us 'The Odd Couple.'"

"Back in those days, a TV executive had bluntly told Reilly, 'We don't allow queers on TV.'" Yet, ironically, Reilly became one of the most prominent faces on television, appearing, for example, as many as a hundred times on the *Tonight* Show with Johnny Carson.

"Charles and I were among Johnny's most frequent guests," Burt said. "Even though I always denied it, Johnny always believed that I let Charles blow me on those trips we took together to Florida."

Reilly also had a serious side as a director, and in that capacity, one of his most noted achievements was casting Julie Harris in the 1976 Broadway production of *The Belle of Amherst,* where she portrayed Emily Dickinson.

Because Big Burt was an outspoken homophobe, Burt was reluctant to bring the two men together. "I was so wrong. My papa and Charles became the best of friends, hugging and kissing each other on the cheek. Dad

Charles Nelson Reilly as a game show contestant.

"None of my studly stable boys in Jupiter were safe when Charles was around," Burt claimed.

never was that intimate with me. Charles talked, acted, walked, and fluttered around like some queen, and he absolutely delighted Big Burt, who was constantly laughing at his jokes. He kept asking me, 'When are you going to bring Charles back to Florida?"

At Burt's theater over the years, Reilly directed seventeen stage productions, some of the most successful ever presented there. "Actors were surprised at how talented he was as a director, having known him only for his frequent, always hilarious, appearances on television."

Burt became so close to Reilly that he gave him the beachfront house in Jupiter where he and Sally Field had lived and loved on their trips to Florida.

When Burt first drove his friend to the property to offer it to him as a gift, he could not bear show him its interior, so he gave him the key and instructed him to enter for a self-guided tour. "It brings back too many memories of my time with Sally. I never want to enter that place again."

"Charles never concealed his gayness, but he never flaunted it either," Burt said. "From 1980 until the time of his death in 2007, he lived with Patrick Hughes, the set decorator and dresser in Beverly Hills, the couple making frequent trips to Florida."

***

If Charles Nelson Reilly and Burt were "The Odd Couple," so were Burt and Bette Davis. He never figured out what drew her to him, either as a man or as an actor. She always applauded his macho charm after sitting through such movies as *Smokey and the Bandit*.

During her later years, in spite of his busy schedule, he saw more and more of her, and was her frequent escort to many parties and gala events. Sometimes, she preferred a quiet dinner at home with him, and she told him stories, both amusing and painful, about her early life.

He wrote many of them down, perhaps thinking he might share them with a biographer one day, because he didn't think what had been written about her up to that moment in time had been accurate.

When he first met her, Burt was amused at her fondness for gossip. "In the 1950s, *Confidential* should have hired her as its Hollywood stringer," he said. "Bette knew every time a cockroach walked across Hollywood Boulevard."

He became aware that her list of enemies was longer than the list of persons she liked and admired. In the early days of her long career, she'd maintained a deep respect for George Arliss, Charles Boyer, James Cagney, Claude Rains, and Spencer Tracy.

A reporter once asked her what actors and actresses she most admired today. "Both Sally Field and I were very flattered that she named us," Burt said. "Others of her favorites included Steve McQueen, Jill Clayburgh, Debra Winger, Sissy Spacek, Meryl Streep, and Paul Scofield."

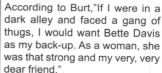

Two views of Bette Davis, upper photo from *All About Eve* (1950). In the lower photo she appears in 1987 with Ronald Reagan, two years before her death.

According to Burt,"If I were in a dark alley and faced a gang of thugs, I would want Bette Davis as my back-up. As a woman, she was that strong and my very, very dear friend."

Bette often talked at length about her least favorite actor, Errol Flynn. "I hated that whoremonger the moment he set foot on the Warners lot, strutting around like some peacock as if he owned the place."

[Burt listened in fascination. His own encounter with Flynn had been brief but memorable.

A stuntman friend of his, who had worked on three of Flynn's epic adventure movies, once escorted Burt to the star's dressing room so that he could meet him. Totally nude, Flynn threw open the door at the very moment he was being serviced by a blonde-haired starlet on her knees. "Come back later, sports," he said. "As you can see, for the moment, at least, I'm busy, unless one of you wants to get on his knees, too. I don't fuck anymore since it interferes with my drinking."

Then he slammed the door in their faces.

Burt and the stuntman never returned.]

Seated in her living room and smoking endless cigarettes, Bette claimed that Flynn was the most beautiful specimen who ever showed up on the Warner lot. "But he had absolutely no talent as an actor. I thought he was an awful choice to star with me in *The Private Lives of Elizabeth and Essex* (1939)."

"My choice for the role was Laurence Olivier," she told Burt, "but Jack Warner wanted Flynn. On bended nylon in his office, I held out for anybody but Flynn. My list included Fredric March, Cary Grant, Henry Fonda, Ray Milland, Joel McCrea, Vincent Price, Ronald Colman, Douglas Fairbanks, Jr...but I was stuck with Flynn."

"The role I most coveted at the time was that Georgia vixen, Scarlett O'Hara. Scarlett was ME right down to her toenails. So even though I'm a New Englander, born and bred, I could say '*fiddle-dee-dee*' better than anyone else alive at the time."

"Jack Warner tried to sell a Warner Brothers package to David O. Selznick, with me as Scarlett, Flynn as Rhett Butler, and Olivia de Havilland as Melanie. Selznick, of course, rejected it and went for MGM's Clark Gable. Only he could play Rhett Butler. Before Vivien Leigh walked off with it, everyone from an aging Tallulah Bankhead to Katharine Hepburn wanted to play Scarlett."

According to Burt, "As much as Bette detested Flynn, she despised Miriam Hopkins even more. Aggressive, blonde, and a die-hard daughter of Georgia, Hopkins fancied the role of Scarlett, too, but she was around 37 at the time, and frankly, Selznick thought she was too old."

According to Bette, "Miriam would have been great as Aunt Pittipat."

Bette's feud with Miriam began when Miriam acquired the screen rights to *Jezebel*, a play by Owen Davis, Jr., who had conceived it as the saga of "a little bitch of an aristocratic Southern girl, Julie Marsden."

Miriam agreed to sell its film rights to Jack Warner with the understanding that she would play the female lead. To her rage and chagrin, Warner double-crossed her, awarding the role to

Jack Warner had his own dream cast for *Gone With the Wind:* "Bette Davis as Scarlett O'Hara and Errol Flynn (depicted above) as Rhett Butler."

Bette, instead. Miriam was enraged once again when Bette won a Best Actress Oscar for her performance. *[Davis' favorite actor, Spencer Tracy, also carried off the gold that year for his performance as a priest in* Boys Town.*]*

When Warners cast Bette and Miriam together in *The Old Maid* (1939), Miriam showed up on the first day of shooting wearing an exact replica of the famous gown Bette had worn in *Jezebel.*

"During the filming of *Old Maid*, Miriam did everything she could to sabotage my performance," Bette told Burt. "She was a brilliant actress, but a complete bitch to work with. I got even by fucking her husband, the director, Anatole Litvak."

When Vincent Sherman was presented with Bette and Miriam as the "pre-packaged" co-stars in *Old Acquaintance* (1943), he said, "I did not direct them. I was the referee."

Burt would continue to see Bette on and off until her death in 1989. "Every night with her, either escorting her somewhere or spending a quiet evening with her, was memorable. She was the ultimate *grande dame* of Hollywood. Once, she told me she wished I had been born before World War I, and that the two of us could have been co-stars in the 1930s."

"I would have snatched you up back then, married you, and you'd never have need of another woman as long as you lived," Bette claimed.

In Burt's limited earlier sexual encounters with the great but fading star, he agreed with those servicemen who sang her boudoir attributes at the Hollywood Canteen during World War II.

Actor Jack Carson phrased it like this: "Bette screws like a mink."

***

Smokey and the Bandit II (1980) reunited the characters from the film's original version. Once again, Burt played opposite Sally Field and Jackie Gleason, alongside a supporting cast that included Jerry Reed, Paul Williams, and Pat McCormick. An added attraction in the reprise was Dom DeLuise.

Stuntman-turned-director Hal Needham was enrolled to helm this latest venture, too. Its plot centers around Bob ("Bandit") Darville (Burt), and Cledus ("Snowman") Snow (Reed), transporting a pregnant elephant, nicknamed Charlotte, from Miami to Dallas for the GOP National Convention.

Gleason was cast again as Sheriff Burford T. Justice and once again, he is in hot pursuit. As a novel twist, he also plays his brothers, Gaylord and Reginald.

DeLuise is an overweight Italian gynecologist. He's been kidnapped to nurse the elephant during her arduous trip.

As anticipated, the second installment of *Smokey* did not generate as much interest or profits as the first version. It earned $66 million on a budget of $17 million. Many of the scenes had been shot in Palm Beach County, often at Burt's Ranch in Jupiter.

The second *Smokey* and Burt's next picture, *The Cannonball Run*, were filmed simultaneously.

Burt did not like the *Smokey* sequel, claiming that it had been "assembled" by Universal purely for profits, with little concern for making a good film.

Thomas Fox in the *Memphis Commercial Appeal* described it as "crude, mindless, scatological, foul-mouthed, and happy. The film bounces along, grabbing every easy laugh and burning up enough diesel fuel to fill a supertanker."

Most critics denounced it, comparing it unfavorably to the original. Roger Ebert said, "There was no need for this sequel. It's just a repeat of the original movie done again, though not as well. How can I say it's lazy when it has 50 trucks doing stunts in it?" Because it takes a lot less thought to fill up a movie with stunts than to create a comedy that's genuinely funny."

Gleason gave his own review, calling it "terrible." He used the same word to describe the third version (*Smokey and the Bandit III; 1983*), too.

[*Burt rejected the lead in* Smokey III, *although he was included in a cameo lounging in a zebra-print hammock, giving the perhaps deliberate impression that he preferred to sleep through it. The major difference is that the few people who saw this version were treated to the sight of Paul Williams in a dress.*]

Smokey III flopped at the box office. On a budget of $9 million, it took in only $7 million.

In 1983, after the wrap of *Smokey III*, Gleason returned to the hospital for the second bypass heart surgery he endured in that year.

After his release, he phoned Burt and said, "I'm in great shape. I've resumed chain-smoking six packs of cigarettes a day, and I can knock off six double scotches in one sitting."

The corpulent actor died in June of 1987 at age 71 at his home in Florida.

***

Burt wanted to be taken more seriously as an actor, which meant no more car-chase films. His longtime friend, stuntman and director Hal Needham, showed him a script for a movie called *The Cannonball Run* (1981). At first, although Burt wanted to help his friend, he rejected it.

Later, however, in reference to the same script, its producer, Albert S. Ruddy, made an offer so generous that Burt accepted. He would get $5 million for two weeks' work, plus a potentially very lucrative percentage of the gross.

"I got involved with the movie for all the wrong reasons," Burt later said. "I never liked it, but I did it to help Hal. I also felt it was immoral to turn down that kind of money. I sold out and deserved the attacks that the critics socked me with."

The script was based on the running, in 1979 of an illegal but real-life cross-country road race, beginning in Connecticut and ending in California.

[One journalist described the real-life contest that inspired the movie as a "strapped down, fueled up, high-tech outlaw enterprise with 2,795 miles of interstate and some 31,000 highway cops between the contestants and the all-time speed record for crossing the American continent on four wheels.]

Filmed in Panavision, *The Cannonball Run* was produced by Hong Kong's Golden Harvest films. Their administration insisted on including Jackie Chan in the cast.

He was one of the most recognizable and influential cinematic personalities in the world. A martial artist, actor, director, producer, stuntman, and singer, he would, in 2015, be named by *Forbes* as the second-highest paid actor in the world, with a net worth of $350 million.

It was clear from the beginning that *The Cannonball Run* would evolve into yet another formulaic "popcorn movie" for Burt. In it, he was cast as auto mechanic J.J. McClure, coupled with his mild-mannered sidekick, Victor (Dom DeLuise). In it, they drive a souped-up, ultra high-octane Dodge Tradesman ambulance.

Burt's co-star was the Londoner, Roger Moore, best known for playing British Secret Agent 007 in seven feature films as James Bond, beginning in 1973 with *Live and Let Die.*

As Seymour Goldfarb, Jr., he drives a silver Aston Martin. In a plot twist, his character suffers from the delusion that he is the real movie star, Roger Moore.

Molly Picon (what is she doing in

No one ever said it would be brainy.

474

this movie?) takes on the role of the original Jewish mother, Mrs. Goldfarb.

Other stars kept popping up in cameo appearances. Burt, as J.J., meets up with two drunken priests, Dean Martin and Sammy Davis, Jr., cast as Jamie Blake and Fenderbaum, respectively. Jamie is a Scotch-swilling con man, and Fenderbaum is his gambling-obsessed teammate, driving a red Ferrari nicknamed "The Flying Fathers."

Jackie Chan with Michael Hui race in a high-tech computer-accessorized Subaru hatchback with a rocket-boosted engine. At one point, the Cannonballers are pitted against a gang of Hell's Angels bikers led by Peter Fonda. *[Fonda and his scary-looking bikers present an excuse for Chan to demonstrate his martial arts skills.]*

Throughout his performance, Fonda pays wistful homage to his big hit film, *Easy Rider* (1969).

James Farr portrays an oil-rich Middle Eastern sheik, driving a Rolls-Royce Silver Shadow. He wants to prove Islamic superiority by winning the race. His sister is portrayed by Bianca Jagger.

Bert Convy, the actor, singer, and game show host, appears as Bradford Compton, a rich but bored executive who makes the Cannonball Run on a motorcycle. He teams with his old friend, Shakey Finch (Warren Berlinger), once the world's greatest cross-country motorcyclist. The two disguise themselves as newlyweds. Lots of celluloid displays their skill at "Wheelies" *[i.e., maneuvers in which a wheeled vehicle is momentarily balanced on its rear wheel or wheels.]*

Jack Elam plays Doctor Nikolas Van Helsing, a proctologist who examines one and all with his index finger. Crazed and hooked on drugs, he performs egregious sight gags.

Pittsburg Steeler Terry Bradshaw wheels with the singer Mel Tillis, each portraying a good 'ol boy. They race together in a Chevrolet Malibu NASCAR Grand National racecar.

Farrah Fawcett, cast as Pamela Gober, and Adrienne Barbeau, playing Marcie Thatcher, provide beauty and boobs.

At one point, Fawcett plays Burt's make-believe patient against his impersonation of an ambulance driver. As an ecologist, she seems to have a prurient interest in trees. For her efforts (or lack thereof), Fawcett won the Razzie Award for "the Worst Supporting Actress of the Year."

Barbeau teams with Tara Buckman as two satin-Spandex-class hotties" who drive a black Lamborghini Countach. In the film, it's pursued by a Nevada Highway Patrol car. When they're stopped, Barbeau does some fancy work with her jump-suit zipper.

In spite of the attacks by critics, *The Cannonball Run* earned $75 million in the U.S. and Canada alone, becoming the sixth-highest grossing film of the year.

Frank Sanello of the *Los Angeles Times* described *Cannonball* as "the ideal movie for the drive-in crowd. It demolishes enough cars to fill a used car lot in Long Beach."

Vincent Canby of *The New York Times* found the film "inoffensive and sometimes funny."

Variety claimed that it was "full of terribly inside showbiz jokes and populated with Burt and Hal Needham's Rat Pack. The film takes place in a redneck Never-Never Land where most of the guys are beer-guzzling good ol' boys and all the gals are fabulously built tootsies."

Roger Ebert claimed "*The Cannonball Run* is an abdication of artistic responsibility at the lowest level of ambition. In other words, they didn't even care enough to make a good lousy movie."

***

Burt's former girlfriend, Adrienne Barbeau, had been cast in *The Cannonball Run*. Also in the cast was the blonde goddess, Farrah Fawcett. Collectively, they represented, at least for Burt, an affair that had ended and another that was about to begin.

According to Barbeau, "When we were in the same movie, it was over for Burt and me. He had made that perfectly clear. I had joined the list of his previous discards like Susan Clark and Brenda Vaccaro, women with whom he had fallen in love, ever so briefly, before walking out the door."

Burt had long admired the charm and vivacity of Farrah Fawcett. He'd first been drawn to her when he bought a copy of that iconic calendar shot, later reissued as a pin-up poster (the best-selling in history) that had launched her to international fame. That had led to her casting in the hit TV sitcom, *Charlie's Angels* (1976-77).

In 1973, she'd married Lee Majors, the film and TV star. After their breakup and divorce, she'd begun a tormented affair with Ryan O'Neal, a romance punctuated with frequent breakups, frequent reconciliations, frequent infidelities, and frequent outbursts, from Ryan, of his violent temper. On and off, their affair lasted from 1979 to 1997, and again from 2001 to 2009, the year of her death from cancer.

As Burt told Hal Needham, "I don't want to exaggerate my affair with Farrah. It consisted of only eight dates, the first just for fun, the second through the seventh leading to her boudoir. On our first date, we both spent an hour talking about Ryan O'Neal, my former co-star and friend of sorts."

According to Fawcett: "I'm not sure two movie stars should ever marry. In a few cases, the union works out but most often, it doesn't."

He wondered if she were talking about her relationship with Ryan, or about his affair with Sally Field.

Whereas many movie stars come from tough backgrounds, Farrah—born in Corpus Christi, Texas in 1947—seemed to have been an adored child. As a high school student and later, college coed, she'd been a beauty contest winner. With her face and figure, she'd become a model and often performed in TV commercials.

In *The Cannonball Run*, Burt is sandwiched between a drunken "priest" (Dean Martin), and a luscious blonde, Farrah Fawcett.

"She let me seduce her but her heart still belonged to Ryan O'Neal," Burt claimed.

"If I had any criticism of Farrah, it was that she spent far too much time fretting over her hair. Not only was it soft to the touch, but it seemed to move as if it had a life of its own. It was very touchable, but often she warned, 'Don't mess up my hair.'"

On their outings, some fans chanted at her, "FARRAH, DON'T CHANGE A HAIR FOR ME."

One night, Farrah told Burt, "I was born under a lucky star. I have never worked hard to make things happen. I'm willing to sit back and watch the events as they unfold. Good things have come my way, with an occasional pitfall such as my break-up with Lee Majors. I take life with a grain of salt and face it with a sense of humor."

"I could never figure out how serious Farrah was," Burt confided to Needham. "She's a bit self-enchanted, always looking at herself in the mirror, but so does virtually every other actress I know. With Farrah, it's that hair, you know."

"My hair stylist told me I was one of the world's most beautiful women," Farrah told Burt. "Right up there with Catherine Deneuve. He also claimed that if I had more teeth, I could race at Hialeah. Do you find my teeth too large and my arms bony?"

"What a question! I don't break you down into parts. Frankly, if I did, I'd vote for the part you keep hidden from the world, the one I'm longing to see right now, the Delta of Venus."

During a conversation about Farrah, Burt told Needham, "I wasn't jealous of her, but of Ryan. It was obvious that she preferred him to me. Some fans thought he was better looking than me, with his blonde curly hair and that toothpaste smile. Here I was with my fake hair."

One night, Farrah upset him over dinner, "My love affair with Ryan is sort of like your affair with Sally. From what I hear, it's marked by infidelity, at least on your part, the same way it was with Ryan and me. Of course, both of you, according to former lovers, have volatile tempers. I hear you also experience a lot of dark moods."

"What are you saying," he asked. "That we're breaking up before we've actually begun?"

"I think so, Burt," she said. "You're a dear and a lot of fun. You make me laugh. But I'm still drawn to Ryan, and it appears we're going to get back together. We'll probably break up again many, many times in the future."

"I have a final request," he said. "Could I have one more just for the road?"

"Of course," she said. "I owe you one for being so understanding."

As he described to Needham, "I just followed that head of hair into her bedroom and seduced her on the same bed where Ryan had made love to her night after night."

"I was out the door and into my car driving home when I realized I'd failed to ask that all-important question: I wanted to know if Ryan's dick was bigger than mine."

***

The next morning, he took a call from his agent, Sue Mengers. "Expect the shit to hit the fan today," she said. "Last night, I heard a rumor that Sally knows about your fling with Farrah. You've cheated on her too many times. The clock is running out for you and Sally."

"Thanks for the wake-up call, Sue," he said sarcastically before putting down the phone.

He had a date with Sally that very evening. Was Mengers telling him the truth? In spite of his constant cheating, he was still in love with Sally.

"What to do?" he asked, as he forced himself to get up and move into a new day.

What would tonight bring?

CHAPTER THIRTEEN

BYE BYE LOVE
SALLY FIELD TIRES OF "BURT THE BANDIT'S" CHEATING HEART
& SUMMONS THE COURAGE TO DUMP HIM FOREVER

PATERNITY
"BURT WANTS TO HAVE YOUR BABY!"
BURT'S ROMANTIC COMEDY ABOUT SURROGATE PARENTHOOD IS A
STILLBORN FLOP AT THE BOX OFFICE

SHARKY'S MACHINE
BURT CONFESSES TO HOW HE PLAYED THE CASTING COUCH
IN HIS SEARCH FOR A LEADING LADY

DOLLY PARTON
PLAYS OPPOSITE BURT AT THE BEST LITTLE WHOREHOUSE IN TEXAS

GOLDIE HAWN & KURT RUSSELL
BURT'S DATING GAME & THE FURIOUS REACTION THAT FOLLOWED

JOAN RIVERS
BURT'S PUBLICLY TELEVISED FOUR-YEAR FEUD

TOXIC REMORSE: "WHAT IF.....?"
"AS AN ACTOR, I CONSISTENTLY MADE STUPID CHOICES.

DONALD TRUMP
"He's destroying our football league"
—Burt Reynolds

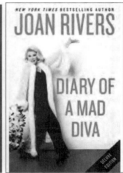

In *Smokey & the Bandit II*, Sally Field and Burt repeated their roles of "The Frog" and "The Bandit." In one of its scenes, Sally's character tells Burt that it's all over between them.

She had requested and received permission from the film's director, Hal Needham, to craft her own dialogue for that scene. After a delay of three days, she presented it to Burt, who read it alone in his dressing room. He was puzzled at the time about whether it reflected a conversation between The Frog and The Bandit; a declaration of intent on Sally's part about ending their love affair; or perhaps a bit of both.

"I knew that as Bandit, I would have a struggle holding my own against a very talented actress, who felt she'd been wronged by both the character I was playing and her lover in real life."

Before the camera, Sally cried real tears as she brought an ending to her character's affair with the Bandit.

According to Burt about the dialogue she'd written, "Those were beautiful words coming from her mouth, each of them designed to cause me pain. Even though we were breaking up, we had the best sex of our lives. Sometimes, angry sex is the best sex of all. During what I feared were our final days together, she seemed to be working overtime to deball me. Ouch! OUCH! She was squeezing those *cojones* with an iron grip. Some women who've been done wrong often possess a strength they didn't know they had."

After *Bandit II* was wrapped, he drove her to the airport for her flight back to Los Angeles. He tried to kiss her goodbye, but she turned her head, and he didn't even get a brush on the cheek. Gazing at him with a stern look he'd never seen in her brown eyes before, she said, "It's all over, pal." Then she turned and boarded her plane.

"And that is what the lady might have written for her farewell scene, not only to the Bandit, but to me, personally."

Apparently, it had all been too much for Sally—Burt's affairs with Adrienne Barbeau and Farrah Fawcett. "She also wasn't too thrilled over my fling with Candice Bergen. Then there was that cheerleader for the Dallas Cowboys, plus countless other one-night stands."

She also blamed me for 'pushing' her into that clunker, *Beyond the Poseidon Adventure* (1979) although she was well paid. I told her to 'take the money and run and that no one would go to see that turkey except Shelley Winters.'"

Sally got mad at Burt when he told a reporter that he felt Catherine Deneuve and Lesley-Anne Down, his co-star in *Rough Cut,* were the two sexiest and most beautiful women in the world. "If women of the world looked like those two, all business would stop," Burt had said. "Men would never want to get out of bed."

After his return to Hollywood, he repeatedly asked to come over to Sally's house, but she consistently turned him down. When the nomination for Best Academy Award for an actress was announced, he called to congratulate her for *Norma Rae* (1979).

She thanked him but also expressed her sympathy that he didn't get a nod for his breakthrough, sensitive performance in *Starting Over* (1979).

[As regards Starting Over, *what was humiliating for him was that both of his co-stars, Jill Clayburgh and Candice Bergen, were nominated for Best Actress and Best Supporting Actress, respectively. Not only that, but Alan J. Pakula received the Best Director nomination, and Dane Wakefield was nominated for Best Screenplay. There was more. Cinematographer Sven Nykvist also got an Oscar nod in his category.]*

Burt extended to Sally three separate invitations to dinner. She finally accepted when he told her, "Even Jesus Christ was given a Last Supper."

The cozy dinner was to be at the Café Four Oaks in Beverly Glen. Companions were to have included Bernie Casey, a native of Wyco, West Virginia, and his wife. Casey was an actor who had once played for both the San Francisco 49ers and the Los Angeles Rams. "He was one of those rare pro footballers who was also adept at writing poetry."

[Burt had reasons for dining with Casey. He wanted a setting where he and Sally would not get into a fight in the presence of their guests, and he also wanted Casey to co-star with him in an upcoming movie, Sharkey's Machine.

There was another reason, too: Two weeks ago, he'd invited Casey to play golf with him on a local course. As Casey was in the shower, the manager told Burt outside, "You are welcome to join our club. However, in the future, you can't bring Mr. Casey."

Burt responded in fury: "Does that have something to do with his skin?"

Moments later, as soon as Casey dressed, he and Burt stormed off in fury, never to return.]

Burt drove to Sally's house at seven o'clock that evening, arriving early because he hoped she might invite him inside for a drink, at which time he could see her two sons as well, but she was ready and waiting by the door. She exited from her house right away and got into his car.

He steered it in the direction of Beverly Glen, and no more than ten minutes later, a terrible argument "the worse we'd ever had" raged.

"The dam broke," he said, "and the flood waters came rushing in. All those resentments and frustrations she'd kept bottled up for months were released."

He couldn't refute her accusations, since they were true. "I had been a rebellious Romeo, but she had other words for it we can't repeat in mixed company."

"But I wasn't gonna sit there and take it," he said. "As a former football player, I wanted to score a few touchdowns of my own, so I went on the offensive. Alas, her case against me was so much stronger than any resentment I harbored against her. What could I accuse her of? One Saturday, we'd had sex twice, and I was ready again before midnight, but she told me she was sleepy and needed her rest."

When they pulled up in front of the restaurant, a valet opened her door. "She sprang from my car like a jackrabbit," Burt said. "I saw her racing down the sidewalk to disappear in the darkness."

Stunned, the valet didn't know what to say. "I'll be back in a second," Burt said. "Don't park the car." He rushed inside the restaurant and headed for the table where Casey sat with his wife. "Forgive me," he said. "Sally's run out on me, and I'm giving chase."

"Go man, go!" Casey said.

"It was dark as I headed north," Burt said. "I finally found her hovering near an alley. She was out of breath and appeared lost, confused, befuddled, not knowing what to do."

"It took some persuading, but I managed to coax her into my car to take her home," he said. "On the way back, I was filled with apologies for my past bad deeds, and she said not one word. Once I arrived at her front door, the jackrabbit

Are they acting, or was it love? Displayed above is a publicity photo for *Smokey and the Bandit*

hopped out of the car and rushed to her door. It must have been left unlocked, because she opened it and rushed right in, slamming it behind her."

Weeks later, he did not plan to attend the Academy Award presentations since he was still angry that he had not been nominated for *Starting Over*. However, late that night and alone in his home, he tuned in to watch the after-Oscar newscasts, learning that Sally had won the Best Actress of the Year award for *Norma Rae*.

Then, to his surprise, the columnist Rona Barrett was broadcast as she interviewed Sally, who was proudly holding her Oscar.

"Would you tell the people what was going on in your head as you rushed down the aisle to receive your Oscar?" Barrett asked.

Sally shot back, "I was thinking '*Fuck you, Burt Reynolds! Fuck you, Burt Reynolds! Fuck you, Burt Reynolds!*"

[Of course, her words had to be bleeped.]

As he remembered it later, he switched off the TV and walked out into his backyard, looking up at the stars. He later told Hal Needham, "I walked out on Dinah Shore who loved me. Now I know what she must have felt. This time, I was the one dumped. I knew in my heart that I'd never forget Sally. My biggest regret is that she never got to experience the best of me. Only the boy, and he was an asshole at times. Now, it was too late."

Sally phoned Burt one final time to tell him that she was marrying the producer Alan Grieseman, a union that in time headed for a divorce court.

Her final words to Burt were, "No man will ever see the Sally Field you saw. Goodbye, Bandit. You stole my heart."

***

David Steinberg, the comedian from Winnipeg, Manitoba, was assigned to direct his first film, *Paternity*, set for a 1981 release from Paramount. Co-producers Lawrence Gordon and Hank Moonjean, who had the same positions on Burt's *Hooper*, once again co-produced *Paternity*, based on a script by Charlie Peters.

After Burt read the script, he said, "Whereas *Starting Over* was very close to the story of my life, *Paternity* IS the story of my life."

In the lead, Burt was cast as Buddy Evans, the super-successful manager of Madison Square Garden in Manhattan. "My character is a man who has everything," he said, "except no wife, no house, no kids, no mortgage."

A confirmed bachelor, he wants to have a son and, thus, begins his search for a surrogate mother to fill the role. The character of Maggie accepts his generous offer to become the mother of his child through artificial insemination of his sperm. A spunky waitress in a coffee shop, she is an aspiring musician, planning to use the money earned through her child-bearing to study in Paris.

The film's producers and director wanted to cast Debra Winger as Maggie, but Burt adamantly refused to go along with their choice.

It was finally decided that Beverly d'Angelo would be ideal in the role. Both Burt and Steinberg had been impressed with her performance as Patsy Cline in *Coal Miner's Daughter* (1981). By 1997, she would begin a long-term love affair with Al Pacino, but at the time that Burt met her, she'd just married Don Lorenzo Salviali.

On the set, Burt had a reunion with top model Lauren Hutton, who was cast once again with him, this time as Jenny Lofton.

Elizabeth Ashley played Sophia, a girlfriend. As Moonjean said, "Elizabeth exuded Southern sex, and Hutton was also on the money. But Beverly outshone both of them."

Burt's buddy in the film was Norman Fell, the veteran actor who had worked with him in the *Dan August* TV detective series.

Inadvertently, Greta Garbo almost made it into the movie. One afternoon, the former silent screen goddess was spotted by Moonjean walking toward the camera. The producer yelled to his cameraman, "Start shooting! It's Greta Garbo!"

"Who in hell is Greta Garbo?" the cameraman asked. Before he could begin filming, the elusive Garbo saw the camera and fled from the scene.

"Too bad," Moonjean later lamented. "*Paternity* might have been billed as Garbo's comeback picture."

Before Burt's character opts for Maggie as his true love, he suffers from an incident of mistaken identity. Lauren Hutton as Jenny, an interior decorator, visits Burt's apartment. Thinking she's an applicant for the "job" of surrogate mother to his child, he asks her to expose her breasts.

Over lunch, Hutton told him that Larry Flynt, publisher of *Hustler,* had offered her a million dollars to pose nude.

"Go for it!" Burt said. "I posed nude for *Cosmo* and didn't get a damn cent."

Steinberg's friend, writer Paddy Chayefsky, arrived on the scene to observe the shooting. He said, "Once again, as in *Rough Cut,* Burt is trying to be Cary Grant in a sophisticated comedy. But Grant didn't

Burt with Lauren Hutton in *Paternity.* "Let me see your breasts."

484

just do Grant, he was a hell of an actor."

"I want to be like Cary Grant, who just might get his tie caught in the tomato soup but will still wind up with the prettiest girl at the table," Burt said.

As proof of his star status, Burt had been assigned a special dressing room—a giant bus the size of a Greyhound Scenic-Cruiser—named "Bandit."

In reference to Burt's skill and talent as an actor, Steinberg said, "I can ask Burt to recreate a moment he did for me five days ago—and after three takes, he can do it. He uses everything—stage technique, recall, working from the inside out, the Method."

The reviews of *Paternity* were among the most hostile of Burt's career. In a moment of truth, Rex Reed tried to explain it to him. "You know, the critics had never been able to hurt you, and that's probably what gets us so angry."

On reflection, Burt said, "I never understood why the critics were so hostile to *Paternity*. I didn't buy a tuxedo to accept an Oscar, but it was not a terrible film. Yet I got the worst reviews I'd had in nine years. Reviews of my movies had usually been bad, but some eighty-five percent of them made money."

"*Paternity* eventually may turn a profit, but what scared me more than anything else was that for the first time, the reviews probably did have an effect on box office. This time, they kept people away."

"Somehow, I've got to live with the brickbats and raspberries," he said. "Sometimes, I have these conversations with God where I say, 'I really do give you all the glory, and I thank you for everything. And then You turn around and have the critics stick it to me. Now either you've got to fix it so that doesn't bother me, or else You've got to drown the critics. I don't care which it is. I do think my time will come."

In spite of its provocative taglines, *Paternity* was not a success.

Immediately after filming, Burt attended the wedding of his best friend, Hal Needham. He married Dani Janssen, the widow of his friend, actor David Janssen. In social circles, she was known as the Queen of Beverly Hills Hostesses."

The wedding's theme was based on

Beverly d'Angelo in *Paternity*, playing a spunky waitress willing to rent out her womb.

Roy Rogers and Dale Evans. Hundreds of guests impersonated them. Burt lent Moonjean a pair of Western boots. According to Moonjean, "They had lifts to make up for his shortness, and I almost tottered over. Those so-called Joan Crawford fuck me high heels would have been easier to walk in."

***

Hank Moonjean's fifth picture with Burt was *Sharky's Machine*. Based on the 1978 novel of the same name by William Diehl, it was scheduled for a release in 1981.

Burt had been drawn to the plot of the novel because it evoked one of his alltime favorite movies, *Laura*, that 1944 classic by director Otto Preminger, staring the beautiful Gene Tierney. In that film, Laura is presumed dead but mysteriously turns up.

As the film's producer, Moonjean hired Burt to both star in and to direct it. Together, they embarked on a search for a leading lady, preferring an actress who was not particularly well known. "Hank and I made good use of the casting couch," Burt told a reporter. *[The reporter couldn't confirm whether Burt was telling the truth or merely joking. Consequently, the remark never got printed.]*

At least three hundred actresses were considered or briefly interviewed for the role of Dominoe, a $1,000-a-night prostitute. The choice eventually narrowed down to Rachel Ward. Burt later asserted that from the moment she entered his office, she had the right look and the sensual appeal of Ava Gardner in the late 1940s and early 50s. But could she talk?

After some conversations, Burt decided that her voice wasn't quite ripe. Then he remembered that Howard Hawks, before hiring model Lauren Bacall, escorted her to the beach, where he instructed her to scream her head off all night. It worked. PRESTO! Bacall's trademark deep voice emerged. After emulating that process, Ward emerged the next day with what

Two household names Down Under: Rachel Ward with her husband, the heartthrob Australian actor, Bryan Brown.

Burt called "a sexy, raspy voice."

Ward was born in England to Australian parents and was twenty years younger than Burt. She had not yet married her first and only husband, Bryan Brown. At the time, she was dating a son of Robert F. Kennedy. As a model, she'd already graced the pages of both *Cosmopolitan* and *Vogue.*

After working with Burt, another big break came in 1983, when she co-starred opposite Richard Chamberlain as the female lead (Maggie Cleary) in the hit TV miniseries, *The Thorn Birds.* That same year, she was voted among the ten most beautiful women in the world.

Sharky's Machine was the first novel written by Diehl, a former journalist. He was fifty-three years old at the time but managed to sell a six-page outline and 120 pages to Delacorte Press for $156,000. He called it, "my fantasy come true."

The book had not sold well in hardcover, but in paperback, became a best-seller. The *Washington Post* has been the first to suggest that "it might make a decent movie, even though it tries to be three or four novels in one—and manages to be none of them."

Burt and Moonjean hired Gerald Di Pego to shape the book into a screenplay after Orion Pictures purchased the movie rights for $400,000. Originally, Burt heard about it when the famous novelist, Sidney Sheldon, read it and sent it to Burt with this cryptic notation: "Highly cinematic."

"I read it in one night, and found it most compelling," Burt said. "I'd done a lot of comedies in the past few years, and people had forgotten about my performance in *Deliverance.* I sent it to John Boorman, who had directed me in that,

Yes, Burt was big in England, too. The poster above advertises *Sharky's Machine's* British release.

Rachel Ward in Burt's arms at the time she was voted one of the ten most beautiful women in the world.

my most acclaimed movie, but he was too busy with *Excalibur*. He suggested I direct it myself, and Hank Moonjean greenlighted me."

In the plot, Burt was cast as Tom Sharky, an undercover Atlanta police detective, who is transferred to the vice squad. He finds himself in a whirlpool of citywide conspiracy, involving corruption, drugs, and prostitution.

"In *Sharky's Machine*, the good guys win," Burt said. "The bad guys, the dopers, lose. That was a big deal for me since I hate dopers. I get mad as hell when I hear that studios are coddling actors who are always high on cocaine."

Rachel Ward was cast in a pivotal role of the jaded call girl, whom Burt, as Sharky, has carefully observed during his extended stake-out. Gradually, and from afar, he falls wistfully, even sappily, in love with her.

He lined up a strong supporting cast. Many of the actors were either friends of his or stars he had worked with before. His favorite actor, Charles Durning, was cast as Friscoe. "He was perfect in *Sharky's*, and I fought to get him cast in my next picture, *The Best Little Whorehouse in Texas.*"

Vittorio Gassman played Victor D'Anton, and Burt admitted that he was a bit intimidated to be helming "The Laurence Olivier of Italy, but he treated me like I was Visconti."

Earl Holliman, as Donald Hotchkins, had been friends with Burt for more than twenty years. Like Burt, he also owned a dinner theater, his in Texas.

Darryl Hickman, as Smiley, had been a child actor, making his film debut as the son of Ronald Colman in *The Prisoner of Zenda* (1937). Burt had worked with Brian Keith before, and greatly respected him as an actor. He considered Keith vital for the role of Papa in *Sharky's*. A former pro-footballer, Bernie Casey, cast as Arch, rounded out the cast.

"Most directors cast actors on the basis of what they had successfully done before," Burt said. "They don't want surprises. That's not how I work. I tell an actor, 'You've done that before. Let's try something else. Surprise the audience this time.' I always wanted directors to say that to me. I had strong ideas of my own, but I always listen to my actors, too. At times, they can be very inventive. There was a wonderful feeling of camaraderie when we were shooting *Sharky's*."

Burt always liked working in Georgia, the state which he had falsely cited as the place of his birth. He'd shot four of his most successful films there: *Deliverance, Smokey and the Bandit, The Longest Yard,* and *Gator*.

Upon its release, most of the reviews were positive—"a big change from what I was used to," Burt said. "Even so, it was a relative disappointment."

Moonjean and Burt had been hoping for a $45 million gross, but *Sharky's Machine* brought in only $15 million.

Roger Ebert wrote, "*Sharky's Machine* contains all of the ingredients of a tough, violent, cynical, big city cop drama, but what makes it intriguing is the way that Burt Reynolds plays against convention. The result of his ambition and restraint is a movie much more interesting than the typical cop thriller."

Janet Maslin in *The New York Times* claimed, "Burt Reynolds establishes himself as yet another movie star who is also valuable behind the camera. *Sharky's Machine* is a tough, loud, bloody movie—and an enveloping one, too. It begins breathlessly, with a chase and a shootout that might serve as the finale for a less eventful film, but, in this case, that simply gets things off to an urgent start."

***

An adaptation of the 1978 Broadway musical, *The Best Little Whorehouse in Texas*, was a 1982 release by Universal that featured an all-star cast: Dolly Parton, Burt Reynolds, Jim Nabors, Dom DeLuise, Noah Berry, Jr., Lois Nettleton, and Charles Durning.

[Durning was later Oscar-nominated as Best Supporting Actor for his role in Whorehouse *as the singing and dancing Governor of Texas.]*

As the female lead, three actresses—Shirley MacLaine, Dyan Cannon, and Jill Clayburgh—had been suggested, but each had been rejected by Universal as "not bankable."

"The brass wanted Dolly Parton," Burt said. "As for the male lead, a number of other actors, including Willie Nelson, were considered, but Universal held out for me. I, too, was considered bankable back then."

Burt was given $3.5 million to star in *Whorehouse,* with Dolly settling for an offer of $1.5 million.

He had a reunion with Dolly, whom he had known casually "ever since she was a chubby-cheeked singer working with Porter Wagoner."

For a pre-production conversation, Burt went to Dolly's suite at the Bel Air Hotel to meet with Tommy Tune and Stevie Phillips. Tune was set to direct the movie version of *Whorehouse.* *[He had, with great success and style, already directed the stage version of* Whorehouse *on Broadway. It had run with huge theatrical acclaim for more than 1,500 performances, many of them with Carlin Glynn or Fannie Flagg as the female lead. None of them had included Dolly. Stevie Phillips had been the producer. Later productions that toured nationwide had starred Alexis Smith and Ann-Margret.]*

In a memoir, Burt later characterized Tommy Tune and Stevie Phillips as "two moonies, talking about the cosmos, spinning bones on rugs, mysterious lights, and astrological shit."

He quickly concluded that Tune might be a brilliant stage director, but was not "in tune" with making movies—"at least not on Earth, perhaps Jupiter."

It appeared that Phillips was convinced that she could persuade Johnny Carson to take the role of the do-gooder broadcaster, but Burt, Carson's close friend, told her, "Johnny won't go for it—so forget it."

Throughout the ordeal, "with these two crazy nuts, Dolly had remained silent, flashing her heavily lipsticked smiles."

A very tolerant vice squad: Comedy team Burt ("*He can sing! he can dance!*") and Dolly ("*It takes a lot of money to look this cheap!*") Parton in *Whorehouse*.

As soon as Phillips and Tune left, Dolly was on the phone to Lew Wasserman, one of the powerhouses at Universal. When he came on the line, she ordered him "to get your ass over to the Bel Air Hotel."

After some strong negotiations, Tune and Phillips were dismissed and Colin Higgins was named as the new director for the film adaptation of *Whorehouse.*

An Australian-American, Higgins was known for his direction of *Harold and Maude* (1971) and for directing *9 to 5* (1980) with Dolly, Jane Fonda, and Lily Tomlin.

Before the debut of filming, Burt flew to Las Vegas to see Dolly perform in one of her very popular stage acts. After the show, she asked him to wait for her in her suite. She arrived with a small entourage, including her makeup woman, her wardrobe lady, and her cameraman.

After hugging and kissing Burt, she revealed what had happened to her the previous night when "this jerk" tried to seduce her.

"He told me he wanted a little pussy," she said, "so I told him, 'So would I. Mine's the size of a god damn Chevrolet.'"

After her assistants left, Burt remained alone with Dolly in her suite. She turned to him and said, "Let's get this humping out of the way, so that in the morning, we can get on with our movie."

490

Carol Hall, who wrote the original music and lyrics for *Whorehouse,* later said, "I think Dolly and Burt did play house, at least for a one-night stand. But it didn't seem to go anywhere. I don't think she was his dream girl, and I don't think he was her dream man.'

Burt was mildly shocked at how self-deprecating Dolly was. "I catch the attention of the public with my big boobs, my big wigs, and my big rear end. It takes a lot of work to look as cheap as I do. I'm a five-foot parody of a trucker's fantasy, an animated dumplin', a cartoon character who looks like a hooker with a heart of goo."

"Dolly is bigger than life, warm and vital," Burt said. "I predict super stardom for her in the movies."

Whorehouse Dolly at the Chicken Ranch as the most likable and lovable Madam since Belle Watling in *Gone With the Wind.*

She told Burt that if she continued to make movies, her greatest dream would be to bring Mae West, the *Diamond Lil* love goddess of the 1930s, to the screen. "I'd get Woody Allen to direct it and be my co-star. I think he's damn cute and sexy."

"Our movie is different from the stage version of *Whorehouse,*" Dolly said. "The two principals had a one-night stand fifteen years ago. In the movie, version, I'll do some rewrites. If you think I'm gonna be in a movie with Burt Reynolds, and not get in a little huggin' and kissin', you're crazy."

As the new film version emerged, Burt was cast as Sheriff Ed Earl Dodd of Gilbert, Texas, who is involved in a long-term relationship with Miss Mona Stangley (Dolly), who runs an illegal brothel outside of town called the Chicken Ranch. It got its name because some of the customers, each a chicken farmer, paid for the brothel's services with live poultry. At this stage in its history, it's a town landmark, its staff and administration tolerated, and by some accounts, respected and beloved.

Disaster arrives in the form of a nosy, big city TV personality, do-gooder Melvin P. Thorpe (Dom DeLuise). It's with the intention of producing a live telecast, in which he'll reveal the existence (and morally reprehensible) role of the whorehouse.

Higgins wanted Mickey Rooney to portray the governor of Texas, but Burt lobbied to get his close friend, Charles Durning, cast in the part instead. "Everyone in the world knows Mickey can sing and dance, but Charles would come as a real surprise," Burt claimed. "No one knows he can sing and dance." Then he turned to Higgins. "You'll look brilliant as a director casting Charles Durning in the role."

Higgins eventually acquiesced to this odd casting choice.

Burt's friend, Jim Nabors, played "Deputy Fred," the town's assistant sheriff. He evoked his familiar role as Gomer Pyle, U.S.M.C., on TV. A native of Sylacauga, Alabama, he told Burt, "I was born to play rednecks."

Rounding out the cast were Lois Nettleton as Dulcie Mae, and Noah Berry, Jr., as Edsel.

One afternoon, Burt spotted "an incredibly handsome guy" (his words) standing at the far end of a movie set, wearing a cowboy hat and a sheepskin jacket. "Who is that good-looking mother-fucker?" he asked Dolly.

"That's my husband, Carl Dean."

"Let's take a picture together," Burt said.

"You do that, little darlin', and I'll kill you," she said.

She'd told *Playboy*, "If my hubby fools around, I don't wanna know. Even if he did—well, I'd feel bad, but the truth is that it really doesn't matter. I don't hang on to people and that includes my husband. I'm very aggressive sexually, and I don't mind being the aggressor if it comes to somethin' I want or need."

She admitted to Burt that she and Carl Dean had an open relationship. "I love Carl dearly. If he ever left me, I'd die."

One night, she invited Burt to dinner, preferring to go to McDonald's for lots of burgers and fries, followed by a pizza or two at a nearby parlor. "We could spend the evening in a movie house munching buttered popcorn and peanuts until the final reel."

Dolly admitted that during the shooting of *Whorehouse*, "I was a real porker, the heaviest I have ever been."

In one scene, Burt had to pick her up, and she heard him groan. The scene had to be repeated for three different takes, and his groaning continued. Finally, after the scene was wrapped, he was rushed to the hospital for a double hernia operation.

"Burt and I were not only two emotionally disturbed individuals, but we were in bad shape physically. At one point, I was bleeding inside, and had to have a couple of D&Cs to avoid hemorrhaging. I began to drink to ease the pain. I finally asked the doctor to tie my tubes so that I could get off birth control pills. In my mind, that was almost the equal of having an abortion. I never consulted my husband about what I had done."

"Each of us, Burt and me, felt sorry for the other one," she said. "The gossip had us having this mad affair. When confronted by the press, I told reporters that Burt and I were too much alike to go at it. We both wear wigs and high heels, and we both have a roll around our middle."

PERRYSCOPE RECORDS RECORDING ARTIST
GREGG PERRY
AVAILABLE ON PERRYSCOPE RECORDS
FOR MORE INFORMATION PLEASE VISIT
WWW.PECKTUNES.COM

Gregg Perry—Was he the love of Dolly Parton's life, or at least the rock that helped her survive Burt Reynolds during the filming of *Whorehouse?*

When Burt read that, he accused her "of destroying the magic. How is the public going to go see us as a romantic couple on screen if you go around bad-mouthing us?"

She pleaded with him not to get angry at her. "It was just a joke," she said.

Dolly recalled that "working on *Whorehouse* was a nightmare. Even before I walked onto the set, several people had been fired. A bumper sticker was printed—"HONK IF YOU'VE BEEN FIRED FROM BEST LITTLE WHOREHOUSE."

"Burt was in pretty bad shape emotionally and physically," she said. "He was still crying crocodile tears over the loss of Sally Field. Sometimes in the middle of one of our scenes, he'd bolt right in the middle of the shoot."

"I'd rush after him, going to his dressing room, trying to give him moral support. But in my case, it was the blind leading the blind. My own life was in upheaval, and I was a nervous wreck. Binge eating most of the time. I'd even started to drink heavily."

Dolly had told Burt that she carried around a small gun in her purse— "a little ol' snub-nose .22 or something. If some sleazy pervert weirdo tries to follow me to my room and knock the door down, he's likely to get filled with lead. Just call me the pistol-packin' momma."

She later admitted she was in an "affair of the heart." She did not name her suitor, but it appeared to be musician Gregg Perry, whom she described as her "ultimate protector, her side-by-side bodyguard, her confidant and companion."

Perry was a singer, songwriter, and producer, whose song "Come Fly With Me" had become a big hit. In time he helped to shape the music and careers of artists who included Freda Payne.

He both wrote and produced many hits for the soul artists of the 1970s, including Mary Wells. *[Perry wrote five of the songs that appeared in her album, In and Out of Love.]*

He was hired to work on the music for *Whorehouse*. At the end of the picture, Perry told Dolly that he "couldn't take the bullshit of the movie business" and enrolled in medical school.

According to Dolly, "He had been put through hell, and I'm sure I was no picnic at the time." She was crushed when he left and poured out her feelings in the song, "What a Heartache You Turned Out to Be."

"Emotionally," she said, "my heart was bleeding."

She admitted that after Gregg left, she contemplated suicide, using that gun she kept. At a crucial moment, her dog, Popeye, ran down the stairs and jumped into her lap. "He saved my life."

But Burt and Dolly felt that their director, Colin Higgins, was a sweet and understanding man. "He did not appear to be in good health," Burt said, "so I knew something was wrong, but I didn't want to pry into his private life. He looked terrible and began to lose weight. I feared for him."

An admitted gay, Higgins died in August of 1988 of an AIDS-related illness.

Whorehouse became the fourth highest-grossing live-action musical film of the 1980s. The hit song of the musical, "I Will Always Love You," became Number One on the country singles chart. It also burst out as an international pop hit for Whitney Houston.

Walter Kerr in *The New York Times* called the musical film "erratic and rambling, though sleekly produced."

One critic wrote that "Burt and Dolly were the best combination since black and white."

Roger Ebert said, "If they ever give Dolly her freedom and stop packaging her so antiseptically, she could be terrific. Both Dolly and Burt in *Whorehouse* never get beyond the concept stage in this movie."

In spite of receiving a number of negative reviews, *Whorehouse* cost $25 million to make and earned more that $70 million at the box office.

***

For another 1982 film release, Burt was offered the male lead in a Technicolor romantic comedy, *Best Friends*, by Norman Jewison, who was both its producer and director. His co-star would be Goldie Hawn, the towheaded, multi-talented actress often cast as a ditzy blonde.

She'd broken into show business as a can-can dancer at the 1965 World's Fair *[in Flushing Meadows Park, Queens, NYC]*, going on to become a go-go dancer during the heyday of disco.

Her greatest breakthrough came when she was cast on TV's *Rowan and Martin's Laugh-In,* in which she played a befuddled, air-headed character.

In 1969, she'd co-starred with Walter Matthau and Ingrid Bergman in *Cactus Flower,* which brought Goldie—as Matthau's suicidal fiancée—a Best Supporting Actress Oscar.

Burt admitted, "I was lovesick crazy for Goldie, finding her a little sexpot as well as the most professional, funniest, and sharpest of all my leading ladies."

He'd first met her during their joint appearance on Johnny Carson's *Tonight* Show. He began dating her that very night, but never revealed how far that "dating" had gone.

At the time he was going out with her, she met actor Kurt Russell, who became her lover and longtime companion. "Kurt wasn't crazy about me," Burt said, "and I'm sure he was jealous, not knowing how far I'd gone with Goldie. Apparently, she'd told Kurt what a wonderful guy I was, and that must have seriously pissed him off."

"Whenever I encountered Kurt, he was very rude to me. Rude as hell, as a matter of fact. I didn't sock him one, preferring to take the high road because of my friendship with Goldie. To tell the truth, I was rather jealous of Kurt myself. In his heyday, that was one good-looking, sexy mother-fucker."

"Perhaps Kurt should also have been jealous of other guys, too—take Tom Selleck and Warren Beatty, for example," Burt said.

The script writers of *Best Friends* were Valerie Curtin and Barry Levinson, who had based the plot on their personal relationship as writers. The couple had married in 1975, but around the time of the release of *Best Friends,* they were in the divorce courts.

Jewison had been impressed with their creative involvement in *And Justice for*

BURT REYNOLDS & GOLDIE HAWN

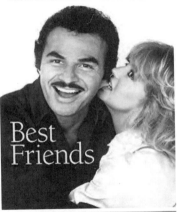

Best Friends and perhaps more?

Although Burt told Loni Anderson that the lower pic, displayed above, of a steamy scene with Goldie Hawn had been issued as a publicity photo by Warner Brothers, it was cold comfort for Loni during her neurotic observations from afar.

All (1979), starring Al Pacino.

"I felt their *Best Friends* script had some problems, but I showed it to Goldie," Jewison said. "She got back to me right away and seemed hot to star in it. I'd admired her talent as an actress not because of her work on *Laugh-In,* but for her role in *Sugarland Express* (1974)."

"Then Burt Reynolds got wind of it and also wanted to star in it," Jewison said. "At that time, no producer said 'no' to Burt Reynolds, still riding high as a box office stud. In 1971, he'd begun a five-year reign as King of the Box Office, beating out all other actors. For thirteen years, he would break records by ranking among the top ten box office stars in the world. No other actor had ever pulled off a feat like that."

"I cast Burt for yet another reason," Jewison said. "I felt he and Goldie would have a sexual chemistry on the screen, shades of Cary Grant and Carole Lombard. When Steve McQueen and Faye Dunaway did *The Thomas Crown Affair,* the screen sizzled with sexual tension. I was hoping that Burt and Goldie would do the same for me."

Before he worked with Jewison, Burt was already familiar with his work, considering *The Cincinnati Kid* (1965), starring Steve McQueen, the best film ever made about gambling. The Canadian director and producer had also been nominated for a Best Director Oscar for *In the Heat of the Night* (1967) and *Fiddler on the Roof* (1971).

Location shooting took place in New York, Maryland, and Washington, D.C. before Jewison ordered cast and crew back to Los Angeles for the wrap-up.

According to the plot, Burt and Goldie were a successful pair of screenwriters and also lovers. Richard Babson and Paula McCullen, who have been living together for five years. As they move along, Burt considers marriage and talks to Goldie about it, although at first, she appears reluctant.

He finally persuades her, and the ceremony is conducted in a bleak, Mexican-American chapel, presided over by a minister who hardly speaks English.

Their boss is Larry Weisman (Ron Silver), an absent-minded, narcissistic producer always demanding rewrites "due yesterday." A New Yorker, Silver had worked with Burt before. In *Semi-Tough,* he had had a minor role as a placekicker.

The family of the characters played by Burt and Goldie have not been informed of their marriage, and they head east to be introduced to their relatives and in-laws. Since the film is a comedy, the viewer can expect sitcom-style disasters. They begin in cold, blustery Buffalo.

Burt meets Goldie's parents, played by the formidable stage actress, Jessica Tandy, and Bernard Hughes. They portray Ellie and Tim McCullen, senior citizens increasingly forced to confront the infirmities of age.

Hughes often played dithering or grandfatherly elders. Burt had seen him in *Midnight Cowboy* (1969), in which he'd appeared with his close friend, Jon Voight.

Burt had always wanted to meet Tandy, having heard numerous tales about her celebrated appearance as Blanche DuBois in the 1947 production of Tennessee Williams' *A Streetcar Named Desire*.

Burt wanted to find out how many of the scandal-soaked behind-the-scenes rumors about that production were true. He still resented Marlon Brando, her co-star, for his rudeness to him and for the inevitable comparisons to his resemblance to the iconic actor.

Burt surprised Tandy by telling her that he thought she was "very, very sexy." He later admitted to that in print.

"His compliment shocked me when I finally figured out he wasn't joking," Tandy told Jewison. "As it turned out, he really did have this thing for older actresses, even Bette Davis. He explained it by telling me of his months-long seduction by an older woman in Palm Beach when he was only fourteen. Burt even propositioned me, and I turned him down, of course, but I was immensely flattered."

When Jewison asked Burt if he had come on to Tandy, he admitted it. "Since I was just a boy growing up in Florida, I've had this thing for older women. I refer to it as 'antique pussy,' a weird perversion of mine. But I don't want the tabloids to get word of this. Bad for my image."

After Buffalo, the newlyweds portrayed by Burt and Goldie travel south to Vienna, Virginia where his parents are living in a high-rise condo. Goldie, as Paula, becomes nervous and agitated during her encounter with Burt's family. Her panic attacks are relieved when Burt gives her Valium, but she overdoses. During a luncheon with her mother-in-law, she falls face first into her salad.

Audrey Lindley was cast as Goldie's mother-in-law, Ann Babson. She was best known for her performances as Mrs. Roper on the hit TV sitcom, *Three's Company*.

Keenan Wynn played Burt's father, who has a habit of forcing sex onto his housekeeper. Burt had known Wynn for years, and once entertained him and his lover, actor Van Johnson, both of whom at

The great stage and screen actress, Jessica Tandy, a few years before her screen gig with Burt.

He found her "very, very sexy."

one time or another had been married to the same woman.

Michel Legrand composed the theme song with lyrics by Marilyn and Alan Bergman. In *Best Friends*, the song was performed by James Ingram and Patti Austin.

"How Do You Keep the Music Playing?" was nominated for an Oscar as Best Song of the Year. It became such a popular standard that some of America's greatest singers recorded it, everyone from Barbra Streisand to Frank Sinatra, as well as Tony Bennett, Céline Dion, Shirley Bassey, and Johnny Mathis.

Best Friends cost Warners $15 million to film and generated $37 million at the box office.

Gary Arnold of the *Washington Post* gave one of the most sensitive reviews, citing Burt and Goldie as "a likably self-effacing comedy team in a new romantic comedy of rare sweetness and intelligence. The film is exceptionally authentic and endearing."   *Variety* called it "a very engaging film, even if it is initially jarring to accept Hawn and Reynolds as screenwriters. They are thoroughly believable as two people struggling to make their relationship work. Hawn especially has kept her customary kookiness in check and conveys her character's plight with maturity and charm."

Janet Maslin of *The New York Times* said that Hawn and Reynolds made "a surprisingly appealing team, a surprise being that two individually stellar comic actors can work so comfortably together. Each of them works on a lower wattage than usual, since the emphasis here is on friendliness, rather than madcap joking."

Pauline Kael of *The New Yorker* wrote, "The script reads fine, but it all plays wrong. The dialogue is too neatly worked out; there's no way to speak it without making us aware of how clever it is—how flip yet knowing."

Roger Ebert found that the plot "sounds like a series of fairly predictable scenes. But they're redeemed by the writing and acting."

Kevin Thomas of the *Los Angeles Times* wasn't willing to rave. He claimed "the movie quickly proves to be the familiar instance of the comedy that presents its central figures in the round only to satirize heavily all the peripheral people, most of whom are weighed down in *schtick*." Gene Siskel of the *Chicago Tribune* sounded a dour note: "Who wants to see such upbeat performers as Hawn and Reynolds bitch at each other for nearly two hours? The casting is wrong here."

***

In 1994, Burt recalled some events that occurred during the premiere

498

(in Austin, Texas) of *The Best Little Whorehouse in Texas*. He feared that many Texans might interpret the film as something that mocked and satirized their state. On opening night, Dolly and Burt sat together, immediately in front of its screenwriter, Larry King.

After the first twenty minutes, in a loud voice, King hissed at Dolly, "You cunt! YOU CUNT! You've ruined my picture!"

Burt was so infuriated, that he was going to attack him. In his words, "I'm gonna hit you so hard that both of your parents are going to die."

Before he assaulted King, two state troopers arrived on the scene to eject the writer from the theater. The next morning, newspapers in Austin carried news of the incident, including Burt's threat of violence.

Whorehouse premiered next in Miami, and Burt offered Dolly and a female associate (unnamed) a ride on his Hawker private jet.

During their flight to Florida, the subject of Joan Rivers came up. Burt criticized her "because her humor is always at the expense of others. Unlike Don Rickles, her attacks are very personal, including all those fatty jokes about Elizabeth Taylor, or whomever."

"You just don't get what she does," the associate said. "I think you're an asshole."

"So I'm an asshole, am I?" Burt said, exploding in anger. He headed for the cockpit, where he ordered the pilot and co-pilot to land the plane immediately.

The pilot protested that they were in the middle of nowhere, but within fifteen minutes, he spotted a small airstrip in a desolated part of Alabama. He surmised that the small plane could land there safely, so he slowly came down for a bumpy landing.

Back in the cabin, Burt flashed anger as he demanded that the associate get off the plane at once.

"You don't mean that," she said.

"Like hell I don't," he answered. "If you don't move your dingleberry-coated asshole off this plane right now, I'll throw you off."

"What about my luggage?" she asked, growing desperate.

"As we take off, I'll throw it off the plane. Now get the fuck out of here."

"C'mon, Dolly," the woman said.

"I didn't call anybody an asshole," Dolly said, "so I'm not budging from my seat."

Dolly and Burt flew the rest of the way to Miami, with no mention made of the incident.

***

But that was hardly the end of it. It was merely the beginning.

"Obviously the bitch, who knew Rivers, told her of the incident," Burt said.

For four straight years, whenever Rivers went on TV, she mocked and ridiculed Burt, getting really personal. During the period when his health deteriorated, she suggested that he might "go the way of Rock Hudson."

"Whenever a leading lady signs to make a film with Burt Reynolds, she has 'no kissing' written into her contract."

In her stage appearances off the TV screen, Rivers got "real down low and dirty," Burt claimed.

A part of her act that infuriated him the most involved her claim that "Burt Reynolds is supposed to be such a stud. It's all pretense. Whenever he seduces a girl, all of them ask the same question, 'Are you in yet?'"

As long as he lived—and he outlived Rivers—he never forgave her for her personal attacks on him, her cruel mockery of his failing looks and thinning hair.

"When my health failed me, she was forever mocking me, a real mean and nasty bitch," Burt said. "She makes her living spreading rumors and making fun of people. Because I criticized her comedy style, she delivered one assault on me after another."

In response, Rivers said, "I've learned to have absolutely no regrets about any of my jokes. If you don't like it, you can tune me out, you can click me off, it's OK by me. I am not going to bow to political correctness. You have to learn, if you want to be a satirist, you can't be part of the party."

"As the decade of the '80s moved on, I was entering the most dismal period of my life," Burt said. "I turned a dark corner and was enveloped in shadows. Regardless of whatever I did on the screen, it was overshadowed by what was happening to me off screen."

***

"On top of my other troubles, I made the biggest career mistake of my life in turning down the role of the retired astronaut, Garrett Breedlove, in *Terms of Endearment* (1983). In Hollywood, there are no rewards for being an idiot."

Larry Brooks had been given the posi-

Joan Rivers in 1987, around the peak of her publicly televised feud with Burt Reynolds

500

tions of director, producer, and writer of the screenplay for *Terms of Endearment*, based on the sensitive and moving novel by Larry McMurtry.

Brooks had met Burt when both of them worked on the set of *Starting Over*. [*Brooks had been both the co-producer and screenwriter.*] Observing Burt closely on the set, noting his movement and his sense of humor, he found him ideal for the role of the retired astronaut, a character who gets involved with the very eccentric Aurora Greenway, which had already been cast with Shirley MacLaine.

Continuing with his tireless reading of novels, Burt had been impressed with the McMurtry novel. He identified with the grounded astronaut, a fallen angel "caught between the worlds of enchantment and disenchantment."

When Brooks approached him with an offer, Burt felt he had to turn him down because he had already committed to film *Stroker Ace* for his longtime friend and director, Hal Needham.

"In looking back, I could have gotten Hal to postpone his film while I worked with Brooks, but I didn't," Burt said. "When I turned down that role, I think my IQ dropped a hundred points. I should have been locked away in an asylum. Oh, the mistakes we make when we try to lose our position as one of the world's top box office champions."

After Burt rejected the role, Brooks asked Paul Newman to star as the astronaut, but he, too, rejected it as "too marginal." Marlon Brando eventually rejected the male lead in *One Flew Over the Cuckoo's Nest*, too.

Brooks then phoned Jack Nicholson, who said, "Hell, yes, I'll do it—that is, if Shirley MacLaine will let me take time off from stud duty to go before the camera."

[Actually, Burt and Nicholson had been considered for the same parts before, beginning back in 1961 when both of them were up for a quickie Western, The Broken Land. *Nicholson got the part because he could ride a horse.*

A decade later, there was talk of replacing Nicholson with Burt in The Last Detail *(1972), the story of two hell-raising shore patrolmen transporting a seaman to the brig. Nicholson was almost too busy to star as Billy ("Bad Ass") Buddusky but managed to pull it off and didn't have to be replaced.*

"Too bad," Burt said at the time in ref-

Above, left, the randy ex-astronaut, Jack Nicholson, in the role Burt raged for having rejected, getting amorous with Shirley MacLaine in *Terms of Endearment* (1983).

erence to The Last Detail. *"It would have been my big break—after all, the word 'fuck' is used 342 times, and all in the first seven minutes."]*

Burt got drunk the night of the Academy Awards when *Terms of Endearment* won Academy Awards for Best Picture, Best Director, and Best Writing on Material from another Medium. MacLaine carried home the gold for her performance, and Nicholson won the Best Supporting Actor Oscar. The role of MacLaine's very hip daughter had been assigned to Debra Winger.

Nicholson only later learned that Burt had been offered his role. "Tough shit he turned it down. It couldn't have happened to a nicer guy."

***

"That elusive Oscar is not resting on my fireplace mantle just because I turned down *Terms of Endearment*," Burt lamented. "I continued to make one stupid blunder after another regarding role playing. I turned down box office gold to settle for movies that were nothing but dirt on which dogs pissed and horses shit. Forgive the blunt language, but I'm still boiling mad at myself."

ACTORS WHO LIVE FAST AND DIE YOUNG, like James Dean,
don't live long enough to confront their mistakes when they're past their commercial primes. That was not the case for Burt, who lived to regret the roles he rejected or missed.

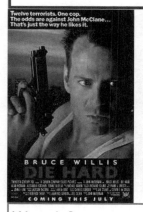

WHAT IF? Burt had accepted roles that were eventually assigned to Bruce Willis (*Die Hard*), Harrison Ford (*Star Wars*), and Richard Gere (*Pretty Woman*). This history of filmmaking in the late 20th Century would have looked very different....

He had been the first choice to play the lead of John McLane in *Die Hard* (1988), the story of a New York cop who happened to be in a Los Angeles high-rise when it's commandeered by terrorist thieves. "Bruce Willis did all right for himself in that one."

"This one you won't believe," Burt said. "I also turned down *Pretty Woman* (1990), the story of a cold-blooded business tycoon who falls for a hooker. The part went to Richard Gere. "There went my chance to make love to Julia Roberts.":

"The beat goes on," Burt said. "I also turned down the role of Han Solo in all the *Star Wars* sequels. Goodbye, millions. I told the producers I wasn't gonna play any damn Space Cowboy."

"Way before I turned down those choice roles, I had been offered the role of the boxer in *Rocky* (1976). The two other actors considered were Ryan O'Neal and James Caan. Sylvester Stallone was parking cars at the time but wouldn't surrender the rights unless he got to play the lead. *Rocky* grossed $250 million and inspired five sequels for more than a cool billion. It also won an Oscar for Best Picture."

"*Rocky* and *Star Wars*...." Burt said. "Had I not been such a jerk, I'd be retired in Florida by now, buying up real estate like this jerk I know, Donald Trump. More about him later."

***

In 1982, Burt made a new friend, John F. Bassett, who had a vision he shared with Burt. That led to his becoming a partner in a new football team and a new league to challenge the NFL.

Before he became a sports industry entrepreneur, Bassett—born in Ontario four years later than Burt—had been a well-known athlete himself when he was only fifteen years old. In 1955, he'd won the Canadian Open Junior Doubles Championship. Not only had he made a name for himself in tennis, but also in squash, football, and hockey at the University of Western Ontario. In time, as president of Amulet Pictures, he also operated as a film producer associated with such movies as *Paperback Hero*, *Spring Fever*, and *Face Off*.

Burt bonded with Bassett immediately. "We talked the same language, although I sorta exaggerated my days as a football hero at Florida State."

Plotting together, and picking up other business partners, they formed their own football team in Tampa, Florida, naming it the Tampa Bandits, a reference, in part, to the character that Burt had portrayed in *Smokey and the Bandit*. Not only that, but Burt became a partner in the newly formed United States Football League (USFL).

Organized in 1983 and nosediving in 1985, it had a short life span. In marked contrast to its massively entrenched rival, the National Football League (NFL), whose games were scheduled for the autumn and winter, it formatted its games for the spring and summer.

Although the USFL was plagued with relocations, merges, and changes in ownership during its brief but eventful lifespan, it eventually embraced eighteen football teams. They included the New Jersey Generals, an organization owned by Donald Trump, who constantly feuded with Bassett.

As Burt hovered in the background, the USFL tried to engage in a bidding war to sign up the era's greatest football players, even if it had to pay them salaries that in time proved too costly.

Burt played a key role in garnering publicity for the Tampa Bandits and launched an aggressive marketing campaign. He used his wide name recognition to garner magazine and newspaper coverage. On the cover of the team's 1983 media guide, he was photographed wearing a Bandits' "trucker hat."

Burt was behind the decision to hire the high-profile Steve Spurrier as head coach of the Bandits. Referred to as "Head Ball Coach," Spurrier was a native of Florida, having been born in Miami Beach at the close of World War II. He attended the University of Florida, where he won the 1966 Heisman Trophy as a college football quarterback with the Florida Gators. The San Francisco 49ers picked him up, which meant that he spent a decade playing in the NFL, mainly as a quarterback and punter.

At the age of 37, he became the youngest head coach in professional football. By 1986, he would be inducted into the College Football Hall of Fame. "I admired Steve's guts," Burt said. "He became known for teasing and needling the rival team, really pissing them off before whipping their asses on the field. He was one of the winningest coaches in Florida history. And we were damn proud of him. Overall, our boy led the Bandits to a 32-21 record before we went belly up."

It was new, it was radical, it defied the conventional wisdom that football should only be played in the autumn and winter. Burt was an investor.

It was the United States Football League, and according to Burt, "Donald Trump helped fuck it up."

Meeting the guys who had formed the Bandits Team evoked memories of Burt's film, *The Longest Yard*, which had been set on the grounds of a prison. "Some of our toughest players, and they were killers on the field, had done time, mostly for armed robbery, but also for rape and stabbings. One big, beefy player from Jacksonville told me he'd done very well in prison."

"I put on a big show for three gay prison guards in the shower room, and I soon became their toy boy. They took care of me real good, giving me special treats. Not only that, I've always been oversexed, and they handled that problem, often at the rate of three blast-offs a day."

For the USFL, both Burt and Bassett wanted "marquee names" such as Reggie White, Mike Rozier, Steve Young, Doug Flutie, and Brian Sipe.

But for Burt, the football hero of them all was Jim Kelly. A native of Pittsburgh, born in 1960, he was strong and beefy, standing 6' 3". He had been a former quarterback for the Buffalo Bills, and he also played two seasons for the Houston Gamblers, which was a member of the USFL.

"Jim was the toughest guy in the USFL—forget that he was a quarterback. He though he was a tackle," Burt claimed.

[In 2002, Kelly would be inducted into the Pro Football Hall of Fame.]

The Bandits played mostly in the Tampa Stadium. nicknamed "The Big Sombrero." Opened in 1967 on the site of Drew Field, an airfield that had flourished during World War II, it had a "fan friendly" seating capacity of 75,000. During its heyday, it was also associated with autumn and winter games of the NFL's Tampa Bay Buccaneers, and hosted two Super Bowls in 1984 and 1991, as well as the 1984 USFL Championship Games. It also hosted concerts, including the record-breaking Led Zeppelin show, drawing 57,000 screaming fans.

In 1999, a dozen years after the demise of the USFL, bulldozers moved in to demolish it.

To the horror of football traditional-

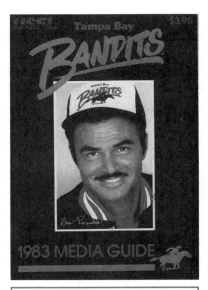

To promote his new football team, the Tampa Bay Bandits, Burt used his macho fame as a screen star to garner publicity.

"I did almost anything for publicity, from staging a Dolly Parton lookalike contest with drag queens to allowing gay photographers to take frontally nude pictures of our players taking a shower."

ists at the NFL, during their inaugural season, the Bandits were a bigger hit than the Buccaneers, the NFL franchise. [*Although both teams shared the "Big Sombrero" as their home stadium, the USFL scheduled its games in the spring and during the oppressive heat of early summer, while the NFL season was in the autumn and winter.*]

Both Bassett and Burt believed that show biz razzmatazz should be injected into USFL games, in marked contrast to what Burt called "the stodgy NFL."

To that effect, he persuaded his friend and former co-star, Jerry Reed, to write and sing the song "Bandit Ball." That term also became the name of the public relations ploy to advertise and promote the team.

"In addition to football, we came up with a lot of gimmicks and did outrageous things. "I even staged a Dolly Parton lookalike contest," Burt said. "What the fans and judges didn't know was that all the contestants in the Dolly lookalike lineup were drag queens."

Whenever they were free, Burt and Loni Anderson appeared at the stadium, signing hundreds of autographs. She posed in one of the club's jerseys and was featured on billboards in a sexy cheesecake shot above the motto—ALL THE FUN THAT THE LAW ALLOWS.

"We welcome one and all, even rowdy thugs, some looking for a brawl after the game," Burt said. "We even hosted gay photographers who wanted to snap frontal nudes of the players in the shower."

"What hastened our demise far before our time came when we brought into our league this rich kid real estate developer from New York, Donald Trump," Burt said. "He swooped down and purchased the New Jersey Generals, which became a member of our league. There are always guys who see a burgeoning business and fly in like vultures. The Donald, as he was known, was the chief offender. He didn't give a damn about the game."

"The Donald thought he knew more about football than Bassett, which, as time soon proved, he did not."

***

"My first introduction to Donald Trump came when he called and invited me to a party at Mar-a-Lago," Burt said. "I drove down from Jupiter. I was very flattered to be invited to the home of this real estate tycoon."

"What I didn't tell him was that for several summers, I got to know Mar-a-Lago on my own terms," Burt said. "In those days, the mansions of the rich folks were boarded up in summer. My gang and I, consisting of both boys and girls, broke into Mar-a-Lago for beer drinking and hot dog roasting, and what horny teenagers sometimes do when they get together. If one of the guys in my gang found a gal they had the hots for, there was a wide choice of bedrooms."

"Long before President Trump threw parties there, my guys and dolls brought in a radio and danced to *Shake, Rattle, & Roll.* I was fifteen years old at the time. The food Trump served sure beat out our hot dogs and beer, but our long ago parties were a hell of a lot more fun than his."

"Donald and I became sorta friends," Burt said. "Of course, I was not stupid. Every time I shook his hand, I kept my other hand on my wallet. To me, he seemed to have a great interest in two things: Money and publicity. As I stood by watching his technique, I saw firsthand that he was brazen with women. In time, some of these gals called it sexual harassment, but he was fairly young at the time, had passable looks, though hardly as good looking as me. Of course, in Palm Beach, if you had a bank account, you immediately became a babe magnet."

"I got to know The Donald a hell of a lot better when we had football teams that were part of the same league," Burt said.

The New Jersey Generals were established to play in the summer of 1983 as part of the USFL. The team played three seasons until 1985, winning 31 regular season games and losing 25 while going 0-21 in post-season competition.

The USFL founder, David Dixon, tapped Trump to become the owner of the Generals. However, as Dixon claimed, Trump backed out after paying an initial installment of the franchise fee. He much preferred a cheap takeover of the struggling Baltimore Colts, which would give him an NFL team. But while in charge of the Generals, he managed to stir up chaos.

He and John Bassett clashed almost from the beginning. Trump tried to lure the legendary coach, Don Shula, from the Miami Dolphins, Shula turned him down. Instead, Trump hired Walt Michaels, the former head coach of the New York Jets.

Bassett told Burt, "Trump's ego transcends his business and political sense. He was born on third and thought he hit a triple. Of course, it helped to be born the son of a multi-millionaire, who staked him and mopped up after his disasters, which included his brief tenure holding the franchise on the Generals."

"His ultimate aim, as it was soon known to me, was to pick up an NFL franchise for a song. I'd call him a shark in a tank of guppies. He knew shit about football and shared none of the passion that Burt and I had for the game."

Although maintaining a surface friendship with Trump, Burt always remained skeptical of him. "I found out that we once took the same gal to bed, a real good looker and blonde. I asked her to rate The Donald's sexual performance, and she told me, 'not much. His dick is slightly deformed.'"

"Whatever in hell did she mean? I didn't want to know more."

Burt recalled the time Trump invited him as a guest to the Trump Tower in Manhattan. "I accepted his generous invitation and really lived it up in this lavish suite—I mean, champagne, steak suppers, a lot of wining and dining. At one point, I invited about ten girls from a Broadway musical and ran up quite a bill. But what in hell did I care? The Donald could afford it. I remember he dropped in, groped a gal or two, and made off with the pick of the litter."

"Then came check-out time, when I asked the clerk to give me a notepad. I wanted to thank The Donald for his generous hospitality. I got the surprise of my life. The bugger presented me with a bill that equaled the national budget of Iran. It was the shock of my life. One night he'd invited me to dine with him in one of his restaurants. Not only was my meal added to my final hotel bill, but his own dinner was on my tab, too. I think added charges were tacked onto the bill, too. Man, The Donald gets his pound of flesh—some friend. I think paying that bill maxed out my Amex credit card."

"Actually, both John (Bassett) and I blamed The Donald for the demise of our league, the USFL," Burt said. "John and I wanted to develop our league and build it up, getting better and better players. But Trump had some sort of get-rich-quick scheme. He came into our league, as he later admitted, because he wanted to shift our season from spring and summer to fall and winter to directly challenge the NFL. I like The Donald, so don't get me wrong. But he fucked us. We weren't ready to compete with the NFL."

Although Trump never got either Bassett or Burt to agree with him, Trump convinced fellow USFL team owners to move to the fall schedule for 1986 as a means of directly competing with the NFL. His thinking was to force a merger with more deeply entrenched football league.

"Trump told me that in a forced merger, his investment would double in value," Burt said.

However, the 1986 season was canceled after the USFL won only a nominal $3 verdict in an anti-trust lawsuit it inaugurated against the NFL. After that, the USFL faded into history. "There went my beloved Tampa Bay Bandits," Burt said.

As the USFL faced Doomsday, it ended owing $163 million.

"I had warned Trump that it was too early to take on the NFL," Burt said, "but he was a very stubborn man, and he defied both John and me. His decision finished us off. I'm sorry it ended that way. I loved being part owner of a football team, and my players were like my sons. It pained me to see them move on."

Bassett was still alive to witness the sad demise of the USFL, and he and Burt had a long drunken night of mourning for the league, which they had hoped would flourish for the rest of their lives…and beyond.

When Burt flew to Canada to make a film in 1986, he phoned Bassett and wanted to get together for a reunion.

"I'm not gonna be around much longer," Bassett told him.

"Well, can I get to see you before you fly away?" Burt said. "Where are you going?"

"Perhaps Mars, or wherever old footballers go to die." Bassett said. "My doctors told me to arrange a burial plot or make a date at the crematorium. I have only days to live."

Like another billionaire, Howard Hughes, Donald Trump did not like to shake hands with anybody, but had to do it anyway. Here, he congratulates footballer Herschel Walker, whom he'd hired for the New Jersey Generals.

Whereas the athlete was thinking of glory on the football field, The Donald was seeking money and publicity.

"On hearing that, my heart was broken," Burt said.

At the age of 47 in Toronto, John F. Bassett passed into football glory, suffering from pneumonia and complications resulting from brain tumors and the side effects of radiation therapy.

***

[Later in his life, Burt also met Bill and Hillary Clinton because of land investments he'd made in Arkansas. Right before she announced a run for the presidency against Barack Obama, Bill and Hillary invited him to a football game in Arkansas. "Not only did I own land there, but I had filmed White Lightning *there in 1973."*

"It was a hell of a lot of fun," Burt said, "and I really dug Bill. Hillary was a lot of laughs. Watching the game with the Clintons was like going back to the future in a time capsule. It was so innocent."

"Hillary was much harder to know that Bill, but I came to dig her, too."

"Instead of Hillary, the guy I'd like to see run for president of the United States would be Jon Voight with Clint Eastwood as sergeant-at-arms," Burt said. "I don't pretend to be in their league when it comes to brain power and being smart.

I like both of these guys very much. We've been close, very close friends for...gosh, how long? More than thirty years. That's amazing."

"When it comes to politics, I take the middle road, not the high or low one," Burt said. "I've always managed to get along with the extreme left or the extreme right in both parties. Once at my home, I invited the ultra-liberal Orson Welles and the ultra-right cowboy conservative, Roy Rogers. Roy is to the right of Goebbels, and Citizen Kane *is a virtual communist in that cowboy's view. When they got into a political argument, I fled into the kitchen."*

"I liked Bill Clinton a lot and identified with him in some ways," Burt said. "We were both good ol' Southern boys and horndogs, and we'd both made Whitewater-type real-estate investments in his native state of Arkansas."

"Hillary was much harder to get to know, but when you cracked her shell, she was a hell of a lot of fun, too."

"I was in a real quandary in 2016 when Hillary announced she was taking on The Donald in the race for the White House. Elections are scary," Burt said. "Especially if you back the wrong candidate. I didn't know who to vote for. I didn't want to sit through four more years of Obama, which was like taking a sleeping pill. I'm not going to say who I voted for—Hillary or The Donald. Perhaps I didn't vote at all."

"We need a strong leader, now more than ever. The world is falling apart. The ice is melting in Greenland; fires are raging in California; tornadoes and earthquakes in Oklahoma; perhaps a war with North Korea or Iran. Many people tell me Trump may start another war."

"Since Trump became president, I'm worried he's gonna start something," Burt said. "There's no question we can't bomb the hell out of a country, but that's not the America I knew. In World War II, we had no choice but to fight for our way of life. We've been the savior of many countries, not the element of their destruction."

"But I hope we don't go to war again and kill a lot of men and women. It seems so unnecessary. When you're the toughest country, you don't have to do that. You just have to have our voice heard a little louder."

"As president, I think Trump has done some good things. But mostly, he acts on his instincts, which aren't good."

"I hope he doesn't do to the United States what he did to our USFL."]

***

Burt had starred in a movie called *The Man Who Loved Cat Dancing* in

510

1973. Now, a decade later, Blake Edwards offered him the role of a sad but amusing Casanova in a comedy / drama *The Man Who Loved Women* set for a release in 1983 by Columbia Pictures.

The movie would feature Julie Andrews, who was hailed in the press as the last of the great musical stars of Hollywood. As the title character in *Mary Poppins* (1964), she'd won an Academy Award. In 1965, *The Sound of Music* made her the most famous woman in the world and rescued 20th Century Fox from possible bankruptcy.

The Man Who Loved Women was not a musical. Blake worked with his psychoanalyst, Milton Wexler, to fashion a new screenplay from François Truffaut's 1977 French comedy, *l'Homme qui aimait les femmes.* Blake's son, Geoffrey Edwards, was also credited as a co-writer of the screenplay. Blake told the press, "The theme for the movie was something I had been kicking around in my head forever, it seemed."

Burt was cast as David Fowler, a womanizing sculptor facing a midlife crisis. His insatiable hunger for beautiful women had rendered him socially, artistically, and sexually impotent. "The hidden joke of the film will be Burt Reynolds as sexually impotent," Burt said. "That will get a big laugh from my fans and half the women in Hollywood."

As the female shrink, Julie Andrews gave perhaps her most low-key performance. As the confirmed bachelor, Burt was the romantic lead with a nod to how he'd played the lead in *Starting Over.* His performance with Andrews, however, didn't reach the level of his earlier movie.

In time, as might be anticipated by the audience, Burt seduces his analyst. On screen, he appears to be not so much a lover of women, but a man obsessed by them—call him "a collector" of women.

Julie even worked with her own analyst to achieve believability in her role of an attractive psychiatrist, Marianna, to whom Burt must confess everything, including his first sexual encounter.

Although reportedly, Julie and Burt liked working together, many viewers of the film found that there was "no sexual chemistry between them whatsoever."

Variety had announced the film in September of 1982, creating

In *The Man Who Loved Women*, Julie Andrews, cast in the role of Burt's psychiatrist, persuaded him to lie down on a couch for counseling and psychoanalysis.

According to Burt, "A surprise in the movie's plot was that I ended up getting my analyst on the couch. too."

some stir among fans in the casting of Warren Beatty in the lead. Actually, Blake had previously approached Dustin Hoffman and offered him the star role, but he had rejected the script. Beatty initially accepted it, but later changed his mind and moved on to another project.

Around Christmas of that year, Burt signed on. He was eager to work with both Blake and Julie, the husband-and-wife team. *[Burt had once been set to work with Blake in his star role in* Rough Cut, *but Blake soon left that assignment.]*

The Man Who Loved Women opens on a sad note, as dozens of women, in all shapes and sizes, attend Fowler's funeral. They tramp across the lawn of a cemetery to pay their final tributes to this now departed Lothario before he's buried.

Before his demise, Fowler (Burt) had spent his entire life letching after women, dreaming of them, pursuing them, and fantasizing about them.

A young Kim Basinger was cast as Louise Carr, a beautiful woman married to a Texas millionaire. She likes to have intercourse in risky public places for added excitement. As one critic wrote, Basinger "drapes her body on Burt Reynolds with a bold sort of leaning maneuver that would create obsession in a man of stone."

Also depicted was his fling with Agnes Chapman (played by Marilu Henner), mistaking her for a woman he spotted on the street whose legs were the only part of her body that he saw.

Sela Ward was cast as Janet Wainwright, another beautiful woman who was loved—ever so briefly—by the Romeo with the roving eye before he moved on.

Denise Crosby (Bing Crosby's daughter) was cast as Enid, a neophyte who was new to the hooker trade. Burt, as Fowler, hires her as a model. He nobly resists acting on his carnal instincts. *[This was Denise in her pre-*Star Trek *days.]*

Much of *The Man Who Loved Women* was shot in Los Angeles on home turf, with location shots in Houston, Texas.

At the premiere (December 16, 1983 in Manhattan) reviews devolved mainly into attacks. Vincent Canby in *The New York Times* had kind words for Burt's performance, but said that the film was "not top-drawer Blake Edwards."

Time Magazine accused Blake of "turning Truffaut's delicious Gallic *soufflé* into a restaurant quiche."

The movie cost $12 million to make, and grossed less than $11 million at the box office. "Another flop for me," Burt said. "I'd better start worrying about my career…and be pretty damn quick about it."

Critic Roger Ebert called the movie "an uncomfortable mixture of psycho-babble, fake sincerity, and scenes we are supposed to take seriously even though they contain obviously impossible elements. This is a portrait of a lonely man. His problem is he loves all women but can never love a woman. When the analyst (Andrews) makes her smarmy little speech about how he really and truly loved all these women, each in her own way, she speaks like no woman I know."

In spite of their failures, Burt enjoyed working with Blake and Andrews. *[In fact he and the director made plans to remake the Laurel and Hardy short,* Music Box, *into a full feature movie.]*

Richard Pryor was tapped to co-star with Burt, but he backed out after only a month. Eventually, Blake, too, abandoned the project, but it was announced that he and Burt would reteam to make *City Heat* in 1984. Blake left that project after only two weeks.

In a retrospective look at Blake's life and career entitled "What Happened to Blake?" a critic wondered why he took the wrong road. "Blake Edwards in the 1960s was an amazing director with a strong visual effect, directing *Breakfast at Tiffany's* (1961) with Audrey Hepburn; *Days of Wine and Roses* (1962) with Jack Lemmon and Lee Remick; and *An Experiment in Terror* (1962), with Glenn Ford and Remick again. But somewhere in all that 'Pink Panthering' he did in the 70s, he lost that visual flair and became boring. The only film in the last thirty years that showed any of the old panache was *Victor/Victoria* (1982)."

The reviewer might have added the provocative *S.O.B.* (also 1982), in which Julie bared her breasts. Both of these movies were shot right before he crafted *The Man Who Loved Women* with his wife, Julie Andrews, and Burt Reynolds.

***

The year of 1984 would end disastrously for Burt, although it started on a more optimistic note. It began when his producer, Albert S. Ruddy, hired him again for a starring role in the sequel, *Cannonball Run II. [The original,* Cannonball Run, *a tale about an illegal cross-country auto race had been a box office hit.]*

Hal Needham was brought back to helm Burt one more time, and, working with his best friend, he assembled a dazzling array of stars, including some of the biggest names in Hollywood and a lot of familiar faces within the "B" movie crowd. Most of the actors in the cast were familiar faces to Burt, many of them friends of his.

The cast included Dom DeLuise, Dean Martin, Sammy Davis, Jr., Ricardo Montalban, Telly Savalas, Marilu Henner, Shirley MacLaine, Catherine Bach, Jackie Chan, Tim Conway, Don Knotts, Jack Elam, Charles Nelson Reilly, Jim Nabors, Molly Picon, Doug McClure, Sid Caesar, Louis Nye, Jamie Farr, Susan Anton, Richard Kiel, Mel Tillis, and Frank Sinatra as himself.

When the movie was released, one critic referred to this roster of stars "as a roll call of shame."

Jaclyn Smith had originally been cast as the female lead but dropped out. Needham claimed it was "because she was scared to death to be up there against Dom and Burt. I didn't want someone on the set who was that scared, so I replaced her with Shirley MacLaine."

"I had long wanted to work with Shirley, and I got my chance," Burt said. "I was not disappointed. I liked her a hell of a lot. I can't say the same for her brother, Warren Beatty. In the early years of my career, he got roles I coveted, and I often got his sloppy seconds in roles he turned down."

"Shirley fitted in well with her Rat Packers of yesteryear, especially Sammy Davis and Dean Martin, with Frank Sinatra soon to jet in."

Martin and Davis returned to their familiar roles of Blake and Fenderbaum, who are in financial trouble with "Don Don Canneloni" (Charles Nelson Reilly), who in turn is in "deep shit" with mob enforcer Hymie Kaplan (Telly Savalas).

Burt found Shirley very candid, even outspoken, especially when she told him, "I have only one vice—fucking. I don't have to worry about my husband growing tired of me since I never see him."

She was referring to what became her thirty-year marriage to film producer Steve Parker, who lived most of the time in Japan.

While he was away, she amused herself with the likes of Alain Delon, Robert Mitchum, Sinatra, Elton John, and Peter Hamill, for whom she competed with Jacqueline Kennedy Onassis.

Martin told Burt, "I love Shirley dearly but her oars aren't touching the water."

Sinatra's appearance in the film reunited him with his fellow Rat Packers, whom he had not worked with or seen for the last three years. *Cannonball II* would mark his last appearance on the screen.

In a private jet, he flew to the desert location outside of Las Vegas for a one-day shoot. Needham said he even showed up a half hour early, at which time Burt, his friend of long ago, also had a reunion with him.

At the end of the shoot, producer Ruddy asked him what he wanted for his appearance. "Just send $100,000 to my favorite charity," Sinatra told him.

In the sequel, Burt reprised his character of J.J. McClure, the cross-country racer, speeding across America with Victor (Dom DeLuise), his familiar sidekick. This movie would mark the end of Burt's appearances in those "formula comedies" like *Smokey and the Bandit*. The cross-country race begins with J.J. and Victor dressed as a U.S. Army general with his driver, a private (DeLuise).

Burt wasn't memorable in *Cannonball Run II*, and the critics eviscerated it, but some of the secondary players were awfully attractive.

Left to right, above: Susan Anton, Joe Thiesmann, and Catherine Bach.

Along the way, they pick up Veronica (MacLaine) and Betty (Marilu Henner). The girls are dressed as nuns for a musical, but soon the habits come off.

Henner had previously worked with Burt on the set of *The Man Who Loved Women*, and he was impressed with her and got Needham to cast her in his latest film.

Veronica and Betty hitch a ride with J.J. and Victor, thinking the guys will win the race and become overnight millionaires.

Burt's longtime friend, Ricardo Montalban, was cast as King Abdul ben Falafel, whose son is Jamie Farr in the role of the sheik. The king wants his countryman to win this Cannonball Run "to emblazon the Falafel name as the fastest in the world." When the Sheik informs him that there is no second *Cannonball Run,* the king simply instructs him "to buy another one."

Added comic relief is provided by Mel Tillis, cast as "Mel" from the first film, this time with Tony Danza as "Tony." They are accompanied by an orangutan, who at times seems to be driving their vehicle.

Another friend of Burt's was Doug McClure, cast as the servant to the Sheik. Call it type casting, but he played an actor who hadn't had a TV series in nine years.

Charles Nelson Reilly, in a performance later reviewed as "pathetic," played the gangster, "Don Don" Canneloni. "He orders his henchmen to kidnap the Sheik and hold him for ransom.

In an attempt to rescue him, J.J., Victor, and Fenderbaum (Davis) infiltrate Canneloni's ranch disguised as belly dancers. The trio of "dancers in drag" appeal to their leader (Sinatra) for help, only to have him jump into the race himself.

At one point, J.J. and Victor picked up Jim Nabors, a stranded soldier cast as Homer Lyle, a spoof of his name in the TV sitcom, *Gomer Pyle.*

The sequel came under heavy fire from the critics, far more than the original. Roger Ebert denounced it as "one of the laziest insults to the intelligence of movie-goers that I can remember. Sheer arrogance made this picture."

Gene Siskel, the co-host of Ebert's TV show, *At the Movies*, labeled *Cannonball Run II* as "a total ripoff, a deceptive film that gives the movies a bad name. It is my least favorite film."

As anticipated by both Burt and Needham, *Cannonball Run II* did not equal the success of the original, making about half the box office earnings as the first version. It did well in Japan, though, perhaps because of Jackie Chan's appearance in a cameo role. The film also earned millions in both Germany and France.

***

According to Burt, "When I left the set of the picture (*Cannonball Run II*), I said goodbye to many old friends whom I would never see again. Something happened to me during the making of my next movie, *City Heat*, and the rumors that were generated, caused many friends not to call on or see me anymore. Many, many people I thought were friends deserted me, but a few remained steadfast and loyal, for which I was forever grateful."

"On top of it all, Loni Anderson became a regrettable fixture in my life, which nearly destroyed me, both emotionally and financially."

Burt claimed that "bottled blondes like Loni Anderson can be dangerous and disruptive to one's bank account."

CHAPTER FOURTEEN

LONI ANDERSON
"A TORRID, TUMULTUOUS, & TERRIBLE" AFFAIR
LONI IS WARNED: "BURT EATS WOMEN AND SPITS OUT THEIR BONES"

CHEESECAKE TO BEEFCAKE: "I WANT TO HAVE YOUR BABY."

BEST FRIENDS
IT WAS THE TITLE OF BURT'S MOVIE WITH GOLDIE HAWN.
WERE THEY MORE THAN FRIENDS?

DORIS DUKE
BURT'S HAWAIIAN FLING WITH THE WORLD'S RICHEST WOMAN
BURT: "I'M NOT INTO BEING ANYONE'S KEPT PLAYMATE."

SUBSTANCE ABUSE & DRUG ADDICTION
BURT'S HELLISH WITHDRAWAL
NIGHTMARISH HALLUCINATIONS OF MAGGOTS DEVOURING HIS FLESH

BURT FEUDS WITH HIS PRODUCERS
STROKER ACE IS A FAILURE, A DUD, A FIASCO, A BOMB.
WHO SHOULD HE BLAME?

DARK MOODS & DEEP DEPRESSIONS
EVEN LONI & HER TRASHY LINGERIE CAN'T LURE HIM BACK TO BED

CITY HEAT
A DANGEROUS STUNT GOES WRONG
BURT GETS SMASHED IN THE FACE WITH A METAL CHAIR

THE AFTER-EFFECTS LEAVE HIM IN PAIN FOR YEARS

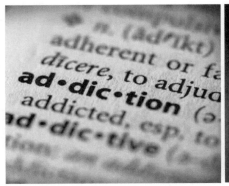

Burt first met Loni Anderson in 1978 when both of them were guests on *The Merv Griffin Show.* She was married at the time to actor Ross Bickell, her second husband, whom she'd wed in 1973. A Virginia-born, classically trained actor, he had studied drama at Boston University.

In reference to her first meeting with Burt, she later claimed, "I found him terrific-looking and the real deal."

He wanted to know how she was handling "all the hoopla connected with her role of the street-smart, secretary in the hit TV sitcom, *WKRP in Cincinnati,* which would be on the air from 1978 to 1982. Burt had seen three episodes of her as the sultry receptionist, Jennifer Marlow ("with all that dyed blonde hair.") He'd also seen best-selling posters of her in both red and white swimsuits that evoked the best of Farrah Fawcett.

The *WKRP* creator, Hugh Wilson, told Burt, "I hired Loni because she had the body of Jayne Mansfield and yet possessed the seemingly innocent sexuality of Marilyn Monroe."

On meeting her, Burt agreed with Wilson's appraisal, finding that she suggested not only Monroe, but "the other great Hollywood blondes like Jean Harlow and Judy Holliday."

"Loni had platinum blonde hair, impossible curves, perfect porcelain skin, and a ten-karat dynamite smile that blinded the male eye. As a Saturday's Hero of yesterday on the football field, I viewed her as the all-time homecoming queen. I'd like to place a crown on her head and something else on her nether regions. Since she wasn't a natural blonde, I wondered if, like Marilyn herself, Loni used bleach down there."

Burt also met her husband, Ross Bickell, that night, hearing he was out of work. He didn't ingratiate himself to Ross by exclaiming, "It's rough, isn't it, being out of work while your wife is shooting to stardom? I experienced the same shit when married to Judy Carne. Hang in there, guy."

Ironically, Ross had tested for a role on *WKRP* opposite Loni, but it had gone to Gary Sandy, who later became her passionate lover.

[Before she got the gig on WKRP, Loni had tested for a role opposite John Ritter in the long-running sitcom Three's Company *(1977-1984), but lost to Suzanne Somers.]*

At first, Loni didn't want to play "another dumb bimbo blonde" on *WKRP*. "My goal was to look like Lana Turner but to be really, really smart."

As in the movie, *A Star is Born*, her star had ascended into the heavens, and Bickell's had fallen to earth. Apparently, he had gotten tired of being referenced as "Mr. Loni Anderson."

Before Burt hooked up with Loni again, she had separated from Bickell and was involved in a torrid affair with actor Gary Sandy, her co-star in *WKRP in Cincinnati*. On TV, he'd played program director Andy Travis. A native of Dayton, Ohio, he was nine years younger than Burt.

"When I took up with Gary, he was receiving hundreds of fan letters every week from horny women across America," Loni said. "After my first night with him" as she revealed in a memoir, "his love-making with me lasted five hours. That guy turned lovemaking into an art form. Getting screwed by him was like an atomic explosion."

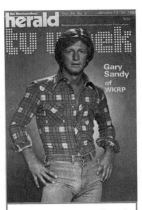

During her first year on *WKRP*, Loni was invited to appear on *The Dinah Shore Show*. "She greeted me with a roaring laugh and a big hug. Really a great broad with a sense of humor. But all that changed in my later appearances on her show. Word reached her that I had the hots for Burt, and all I got this time was a limp handshake."

Before there was Burt in Loni's life, there was Gary Sandy, "an atomic explosion in bed."

"I suspected Dinah also had her eye on Gary Sandy, who was shacked up with me at the time," Loni said. "So Dinah had a double reason to view me as a rival."

While being bedded by Gary, Loni was also being wooed through a representative of Burt's. He kept calling her, asking her if she'd go out to dinner with his star. "I kept putting him off, telling him I was involved with Gary Sandy. But the calls kept coming in, making me wonder why Burt couldn't phone for himself. Of course, I had to

Howard Hessamann, Loni Anderson, & Jan Smithers as work colleagues and sitcom icons.

consider the invitations. After all, he was THE Burt Reynolds, the biggest box office attraction in America." Dumping Bickell, she found Gary a "romper and a stomper, with a hefty temper and a smile that could charm pictures off the wall."

"I was thirty-five years old, and couldn't keep my hands off this guy," she said. "I was possessed, sexually addicted."

In time, as was almost inevitable, there was trouble in paradise between Gary and Loni. First, he learned she was making far more money than he was in their TV sitcom. Later, when she was nominated for an Emmy, and he was overlooked, he exploded in anger. Not only that, he suspected she was slipping around and seeing other men.

At this time in her life, the tabloids had headlined *WKRP NO LONGER ONE BIG HAPPY FAMILY.* Gary and Loni became known as the "Battling Andersons," their constant bickering named after her. She claimed, "Gary yelled, slammed doors, kicked things, stomped his boots."

She finally fought back as their relationship neared a bitter end. He constantly attacked her celebrity. She finally claimed, "I felt he was disgusted with me, especially the acclaim from my fans."

***

Three years had passed, and Burt had been nominated as "Entertainer of the Year," at a big televised gala that even attracted President Ronald Reagan and one of Burt's best friends, Clint Eastwood. Big Burt and Fern flew in for the occasion, and watched as Big Burt's favorite actor, James Stewart, presented Burt with the award.

At the Variety Club, the children's charity honoring Burt, Loni showed up "poured into a voluptuous gown." He noticed her as she worked the room, mingling with A-list stars such as Lucille Ball, Jack Lemmon, even Cary Grant. Her task that night was to introduce Jim Nabors.

Loni was seated at a table with David Gershonson, Burt's manager, and his former agent, Dick Clayton. Burt waved to her from a nearby table, as he was greeted by Jackie Gleason, Brian Keith, and Madeline Kahn. Loni wondered if Burt were still interested in dating her, and she was determined to find out.

As the night wore on, Loni came over to Burt. As he later confessed, "She snuggled up to me

Burt captures Miss America of 1976. Tawny Godin (aka Tawny Little) on the cover of *Seventeen.*

and, in a breathy voice, whispered in my ear: 'I want to have your baby,' she cooed."

She had been prompted to whisper about a possible baby with him because she'd seen him in repeated visits on television, especially on Johnny Carson's *Tonight* Show, where he had often expressed his desire to father a son. One night, as a joke, Carson presented him with a live baby on the air as the kid's mother watched anxiously from backstage.

He called the next day, inviting Loni to spend New Year's with him in Florida.

After mulling it over for two days, Loni returned Burt's call, accepting his invitation for the New Year in Florida. Arrangements were made, and she had to work hard to conceal her excitement. Christmas had been spent with Gary and her family, and she dreaded telling him she was flying to Florida to be with Burt.

As anticipated, his temper flared up, and he warned her, "Burt Reynolds will eat you alive. He devours women and spits out their bones."

Ironically, as she was watching television, she saw Tawny Little being interviewed by Regis Philbin and Kathie Lee Griffin. Tawny, Miss New York of 1975 and Miss America of 1976, told the TV hosts how exciting her life had become now that she was seriously dating Burt Reynolds.

Loni was stunned, phoning Burt that she was reconsidering flying to Florida to be with him. She challenged him about his relationship with Tawny.

"There's nothing to it," he assured her, "A few dates, a few dinners. We've never been more intimate than a kiss on the cheek."

She was not sure if she believed him. That was certainly not the spin Tawny had given on TV.

It wasn't until 1994 that Loni learned the truth when she read a memoir by Elaine Hall, who had been Burt's assistant for many years.

As Loni found out, Burt had a most serious romance with Tawny, with plenty of talk about marrying her and having children. Unknown to Loni at the time, Burt had put her on a plane to New York only one hour before he greeted Loni after the landing of her plane from Los Angeles.

He'd told Tawny that he wanted to be alone with Big Burt and Fern for a family reunion, hoping she would understand. It was through tabloid coverage that the former beauty contest winner, and later TV personality, learned about Burt's blossoming affair with Loni.

[*One should not necessarily feel sorry for Tawny. Soon after that, in 1983, she began dating "that handsome blonde stud," John Schneider, the star of TV's hit sitcom,* The Dukes of Hazzard. *She married him, their union lasting for three years.*]

At the Miami Airport, Burt greeted Loni with a hug and a kiss before they boarded his private helicopter, manned by two young pilots, for a flight up the Gold Coast to Jupiter. The sun had set, and the twinkling lights were aglow below. Burt held her hand and looked dashing in his aviator jacket, evoking Robert Taylor in one of his war movies. As they flew above the Intercoastal Waterway, she found the Christmas lights dazzling.

Finally, the helicopter set down on a tennis court at Valhalla, his eight-acre estate on Hobe Sound fronting the Intercoastal.

He ushered her into a home he owned there, allowing her to settle into a beautifully furnished bedroom where she found all the conveniences, including a large supply of cosmetics and beauty aids.

Fresh flowers had been placed throughout the house, and she descended the steps in an evening gown. He pronounced her appearance as "stunning."

The catered dinner of fresh lobster had gone smoothly, as they talked, just getting to know each other. For the first time, he became aware that she had been married and divorced before Ross had come into her life. In 1964, she'd wed Bruce Hasselberg, "who was in sales or something."

She met him the night his sister, Barbara Hasselberg, had been crowned Miss Minnesota, with Loni being runner-up. "Bruce was my consolation prize that night," Loni said. "Three weeks after I met him, we eloped. I was sweet eighteen."

Burt also learned that Bruce and Loni, during their two-year union, had produced a daughter, Deidra.

Loni tried to explain to Burt that they never actually had penetration, and her doctor had to break her hymen to discover she was pregnant. Burt didn't want to hear a medical explanation as to how "young sperm managed to seep through."

"My young husband suggested an immaculate conception like the Virgin Mary," Loni said.

Burt was completely baffled but didn't pursue it further. "I want to meet Deidra when it's convenient," he said.

Back in Hollywood, Deidra had already delivered her review of Burt: "I think he's cuter than Robert Redford."

Before Deidra's endorsement, Loni told *Playboy* that she thought, "Burt Reynolds is the handsomest actor in Hollywood."

Since he had many events planned for the following day, he decided to leave early, settling for a light kiss on her lips as he departed.

The next morning, he arrived early and drove her to his dinner theater, where he was directing one of his favorite plays, *One Flew Over the Cuckoo's Nest*. He told her he'd wanted to star in the movie version, but producer

Michael Douglas, after turning down his father, Kirk ("too old"), awarded the role to Jack Nicholson.

Burt introduced Loni to the stars, Martin Sheen and Adrienne Barbeau. Loni was not aware that Barbeau and Burt had had an affair. The stars concealed their surprise. Only the day before, Burt had showed up with Tawny Little, suggesting they were so much in love they'd have to get married.

Loni watched as Burt directed the cast and was astonished at how good he was. Later, he drove her to his ranch where she met Big Burt and Fern. His parents welcomed her warmly and served her a home-cooked dinner.

For New Year's Eve, he took her to Palm Beach for a lavish dinner and show, and they attended a party where she met the reigning socialites with a scattering of the Hollywood elite. One observer later reported, whether it was true or not, that she saw a drunken Teddy Kennedy flirting with Loni.

That night, enclosed within the cozy walls of Valhalla, Burt and Loni made love for the first time. She would later recall it as "the most romantic evening of my life."

In bed, she might have anticipated that the reigning male sex symbol of American would be, in her words, "a macho, thrash-and-bash guy," but she found him a tender, gentle lover.

She later wrote that he was "the most beautiful man I had ever seen," commenting on his broad shoulders, muscled arms, great butt, and wonderful strong legs. "He was no Arnold Schwarzenegger, but more like a classic Greek statue, perhaps Adonis."

She made no reference to that part of his anatomy concealed from *Cosmo* readers in his nude centerfold.

That night, they even found "our song," which came from the Jerry Herman musical, the Broadway flop, *Mack and Mabel,* a reference to Mack Sennett and the silent screen star, Mabel Normand. The song they adopted as their own was the bittersweet love song, "I Won't Send You Roses."

She did admit later that the hot sex and unbridled passion she'd known "with both Ross (Bickell) and Gary Sandy wasn't there with Burt, but it was nice."

She was due back on the set of *WKRP*. Before departing, Burt promised he'd give up all other women. "Why will I do that?" he asked. "Because I'm falling head over heels in love with you. What will I need with someone else? There's only you. From this day forth, call us a team."

Within a month, Burt's fledgling relationship with Loni graced the covers of at least ten magazines which hailed them as "the power couple," and as two stars at the peak of their careers.

Burt told *People* magazine: "Whether my relationship with Loni will go any further than it is right now, I have no idea. Loni and I are both trying very hard to get acquainted and to like each other without too many explosions and too many broadsides from the press."

***

Back in Hollywood, awaiting Burt's return, Loni had cause to wonder, as she later claimed, "Had she fallen in love with Burt Reynolds' screen image, or the man himself?"

[It was not uncommon for a man or woman falling for a movie star to be enthralled by who they were on the screen and not in real life. Rita Hayworth expressed it best when she was quoted as saying, "Men fall in love with Gilda and wake up in bed with me."]

Two polls named Loni Anderson and Burt Reynolds—hailed as "the power couple"—as the most beautiful male and female stars in Hollywood.

A day after her return, Loni reported to work on the set of *WKRP in Cincinnati*. There, she confronted Gary Sandy, her former lover, and she had to tell him what had happened in Florida, expressing it bluntly. "I'm sorry but Burt and I are now together."

She was soon greeted with a tabloid headline—BURT REYNOLDS DUMPS MISS AMERICA, TAWNY LITTLE.

Another headline blared—LONI ANDERSON DUMPS HEARTBROKEN GARY SANDY AS 'BANDIT' STEALS HER HEART.

People magazine called them "the perfect blend of cheesecake and beefcake."

In the fourth and final season of *WKRP*, Loni found it increasingly difficult to work with Gary. "I had to put up with a lot of 'fuck you's,'" she said.

Her on-set tension was relieved somewhat when Burt flew back to the coast, bringing with him a garnet ring surrounded with diamonds. When he was at work, he often phoned her two or three times a day, during which he would rave about one of her body parts—"Yes, that one, too."

"One part I found worthy of praise was the area behind her right knee," he claimed.

Flowers arrived daily, often two or three deliveries, showing his preference for red roses. He continued to woo her with gifts that included an

Hermès scarf, a diamond-and-ruby necklace, gold slippers, a shocking pink satin gown that required almost no alteration, and sometimes, something simple like a box of chocolates or a bottle of Chanel No. 5.

After he'd been back for a week, Loni invited him to her home for dinner and to meet her mother, Maxine, and her daughter, Deidra. "He was charming and gracious," Loni said, "and my gals seemed to like him a lot, Deidra for his looks and Maxine for his sense of humor."

After he'd left, Maxine said, "He's not Clint Eastwood, but he'll do."

When Burt had to go to the hospital for a hernia operation, Loni was there to comfort him. After he was released, he asked her to fly to Hawaii with him for a much-needed vaca-

Burt competed fiercely with Tom Selleck (depicted above) as Hollywood Hunk of the Year.

tion. His manager had already rented a luxurious vacation retreat for them near Diamond Head, just outside Honolulu. [It was modestly called The Grass Shack.] It stood between the homes of Jim Nabors and the tobacco heiress, Doris Duke.

One night, Burt invited Tom Selleck, who was nearby, filming an episode of *Magnum P.I.*

Burt's recovery from his operation was rapid, and soon, he was making love two or three times a day, as he relayed to Jim Nabors.

Loni defined her time with him in Hawaii as "the most romantic vacation of my life." To top it off, he brought in the best jeweler from Honolulu to design, for her, a diamond bracelet and a necklace depicting a Hawaiian fertility goddess.

Back in Los Angeles, she starred in the final episodes of *WKRP*, which was going off the air. Gary remained as belligerent as ever, but, even so, she was sorry to see the series come to an end. It had made her famous, and she had bonded with the crew, indulging in one of the most passionate affairs of her life, until she tossed Gary over for Burt.

After a final night with Burt, he flew to Buffalo for location shooting with Goldie Hawn in their co-starring vehicle, *Best Friends* (1982). Rumors reached Loni in Los Angeles that he was engaged in an affair with Goldie.

When she was free, Loni flew to Buffalo to join him. Their reunion got off to a bad start when he threw open the door to their suite. Clouds of smoke billowed outward into the hallway, and he was immediately covered with soot and a heat so intense that the front of his hairpiece melted. He had wanted to have all three of the fireplaces blazing for her arrival, but the chimneys had backed up, and smoke was everywhere.

When the air finally cleared and he emerged from the shower, they made love.

The following evening, he invited her to see Richard Harris, the Irish actor and hellraiser, perform as King Arthur in a traveling roadshow version of *Camelot*.

A royal command for a *ménage à trois* with Loni and Burt: Richard Harris as King Arthur in *Camelot*

After the show, they dined with Harris, who started to drink heavily. When Loni excused herself to go to the women's toilet, Harris leaned over to Burt with an invitation: "After dinner, let me join you in your suite for a three-way."

Harris later said, "Burt turned me down and didn't take offense. I guess I had heard all the wrong rumors. I'd been told they were two wildcats, and the more in their bed the merrier. Too bad. It could have been fun."

Before Loni flew out of Buffalo, she and Burt made a vow. "We must never be apart for more than a month at one time," he said. "We'll adjust for location shoots."

That afternoon, under the overcast gray skies of Buffalo, they embarked on a tumultuous relationship that would last for eleven and a half years, only some of which were spent as man and wife.

***

One early afternoon when Loni went shopping, Burt remained behind. What he didn't mention was that he'd received an invitation to go for a swim in the ocean with Doris Duke, the tobacco heiress, and presently, his neighbor.

Her home near Diamond Head outside Honolulu had been built right before World War II and was the most luxurious residence in the area. Burt once went on a tour of the home with Duke, who had filled it with treasures from Iran, Morocco, Turkey, Spain, Syria, Egypt, and India.

[*Since Miss Duke's death in 1993, the Shangri La Museum of Islamic Art, Culture & Design has been owned and operated as a public museum of the arts and cultures of the Islamic world by the Doris Duke Foundation for Islamic Art.*]

Burt met her on the beach at her favorite spot and appraised her still slim figure. He complimented her, telling her she had "the world's most beautiful legs."

"Both Cary Grant and Errol Flynn once told me the same thing," she said. That caused him to decide that Duke was not the modest type.

He'd long followed the scandal-filled life of the heiress as she was involved in one affair after another. Her bedfellows were legendary, a bizarre but fascinating collection that included General George C. Patton, Elvis Presley, and Aristotle Onassis. She'd once been married to Porfirio Rubirosa, the playboy from the Dominican Republic who was celebrated for his endowment. Author Truman Capote had labeled it "a foot-long octoroon dick."

Burt had also heard of her affair with Marlon Brando. A sharp-eyed observer had spotted Duke and Burt cavorting on the beach and must have called in an item to the local gossip columnist. She wrote, "Once Doris Duke roamed a nearby beach with Marlon Brando. Now she's been seen with his lookalike, Burt Reynolds."

"Except for me, the big names seemed to have wandered out of Doris' life," Burt said. "But from what I'd observed out my window, she was not lonely. A parade of muscular young Hawaiian boys could be seen coming and going from her estate. The word was out…she preferred dark meat."

Burt apparently succeeded in keeping his friendship with Duke a secret except when he and Loni entertained her.

Back in Hollywood, he told agent Sue Mengers, "That item about Duke and me keeps perpetuating my attraction to older women. If so, Doris sure fits the bill. She was born in 1912, and I didn't pop out of the womb until 1936. She's in great shape, and I could live in luxury as her in-house sex slave."

"At least Doris can afford you, and you could stop spending all your hard-earned cash buying jewelry for Loni," Mengers said. "You wouldn't have to work so hard if you became her kept boy."

"It wouldn't work sexually," he revealed. "She wants to have her toes tongued and sucked voraciously."

For a while, at least, tobacco heiress Doris Duke, the richest woman in the world, toyed with the idea of supporting Burt as her kept boy.

***

The stay in Hawaii had at first seemed idyllic, but soon there was trouble in paradise. It stemmed from Burt's long history of violent ac-

527

cidents. He had lost his spleen in a car accident when he was a teenager, and he'd sustained many injuries during his brief stint as a college football player. As a longtime stuntman, he had suffered numerous other injuries, and as an actor in films—notably in *Deliverance*—he had almost drowned.

Loni was unfamiliar with drugs, but she soon became aware of how dependent her new boyfriend was on painkillers. He regularly ingested such pharmaceuticals as Percodan, Compazine, and Valium, and was particularly addicted to the latter as a mean of alleviating anxiety attacks.

At times, he clutched his chest and could hardly breathe. He would go into a fit of hyperventilating. To revive himself, he kept stashes of small paper bags throughout any house he lived in, breathing in and out of them as a means of restoring his breathing to normal.

He explained to her that he had no need for recreational drugs such as heroin and cocaine, but that he turned to pharmaceuticals to ease his almost constant pain. He never smoked cigarettes and had only wine on occasion, perhaps champagne if the event were festive. Otherwise, he shunned liquor.

Loni began to discover more about the man with whom she shared a life as he continued to make love to her.

As months went by, he became increasingly jealous of her and very possessive. He particularly didn't want to hear about Gary Sandy or Ross Bickell, her second husband. He certainly didn't want her to speak of her first husband, Bruce Hasselberg, the father of her daughter Deidra.

Of course, she knew that much of his own past had been notorious, but he never wanted her to refer to his former loves, particularly Dinah Shore or Sally Field. He even resented time Loni spent with her mother or daughter.

On certain days, dark moods would overtake him as Dr. Jekyll became Mr. Hyde. On such occasions, he would retreat from the world and didn't want anyone to intrude on him.

One night in Jim Nabor's home, Burt became violently ill, clutching his stomach before vomiting on the floor. She rushed to the phone to call a doctor, but he screamed at her not to. "The tabloids will go wild, you fool," he shouted at her.

A doctor was summoned to the house, one who also attended Doris Duke and was known for his discretion. After a careful review, the doctor determined that Burt was addicted to Percodan and that that and other drugs were eating away at the delicate lining of his stomach. She'd noticed that when he woke up in the morning, he often vomited a yellowish bile into the sink when trying to brush his teeth.

The doctor requested that Burt enter a hospital for treatment immediately, but he refused, again citing possible bad publicity if word reached the press.

It was then determined that he should begin a period of withdrawal which would mean a minimum of three days and nights. "It'll be a living hell for Mr. Reynolds," the doctor warned Loni. Before departing, the doctor recommended that Loni lock herself in a room in case Burt turned violent during withdrawal. "He is likely to enter periods of hallucination."

In the doctor's final session with Burt, he was very blunt. "If you don't go through this hellish withdrawal, you will die! You're gradually killing yourself and if you continue your present addiction, you won't last even one year."

For the next three days and nights, Burt managed to drink only weak tea, which at first his stomach rejected. "It was hell on earth," she said.

Burt later told Jim Nabors that it had been a time of hallucinations in which he imaged "giant caterpillars devouring my flesh. Night sweats. Stomach cramps. Hot baths didn't seem to do much good. Nightmares. Sleep for only three minutes at a time. Hot flashes. At one point, I was on fire, evoking an old stunt I'd once performed on TV in New York. The most horrible of all, large maggots were devouring my intestines."

She stood by him like a loyal friend and saw him through his ordeal. One morning, he managed to keep down tea, toast, and even some orange juice.

He'd lost weight. He began to swim laps in Nabor's pool, preparing himself for a return to Los Angeles to make a new film.

She hated to leave him alone, but she had to fly away in August of 1982. She'd been cast in *Country Gold* (1982), to be shot in Nashville, starring Burt's close friend, Earl Holliman and former co-star. There, Dolly Parton shared memories of making *The Best Little Whorehouse in Texas* with Loni.

Burt flew into Nashville within the week and had a reunion not only with Parton and Holliman, but with Mel Tillis, another friend and co-star of his.

It was during this period that Loni claimed that Burt proposed marriage to her, thanking her for "standing by me in my darkest hour."

Later, Burt had a different recollection, writing that he did not remember ever proposing to her. "Almost every day, I told myself I didn't really like her—I mean the sex thing was okay, but liking, much less loving, did not exist in my heart. Besides, she wore too much makeup. When she kept pestering me to marry her, I said I would as soon as I built a chapel on my estate in Jupiter. I made sure I didn't finish that damn chapel for four more years."

Back in Los Angeles, Loni became increasingly aware of one of Burt's better qualities, and that was his loyalty to his friends, including newly minted ones like Ann-Margret and her husband and manager, Roger Smith.

A parade of these friends came and went from Burt's residence: Charles Nelson Reilly, James Best, Dom DeLuise, Charles Durning, Doug McClure, singer Jerry Reed, and even Ernest Borgnine. Ned Beatty was also a regular, as was Esther Williams.

Loni perhaps had heard rumors of a long-enduring affair between Burt and the swimming star, but she seemed devoted to her husband, Latin lover Fernando Lamas, so such gossip was usually discounted.

Burt loved his new home that he shared with Loni and was even fond of his neighbors. "In case I wanted to hear a great voice, I could walk down the street, knock on Barbra Streisand's door, and she'd give me a concert."

Surely Burt was exaggerating, He could also visit the rocker next door, Rod Stewart.

When tired of music, he could call on another neighbor, Gregory Peck. "He was one good-looking guy, but at times, I felt we had only one thing in common: We'd both fucked Ingrid Bergman at different stages in her life."

"It was a turning point in my life," Burt recalled. "Loni, whom I continued to call The Countess, had a career that was starting to take off. As for me, I desperately needed a hit, having had two box office flops in a row, which has been known to derail many a movie career. Even Julie Andrews couldn't rescue our turkey, *The Man Who Loved Women* (1983).

To reward Loni for helping him through his withdrawal from drugs, he presented her with a shiny, emerald-green Rolls-Royce. Its license plate read MISS A.

The time had come for both Burt and Loni to go back to work, and they had dinner with Hal Needham, still one of Burt's best friends and his frequent director.

It was on that night that Needham pitched a new script, not only for Burt to star in, but for Loni to take the role of the leading lady.

***

Burt's first movie for 1983, *Stroker Ace,* in which he was cast in the title role, marked the first rung on the ladder as he headed down from the top of "the dung heap," he called Hollywood.

He played a popular race car driver from Waycross, George, which he had long—and wrongly—alleged as his birthplace. In the role, he portrayed a three-time champion on the NASCAR circuit, driving a #7 Ford Thunderbird. He was called "an all-or-nothing man who wins if he does not crash."

In 1977, First Artists had announced that it had acquired the rights to the 1974 novel, *Stand On It,* by William Neely, as a vehicle for Paul Newman.

The New York Times had taken a harsh view of the novel, wondering how "this one found its way into hardcover and didn't go immediately to paperback." But the *Chicago Tribune* suggested that the movie version of *Stroker Ace* might do for stock-car racing what Burt's *Semi-Tough* had done for football.

The Newman deal fell through, and executive producer Walter Woods acquired the rights, hiring two of Burt's friends to oversee the film, with Hank Moonjean as producer and Hal Needham as Burt's director once again.

Wood predicted "Burt 's loyal fans will turn out. For the past five years, he's been number one at the box office, in spite of the fact he's never gotten a good review."

Wood admitted that he'd never seen a stock-car race, although later he would own part of a stock-car franchise. "We didn't set out to make a racing film, rather, a light comedy. Based on their previous films with Burt, I knew Hank and Hal could pull it off," he said.

Burt wasn't that turned on by the screenplay Needham had written for him, but he found his $5 million salary "a juicy piece of steak." Financing was arranged in a joint deal with Universal and Warners.

Stroker's rival is Aubry James (Parker Stevenson), an ambitious young driver who propels a #10 1982 Buick Regal.

The next lead was played by Ned Beatty, Burt's longtime friend and former co-star of *Deliverance* (1972). He became the scene stealer of the movie, cast as Clyde Torkel, a blithering idiot who is Stoker's sponsor. He signs a contract with Stroker to promote his chain of fast-food fried chicken restaurants. The label they'll attach to both their driver and the product he's promoting is "The Fastest Chicken in the South."

Stroker's contract calls for him

Jim Nabors, Loni Anderson, and Burt dressed up in chicken feathers in *Stroker Ace.*

531

to make frequent appearances dressed in a feathery chicken outfit that includes giant chicken feet.

Another of Burt's friends, Jim Nabors, played his crew chief, Lugs Harvey, doing his best Gomer Pyle impersonation.

Loni Anderson was cast as Pembroke Feeny, doing her best Marilyn Monroe imitation, although Burt found her "more Mamie Van Doren."

She portrays a Sunday school teacher and a virgin. When Burt heard that, he told Needham, "Casting Loni as a virgin is like casting Marilyn Monroe as the Virgin Mary."

In the script, Stroker is a ladies' man who tries to seduce Pembroke, but she spurns his advances. After getting her drunk one night on champagne, he removes her clothing but decides not to take advantage of her.

At least that was what the script called for. But that was hardly the situation in real life. Needham and most of the cast and crew took note of the powerful sexual chemistry between Burt and Loni.

Stroker Ace drew some of the most critical reviews of Burt's career. This time, bad reviews made a difference. On a budget of $16.5 million, the film took in $11.4 million at the box office.

The film did receive awards, however, Golden Raspberries naming it Worst Picture. Needham got Worst Director, Loni earned the Worst Actress, and Worst New Star Award, and Nabors won for Worst Supporting Actor.

Critic Gary Arnold was the kindest, calling it "a knuckle-headed but amiable summer trifle." Vincent Canby of *The New York Times* labeled it "the must-miss of the summer. It's a witless retreat of the earlier, far funnier road-movie collaborations of Needham and Reynolds."

Gene Siskel wrote, "Reynolds' reputation as a serious actor is virtually destroyed with this miserable picture. He's sending only one message here. Fans, I'm in it only for the money." *Variety* wrote that the Reynolds-Needham team was "Just coasting in circles, trying to pick up whatever prize money might be attracted by their track record." Sheila Benson of the *Los Angeles Times* described Burt as "ambling through the film as if it were a colossal in-joke, which, of course, it must be, since it isn't perceptibly funny to anyone outside the immediate circle of Needham and Reynolds."

Roger Ebert claimed, "to call the film lightweight, bubble- headed summer entertainment is not criticism but simply description."

***

Burt had first met actress Kirstie Alley on the set of *Stroker Ace* in which he was co-starring with her real-life love interest, Parker Stevenson. He didn't know who she was, but before the end of the decade, all of America could identify her. From 1987 to 1993, she played Rebecca Howe in the hit TV sitcom, *Cheers*.

Attracted to her sexy figure and good looks, Burt asked, "And who in hell might you be, little darlin'?"

In her sexy voice, she answered, "I'm just here to fuck Parker."

From the beginning, he got a taste of Kirstie's ribald humor. He later asserted, "She even beat mine!"

Two nights later, he invited Parker and Kirstie to join Loni and him for dinner. He ordered raw oysters for the entire table, but mainly for Parker. "I always heard that oysters made a man more potent and, faced with a gal like Kirstie in bed, I suspected that he'd need a double or triple dose of testosterone."

"As appetizers were served, I got turned on watching Kirstie down a succulent oyster," Burt said. "Then she surprised the table and turned to Loni."

"Have you ever gone by a construction site and wanted to take every rugged hunk home with you to fuck?"

Between oysters, Parker just puffed on his cigar and proclaimed, "What a gal!"

In contrast, Loni became tongue-tied. Burt tried to read her face. Had Kirstie tapped into Loni's ultimate fantasy? Perhaps one about construction workers?

"Maybe if I had read Loni's face more carefully that night, I would be a hell of a lot richer," he told Hal Needham years later during their discussions of that memorable night.

Burt later persuaded Parker and Kirstie to co-star in the play, *Answers*, at his theater in Jupiter.

Kirstie married Parker in 1983, a turbulent union that made it until a divorce in 1997.

"I finally realized what had attracted Kirstie to Parker," Burt said. "On her third try for an Emmy for *Cheers,* she finally won. I was watching her give her acceptance speech."

She publicly thanked Parker, claiming "He is the man who has been giving me the big one for the past eight years."

"I bet after that endorsement, Parker's phone must have been ringing at all hours of the day and night," Burt said. "All the size queens in Hollywood, both male and female, must be trying to hook up with him."

Kirstie Alley in *A Bunny's Tale*, a 1985 Made-for-TV movie about Gloria Steinam's infiltration of the Playboy Club.

More trouble arose between Burt and Loni during and after the filming of *Stroker Ace.* Since the movie was shot in Atlanta during the long, hot summer of 1983, Burt rented a lakeside house for them for some respite from the heat. He also informed her for the first time that he had a vacation retreat in the mountains of North Carolina, at which they could go after scenes were shot at the Charlotte Motor Speedway.

In the middle of the shoot, Loni's daughter, Deidra, and her boyfriend Bobby came to visit Loni.

Burt seemed to resent the presence of Loni's daughter, and after three days, he threw a temper fit that "left Deedee in tears," Loni claimed.

Burt seemed riddled with anxiety, and he was always nervous and quick to flare into a rage over what he perceived as the slightest infraction. At one point he collapsed in their rented villa and fell down on the floor, clutching his stomach again. It was on that night that she discovered he was back on pills again, swallowing an excessive number of Percodan. He promised her he would drop the pills as soon as *Stroker Ace* was wrapped.

He also suggested that for greater harmony, it would be a good idea for Deidra and her boyfriend to return to Los Angeles.

His mood only worsened as the film neared the end of its shooting. Late one afternoon, he was in a car with two of his male assistants, driving to his lakeside retreat, when he burst into a rage.

The driver later characterized it as a jealous fit. "John Byner was working on our movie, and Burt accused Loni of renewing her affair with him. Apparently, she had once dated this man, whoever he was. I didn't know. Or maybe it was someone else. Burt just seemed to suspect it was someone either in the cast or crew."

She denied any involvement, but he accused her of being a liar. He grabbed hold of her wrist, twisting it so hard he broke the skin, leading to her bleeding. Ultimately, her wrist was sprained and she seemed in agony.

Back at the lake house, he seemed remorseful and begged her to forgive him. He put ice on her wound, hoping to bring some relief and to prevent swelling. She was due on the set in the morning, and she'd get makeup men to conceal he injury.

"The mere thought of you with another man drives me wild," he claimed."

That night was the first time he'd ever been violent with her, and she remembered hearing of Judy Carne's accusation that he was a "wife beater."

Before dawn, after much pleading from him, she decided to forgive him, blaming it on the pressure he was under. "He was fearful that his movie career would go down the tubes if *Stroker Ace* weren't a hit."

Cast and crew headed for Western North Carolina. After filming was wrapped in Charlotte, Burt went ahead of Loni to open his vacation home in the Blue Ridge Mountains. She drove up two days later.

On their first night together in the house, a "deep, dark mood" descended on him. As their voices of accusation against each other grew louder, he lunged toward her as if to strike her. She ducked under his arm, raced to the bathroom, and locked the door. He screamed and yelled for about a half hour, threatening to kick the door in.

Finally, he left, but returned about an hour later, sobbing and begging her to forgive him. After an hour, she decided to open the door, and he fell into her arms.

The tension between them was still high, although there were no more violent scenes. They parted, both agreeing to take a "breather" from each other. She flew back to Los Angeles, and he winged his way to Palm Beach and drove to Jupiter to see Big Burt and Fern.

With his parents, he poured out his frustration for having hooked up with Loni. He described one detail after another where he found her objectionable. He cited giving her a credit card with a $45,000 limit. "In one hour, she maxed it out. She buys everything in triplicate—dresses, jewelry, china, linen."

She'd told him, "Once I've been photographed in a dress, I can't wear it again, but I have to buy something new. After all, I have to dress like a star."

Before his return to Los Angeles, Burt told his parents that he was "giving Loni her walking papers and kicking her out of his home."

Fern told him, "You deserve someone better, Buddy. She's not the right gal for you."

Big Burt chimed in, "I don't like her. She's a painted woman, and that's the last thing you need in your life."

***

While maintaining an on-again, off-again affair with Loni, Burt turned forty-seven, a dangerous age for a male movie star, and one almost disastrous for an aging actress. His goal was to stay relevant in the 1980s when he would turn fifty.

Burt's career as a good ol' Southern boy/bootlegger fleeing the sheriff was coming to an end. He concluded that new and different stars were emerging in the 1980s, and he feared competition from Tom Cruise and Sylvester Stallone. Muscleman and Mr. Universe title holder, Arnold Schwarzenegger, was also emerging as a threat. He'd gone to see *The Jayne Mansfield Story* (1980), in which Loni had impersonated the tragic star. The Austrian bodybuilder had been cast as her husband, another muscleman and title holder, Mickey Hargitay, Jane's real-life husband. "I suspected Arnold asserted his conjugal rights to his on-screen wife—that is, my dear, Loni. It made me mad as hell just thinking about it." He pondered beating the truth out of her one night but rejected such a move.

He spent his first week back in Los Angeles alone except for one visitor, who arrived disguised under the cloak of darkness. He was relieved that the husband of Esther Williams, his former co-star Fernando Lamas, was out of town. That way, he and "Neptune's Daughter" could go for a nude midnight swim.

By the second week, he began to miss Loni and called her for an invitation to dinner in a quiet, dimly lit bistro in Beverly Hills. She not only accepted his invitation but another invitation as well, which involved spending the Christmas holiday outside Atlanta, from which they had recently retreated.

He told her he owned a lovely old home outside Atlanta, which he'd named "Tara," since it evoked Scarlett O'Hara's home in *Gone With the Wind*.

He suggested they extend invitations to Deidra and her boyfriend, Bobby, as well as to Jim Nabors and his lover in Hawaii, even to tobacco heiress Doris Duke, although it was doubtful she'd attend.

When Loni arrived at Tara, she found it furnished with props from *Sharky's Machine*. But it possessed not one of the accessories needed to run a household, including bed linens for six rooms, bathroom accessories, silverware, towels, cleaning supplies, and the other items needed to entertain holiday guests over an extended holiday getaway. Fortunately, Burt had given her his credit card, and she was seen in the stores of Atlanta, filling up shopping carts with a seemingly endless array of items.

That Christmas turned out to be one of the best and most memorable of her life, complete with lavish gifts, blazing fireplaces, a bounty of her home-cooked meals, and even the singing of Christmas carols.

Trouble began when they flew to Florida for New Year's. Big Burt and Fern were having a family reunion, inviting an array of relatives and a few family friends. For reasons never truly explained, Burt asked Deidra and Bobby not to attend, but to remain at Valhalla.

Deidra was so infuriated that she never forgave Burt for the slight, and she and Bobby flew back to Los Angeles.

When Burt returned to California, he tried to make amends by presenting Deidra with a Mercedes convertible. She rejected it, sending word to him that she preferred to drive the Datsun Loni had given her when she was graduated from high school.

***

In the wake of their filming of *Stroker Ace,* a lot of problems—physical, emotional, and financial—tainted the lives of both Burt and Loni.

During her second marriage, both she and Ross Bickell had turned over their financial affairs to a business manager. Many stars, such as Kirk Douglas and Doris Day, had made the same mistake in years gone by.

When she went to check up on her finances, including her salaried appearances on *WKRP,* she found that instead of having a million dollars in the bank, she owed a million dollars, mainly to the Internal Revenue Service, which was demanding payment.

Burt, meanwhile, had returned to his pill popping, and allowing his body to grow a bit flabby. He feasted on favorite foods that Fern used to prepare for him, especially Southern fried chicken with lots of creamy gravy.

Sometimes, he'd go a week and be all right, but then dark moods would return. He often claimed he was almost having a stroke, but Loni felt it was another one of his anxiety attacks. He would lock himself away for days before getting up to go see one of his "Dr. Feelgoods" for more prescriptions for pills.

In the early days of their relationship, he had been an ardent, passionate lover, but now he hardly touched her. She dressed in "trash lingerie" (her words) but even that didn't entice him.

When she complained about the lack of sex in their relationship, he shot back, "Who in hell do you think I am? Some fucking stud service at your beck and call?"

Their relationship deteriorated to such an extent that one morning when she got up, she was determined to move out. When he was away, she arranged for two men from a trucking service to pack up her possessions and return them to her own home.

Loni needed money, and show-biz gigs weren't coming her way. One afternoon, a friend from yesterday called. It was the actor Robert Hays, who had had two big film hits, *Airplane* (1980) and *Airplane II—the Sequel* (1982). He wanted to meet with her about co-starring with him in a feature film, *Fast Eddie.*

After talking over the movie, he noticed that she was wallowing in gloom over the personal disaster of her life and her ever-increasing financial woes. He asked her to spend the afternoon with him at Hollywood Park, enjoying horse races.

She agreed and descended with him on the park. There, she was seated with Hays on an upper balcony when she noticed a stirring in the bleachers right below her. Arriving were Cary Grant and his wife, Barbara Harris Grant [married 1981-1986], accompanied by Burt and Dinah Shore.

Hays spotted Burt and wanted to go down to shake his hand. He had just returned from Jupiter, where he had starred at Burt's dinner theater. Loni nixed the idea of accompanying Hays in his pursuit of the meet-and-greet.

Not once did Burt look up at her, which allowed her to observe the famous quartet. At one point, she saw Cary Grant and Burt heading off together for the men's room, where they were gone for a long time.

When not engaged in an animated talk with Grant, Burt had his arm around Dinah. They were laughing and talking like they had at the apex of their affair.

Dinah, of course, was much older now, but appeared slim, attractive, and in good physical condition. Loni assumed, rightly or wrongly, that Burt had resumed his affair with her.

Two weeks went by before she picked up the phone to discover Burt on the other end. He talked to her for an hour, turning on all "that macho charm" that had attracted her to him in the first place.

She seemed reluctant to rush back into his arms, and there were some recriminations about his seeing Dinah again. He made some accusations about Robert Hays, but the phone call ended well. They agreed to get together for dinner. To cap the following evening, he took her to bed and made love to her. By morning, the Burt/Loni love affair had resumed.

She had only one day to enjoy the good news before trouble descended. Hays called to tell her the producers had pulled the plug on *Fast Eddie.*

That very afternoon, she drove to her doctor's office for her annual gynecological exam, the results of which horrified her. He had discovered that she had six fibroid tumors, one a fast-growing one the size of a grapefruit. An operation was needed, a surgery that he reported might lead to a hysterectomy. She was alarmed at that, for, at the age of thirty-seven, she was still talking about having Burt's baby.

To see her through her surgery, Loni's mother, Maxine, flew in from Arizona. But, to her disappointment, Burt did not stay around but called from Florida to find out how the surgery had gone.

She reported that the tumors had been benign and had been successfully removed, and that the hysterectomy had not been needed. She told him, "Now we can have our baby."

"Burt told me he was planning to have a family with Loni," James Best said. "I didn't want him to hear it from me, but I felt marriage to her would be a disaster waiting to happen. They were not compatible, all of Burt's friends told him that, but he was so god damn stubborn and wouldn't listen."

After a brief recuperation at Jim Nabors' home in Hawaii, Loni returned to Los Angeles and then flew to join Burt in Jupiter, staying at his property, Valhalla.

She was back in his "loving arms," as they plotted their future together, although she was still burdened with financial problems.

She needed work, and her agent called with a gig for her to fly to San Francisco at once to begin work on a made-for-TV movie, *My Mother's Secret Life*. Burt's former girlfriend, Farrah Fawcett, suddenly dropped out of the cast. Loni had been hastily hired to replace her.

Telling Burt goodbye, Loni flew to San Francisco to begin work on this drama about a sixteen-year-old girl who discovers that her mother is a high-priced call girl.

The cast and crew were given a break to celebrate Thanksgiving, and she flew back to Los Angeles to spend the holiday with Burt.

Thanksgiving went smoothly, and she found her first night back with him "very romantic." Trouble began the next afternoon when she was showering, and he began to rumble through a chest of drawers in her bedroom. In it she had stuffed memoirs, letters, a diary, and other tokens of her past life without any attempt to go through the materials for an "edit."

Apparently, he uncovered what he thought was "gotcha evidence" that she was having affairs on the side, although this had not been the case.

She emerged from the bathroom with her hair dripping wet and a large bath towel covering her torso. Suddenly he started yelling at her, and with no evidence whatsoever, denouncing her as a "whore."

He grabbed her by her shoulders, digging his fingers into her soft flesh, causing bruises. In one fit of anger, he used all the power in his body to shove her against a wall. The impact was devastating to her physically, and she collapsed on the floor.

That night, without a reconciliation, she flew back to San Francisco to resume shooting.

Her body revealed several black-and-blue bruises, which the makeup men had to cover up since scenes of her as a call girl required that she wear a *négligée* and other flimsy lingerie.

An avid reader of novels, Burt read in *The New York Times* a review of Elmore Leonard's most recent novel, *Stick,* the name taken from the lead character, "Stick" Stickley, a former thief released from prison after serving a seven-year sentence for armed robbery.

"As soon as I read the book, I wanted to direct and star in the movie," Burt said. "I like Leonard's work, and I felt I knew its all-too-familiar backdrop of Florida and the life depicted there. I was Stick!"

The *Times* review convinced producers Jennings Lang and Robert Daley to raise the money to turn the novel into a movie. Leonard was a big winner when they offered him $350,000 to write the screenplay. He was known as a "hard-boiled" writer of gutsy fiction.

As the plot unfolds, Stick, a free man at last, is immediately lured back into crime. His former friend, Rainy (José Perez), entices him into an illegal drug pickup in the Florida Everglades.

Burt cast Charles Durning, his longtime friend, as the villain, "Chucky," attired him in the loudest, campiest wardrobe ever seen in the state of Florida.

His chief henchman is "Moke" (Dar Robinson), an albino killer who fatally shoots Rainy. He would have killed Stick, too, but he flees.

Along the way, he meets Barry (George Segal), a rich but eccentric playboy, in a part critics labeled "Increasingly insufferable."

The *Chicago Tribune* wrote, "Segal's career decline has matched that of Burt Reynolds in velocity. In the mid-1960s, he was appearing in such quality pictures as *Who's Afraid of Virginia Woolf?* A decade later, he's reduced to mugging his way through *Stick.*"

Segal told the press, "If you had asked me if I'd ever be in a Burt Reynolds movie, I would have said, 'No way!' As it turned out, he was a wonderful director."

For the role of Kyle, Stick's leading lady, Burt hired his longtime friend and rumored lover, Candice Bergen. Unconfirmed reports reached Loni in Hollywood that Burt had resumed his affair with her.

In the film, she played a business advisor to Barry (that is, playboy Segal). While doing so, she ignites "a flame in Stick's heart."

Burt, cast as a gritty ex-con in *Stick*, takes time out to make love to Candice Bergen.

Most critics found Bergen's role disappointing, often commenting on her "wooden acting." One critic wrote, "This is Bergen's most lifeless role to date, and that includes her TV work on *Hollywood Wives.*"

Filming began in Florida in October of 1983, but because of many delays, even reshooting half the film, *Stick* was not released until 1985.

When he finished his final cut and sat through it, Burt was pleased with the result. "We made a pretty good flicker," he told the producers.

But within a week, "those dudes in the Black Tower sabotaged *Stick.*" *[Burt was referring to the tower that housed the head office of Universal.]*

A call came in from Sid Steinberg, the CEO of MCA. "I hated that fucking piece of shit you turned out," he yelled at Burt. "It's so bad I've ordered the latter half of it rewritten and reshot."

Burt was summoned back to the studio and carried out his orders, although raging and fuming as he did so. "I gave up and didn't go to war with the jerks at Universal. I just went through the motion and reshot half the picture, the last I would direct for another four years. I kept my mouth shut and swallowed my pride. But I was devastated."

No one was more disappointed with the film that Leonard himself. "When I sat through this stinker, I did not recognize my screenplay. Reynolds even hired another writer to come up with a new draft, adding more action. As for our director and star, he was just playing Burt Reynolds, not my character of Stick."

Nearly all the reviews were negative. Even so, Burt's fading box office clout led to a strong opening week, which quickly faded, and *Stick,* playing to empty theaters, soon faded into oblivion. It had cost $22 million to make but had a box office gross of only $8.5 million. "Another flop for me," Burt lamented. "Pretty soon, I'll be labeled "The Flopper in Hollywood.""

Critic Gene Siskel wrote: "The guilty party of this disaster is Burt Reynolds, who continues to deliver one bad movie after another, this time serving as his own director, a case of the blind leading the blind. He's made it part burlesque, part conventional chase movie. His portrayal of Stick, a gritty ex-con out to avenge a friend's murder, is not much different from his good old boy persona in the *Cannonball Run* films."

***

Back in Hollywood, after having shot *My Mother's Secret Life,* Loni received a call from her friend, Karen Valentine. At one point in their talk, she told Loni that she was looking forward to flying down to Florida with her on the private plane Burt had chartered for his friends. "All of us are going down for the premiere of *The Man Who Loved Women.*" She was referring, of course, to the movie Burt had made with Julie Andrews.

Loni knew nothing of this flight or the premiere. After placing a number of calls to Florida, she reached Burt on the set where he was reshooting half the scenes of *Stick*.

"You know, honey," Loni said. "You forgot to extend an invitation to Florida for your guest of honor, namely me. How could you overlook the most important woman in your life, your beloved?"

"Oh, I've been meaning to phone but I've been too damn busy," he said. "I do have something to tell you, but I don't think you're gonna want to hear it."

"Is it about you and Candice Bergen getting serious?" she asked.

"Not Candice," he said. "Sally Field."

She heard the news as if "a bolt of electricity had shot through my body."

"Sally and I have been talking," he said. "Serious talks. We both agreed I'd made a lot of mistakes, but that I've grown since then. We've agreed to get back together. She's going to give me a second chance. We still love each other very much. I'm her man, and this time it's for keeps. So sorry, Loni. I know you don't deserve this."

Unable to speak, Loni put down the phone and didn't answer a series of repeated callbacks, letting her answering service take the messages.

It seemed only yesterday that he had proposed marriage to her. What was a jilted girl to do? She headed for the refrigerator where the champagne was chilling.

The tabloids had been tipped off, and the next day, stories of the reunion of Burt and Sally were splashed across their pages in supermarkets across the country.

Pictures of these "two lovebirds," as they were called in the press, sickened Loni.

It was at this crucial time that she received a call from actress Lynda Carter, who told her that Johnny Carson's production company wanted to cast both of them in co-starring roles

Burt and Loni co-starred in that colossal flop, *Stick*, but were still a hot item in the tabloids and gossip magazines. Then the news burst out: Burt and Sally Field were back together.

in a TV series, *Partners in Crime* (1984). The producer for NBC would be Leonard Stern, who had produced Rock Hudson's six-year run of *McMillan and Wife.*

Carter had been crowned Miss World United States in 1972 and was widely known for starring in the hit TV series, *Wonder Woman* (1975-1979) for CBS.

Partners in Crime would air from September to December in 1984 but was canceled after only 13 episodes. At first, Loni was overjoyed at the offer, knowing she would be well paid for her services, perhaps enough to get the IRS off her back.

Glad to be employed as an actress, she still felt hurt and vulnerable in her private life.

It was at this very time that she ran into an actor she called "Mr. X," preferring not to name him because of another romantic involvement he had.

They'd last seen each other eight years ago, and he had become a well-known actor on TV. Some speculated that the mystery man was actor Doug McClure, but that was never confirmed—it was, in fact denied.

Mr. X and Loni agreed to have dinner that night, which was followed by an evening of lovemaking. She later praised him for "awakening every nerve in my body. Suddenly, I felt wanted and desirable again as a woman."

But over morning coffee, reality set in. Her relationship with Burt had not officially ended, and Mr. X confessed that he was in love with another woman.

Based on their respect for his evolving romance with someone else, they agreed not to launch an affair. "Perhaps we'll meet some night at a party, and across a crowded room, we'll give each other a knowing smile to remember our night of unbridled passion," he said.

They parted that morning.

Finally, after repeated attempts, Burt got Loni on the phone. "I've been a fool," he claimed. "I've made a real stupid mistake. I realize now that it was

It's hard to make a living in TV Land, even when you're gorgeous!

Partners in Crime with *Wonder Woman* Lynda Carter (left) and Loni Anderson.

you, not Sally, I love. It's been you all along. Sally and I thought we could walk down memory lane, but the path was too rocky for both of us. We've called it quits for good. Your errant boy wants to return home and make it up to you."

She listened in astonishment at this sudden change of heart. He invited her to fly to Florida and spend New Year's with him at Jupiter.

"It'll be like a scene in my movie, *Starting Over*," he said. "But this would be real life, not make believe. What we need is a fresh start, forgetting past mistakes."

"You've put me through hell," she charged. "Now you expect me to come running back to your arms? I assume it was Sally who got cold feet. If she hadn't, and for all I know, you'd be with her right now. I've got to think about it. Don't call me. I'll call you if I change my mind."

Throughout the night, she let the answering service pick up his messages.

When morning came, she felt she could never trust Burt again. How could she possibly build a future with a man so unreliable?

***

City Heat (1984), an action crime-comedy, almost ended Burt Reynolds' movie career. It began as the brainchild of Blake Edwards, who wrote the original screenplay.

While living in Switzerland with his wife, Julie Andrews, he created the drama, which he called *Kansas City Blues*, a re-creation of that city as it looked in the prohibition year of 1933.

He gave it to his wife, Julie, to read, and she told him, "It's the very best thing you've ever written."

Both of them had filmed *The Man Who Loved Women* (1983) with Burt.

The plot revolved around two strong men, Police Lieutenant Speer, and the secondary role of Mike Murphy, who had been on the police force but was now a private eye.

These were two strong macho roles, and both Andrews and Edwards thought Burt would be ideal cast as Mike.

Burt had once told Edwards that he'd always wanted to make a movie with his friend, Clint Eastwood. When Warners expressed interest in the script, these two "macho honchos" were recommended as the leads.

Burt was a friend of both Eastwood and Edwards, so he set up a pre-production confab to discuss the picture. Edwards wanted to direct both actors in the film version of his screenplay.

The meeting between these two powerful guys lasted about thirty minutes," Burt said. "It was like Custer meeting Geronimo. Blake was champagne and caviar, Clint beer and pretzels. Blake was elegant and talked on and on, with Clint occasionally interjecting a Gary Cooper 'yup' or 'nope.'"

After Edwards left, Burt turned to Eastwood, knowing how unsuccessful the meeting had been. "This Edwards guy is from another planet, perhaps Jupiter," Eastwood said. "No, not that, but definitely Pluto."

"Does that mean you're out of the picture?" Burt asked.

"No, I'm being paid $4 million, and I'm doing it," Eastwood said. "Edwards is off the picture, but he's getting $3 million for his screenplay, so don't feel sorry for him."

In the next few weeks, the script was so greatly altered that Edwards demanded that his name be changed to "Sam O. Brown" in the film credits. Joseph C. Stinson was the co-writer of the revised screenplay.

Within a few days, Eastwood phoned Burt to tell him that Richard Benjamin had agreed to direct *City Heat*.

Critics were amused to watch Clint Eastwood and Burt engage in "The Battle of the Phallic Pistols," as if boasting about which of them had the larger penis.

City Heat, however, almost cost Burt his life.

Married to actress Paula Prentiss, Benjamin was an actor himself, having starred in such well-known movies as *Goodbye, Columbus* (1969), based on the Philip Roth novel, and also in *Catch-22* (1970), from the Joseph Heller bestseller. Benjamin's first time as a director was helming the comedy, *My Favorite Year* 1982), starring Peter O'Toole.

The two leading ladies had to be cast. Burt's character of Mike, a private eye, had a secretary, Addy. There was talk of using Julie Andrews as the secretary. Burt did not want her, feeling the role was "not suited for Mary Poppins." Later, both Eastwood and Burt agreed on Jane Alexander for the role. In the plot, she's attracted to both men.

Alexander, a Bostonian, was both an author and an actress. In 1993,

Bill Clinton would name her Chairwoman of the National Endowment for the Arts. Before working with Burt, she had starred in several films, including *All the President's Men* (1976) and *Kramer vs. Kramer* (1979). She'd also portrayed Eleanor Roosevelt in two TV productions in 1976 and '77.

As Mike, Burt also develops a romantic interest in a rich socialite, Caroline Howley. Burt wanted Madeline Kahn to play Caroline, the socialite. He had admired her talent when he'd worked with her on *At Long Last Love* (1975), even though the picture had flopped.

Cast as two over-the-top gang bosses were Tony Lo Bianco and Rip Torn, who had been Burt's roommate in New York during their early days as struggling actors.

Burt had admired Benjamin's talent as a director in *My Favorite Year* (1982), but found him "a sterile wimp in dealing with Clint. When he walked onto the set, Benjamin's backbone turned to Jello. Whatever Clint said, it was 'yes, sir, I'll do it.' Benjamin was almost petrified in Clint's presence."

The plot was convoluted, and included the theft by Mike (Burt) of certain underground financial records. But most of the attention in the script focused on the rivalry between the characters portrayed by Burt and Eastwood. In one of the most amusing scenes, they indulge in one-upmanship with their "phallic pistols," as if mocking their own macho mystiques. The hipper members of the audience got the point that their pistols were symbols of their penises.

The film opens with a fight scene in a coffee shop. Speer (Eastwood) and Mike (Burt) had once been friends until Mike left the force. Speer is sipping his coffee as two goons arrive to beat up Mike. Speer doesn't' intervene until one of the goons causes Speer to spill his coffee. Both goons are thrown through the front door, and Mike sarcastically thanks Speer for saving his life.

What Eastwood didn't know at the time was that Burt had been almost fatally struck down during the fight scene.

As Burt recalled, "In the beginning, the scene had been magical. The timing was perfect, and the jokes were working. All of us, even Clint, were having fun."

"An extra, cast as one of the goons, was supposed to pick up this breakaway chair made of balsa wood and smash it in my face," Burt said. "Instead, the jerk made a mistake that almost cost me my life and certainly derailed my movie career. He picked up a metal chair by mistake and slammed it into my face."

"He caught me flush on the jaw," Burt said. "Although I didn't realize how serious it was."

Instead of crying out and halting the shoot, Burt bravely carried on, even though he had a ferocious headache, and there was a ringing in his ears. He had flashes of blindness before his sight came back.

"On reflection, I should have gone immediately to the hospital," Burt said. "When I learned how serious my injury was, I should also have dropped out of the picture instead of seeing it through like the fool I was. I knew at some point I would have to have surgery, maybe a serious operation, but I postponed that horror."

He recalled his first night alone as "burning in Hell's fire." Heavy drugs put him to sleep for about three hours. "When I woke up, I knew I was in deep shit," he recalled. "I felt I was being stabbed by a butcher knife. I was dry heaving on an empty stomach, spitting up bile. My head was swimming. I was staggering about with motion sickness. Idiot that I was, I didn't summon help, but reported to work that day. Come hell or high water, I was determined to complete *City Heat*."

He turned to his painkillers, and also took Compazine pills to stave off nausea. "I had this constant feeling I wanted to vomit, even though there was nothing on my stomach. The next day, I had to drink milkshakes to keep from starving, as I could not chew. I looked pasty-faced. One of my plights was to stave off vertigo, as I was almost constantly dizzy and afraid I would fall."

"Every time I spoke, my face clicked," he said. "A real lopsided bite. I was in agony before the cameras but tried not to show it. I was overcome with fear that I was ruining Clint's movie, but never once did he confront me. He gave me some time off, even though it was increasing the budget by thousands of dollars. In fairness to him, he didn't know how serious my injury was."

By the time the film had wrapped, Burt's weight had dropped by thirty pounds, with more weight loss to come. "I looked gaunt, like a starving goat with its ribs showing. I had all the energy of a wounded animal."

Ten days into the shoot, Burt claimed, "I knew I was going to be roasted by the critics," he said. "I was impersonating Jack Lemmon in this weird flick where people were getting blown away. The public wanted to see Clint and me in *Boom Town* or see us in a modern movie."

[Burt was referring to the 1941 movie that had starred Clark Gable and Spencer Tracy as supportive pals seeing each other through various setbacks and disasters.]

"What movie-goers got was 'Dirty Harry vs. The Wimp,'" Burt said. "It's regrettable that our movie sucked. Hollywood biggies will see that Clint and I never work together again."

Upon its release, *City Heat*—made for a budget of $25 million—took in $38 at the box office. Warners distributed the film during the Christmas season of 1984.

As predicted, most of the reviews were negative. *Variety* claimed that "*City Heat* will hardly go down as one of the highlights of the careers of Clint Eastwood and Burt Reynolds. There remains a certain pleasure just in seeing them square off together in a good-natured arm-wrestling match of charisma and star voltage. Nevertheless, one might have hoped for material more exciting than this hokum."

Alexander Walker in the *Evening Standard* in England wrote, "Too often, *City Heat* is like watching a couple of cash registers upstaging each other."

In Chicago, Roger Ebert wrote, "How do travesties like *City Heat* get made?" In the same city, his rival, critic, Gene Siskel, claimed, "Except for two moments where Eastwood does an amusing parody of his angry stint, *City Heat* is devoid of humor, excitement, and amazingly, a comprehensible story."

Janet Maslin said, "The screenplay, which is part *Sting*, part *Sam Spade*, and part kitchen sink, is either a hopelessly convoluted genre piece or a much too subtle take-off on the same. A dramatic streamlining is badly needed."

Kevin Thomas in the *Los Angeles Times* wrote that "Eastwood and Reynolds were in fine fettle on their own and together, playing off each other beautifully. But the pleasure derived in watching them poke fun at themselves and each other in this period gangster comedy which is spoiled by a numbing display that is far too literal for such hokum."

The Washington Post criticized the "embarrassingly broad comedy and director Benjamin's smarmy fealty toward his leads. Inside this star vehicle, there's a real movie screaming for air."

***

As Burt's weight continued to drop, his body became that of a skeleton, and he looked increasingly gaunt. Around this time, the AIDS epidemic descended on the world.

The gossip began in Hollywood and quickly spread, even appearing in tabloid headlines:

BURT REYNOLDS HAS AIDS.

CHAPTER FIFTEEN

ADDICTION & WITHDRAWAL

Enduring the Agonies of the Damned,
Burt Becomes a Pill-Popping Addict
to Ease the Constant Pain of a Broken Jawbone.

RUMORS

Suffering a Daunting Weight Loss,
"Half of America Thought I was Gay,
and the Other Half Claimed I Had AIDS"

THE PARADE PASSES BY

Millions of His Fans Move On to Other Screen Heroes.

GRIT & RESILIENCY

Burt Comes Back Again, and Again...and Again, and Again.

LONI & BURT: MAKING IT LEGAL

In a Wedding Delayed for Years,
Burt & Loni Anderson Finally Wed
After Some Pre-Nup Squabbles

QUENTIN

Unable to Conceive, the Newlyweds Adopt
"My Future Little Linebacker,"
Quentin Reynolds.
"I'll be the Father to Him My Father Never Was to Me,"
Burt Vows.

"After limping through *City Heat* with Clint Eastwood, I felt like an animal who'd been shot by a hunter in the forest but wasn't quite dead yet," Burt said.

"Back at Carolwood *[Burt's estate in Beverly Hills]*, I locked myself in my bedroom and pulled all the draperies because daylight made me feel like needles were penetrating my eyeballs. I had to take out my phone because I could not tolerate noise. If I stood up, my head started spinning like I was some runaway merry-go-round."

"If I had known back then that I would suffer this incredible pain for the next two years, I think I would have chosen to end it all on my first day back," he said. "But I felt I could find the right doctor who would ease my pain and get my jawbone adjusted again."

"Then I did something stupid," he said. "I flew on an airplane to Fort Lauderdale for the opening of Burt and Jack's, a restaurant in which I had heavily invested. The altitude of the flight caused my head to explode. Once on the ground, I headed to Valhalla, where I collapsed and summoned a doctor."

The doctor who examined Burt's facial structure was aware of his broken jaw, but he didn't really seem to know what to do other than recommend something new on the market: the drug Halcion. This central nervous system depressant tranquilizer had gone on sale in the United States in 1982. It was usually used for short-term treatment of acute insomnia, which was plaguing Burt.

"I began a love affair with these little blue pills, and on days of my greatest pain, I took as many as twenty. I was in love with Halcion. Call it an addiction if you will."

"For the next weeks, even months, I went from doctor to doctor. At least I found out what in hell was the matter with me."

He had been diagnosed with a temporomanidibular disorder, or TMD, or TMJ disorder. TMD is a hinge that links one's jaw to the temporal bones of one's skull, which are in front of each ear. It allows a person to move his or her jaw up and down and side to side, so one can talk, chew, or yawn. The doctor explained Burt's broken jaw affected his sense of balance and sensory perception, a condition like being perpetually seasick and nauseous and in constant pain from inner ear damage.

As if all that weren't difficult enough to learn, he was also made aware of news that was even worse: TMD affected thousands upon thousands of people. "So I was not alone in my suffering," Burt said. "But here's the catch. There is no known cure. After suffering year after year, many victims of TMD commit suicide."

"I began to visit doctor after doctor, as one specialist after another was recommended to me," Burt said. "One doctor suggested experimental surgery such as implanting a metal hinge on my jaws. I was told it might not work. In that case, the hinge could not be removed."

"Fuck that!" he told the doctor before storming out of his office.

"I couldn't chew food and survived on liquids," Burt said. "I tried to bite into something solid but my bite was out of alignment, so much so it crushed my Eustachian tube. Sometimes known as the auditory tube, it links the nasopharynx to the middle ear."

"My ears exploded if I traveled by plane, so I took the train or else motored somewhere, even though any motion made me nauseous."

In search of a cure, he traveled from city to city, from Chicago to New York, from Philadelphia to Miami, all to no avail.

He'd heard about this specialty dentist in Beverly Hills and went to see him. "I had a great set of bottom dentures. He shaved them off, every one of them. I was knocked out cold while he did that. When I came to and saw what he'd done, I exploded 'What the Hell!' I'll go through the rest of my life playing Walter Brennan roles. 'You've really fixed me good, you bastard,'" he shouted at the dentist.

He stormed out of the office and found another dentist who capped all his lower teeth.

"It served a cosmetic purpose, but I still couldn't chew anything, not even a water-

Burt and his backers assumed that diners would be enchanted by PoFolks and its homespun charm. They weren't.

melon," he said.

"I assumed I would never work again," Burt said. "I got lured into backing a new set of restaurants in the South called "PoFolks."

The chain specialized in familiar good ol' home-cooked Southern favorites: collard greens cooked in bacon fat, hush puppies, catfish, grits and gravy, fried chicken, pinto beans, pork chops, pecan pie, and overly sugared iced tea.

The franchise opened its first restaurant in Nashville, expanding to Arkansas and later Texas. "With no movie roles coming in, I thought I had it made for life, enough money to retire on. But, alas, PoFolks went belly up, mired in million of dollars of debt and endless lawsuits. Thank God for those Halcion pills, which kept me floating on a pink cloud. When I could get out of bed, I stumbled around like a zombie."

***

Loni Anderson had not seen Burt since their estrangement at Thanksgiving, 1983. After that, they had a few casual chats on the phone, nothing else. Then, in February of 1984, he placed an urgent call to her, pleading with her to come at once to Carolwood. Within the hour, she pulled up at his door.

His physical appearance shocked her, as he'd lost at least fifty pounds, perhaps a lot more. He was shirtless, and his ribs were showing.

He explained his condition of a broken jawbone and all its side effects left over from his fight scene in *City Heat*. He told her that his pain had not let up night or day, and he could sleep for just minutes at a time before waking up in agony.

As an hour or so went by, he grew more and more agitated after pleading endlessly for her to move back into Carolwood. At one point, he broke down and sobbed uncontrollably. When he still could not get a commitment from her, he went over to a drawer and removed a gun. He pointed it at his temple, threatening to commit suicide if she did not return to him.

On looking back, he claimed to understand completely why she did not want to commit to him at first. "I desperately needed to put some flesh back on my rapidly shrinking body. No more nude centerfolds for me. I'd also gone through my money so that was no longer an allure. No one wanted to hire me in Hollywood. I'm sure a producer could not get an insurance policy on me. I looked like a pile of shit. Half of America thought I was gay, the other half that I was dying of AIDS."

Loni was in a dilemma, not knowing how to handle "Mr. Skin and Bones." Before he did something drastic and really harmed himself, she decided to come back into his life.

He suggested a kind of honeymoon in Acapulco, where MGM executives had given him access to a beautiful vacation home owned by the studio. Many of its biggest stars had rested there during the Golden Age of Hollywood.

Burt and Loni flew there aboard MGM's private jet, where they were met by a chauffeur and a limousine. Las Brisas lived up to its glamourous reputation and was staffed with servants.

After four days, he grew restless and wanted company, calling his close friend Ricardo Montalban and his beautiful wife, Georgiana, inviting them to fly down. Some admirers such as Orson Welles, former husband of screen goddess Rita Hayworth, considered Georgiana "the most beautiful woman in Hollywood." She was the sister of screen legend Loretta Young.

In spite of his dire condition, Burt overruled Loni and decided to drive their rented Jeep to the airport to pick up his guests.

She was afraid that in his condition, he would wreck the Jeep—and he almost did. When Georgiana and her husband finally arrived at Las Brisas, she ran into the house to confront Loni: "I will never ride in the same car with your madman boyfriend. Burt almost killed us eight times and nearly slaughtered at least two dozen Mexicans."

Burt had promised beach picnics, aerial balloon rides over the bay, fishing from aboard a yacht, and motor tours of the environs, but he was far too weak for that. Throughout their visit, all he could manage was to sit with them beside the pool as Ricardo swam laps.

Before flying back to Los Angeles, Georgiana gave Loni some advice: "Ricardo and I love Burt dearly, but he doesn't need a girlfriend or wife. What he needs is an around-the-clock nurse."

Three nights later, Burt seemed in a better mood. After their departure, he'd been in one of his bad moods and stayed in a darkened room, complaining of any outside noise. But on that night, he seemed more upbeat than he'd been in days, as if returning to the man she had once known.

Late that afternoon, she noticed a plate of fudge brownies left in the refrigerator, and she assumed that the Mexican cook had left them for the evening they'd planned in front of the television set.

Ricardo Montalban and his wife, Georgiana Young, in 1950.

553

On the sofa, he became amorous for the first time since she'd come back into his life. Suddenly, she found him kissing her passionately and exploring her neck with his tongue. That led to lovemaking. She claimed that "the earth moved. I was ecstatic."

Later that evening, it was time for those fudge brownies in the fridge. Each of them ate two brownies with glasses of milk.

Within a half-hour, her head was spinning. Whereas that was commonplace for Burt, it was very rare for her. "You're drugged," he told her. "Those are Alice B. Toklas brownies."

Literature's most famous lesbian lovers, Gertrude Stein (left) and Alice B. Toklas, who entertained Ernest Hemingway with her marijuana-laced brownies.

[He had to explain who Toklas was. The lesbian lover of the literary giant, Gertrude Stein, with whom she lived in Paris in the 1920s and 30s, she had published a recipe for marijuana brownies. In the 1960s, it became legendary in America as thousands of people baked and consumed them.]

That night marked Loni's first consumption of what she called "the devil weed." She was high for the rest of the night, eventually passing out on the bed beside Burt. She slept soundly and didn't awaken until late the next morning. She turned over to see him still asleep beside her. On the nightstand was the empty plate that had held the brownies Apparently, he'd consumed all of them before falling into a deep, coma-like sleep.

She kept checking on him throughout the day. She determined that his breathing was regular. She tried, at various times, to wake him up, but it was of no use. Finally, after a deep sleep of thirty-six hours, he woke up and headed for the shower.

Lynda (Carter) and Loni (Anderson) as glam detectives in *Partners in Crime*.

Back at Carolwood, his condition worsened again, and so did his excessive use of painkillers. He was drugged day and night.

Loni had to fly with Linda Carter to San Francisco to shoot episodes of their ill-fated TV drama, *Partners in Crime*. On some days, he phoned her eight times, pleading, "Don't ever leave me. Please, don't let me end up like Elvis."

She flew back every weekend to spend time with him, but his condition seemed to be worsening.

There was more bad news on the way. When she arrived back in Carolwood, Burt greeted her with Valium, suggesting she take some pills before he told her the news.

"Are you going back to Sally Field?" she asked.

"No, not that, but your mother is dying of cancer. The doctor has given her less than six weeks to live."

Loni rushed to her mother, Maxine, and tried to save her life, arranging for whatever treatment was available at that time. Maxine seemed to rally on some days, but the medical forecast was gloomy.

Loni prevailed on Burt to pull himself together and pay a final *adieu* to Maxine. The visit went well, and he laughed and joked for a while with her before both of them grew faint and tired.

Loni asked Burt to remain behind for a few minutes so that she could talk privately to her mother. During their conversation, Maxine warned, "Don't marry that man. He thinks only of himself, not you. If you marry him, you'll regret it for the rest of your life."

On the way back, Loni predicted, "Maxine has only days to live."

"Well," he answered, turning to her in anger. "I'm dying, too. What about me? I need some loving care, too."

On March 1, 1985, Maxine died at the age of sixty.

Burt skipped her funeral in Minnesota and flew to Jupiter to spend some time with Big Burt and Fern. He told Loni, "My own parents are getting old, too. They'll soon be dying."

To recover from her mother's death, Loni and her daughter, Deidra, flew to Florida even though Deidra had never liked Burt.

When Loni arrived at Valhalla, she found two paramedics hovering over Burt. He seemed to have lapsed into a coma and could not be revived.

She ordered his assistant, Elaine Hall, to call on ambulance at once. "Burt would never want that, the publicity, you know," Hall claimed.

"Fuck the publicity!" Loni said. "Can't you see, he's dying? At least summon a doctor!"

When a doctor arrived shortly thereafter and examined Burt, he ordered Loni to "Get him to the hospital at once—or else he'll be dead within the hour."

At the hospital in Jupiter, he was examined by a specialist, who demanded to know the list of drugs Burt had ingested. Loni named them.

His drug of choice was Percodan, a widely used painkiller. He also took daily dosages of Prochlorperazine, which was said to treat nausea, schizophrenia, migraines, and anxiety.

"I see you've registered him under the name of Ralph Jeffries," the doctor said. "He bears an amazing resemblance to the movie star, Burt Reynolds. As for you, Mrs. Jeffries, you look very much like that blonde star of *WKRP in Cincinnati* on TV. You know, Loni Anderson."

"Everybody tells me that," she said.

"He looks like he was a bit beefy at one time," the doctor said. "Now he weighs 125 pounds and resembles one of the Jews released from a Nazi concentration camp in the spring of 1945."

That night, a false bulletin went out over the wires: BURT REYNOLDS IS DEAD.

Within fifteen minutes, the bulletin was withdrawn and didn't appear in any of the morning papers.

Two days later, when Burt came out of his coma, the doctor suggested that he commit himself to a rehab center at once.

"I can't do that," Burt protested. "The press, the bad publicity, the fake news will have me seeking treatment for AIDS."

"To hell with that," the doctor said. "You've got to give up your dependency on drugs—or you'll die. Your choice."

Back at Valhalla, Burt went into withdrawal, suffering "days and nights in hell," as he took doses of phenobarbital.

When he had recovered from the worst of his withdrawal, he was weak and wobbly on his legs. He didn't want to be photographed passing through an airport, so he chartered a private plane for the cross-country trip back to California.

For a week after his return to Carolwood, Loni hired male nurses to administer around-the-clock care. "He looked like the skin had been peeled from his bones."

She had to fly to Canada to film a made-for-TV movie, and when she returned, she found him in better condition.

That marked a shift in their relationship, as he had begun to recover. They did virtually nothing but lounge around, watching his favorite black-and-white classics on TV, especially movies that starred Cary Grant. He often discussed his life, including his football days and his doomed affairs with Judy Carne, Dinah Shore, and Sally Field.

She said, "I had fallen out of love with him, but now found myself falling in love with him all over again. He dragged me through an emotional swamp but seemed to be emerging from it."

A tabloid published an article from a psychic, and she showed it to him. It seemed that in a former life, she had been his mother, giving birth to her son, "a demon seed."

"During all my time with Burt," Loni said, "he was drugged. I didn't get to know who Burt Reynolds was. Now I wanted a chance to find out who the real man was."

***

Like a California wildfire, rumors spread across the country that Burt had AIDS. His rapid weight loss had led to that gossip. "People I thought were my friends were no longer home when I called. When you're a box office champ, so-called friends arrive in herds. But when you're down and out, they also flee in droves."

"Some of the people I had considered as friends ran like rats fleeing the *Titanic*," Burt said. "I'll never forgive those traitors. Fortunately, a few friends remained, and I'll be forever grateful to them."

He cited Dinah Shore as chief among them, but not Sally Field. She angered him when she was interviewed by *Playboy*. The reporter asked her, "Does Burt Reynolds have AIDS?"

"I don't know," Sally said. "There's always been something going on around Burt."

When her remarks were published, Burt exploded in anger. "Instead of defending me and dismissing the rumors as ridiculous, she left it hanging. That only increased speculation about me. I don't think I can ever forgive her for that."

Fortunately, I found out who were my good and true friends, and they stood by me, for which I will be eternally grateful."

He cited Charles Nelson Reilly, Hal Needham, Clint Eastwood, Jon Voight, Charles Durning, Jim Nabors, James Best, Dom DeLuise, Ricardo Montalban, Esther Williams, Angie Dickinson, and "500 stuntmen."

He was particularly impressed with the loyalty of two newly minted friends, Ann-Margret and her husband and business manager, Roger Smith. She and her husband had met him on a few previous occasions, beginning with *The Dinah Shore Show* and had spoken to him at various events. But it was one night at a dinner to which they invited him in Toronto (they happened to be staying in the same hotel) that they bonded.

The trio found they shared a mutual love of sports, and in a few days, he had chartered a jet and flown them to watch Florida State University, his alma mater, play a game.

Burt had nothing but praise for the sexy Swedish actress, singer, and dancer, who was hailed as "the female Elvis Presley." She'd become romantically involved with Elvis while making *Viva Las Vegas* in 1964 but had married the actor Roger Smith in 1967.

Burt also like Ann-Margret's sultry, vibrant contralto voice, and had long admired her screen presence in such films as *Bye Bye Birdie* (1963); *The Cincinnati Kid* (1967); and *Carnal Knowledge* (1967).

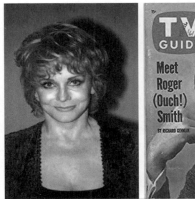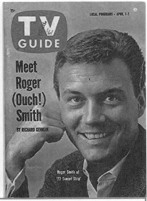

In an troubled period when many of other acquaintances abandoned or shunned him, Ann-Margret (shown left in 1997) and her husband, Roger Smith (shown during his 77 *Sunset Strip* heyday on the cover of *TV Guide*) remained steadfast, available, cheerful, supportive, and loyal.

"For such a hot tamale, she had been born in the land of lumberjacks and farmers north of the Arctic Circle," Burt said. "What a wonderful woman she was, and such a good friend who stood by me when I was in my worst days."

After they were collectively reassembled in California, Burt, Ann-Margret, and Roger began assembling on weekends to watch televised weekend football games at Carolwood, where Burt always had a lavish dinner prepared for them.

When Ann-Margret learned of his drug dependencies, she stepped in and tried to help him. She was sympathetic became of her own problems with alcohol.

"Call me every time you want to take another pill," she told him.

"I'll be calling you a lot," he answered.

She later wrote, "Burt is a real guy, one hundred percent macho on the outside, but a pussycat with a big heart inside. I saw that closely guarded sensitive side surface. I pushed him to take control of his life, to seek professional help—and I'm glad I did."

Elizabeth Taylor also stood by Burt, as she had her dear friend Rock Hudson, her co-star in *Giant* (1956). He had contracted AIDS, which would lead to his death in 1985.

Taylor phoned Burt and asked if he'd appear at a fund-raiser for AIDS victims. "Of course I will," he told her.

The big event on September 19, 1985 was opened by Burt Lancaster, who read a letter written by Hudson weeks before his death.

Then Burt came out and read a letter from President Ronald Reagan, who so far during his administration had not dared to even mention AIDS.

Perhaps at the urging of First Lady, Nancy, he had begun to realize that another Black Plague had descended on the world.

During his reading of the Reagan letter, Burt was booed. "I knew they weren't booing me, but Reagan himself because of his reluctance to get on the fund-raising bandwagon for AIDS sufferers."

In the middle of the AIDS crisis and in the wake of Hudson's death, it was assumed that Burt was the latest male movie star to succumb to the deadly disease. His weight loss was not attributed to his broken jawbone, but to AIDS. In the mid-1980s, Burt was accused of being a closeted homosexual, since thousands of people thought straights were immune.

"To complicate matters, some lookalike was impersonating me, going to clinics and registering under my name."

In desperation, Burt called Nancy Reagan at the White House, getting her secretary. Within the hour, the First Lady returned his call, since they had been friends.

He explained to her what this imposter was doing, and she promised to get back to him after she ordered an investigation. Four days later she phoned him and told him that some man, suffering from AIDS, was, indeed, impersonating him. The stunt was believed to have been instigated by a right wing senator, who was advocating that all gay men in America be rounded up and put into isolation, almost like a concentration camp.

"To get publicity, this group needs another high-profile movie star to get AIDS like poor Rock," Nancy said. "I don't think we can stop their stunt, but at least we know what they're trying to pull. Hang in there and get well and start putting on some weight again. You can defeat these goons by getting well and healthy."

One night at Carolwood, Burt began to hyperventilate, as he so often did. But this time the paper bag trick did not work, and in desperation, he called for an ambulance. After a long delay, it finally passed his house three times. The two attendants, as it turned out, did not want to pick him up since they had heard all the AIDS rumors. Finally,

"Hellcat" Ronald Reagan and Nurse Nancy co-starred in a jingoistic wartime potboiler, *Hellcats of the Navy* in 1957.

She confessed to Burt that she had to "drag Ronnie kicking and screaming to the podium to even address the AIDS issue during his presidency." He shied away from it because of its links to gay men.

he hobbled to the street and had to hail them down.

At the hospital, he was put in a ward devoted to AIDS victims, and was truly exposed to their plight, which made him forever sympathetic to victims of the disease.

"Being in the hospital ward, and being with these victims, I think I reached the bottom pit of my life," Burt said.

Because Loni had been romantically linked to Burt, it was commonly assumed that she might be contagious. She came in one afternoon to confront Burt at Carolwood. Her hairdresser had refused to do her hair, and her manicurist had refused to touch her nails.

Then, at least two dozen homosexuals approached the gay tabloids distributed along Hollywood Boulevard, each giving a detailed account stating that Burt had paid them to have sex with him. One underground paper ran reports that he had long been known for picking up hustlers along Santa Monica Boulevard.

There was even a published report that Burt and Rock Hudson had been lovers, and that Burt had contracted the disease from this fallen star. Another underground paper published a report on Burt, alleging that he had had a long-term affair with his friend and frequent co-star James Best. It was also alleged that Burt and Jan-Michael Vincent had been lovers.

Although Burt kept protesting, "I'm not gay," one tabloid reported, "The lady doth protest too much."

"Time and time again, I told the world my weight loss was because of that broken jawbone. Except for a few dear friends, no one wanted to believe me. Then word got out: If I were ever again cast in a movie with a kissing scene, no actress in Hollywood would ever kiss me on camera. Even dentists started refusing to take me as a patient—all except one."

Burt described the dentist, Gus Schwab of San Diego, as "a cranky old coot who charges thousands and thousands of dollars. But he came through for me, realigning every tooth in my mouth. I began to get better and in time, could chew again."

Johnny Carson had phoned several times, inviting Burt to appear on *The Tonight Show* to dispel rumors that he had AIDS. At first, Burt was reluctant to appear because of his gaunt appearance and weight loss.

Finally, he went on the show, projecting as much health and vitality as he could. He won over the audience with his humor and had them applauding.

"Johnny saved my career," Burt recalled. "Film offers had dried up, but then some movie roles came in. Let's face it: None of the roles was *Deliverance,* but I was glad to get work because I needed the money...and how!"

"If I really had AIDS, I would have come clean with the public," Burt said. "Like Magic Johnson, I would have used my affliction to educate the public and fund-raise for victims of the disease."

"Some idiots believed that only gay men got the disease. Any fool should have realized that if you had a blood stream, you were a target for AIDS, especially if you fucked around. In a few years, even the idiots got the message, as millions of men, women, and even children got AIDS. Some poor babies were born with it because their mothers had it."

***

Back at work making movies again, Burt made three action films in 1986 and 1987. "They weren't great in any way, but I took the roles to combat those rumors that I had AIDS. I wanted to appear on the screen again and show the world I was still in there kicking."

During his long confinement in his bedroom, Burt had continued to read novels, looking for a property whose film adaptation might be suitable for him to star in. He'd read William Goldman's 1985 novel, *Heat*, and thought it could be adapted into an award-winning film.

He saw himself as the male lead, an ex-mercenary soldier of fortune, Nick ("Mex") Escalante, working as a bodyguard in Las Vegas. The character was described as "so tough that hunks twice his size turn to jelly at his frown, yet so lovable that little girls blow kisses at him."

A budget of $17 million was raised with distribution arranged through New Century Vista. Even though Burt's box office clout was but a memory, the producers still offered him $2 million for his star role.

Burt was delighted when Robert Altman agreed to direct it. But, to Burt's dismay, Altman dropped out after only one day on the set.

As a replacement for Altman, Dick Richards came in as a director. He and Burt immediately tangled and then continued with one argument after another. Their feud got so intense that at one point, Burt struck him.

The director later filed a $25 million lawsuit against Burt. The case was settled when a judge ordered Burt to pay half a million in damages. He later lamented, "I spent $500,000 for that punch. If I hit a guy, it's certain that he'll later run a studio or become a bigtime director. Just my luck!"

Another director, Jerry Jameson, was brought in, but when that didn't work out, the producers brought back Richards, despite the legal hostilities between Burt and him. Eventually, Richards fell from a camera crane and wound up in a hospital. Before the film was wrapped, a total of six directors had become involved, usually unsuccessfully or disastrously, with some aspect of its production.

Karen Young, cast as Holly, was Burt's leading lady. She plays a prostitute who is sadistically beaten up while on a date with Vegas high roller and mob boss, Danny Del-Marco (Neil Barry). Nick sets out to revenge her beating, which leads to a violent confrontation. Holly arrives at DeMarco's suite, finding him tied up. She cuts off the tip of his penis, mocking it as being so small.

Peter MacNichol had the third lead as Cyrus Kinnick, a rich gambler who hires Nick to teach him how to be tough. Burt, as Nick, goes after the villains, managing to get them "crushed, electrified, speared, fried, and parboiled in slow motion."

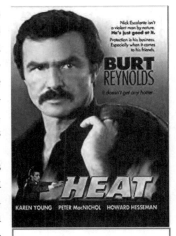

"At least I wasn't the poor bastard who got the tip of his penis clipped off," Burt said. "The villain of *Heat* had to suffer through that."

The reviews were disastrous. *Heat* generated no heat at the box office, taking in only $2.5 million. Burt's reaction? "At least I didn't have Sheriff Jackie Gleason chasing my car across the South."

Walter Goodman of *The New York Times* wrote, "SO, you think Charles Bronson is the most lethal object on two feet? That's because you haven't seen *Heat*."

***

Burt reinforced his self-image as "The Comeback Kid" after arranging a deal for which he was paid "a cool $3 million" to star in an action-thriller entitled *Malone* (1987). Christopher Frank wrote the hackneyed screenplay based on William Wingate's novel, *Shotgun*.

Harley Cokeliss was hired to direct this poorly paced narrative and to deal with the always temperamental Burt. He told Burt, "If you want to plow your fist into my face, go ahead. I could use the extra half million in a lawsuit your last director got."

According to Burt, "I signed to make *Malone*, shot in Henley, Canada, in 1986, because I thought there was a chance that it might be about more than a guy running away from his past. I was cast as a former CIA hitman who flees from his former job and ends in a small town after his car breaks down."

There, he meets and befriends a kindly mechanic, Paul Barlow (Scott Wilson), and his daughter, Jo Barlow (Cynthia Gibb).   This father and daughter are being menaced by a scary right-wing fanatic portrayed by Cliff Robertson, who gives a smarmy performance as a rich, empire-building ultra-nationalist who buys up local property, forcing the owners to sell…or else.

Cast as Jamie, top model Lauren Hutton had co-starred with Burt before, and perhaps done more than co-star. She played Malone's "playful playmate," who incidentally, has been instructed to kill him.

"I'm not doing Clint Eastwood in *Pale Rider,*" Burt said. "There's a little bit of Stallone in *First Blood,* but I'm not damaged goods like Sly was in *Rambo.*"

"At various points in time, both Gerard Depardieu and Christopher Lambert were to star as *Malone,*" Burt said. "I wonder how this guy got rewritten into me. There's something in all of us that responds to the sight of an avenging angel destroying bullies and the forces of evil."

Filmed on a budget of $10 million, *Malone* took in only $2.5 million at the box office.

In *The New York Times,* Walter Goodman said, "What is there about a Burt Reynolds movie these days that gives you the feeling of having seen it before, once or a dozen times? Maybe it's the role into which Reynolds seems to have settled, a master of mayhem facing a midlife crisis. *WHACK! CRACK! GRUNT! GROAN!* It's just a question of the ways devised for Malone to kill."

***

Burt's third flop in a row was *Rent-a-Cop* (1987), an American comedy/crime thriller that reunited him with Liza Minnelli, his friend and former co-star from *Lucky Lady,* one of their most dismal commercial failures.

"I did *Rent-a-Cop* because my bank account was running on empty," Burt said. "I was becoming an endangered species: An old actor. When you're the box office champ of the world, you can be artistic, but an aging Romeo like me has to be realistic."

Although Liza had maintained her friendship with Burt, she had not made a movie in five years. Not having seen her in a while, he found her "looking youthful, gamin-like, wide-eyed, and lovable." She emerged

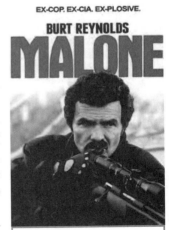

EX-COP. EX-CIA. EX-PLOSIVE.

BURT REYNOLDS

MALONE

Formulaic? Even for Burt's most ardent fans, his later string of action-adventure movies began to resemble each other.

from the Betty Ford Clinic in 1984 after going through rehab for drug abuse. "Liza and I had something in common," Burt said.

"The producers and the director, Jerry London—this was his first feature film—made me an offer I could not refuse, a cool three million bucks, which I badly needed."

In the screenplay by Michael Blodgett and Dennis Shryack, Burt was cast as Tony Church, a disgraced and "defrocked" Chicago police detective now working as a security guard. Liza was cast as Della Roberts, a high-priced hooker, who has witnessed a killing and is in need of protection.

"The story of the cop and the prostitute was familiar fare to movie-goers," Burt said. "The story is always that the cop hates the girl, and the hooker hates the cop, but they need each other for whatever reason. Of course, it's in the script and all too predictable: They fall in love."

The third lead, the role of "Dancer," a sadistic killer, went to James Remar. Burt was instrumental in getting two of his friends, Robby Benson and Bernie Casey, cast in the film as well. The singer, Dionne Warwick, had a cameo appearance as "Beth."

On her first day back with Burt, Liza told him, "Everybody I know, including not only myself, but my mother, even you, gets into trouble from time to time. When you dole out too much credit to public opinion, when your sense of self grows blurry, when you feel that what people think of is more important than how you feel, that's when it's dangerous and that's an easy thing to happen...to me, to a housewife. That's when you worry about getting enough sleep, so you take a sleeping pill. When other people think you're overweight, you take a diet pill. And then you wind up in rehab."

"Been there, done that," Burt said. "You're preaching to the choir."

The director felt the sexual chemistry between Liza and Burt was "explosive."

In his second movie with Liza Minnelli, Burt played a cop and Judy's daughter played a prostitute. She rents him, not for stud services, but to protect her from killers out to do her in.

The location shooting for *Rent-a-Cop* was in Chicago, but for the studio shots, London flew cast and crew to Rome. Liza found the Eternal City cold and gray in December, and she took a lot of Vitamin C to stave off the flu.

Loni Anderson had never been to Rome, so she flew there, telling London, "I spent $8,000 of my own money to get here."

She found Burt in a foul mood, and he seemed to pick arguments with her. Once, when she'd either misplaced or lost a pair of expensive gloves she'd purchased on the via Sistina, he attacked her in front of cast and crew. A cameraman claimed, "He was shoving and pushing Loni around. I took a chance and came up to him, telling him, 'Get a grip, man!' It's a wonder he didn't knock my face in.'"

Loni flew back early but joined Burt in Florida for Christmas. He also invited Liza and her husband, Mark Gero *[they were married from 1979–1992]*, along with Lorna Luft *[Burt's former girlfriend]* and her husband, Jake Hooker.

Burt was in a foul mood all during Christmas, and Liza took note. "I love Burt like a brother," she told Loni, "But I don't know how you take the abuse."

"There was nothing merry about that Christmas," Loni said.

For the New Year, Loni and Burt flew to Venice for "a gathering of the world's millionaires," at which he gave a short but witty speech.

They were booked into the deluxe Cipriani in a suite once occupied by Ernest Hemingway.

Their party was joined by Charles Nelson Reilly, who came alone but met up with a handsome young gondolier. Joining the party was Vic Prinzi, one of Burt's oldest and dearest friends, dating from his college days, along with Prinzi's wife, Barbara.

Getting ready for a gala night on the town, Loni emerged from a shower in the bathroom with one of the hotel's big towels wrapped around her. Burt turned on her, claiming she had paraded in front of the windows to attract the attention of tourists and locals on boats traversing the Grand Canal.

"You look disgusting," he shouted at her. "From now on, I want you to appear dressed. If getting ready to go to bed, wear a nightgown. I don't want to see you completely naked ever again. A nude woman has no mystery, no sex appeal."

Aboard the *Orient Express* leaving Venice for Paris before their return to America, Loni was fully clothed.

London had high hopes for *Rent-a-Cop*, claiming "Burt has delivered his best performance in several years. I think our film will be a big, big hit.

Audiences will emerge from the theater with a warm glow that Burt has given them."

That prediction was too optimistic, since very few audiences saw the film. It generated only $295,000 at the box office, an astounding financial disaster for its backers, who lamented giving Burt his $3 million salary.

Reviews were negative, Roger Ebert writing, "*Rent-a-Cop* is a collision between a relationship and a cliché—and the cliché wins. The cop and the hooker yarn is strictly off the assembly line and contains few surprises. There is no reason to see it."

Walter Goodman in *The New York Times* called the plot "sloppy and the direction efficient and uninspired."

Both Burt and Liza were nominated for the 1988 Golden Raspberry Awards for the Worst Actor and Worst Actress of the Year Awards. She won the dubious prize.

***

The Front Page, by Ben Hecht and Charles MacArthur, was the most famous newspaper comedy ever written. It had been a hit on Broadway before being turned into a box office bonanza in 1931, co-starring Adolphe Menjou and Pat O'Brien.

Nine years later, Howard Hawks updated it, transforming one of the reporters in the pressroom into a woman. Under the title of *His Girl Friday*, it became a starring vehicle for Cary Grant as a conniving editor, with Rosalind Russell cast as his star reporter (and ex-wife). Ralph Bellamy completed a sort of love triangle as a mama's boy.

In 1974, the noted director, Billy Wilder, used the original title for another screen adaptation, this one starring Jack Lemmon, Walter Matthau, Carol Burnett, and Susan Sarandon.

For yet another variation, this one called *Switching Channels* (1988), director Ted Kotcheff and producer Martin Ransohoff had screenwriter Jonathan Reynolds update the script.

In the new version, Burt Reynolds was cast as John L. Sullivan IV, nicknamed "Sully." He is the operations manager of Satellite News Network, a fictitious cable TV news channel. He tries to prevent the upcoming marriage of Christy Colleran (Kathleen Turner), his star reporter and ex-wife, by keeping her on location and on the job during the critical news coverage of an upcoming execution and prison break.

She has fallen in love with Blaine Bingham (Christopher Reeve), the owner of an international sporting goods company.

The male lead was to have been played by Michael Caine, but he was delayed, filming *Jaws: The Revenge* (1987). In his place, Burt was assigned Caine's role but was angered when informed that Turner would take star billing over him.

He recalled, "I wasn't doing anything other than sitting around mulling over the lint in my belly button. I've always been a fan of Ted Kotcheff, and I had really liked *North Dallas Forty* (1979). That movie had starred Nick Nolte and my buddy, Charles Durning. Some critics hailed it as the best gridiron film ever made. Those jerks, of course, had never seen *The Longest Yard*."

"I'd seen Cary Grant in *His Girl Friday* (1940), and I hoped that Grant wouldn't be turning over in his grave when he saw our version. I was told we were going to keep it fast and talky, some scenes being eight pages of dialogue."

It was never known why Reeve accepted the rather wimpy third lead. Perhaps he wanted to work with Caine again, since they had starred together in *Deathtrap* (1982).

This New Yorker had shot to fame as *Superman* in 1978. He had been

Switching Channels was the fourth remake of the hit newspaper comedy *The Front Page*.

In it (lower photo), Christopher Reeve (left), Kathleen Turner, and Burt form a love triangle. Off screen, he disliked Turner intensely.

careful about selecting roles and had turned down *American Gigolo, The World According to Garp, Fatal Attraction, Pretty Woman, Romancing the Stone, Lethal Weapon,* and *Body Heat*.

Reeve made the claim that he'd based his performance on a bizarre coupling of two radically different people: Cary Grant in *Bringing Up Baby*, a film he had made with Katharine Hepburn in 1938; and the persona and antics of Donald Trump, a real estate developer in Manhattan.

Ned Beatty, Burt's longtime friend, was cast as Roy Ridnitz, the state's Attorney General, who is running for governor and who has convicted an innocent man about to be sent to the electric chair.

During the making of the movie, there were press reports that Burt and Turner were engaged in a feud. She told the press, "Working with Burt Reynolds was terrible. The first day he made me cry. He said something about not taking second place to a woman. His behavior was shocking. It never occurred to me that I wasn't someone's equal. I left the room sobbing. I called my husband and said, 'I don't know what to do.' He said, 'You just do the job.' It got hostile as the crew took sides during our feud. For my performance, I was able to put the negativity aside. I'm not convinced Reynolds could do that."

On TV in 2018, shortly before Burt died, talk show host Andy Cohen asked Burt, "Who was the most overrated star of the 1970s and '80s?" Burt cited Kathleen Turner.

Switching Channels came in for attacks from the critics and was a financial disaster. It had been made on a budget of $19 million, but generated only $9 million at the box office.

Vincent Canby of *The New York Times* wrote: "The new movie is an utter waste of time. Burt Reynolds acts less an obsessed, power-driven editor than a movie star making an appearance on a talk show, trading quips and making sure that his hair remains in place."

Desson Howe in *The Washington Post* said, "Reynolds' high jinks and cheap gags can't replace Cary Grant's suavity. Turner roundly blunts Rosalind Russell's biting, mile-a-minute Hildy. She's always out of breath, she asks atrocious questions, and her voice honks with fatigue."

The film was nominated for two Golden Raspberry Awards, Burt for Worst Actor and Reeve for Worst Supporting Actor. Both them lost, Burt to Sylvester Stallone for *Rambo III* and Reeve to Dan Aykroyd for *Caddyshack II.*

***

In July of 1987, Loni told friends that she believed Burt and her would separate after she pulled off the lavish wedding of her daughter, Deirdra, to her boyfriend, Charles Hoffman. She'd met the young man at UCLA, and they had been living together for two years.

The Florida wedding was preceded by two lavish showers in Los Angeles. The first was at Burt's Carolwood, with a Venetian theme cast with costumed gondoliers. The second was at the elegant home of Ricardo Montalban.

For the Florida wedding, although Loni knew she'd infuriate Burt, perhaps even catalyze a jealous fit from him, she invited her two former husbands to the wedding. Bruce Hasselberg, whom she'd divorced in 1966, showed up, since he was Deidra's biological father. Ross Bickell, whom she'd divorced in 1981, also arrived. Burt wanted to avoid each of them.

He eventually withdrew from all of the wedding plans but agreed to finance half the cost of the couple's honeymoon in Hawaii.

After Deidra's wedding, Loni was set to appear in the film *Stranded* (1986) with Perry King. Burt "threw a fit," and made a lot of accusations about King and Loni. He seemed to accuse her of having an affair with almost any man she knew, even her druggist.

Originally, Loni had been flattered by Burt's possessiveness and jealousy, but after years of it, it had become an irritant. She told friends that she didn't see much of a future with Burt.

He had promised to marry her as soon as he completed the chapel on his ranch in Jupiter, After many delays, and although it was rarely used or visited, the chapel was now ready for a ceremony.

In the meantime, Burt agreed to return to the screen again after a series of flops.

"I still have a few faithful fans out there, a sea of blue hair," he said. "I'm grateful for them, thankful they're still around. They continue to appreciate me as I struggle along. I regret that I don't have the dignity of Ricardo Montalban, the class of Dean Martin, or the humor of Bill Cosby."

***

For 1989 releases, Burt starred in two movies, beginning with *Breaking*

Q: What red-blooded American guy wouldn't want to be stranded on a desert island with her?

A: Her ex-boyfriend!

STRANDED

A wet and wild romantic comedy

Starring
LONI ANDERSON
and
PERRY KING

WORLD PREMIERE MOVIE! TELECAST IN STEREO
9PM° 4;13;22,33;35
HOMECOMING WEEK!

In 1986, Loni had starred with Perry King in a sexually provocative movie called *Stranded*.

Who knows what professional and personal rivalries threw Burt into his orgies of possessive rage in the months and years that followed?

569

In, a crime comedy about how professional small-time criminals live and practice their trades.

The Scottish director, Bill Forsyth, cast Burt in the lead role of Ernie Mullins, an old New York professional safecracker, now operating out of Portland, Oregon. He teams up with Casey Siemaszko, cast as Mike Lafeye, a "noisy, amiable kid," who becomes his apprentice and lookout during a robbery.

Ernie has a steady "love-for-sale" girlfriend, "Delphine the Hooker" (Lorraine Toussaint). The movie also stars two famous actors of yesterday, Albert Salmi and Harry Carey, as Ernie's card-playing chums.

"This was my first character role, a preview of my future career in films, if I were meant to have a future," Burt said. "No more $3 million film roles for me. I worked on *Breaking In* for SAG scale."

Forsyth held out hope for the movie: "There was so much compromise, so much duplicity in the script by John Sayles. There was a lot of blackmail going on, too, so I had a lot of themes to explore."

Roger Ebert wrote, "*Breaking In* has been billed as a comeback for Reynolds, but maybe it's simply a well-written, well-directed picture. He has a comfortable screen presence and can act, when that seems appropriate, but he derailed his career with a series of lame-brained, action comedies directed by and co-starring his pals. This time in the Forsyth universe, he shows the warmth and quirkiness that made him fun to watch in the first place."

Breaking In turned out to be another box office dud for Burt. On its limited budget of $5 million, it took in only $1.8 million at the box office.

As a teenaged burglar, Casey Siemaszko (left) teams with a real pro, Burt, who received a lot of publicity because *Breaking In* was the first time he played a character defined as "an older man."

***

Jagged Edge (1985), starring Jeff Bridges, Glenn Close, and Robert Loggia, had done well at the box office. It was a suspenseful tale of a private investigator framed for a murder. He's assigned an attractive female lawyer to defend him, and she falls in love with him.

David Puttman, the new CEO, had taken over at Columbia, and he rejected the sequel to *Jagged Edge,* reportedly exclaiming, "I don't like sequels."

But the producer, Martin Ransohoff, proceeded with the project anyway, hiring Bill Phillips and Steve Ransohoff to fashion a screenplay He signed Michael Crichton to direct, and this would turn out to be the last movie he'd direct.

Originally entitled *Smoke,* the title was later changed to *Physical Evidence.* Ransohoff had produced *Switching Channels* starring Burt, and he thought he'd be ideal in the lead role of Joe Paris, a beleaguered ex-police officer, who has a history of violence. He wakes up one morning with a splitting headache and blood on his shirt but cannot recall the events of the night before. His fingerprints are discovered at a murder scene.

"Joe Paris is a ballsy character," Burt said. "A kind of Dirty Harry gone amok. He's on the verge of a nervous breakdown, but he has a strange sense of humor about it all. I was hot to play him."

Filming began in September of 1987 in Boston, with the cast and crew later transferred to that area between Montreal and Toronto as the cold autumn winds blew across the Canadian landscape.

In this new spin-sequel, an attractive female lawyer, Jenny Hudson (played by Theresa Russell), is assigned as a public defender for Joe Paris. She comes on cocky and self-assured, but he suspects she's not up for the job. Gradually, she falls in love with him.

Cast as the state's attorney, Burt's longtime friend, Ned Beatty, played James Nicks. On the set, Burt greeted Beatty with a joke. "Don't get your hopes up this time," he said. "No guy's gonna rape you." *[He was, of course, referencing the now famous rape scene in* Deliverance.*]*

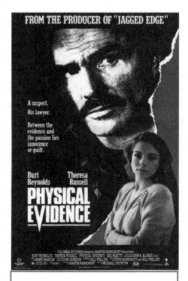

Roger Ebert wrote, "Burt Reynolds is given a few moments when he projects some menace and mystery, just enough for us to suspect he really may have committed the crime. But then the plot doesn't follow through on that, and before long, the story has settled into familiar patterns. The movie's basic idea is role reversal in the Hepburn and Tracy mold, with Reynolds as the untamed ruffian and Russell as the no-nonsense lady who will love him only if it straightens out. The problem is that there is no sexual chemistry between Russell and Reynolds. They don't budge the needle on

Critics labeled its plot "right out of the recycling bin...It's been done before...and better."

571

the romantic voltmeter."

The *Los Angeles Times* found it "flat and remote, a thriller that doesn't thrill." The *Chicago Tribune* labeled it "a feeble thriller, the worse case of filmmaking-by-numbers, reflecting not an ounce of commitment or conviction."

Made for a budget of $17 million, *Physical Evidence* took in only $3.5 million at the box office.

***

Over the course of their long affair, Burt and Loni often discussed marriage, the talk coming mainly from her. Not only that, but they occasionally spoke of their desire to have a child. He noted that she'd already had a daughter, Deidra, who seemed happily married and was doing well professionally.

"I was in my fifties, and I knew the clock marked 'Father Time' was ticking away," Burt said. "My time to have a child, boy or girl, was now or never. My preference was for a Tom Sawyer-like boy, with whom I could play baseball or else cheer him on as he raced across the finish line to score the winning touchdown."

"As 1985 came to an end, I had recovered for the most part from that near-fatal accident I had suffered on the set of *City Heat*," he said. "I had returned to Loni's bed after a long absence. Try though we might, we could not conceive. I labored hard to make her pregnant—no such luck. Was it her fault or mine? She'd had a child before, so I feared it might be me."

Burt made an appointment with a fertility specialist in Beverly Hills. Inside his office, a nurse, who reminded him of Nurse Ratched in *One Flew Over the Cuckoo's Nest*, handed him a copy of *Playboy* and a small cup and pointed him in the direction of the toilet. "Bring it back as soon as you finish, and we'll rush a sample of your semen to the lab."

He was so put off by this sex-on-demand request that he refused. Nurse Ratched then suggested that he have sex over the course of the next few mornings with Loni, using a condom. Then he was to rush the semen-filled condom to her office, where she would send it immediately to the lab.

This went on for about a week, as Burt did the mandatory morning *schtupping* with Loni, and then drove to the doctor's office in Beverly Hills, handing the sample over to Nurse Ratched, who held it up for a quick eye examination before rushing it to the lab.

In a week, the results came in, and Nurse Ratched gave him the news: "Your sperm is pretty much that of a normal man, although I've seen far bigger loads for the lab to examine."

Loni, too, went to a fertility specialist, enduring a laparoscopy and having her Fallopian tubes flushed. The doctor found no reason she could not conceive at her age, as she had more than twenty years before.

She asked Burt to have sex with her the following morning, using a condom. She took the semen-filled condom to her own specialist, who sent it off to a lab. The result that came back declared that Burt's sperm count was very low. The doctor attributed that to both his age and his excessive drug use (and abuse) over the years.

After their failed attempts to conceive, both of them talked of adoption. A politician friend of the Reynolds family from decades ago phoned Burt when he heard, on the Johnny Carson Show, how much he wanted to be a father.

He met with Burt for a very private conversation and an offer. A friend of his was a well-known football player whose exploits on the field often ended up in the sports pages. "He looks so much like you that his teammates have nicknamed him 'B.R.'" The football player was married but had had a one-night stand with a teenage girl who had been the family's babysitter.

As the politico explained it, the girl lived with her father, having lost her mother. She was drug-free and apparently had never had sex before she was seduced and overpowered by her employer, the football star. She wanted to have the child, and then get on with her own life, perhaps marrying the boyfriend she had been dating.

The politician showed Burt a photograph of the young girl, who looked attractive, healthy, and wholesome. Burt was assured that she was religious and had never been in any sort of trouble before.

Burt talked it over with Loni, and both of them decided that if they opted to adopt a child, it would be better if they were married.

Although Burt was still unwilling to submit to marriage, he felt, "I owed Loni one. After all, she had stood by me during my total physical breakdown, all the violence, the pill popping, and my total lack of interest in having sex, which went on for many months."

He had another lingering fear about a marriage to Loni: He didn't trust her to be faithful to her marriage vows. Goldie Hawn, his co-star in *Best Friends*, had phoned him, telling him that she had introduced Loni to Warren Beatty. "Loni made goo-goo eyes at Warren, while I had to go powder my nose. I don't know if they set up a rendezvous, but I wouldn't trust her. Reconsider your plans to get married. That's my advice."

He thanked her for the tip, knowing that his former rival, Warren, could have almost any girl he wanted.

Loni had to leave to film a made-for-TV movie, *Whisper Kills* (1988).

She later claimed that her co-star, Joe Penny, and herself "indulged in the sexiest scenes ever shown in a feature film. He is also the greatest on-camera kisser in the history of Hollywood, and that includes Burt Reynolds."

Apparently, Burt never heard that comment.

In spite of advice he was getting from friends, Burt proceeded with his marriage plans anyway, informing his parents of "the bad news." Both of them opposed the marriage but had little choice but to give in to his wishes since power in their family had totally shifted to their son. He was in control of their lives, and they depended on him for their survival.

Lawyers for both Loni and Burt went to work on a pre-nup, which led to a number of bitter arguments. "I wasn't the millionaire I used to be, and I had been forced to sell a lot of my property, including my Tara outside Atlanta. But I still had a lot of assets, so I wasn't exactly having to use a shithouse with a half-moon carved on the door. I still had some dough in the bank I had left over from the $3 to $5 million picture deals I'd made. Too bad the films lost millions for their backers. I felt guilty about that."

As the lawyers bickered, he later recalled, "I had no idea that Loni was rewriting the *Magna Carta*. There was a catch. If we had a child, then the agreement would be voided. I misunderstood. That also pertained to our having adopted a child. In other words, I would get fucked."

On April 29, 1988, Burt was getting dressed in his bedroom with his longtime friend, Vic Prinzi.

Prinzi warned him, "Why not become the runaway groom? Let's get the hell out of here and race toward Miami and have a blast. Leave Loni stranded at the altar."

"I should have listened to my good pal, Vic," Burt said. "He sure knew what he was talking about. I was a dumbass to marry an actress. Almost from the beginning, my marriage was not lollipops and roses. In fact, I didn't know if I really liked her, except for the sex thing."

On the occasion of his wedding, Burt entered the chapel he had built and walked down the aisle with Prinzi and his neighbor, singer Perry Como. As he strolled by, he flashed his now-famous smile at his sixty-five invited guests.

Fern had broken her hip and had been placed near the front, in a wheelchair. As her eyes met her son's, she signaled to him, "No! No! No!"

Seated in the chapel were some of his best friends, including Robby Benson, Ann-Margret, and her husband, Roger Smith. He waved at Dom DeLuise and Bert Convy. Jim Nabors was there, and he would later sing "The Lord's Prayer" and "Our Love Is Here to Stay."

"As it turned out," Burt said, "Jim boy was a lousy prophet."

As Loni's parents were both deceased, she came down the aisle on the arm of Big Burt, who only the night before had lectured his son not to marry her. She looked stunning in a leg-baring, lacy white gown.

Fern could be heard telling the preacher, the Rev. Jess Moody, "to get on with this thing."

The one part of the ceremony that seemed to thrill Loni the most was when Burt presented her with a whopping, seven-carat diamond ring.

After the wedding, the bride and groom moved into the flower-filled helicopter hangar for the reception. A banquet had been laid out, including Florida lobster and crab, beef Wellington, and a flotilla of Burt's other favorites, including Southern fried chicken.

Def Leppard, Yves Montand, a new Hulk & those darn Batemans

Her Royal Pregnancy

Exclusive

BURT & LONI

THE WEDDING, THE PARTY, THEIR OWN PHOTO ALBUM

"I feel like Cinderella who has married Prince Charming," Loni said.

Burt said, "I've married my best friend."

Overhead, an "armada" of helicopters filled with reporters and photographers drowned out conversation. This invasion so angered Big Burt that at one point, he threatened to get his rifle and shoot them out of the air. Burt restrained him.

After the banquet, guests entered a gazebo where a heart-shaped, three-tiered wedding cake in pink and white icing awaited them.

Before the wedding, Burt had already planned a way to deflect the paparazzi: Ann-Margret and Roger Smith boarded Burt's familiar black-and-white helicopter and flew south to Miami. Many of the encircling aircraft followed them. When they disembarked, fury stirred among the reporters and photographers who had been tricked.

In the meantime, Burt and Loni flew to Key West aboard millionaire Bernie Little's jet copter, landing at the airport there, where a limousine awaited to take them to the yacht basin.

There, they boarded a lavish, 125-food luxury yacht, the *Golden Eagle,* for a tour of the southern Bahamas, with a stopover in Turks & Caicos. As they set out, they experienced rough waters, and soon Loni came down with "the world's worst case of sea-sickness."

Burt ordered the captain to turn back to Key West, where they spent a couple of days sailing through the calmer waters of the Florida Keys, stopping for dinner one night at Marathon. After leaving the Keys, they cruised up the Intercoastal Waterway to Jupiter.

Their major concern after their honeymoon was not their marriage, but the prospect of becoming adopted parents of a little baby boy—or would it be a girl? Loni started buying both pink and blue accessories.

Burt predicted, "The kid's got to be either a boy or a girl. So we seemed prepared to meet either gender."

***

The multi-talented Robby Benson had long been a friend of Burt's and had attended his wedding. When Burt was a big name, the handsome young actor had appeared on the screen with him before, notably in the movie called *The End* (1978).

At Burt's wedding reception, Robby was a bit hesitant, but asked Burt if he'd appear in a brief role in his latest movie, *Modern Love* (1990). It was a story about love, marriage, and parenting from various angles and perceptions. Filming would be in South Carolina, where Benson was teaching moviemaking to a university class.

Burt was agreeable to work with Robby again on *Modern Love*, in which the young actor was the producer, director, and star. He had already rounded up a talented roster of actors, including, among others, Rue Mc-Clanahan, famous for *The Golden Girls*, Frankie Valli, Kaye Ballard, and Louise Lasser.

[It might have been called "A Family Affair," since Benson used his own wife, Karla DeVito, as his girlfriend (and later, wife) in the movie. He also cast their daughter, Lyric Benson, as Chloe, who played their offspring.]

Burt was assigned the small role of Col. Frank Parker, and some critics claimed that Benson, as director, brought out a sensitive side of Burt not usually seen on the screen. One critic even called him "classy." Once scene in particular was notable when actor Bill Arvay, cast as a doctor, tells Burt that his wife did not survive surgery.

Modern Love had limited distribution when it opened in April of 1990 and disappeared quickly from the screen.

Beginning in 1984, Robby had undergone the first of four open-heart surgeries to fix a heart valve defect. This turned him into an activist and fundraiser for heart research, to which Burt contributed.

***

Burt waited anxiously for the birth of the child he was set to adopt with Loni, who was now his wife. His greatest fear was that at the last

576

minute, the infant's mother, an unmarried teenager, would see the newborn and decide she wanted to keep it.

At long last, as agreed upon, her doctor put through the call that Burt had waited for for so long. "You've got a little linebacker," he told Burt.

"I cried with joy," Burt said. "I would have loved a little girl and protected her, but it was a boy I really wanted," he said.

He brought the news to Loni, telling her, "He's gonna be the greatest football player in the history of the NFL."

"How do you know that?" she reportedly asked. "He might grow up to be a ballet dancer."

For a name, both of his new parents

Robby Benson with his wife, Karla DeVito in *Modern Love*. In the movie, he meets her as a doctor who has to examine his penis.

agreed on Quentin Reynolds, in ways that evoked the famous journalist (1902-1965) and World War II correspondent The name also derived from "Quint," the character Burt had played on the long-running TV series, *Gunsmoke*.

On the third day after Quentin's birth, Burt was holding the infant boy in his arms "with that hair growing on his head, I can tell he's part Cherokee, just like his dad, the same blood flowing through his veins." He seemed to forget that Quentin didn't have any direct biological link to his bloodline.

Looking into the eyes of this three-day-old son, he later claimed, "I saw something beautiful there, something timeless and wonderous, even profound. In time, this little boy I held in my arms would force me to grow up and become an adult male for the first time in my life. My day of being a notorious boy/man out for his next adventure had come to an end. I had the responsibility of a parent, and I was determined to live up to what was needed and wanted from me."

"I was no longer the greatest thing on the screen, but in Quentin's eyes I was still number one at the box office. I was his Da-Da, the greatest role I would ever play."

He later claimed, "Loni didn't take to motherhood as I did to fatherhood. She didn't seem to want him to grow up to be a football hero. But I'd already gone ahead and arranged a four-year scholarship for my boy at Florida State. I'm sure that in 2006 he'll be the star halfback."

At the age of ten months, Quentin took his first steps toward his Da-

Da. A few weeks later, he uttered his first words. Predictably, they were "Da-Da." When he got older, Burt spent $10,000 to buy the boy a rocking horse.

Loni, according to Burt, arose at eleven every morning, and often spent the afternoon shopping in the boutiques along Worth Avenue in Palm Beach.

Big Burt seemed delighted with his new grandson. "He was kissing the boy all the time, making me wonder why he'd never kissed me when I was growing up."

"I was a very possessive father, smothering Quentin with love. As he grew older, he pretended not to like it, but I think in his heart he welcomed my devotion to him."

"In the meantime, with money dwindling, I had to cut back," Burt said. "I sold my home, Carolwood, on the most expensive street in Beverly Hills, and got a good price for it. Soon, my beloved theater in Jupiter would be lost, too."

***

The Burt Reynolds Theatre in Jupiter had been his dream, and for more than a decade, he'd seen it through the high times and its low points.

But by August 5, 1989, he was not able to funnel more money into it. The curtain fell that night on its last stage play, a revival of the Broadway hit, *A Funny Thing Happened on the Way to the Forum.*

Originally, he announced that he was donating the theater—valued at $4.5 million—to the Palm Beach Community College for use as a performing arts and educational facility. However, the governor of Florida nixed the deal, because there was a $2 million mortgage on the property. Not only that, but Burt had run up another $2 million in debts that it owed.

Burt then made a deal to sell the theater for $2 million, the price he'd paid to

Two very public views of Baby Quint in different eras of his parents' joy and later marital anguish.

construct it, to Richard Atkins Productions.

Records at the time revealed that the theater had never made money except for two seasons, 1981 and 1985. That was because its break-even point was 95% capacity. Ticket prices, as dictated by Burt, were kept so low that the theater could not make a profit on a show.

Christine Arnold Dolen in *The Washington Post* analyzed the problem. "Tourists once flocked by the busloads to obscure little Jupiter, imagining that Burt Reynolds himself might greet them at the door. The big stars that originally attracted them have been sticking to films and TV."

The theater in time found it increasingly difficult to attract stars like Burt originally did, hiring Carol Burnett, Farrah Fawcett, Ossie Davis, Kirstie Alley, and Dom DeLuise.

The last big-name stars to appear were Desi Arnaz, Jr., comedian Rip Taylor, and Marie Windsor. In her article, Dolen asked: "Where were the likes of Michelle Pfeiffer, Jeff Goldblum, or Gregory Hines? In Central Park working for Joseph Papp for a few weeks."

Atkins operated the theater until 1996 when he, too, suffered a financial disaster and had to get rid of it.

After several other upheavals and more money problems, the complex eventually morphed into the Malitz Jupiter Theatre, opening in February of 2004. Today, it's one of Florida's most pre-eminent professional theaters.

***

Burt had vowed, "no more television, no more detective roles." But after his last string of films flopped, he needed money and changed his mind.

His rival of yesteryear, Tom Selleck, phoned. He was the executive producer of a new TV detective drama, *B.L. Stryker,* and he wanted Burt to play the title role of Buddy Lee Stryker (aka B.L.), a Vietnam war vet and retired New Orleans police officer who has moved to the other side of the tracks in Palm Beach and is now working as a private investigator, living on a houseboat and driving an old Caddy.

As the cynical detective, Burt, in the view of some critics, evoked Humphrey Bogart in those *film noir* movies he'd made in the 1940s.

Burt's inseparable friend in the series was Ossie Davis, who was also his close friend in real life. The African American actor played a former boxer, Oz Jackson. Another friend, Rita Moreno, portrayed Kimberly Baskin, Stryker's ex-wife, in six episodes.

B.L. Stryker was part of the *ABC Mystery Movie* umbrella group, along with *Columbo, Kojak,* and *Gideon Oliver.* Selleck wanted Burt to direct some of the episodes himself.

The TV drama aired from February 13, 1989 to May 5, 1990.

Burt was suddenly in a position to find employment for some of his friends, including country singer Jerry Reed, Dom DeLuise, Ricardo Montalban, and even his wife, Loni Anderson.

In her episode, *Grand Theft Hotel*, Stryker is hired as the head of security at a posh Bahamian resort. There, he becomes involved with a beautiful blonde (Loni, of course), and solves the murder of the rich friend of his ex-wife (Rita Moreno).

Burt and Moreno co-starred again in another episode of *Stryker* entitled "High Rise" with Ossie Davis. They are held captive by bank robber Montalban.

Burt had high hopes for the series, which was, for the most part, well reviewed. He had hoped that it would put him back on his feet financially, thinking it might run for five years. He said, "I'll be able to retire for life."

But B.L. Stryker was canceled after the first season.

***

"Having done a ton of television shows and more feature films than I can count, I'm tired of having some filmmaker younger than some sandwiches telling me to turn left at the sofa," Burt said. "Among these young jerks, there is no appreciation and no sense of Hollywood history and time-sharpened techniques. Some of these guys don't even know that Ronald

Even during the depths of their marital dischord, the networks continued to push Burt together with Loni in episodes of a TV series that reminded viewers of their links and kept them firmly in the tabloids as a dysfunctional team.

Reagan used to be a movie star."

"A case in point is Henry Winkler, the director of a movie I made in 1993 called *Cop and a Half*. He and I fought for most of the shoot. That was in 1993. I did not only the cop comedy but another four or so pictures, each a stinker. I barely recall them."

In *Cop and a Half*, Burt starred as the veteran detective Nick McKenna, who is forced to work with an eight-year-old, an eyewitness to murder. He and Burt need to track down the killer and the drug kingpin who ordered the hit.

The kiddie role was originally offered to Macauley Culkin, but he turned it down. The part of Devon Butler was then cast with Norman D. Golden II, an African American actor born in 1984. After working with Burt, Golden would co-star with Oprah Winfrey, Joan Plowright (Mrs. Laurence Olivier), Wesley Snipes, and Patrick Stewart.

BURT REYNOLDS
COP
~AND~
A HALF

"My advice to an actor: Never star in a movie with a kid. Norman D. Golden II stole every scene I was in."

Originally, Winkler offered Burt's role to Kurt Russell, but he bowed out. "I wonder if Kurt is still mad at me for making a play for Goldie Hawn?" Burt said to Winkler.

He was delighted to work with Ruby Dee, the wife of Ossie Davis, cast as Rachel Baldwin. "I tried to do every scene I could with her, since I had a crush on her. Ossie wasn't too happy about that."

Made for only $4 million, this movie was a surprise hit, earning $41 million at the box office.

Jay Boyart of the *Orlando Sentinel* gave one of the best reviews of Golden. "He is genuinely cute and a pretty good actor, besides."

Other reviews were more devastating. Leonard Maltin gave "a hemorrhoid-and-a-half to anyone who sits all the way through the film, an abjectly painful comedy, which does for Reynolds as much as *Stop! Or My Mom Will Shoot* did for Sylvester Stallone."

Gene Siskel in Chicago accused Burt of "artistic bankruptcy," calling it "the worst film made in 1993."

Both Burt and Golden were nominated for Worst Actor in the Stinker Bad Movie Awards. Burt beat out Golden for the dubious Golden Raspberry Award for Worst Actor of the Year. Golden was also nominated for Worst New Star.

***

Before 1993 ended, Burt starred in another made-for-TV comedy/drama, *The Man from Left Field*. He was both the director and the star, hiring the singer Reba McEntire as the leading leady.

Cast in small roles were Burt's friend Charles Nelson Reilly and Dale Robertson. Robertson, a former boxer, football player, and soldier, had had a film heyday in the 1950s working with Joan Crawford, Marilyn Monroe, Jeanne Crain, and Betty Grable.

Singer Randy Travis was the real star of this "movie within a movie" about the making of a movie. The singer befriends a runaway orphan and also gets to live his long-time dream by landing in a film about the untamed West.

There is a lot of singing and fighting going on. Burt joins in the fighting. Chuck

Burt co-starred with singer Reba McEntire in *The Man from Left Field*. "She's quite a woman and a hell of an actress," he said.

She offered Burt her love and prayers during his widely publicized divorce from Loni.

Norris, in a cameo, said, "I was in the cast just to kick Randy's ass in this cool fight scene."

Burt's final verdict? "I think our movie did more for Randy's singing career than it did for my career either as an actor or star."

***

"While I was busy editing *The Man from Left Field,* I didn't realize that 'my beloved wife,' Loni Anderson, was kidnapping our son, Quentin and flying him to Los Angeles. Once there, she would make the poor kid a pawn in our long-drawn-out divorce, which would make tabloid headlines across the nation."

CHAPTER SIXTEEN

EVENING SHADE

BURT PLAYS OPPOSITE "THE SEXIEST WOMAN ON EARTH" IN A TELE-
VISED ODE TO SMALL TOWN AMERICANA.

PSSSST! Its Title Was Suggested by Hillary Clinton

HOW

TERRY WARREN,

A "VERY SEXY" ATHLETE, SINGER, & ACTOR, POURED GASOLINE AND
FLAMES ON THE DISINTIGRATING DOMESTIC LIFE OF BURT & LONI

PAMELA SEALS

"THAT COCKTAIL WAITRESS,"
THE LAST OF BURT'S MAJOR-LEAGUE AFFAIRS.

HOLLYWOOD'S UGLIEST DIVORCE

IN COURT AND IN THE TABLOIDS,
BURT & LONI HURL MUTUALLY DESTRUCTIVE ACCUSATIONS

BANKRUPTCY

BURIED UNDER MOUNTAINS OF UNPAID BILLS,
BURT ENDURES UNWANTED HEADLINES FROM ACROSS THE NATION

BOOGIE NIGHTS

BURT INSISTS THAT HE HATES IT,
BUT THIS BEHIND-THE-SCENES LOOK AT THE PORN INDUSTRY OF THE
70S BECOMES THE AWARD-WINNING HIGH OF HIS CAREER.

The 1990s were a ten-year span of struggle and turmoil, characterized mainly by Burt's divorce proceedings from Loni Anderson and their flame-throwing wars over money.

As it applied to his movie career—with the noted exception of *Boogie Nights* (1997) and the TV sitcom, *Evening Shade*—it was a decade of mainly flops. *Evening Shade,* however, a series that aired from 1990 to '94, would win him an Emmy, a Golden Globe, and a People's Choice Award for its 98 episodes. During his tenure as its star, Burt would lease a palatial mansion on five manicured acres in Bel Air.

The title for *Evening Shade* was suggested by the soon-to-be-First Lady of the United States, Hillary Clinton. The creators of the show, a man-and-wife writing team, Harry Thomason and Linda Bloodworth-Thomason, were described by Burt as "Hillary's cronies." Both the dynamic duo had achieved great success with another TV sitcom, *Designing Women,* which had aired from 1986 to 1993.

Burt met with them to hear their pitch for a new series. When it was suggested that his character of Woodrow ("Wood") Newton would be a small-town newspaper publisher in rural Arkansas, he objected. "I won't play a newspaperman or a lawyer, two breeds of men I detest."

He suggested (and prevailed) that he portray the head coach of a losing high school football team that's notorious for being defeated at every game. As a former Pittsburgh Steelers Quarterback, he takes over the team, as it has a 30-game-and counting losing streak.

As the writing team, now in creative dialogues with Burt, evolved the lead character, it was suggested that he play it "a bit like Jimmy Stewart, with a dose of Andy Griffith from the hick town of Mayberry, but with more sophistication."

As their discussions evolved, the supporting characters were created, beginning with Wood's wife, Ava Evans Newton, whom he'd married when she was only eighteen. The role went to Burt's former co-star, Marilu Henner. "She's got that twinkle in her eyes and knows how to twist men around her finger," Burt said. "She is, without a doubt, one of the sexiest women known to have inhabited Planet Earth."

Her father, Evan Evans, the owner of the local newspaper, was cast with Hal Holbrook. He would be killed off when he had to bow out to star in another TV series.

One night, Burt was watching the Tony Awards where he saw Michael Jeter win for his poignant performance as a dying bookkeeper in the 1990 stage version of *Grand Hotel*. Burt thought he'd be the best choice for Herman Stiles, "A Barney Fife type." That was a reference to Don Knotts, Andy Griffith's deputy in Mayberry. Jeter would play a wimpy-looking math teacher who signs on as Wood's assistant coach.

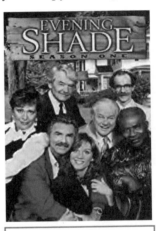

That same night Burt watched his friend, Charles Durning, also win a Tony for his interpretation of Big Daddy in *Cat on a Hot Tin Roof*. Burt phoned and asked him to play the role of the town doctor, Harlan Eldridge. "The part calls for you to be outsized, so you don't have to go on a diet, Charlie," Burt assured him.

The doc's sexy wife, Marleen, was portrayed by Ann Wedgeworth. Burt had met her when she was pregnant and just eighteen, having married his long-ago roommate, actor Rip Torn.

"Crazy Elizabeth" signed on too," Burt said. He was referring to his former co-star Elizabeth Ashley, who was cast as a Southern Diva, Frieda Evans. She told Linda Thomason, "Hollywood is a sea of assholes, but Burt Reynolds is an island. Count me in."

A young Hilary Swank appeared in some episodes as Aimee Thompson.

Burt poses with the cast of the TV sitcom, *Evening Shade*, one of his biggest all-time hits. In his arms is Marilu Henner,

"If she were my real wife, I would never have gotten out of bed," he said.

On the right is Ossie Davis, cast as Ponder Blue, the king of barbecue.

585

Burt called his longtime friend, Ossie Davis, and asked him if he'd star in the key role of Ponder Blue, the African American owner of the local barbecue pit, a hangout for locals. His character doubles as the narrator who—in a style akin to the structure of *Our Town*—frames most of the episodes.

At first, perhaps for artistic reasons, Davis was reluctant, telling Burt, "My feet are too big and my head is too solid. I can't float on the surface that sitcom tends to generate."

"Whatever in the fuck are you talking about? Burt asked. "I'm signing you on!"

Burt directed some of the episodes himself, and on a few occasions, brought in his friend, Charles Nelson Reilly, to helm various sitcoms.

A roster of guest stars came and went, including Kenny Rogers singing "Twenty Years Ago," as well as Alice Ghostley, Terry Bradshaw, Tammy Wynette, Willie Nelson, Tony Bennett, and even Richard Simmons in a hilarious segment.

"All in all, *Evening Shade* was the most satisfying thing I ever did on television," Burt said.

***

"During my two-year (so far) marriage to Loni Anderson, she and I had our arguments—let's call them knock down, drag out events," Burt said. "I knew Doris Duke, with her tobacco millions, but I think Loni must have thought I was Doris' heir. She certainly spent like I was."

"Her clothing bill ran to more than $10,000 a month, and she already owned half the designer dresses and gowns in Beverly Hills. When I bitched about the bills, her excuse was always the same: 'It's vital for me to always look like a star when I go out.'"

"Since she wore an outfit only once, I don't know what she did with them," Burt said. "I suggested she present them to Jacqueline Kennedy Onassis."

"I regretted many decisions I made during my marriage to Loni," he said. "I turned down the lead in *Soapdish* (1991), which would have reteamed me with Sally Field. It was a hard decision, because the producers were offering the salary I had drawn when I was box office champ."

"Loni told me it would be like stabbing a knife in her heart if I worked with Sally again," he said. "*Soapdish* was a big hit, and it might have ignited my fading screen career. The role went to Kevin Kline. I never forgave Loni for talking me out of uniting the Frog and the Bandit on the screen for a final time."

"As I grew older, Loni grew younger every month," he claimed. "Cellulite was just one of the ingredients used to stave off the march of Father Time. If our marriage endured long enough, and that was highly unlikely, I'd one day be accused of taking on a child bride."

When he thought life with Loni couldn't possibly become more difficult, it did. "He likened the turmoil to "a tornado that seems to come out of nowhere in Oklahoma and lifts the roof right off your home."

Sally Field and Kevin Kline in this publicity shot for *Soapdish*, the role Burt abandoned, based on what he defined as loud opposition from Loni Anderson

One afternoon, he returned home early, having wrapped an episode of *Evening Shade* three hours in advance. "It was one of those rare afternoons when everything—the cameramen and our stars and regulars—were all right on the mark. I decided to come home early to spend a quiet evening with Quinton and Loni, especially Quinton."

He didn't call Loni to tell her he'd be on the way. Nothing needed advance preparation, since it was already understood that he'd invite her that evening to one of his favorite bistros in Beverly Hills, and that they'd drive off for dinner together after he'd read a bedtime story to Quinton. On his way home, he stopped at a toy store to make some purchases for his son. A few minutes after he

A former linebacker for the FSU team, Terry Warren entered the troubled lives of Burt and Loni Anderson.

It became a sort of game between them: Who would take possession of the stud?

flashed his credit card, the clerk went aside to make a phone call and then reported, "Your card has a $25,000 limit, but that has been exceeded. Sorry, Mr. Reynolds."

He'd given the new card to Loni only that morning.

It was early October but still scorching hot when Burt returned home early. He looked through the glass doors and spotted Terry Warren and Loni in a cozy embrace beside the pool, each of them wearing skimpy bikinis.

Burt had first met Warren when he was a student at the Institute of

Theater Training in Jupiter. He noticed that the girls found this former Florida State University linebacker, "very, very good looking and even more than looks, very very sexy." He told Terry, "The gals used to go for me like that not so long ago. Enjoy it while you can."

Burt interpreted him as one of his best students, as he preferred acting instead of football. Soon he made him one of his personal assistants and brought him to live and work with him in Los Angeles.

He admitted he had been suspicious of Terry and Loni before, since he often filled in for Burt when he was working, escorting her out to dinners and parties.

That afternoon, Burt decided to "step out and confront the cozy love-birds," as he described them. The couple immediately separated. "Terry may have thought I was going to rip off his dick, and Loni might have feared I'd rip off that head of hair. But for once in my life, I controlled my temper and went back inside."

He ordered Terry out of his house, and later, when Loni came in, he confronted her, too. "Get out of here and take your god damn clothes with you. Otherwise, I'll throw them out on the lawn and turn the hose on them." He recalled that would take some doing, since her closets held the equivalent of MGM's wardrobe inventory during the Golden Age of Hollywood.

"Go to Terry," he commanded, "although I don't know how in hell the kid can afford you. He depends on me for his eats, his clothes, and he even drives one of my cars. All he can give you is a permanent hard-on."

She pleaded with him, claiming, "It'll never happen again. He's just a boy. I was flattered by his attention. It told me I was still attractive."

"She begged, she crawled, she wept," Burt said. "She made promises."

"I need you," she sobbed. "Need you in my life."

Finally, and with Terry gone, Burt admitted, "I did the really stupid thing. I took her back on my own terms. We would reconcile in name only. That is, showing up smiling and holding hands at premieres or at parties."

After a few days, when she became amorous, he looked at her sharply. "I don't know if I will ever make love to you again."

And he never did. Or so he said.

That might have been the way Burt filtered the story for his friends. But as in most man-and-wife confrontations, there were other sides, including the point of view of his spurned wife.

***

Evening Shade had been a big hit on TV, and Burt owned a part of it.

He expected to make enough money when it was sold in syndication that he could retire in comfort in Jupiter, working only if he wanted to, never out of necessity.

He believed in the TV series so much that he borrowed $4 million to become part owner of it. But the powers at CBS, which held controlling interest, sold it for syndication for only $150,000 per episode, despite Burt's demand that they charge $1 million for each showing. "Instead of those millions I dreamed about, I ended up owing that killer sum. I got robbed. Not only that, but in spite of its high ratings, CBS canceled the series. That's show biz!"

He suffered additional financial setbacks when he lost a lucrative $500,000 contract from the Florida Citrus Commission, as well as his long-running ad campaign with Quaker State Motor Oil.

More bad news was on the way. One morning in the spring of 1992, he was awakened to hear that in Florida, Fern had been rushed to the hospital.

Dressing quickly, he put the pedal to the metal, racing to the hospital to be at her bedside. She'd been alerted to his visit, and was sitting up in bed, having applied lipstick.

Their reunion was brief. She told him, "You were the greatest thing that ever happened to me in my whole life. I love you. Now get out. I've got to go to sleep."

He had to fly back to California, but Fern clung to life for another six months. He buried her behind the chapel where—against her advice—he'd wed Loni. "I should have listened to Mother."

***

A few days after he was evicted from Burt's rented home in Los Angeles, in response to Burt's accusation that he'd been *schtupping* Loni, Warren phoned Loni to relay some scandalous information. Warren revealed that Burt had sustained a long-running affair that dated from 1988, the first year of their marriage.

Terry told Loni that whereas he was not proud to reveal this information, he regretted having aided and abetted Burt's intimacies with Pam Seals, an attractive blonde cocktail waitress whom he'd met at Malio's, a popular sports bar in Tampa, when he was invested in the Tampa Bay Bandits. Seals had been a former cheerleader for the Tampa Bay Rowdies, a soccer team.

"Pam was always in the background," Warren allegedly told Loni. "I call her Burt's shadow. She was even an extra in a movie you and Burt made. I arranged hotel rooms for her and often served as her escort to throw the attention off Burt. She showed up in every city Burt visited. Often in a theater at a premiere, or whatever. Usually, she sat three or four rows behind you. I took her out when Burt was involved with you. Every thirty days, he writes her a big monthly check."

When production of *Evening Shade* went into its summer shutdown, Seals followed Burt from city to city as he delivered his one-man show, *An Evening with Burt Reynolds*. According to Warren, "She was always there in the same bed with him. He usually booked a two-bedroom suite, and I lived with them."

Pamela Seals was a sexy blonde cocktail waitress Burt met in Tampa when he was part owner of a football team.

She would become the last of his many long-lasting affairs. But there was trouble ahead in paradise.

To her horror, Loni learned that even Quinton had met Seals during some of his sojourns with his father in Jupiter. Warren claimed, "I heard her tell your son, 'Better get used to me, 'cause I'm gonna become your new momma,'"

After Burt fired (and evicted) Warren from his life, he and Loni continued to stay together for a few more months, putting up a good front at public events for reporters and photographers. They became "resocialized" as Hollywood's most loving couple, although they were anything but.

Loni later claimed that when they were out of the public eye, a very different man emerged, one of dark moods and violent tempers. She asserted, publicly and privately, that he had fallen victim to his addictions again: Prozac, Valium, Didrex, Compazine, and Vicodin.

When Loni later published her memoirs, she painted a gloomy picture of a very disturbed husband, who often resorted to physical violence, shoving her against a wall or bouncing her off the furniture.

Their most horrific fight occurred one night when he went to a drawer and removed a loaded pistol before returning to confront her. At first, she might have thought he was planning to shoot her, but he had a different idea. He handed her the gun, telling her, "Why don't you shoot yourself—fatally, that is—and put all of us out of our misery?"

One weekend, he suggested they fly to Florida, this time for a stay at Valhalla. He hardly spoke to her once they arrived and locked himself away for the rest of the day.

That night, he entered their bedroom at Valhalla, telling her, "I'm going to the ranch tonight. I want to be alone. Don't ask any questions. You'll find out tomorrow."

With that foreboding prediction, he fled.

The next morning, two officers from the sheriff's department arrived to serve her with divorce papers.

She quickly realized that their flight from Los Angeles had been part of a set-up. [*Loni came to believe that Burt had tricked her by flying to Florida, where he planned to file for divorce since that state's community property laws were far more lenient than those of California. The custody battle for Quinton, however, would be fought in the courts of California.*]

That very morning, CNN led with the news of Burt's filing for divorce. By ten that morning, helicopters were flying over Valhalla, and paparazzi had assembled with reporters at its entrance. She later compared all this hysteria to a scene from *Apocalypse Now* (1979) starring Marlon Brando.

Burt admitted that one of the most difficult tasks involved confronting Quinton with news that he'd be divorcing his mother. He walked with his son along the beach, finding it difficult to tell him.

Apparently, he already knew. Quinton took his hand and asked, "Dad, is the dance over?"

"It is, son. The marriage didn't work out. Now the nasty days begin. You'll be reading a lot about us in the papers, a lot of lies. Maybe the boys at school will mock you. I'm sorry."

"It'll be okay," the boy said. "I can take it, and I know you can, too. We're two strong guys."

When Loni flew back to California with Quinton, calls from both the press and friends or acquaintances kept the phones ringing constantly. Even singer Robert Goulet phoned, asking Loni, "Is Burt going through mid-life crisis or is it something else?"

As the months went by, the story of Burt and Pam Seals went public. The *Globe* ran a story called "MEET THE WOMAN I LOVE." In it, Seals was quoted as saying, "Burt Reynolds as a lover is every woman's dream." A photographer snapped a picture of them together in a hot tub.

"My marriage to Loni has been an empty shell for two and a half years," Burt told the press. "Now Pam and I don't want to hide in the shadows anymore. I want to be able to take Pam out in the public without everyone speculating about who that beautiful woman with Burt is."

"We're very much in love," Seals asserted. "The first time Burt kissed me, his lips just melted into mine."

Burt, in a garish suit dyed a purple eggplant, appeared on *Good Morning America*. His appearance on that show became notorious. Susan Schindehette, a journalist specializing in human-interest stories, described his look: "He came out looking more like an apparition from Madame Tussaud's waxworks than a movie star—complexion wan, speech slurred, face puffy under a heavily applied mask of makeup, lip shorn of its familiar mustache."

In the statements he made on TV, Burt was so candid he shocked millions of viewers. He admitted that he and Loni had not had sex in three years, and he accused her of having "many lovers on the side."

He admitted to an involvement with another woman, an obvious reference to Seals. However, he claimed it was Loni who had been unfaithful first, alluding to Terry Warren, though not actually naming him.

"I caught her cheating on me," he told TV cameras. "So I just…I made the decision to call off our marriage." He didn't stop there: "Loni Anderson is an underemployed actress suffering from low self-esteem. She is not a good mother."

He challenged Loni to join him in a sodium pentathol test to determine who cheated first. "If she wins, I will give her everything I own, including my ranch, my house, a lot of Western art she doesn't want, and the $13 million she's asking for. If I win, I get Quinton—that's all I want."

When besieged by reporters, Loni announced, "I do not intend to engage in a media war. I have to consider the welfare and best interests of my little boy."

That same day, Burt was asked by a reporter if Loni had been the love of his life. "Not at all! NO WAY! The love of my life was Sally Field, a lady who stole my heart. I really cared for Sally, as she is very, very special. I'm not certain if I ever loved Loni Anderson. She's not very lovable, you know. Most so-called 'sex kittens' aren't, or so I've found."

Later, Loni countered Burt's depiction of her as an "adulterous conniver and an indifferent mother." After she was assigned a role as a hospital administrator in the final season of NBC's sitcom *Nurses* (1991-1994), she gave an interview in which she claimed, "I never looked at another man. I'm a blameless victim of a middle-aged egomaniac run amok."

***

Somewhere along the way, Burt and Terry Warren made up. Burt phoned him and invited him to Jupiter. Burt wanted a favor, offering to pay him to write an "I Saw" article in the *Enquirer*, with the understanding that it would allege that Loni had made repeated sexual overtures to him.

In return, Burt promised Terry that he'd use his influence to promote Terry's acting and singing career.

Warren agreed to it, little knowing at the time that the article he'd write would lead to unintended consequences.

[Burt had been captivated by Warren when he sang the national anthem at FSU's homecoming game against Tulane. That afternoon, Burt met the All-America linebacker, and seemed enchanted by what he called his "big, sincere smile and winning personality. He was also a good singer and great on the football field. I envied his sex appeal."

He and Burt bonded that day, and Burt took him to Jupiter and enrolled him in his theater training school. He also invited Warren to come and live with him in both Florida and California.]

Photo above is a screen shot from a rather odd, utterly humorless videotaped endorsement Burt crafted, wherein he testified to Terry Warren's singing talent.

Throughout most of the clip, Warren remained silent and looked uncomfortable.

Burt kept his promise and got Warren booked on his *Evening Shade* TV series and in small roles in a string of his movies. When Burt went on the road, Warren was with Burt as well as Pamela Seals. The bonding gave rise to the charges of Burt's bisexuality, which soon evolved into tabloid gossip that Burt was gay, a rumor that had spread across the country in the mid-80s. Charges became so pronounced that Burt appeared on television, denying he was a homosexual. "I've had so many lies spread about me," he told TV audiences. "I guess I can live with these latest batches of lies, too."

His close friends claimed that Burt was afraid that gay rumors would destroy his remaining fan base. Some of his closest friends rushed to defend him, including Bernie Little, a Lakeland (Florida)-based beer distributor. "Burt is a man's man. He is just a country boy who likes boiled peanuts. There is one thing he is, a real man, and he isn't gay."

But the defense was met with increasing charges he was gay. A former assistant, Brian Todd, said, "Burt's rage against Loni was in large part because she tried to steal Terry from him. The battle raged as to who would win this prize stud."

***

For the next two years, Loni and Burt became "tabloid fodder," the stories growing more libelous, ridiculous, and outrageous. As legal battles continued, Burt spent at least a million dollars in lawyers' fees—perhaps a lot more—and it is estimated that Loni spent at least half of that, too.

After his failure to pick up a bundle from the syndication of *Evening Shade*, Burt threatened to declare bankruptcy. He was hovering on the brink, as a mountain of unpaid bills grew higher and higher.

As the feud between Loni and Burt continued, much of it played out in public, a messenger delivered a handwritten letter to her from Burt. She found its language "abusive and obscene." In it, Burt declared World War III "like you've never seen."

He claimed that the *Enquirer* was ready to publish a three-part series in which, among other allegations, it would be claimed that she had affairs with three married men during the course of their marriage.

The letter ended with this threat: "Never think that I'm too much of a gentleman to destroy you, everything, every person, who respects you. If you doubt it, you are very wrong. I will. I will!" She sent the threatening letter to her lawyers, hoping it could be used against Burt in their custody battle.

At the time of their marriage, Loni was worth $1 million, in contrast to Burt, who had a net worth of $15 million.

She asked the court for $75,000 a month, claiming, "I haven't funds with which to support myself and Quinton."

At this point, there wasn't a lot left in Burt's bank account(s) and he made a settlement of $1.9 million from his resources, which were meager at the time. He claimed, "I had to pay the third highest child support ever recorded in the history of the State of California."

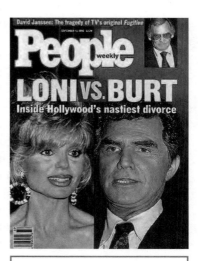

In 1993, the year of her divorce, Loni went public with her love affair with Geoffrey Brown, one of her lawyers, who had stood by her during her darkest days battling Burt in court.

She described him as "being more than six feet tall, with a touch of gray at the temples, and the bluest eyes I've ever seen." Before practicing law in California, he had worked for naval intelligence during the Vietnam War.

The breakup of the marriage of Burt to Loni Anderson was largely played out in the tabloids, even in *People* magazine (above).

Burt told the press, "Her financial demands are outrageous. She wants everything I have."

That November, *People* magazine pictured Loni Anderson with Geoffrey Brown on its cover. That led to an avalanche of mail pouring into Brown's office, with all sorts of proposals.

Burt allegedly spread the story that Brown was "light on his loafers," a veiled suggestion that he was gay. In contrast, it was also rumored that he had two other mistresses stashed away in Los Angeles.

"All these lies were ridiculous," Loni said. "I hoped this avalanche of lies wouldn't have him fleeing from me."

It was widely predicted that Loni and Brown would get married, but they did not. She would eventually take a fourth husband but not until May 17, 2008 when, as she admitted, "I was no spring chicken." She wed musician Bob Flick, one of the founding members of the Brothers Four. The couple had first met at a movie premiere in Minnesota in 1963.

After his second marriage, Burt would never wed again.

In the summer of 1995, Burt read that Loni was performing as part of a summer tour through Ohio, appearing with the Kenley Players, as he had done in years gone by. She starred as Lorelei Lee, the role made famous by Marilyn Monroe in *Gentlemen Prefer Blondes* (1953).

"Gentlemen might prefer blondes, but they should never marry one," Burt said. "Most of those bottle blondes in Hollywood are hookers, willing to bankrupt you. I'm not singling out any one blonde, of course."

The battle of Burt and Loni would continue on and off for years, as he experienced increasing financial difficulties. He fell behind in his payments to her. There had been many disputes over who owned certain automobiles, furnishings, and paintings, many of which just "disappeared."

In a memoir, Burt cited an old debt that led to a conflict with Loni around 2014. She'd gotten an order from a judge which forced him to sell off a lot of the personal memorabilia which he had spent years collecting.

The sale even included his high school football trophies and also his Golden Globe for *Boogie Nights*. His Western art also went on the auction block, which he described as "a yard sale in Las Vegas."

Out with Burt Reynolds and in with the new.

Loni Anderson goes public in *People* magazine with her new love, Geoffrey Brown, one of her lawyers. "He is all the wonderful things Burt was not," she claimed.

"I'm a Pack Rat, and the auction forced me to say goodbye to many of my most treasured possessions, even all those cowboy boots I used to own."

"I was surprised to find that I had so

many fans willing to pay a lot of good money for a token of me," he said. "Sometimes, they paid three or four times more than what any item was worth. I guess if things get really tough, I can sell my jockstraps to any gay guys who still dig me."

***

Quinton lived across from his mother in California, and Burt resided in Florida. "We didn't get to see much of each other," Burt said. "I warned him not to go into show biz, claiming it might break his heart, but he became a film editor."

"Over the years, we didn't have the father-son relationship I had dreamed we would. I love the boy dearly, however. Who ever promised you'd get what you want out of life?"

***

In 1995, recovering from his divorce and eager to work after the demise of *Evening Shade*, he appeared briefly in the TV series, *Hope and Gloria*, cast as himself, in an episode called "Sisyphus, Prometheus, and Me." [*"Or was it called 'Syphilis, Promiscuity, and Me'" he said, jokingly.*]

In *Hope and Gloria*, Hope was the producer of a local TV show. Her cheating husband had left her a decade earlier. Gloria was a streetwise single mother and hairdresser who's the sole supporter of her young son. These women share the highs (there are only a few of those) and the downs of their complicated yet humorous lives.

Burt, in the same year of 1995, was cast once again with Cybill Shepherd. Reunited on a film set, they ruefully recalled their disastrous flop of twenty years before, *At Long Last Love* (1975). "You've bounced back," he said.

Her TV sitcom, *Cybill* (1995-'98), was already a hit on CBS. It revolved around a struggling actress, a down home girl from Memphis

Burt from around the era he played in a single episode of the TV sitcom *Hope and Gloria*.

in her 40s, who has never risen to stardom. Her career has consisted mainly of TV commercials, soap operas, and B movies.

As part of her *schtick*, Cybill rants about female sexuality with occasional bouts of outrage and hysteria. She told Burt that the plots of many of the episodes of her show "were mined from her own family, marriage, and experiences."

Burt appeared in only one segment with her, portraying himself as a guest at her party in *The Cheese Stands Alone*, in which she gets a job on TV in a cheesy sitcom.

***

By the end of 1995, Burt was offered a star role in *The Maddening*, an erotic psychological thriller referred to later as a "direct-to-video creepfest." The only good thing for him was that he worked with one of his dearest and most supportive friends, Angie Dickinson. "We've seen better days," he told Angie. Perhaps with a certain bitter irony, she agreed, of course.

The plot swirls around the kidnapping of a young mother, Cassie Osborne (Mia Sara), and her five-year-old daughter.

Cassie stops at a seedy gas station run by Roy Scudder (Burt), who rigs her vehicle to break down a short distance down the road. He then lures mother and daughter back to his home where they meet Georgina (as portrayed by Dickinson), his insane wife.

At one point, Roy (Burt) rapes his captive, and chains her to a bed. The plot got so complicated that even Burt had a hard time following it to its final bitter conclusion.

What was even more "maddening" than the title of the movie was that it generated only $5,000, the lowest box office receipt of any film Burt ever made.

***

For a 1996 release of *Citizen Ruth*, a comedy/drama, Alexander Payne made his directorial debut, tackling head-on the subject of abortion. *[The very mention of an abortion in a movie was once forbidden by the long-abandoned Production Code.]*

Laura Dern was its star, cast in the title role of Ruth Stoops, a poor, irresponsible, and

A Maddening Plot. A Maddening work environment on the set. And Maddeningly unprofitable.

pregnant druggie. After having intercourse in a flophouse with a stranger, she gets pregnant for the fifth time.

Burt was assigned the role of an anti-abortionist, Blaine Gibbons, a character he hated. After years as a romantic lead, Burt was reduced to eleventh billing.

The film depicts the escalating battle between the pro and anti-abortion forces. Both sides engage in deceitful practices. Payne insisted that his film was really about the human side of fanaticism.

Shot on a budget of $3 million, it generated $285,000 at the box office.

Citizen Ruth with a photo of Burt as an anti-abortionist with eleventh billing.

***

At last, Burt finally got a key role in a 1996 erotic black comedy that actually made money at the box office. *Striptease* was both directed, co-produced, and written by Andrew Bergman, who cast Demi Moore as the lead. She plays an FBI secretary-turned-stripper who gets embroiled in both a child custody case dispute and corrupt politics. For her starring role, she was paid an astonishing $12.5 million, making her the highest-paid actress in film history. At the time Burt met her, she was married to her second husband, actor Bruce Willis.

Burt was cast in his most colorful role of the decade, that of the unhinged politician, Congress David Dilbeck. He visits The Eager Beaver, a strip club in Miami, and becomes enchanted with Demi's character of Erin Grant.

When his political enemies plot to expose him, they end up murdered. Dilbeck invites Erin to perform privately for him, and even asks her to become his lover (later, his wife). Fearing a scandal, his political backers debate whether they should kill her.

Erin, along with police officer Lt. Al Garcia (Armand Assante), concocts a plan to bring the congressman and Erin's potential assassins to justice.

The reception of *Striptease* was mixed, opening to bad reviews and poor box office—at least in the U.S. Made for $50 million, it generated $113 million, mainly in Europe.

It also won the Golden Raspberry Award as Worst Picture of the Year. Moore's overpaid starring performance marked the beginning of a massive downturn in her career.

Striptease with Demi Moore.

Right photo, Burt—never afraid to self-satirize—as a lecherous congressman head over heels in love with Moore and slathered in Vaseline.

***

In an offbeat, rarely seen film, *Frankenstein and Me* (1996), Burt had a co-starring role in this 91-minute movie shot at Trimark Studios and directed by Robert Tinnell.

The setting is the small desert town in the Mojave Desert. There, a 12-year-old boy, Earl Williams, is obsessed with monsters in horror movies.

Frankenstein is his favorite monster, and his fantasies are supported by his father, Lee Williams (Burt). A failed Hollywood actor (Burt called it "type casting"), he is also a dreamer. When he dies, Earl's mother doesn't know what to do with her son.

When the traveling carnival comes to town, Earl wanders into the House of Mysteries, where he meets what the carnival's hype defines as "the actual and authentic Frankenstein Monster."

When its local gig is over, the carnival leaves town. As Earl watches its vehicles go, the inanimate replica of the "monster" falls out of the back of a truck. Earl spends the

Poster for *Frankenstein and Me*.

It was the first time in recent memory when promoters of a Burt Reynolds film did not include his photographic likeness on the movie poster.

rest of the movie trying to bring it back to life.

When Burt sat through the final cut, he said, "I'm not writing an acceptance speech for the Academy Award."

***

Mad Dog Time (aka *Trigger Happy*) was a 1996 crime/comedy oddity mainly because of its cast of well-known actors and cameo appearances by a number of stars.

Director and scriptwriter Larry Bishop shoehorned and hired a high-profile roster of talented and widely popular actors—Ellen Barkin, Diane Lane, Gabriel Byrne, Richard Dreyfuss, Jeff Goldblum, Gregory Hines, and, finally, Burt himself—into the lead roles.

Some of the drama unfolds in a swanky, mob-patronized nightclub where gangsters listen to Rat Pack music when they're not shooting and killing each other.

Mickey Holliday (Goldblum) is the top enforcer for Vic (Dreyfuss), the mob boss, a sort of John Gotti figure. Rita and Grace (Barkin and Lane) are the gun molls, a pair of sisters. A lot of the cast gets bumped off, including "Wacky Jackie" Johnson (Burt himself) who makes dying look fun.

Christopher Jones, that heartthrob of yesterday, made his final screen appearance—his first in twenty-five years. Discovered by Shelley Winters in the 1960s and married for a while to Susan Strasberg, he was once hailed as "the New James Dean." His film career had sputtered and died, to some degree in the wake of his personal depression, after David Lean, the deeply respected director of *Lawrence of Arabia* (1962) and *Doctor Zhivago* (1965), cast him as the romantic lead in *Ryan's Daughter* (1969).

Paul Anka entertains as "Danny." Richard Pryor appears as "Jimmy the Gravedigger." He is seen in a wheelchair and speaks in a garbled voice. "Poor Richard looked like he was en route to the graveyard," Burt said.

Joey Bishop speaks one word ("hello"), and Bob Reiner is a limo driver.

On a budget of $8 million, the film made only $108,000. Reviews were hostile, *The New York Times* defining it as "a rat's nest of

Film critic Roger Ebert said, "*Mad Dog Time* is the first movie I have seen that does not improve on the sight of a blank screen viewed for the same length of time. "

600

hip pretensions posing as a comedy." *Entertainment Weekly* described it as "jaw-dropping incoherence." Both Roger Ebert and Gene Siskel nailed it as "the worst film of the year."

Christopher Jones in 1962 in *The Night of the Iguana.*

Tennessee Williams exerted "playwright's privilege" and seduced the handsome young star.

***

Director Russel Solberg asked Burt to star in a new action film, *Raven* (aka *Raven Team*). He played Raven Katz, with a supporting cast of Matt Battaglia as Duce Grant and Krista Allen as Cali Goodwin.

"I was given a script by Jacobsen Hart, but I changed all my lines," Burt claimed. "The really talented ones understand that filmmaking is a collaborative effort. If you say something funny, they say, 'I wrote that.'"

"Raven is very much a copy of that John Travolta movie, *Broken Arrow* (1996) with me playing his part."

[Burt was referring to the film in which Travolta co-starred with Christian Slater. It was about a high security, high-tech Air Force pilot who deliberately crashes a plane in Utah to hold its nuclear weapons for ransom.]

Burt's version of this saga went direct to video, although it did briefly open in theaters right before Christmas in Germany.

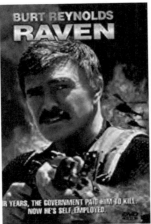

BURT REYNOLDS
RAVEN

R YEARS, THE GOVERNMENT PAID HIM TO KILL. NOW HE'S SELF-EMPLOYED.

"In *The Raven*, I got the star role once again, and I was even featured as the action star on the movie poster," Burt said.

"Only trouble was, no one wanted to see me in this dud."

***

For his final film in 1996, Burt took the third lead in *The Cherokee Kid,* a Western made for HBO, a picture directed by Paris Barclay.

It starred "Sinbad," who portrayed Isaiah Turner, a naïve farm boy who's transformed into a confident Old West gunslinger after the traumatizing murder of his parents. Born David Adkins, "Sinbad" was mainly a stand-up comedian known for his mocking commentaries on race relations and racism. That same year he worked with Burt, Sinbad toured with First Lady, Hillary Clinton, in a USO tour through Bosnia and Herzegovina.

Cast into a lesser role was James Coburn. Burt had envied his performances in films that included *The Magnificent Seven* (1960) and *Hell is for Heroes* (1962). Along with Lee Marvin, Steve McQueen, and Charles Bronson, the Nebraska-born Coburn was known as one of the most prominent "tough-guy" actors of his day. Film critic Pauline Kael claimed, "He looked like the child of a liaison between Lt. Pinkerton and Madame Butterfly."

The Cherokee Kid was the second picture Burt made with Gregory Hines, the African American dancer, actor, singer, and choreographer. He told Burt that at the age of two, he was tap dancing in Harlem.

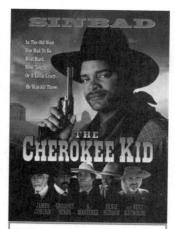

Sinbad—a new genre of action-adventure hero. In private, he said, "I traveled abroad with Hillary Clinton, but I never seduced her."

"I visited the dying bed of your friend and mine, Sammy Davis, Jr. in 1990," Hines said to Burt. "The throat cancer was advanced, and he couldn't speak. He made a gesture to me, as if passing a basketball...and I caught it. I'll carry on from where Sammy left off."

The Cherokee Kid begins with Sinbad's showdown with "The Undertaker (Hines) in Larabee, Texas. In the gunfight, the Kid falls, much to the delight of land-grabber Bloomington (Coburn), who has grown rich by forcing Native Americas to sell their land for almost nothing.

After the Kid's eulogy, the film drifts back to his journey in life.

As a child, to escape death from Bloomington (Coburn), the Kid flees and finds refuge in the wagon of Otter Bob (Burt), a lonely mountain man. A bond forms between them, as the Kid teaches Otter Bob to read, and Otter Bob teaches the Kid how to survive as a mountain man.

Other gunfighters overtake them for a

Burt, in his role of "Otter Bob" in *The Cherokee Kid,*" claimed, "I modeled my character after Gabby Hayes, that crusty old codger in all those Roy Rogers movies. Except Gabby had no teeth, and I flashed a mouthful entirely crafted by my dentist."

final battle, and Otter Bob sacrifices his life to save the Kid.

In a screening room, Burt sat through the film until his death scene. Then he abruptly got up from his seat and left the theater. He had something more important do to: He had to file for bankruptcy.

***

Sharon Waxman, a writer for *The Washington Post* said: "One day you're a movie star jetting across the country in a private plane, drinking champagne in your hot tub with a bunch of buddies and some lady friends. You've got five houses, a ranch, and some hundred-some horses."

"The next day," she continued, "You're making headlines. Divorced. Sued. Deeply in debt. Suddenly, the world knows you owe your toupee maker $121,797. Visa Gold has been withdrawn. Network CBS wants back that $3.7 million it lent you. *Now.*"

"No question about it: It's more fun being rich and famous."

Ken Kragen, Burt's business manager in 1991, said, "Many stars including Burt, feel invincible in their heyday. Even when things cool off, they still try to live the lifestyle of their glory days. Often, their business men don't challenge them out of fear of getting fired. Burt tried to live up to his old image long after his day as box office champ had passed."

At the time Kragen said that, it was estimated that at least a dozen top Hollywood stars, both women and men, were hovering on the brink of bankruptcy.

From prizefighters such as Leon Spinks, Sugar Ray Seales, or Michael Nunn, as well as movie stars, many celebrities have filed for bankruptcy, including a future president, Donald Trump. Stars who bit the bullet included M.C. Hammer, Kim Basinger, Lynn Redgrave, Dorothy Hamill, Merv Griffin, and Wayne Newton.

Time and time again, Burt was asked, "What did you do to dump millions of dollars?" Hal Needham said, "You could have bought Jackie Onassis for that."

"I hate looking like a deadbeat, but I've had a lot of shits dipping into my pot of gold over the years." Burt said.

Burt talked with many of his friends about how painful it was for him to file Chapter 11. "It's ripping me apart, because I always paid my bills. I'm no Donald Trump skipping out. I have hopes for tomorrow. I've been rich, and I've been po'. Maybe I can rise again. Of course, maybe not at my age."

For a long time, Burt's lawyer, Robert Montgomery (not the famous movie star, of course), had urged him to file for Chapter 11. "I cajoled, implored, did whatever I could, and the answer was always 'no.' Finally, Burt was faced with no other choice. In language not very legal, he was going belly up."

In 1996, when Burt filed for bankruptcy, he possessed assets of $6.5 million, but owed some $12 million in debts.

Millions had poured into his coffers between 1978 and 1982, when he was a box office champ, releasing such mega-hits as *Smokey and the Bandit*, his all-time box office grosser.

At his peak earning power, his accountant listed his net worth as $60 million, which in today's dollars would be at least $150 million.

He lived lavishly, buying mansions and vacation retreats. They included properties in North Carolina, Georgia, Texas, Florida, Arkansas, and Beverly Hills, plus a 160-acre ranch in Jupiter complete with 150 horses. He spent millions on a private jet and a helicopter with two co-pilots standing by to take off at any time.

"I should never have listened to those jerks who lured me into those restaurant chains," Burt claimed. "I also invested in something called Daisy Diner, which ended up costing me another $15 million. Some jerk from Daisy phoned once a day, telling me he needed another $1 million in cash. On my worst day, he demanded $5 million in cash."

His restaurant chain, PoFolks, ended up with $30 million in unpaid bills.

By the time he married Loni Anderson in 1988, his fortune had dwindled to $15 million, and the divorce court took a chunk of that. The court denied her request for $75,000 monthly for child support for Quinton, their adopted son, lowering the figure to $15,000 a month.

There was also a $1.9 million mortgage on her home to pay off.

Creditors who wanted to seize his assets included CBS, Chase Manhattan Bank, First Union Bank in Nashville, William Morris, International Creative Management, and agents for Creative Artists. Of course, ex-wife Loni wanted her share, too.

Burt's bankruptcy did not mark the end of his financial woes. Even when it was over, a bank foreclosed on one of his properties, and he continued his battles with the IRS over unpaid taxes.

***

As the 1990s moved on, and as Burt continued to find work, his agent summed up how he was viewed in Hollywood. "There's a split between the executives in town who are under forty and those who are over forty.

The younger executives are more open to Burt because they grew up loving *Deliverance*. But the older ones remember how crazy he was, and they are less receptive."

He viewed his next film as "merely taking home a paycheck." He was referring to the 1997 comedy, *Meet Wally Sparks*, directed by Peter Baldwin. The comedian, Rodney Dangerfield, was not only the star but the co-writer of the screenplay.

Other than Burt, supporting players included Debi Mazar, cast as Wally's (i.e., Rodney's) producer, Sandy Gallo.

Sparks is the host of a sleazy, tabloid-style TV talk show which "would make Jerry Springer look like Mother Theresa, and Joan Rivers look like a Sunday school teacher."

His ratings are nose-diving and the head of the network, Lenny Spencer (Burt) gives him an ultimatum, "Clean up your ratings in a week, or you're out the door."

RODNEY DANGERFIELD
He's a menace to High Society.

As a team, Baldwin and Dangerfield persuaded a lot of big names to appear in cameos, including Jerry Springer himself. Also appearing were Jay Leno, Geraldo Rivera, Roseanne, Morton Downey, Jr., Sally Jesse Raphael, and even Burt's co-star of yesterday, George Hamilton.

Look for Tony Danza as a New York cabbie. The porn star, Ron Jeremy, appears as himself. "He didn't display his thick nine-inch cock," Burt said, "and we can be grateful for that."

Garnering largely negative reviews, the film had a strong box office opening weekend. Its numbers quickly dwindled. Its final gross was around $4 million.

***

Burt's next film was *Bean* (aka *Bean: The Ultimate Disaster Movie*). Although it was a hit in both America and in England, its success had nothing to do with Burt's star power.

In *Meet Wally Sparks*, Burt looked distinguished as the CEO of a network TV studio. "This was Rodney Dangerfield's show," Burt said. "The rest of the cast, including myself, were mere mannequins."

It was based on the British TV series, *Mr. Bean*. Rowan Atkinson was cast as Mr. Bean, supported by Peter MacNicol, Pamela Reed, Harris Yulin, and Burt himself.

Mr. Bean is a well-intentioned but hopelessly clumsy security guard at the Royal National Gallery in London. He is put in charge of a transfer of the portrait, *Whistler's Mother*, to the Grierson Art Gallery in Los Angeles, following its purchase by philanthropist General Newton (Burt) for $50 million.

Expect the usual mishaps and disasters, enough to attract audiences who shelled out $251 million to see this improbable farce.

***

Despite the much-fallen state of his acting career at this stage of his life, Burt was occasionally assigned the lead in a low-budget quickie. Such was the case when he starred in *Big City Blues* (1997) directed by Clive Fleury, who had also written the script.

It focuses on a bizarre cast of characters who unknowingly cross paths during a night in "the Big City."

Burt and William Forsythe were cast as hitmen who receive their murder contacts from an Englishman.

Dreaming hopelessly of a career as a model, Angela is a beautiful prostitute. She is searching for her *doppelgänger* and gets involved with two trannies, Georgie and Babs.

***

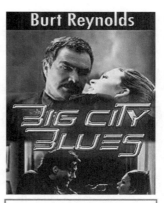

Burt Reynolds

"*Boogie Nights*, a 1997 drama distributed by New Line Cinema, was the worst experience I ever had making a film," Burt said. "I clashed with the director (Paul Thomas Anderson) on several occasions, and felt I was on some level the victim of a gimmick."

[In making that statement, he ignored the fact that it was the most lauded performance of his life—it even received an Oscar nod—and that it revived his sagging film credits.]

Boogie Nights also helped establish the successful screen career of actor and hip-hop

No longer in his familiar role of a police detective, Burt was cast as a hitman in *Big City Blues*.

"It was my big chance to work with a pair of trannies," he said.

606

singer Mark Wahlberg—previously known as "Marky Mark" and the Funky Bunch—and for posing almost nude for Calvin Klein underwear ads showing off his bulging basket.

The film was the brainchild of Paul Thomas Anderson, who wrote, produced, and directed it. He based it on a short "mockumentary" he created in high school called *The Dirk Diggler Story.* That short was originally based on a 1981 documentary: *Exhausted: John C. Holmes, The Real Story.* It was about the life and times of the most famous male porn star of the 1970s, John C. Holmes, known for his exceptional endowment. At the apex of his career, he had starred in some 560 adult films and was said to have had sex with some 14,000 women and a scattering of gay men.

For extra money, he charged rich gays $1,000 for his sexual intimacies. He made only one full-length gay movie, but a number of short "anal loops" with young actors serving as bottoms. During the course of his career, he was said to have caused the death of two young boys on whom he performed sodomy, but that may be just an urban, or porn-industry, myth.

Cinematographer Bob Vosse, in the documentary, *Wadd: The Life and Times of John C. Holmes,* claimed, "Holmes was to the adult film industry what Elvis was to rock 'n' roll. Holmes simply was the King of Porn."

In 1971, Holmes launched his career in porn through a series of hard-core movies centered on a private investigator named "Johnny Wadd."

Holmes died of AIDS in March of 1988.

Writer/director Anderson, known as a *wunderkind* and a native of Los Angeles born in 1970, would, over the course of his career, be nominated for 25 Academy Awards, winning three for members of his cast and crew.

He directed his first feature film, *Hard Eight,* in 1996, the year before he shot *Boogie Nights.* Roger Ebert, writing about *Hard Eight,* said, "Such movies remind me of what original, compelling characters the movies can sometimes give us."

For *Boogie Nights,* Anderson wound up with one of the most tal-

Burt "directs" Mark Wahlberg in *Boogie Nights.* As the porn director, Burt jokingly told the former Marky Mark: "At the end of our movie, you've got to unzip and show at least fourteen inches flaccid."

"If you're not hung that well—flaccid, that is—the prop department will use a prosthetic."

ented coven of actors in the 1990s. Ironically almost none of the members of the final cast had been his first choices. Long before he cast Burt as porn director Jack Horner, he pitched the part to Bill Murray, Harvey Kietel, Warren Beatty, Albert Brooks, and Sydney Pollack.

Julianne Moore and Mark Wahlberg prepping for an off the record porn scene in *Boogie Nights*. Many critics wondered why such a distinguished and talented actress as Moore was doing porn.

The role of Dirk Diggler was originally offered to Leonardo DiCaprio, but he had signed to film the blockbuster *Titanic*. Anderson then offered the role to Joaquin Phoenix, who seemed not too happy with his casting as a porn actor. It was DiCaprio who suggested Mark Wahlberg.

Both Drew Barrymore and Tatum O'Neal were considered for the role of Brandy ("Rollergirl"), who does everything, even have sex, on skates. Heather Graham was eventually cast in the part.

"Initially, I felt *Boogie Nights* would be the film disaster of the '90s," Burt said. "I kept turning it down but Anderson was persistent. I was told he wanted to be the hot fucking dog of American movies in the '90s."

"At our first reading, I met Mark and he came over to me and said, 'How you doing, Dad?'"

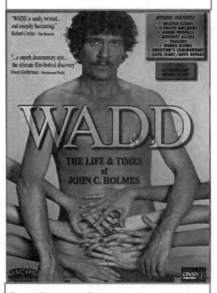

Porn King John C. Holmes, appearing on screen as Johnny Wadd, boasted: "It took a lot of female hands to cover up my horse-like junk."

"Our father-son relationship remained so throughout the shoot."

One reviewer commented on Burt as "Papa Bear to a dysfunctional family of misfits and good-natured sex perverts."

In the film, Burt was viewed as "a low-rent Hugh Hefner, who, smoking a Tiparillo, views a sex scene with the detached eye of a judge at a livestock show."

Boogie Nights opens in 1977 when Eddie Adams (Wahlberg), a seventeen-year-old high school dropout, is working at a nightclub as a busboy.

There, he meets Jack Horner (Burt).

He auditions him by watching him have sex with the Rollergirl (Graham), who acts her part with "zonked-out grace." Horner thinks the secret of Eddie's success in porn lies in that "something special he has between his legs, an enormous penis."

Colonel James (Robert Ridgely) meets Eddie—now billed as Dirk Diggler—at a party at Jack's house. He demands the teenager show him his junk. Dirk obliges, opening his trunks to give the financier a preview.

Before the film ends, the entire audience will get to see what made the Colonel stare. There is no longer any illusion as Dirk unzips and dangles his genitalia for the world to see. Of course, it was prosthetic.

In one of her best-ever performances, Julianne Moore had the second lead, cast as Maggie, whose porn name was "Amber Waves." She is Burt's "wife," and a sort of mother figure earning a living, among other pursuits, by going down on Diggler's mammoth appendage. One critic claimed that Moore "pierces the heart as Amber, who buries her agony in cocaine and parental role playing with Dirk and Rollergirl."

Others in the talented cast include William H. Macy as "Little Bill" Thompson, Jack's assistant director. He has to stand idly by at sex parties watching his wife, Nina Hartley, get it on with any man she can.

Dirk's new best friend is Reed Rothchild (John C. Reilly), who develops a crush on him.

Philip Seymour Hoffman appears as "Scotty J.," Dirk's most ardent admirer. Buck Swope (Don Cheedle) is a second-tier actor and would be high-fi salesman.

As *Rolling Stone* noted, Burt "blends crack comic timing with unexpected sincerity, hitting a career high as the director who thinks he can turn porn into art."

The action takes place during the waning years of the decadent 1970s and the advent of the early '80s where the home video revolution shakes up the porn industry's *modus operandi* and upsets everyone's lives and incomes.

As the movie rolls along, *Boogie Nights* shifts gears, revealing the dark, disastrous side of fame, power, and sex. Drugs, jealousy, and big business take their toll as lives are devastated.

When Burt sat through the final cut of *Boogie Nights*, he was so outraged that he fired his agent.

Although Burt may have despised his young director, Anderson was obviously pleased with Burt's performance, because he asked him to join the cast of *Magnolia* (1999) a "mosaic of misery" with many of the same actors who had appeared in *Boogie Nights*, i.e., Julianne Moore, John C. Reilly,

William H. Macy, and Philip Seymour Hoffman. Tom Cruise, cast in the lead of *Magnolia*, had been a fan of *Boogie Nights*.

Boogie Nights took in a worldwide gross of $45 million and for the most part garnered rave reviews.

Janet Maslin of *The New York Times* praised Burt's work, claiming, "It is his best and most suavely funny performance in many years. Like Jerry Lewis in *The King of Comedy*, Reynolds gives the role an extra edge by playing a swaggering, self-important figure very close to the bone. The movie's special gift is Mark Wahlberg as Dirk Diggler, his *nom de porn.*"

Roger Ebert wrote, "*Boogie Nights* is an epic of the low road, a classic Hollywood story set in the shadow instead of the spotlight but containing some of the same ingredients: Fame, envy, greed, talent, sex, money. The movie follows a large, colorful, and curiously touching cast of characters as they live through a crucial turning point in the adult film industry."

Mick LaSalle of the *San Francisco Chronicle* claimed that *Boogie Nights* "is the first great film about the 1970s, capturing the decade's distinct, decadent glamour." Andrew Johnson in *Time Out New York* said, "The porn milieu may scare some folks off, but the movie offers laughs, tenderness, terror, and redemption. The Academy really should have the balls to recognize it."

At Oscar time, Burt was nominated for Best Supporting Actor, joining Moore, who was nominated for Best Supporting Actress. Anderson was nominated for Best Original Screenplay.

Burt had never been given many awards—and would never be so honored again. He was also nominated Best Actor by the Screen Actors Guild. He also won a Golden Globe and the Awards of the New York Film Critics Circle and the National Society of Film Critics.

He said, "Often, actors don't get the awards they deserve. Take Clark Gable as Rhett Butler in *Gone With the Wind*. I can't find one flaw in his performance, but everyone else but him won awards. He walked away with nothing. I'm not comparing myself to him, but I think that once you get into a certain category, people just take you for granted. They look at my work and they say, 'How can we put cotton candy under a microscope.' Well, you don't have to unless the cotton candy has somehow shown an incredible resiliency. It's managed to survive where all odds are against it."

CHAPTER SEVENTEEN

A LION IN WINTER

Burt Hobbles from One Film Disaster to Another...
"But Still In There Kicking Ass!"

A Fan Claims that Burt was
"Cary Grant Crossed with Tom Jones"

"I'm going to keep working until they shoot me and take me off and bury me— and I hope they film it."

"I should write a book and call it 'The Forgotten Films of Burt Reynolds.'"

MORE ABOUT PAMELA SEALS

Burt's Long-Time Mistress Sues for Half of His Assets
Plus Lifetime Support for Herself and Her Mother

BURT & SYLVESTER STALLONE

Are Voted "Worst Screen Couple of the Year" When They Lose the Race in *Driven*, A Film Defined by Critics as "A FLOP CATASTROPHE"

"GOODBYE BANDIT"

The Final Curtain:
Burt Collapses and Dies
of a Heart Attack in Florida

To Baby Boomers who flocked to the movies of the 1970s and '80s, Burt Reynolds remains a screen legend. To the generations that followed, he is an obscure footnote in Hollywood history, a faded box office champ of yesterday. Nonetheless, he left an indelible legacy.

"Today, if devotees of Turner Classics are in the market for 1970s sleaze, turn to me," Burt said. "There was no actor better at depicting it than me. My greatest fun was working with fat boy, Dom DeLuise. He and I were what Hope and Crosby were to audiences of the 1940s."

In the *National Review,* Kevin D. Williamson wrote: "At the end of his life, Burt Reynolds reminded me a little bit of sainted Pope (1978-2005) John Paul II, who was an actor early in his life. Reynolds kept working. He was very old, and in poor health, and he declined in full view of the public, subject to that public's habitual cruelty, against which he made no defense other than his own wry self-deprecation. He preached no sermons and invoked no higher power. He just kept going, kept working. Maybe he didn't want to sit around waiting to die."

"Time may have stripped him of some of his bravado and virility, but simple endurance is a manly virtue, too, one that is undervalued at the moment."

Burt himself was disarmingly frank about the peaks and valleys of his incredible life. "I'm the world's worst sucker when it came to handling money. Some actors—at least a few—are brilliant about making investments and piling up the loot. Those guys—and I won't name them—happen to be lousy actors, but great businessmen."

When he was asked at century's end if he had any regrets, he said, "I wish I'd spent even more money and had a lot more fun. There were many available female stars in Hollywood that I never got around to."

***

In the late 1990s, Burt, along with co-star Rob Lowe, entered the sometimes bizarre postmodern world of director Albert Pyun. Pyun was best known for his low-budget, direct-to-video 'B' movies. He had carved out a Hollywood niche for himself by blending martial arts (especially kickboxing) with sci-fi and dystopian or post-apocalyptic themes.

Some of Pyun's best-known films included *Brain Smasher...A Love Story* (1993) with Andrew Rice Clay; *Captain America* (1990) with Matt Salinger; and *Postmortem* (1998) with Charlie Sheen, the disgraced party boy.

Pyun was also known for casting actors past their prime—hence the teaming of Burt with Rob Lowe for the 1997 video release of *Crazy Six.*

Crazy Six takes place a decade after the fall of Communism in some unnamed Eastern Bloc country. Powerful clan families have emerged from the anarchy to vie for control of the lucrative arms trade.

Cast as Dakota, Burt is a grizzled and very cynical cop wearing a gigantic cowboy hat and having nothing to lose except perhaps his life.

Lowe played a grunged-up crackhead gang leader working alongside his frenemy, a French-accented, dog-stroking mobster, Dirty Mao, as played by Mario Van Peebles.

One reviewer was taken with the "Kool-Aid colors" of blue, green, yellow, red, and fuschia. Another reviewer defined *Crazy Six* as "an unwatchable mess, a dull perfume commercial from hell that even wastes Burt Reynolds." Yet another critic claimed, "*Crazy Six* is the best-photographed and most poorly written film ever made."

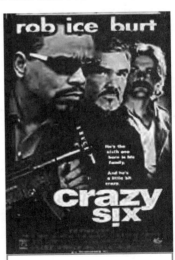

In a place called "Crimeland," all hope is gone and dark visions rule as Ice-T, Burt, and Rob Lowe co-star in *Crazy Six.*

Burt was very sympathetic to Lowe, since each of them had been recent victims of widely distributed tabloid scandals. In 1988, a sex tape of Lowe had been leaked to the public and been widely viewed across the world. At the Democratic National Convention, Lowe had campaigned for Michael Dukakis. Then, as part of some political revenge that might have been associated with his endorsement of Dukakis, Lowe had appeared on a television tape having sex with a sixteen-year-old.

Then, another sex tape was released. It had been filmed in a hotel room in Paris, showing Lowe and Justin Morritt having both oral and vaginal sex with an unidentified girl. Even more than the events associated with the first scandal, these sex tapes damaged Lowe's public image and his film career.

When asked about the sex tape indiscretions of his co-star, Rob Lowe, Burt responded jokingly. "If that sexy guy and I did a sex tape with just the two of us, it would outgross Linda Lovelace's *Deep Throat*. We'd make enough money to retire in luxury for life."

When Rob Lowe made a "comeback" after public disgrace for his involvement in some porn films, every actor in Hollywood, on the rise or on the decline (i.e., Burt Reynolds) took notice.

***

"My success with *Boogie Nights*, and with all those awards it generated, revealed to the world I was still alive and in there, ass-kicking," Burt said. "TV and movie offers were coming in, and I went for a trilogy from TNT where I would play a detective again in something akin to what I'd done in my TV series, *Dan August* (1970-71)."

The provisions of his contract allowed him to direct the first movie within the package. It was *Hard Time* (1988). "My character was called Conrad Logan, but I changed the name to Logan McQueen in honor of Steve McQueen."

"I enjoyed directing," Burt said. "It's the difference between being a chess player and a chess pawn."

"The series was a chance for me to do something that the Turner Network had never done before," he said. "That was to take a few characters and star them in all three films. But they would change their personalities in every episode of the trilogy."

Once again, Burt brought in his longtime pal, actor Charles Durning, cast as Det. Charlie Duffy. *Variety* was a bit cruel in its review of this pairing. "Reynolds cruises the mean streets of Miami *[actual shooting was in Los Angeles]* with his partner, Charles Durning. Welcome to the Geritol School of Law Enforcement. We see 62-year-old Reynolds sprinting after some low-lives, wheezing and appearing on the verge of collapse. At this pace, his only arrest is liable to be of the cardiac kind. Apparently, he is determined to show the world he's still as macho as ever, since his character later beats the crud out of a couple of thugs, blowing holes through chests using weapons powerful enough to bring down a superpower. Even the 75-year-old Durning gets to rough up some undesirables."

In other key roles were Robert Loggia as bad guy Connie Martin, and Billy Dee Williams as a politically motivated prosecutor.

Mia Sara, as the female lead, has the camera panning up her shapely, pantyhose-clad leg, signaling she's the *femme fatale* of the piece.

A critic wrote, "Reynolds has enough charisma to pull off the cranky cop *schtick* despite his whitened hair and world-weary countenance."

Reteaming Burt with Durning, *Hard Time: The Premonition* (1999) was the second film within TNT's trilogy. Burt's longtime crony, Hal Needham, was called in to direct. Bruce Dern had the third lead in yet another detective yarn whose plot was so familiar it was quickly forgotten.

For the final episode, *Hard Time: Hostage Hotel*, Burt was directed by Needham, with Durning cast as his sidekick detective. This episode was more memorable and had the added advantage of the casting of the third lead with Keith Carradine, an actor, singer, songwriter, and the son of the famous star, John Carradine.

One critic called the last of the *Hard Time* trilogy "a bargain-basement *Die Hard*." Carradine was cast as a vengeance-seeking Vietnam vet, Arlin Flynn, who takes over a landmark hotel in Los Angeles, which he has booby-trapped at strategic locations.

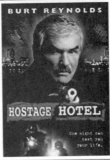

Congressman Robert Sinclair (David Rasche) is delivering a speech in the main ballroom, and Flynn not only kidnaps his family, but Burt's detective sidekick, Durning, too.

Burt has to work his way through all those booby traps for the inevitable rescue.

A formulaic triology, a "bargain-basement *DIE HARD*" reteamed Burt with his faithful pal, Charles Durning, in what detractors called the "Geritol School of Law Enforcement."

***

Director Richard Weinman united Burt and Keith Carradine once again in *The Hunter's Moon* (1999), an action drama. Alaska-born Hayley DuMond had the third lead. The movie opened in only a few theaters with mostly empty seats. After that, it went to video.

The plot takes place in the Depression era when Turner (Carradine), a World War I vet, returns to the States with other members of his "Lost Generation." Once there, he stumbles upon a backwoods mountainside community where he falls in love with the daughter of a tyrannical landowner, Clayton Samuels. Naturally, to stir up the plot, this cranky old man (Burt) will stop at nothing to prevent his daughter from running off with Turner.

During its filming, Carradine was in the midst of divorcing his first wife, Sandra Will, and he fell for his co-star, DuMond, although he would not marry her until 2006.

***

As he rushed from one picture to another, the closing year of the 20th Century was one of the busiest of Burt's career. *Pups* was directed by a Londoner, Ash Baron-Cohen, who billed himself only as "Ash."

He was also the writer of this independent drama about two 13-year-olds, a boy and a girl, who spontaneously decide to rob a bank one morning on their way to school. That morning Stevie (Cameron Van Hoy) discovered a .44 Magnum in his mother's closet. He entices his girlfriend Rocky (Mischa Barton) into the scheme.

The two of them were later labeled "the Bonnie & Clyde of the MTV Generation." In some ways, *Pups* evokes the film *Dog Day After-noon* (1975) starring Al Pacino.

The alarm at the bank brings the police rushing to the scene, along with a SWAT team and helicopters overhead. Directing the operation is FBI

In *The Hunter's Moon*, Burt Reynolds plays a tyrannical landowner in a backwoods settlement who will "stop at nothing" to break up his daughter's love affair.

In *Pups*, Burt is an FBI agent facing two 13-year-old bank robbers (a boy and a girl).

Irked by his importunate superior and repeatedly interrupted by cellphone calls from his family, he wants to end the stand-off without bloodshed.

He does not get his wish.

616

agent Daniel Bender (Burt), whose job is to try to get the young bank robbers to give themselves up or at least to release the hostages. During the ordeal, he fulfills requests (everything from food to condoms) from the young robbers inside.

Finally, near the end, Stevie surrenders. As he leaves the bank, he attempts to remove a flower from his pocket, but is fatally shot by a member of the SWAT team posted on a nearby roof.

Burt, as Bender, yells, "Get that motherfucker down from the roof."

It is too late.

Burt played his role with what was called "a workmanlike mixture of toughness, irascibility, and mission." Robert Koehler of *Variety* said, "Reynolds works against his character's *clichés* and indicates that *Boogie Nights* was no fluke." *Entertainment Weekly* praised Burt's "energized performance."

Pups really belongs to Cameron Van Hoy as Stevie, who was called "amazing, like a game boy junkie turned into a virtual James Cagney." One critic said he was a "volatile, fast-talking compendium of pop culture, childish rage, adolescent mischief, and adult stupidity and remorse."

Politically, *Pups* could not have opened at a worst time. It held its premiere only two days before the Columbine High School massacre in Littleton, Colorado, which led off the evening news every night for at least a week.

[*In* Pups, *Adam Farrar, the 28-year-old brother of Leonardo DiCaprio, played a paraplegic Gulf War veteran. He made headlines when he was arrested and later released for his allegedly threatening to kill his girlfriend at Marina Del Rey.*]

***

Burt hardly remembered making *Stringer* (also 1999), in which he played a cynical "news hound" named Wolko. The plot takes a harsh view of "stringer journalism."

As a bureau chief of a local news outlet, Wolko sends a stringer to the site of high-visibility fires, accidents, rapes, and robberies. He turns his camera on rape victims, burning firemen, dying supermarket guards, and car crash victims. The sensation-seeking Wolko, as time goes by, demands ever more sensational im-

In *The Stringer*, Burt played cynical Wolko, a sensation-demanding newspaper bureau chief who goads his stringer into more and more shocking images.

It's a bitter examination of the worst side of so-called journalism.

ages for his newspaper.

***

For his final film release in 1999, Burt was assigned a minor role in a Russell Crowe comedy-drama, *Mystery, Alaska*. Directed by Jay Roach, this was the tale of an amateur ice hockey team from the fictional town of Mystery that plays an exhibition game against the National Hockey League. The movie was shot in the Banff National Park outside Canmore, Alberta.

Crowe played Sheriff John Biebe, who is married to Donna (Mary McCormack).

At one point, the hockey team's star player, Connor Banks (Michael Buie), shoots a local, Judge Burns (Burt) holds a trial but the jury finds him not guilty, not wanting him to miss an upcoming game. Judge Burns angrily addresses the townspeople, telling them they have exalted the hockey star over what is right, and they have disgraced themselves and his courtroom.

Made for $28 million, the film earned $9 million at the box office. The lack of hockey action and authenticity left most critics cold.

***

Burt launched himself into the 21st Century by co-starring with Richard Dreyfuss in *The Crew* (2000), a black comedy crime drama directed by Michael Dinner. It was the story of four retired mobsters who choreograph one last crime as a means of saving their home on South Miami Beach.

Two pros: Russell Crowe with Burt in Mystery, Alaska. a town that wants to win at hockey at any cost.

RICHARD DREYFUSS   BURT REYNOLDS

THE CREW

DAN HEDAYA   SEYMOUR CASSEL   CARRIE-ANNE MOSS   JENNIFER TILLY

Richard Dreyfuss, Burt, Dan Hedaya, and Seymour Cassel plan one last crime.

It leads to their entrapment in a Columbian drug-smuggling ring.

Dreyfuss had seen better days on the screen, having starred in such hits as *American Graffiti* (1973), *Jaws* (1975), and *Close Encounters of the Third Kind* (1977). In *The Crew,* he plays Bobby Bartellemo, the leader of the criminal quartet.

Bert was cast as "Bats," a cantankerously aging man with a short fuse and a pacemaker. "I knew the character I wanted to play because I understand this guy very well. He goes from being perfectly sane to, within a quarter of a second, choking you to death and banging your head against the floor. I've played wise guys before, but I've never played a wise guy who is demented. That's the reason they call me Bats."

The other two criminals are "Mouth" (Saymour Cassel), a ladies' man many years past his prime, and "The Brick" (Dan Hedaya), a nice but dim-witted gangster from yesterday.

The unholy four steal a corpse from the mortuary to use as a "victim" in a staged murder scene. From that point on, the script becomes entangled in a zany blend of drug lords, burning buildings, kidnappings, and a young stripper, Ferris (Jennifer Tilly).

Reviews were mostly negative, many critics citing *The Crew's* similarity to Clint Eastwood's *Space Cowboys* (2000), which involved four crabby retirees who reassemble for one final and dysfunctional flight into space.

The Crew was dismal at the box office, earning back only $13 million from its production cost of $38 million.

***

Burt had accepted the male lead in *Waterproof,* with shooting completed in 1998. But this Barry Berman-directed film could find no distributor until Cloud Ten Pictures bought the rights in 2002. Even so, the company didn't hold its premiere until August of 2001 at the Urbanworld Film Festival.

Cast as a store owner, Eli Zeal, Burt is shot by an eleven-year-old boy trying to rob him. His mother, Tyree Battle (April Grace), takes him to their hometown to nurse him through his recovery and to protect her son from the police.

At their home in Waterproof, Louisiana, a complicated melodrama unfolds as the lives

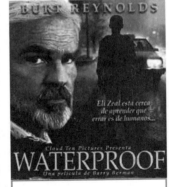

As the gunshot victim of an attempted robbery of his store by an 11-year-old boy, Burt gets involved in the complicated lives of the inhabitants of Waterproof, Louisiana.

of the locals and their problems may—or possibly not—interest the average viewer.

Most of the filming took place in Wilmington, North Carolina. Before the role was offered to Burt, Paul Newman, Gene Hackman, and Jack Lemmon wisely rejected it.

The kindest review was from Ken James in the *Christian Spotlight*. "Technically, it is well done and on par with most other indie films. The acting is convincing and the story strong enough to captivate those willing to sit through some initially slow drama."

***

The final film in which Burt would both star and direct was *The Last Producer (aka The Final Hit)*, released in 2000. The movie had certain autobiographical overtones for him and became a special favorite of his. He employed a number of friends, especially Ann-Margret cast as his pill-popping wife, Mira Verder. The leading supporting players were Rod Steiger and Benjamin Bratt.

Burt cast himself as Sonny Wexler, a washed-up veteran producer nominated long ago for an Oscar. He's fallen on bad days and labeled as a has-been. Desperate for a comeback, he feels he's got to make it with this last film, or else end up like hundreds of others walking down the Boulevard of Broken Dreams.

A new generation has taken over in Hollywood, as personified by Damon Black (Bratt) who wants to shove Sonny out the door. He has only seventy-two hours to raise money for the script he's desperate to produce, and he turns to the Mafia, borrowing $50,000.

Burt worked alongside such friends as Charles Durning, cast as Syd Wold, and also Robert Goulet and Angie Dickinson, his former co-star. Familiar faces, each cast as a poker player, included James Farentino, Shelley

Burt's star role in *The Last Producer* did not attract the attention the producers wanted.

In a desperate move, they changed the name of the film to *The Final Hit*, hoping to generate more box office. That, however, failed too.

Berman, and the comedian, Shecky Greene.

The Last Producer was first released on home video in Iceland and Argentina before being aired on American television.

***

The badly titled *Driven* (2001), an action sports film about car racing, had been a pet project for its star and screenwriter, Sylvester Stallone, for four years, during which he tried to get it financed, churning out twenty drafts of his screenplay.

When it was finally approved, Stallone turned to Renny Harlin to direct *Driven* and co-produce it. These men had previously teamed together during production of the film *Cliffhanger* (1993) in which Stallone was pitted against a ruthless gang in search of $100 million stashed in the Rockies.

In *Driven*, Stallone played Joe Tango, a former driver and Champ Car Champion. The paraplegic team owner, Carl Henry (Burt), convinces him to come out of retirement to serve as a mentor for Jimmy Bly (Kip Pardue), a hot shot in the racing world.

From that point on, *Driven* needs a "road map" to follow its tortuous turns and romantic complications.

Most of *Driven* was shot in Toronto, and scenes from a variety of worldwide races were interjected. The premiere took place at Grauman's Chinese Theatre in Hollywood and received negative reviews. Appearing on the TV show, *Ebert & Roeper,* Jay Leno described *Driven* as the worst car-racing film ever made. It was a commercial failure, grossing only $32 million on a budget of $72 million.

At the 22nd Golden Raspberry Awards, *Driven* received seven nominations, including Worst Picture, Worst Director,

In the ill-fated *Driven*, Sylvester Stallone (left) and Burt had seen better days.

As Stallone told him, "We can't always be No. One at the box office. You just can't be the guy in front all the time."

Worst Screenplay, and Worst Screen couple (Burt and Stallone). Burt was also nominated for Worst Supporting Actor.

Stallone summed it up: *"Driven* didn't do for me what *Rocky* did. I regretted making it."

Burt had his own summation: "I'm sorry I didn't pursue more aggressively the role of *Rocky* when it was first offered to me."

***

Tempted (2001) was an Australian-French-American thriller better than most fare that Burt was churning out at the time. In a nutshell, he starred as Charlie LeBlanc, a wealthy businessman dying from a brain tumor. He is married to Lilly LeBlanc (Saffron Burrows), thirty years his junior, and he wants to test her fidelity to see if she's worthy of inheriting his vast fortune.

He hires her handsome young law student, Jimmy (Peter Facinelli), to see if he can seduce Lilly. His looks were frequently cited by viewers as evoking a young Tom Cruise. For his services, Burt, as Charlie, offers the boy $50,000.

Things start to go wrong after Jimmy confides to his gay friend, Ted (Eric Mabius), about what the dying man is up to.

In the meantime, Charlie has hired a private eye to videotape everything going on behind locked doors. Soon there is a lot of incriminating evidence on tape.

The setting of New Orleans adds a touch of mystery and glamour to the backdrop.

The drama was both directed and written by Bill Bennett. A critic wrote that Bennett was one of those directors like Stanley Kubrick, who insists on exploring different genres to see if he could pull it off. Cited were

A critic at Fantasy Filmfest in Cologne, Germany, wrote: "*Tempted* always stays believable as the plot and characters are concerned. The thriller plot makes it very moody. The interaction between Burrows and Fascinelli is sexy—not to mention Burt Reynolds' great performance."

his Australian road movie, *Kiss or Kill* (1997); his period anthropological drama, *In a Savage Land* (1999) set in New Guinea, and his broad, gold-digging comedy *The Nugget* (2002).

Tempted was generally well received, though one reviewer recommended it only for "crime junkies, those intrigued by *film noir* flicks about infidelity, jealousy, deceit, temptation, deceit, and murder."

***

Director Mike Figgis, in pitching *Hotel* (2001) to Burt, described it as a "Dogme film-within-a-film." Burt really didn't know what he was talking about but took the seventh billing as the manager of the Flamenco Hotel.

As he read the script, it involved a hit man, a call girl, and a Hollywood producer. His strange hotel staff shares meals consisting of human meat.

Once again, as in *Tempted*, he appears with Saffron Burrows, cast as the Duchess of Malfi in Venice. [*A British film crew is shooting a celluloid version of the* Duchess of Malfi. *By John Webster, and published in 1623 as* The Tragedy of the Dutchesse of Malfy, *it has been interpreted as one of the greatest tragedies of English Renaissance drama.*]

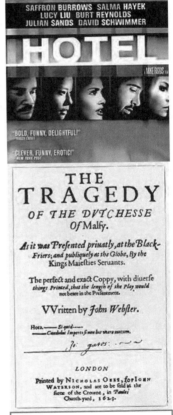

In turn, the British filmmakers are being filmed by a sleazy documentarian primadonna.

Supporting players include Lucy Liu, John Malkovich, David Schwimmer, and Salma Heyek.

Roger Ebert tried to sum up what was happening: "Many critics have agreed that *Hotel* is not successful. Not successful at what? Before you conclude that the movie doesn't work, you have to determine what it intends to do. This is not a horror movie, a behind-the-scenes movie, a sexual intrigue, or a travelogue, but all four at once. Elbowing one another for the screen time, it reminds me above all of a competitive series of jazz improvisations, in which musicians quote from many sources and the joy comes

Not Saffron Burrows, Not Salma Hayek...Not even Burt. None of them could save this misfire, even though some critics reviewed it as "bold, funny, delightful, clever, and erotic."

in the way they're able to keep their many styles alive in the same song. The movie has to be pointless in order to make any sense."

A confused mess, *Hotel* (2001) took in only $29,000 at the box office.

***

Another role for Burt in 2001 was *The Hollywood Sign,* a comedy/suspense drama directed by Sönke Wortmann and written by Leon de Winter. Tom Berenger, Rod Steiger, and Burt play a trio of washed-up actors risking their lives to make a comeback in Tinseltown. This trio of bumbling has-beens try to con a coven of gangsters into believing that they are cops. Steiger was particularly effective in one of his last screen roles.

The female lead went to Jacqueline Kim, cast as the confident, intelligent Paula Carver. Critics found she came off best when wearing little or no clothing.

The three film stars of yesteryear meet at the funeral of a legendary Hollywood agent, and soon, their alcoholic reunion has them visiting Los Angeles' famous H-O-L-L-Y-W-O-O-D Sign. There, they discover a corpse, which leads them to uncover an in-progress scam for stealing millions from a Las Vegas casino. The plot grows complicated at this point. Not only is it far-fetched, but filled with improbable coincidences and weird scams.

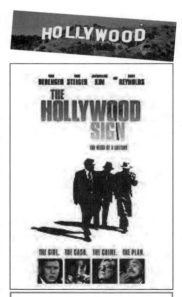

In a nutshell, the actors use a movie screenplay as the blueprint for the Vegas casino ripoff. A tender moment for Burt, cast as Kage Mulligan, occurs when he's seen watching himself on the screen in a flashback to a long-forgotten Western.

To end busy 2001, Burt appeared in an episode of the ill-fated TV series, *Emeril,* a sitcom starring cable TV celebrity chef Emeril Lagasse. Ten episodes were filmed, but only seven were aired from September to November of 2001.

Its creator, Linda Bloodworth-Thomason, had hoped that the series "would do for men what her other series, *Designing Women,* had done for women."

While filming was taking place, the Sep-

One critic wrote: "Everyone in this unfortunate flick seems to be waiting for the cue to drop. Performances are hickory; the screenplay is clumsy, timing is *waaaaay* off, and god knows where the director was during filming."

tember 11 terrorist attacks had occurred on the World Trade Center in Manhattan. The premiere was postponed but when it was finally shown, the opening sequence featured the doomed buildings standing erect.

Burt starred as himself in an episode called *The Sidekick*. He was sorry to see the series go off the air. The *Los Angeles Times* referred to it as "pretty dreadful."

***

Burt had long admired the acting of British star Julie Christie, an icon of "Swinging London in the 1960s." He looked forward to working with her when Director Rudolf van den Berg (who also co-wrote the script) cast them in *Snapshots* (2002), which was filmed in both Morocco and Amsterdam.

"I would have married Julie Christie, but Warren got to her first," he told his director.

He was referring to her affair with Warren Beatty, whom Burt continued to regard as a rival. Her intermittent relationship with Beatty ran between 1967 and 1974.

Born in British India, Julie had been considered for the role of Honey Rider in the first James Bond film, *Dr. No* (1962), but producer Albert R. Broccoli thought her breasts were too small.

Her breakthrough role had come playing the would-be lover of Tom Courtenay in *Billy Liar* (1963), but her real success came when John Schlesinger cast her as an amoral model in *Darling* (1965), resisting the studio's wish to star Shirley MacLaine, Beatty's sister. Julie won the Oscar that year for Best Actress. That same year, she played Lara Antipova in David Lean's *Doctor Zhivago*. Burt had also seen all the movies she'd made with Beatty, including when she played a brothel madam in Robert Altman's postmodern western, *McCabe & Mrs. Miller* (1971).

In *Snapshots*, Burt was cast as Larry Goldberg, in this story of first loves and second

Snapshots.

Lower pic: Julie Christie, one of the most recognizable cinematic beauties of the 60s, shown here in a publicity photo for *Dr. Zhivago* (1965)

chances. He is the hermit-like owner of a secondhand bookstore in Amsterdam, having lived there for three decades. A former poet, he still carries wounds from a past love affair with Julie, who was oddly cast as Narma, a Moroccan woman.

One day Aïsha (Carmen Chaplin) walks into his bookstore. In the movie, she looks like Larry's lost love from Morocco—indeed she is Narma's daughter. *[In real life, Carmen is the granddaughter of Charlie Chaplin.]*

The girl makes Larry rethink his life. In this tale of redemption and lost love, his old flame's daughter is out to "discover" her purpose in life, similar to what Burt's character is doing in flashbacks. He doesn't realize he is drawn to the girl because she reminds him of Narma. Carmen has dark features, twinkling blue eyes, and a slender, lithe body.

In her self-discovery, she is taking snapshots of herself, a series of black-and-white nude studies—hence the title of the movie.

Upon its release, *Snapshots* went directly to video. It developed a small following who appreciated its offbeat charm, although it suffered the usual brickbats.

"Burt Reynolds was out of his element," wrote one critic. "He's just not believable as an old hippie in Amsterdam—even smoking a joint. The story is a little too *clichéd* — coming of age, reuniting old loves, even flirting with 'older man falls for sweet young thing who may be his daughter.' But still, *Snapshots* holds my interest."

Another critic wrote, "This corny and awkward little flick has too many deficits. Suffice it to say that in the grand scheme of cinema, it's crap! However, as a no-brainer for sentiment watching for the zoning sofa spud, it squeaks by as nominal fluff. Recommended for fans of the players or anyone who can't find anything better on the channels."

***

The X-Files was a science fiction TV series created by Chris Carter that first aired from September of 1993 to 2002 on Fox, a total of 202 episodes, only one of which starred Burt. By the time it went off the air, it had become the longest-running sci-fi series in television history.

The plot spun around FBI special agents, Fox Mulder (David Duchovny) and Dana Scully (Gillian Anderson), who are assigned to probe paranormal phenomena. Mulder believes in the existence of aliens from Outer Space, whereas Scully is a medical doctor and a skeptic assigned to analyze Mulder's discoveries of the paranormal.

In the 13th episode of the ninth season, Burt starred in "Improbable" in which he was cast as God himself. Burt jokingly referred to it as "type casting." It is estimated that he was seen by nine million people out there in TV land.

Burt had told one of the *X-Files* stars, Robert Patrick, that he wanted to appear on the show. Patrick said, "As a young man, I had thrilled to Burt's movies. I found the chance of working with him surreal. We had a great time, and everybody in the cast loved him."

The show featured a very elaborate special effects gimmick in which the image of Burt's face appears in the sky above. This image was superimposed in the clouds over the cityscape by special effects artist Mat Beck, "I added a blue effect to make Burt look godly," he said.

That scene came at the end. Burt's first appearance was less than godly, as "God" shows up in a casino bar as a mysterious, mustachioed man speaking in an enigmatic way.

The truth is still out there.

THE X FILES
EVENT SERIES

FBI Special Agents David Duchovny and Gillian Anderson discover an agenda of the U.S. government to keep the existence of extra-terrestrial life a deep, dark secret.

***

After appearing in *The X-Files*, Burt was given the lead in a feature film, *Time of the Wolf* (2002), directed by Red Pridy and co-starring Marthe Keller and Devin Douglas Drewitz, a child actor.

Filmed in Ontario, the plot centers around an orphan boy who goes to live

Can you see the face of Burt (aka the face of God) in the mosaic-inspired cityscape laid out above?

The producers of *The X-Files* built an entire episode around it.

with his surviving relatives, an estranged aunt and uncle, Archie and Rebecca McGregor.

In the role of Aaron, Drewitz steals the picture when he bonds with a white wolf in the forest. *[The boy had previously appeared in two episodes of the Stephen Spielberg sci-fi TV miniseries,* Taken *(2002).]*

Also in the cast was Jason Priestley as Mr. Nelson, the schoolmaster.

[Time of the Wolf is not to be confused with the French suspense drama le

temps du Loup, starring Isabella Huppert and released around the same time.]

***

As the third lead, Burt joined a major cast to film the made-for-TV movie, *Johnson County War* (2002), shot in the untamed wild scenery of Wyoming. This epic picture of the Old West dramatized the infamous conflicts between 1889 and 1893 where ranchers and their hired guns battled the more innocent settlers, often hanging them.

The events that occurred during those horrendous days have been fodder for popular novels, films, and TV epics, presenting a highly mythologized and symbolical story of 19th Century North America's battles over land rights.

The Pulitzer Prize-winning author, Larry McMurtry, was mainly responsible for the screenplay. He is known for his romanticized adaptation of such legendary figures as Billy the Kid, Calamity Jane, and Wild Bill Hickock explored in such works as *Lonesome Dove* and *Buffalo Girls*.

Rachel Ward was cast as Queenie, a tough but highly likable prostitute.

Along with fellow ranchers, the trio of Hammett brothers are trying to protect their homestead property from the rich and powerful ranchers determined to drive them out, if not kill them. They are willing to commit whatever devious means are necessary.

This epic was presented against the backdrop of some of the most dramatic scenery in Wyoming.

***

A Touching Bond Between Boy and Beast

"I was the estranged uncle of this boy, as played by Devin Douglas Drewitz," Burt said.

"If an actor wants to get noticed, never star in a picture with a cute kid and a white wolf."

Burt joined with co-stars Tom Berenger and Luke Perry to re-fight the late-19th Century Wyoming Wars between cattle barons and the more innocent settlers seeking a homestead.

Burt met Mary Tyler Moore when she was a recovering alcoholic cast opposite him in *Miss Lettie and Me* (2002), a soapy made-for-TV drama based on Katherine Paterson's short story, *Poor Little Innocent Lamb.*

When director Ian Barry presented Burt with the script, and he read it, he phoned the next day. "I'll do it but it sure ain't *Deliverance* unless you want to throw in a male rape scene to enliven things a bit."

Burt had long admired the talent of Moore, who was born in Brooklyn the same year he was. He especially liked some of her episodes on *The Mary Tyler Moore Show,* which ran on TV from 1970 to '77. Critics hailed her for "defining a new version of American womanhood."

Burt admired her acting even more in *Ordinary People* (1980), a coming-of-age drama about a dysfunctional family and a mother who grieves for one son who died and another who has attempted suicide. She was Oscar-nominated for her remarkable performance.

[When Burt was introduced to her, he reverted to his impish self, asking, "Did Elvis get to hump you when you played a nun opposite him in Change of Habit *(1969)?"]*

In *Miss Lettie and Me,* Tyler, in the title role, played an embittered woman who has cut herself off emotionally after years of heartache. Cast as Samuel Madison, Burt is her one-time love. The plot picks up when the nine-year-old daughter of Lettie's estranged aunt arrives on her farm. That winning role of Travis starred Holliston Coleman.

The movie was shot at the historic Brookfield Plantation outside Griffin, Georgia.

Variety claimed that "This Johnson & Johnson Spotlight presentation for TNT is as fluffy and sterile as its sponsor's cotton swabs. Moore and Reynolds, the top-billed stars, aren't utilized to their full potential. By the predictable climax, all that's missing is Tiny Tim and a Christmas goose."

The taming, domestication, and neutering of Burt Reynolds are depicted in such family-friendly-icky movies as *Miss Lettie and Me.*

***

In the last film directed by Frank Q.

Dobbs, he tapped two longtime friends, Burt Reynolds and Bruce Dern, to play the leads in this made-for-TV western, *Hard Ground* (2003).

Upon its release, it was said to be the most violent movie ever shown on the Hallmark Channel.

Burt, as "Chili" McKay, and Dern, as Sheriff Hutch Hutchinson, are friends, enemies, and brothers-in-law tracking down a savage killer who murders men, women, and kids any time the mood overcomes him. He is backed up by a coven of bad guys and a corrupt Mexican general.

Billy Bucklin (David Figioli) is the rotten-to-the-core psycho being pursued.

For female relief, Amy Jo Johnson was cast as Elizabeth Kennedy, packing a 10-guage double-barreled shotgun in case any rapist gets the wrong idea.

Many viewers claimed that *Hard Ground* was in the genre of Larry McMurtry's four-part TV miniseries, *Lonesome Dove* (1989), The time line for *Hard Ground* moves the *Lonesome Dove* era into the 20th Century—or at least 1901.

Reviews were mixed, one critic writing, "I didn't think really good Westerns were made any more, but I give this one nine out of ten."

Major dissent was echoed by another reviewer, who called the acting atrocious. "I thought Reynolds would be good in a Western, but he is bland and boring. The whole cast sucks, shotgun-wielding Amy Jo Johnson was absurd and badly cast."

Another attack claimed, "For two big screen greats like Burt Reynolds and Bruce Dern, *Hard Ground* was disappointing. I expected more, but got less. If I were Reynolds or Dern, I'd be ashamed to show my face after appearing in this stinker. If they were younger, this movie would have derailed their careers, from which they could never rebound."

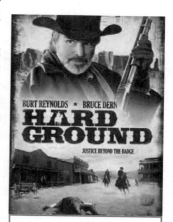

***

In his late sixties, Burt faced his last tabloid scandal involving a spurned lover. He and Pamela Seals, the ex-cocktail waitress from Tampa, filed elaborate and genuinely bitter charges and countercharges, their accusations becoming tabloid fodder, something

Starring Burt Reynolds and Bruce Dern, *Hard Ground*, as stated by one critic, "has all the overused hallmarks of a typical "Shoot 'Em Up: Save the girl, ride off with grandiose parting words of wisdom, fading into the sunset-like Westerns of the 1960s and '70s."

he hadn't experienced since his scandalous divorce from Loni Anderson.

Seals had first met Burt in 1988, and their affair was said to have lasted for sixteen years, twelve of which they actually lived together.

Burt's first lawsuit against her was filed in November 2004 in Palm Beach. It accused her of trying to "extort millions" from him and of threatening to go to the tabloids with allegations of physical abuse and drug addiction.

To counter Burt's suit, Mark Maynor, Seals' attorney, denied any charges of blackmail. "My client wants to recover what was promised to her and also to be paid back $50,000 which she incurred in a credit card purchase for him."

Burt claimed he had purchased a condo for her costing $500,000 in the gated compound of Marina Gardens in Palm Beach Gardens. However, as her suit charged, he did not continue with the monthly mortgage payments, which she could not afford.

Seals, 48, claimed that at one point, she had been engaged to Burt and had endured "both physical and verbal abuse" from him. As had been alleged before by other women, he often underwent violent mood swings, during which time he might resort to physical attacks.

Quoted in the press, Seals said, "I have done everything I can to keep Mr. Reynolds out of the public eye so he would not face exposure in the tabloids. It is not my intention to hurt him. But I do want what is coming to me, what I deserve, and what was promised to me."

Burt's attorney, Robert Montgomery, in papers filed in Palm Beach, alleged that his client had given Seals vast amounts of cash, expensive clothing—enough to fill a dress shop—and "a ton" of jewelry, plus providing a lavish residence for her, servants, and travel aboard his private jet.

In defending Burt, Montgomery said that Burt was threatened by Seals, who told him that if he did not give in to her demands, she was prepared to give "false, spurious, deceitful, and scandalous allegations" against him. "When Mr. Reynolds and Miss Seals

Daily Mail

Broke Burt Reynolds to be kicked out of home

SEE PAGE 13

Back in the tabloid headlines again, Burt had a painful, costly breakup with his longtime mistress, Pamela Seals.

Here, he and his bosomy girl friend appear on the front page of London's *Daily Mail* on August 17, 2011.

separated," Montgomery said, "he was under the impression that the matter between them had been concluded, considering the extraordinary amount of money he had lavished on her during their years together."

Seals also filed suit in California, claiming that she resided there at times with Burt at his home. The suit was filed because, unlike Florida at the time, California recognized "palimony," as Burt's good friend, Lee Marvin, painfully found out. [*Palimony, of course, awards one member of an unmarried couple after their separation if they had lived together for a period of time like a man and wife.*]

In her suit, Seals sought half of Burt's assets, including his home in Florida, valued at $2.5 million. Montgomery also claimed that Seals was demanding "lifetime support" for both herself and her aging mother.

In a countersuit filed in Los Angeles, Burt's attorney sought to bring an injunction against Seals for moving ahead with a suit in California because both of them were residents of Florida. J. Michael Kelly, a California lawyer, claimed he didn't think Seals would have much of a case to pursue in California. Over the years, he had represented celebrities ranging from Elvis Presley to Anthony Hopkins.

"It's doubtful if Seals can meet the legal standard of palimony in California," Kelly claimed. "It would require that Burt and Seals present themselves as man and wife in this state, which was not the case."

Montgomery weighed in, claiming that Burt had made every effort to avoid litigation, even offering to give her a million dollars. "But Miss Seals kept demanding more and more and more."

In June of 2015, it was announced that Burt and Seals had reached a settlement, the terms of which were not announced.

John McGovern, Burt's attorney in Palm Beach, said, "Neither side admitted to the allegations in their separate lawsuits, but both parties are committed to putting this matter behind them and moving on to whatever the future holds. Mr. Montgomery, my fellow attorney, still believes the matter should not have been settled, because Mr. Reynolds has done no wrong, but in these cases, it is the client who can bring an end to litigation if a settlement can be reached that is satisfactory to him. Both Mr. Reynolds and Miss Seals want the matter settled and done with."

Marvin Gross, the attorney for Seals in Los Angeles, said, "The case my client has against Mr. Reynolds has been resolved to everyone's satisfaction. Our agreement settles both the lawsuits in California and Florida."

***

Without a Paddle, Burt's final 2004 release, was a drama mixed with bawdy comedy that some viewers found offensive. When Burt met with director Steven Brill, and agreed to play a supporting role in it, he told the director that *Without a Paddle* in some respects evoked memories of *Deliverance* (1972) in that friends go on a dangerous rafting trip together.

Without a Paddle was filmed in the interior of the North Island of New Zealand, on rivers just north of Wellington.

The story was inspired by a real event. D.B. Cooper was the name reporters gave to a young man who, in 1971, hijacked an airliner, extorted $200,000 from its owner (Northwest Orient), and parachuted off the airborne plane with 21 pounds of $20 bills strapped to his body. He was never found, and it is generally assumed that he did not survive the parachute landing. In July of 2016, the F.B.I. officially closed the case.

The star roles went to three young men cast as high school friends: Seth Green as Dan Mott, Matthew Lillard as Jerry Conlaine, and Dax Shepard as Tom Marshall. Burt had the fourth lead as Del Knox.

The trio find a map leading to Cooper's lost treasure in dangerous, foreboding terrain, and they set out to recover the money. Thus, their adventure begins, filled with plenty of danger and comedy, too, a lot of it what critics call "the toilet variety."

An amorous but deadly grizzly bear is just one of the menaces they face, as well as two gun-toting, pot-growing rednecks reminiscent of the villains in *Deliverance*.

In one scene they fall off a waterfall, which destroys their canoe—hence, another page torn from the script of *Deliverance*. The adventurers meet up with two hippie girls, Flower and Butterfly (Rachel Blanchard and Christina Moore).

In the midst of their entrapment, they are saved from a thunderstorm by a mountain man—Burt, in his role of Del Knox. He turns out to be Cooper's partner from the era just before his para-

Burt, looking rather grotesque as a secretive and reclusive hermit, had a supporting role in this *Deliverance*-like film, *Without a Paddle*.

The leads were played by Seth Green, Matthew Lillard, and Dax Shepard.

chute death.

When the menacing rednecks continue their malfeasance the next morning, Knox shoots them with his dual wield revolvers. The men later find Cooper's decayed corpse and the suitcase that held the ransom money. But a part of the loot has been burned.

Before the end, they have to face a menacing sheriff and Brigg (Ray Baker) who works for pot dealers.

After its release, the film took in $70 million on a budget of $19 million.

Some reviewers suggested the movie was for "the stone crowd, members of which should smoke a joint or two before sitting through it."

It was noted that Dax Shepard assumed the role Burt had played in *Deliverance.*

One reviewer said, *"Without a Paddle* is funnier than hell—and not all about tits, dicks and feces." The authors of this book found Burt's monologues about the aging process and the passage of time especially poignant.

***

The year 2005 turned out to be busy, career-wise for Burt. It began with his taking the role of Coach Walcott in the hit TV series, *The King of Queens.*

This sitcom starred Kevin James as Doug Hefferman, with Leah Remini cast as his wife, Carrie. They are a blue collar working-class couple with Doug as a delivery driver. Their lives are complicated by her father, Jerry Stiller, cast as the forever funny and meddlesome Arthur.

Burt appears when Doug delivers a package to his old high school, where he reunites with Burt, his former coach. As memory serves, Doug was a disaster as a footballer.

"I must have been desperate for a gig when I appeared in *The King of Queens* with the portly parcel deliveryman, Kevin James, and his nagging father-in-law."

Pictured above is the trio of regulars on this sitcom: Leah Remini, Jerry Stiller, and James.

That same year, Burt was offered one of his most colorful roles when he appeared in an episode of *The Dukes of Hazzard,* a hit TV sitcom. He played Jefferson Davis/Boss Hogg, a role that got him assigned the most riveting dialogue of any movie in which he appeared during the 21st Century.

He and his best friend of yesterday, James Best, were reunited, since the years had separated them. In the series, Best had become a household name by appearing in his most memorable role, that of Rosco P. Coltrane, a bumbling and corrupt "law enforcer."

Burt appeared as the white-suited Jefferson Davis (Boss Hogg) in *The Dukes of Hazzard* (2005), a not-particularly-ambitious or well-received movie inspired by the success of the long-running TV series.

"I modeled my character on Huey Long, the most notorious governor in the history of Louisiana," Burt said.

The action comedy aired on CBS from 1979 to 1985, spanning six seasons. It focused on the adventures of the Duke Boys, notably Bo Duke (John Schneider). The boys live on a family farm in the fictional Hazzard County, Georgia. There, they are in constant conflict with the crooked and corrupt county commissioner, Boss Hogg (Burt).

He loved his dialogue, such as "As long as I'm the County Commissioner in the great state of Georgia, you two are gonna rot in the penitentiary. Cuff 'em!"

In a 2006 comedy, *Forget About It*, Burt appeared in the star role, cast with familiar faces of yesterday, including his leading lady, Raquel Welch. The director, B.J. Davis, claimed, "I think Raquel and Burt have buried the hatchet."

He co-starred once again with Robert Loggia, and also with his most frequent co-star, Charles Durning.

They played a trio of retired military men who find a suitcase filled with money near their trailer park in Arizona. Little did they know that it belongs to a former gangster on the witness protection plan. The old man's neighbor is the sexy Christine Delee (Miss Welch).

Forget About It was first screened in May of 2006 at the New Jersey Film Festival, winning the Best Movie Award for the year. That was fol-

"Once again, I was cast opposite one of my least favorite actresses," Burt said. "Miss Raquel Welch. We never had any screen chemistry."

lowed by its premieres in Waterbury, Connecticut, and Phoenix, Arizona.

***

For his next movie, *Grilled,* released in 2006, Burt went from the star role to playing a character called "Goldbluth" in 12th billing.

Directed by Jason Ensler, the film starred Ray Romano as Maurice and Kevin James as Dave. Burt had worked with James before when he appeared in an episode of *The King of Queens.*

Maurice and Dave are failures, trying to sell steaks door to door. They fail but along the way, they encounter Loridonna (Sofia Vergara). Loridonna is on the phone with her friend Suzanne (Juliette Lewis), who has swallowed a fish. Suzanne, as it turns out, is a Mafia princess. Maurice and Dave meet gangland boss, Tony (Kim Coates).

That leads to complications later on when Tony, Suzanne's husband, catches Maurice and Loridonna making love. He's quite casual about it, telling Maurice that the woman he's balling used to be a man. That seems to disgust Maurice.

The plot grows more complicated when Tony suspects Dave of having sex with his wife, Suzanne. Tony goes after him, planning to kill him, but soon, he's mowed down himself by two hitmen.

Dave and Maurice then encounter Goldbluth (Burt) who is also being sought by hitmen, He agrees to purchase $21,000 of steaks from them, but he also has to fight off hitmen, emerging without a scratch.

Not only is Goldbluth's life saved, but so is Dave and Maurice's job as salesmen. The film ends as steaks are on the grill for a barbecue in Dave's backyard.

Originally entitled *Men Don't Quit,* the film was scheduled for a nationwide release in 2005, but test screenings generated such a negative response that it was sent directly to video under the new title of *Grilled.*

Ray Romano (right) and Kevin James had the male leads in *Grilled,* with Burt in a very secondary role as Goldbluth.

"The original title, *Men Don't Quit* might have been the title of my 21st Century biography, a story of an actor who would not give up," Burt said.

***

Burt made one more film in 2006, a music drama, *Broken Bridges*.

Distributed by Paramount Classics, *Broken Bridges* starred Bo Price (Toby Keith) as a down-and-out country singer returning home for his brother's funeral, following a military training accident. Once back on his native soil, with its many memories of yesterday, he meets his lost love, Angela Delton (Kelly Preston), a Miami news reporter. He also meets her sixteen-year-old daughter, Dixie Leigh Delton (Lindsey Haunt).

The former drunkard, now sober patriarch of the Deltons, is none other than Burt, cast as Jake Delton. Her father's "musical blood" is said to run through Dixie's veins.

Toby Keith and Kelly Preston were the stars of *Broken Bridges*, with Burt in a supporting role.

Many critics commented on the blatant product placement by Toby Keith's sponsor, Ford, as a major detriment to the film.

Willie Nelson, a longtime friend of Burt's, was cast as himself.

Made for a budget of $11 million, the film opened to a box office gross of $253,000, but earned $8 million in DVD sales.

***

Directed and produced by Uwe Boll, *In the Name of the King: A Dungeon Siege Tale* was a 2007 German-Canadian-American action fantasy starring Jason Statham as Camden Konreid in the Kingdom of Ebb. Burt had ninth billing as King Konreid in this fantasy inspired by the *Dungeon Siege* video game series.

The movie was shot in the westernmost area of Greater Victoria in British Columbia, where many locals were recruited as extras.

"I never bothered to read the whole script," Burt said. "Too complicated for me. All I know is that at one point, Camden is revealed to be the heir to my throne, which solves the problem of who to pass my crown to. That's was good because later, I'm mor-

"I'd already played God on the screen, and now *In the Name of the King*, I was some medieval royalty," Burt said.

"If you live long enough, you get to experience everything."

tally wounded."

On a budget of $60 million, *In the Name of the King* flopped at the box office, taking in $13 million.

Not only that, but the movie was critically panned, ranking among the 100 worst films made in the 21st Century. One critic wrote, "*Lord of the Flies* it ain't." Attacked by most critics, were the "wooden performances, laughable dialogue, and shoddy production values."

There's more. Much to his fury, Burt was voted the Worst Supporting Actor of the Free World.

***

In 2008, Burt was cast in an MGM poker drama, *Deal*, in which he co-starred with Bret Harrison under the direction of Gil Gates, Jr., who also co-wrote the screenplay. Burt's frequent co-star, Charles Durning, was given the third lead.

In a nutshell, it was the drama of a former poker-playing ace, Tommy Vinson (Burt), passing his skills onto a younger player, Alex Stillman (Harrison), as he sees great potential in the player.

At first reluctant, Alex joins Burt with the deal that they would split his earnings 50/50.

Tommy has to face such card sharpies as Karen "The Razor" Jones (Jennifer Tilly). Romantic interest for Alex comes in the shapely form of Shannon Elizabeth as "Michelle." Only later, he finds out she is a prostitute.

At the climax, Alex competes in the World Poker Tournament in which Tommy (Burt) also competes. Even though he has the winning hand, Tommy lets his former *protégé* win the tournament.

"Guess what?" Burt said. "For my act of generosity at the poker table, I was nominated for a Razzle as the Worst Supporting Actor of the Year."

In this poker drama, *Deal*, Burt was cast as a veteran card sharpie, teaching his *protégé*, Bret Harrison, the secrets of how to emerge with a winning hand.

***

Shot on the Isle of Man off the coast of England, *A Bunch of Amateurs* (2008) was a British comedy that pitted Burt in the lead

"It sure was no winner for me," Burt lamented. "I almost won a Razzie as Worst Supporting Actor of the Year."

role of Jefferson Steel with the great Derek Jacobi cast as Nigel Dewberry, his bitchy rival.

Burt as Steele was a washed-up Hollywood star who flies to England thinking he is to play the title role of King Lear at "Stratford," believing the setting is Stratford-upon-Avon, the birthplace of William Shakespeare.

Once abroad, he finds out that he has signed to be one of the Stratford Players in the little Suffolk village of Stratford St. John. He considers himself too big for such a lowly set-

"In *A Bunch of Amateurs*, I got to play King Lear on the screen, albeit very briefly," Burt said.

"I can only hope I amused Prince Philip and Queen Elizabeth, who were sitting in the royal box at the film's premiere in London."

ting—hence, the drama begins. The transition from this snobbish movie star to humble "member of the ensemble" takes some time, but eventually he is reconciled with his amateur colleagues.

Once again, Burt found a role for his longtime friend and co-star, Charles Durning, cast this time as Charlie Rosenberg.

Many critics found *A Bunch of Amateurs* to be Burt's best performance since *Boogie Nights*. Most of the acclaim went to Imelda Staunton in her role of Mary. She plays Steele's adoring, then disillusioned fan. Samantha Bond, as Dorothy Bettle, was hailed as a *tour de force* as the enchanted director.

Many British critics claimed Burt handled his King Lear lines very well, though no one thought he was Laurence Olivier or John Gielgud. Several comments were made about Burt's recent "bad plastic surgery."

The film was given the royal seal of approval at the Royal Film Performance at London's Leicester Square attended by Queen Elizabeth II and Prince Philip. Her Majesty later told Samantha Bond that she found the plot "quite amusing."

***

On heavy medication, Burt, 73, fell down the stairs at his elegant home on Hobe Sound in Florida. Fearing he might have broken his hip—or worse—he was asked to be taken to Hanley Center—a hospital and drug rehabilitation center in Palm Beach County with special emphasis on late-in-life addictions—in August of 2009.

After undergoing painful back surgery, he had become too reliant on painkillers, and was popping pills day and night until he was seriously addicted once again. On entering rehab, he told his doctors, "I want to regain control of my life. I'm a prisoner of prescription drugs, and I need help."

He began a month-long detox program during that hot summer. There were unconfirmed reports that the doctors were not only alarmed by his deteriorating physical condition, but by his state of mental health, too, as he appeared irrational at times.

On one occasion, he refused to eat because he claimed that some enemy of his had bribed one of the center's cooks to poison him.

Upon his release, he wanted the word to get out that he had stabilized his physical and mental condition and was ready to work again. With the understanding that it would be shot in his native state of Florida, he accepted the first film offer that came in.

He was cast in an episode of *Burn Notice* (2010), a TV series aired on the USA Network for seven seasons that had first been shown in 2007. The series starred Jeffrey Donavan as Michael Westen, a former U.S. Army Ranger and current CIA operative based in Miami. The title of the series referred to "burn notices" issued by intelligence agencies to discredit agents considered unreliable.

Burt played Paul Anderson, an ex-CIA agent. Weston tries to deliver Burt safely into government protection while a well-armed Russian "black-ops" team chases after them.

Back at work, Burt told the press, "I forgot how hard you work on one of these series. The hours are unbelievably long. The guys like to horse around. You'll die in the heat if you don't get a laugh or two."

Burt felt his performance paid homage to such past pictures of his as *Operation C.I.A.* (1965) and *Malone* (1987).

Returning to work again after rehab, Burt said, "I was very happy to be working with the boys on *Burn Notice*. I had several scenes with the guys, Jeffrey Donavan and Bruce Campbell. Maybe it's because I'm old, but they were very sweet, I had a lot of fun working with them."

"My character is flawed, one of the walking wounded. That's the real me. The writers wrote a lot of my own *persona* into the Paul Anderson character. I felt in his skin as I played him."

***

In 2010, Burt was rushed to the hospital for a quadruple heart bypass, but after he recovered from surgery, he wanted to return to work.

He was assigned a small role, identified only as "Pops," in a made-for-TV movie entitled *Category 5*.

Soon after it opens, audiences learn that a family has just survived Hurricane Katrina. Then Charlie DuPuis (C. Thomas Howell), his wife, Ellie, and their son, Danny, and Charlie's father (Burt) find there is another storm on the way, except this one may be even more disastrous.

As one critic wrote, "Burt is not looking his best these days, but he brings a certain panache to his role. He is certainly the most believable actor in the film, and, in fact, is the only reason to watch it."

***

"I thought I was a goner when I was rushed to the hospital for heart surgery,: Burt said. "But I survived to work again in *Category 5*, the perfect storm and the 'ultimate' hurricane movie."

Burt played a codger with a gun who refuses to leave his house.

One critic attacked the film for its "silly dialogue, poor acting, and cliché-ridden plot."

Not Another Not Another Movie, with its dreadful title, was a 2011 direct-to-video release, co-starring Bury with Chevy Chase, supported by Michael Madsen. Directed by David Murphy, it was a movie Burt wanted to forget.

Viewers follow the exploits of Sunshine Studios, called "the absolute worst film company on the planet," known for churning out such cheesy fare as *Attack of the Bulldozer* or *Vampires in Mexico 2*. When it's faced with bankruptcy and desperate to generate a hit, the company puts everything on the line to make the biggest parody of all time. With no script, no name, and no idea of what they're doing, they begin *Not Another Not Another Movie.*

Burt was cast as the CEO of Sunshine. At the opening, in a voice of weary resignation, he announces: "This is stupid! The whole movie is just stupid! Makes perfect sense why I'm here. I'm directing. I play this guy from the Mafia" He then reverts to his Marlon Brando impersonation from *The Godfather.* "You might think it's a great opportunity, but it's not. Who cares? I'll just bite my tongue, think happy thoughts, and get through this. Who am I kidding? I'm screwed."

When it was released, and reviewing Burt's role in it, one critic wrote: "Oh, how the mighty have fallen."

***

Burt made one more movie in 2011, a forgettable piece called *Reel Love,* produced by Entertainment One for an airing on CMT that November. It is not to be confused with *Reel Love* produced by GMA Network in the Philippines.

Brian K. Roberts, based on a script by Sharon Weil, cast Leanne Rimes in the star role of Holly Whitman, who returns from New York, where she is trying to make it as an actress. She's back in her small hometown when her father, Wade Whitman (Burt), is rushed to the hospital after suffering a heart attack. This former "ladies' man" may be experiencing his last days.

Back at home, Holly goes on a soulful journey to reconnect with family and friends, and, as might have been predicted, romance enters her life.

***

One critic wrote, "*Not Another Not Another Movie* is a classic bait and switch. It professes to be a parody of parody movies when, like the films it pretends to imitate, it does not seem to have any idea what parody entails. Burt Reynolds is simply picking up a paycheck by appearing in this crap."

A critic wrote of *Reel Love,* "The centerpiece of the film is its acting. Three performances stand out, notably Burt Reynolds playing a Lothario of yesterday. But this is not a great movie."

Those two heartthrobs of yesterday, Rob Lowe and Burt Reynolds, were united again in yet another film, the badly titled *Pocket Listing*. This was a *neo-noir* black comedy acquired by MGM and Orion Pictures for a limited theatrical release before going to video on demand in December of 2011.

Directed by Conor Allyn, it had a screenplay by newcomer James Jurdi, who was also the star. He played Jack Woodman, a disgraced Los Angeles real estate broker hired to sell the Malibu villa of Frank Hunter (Lowe) and his sexy wife Lana (Jessica Clark). Woodman is also framed by Burt's menacing, drug-addled son Aaron (Logan Fahey).

The film was an oddity in that it featured a real estate agent as a kind of hero. "I don't just sell houses, I deal in dreams," claims Woodman. As portrayed by Jurdi, his role was referred to as a "super-hot, ultra-slick shark, who experiences a rise, a fall, and ultimately, redemption."

In the high-ticket world of Beverly Hills real estate, expect double crosses, mistaken identities, crooked deals, *femme fatale* bombshells, Russian *Mafiosos*, and Mexican gangsters.

Jurdi goes from hot-tub orgies to cleaning toilets. He fills the bill as a gaudy, smooth-talking Los Angeles realtor who knows the message: In his profession, you're only one deal away from either hitting the jackpot or going bust.

Lowe is a real badass in his strong role as the villa owner. In his hipster wig, he is a welcome return to the kind of raspy voice, cool-as-ice villain he perfected in such comedies as *Tommy Boy* (1995) and *Wayne's World* (1992).

Lana (Clark) is the ultimate seductress. Like her namesake of yesterday, Lana Turner, she chews up the scenery.

In the words of one hot-to-trot critic, "I can't decide which star I have the bigger crush on—Jessica Clark, James Jurdi, or Rob Lowe—perhaps all three at once."

Some of the characters are filthy rich, others dirt poor, and a few may be criminal, but they are all chasing the American dream of infinite excess and uninhibited

James Jurdi, Jessica Clark, Rob Lowe, and Burt Reynolds starred in *Pocket Listing*. The film dealt with the intricacies of the tawdry, high-leveraged real estate world in Beverly Hills.

"When I siged to do the film, the director assured me there would be a torrid love scene between Rob and me," Burt said. "I was double-crossed—no love scene."

desires.

Its most insightful review found *Pocket Listing* "a winning cocktail of *Body Heat, The Player, Get Shorty,* and *Million Dollar Listing.* It's a genre cocktail, mixing Scorsese light material excess with reversal of fortune drama and high stakes, sexy con man *noir.* But it works largely in part to solid performances from Jurdi as an amiable anti-hero. Clark is an irresistible charmer straight out of a 1950s Orson Welles crime yarn. Wish Burt had more of a presence here, though, but just happy to see him in something legit.

***

Hollow Creek (2016) was obviously inspired by the thriller/mystery writings of Stephen King. The plot focuses on an adulterous couple—Blake Blakeman (Steve Daron) and Angelica Santo (Giusela Moro)—who retreat to a remote cabin in the Appalachian Mountains, where he plans to complete a new horror novel. She is a book illustrator.

Once in residence, they learn that several boys have gone missing in the area. The couple hears strange noises in the woods near their cabin. When Angelica follows a lead to one of the missing boys, she mysteriously goes missing herself, and Blake becomes the prime suspect.

The town is filled with country folk, some of whom appear a bit deranged, including law enforcement. The trail leads to Burt, cast as Seagrass Lambert. He has the most intriguing cameo in the film, and, as a critic, pointed out, "Gets the most dramatic chunk of the writing. But even Burt can't save this movie."

Moro was not only the movie's lead actress, but also its writer and director. In a review, Mariam Bastani wrote: "Overall, *Hollow Creek* doesn't deliver the thrills expected and the compelling elements are far too short. It is a thriller with too many themes. No doubt disappearing children is terrifying, but *Hollow Creek* is just not scary. It's like a TV rendition of a true crime story as a soap opera with some ghosts and fucked-up families mixed in."

Hollow Creek was influenced by the novels of Stephen King, *and* starred Guisela Moro, Steve Daron, and Burt Reynolds.

A critic wrote, "This movie tries to cover too much ground. Is it a thriller? Is this about abduction? Is this about deranged country folk? Is this about the moral pitfalls of adultery? Is this a ghost story?"

***

Around the same time for yet another 2016 release, Burt played Grandpa Barnes in *Elbow Grease*, another Southern romantic comedy. It takes an inside look, filled with humor and craziness, into the everyday life of the Barnes family.

Billy's marriage to Ellie is going through rough times. His wayward brother arrives and manages to stir up trouble not only in the family, but through the entire town of Guppie, South Carolina.

The movie opened at the Sarasota Film Festival, but never found a national distributor.

***

Burt's most profitable gig for 2016 was when he was cast as Ron Wilcox in the TV series, *Hitting the Breaks*. This was the story of the Wilcox family's move from Atlanta to a small town in the Rocky Mountains of Colorado.

Most of the plot focuses on Randy Wilcox, an ex-race car driver who inherits the Serenity Inn, a struggling bed-and-breakfast previously owned by his parents. The series examines a medley of eccentric locals. Burt appeared in episodes such as "Home Alone on the Range,"" Beautify Long Drop," and "Mitch Ado About Nothing."

***

Although 2017 would be the last complete year in Burt's life, he worked steadily throughout, turning out six movies, beginning with *Apple of My Eye*.

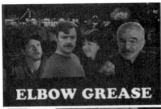

Passing the torch to a new generation of Hollywood actors, Burt, on the set of *Elbow Grease*, chats with Michael Provost.

Elbow Grease is a romantic comedy that embodies everyday life in a turn-of-the-20th-Century remote backwater of South Carolina.

"By the time I had this small gig in some flick called *Hitting the Breaks*, I felt my life had come full circle," Burt said.

"Gone was most of my money. Faded with the summer wind, a string of lovers, some of whom were getting as old as I was—if they hadn't already arrived where faded movie queens go when they die."

This is the tender story of a teenager who loses her sights after a riding accident. A guide dog trainer decides to train an adorable miniature horse to be both her companion and surrogate eyes.

Two veteran actors, Amy Sart as the Mom and Burt as the dog trainer, glide through their roles with ease and believability. The story is, in the words of a critic, "Overly simple but the acting is straightforward."

***

In the final months of his life, Burt entered the "Lion in Winter" stage of his long career. There was still the faintest glimmer of the former Burt Reynolds, who, in the words of one fan, was "Cary Grant crossed with Tom Jones."

Kevin D. Williamson wrote about Burt's Third Act: "He kept working, beaten down by age as he was, shockingly frail-looking, diminished, nothing like the man on the bearskin rug titillating the readership of *Cosmo*. He kept his sense of humor—about himself, above all. He could have ended his cinematic career on the sweet high note of *The Last Movie Star*, but he didn't. This broken-down Hollywood Lothario of yesterday had a few more films in him before he faced the final curtain."

In reference to *Apple of My Eye*, a critic wrote, "The story unfolds without a single emotional outburst or anything that might scar the young ones. In this world, going blind carries with it the same inconvenience of having to take out the trash or do the dishes. Bette Davis did it better in *Dark Victory* (1939)."

***

Burt's only critically acclaimed film of the 21st Century was the semi-autobiographical *The Last Movie Star*, an American drama released in 2017 and directed by Adam Rifkin (*Detroit Rock City; 1999*). Burt played the lead, supported by actors Ariel Winter, Clark Duke, Ellar Coltrane, and Chevy Chase.

After holding its world premiere at the Tribeca Film Festival in Manhattan, *The Last Movie Star* was previewed through DirectTV Cinema in February of 2018 before its limited release in theaters. After that, it went to video on demand.

As Vince Edwards, fading movie star of yesterday, Burt attends a small local film festival in Nashville. But it's more than that: He goes through a

646

journey into his past, as he faces the fact that his glory days are behind him. From now on, everything will be downhill, anti-climactic, and a failed ode to yesteryear.

Originally entitled *Dog Years*, most of *The Last Movie Star* movie was shot in Knoxville, Tennessee. As *Dog Years*, the movie won the Chairman's Award at the San Diego International Film Festival.

Rifkin later admitted that whereas at first, he had feared that the script would hit too close to Burt's inner core, he was more than open to reveal his vulnerability. "He assured me that he was fully prepared to face his regrets and let his real life *persona* shine through."

Burt's favorite line in the movie was, "When you're famous, everybody wants to screw ya."

One fan wrote: "Burt Reynolds gives a deeply touching performance with an emotional roller-coaster masterpiece. This movie was brilliant and beautifully written, a bold film that captures the frightful reality of himself growing old and coming to terms with the irretrievable loss of youth."

As the flamboyant Lil, Ariel Winter walks away with some of the best scenes in the flick.

A young actress, Ariel Winter, gave a striking performance as Burt's off-beat hostess at the meager film festival honoring the fading actor in *The Last Movie Star.*

She bombards every episode in cut-off jeans that barely conceal her crotch. Her character's duties involve transporting Burt—as a crotchety and ill-tempered movie star—to appointments and photo ops during the course of his involvement at the rinky-dink film festival that's honoring him.

When Burt arrives at the "festival," he sees that it is a small-time, back-of-the-bar affair, organized by a group of overzealous fanboys led by Clark Duke and Ellar Coltrane.

Rotten Tomatoes posted its summation: "*The Last Movie Star* has a few poignant moments thanks to Reynolds and Ariel Winter, but their performances are stranded in a middling drama unworthy of their efforts."

Scott Tobias of NPR wrote: "Though Adam Rifkin's heart is in the right place, there is not a moment in the film that isn't overplayed. Had he been willing to dial down the soppiness even a little, there's potential in *The Last Movie Star* to double as a tribute and a cautionary take on the perils of fame."

David Ehrlich wrote, "The message comes through loud and clear: Burt Reynolds is communing with his past and coming to grips with the images that continue to haunt him, but he's also adding one more (or one last) character to his wrinkled body of work. Unfortunately, while either one of those ideas might have made for a fun movie on its own, the corny and haphazard ways that Rifkin smushes them together results in a well-intentioned but tedious tribute that's too generic to take advantage of its introspective lead performance."

"In the TV show, *In Sanity, Florida*, I played a retired movie star," Burt said.

"I was wrong for the part. I sure as hell wasn't retired."

***

Perhaps Burt should have let *The Last Movie Star* be his swan song. But in the months leading up to his death, he stumbled in and out of more movies beginning with *In Sanity, Florida,* a 2017 TV series.

Burt appeared as himself, a retired movie star in an episode entitled "The Town Is Small, the Crazy Isn't."

The setting appears like a throwback to a small town in the 1930s. The set in Yesteryear Village at the Palm Beach County Fairgrounds was used as the backdrop.

***

That movie was followed by direct-to-video *Hamlet & Hutch,* where Burt was cast as Papa Hutch, a former Broadway star long past his days of glory on the stage. Struggling with Alzheimers, he relocates to the South to live with his granddaughter, Tatum (Terri Vaughan), and her ten-year-old daughter Liz (Emma Rayne Lyle).

The title derives from the small-town production of the Shakespeare classic, *Hamlet.* Burt's character of Papa Hutch has volunteered his services as the actor who'll play the Prince of Denmark in an upcoming small-town revival.

In *Hamlet and Hutch*, the plot focuses on an aging man's struggle with Alzheimer's and his immediate family's difficulty in taking him in to care for him.

***

Burt went on to accept the lead in *Miami Love Affair* (2017). Directed by Ralph Kinnard, it's a romantic comedy in which Burt plays a rich businessman and art dealer, who is also the narrator. The plot follows a trio of young love affairs during the Art Basel Fair in Miami.

Kinnard said, "This film starring Burt is an homage to Miami, a romantic comedy that makes viewers experience a struggle for greatness in the exciting world of art while following the never-ending quest for true love."

***

Burt's next film was *Henri* (2017). The character he played grew up in a monastery in the Far East but has moved to the Deep South of the U.S.A. A man of peace, he seems to attract trouble. In the words of one critic, "Expect love, action, suspense, and adventure."

In *Miami Love Affair*, Burt both appeared on the screen and narrated its background.

"Everybody on the screen fell in love—all except me," Burt said.

***

Burt marked the last year of his life starring in *Shadow Fighter* cast as Paddy Grier, It's the story of a homeless ex-boxer, (Burt) and an inner city kid. As a team, they form an odd coupling, facing their futures while fighting the tragedies of their past.

In the words of one critic, "It's the story of a single mom trying to raise kids; drug dealers, bad cops, good cops, and

"In *Shadow Fighter*, I played a former boxer forced to live on the street," Burt said. "I feared that if my finances got any worse, I, too, would be without a roof over my head."

In *Henri*, the secondary tagline was, ""For the sake of love and justice."

Reynolds playing a feeble boxing trainer with plenty of fire still in his gut."

***

Two films were set for a 2019 release after Burt's death. They marked his final appearances on the screen, beginning with *An Innocent Kiss* in which he played Grandpa Barnes.

This is a chaotic film about a typical day in the life of the dysfunctional Barnes household, where family members deal with financial woes, a boy caught masturbating, a rocky marriage, and a face-off against an old wrestling foe. Burt plays the father of Billy and Randy, sons worthy of every gray hair on his head.

Not released at the time of Burt's death, *An Innocent Kiss* was a chaotic movie about a dysfunctional family. As the grandfather of the brood, Burt remarks, "The only perfect families are found in the movies."

Defining Moments, released in the spring of 2019, marked Burt's final appearance on the screen. In it, he was cast as Chester, the male lead.

The film's writer, director, and producer, Stephen Wallis, said, "Our movie follows the intertwining stories of several families when faced with the most important moments of their lives. From birth to death, *Defining Moments* is a reflection of the journeys all of us take—whether we choose to or not."

In Burt's role of Chester, he is a man with a distant relationship with his daughter, who hopes to have a reconciliation before he dies.

The movie was wrapped in September of 2017 in Ontario, Canada.

In his last interview, a reporter asked Burt what he would be most remembered for.

Replying with a smirk, he said, "I'll be forever known for sleeping with Jack Nicholson."

***

Right before he died, Burt had accepted a role in the upcoming Quentin Tarantino film, *Once Upon a Time in Hollywood,* set for a summer release in 2019.

The film teamed Brad Pitt and Leonardo DiCaprio with Margot Robbie cast as Sharon Tate, who was murdered by the Charles Manson crazies.

Bruce Dern replaced Burt in the role of George Spahn, an 80-year-old, nearly blind man who rents his Los Angeles ranch as a location for Western films.

In the film, the insane Manson convinces Spahn to allow him and his followers to camp out at his ranch. Manson orders his female followers to have sex with the aging man and to serve as his seeing-eye guides.

***

On September 6, 2018, a spokeswoman for the Martin County Sheriff's Office in Florida told reporters, "Mr. Burt Reynolds, age 82, the movie star, has passed away at the Jupiter Medical Center. He was taken there by men from the Fire Rescue Department. A caretaker at his home on Hobe Sound reported that the actor had collapsed from chest pains. An ambulance was summoned. It was too late."

Tributes poured in from all over the world, the *New York Daily News* ran his image on its frontpage under the "Second Coming" headline—FAREWELL BANDIT."

In story after story, quotes both old and new were published in international newspapers. In London, an appraisal from Freddie Mercury was dug up from the files. "Forget about that ever-present hairpiece," the singing star had said. "Burt Reynolds defined masculine beauty in the 1970s, hairy chest and all. The former football halfback would be my ultimate dream-date."

Robert Redford, Clint Eastwood, Jack Nicholson, Al Pacino, and Robert DeNiro are towering figures in the history of cinema. But Burt Reynolds owned the 1970s and early '80s as a genuine movie star and box office champ.

The time had come for Burt Reynolds to put the pedal to the metal with that incredible horsepower under the hood of his Pontiac Trans-Am, and to leave all of us, including Sheriff Burford T. Justice, in the dust.

In his final interview, Burt said, "I have no life regrets. There's nothing I can do about things that weren't happy or good. I just try not to dwell on those. Regrets are not healthy. All of my experiences, good or bad, made me who I am today, and I'm grateful for the positive ones. I don't think of my past as anything negative. If it is negative, I've forgotten it."

IN AFFECTIONATE MEMORY OF

BURT REYNOLDS
1936-2018

A GREAT AMERICAN MOVIE STAR

FROM HIS THOUSANDS OF FANS, WHO PRAY
That HIS NIGHTS WILL ALWAYS BOOGIE,
THAT HIS PEDAL WILL ALWAYS REACH THE METAL,
THAT HIS RUBBER WILL ALWAYS HIT THE ROAD,
THAT HE RECEIVE DELIVERANCE FROM HIS BURDENS, &
THAT HE WILL ALWAYS REST IN PEACE

Putting the Pedal to the Metal:
MEET THE AUTHORS

DARWIN PORTER

As an intense nine-year-old, **Darwin Porter** began meeting movie stars, TV personalities, politicians, and singers through his vivacious and attractive mother, Hazel, an eccentric but charismatic Southern girl who had lost her husband in World War II. Migrating from the Depression-ravaged valleys of western North Carolina to Miami Beach during its most ebullient heyday, Hazel became a stylist, wardrobe mistress, and personal assistant to the vaudeville *comedienne* **Sophie Tucker**, the bawdy and irrepressible "Last of the Red Hot Mamas."

Virtually every show-biz celebrity who visited Miami Beach paid a call on "Miss Sophie," and Darwin, as a pre-teen loosely and indulgently supervised by his mother, was regularly dazzled by the likes of **Judy Garland, Dinah Shore,** and **Frank Sinatra.**

It was at Miss Sophie's that he met his first political figure, who was actually an actor at the time. Between marriages, **Ronald Reagan** came to call on Ms. Sophie, who was his favorite singer. He was accompanied by a young blonde starlet, **Marilyn Monroe.**

At the University of Miami, Darwin edited the school newspaper. He first met and interviewed **Eleanor Roosevelt** at the Fontainebleau Hotel on Miami Beach and invited her to spend a day at the university. She accepted, much to his delight.

After graduation, he became the Bureau Chief of *The Miami Herald* in Key West, Florida, where he got to take early morning walks with the former U.S. president **Harry S Truman**, discussing his presidency and the events that had shaped it.

Through Truman, Darwin was introduced and later joined the staff of **Senator George Smathers** of Florida. His best friend was a young senator, **John F. Kennedy.** Through "Gorgeous George," as Smathers was known in the Senate, Darwin got to meet Jack and Jacqueline in Palm Beach. He later wrote two books about them—*The Kennedys, All the Gossip Unfit to Print,* and one of his all-time bestsellers, *Jacqueline Kennedy Onassis—A Life Beyond Her Wildest Dreams.*

For about a decade in New York, Darwin worked in television journalism and advertising with his long-time partner, the journalist, art director, and arts-industry socialite **Stanley Mills Haggart.**

Stanley (as an art director) and Darwin (as a writer and assistant), worked as freelance agents in television. Jointly, they helped produce TV commercials that included testimonials from **Joan Crawford** (then feverishly promoting Pepsi-Cola); **Ronald Reagan** (General Electric); and **Debbie Reynolds** (Singer sewing machines). Other personalities appearing and delivering televised sales pitches included **Louis Armstrong, Lena Horne,** and **Arlene Dahl,** each of them hawking a commercial product.

Beginning in the early 1960s, Darwin joined forces with the then-fledgling **Arthur Frommer** organization, playing a key role in researching and writing more than 50 titles and defining the style and values that later emerged as the world's leading travel guidebooks, *The Frommer Guides,* with particular emphasis on Europe, New England, and the Caribbean. Between the creation and updating of hundreds of editions of detailed travel guides to England, France, Italy, Spain, Portugal, Austria, Hungary, Germany, Switzerland, the Caribbean, and California, he continued to interview and discuss the triumphs, feuds, and frustrations of celebrities, many by then reclusive, whom he either sought out or encountered randomly as part of his extensive travels. **Ava Gardner, Debbie Reynolds,** and **Lana Turner** were particularly insightful.

It was while living in New York that Darwin became fascinated by the career of a rising real estate mogul changing the skyline of Manhattan. He later, of course, became the "gambling czar" of Atlantic City and a star of reality TV.

Darwin began collecting an astonishing amount of data on Donald Trump, squirreling it away in boxes, hoping one day to write a biography of this charismatic, controversial figure.

Before doing that, he penned more than thirty-five uncensored, unvarnished, and unauthorized biographies on subjects that included **Kirk Douglas, Playboy's Hugh Hefner, Debbie Reynolds and Carrie Fisher, Bill and Hillary Clinton, Ronald Reagan and Nancy Davis, Jane Wyman, Jacqueline Kennedy, Jack Kennedy, Lana Turner, Peter O'Toole, James Dean, Marlon Brando, Merv Griffin, Katharine Hepburn, Howard Hughes, Humphrey Bogart, Michael Jackson, Paul Newman, Steve McQueen, Marilyn Monroe, Elizabeth Taylor, Rock Hudson, Frank Sinatra, Vivien Leigh, Laurence Olivier, the notorious porn star Linda Lovelace, Zsa Zsa Gabor and her sisters, Tennessee Williams, Gore Vidal,** and **Truman Capote.**

As a departure from his usual repertoire, Darwin also wrote the controversial *J. Edgar Hoover & Clyde Tolson: Investigating the Sexual Secrets of America's Most Famous Men and Women,* a book about celebrity, voyeurism, political and sexual repression, and blackmail within the highest circles of the U.S. government.

Porter's biographies, over the years, have won thirty first prize or "runner-up to first prize" awards at literary festivals in cities or states which include New England, New York, Los Angeles, Hollywood, San Francisco, Florida, California, and Paris.

Darwin can be heard at regular intervals as a radio and television commentator, "dishing" celebrities, pop culture, politics, and scandal.

A resident of New York City, Darwin is currently at work on a startling new mother-daughter biography of two of the most remarkable divas in show-biz history, **July Garland and Liza Minnelli.**

DANFORTH PRINCE

The co-author of this book, **Danforth Prince** is president and founder of Blood Moon Productions, a publishing venture that's devoted to salvaging and compiling the oral histories of America's entertainment industry.

Prince launched his career in journalism in the 1970s at the Paris Bureau of *The New York Times*. In the early '80s, he joined Darwin Porter in developing first editions of many of the titles within *The Frommer Guides*. Together, they reviewed and articulated the travel scenes of more than 50 nations, most of them within Europe and the Caribbean. Authoritative and comprehensive, they became best-selling "travel bibles" for millions of readers.

Prince, in collaboration with Porter, is also the co-author of several award-winning celebrity biographies, each configured as a title within **Blood Moon's Babylon series.** These have included *Hollywood Babylon—It's Back!; Hollywood Babylon Strikes Again; The Kennedys: All the Gossip Unfit to Print; Frank Sinatra, The Boudoir Singer, Elizabeth Taylor: There Is Nothing Like a Dame; Pink Triangle: The Feuds and Private Lives of Tennessee Williams, Gore Vidal, Truman Capote, and Members of their Entourages;* and *Jacqueline Kennedy Onassis: A Life Beyond Her Wildest Dreams.* More recent efforts include *Lana Turner, Hearts and Diamonds Take All; Peter O'-Toole—Hellraiser, Sexual Outlaw, Irish Rebel; Bill & Hillary—So This Is That Thing Called Love; James Dean, Tomorrow Never Comes; Rock Hudson Erotic Fire; Carrie Fisher and Debbie Reynolds, Princess Leia & Unsinkable Tammy in Hell, Playboy's Hugh Hefner, Empire of Skin,* and *Kirk Douglas: More Is Never Enough.*

One of his recent projects, co-authored with Darwin Porter, is *Donald Trump, The Man Who Would Be King.* Released directly into the frenzy of the 2016 presidential elections, it won three literary awards at book festivals in New York, California, and Florida. It's a celebrity exposé of the decades of pre-presidential scandals—personal, political, and dynastic—associated with **Donald Trump** during the rambunctious decades when no one ever thought he'd actually get elected.

Prince is also the co-author of four books on film criticism, three of which won honors at regional bookfests in Los Angeles and San Francisco.

A graduate of Hamilton College and a native of Easton and Bethlehem, Pennsylvania, he is the president and founder of the Georgia Literary Association (1996), and of the Porter and Prince Corporation (1983) which has produced dozens of titles for Simon & Schuster, Prentice Hall, and John Wiley & Sons. In 2011, he was named "Publisher of the Year" by a consortium of literary critics and marketers spearheaded by the J.M. Northern Media Group.

He has electronically documented some of the controversies associated with his stewardship of Blood Moon in at least 50 documentaries, book trailers, public speeches, and TV or radio interviews. Most of these are available on **YouTube.com** and **Facebook** *(keyword: "Danforth Prince")*; on **Twitter** *(#BloodyandLunar)*; or by clicking on **BloodMoonProductions.com.**

Do you want to meet him, up close and personal? Prince is also an innkeeper, running a historic bed & breakfast in New York City, **Magnolia House (www.MagnoliaHouseSaintGeorge.com)**. Affiliated with AirBnb, and increasingly sought out by filmmakers as an evocative locale for moviemaking, it lies in St. George, at the northern tip of Staten Island, a district that's historically associated with Henry James, Theodore Dreiser, the Vanderbilts, and key moments in America's colonial history.

Set in an elaborately terraced garden, and boasting a history of visits from literary and show-biz stars who have included Tennessee Williams, Gloria Swanson, Jolie Gabor, Ruth Warrick, Greta Keller, Lucille Lortel, and many of the luminaries of Broadway, the inn is within a ten-minute walk to the ferries sailing at 20- to 30-minute intervals to Lower Manhattan.

Publicized as "a reasonably priced celebrity-centric retreat with links to the book trades," and the beneficiary of rave ("superhost") reviews from hundreds of previous clients, **Magnolia House** is loaded with furniture and memorabilia that Prince collected during his decades as a travel journalist for the Frommer Guides.

*Stay with Us! Learn more about "Celebrity-Centric Sleepovers" at Blood Moon's **Magnolia House**, a historic and moderately priced "Airbnb" in New York City.*

For more information about the hospitality that's waiting for you in NYC at the Bed and Breakfast affiliate of Blood Moon Productions, click on
MagnoliaHouseSaintGeorge.com

657

Now, There's a GUIDEBOOK to accompany your visit to one of Staten Island's Most Intriguing Landmarks:

Blood Moon Productions proudly announces the release of an illustrated history of **Magnolia House**, a historic home that's internationally famous for its associations with celebrities.

It's the first in the authors' series about how travel writing for **THE FROMMER GUIDES** evolved into a celebrity adventure directly linked to show-biz.

As stated by Danforth Prince, "It's been a helluva ride, 'lo these many years, churning out travel guides and the traumatic, sometimes tragic, life stories of the notorious and merely famous celebrities we've written about. Magnolia House with its affordable overnight accommodations presents us with the opportunity of meeting some of the fans of the subjects we've 'exposed' in print."

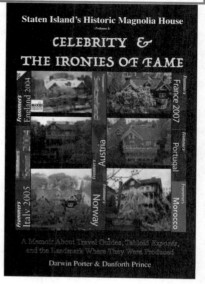

Staten Island's Historic Magnolia House
(Volume I)
CELEBRITY &
THE IRONIES OF FAME

A Memoir About Travel Guides, Tabloid Exposés, and the Landmark Where They Were Produced.

Darwin Porter & Danforth Prince

STATEN ISLAND'S HISTORIC MAGNOLIA HOUSE, VOLUME ONE
CELEBRITY & THE IRONIES OF FAME:
A MEMOIR ABOUT TRAVEL GUIDES, TABLOID EXPOSÉS, & THE LANDMARK WHERE THEY WERE PRODUCED.

Softcover, 6" x 9", with 230 pages, at least a hundred photos, and scads of gossip about who did what to whom during the course of 50 years as the world's preeminent travel journalists. Available everywhere online through Amazon.com, BarnesandNoble.com, or as a free giveaway to overnight guests. ISBN 978-1-936003-65-5.

WHAT IS MAGNOLIA HOUSE? The name it bears has been on record with Staten Island's Borough Hall for at least a century, as it's a byproduct of owners who, in the immediate aftermath of the Civil War, gave it a name that evoked their native Virginia. Dating from the 1830s, it's a *Grande Dame* with a knack for nourishing high-functioning eccentrics. Many of them have lived or been entertained here since New York's State Senator Howard Bayne, a transplanted Southerner, moved in with his wife, the daughter of the Surgeon General of the Confederate States of America, in the aftermath of that bloodiest of wars on North American soil, the War between the American States. Since then, many dozens of celebrities—some of them notorious—have whispered their secrets and rehearsed their ambitions within its walls.

This is the story of how this "Wise Victorian Lady"—in its role as the editorial headquarters for many of THE FROMMER GUIDES and later for BLOOD MOON PRODUCTIONS—adapted to America's radically changing tastes, times, circumstances, and values.

LOVE TRIANGLE:
RONALD REAGAN
JANE WYMAN, & NANCY DAVIS

HOW MUCH DO YOU REALLY KNOW ABOUT THE REAGANS? THIS BOOKS TELLS EVERYTHING ABOUT THE SHOW-BIZ SCANDALS THEY DESPERATELY WANTED TO FORGET.

Unique in the history of publishing, this scandalous triple biography focuses on the Hollywood indiscretions of former U.S. president Ronald Reagan and his two wives. A proud and Presidential addition to Blood Moon's Babylon series, it digs deep into what these three young and attractive movie stars were doing decades before two of them took over the Free World.

As reviewed by Diane Donovan, Senior Reviewer at the California Bookwatch section of the Midwest Book Review: *"Love Triangle: Ronald Reagan, Jane Wyman & Nancy Davis may find its way onto many a Republican Reagan fan's reading shelf; but those who expect another Reagan celebration will be surprised: this is lurid Hollywood exposé writing at its best, and outlines the truths surrounding one of the most provocative industry scandals in the world.*

"There are already so many biographies of the Reagans on the market that one might expect similar mile-markers from this: be prepared for shock and awe; because Love Triangle doesn't take your ordinary approach to biography and describes a love triangle that eventually bumped a major Hollywood movie star from the possibility of being First Lady and replaced her with a lesser-known Grade B actress (Nancy Davis).

"From politics and betrayal to romance, infidelity, and sordid affairs, Love Triangle is a steamy, eye-opening story that blows the lid off of the Reagan illusion to raise eyebrows on both sides of the big screen.

"Black and white photos liberally pepper an account of the careers of all three and the lasting shock of their stormy relationships in a delightful pursuit especially recommended for any who relish Hollywood gossip."

In 2015, LOVE TRIANGLE, Blood Moon Productions' overview of the early dramas associated with Ronald Reagan's scandal-soaked career in Hollywood, was designated by the Awards Committee of the **HOLLYWOOD BOOK FESTIVAL** as Runner-Up to Best Biography of the Year.

LOVE TRIANGLE: Ronald Reagan, Jane Wyman, & Nancy Davis
Darwin Porter & Danforth Prince
Softcover, 6" x 9", with hundreds of photos.   ISBN 978-1-936003-41-9

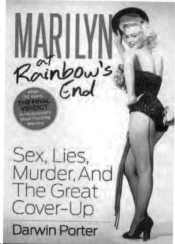

CARRIE FISHER & DEBBIE REYNOLDS
PRINCESS LEIA & UNSINKABLE TAMMY IN HELL

It's history's first comprehensive, unauthorized overview of the greatest mother-daughter act in showbiz history, **Debbie Reynolds** ("hard as nails and with more balls than any five guys I've ever known") and her talented, often traumatized daughter, **Carrie Fisher** ("one of the smartest, hippest chicks in Hollywood"). Evolving for decades under the unrelenting glare of public scrutiny, each became a world-class symbol of the social and cinematic tastes that prevailed during their heydays as celebrity icons in Hollywood.

It's a scandalous saga of the ferociously loyal relationship of the *"boop-boop-a-doop"* girl with her intergalactic STAR WARS daughter, and their iron-willed, "true grit" battles to out-race changing tastes in Hollywood.

Loaded with revelations about "who was doing what to whom" during the final gasps of Golden Age Hollywood, it's an All-American story about the price of glamour, career-related pain, family anguish, romantic betrayals, lingering guilt, and the volcanic shifts that affected a scrappy, mother-daughter team—and everyone else who ever loved the movies.

"Feeling misunderstood by the younger (female) members of your gene pool? This is the Hollywood exposé every grandmother should give to her granddaughter, a roadmap like Debbie Reynolds might have offered to Billie Lourd." **—Marnie O'Toole**

"Hold onto your hats, the "bad boys" of Blood Moon Productions are back. This time, they have an exhaustively researched and highly readable account of the greatest mother-daughter act in the history of show business: Debbie Reynolds and Carrie (Princess Leia) Fisher. If celebrity gossip and inside dirt is your secret desire, check it out. This is a fabulous book that we heartily recommend. It will not disappoint. We rate it worthy of four stars."
—MAJ Glenn MacDonald, U.S. Army Reserve (Retired), © MilitaryCorruption.com

"How is a 1950s-era movie star, (TAMMY) supposed to cope with her postmodern, substance-abusing daughter (PRINCESS LEIA), the rebellious, high-octane byproduct of Rock 'n Roll, Free Love, and postwar Hollywood's most scandal-soaked marriage? Read about it here, in Blood Moon's unauthorized double exposé about how Hollywood's toughest (and savviest) mother-daughter team maneuvered their way through shifting definitions of fame, reconciliation, and fortune."

—Donna McSorley

Another compelling title from Blood Moon's Babylon Series
Winner of the coveted "Best Biography" Award from the 2018 New York Book Festival

CARRIE FISHER & DEBBIE REYNOLDS,
UNSINKABLE TAMMY & PRINCESS LEIA IN HELL
Darwin Porter & Danforth Prince

630 pages Softcover with photos. Now online and in bookstores everywhere
ISBN 978-1-936003-57-0

This is What Happens When A Demented Billionaire Hits Hollywood

HOWARD HUGHES

HELL'S ANGEL

BY DARWIN PORTER

From his reckless pursuit of love as a rich teenager to his final days as a demented fossil, Howard Hughes tasted the best and worst of the century he occupied. Along the way, he changed the worlds of aviation and entertainment forever.

This biography reveals inside details about his destructive and usually scandalous associations with other Hollywood players.

"The Aviator flew both ways. Porter's biography presents new allegations about Hughes' shady dealings with some of the biggest names of the 20th century"

—New York Daily News

"Darwin Porter's access to film industry insiders and other Hughes confidants supplied him with the resources he needed to create a portrait of Hughes that both corroborates what other Hughes biographies have divulged, and go them one better."

—Foreword Magazine

"Thanks to this bio of Howard Hughes, we'll never be able to look at the old pinups in quite the same way again."

—The Times (London)

Winner of a respected literary award from the Los Angeles Book Festival, this book gives an insider's perspective about what money can buy —and what it can't.

814 pages, with photos. Available everywhere now, online and in bookstores.

ISBN 978-1-936003-13-6

LANA TURNER

THE SWEATER GIRL, CELLULOID VENUS, SEX NYMPH TO THE G.I.s WHO WON WORLD WAR II, AND HOLLYWOOD'S OTHER MOST NOTORIOUS BLONDE

BEAUTIFUL AND BAD, HER FULL STORY HAS NEVER BEEN TOLD.
UNTIL NOW!

Lana Turner was the most scandalous, most copied, and most gossiped-about actress in Hollywood. When her abusive Mafia lover was murdered in her house, every newspaper in the Free World described the murky dramas with something approaching hysteria.

Blood Moon's salacious but empathetic new biography exposes the public and private dramas of the girl who changed the American definition of what it REALLY means to be a blonde.

Here's how **CALIFORNIA BOOKWATCH** and **THE MID-WEST BOOK REVIEW** described the mega-celebrity as revealed in this book:

"Lana Turner: Hearts and Diamonds Take All belongs on the shelves of any collection strong in movie star biographies in general and Hollywood evolution in particular, and represents no lightweight production, appearing on the 20th anniversary of Lana Turner's death to provide a weighty survey packed with new information about her life.

"One would think that just about everything to be known about The Sweater Girl would have already appeared in print, but it should be noted that Lana Turner: Hearts and Diamonds Take All offers many new revelations not just about Turner, but about the movie industry in the aftermath of World War II.

"From Lana's introduction of a new brand of covert sexuality in women's movies to her scandalous romances among the stars, her extreme promiscuity, her search for love, and her notorious flings - even her involvement in murder - are all probed in a revealing account of glamour and movie industry relationships that bring Turner and her times to life.

"Some of the greatest scandals in Hollywood history are intricately detailed on these pages, making this much more than another survey of her life and times, and a 'must have' pick for any collection strong in Hollywood history in general, gossip and scandals and the real stories behind them, and Lana Turner's tumultuous career, in particular."

Lana Turner, Hearts & Diamonds Take All
Winner of the coveted "Best Biography" Award from the San Francisco Book Festival
By Darwin Porter and Danforth Prince
Softcover, 622 pages, with photos. ISBN 978-1-936003-53-2
Available everywhere, online and in stores.

DONALD TRUMP
IS *THE MAN WHO WOULD BE KING*

This is the most famous book about our incendiary President you've probably never heard of.

Winner of three respected literary awards, and released three months before the Presidentail elections of 2016, it's an entertainingly packaged, artfully salacious bombshell, a scathingly historic overview of America during its 2016 election cycle, a portrait unlike anything ever published on CANDIDATE DONALD and the climate in which he thrived and massacred his political rivals.

Its volcanic, much-suppressed release during the heat and venom of the Presidential campaign has already been heralded by the *Midwestern Book Review, California Book Watch, the Seattle Gay News*, the staunchly right-wing **WILS-AM radio**, and also by the editors at the most popular Seniors' magazine in Florida, *BOOMER TIMES*, which designated it as their September choice for **BOOK OF THE**

TRUMPOCALYPSE: *"Donald Trump: The Man Who Would Be King* is recommended reading for all sides, no matter what political stance is being adopted: Republican, Democrat, or other.

"One of its driving forces is its ability to synthesize an unbelievable amount of information into a format and presentation which blends lively irony with outrageous observations, entertaining even as it presents eye-opening information in a format accessible to all.

"Politics dovetail with American obsessions and fascinations with trends, figureheads, drama, and sizzling news stories, but blend well with the observations of sociologists, psychologists, politicians, and others in a wide range of fields who lend their expertise and insights to create a much broader review of the Trump phenomena than a more casual book could provide.

"The result is a 'must read' for any American interested in issues of race, freedom, equality, and justice—and for any non-American who wonders just what is going on behind the scenes in this country's latest election debacle."

Diane Donovan, Senior Editor,
California Bookwatch

DONALD TRUMP, THE MAN WHO WOULD BE KING
WINNER OF "BEST BIOGRAPHY" AWARDS FROM BOOK FESTIVALS IN
NEW YORK, CALIFORNIA, AND FLORIDA
by Darwin Porter and Danforth Prince
Softcover, with 822 pages and hundreds of photos. ISBN *978-1-936003-51-8*.

**Available now from Amazon.com, Barnes&Noble.com,
and other internet purveyors, worldwide.**

LINDA LOVELACE

INSIDE LINDA LOVELACE'S DEEP THROAT
DEGRADATION, PORNO CHIC, AND THE RISE OF FEMINISM

THE MOST COMPREHENSIVE BIOGRAPHY EVER WRITTEN OF AN ADULT ENTERTAINMENT STAR, HER TORMENTED RELATIONSHIP WITH HOLLYWOOD'S UNDERBELLY, AND HOW SHE CHANGED FOREVER THE WORLD'S PERCEPTIONS ABOUT CENSORSHIP, SEXUAL BEHAVIOR PATTERNS, AND PORNOGRAPHY.

Darwin Porter, author of some twenty critically acclaimed celebrity exposés of behind-the-scenes intrigue in the entertainment industry, was deeply involved in the Linda Lovelace saga as it unfolded in the 70s, interviewing many of the players, and raising money for the legal defense of the film's co-star, Harry Reems.

In this book, emphasizing her role as an unlikely celebrity interacting with other celebrities, he brings inside information and a never-before-published revelation to almost every page.

"This book drew me in..How could it not?"
Coco Papy, *Bookslut.*

THE BEACH BOOK FESTIVALS GRAND PRIZE WINNER FOR "BEST SUMMER READING OF 2013"

RUNNER-UP TO "BEST BIOGRAPHY OF 2013" *THE LOS ANGELES BOOK FESTIVAL*

Another hot and insightful commentary about major and sometimes violently controversial conflicts of the American Century, from Blood Moon Productions.

Inside Linda Lovelace's Deep Throat, by Darwin Porter
Softcover, 640 pages, 6"x9" with photos.
ISBN 978-1-936003-33-4

PINK TRIANGLE

THE FEUDS AND PRIVATE LIVES OF

TENNESSEE WILLIAMS, GORE VIDAL, TRUMAN CAPOTE,

& FAMOUS MEMBERS OF THEIR ENTOURAGES

Darwin Porter & Danforth Prince

This book, the only one of its kind, reveals the backlot intrigues associated with the literary and script-writing *enfants terribles* of America's entertainment community during the mid-20th century.

It exposes their bitchfests, their slugfests, and their relationships with the *glitterati*—Marilyn Monroe, Brando, the Oliviers, the Paleys, U.S. Presidents, a gaggle of other movie stars, millionaires, and international *débauchés*.

This is for anyone who's interested in the formerly concealed scandals of Hollywood and Broadway, and the values and pretentions of both the literary community and the entertainment industry.

"A banquet... If PINK TRIANGLE had not been written for us, we would have had to research and type it all up for ourselves…Pink Triangle is nearly seven hundred pages of the most entertaining histrionics ever sliced, spiced, heated, and serviced up to the reading public. Everything that Blood Moon has done before pales in comparison.
Given the fact that the subjects of the book themselves were nearly delusional on the subject of themselves (to say nothing of each other) it is hard to find fault. Add to this the intertwined jungle that was the relationship among Williams, Capote, and Vidal, of the times they vied for things they loved most—especially attention—and the times they enthralled each other and the world, [Pink Triangle is] the perfect antidote to the Polar Vortex."

—Vinton McCabe in the NY JOURNAL OF BOOKS

"Full disclosure: I have been a friend and follower of Blood Moon Productions' tomes for years, and always marveled at the amount of information in their books—it's staggering. The index alone to Pink Triangle runs to 21 pages—and the scale of names in it runs like a Who's Who of American social, cultural and political life through much of the 20th century."

—Perry Brass in THE HUFFINGTON POST

"We Brits are not spared the Porter/Prince silken lash either. PINK TRIANGLE's research is, quite frankly, breathtaking. PINK TRIANGLE will fascinate you for many weeks to come. Once you have made the initial titillating dip, the day will seem dull without it."

—Jeffery Tayor in THE SUNDAY EXPRESS (UK)

PINK TRIANGLE—*The Feuds and Private Lives of Tennessee Williams, Gore Vidal, Truman Capote, and Famous Members of their Entourages*
Darwin Porter & Danforth Prince
Softcover, 700 pages, with photos ISBN 978-1-936003-37-2 Also Available for E-Readers

ROCK HUDSON EROTIC FIRE

Another tragic, myth-shattering, & uncensored tale about
America's obsession with celebrities, from Blood Moon Productions.

In the dying days of Hollywood's Golden
Age, Rock Hudson was the most celebrated
phallic symbol and lust object in America.
This book describes his rise and fall, and the
Entertainment Industry that created him.

Rock Hudson charmed every casting director in
Hollywood (and movie-goers throughout America) as the mega-star they most wanted to share
PILLOW TALK with. This book describes his
rise and fall, and how he handled himself as a
closeted but promiscuous bisexual during an age
when EVERYBODY tried to throw him onto a
casting couch.

Based on dozens of face-to-face interviews with
the actor's friends, co-conspirators, and enemies,
and researched over a period of a half century,
this biography reveals the shame, agonies, and
irony of Rock Hudson's complete, never-before-
told story.

In 2017, the year of its release, it was designated
as winner ("BEST BIOGRAPHY") at two of the
Golden State's most prestigious literary competi-
tions, the Northern California and the Southern
California Book Festivals.

Rock Hudson Erotic Fire

Darwin Porter & Danforth Prince
Another Outrageous Title in Blood Moon's Babylon Series

It was also favorably reviewed by the *Midwestern
Book Review, California Book Watch, KNEWS RADIO,* the *New York Journal of Books,* and the
editors at the most popular Seniors' magazine in Florida, *BOOMER TIMES.*

ROCK HUDSON EROTIC FIRE
By Darwin Porter & Danforth Prince
Softcover, 624 pages, with dozens of photos, 6" x 9"
ISBN 978-1-936003-55-6

Available everywhere now, online and in bookstores.

HOLLYWOOD BABYLON

It's Back! (Volume One) and
Strikes Again! (Volume Two)

Profoundly outrageous, here are Blood Moon's double-header spins on exhibitionism, sexuality, and sin as filtered through 85 years of Hollywood indiscretion

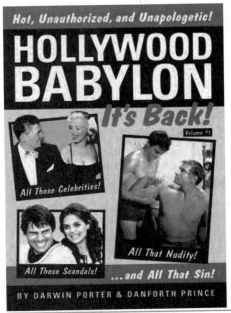

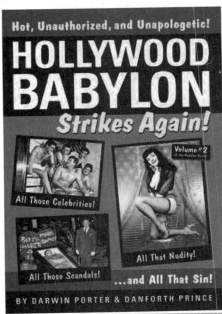

Winner of the Los Angeles Book Festival's Best Nonfiction Title of 2010, and the New England Book Festival's Best Anthology for 2010.

"If you love smutty celebrity dirt as much as I do, then have I got some books for you!"
The Hollywood Offender

"These books will set the graves of Hollywood's cemeteries spinning."
Daily Express

"Monumentally exhaustive...The ultimate guilty pleasure"
Shelf Awareness

Hollywood Babylon It's Back!
& Hollywood Babylon Strikes Again!

Darwin Porter and Danforth Prince
Hardcover, each 380 outrageous pages, each with hundreds of photos

[Whereas Volume One is temporarily sold out, and available only as an e-book, Volume Two, also available as an e-book, still has hard copies in stock]

ISBN 978-1-9748118-8-8 and ISBN 978-1-936003-12-9

PETER O'TOOLE

HELLRAISER, SEXUAL OUTLAW, IRISH REBEL

At the time of its publication early in 2015, this book was widely publicized in the *Daily Mail*, the *New York Daily News*, the *New York Post*, the *Midwest Book Review*, *The Express (London)*, *The Globe*, the *National Enquirer*, and in equivalent publications worldwide

One of the world's most admired (and brilliant) actors, Peter O'Toole wined and wenched his way through a labyrinth of sexual and interpersonal betrayals, sometimes with disastrous results. Away from the stage and screen, where such films as *Becket* and *Lawrence of Arabia*, made film history, his life was filled with drunken, debauched nights and edgy sexual experimentations, most of which were never openly examined in the press. A hellraiser, he shared wild times with his "best blokes" Richard Burton and Richard Harris. Peter Finch, also his close friend, once invited him to join him in sharing the pleasures of his mistress, Vivien Leigh.

"My father, a bookie, moved us to the Mick community of Leeds," O'Toole once told a reporter. "We were very poor, but I was born an Irishman, which accounts for my gift of gab, my unruly behavior, my passionate devotion to women and the bottle, and my loathing of any authority figure."

Author Robert Sellers described O'Toole's boyhood neighborhood. "Three of his playmates went on to be hanged for murder; one strangled a girl in a lovers' quarrel; one killed a man during a robbery; another cut up a warden in South Africa with a pair of shears. It was a heavy bunch."

Peter O'Toole's hell-raising life story has never been told, until now. Hot and uncensored, from a writing team which, even prior to O'Toole's death in 2013, had been collecting under-the-radar info about him for years, this book has everything you ever wanted to know about how THE LION navigated his way through the boudoirs of the Entertainment Industry IN WINTER, Spring, Summer, and a dissipated Autumn as well.

Blood Moon has ripped away the imperial robe, scepter, and crown usually associated with this quixotic problem child of the British Midlands. Provocatively uncensored, this illusion-shattering overview of Peter O'Toole's hellraising (or at least very naughty) and demented life is unique in the history of publishing.

PETER O'TOOLE: *HELLRAISER, SEXUAL OUTLAW, IRISH REBEL*
DARWIN PORTER & DANFORTH PRINCE
Softcover, with photos. ISBN 978-1-936003-45-7

HUMPHREY BOGART

THE MAKING OF A LEGEND

DARWIN PORTER

A "CRADLE-TO-GRAVE" HARDCOVER ABOUT THE RISE TO FAME OF AN OBSCURE, UNLIKELY, AND FREQUENTLY UNEMPLOYED BROADWAY ACTOR.

Whereas **Humphrey Bogart** is always at the top of any list of the Entertainment Industry's most famous actors, very little is known about how he clawed his way from Broadway to Hollywood during Prohibition and the Jazz Age.

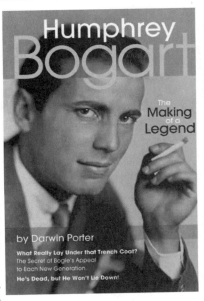

This pioneering biography begins with Bogart's origins as the child of wealthy (morphine-addicted) parents in New York City, then examines the love affairs, scandals, failures, and breakthroughs that launched him as an American icon.

It includes details about behind-the-scenes dramas associated with three mysterious marriages, and films such as *The Petrified Forest*, *The Maltese Falcon*, *High Sierra*, and *Casablanca*. Read all about the debut and formative years of the actor who influenced many generations of filmgoers, laying Bogie's life bare in a style you've come to expect from Darwin Porter. Exposed with all their juicy details is what Bogie never told his fourth wife, Lauren Bacall, herself a screen legend.

Drawn from original interviews with friends and foes who knew a lot about what lay beneath his trenchcoat, this exposé covers Bogart's remarkable life as it helped define movie-making, Hollywood's portrayal of macho, and America's evolving concept of Entertainment itself.

This revelatory book is based on dusty unpublished memoirs, letters, diaries, and often personal interviews from the women—and the men—who adored him.

There are also shocking allegations from colleagues, former friends, and jilted lovers who wanted the screen icon to burn in hell.

All this and more, much more, in Darwin Porter's *exposé* of Bogie's startling secret life.

WITH STARTLING NEW INFORMATION ABOUT BOGART, THE MOVIES, & GOLDEN AGE HOLLYWOOD

542 PAGES, WITH HUNDREDS OF PHOTOS **ISBN** 978-1-936003-14-3

PAUL NEWMAN

THE MAN BEHIND THE BABY BLUES
HIS SECRET LIFE EXPOSED

Drawn from firsthand interviews with insiders who knew Paul Newman intimately, and compiled over a period of nearly a half-century, this is the world's most honest and most revelatory biography about Hollywood's pre-eminent male sex symbol.

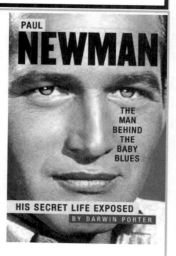

This is a respectful but candid cornucopia of once-concealed information about the sexual and emotional adventures of an affable, impossibly good-looking workaday actor, a former sailor from Shaker Heights, Ohio, who parlayed his ambisexual charm and extraordinary good looks into one of the most successful careers in Hollywood.

Whereas the situations it exposes were widely known within Hollywood's inner circles, they've never before been revealed to the general public.

But now, the full story has been published—the giddy heights and agonizing crashes of a great American star, with revelations and insights never before published in any other biography.

"Paul Newman had just as many on-location affairs as the rest of us, and he was just as bisexual as I was. But whereas I was always getting caught with my pants down, he managed to do it in the dark with not a paparazzo in sight. He might have bedded Marilyn Monroe or Elizabeth Taylor the night before, but he always managed to show up for breakfast with Joanne Woodward, with those baby blues, looking as innocent as a Botticelli angel. He never fooled me. It takes an alleycat to know another one. Did I ever tell you what really happened between Newman and me? If that doesn't grab you, what about what went on between James Dean and Newman? Let me tell you about this co-called model husband if you want to look behind those famous peepers."

—Marlon Brando

Paul Newman, The Man Behind the Baby Blues,
His Secret Life Exposed, **by Darwin Porter**
Recipient of an Honorable Mention from the New England Book Festival
Hardcover, 520 pages, with dozens of photos.
ISBN 978-0-9786465-1-6   **Available everywhere, online and in bookstores.**